Network Management

Benoit Claise, CCIE No. 2686
Ralf Wolter

Cisco Press

Cisco Press
201 West 103rd Street
Indianapolis, IN 46290 USA

Network Management

Benoit Claise, CCIE No. 2686, Ralf Wolter

Copyright© 2007 Cisco Systems, Inc.

Published by:
Cisco Press
800 East 96th Street
Indianapolis, IN 46240 USA

Printed in the United States of America 1 2 3 4 5 6 7 8 9 0

First Printing June 2007

ISBN-10: 1-58705-198-2

ISBN-13: 978-1-58705-198-2

Library of Congress Cataloging-in-Publication Data

Claise, Benoit.

  Network management / Benoit Claise, Ralf Wolter.

      p. cm.

  ISBN 978-1-58705-198-2 (hardcover)

1. Computer networks--Management. I. Wolter, Ralf, 1926- II. Title.

  TK5105.5.C544 2007

  004.6068--dc22

2007018567

Warning and Disclaimer

This book is designed to provide information about accounting and performance strategies for network management. Every effort has been made to make this book as complete and accurate as possible, but no warranty or fitness is implied.

The information is provided on an "as is" basis. The authors, Cisco Press, and Cisco Systems, Inc. shall have neither liability nor responsibility to any person or entity with respect to any loss or damages arising from the information contained in this book or from the use of the discs or programs that may accompany it.

The opinions expressed in this book belong to the authors and are not necessarily those of Cisco Systems, Inc.

Corporate and Government Sales

The publisher offers excellent discounts on this book when ordered in quantity for bulk purchases or special sales, which may include electronic versions and/or custom covers and content particular to your business, training goals, marketing focus, and branding interests. For more information, please contact:

U.S. Corporate and Government Sales

1-800-382-3419
corpsales@pearsontechgroup.com

For sales outside the United States please contact:

International Sales

international@pearsoned.com

Trademark Acknowledgments

All terms mentioned in this book that are known to be trademarks or service marks have been appropriately capitalized. Cisco Press or Cisco Systems, Inc., cannot attest to the accuracy of this information. Use of a term in this book should not be regarded as affecting the validity of any trademark or service mark.

In addition, this book includes excerpts from the following copyrighted documents:

RFC 3954, *Cisco Systems NetFlow Services Export Version 9*. Copyright © The Internet Society, 2004.

RFC 2863, *The Interfaces Group MIB*. Copyright © The Internet Society, 2000.

RFC 2924, *Accounting Attributes and Record Formats*. Copyright © The Internet Society, 2000.

RFC 2578, *Structure of Management Information Version 2 (SMIv2)*. Copyright © The Internet Society, 1999.

RFC 1213, *Management Information Base for Network Management of TCP/IP-based Internets: MIB-II*. Copyright © The Internet Society, 1991

RFC 3813, *Multiprotocol Label Switching (MPLS) Label Switching Router (LSR) Management Information Base (MIB)*. Copyright © The Internet Society, 2004.

RFC 3812, *Multiprotocol Label Switching (MPLS) Traffic Engineering (TE) Management Information Base (MIB)*. Copyright © The Internet Society, 2004.

RFC 4293, *Management Information Base for the Internet Protocol (IP)*. Copyright © The Internet Society, 2006.

RFC 2932, *IPv4 Multicast Routing MIB*. Copyright © The Internet Society, 2000.

RFC 2579, *Textual Conventions for SMIv2*. Copyright © The Internet Society, 1999.

RFC 3919, *Remote Network Monitoring (RMON) Protocol Identifiers for IPv6 and Multi Protocol Label Switching (MPLS)*. Copyright © The Internet Society, 2004.

RFC 4149, *Definition of Managed Objects for Synthetic Sources for Performance Monitoring Algorithms*. Copyright © The Internet Society, 2005.

RFC 4150, *Transport Performance Metrics MIB*. Copyright © The Internet Society, 2005.

RFC 4710, *Real-time Application Quality-of-Service Monitoring (RAQMON) Framework*. Copyright © The Internet Society, 2006.

RFC 2869, *RADIUS Extensions*. Copyright © The Internet Society, 2000.

RFC 2865, *Remote Authentication Dial In User Service (RADIUS)*. Copyright © The Internet Society, 2000.

Additional material in this book has been reproduced by kind permission of the ITU-T, TMF, and IPDR.

Feedback Information

At Cisco Press, our goal is to create in-depth technical books of the highest quality and value. Each book is crafted with care and precision, undergoing rigorous development that involves the unique expertise of members of the professional technical community.

Reader feedback is a natural continuation of this process. If you have any comments about how we could improve the quality of this book, or otherwise alter it to better suit your needs, you can contact us through e-mail at feedback@ciscopress.com. Please be sure to include the book title and ISBN in your message.

We greatly appreciate your assistance.

Publisher	Paul Boger
Associate Publisher	Dave Dusthimer
Cisco Representative	Anthony Wolfenden
Cisco Press Program Manager	Jeff Brady
Executive Editor	Mary Beth Ray
Managing Editor	Patrick Kanouse
Senior Development Editor	Christopher Cleveland
Senior Project Editor	San Dee Phillips
Copy Editor	Gayle Johnson
Technical Editors	Alexander Clemm, Chris Elliot, Simon Leinen, John Strassner, Emmanuel Tychon, Jan Bollen, Michael Behringer
Editorial Assistant	Vanessa Evans
Book and Cover Designer	Louisa Adair
Composition	Mark Shirar
Indexer	Tim Wright
Proofreader	Molly Proue

Americas Headquarters
Cisco Systems, Inc.
170 West Tasman Drive
San Jose, CA 95134-1706
USA
www.cisco.com
Tel: 408 526-4000
800 553-NETS (6387)
Fax: 408 527-0883

Asia Pacific Headquarters
Cisco Systems, Inc.
168 Robinson Road
#28-01 Capital Tower
Singapore 068912
www.cisco.com
Tel: +65 6317 7777
Fax: +65 6317 7799

Europe Headquarters
Cisco Systems International BV
Haarlerbergpark
Haarlerbergweg 13-19
1101 CH Amsterdam
The Netherlands
www-europe.cisco.com
Tel: +31 0 800 020 0791
Fax: +31 0 20 357 1100

Cisco has more than 200 offices worldwide. Addresses, phone numbers, and fax numbers are listed on the Cisco Website at **www.cisco.com/go/offices.**

About the Authors

Benoit Claise, CCIE No. 2686, is a Cisco Distinguished Engineer working as an architect for embedded management and device instrumentation. His area of expertise includes accounting, performance, and fault management. Claise is a contributor to the NetFlow standardization at the IETF in the IPFIX and PSAMP working groups. He joined Cisco in 1996 as a customer support engineer in the Technical Assistance Center network management team. He then became an escalation engineer before joining the engineering team.

Ralf Wolter is a senior manager, Consulting Engineering at Cisco Systems. He leads the Core and NMS/OSS consulting team for Europe and works closely with corporate engineering, as well as supporting large customer projects. His special field of interest is device instrumentation, related to accounting and performance management. He joined Cisco in 1996 as a systems engineer. He has provided technical leadership for many large network management projects in Europe, the Middle East, and Africa. Before his current position, he worked as a networking consultant at AT&T/NCR, focusing on the design and management of data networks.

About the Technical Reviewers

Dr. Alexander Clemm is a senior architect with Cisco. He has been involved with integrated management of networked systems and services since 1990. He has provided technical leadership for many leading-edge network management development, architecture, and engineering efforts, from conception to delivery to the customer. His current responsibilities involve embedded management and instrumentation of devices for management purposes. Outside Cisco, Clemm is on the organizing or technical committees of the major IEEE management-related conferences. He is the author of the Cisco Press book *Network Management Fundamentals*.

Chris Elliott, CCIE No. 2013 in Routing and Switching, has recertified in NMS and security, among other topics. He has extensive expertise in all aspects of networking, starting 30 years ago with ARPA-net. He has focused on network management for the last 17 years and is involved in several IETF protocol standardization efforts. He is the author of the book *Performance and Fault Management*. In addition, he is the developer and presenter of several in-depth technology discussions presented at NetWorld+Interop, Networkers at Cisco Live, NANOG, and elsewhere.

Simon Leinen has been working since 1996 as a network engineer for SWITCH, the Swiss education and research network operator. He helps build network monitoring and accounting systems. He has participated in several joint European research projects. Other activities include IETF standardization work—in particular, in the IPFIX and NETCONF working groups—and the development of the Performance Enhancement and Response Team (PERT), a service addressing end-to-end performance issues experienced by research network users.

John Strassner is a Motorola fellow. He is also the Director of Autonomic Computing Research at Motorola, where he is responsible for directing Motorola's efforts in autonomic computing, policy management, knowledge engineering and identity management. Previously, John was the chief strategy officer for Intelliden and a former Cisco fellow. John invented DEN (Directory Enabled Networks) and DEN-ng as a new paradigm for managing and provisioning networks and networked applications. John is the chair of the ACF and vice-chair of the Reconfigurability and Autonomics working group of the WWRF. He is the past chair of the TMF's NGOSS metamodel, policy, and Shared Information and Data modeling work groups, as well as being active in the ITU, OMG, and OASIS. He has authored two books (Directory Enabled Networks and Policy Based Network Management), written chapters for three other books, and has authored over 145 refereed journal and conference publications. Finally, he is an associate professor at Waterford Institute of Technology in Ireland.

Dedications

Benoit:

First, and most important, I would like to thank my family for their ongoing support during the very long journey of writing this book. Expressed differently: "Lore, Julien, and Jocelyne, please accept my apologies for the multiple evenings and weekends I should have spent with you."

I also would like to thank Luc David and Frank Van Steenwinkel—respectively, my manager and director when I was at the Technical Assistance Center—for giving me the freedom to do what is important.

Finally, I express my gratitude to the numerous people who encouraged me during the first stage of the project and throughout the completion of the book: some by reviewing the text, some by testing in the lab, and some simply for offering kind words. Special thanks for the always-positive attitude of Ralf, my coauthor.

Ralf:

First, I thank my wife Miriam for her love and patience during the course of this book. Without her commitment to me and the kids, I would not have been able to succeed in my professional life, and this book would have remained a nice dream. Instead, it became real! I also want to thank my children, Lydia and Henry, for releasing me during uncountable weekend hours. I'm looking forward to the day when they can read and understand this book.

Next, I want to thank my coauthor, Benoit, for his commitment and for constantly reminding me that quality and consistency cannot be neglected, even for the price of missing a deadline. Taking this journey together is an experience I will never forget.

Finally, and certainly most important of all, I give all thanks to God the Father, the Son, and the Holy Spirit for all that I am.

Acknowledgments

This book is the result of a team effort, finally during the writing and before throughout years of teamwork and cooperation in driving the technology. We would like to acknowledge those who made it possible to write this book.

A big thank-you goes to several Cisco colleagues for their support, encouragement, and constructive feedback during the reviews, especially Marisol Palmero for the Data-Collection MIB, Bulk-MIB, and NBAR; Emmanuel Tychon for IP SLA; Alex Clemm for the scenarios; Jan Bollen for voice management; Michael Behringer for security; Chris Elliot for SNMP; Greg Weber for IPDR; and Stuart Parham for lab support. Their professional input helped add the missing pieces.

We would like to say a special thank you to Simon Leinen and John Strassner for their due diligence and encouragement during the writing and reviewing of the book. We really appreciate your constructive feedback!

A special thanks to our senior development editor, Christopher Cleveland, for the right combination of pushing and patience, and to our executive editor, Mary Beth Ray, for being flexible and always supportive and encouraging.

This Book Is Safari Enabled

The Safari® Enabled icon on the cover of your favorite technology book means the book is available through Safari Bookshelf. When you buy this book, you get free access to the online edition for 45 days.

Safari Bookshelf is an electronic reference library that lets you easily search thousands of technical books, find code samples, download chapters, and access technical information whenever and wherever you need it.

To gain 45-day Safari Enabled access to this book:

- Go to http://www.ciscopress.com/safarienabled
- Complete the brief registration form
- Enter the coupon code GLFI-9ZBE-C2WM-CWEP-7I1E

If you have difficulty registering on Safari Bookshelf or accessing the online edition, please e-mail customer-service@safaribooksonline.com.

Contents at a Glance

Contents

Icons Used in This Book

 File Server

 Communications Server

 Firewall

 Network Management Appliance

 Laptop

 Web Server

 PC

 Modem

 Workstation

 CiscoWorks Workstation

 CiscoCA

 Cell Phone

 Cisco IP Phone 7970

 Satellite

 Phone

 Router

 Voice-Enabled Router

 Multiservice Switch

  NetFlow Router

 Access Point

 Multilayer Switch without Text

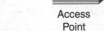 Route/Switch Processor w/ Si

 ATM Switch

  Network Cloud, Standard

 Line: Ethernet

Line: Serial

Wireless Connection

 Database

  Cluster Controller

 Front End Processor

  CallManager

 Cisco 1000

  Switch

 Signaling Copntroller

Command Syntax Conventions

The conventions used to present command syntax in this book are the same conventions used in the IOS Command Reference. The Command Reference describes these conventions as follows:

- **Bold** indicates commands and keywords that are entered literally as shown. In configuration examples and output (not general command syntax), bold indicates commands that are manually input by the user (such as a **show** command).

- *Italic* indicates arguments for which you supply actual values.

- Vertical bars (|) separate alternative, mutually exclusive elements.

- Square brackets ([ ]) indicate an optional element.

- Braces ({ }) indicate a required choice.

- Braces within brackets ([{ }]) indicate a required choice within an optional element.

Introduction

For today's network operators, understanding the performance and effectiveness of their networks is critical to business success. The age of largely overprovisioning networks to boost bandwidth already seems like the distant past. The economic climate has moved toward maximizing the return on investment into the network infrastructure. At the same time, as the wide adoption of network applications seamlessly converges business-critical data, voice, and video into the same network infrastructure, any performance degradation and downtime can cost businesses tens of thousands of dollars each hour. In addition to performance issues caused by failures, outages, and misconfigurations, peer-to-peer traffic increases almost daily.

From a business perspective, enterprises need to ensure that business-critical applications receive proper treatment, defined by a service-level agreement (SLA), and keep the networking infrastructure in an appropriate balance between costs and benefits. Service providers generate revenue by delivering connectivity, potentially bundled with value-added services. They can differentiate themselves either through cheaper prices or by offering their customers better SLAs, proactively monitoring them, and notifying customers about outages and potential bottlenecks. From the enterprise perspective, this is a major step toward increasing application reliability and organizational efficiency and productivity.

Accounting and performance management applications are vital to network efficiency. For example, these tools can identify underused network paths or nodes, the most active routes through the network, and points where the network is overloaded. For optimal use, operators need to tune their networks and corresponding service parameters based on a detailed picture of the networks' characteristics, achieved through accounting and performance management. There is a close relationship between accounting and performance management, which is the justification for combining these two areas in this book.

This book's focus is on accounting and performance device instrumentation. It delves into the details of the Cisco device features related to accounting and performance management, with limited emphasis on applications, mediation devices, and higher-level functions. Accounting and performance management help you understand these data collection concepts and distinguish the different methods. In addition, detailed guidance and scenarios help you apply these concepts.

Goals and Methods

Why should you read this book? The objective is to set the foundation for understanding performance and accounting principles, provide guidance on how to do accounting and performance management, and to illustrate these with real-world examples and scenarios so that you can apply this knowledge in your own network.

This book can be a reference for experts as well as a "read it all" book for beginners. Its objectives are as follows:

- To help you understand the relationship between accounting and performance and to teach you how to use them in conjunction with each other.
- To address both enterprises and service providers. Basically, both groups can collect similar types of data with potentially the same accounting features, while targeting different goals. An example is gathering NetFlow data for monitoring purposes for an enterprise customer while a service provider collects similar NetFlow records for billing purposes.

- To offer guidance in choosing the "right" features and applying them using best practices.
- To provide an in-depth description and comparison of the various accounting and performance methods. This helps you clearly distinguish the various methods and choose the right method for your network and the problems you need to solve.
- To briefly describe accounting and performance scenarios and examples, such as IP telephony, security, traffic engineering, and billing.

Who Should Read This Book?

To get the most out of this book, you should have a basic understanding of NMS and OSS concepts and be familiar with the command-line interface of Cisco devices. The primary audience for this book includes the following:

- NMS/OSS architects and network designers, operations people, service designers, network management administrators, accounting and billing operations/IT department, capacity planning department, security department
- Students with a general interest in network management and a special interest in accounting and performance strategies

How This Book Is Organized

When developing the outline for this book, we had two different groups of readers in mind: beginners and experts. You can read this book from cover to cover and get a good understanding of accounting and performance management. You also will learn how to implement the described solutions in your network. The chapter structure follows a logical path for newcomers to accounting and performance management. If you are already familiar with the basic technologies and are more interested in the implementation details and how to apply them, you can jump directly to the chapter of your main interest. Last but not least, we would like this book to become a reference and "dictionary" for performance and accounting techniques, allowing an easy comparison of features.

Figure I-1 provides a map to help you quickly make your way through the large amount of information provided.

Figure I-1   *How to Read This Book*

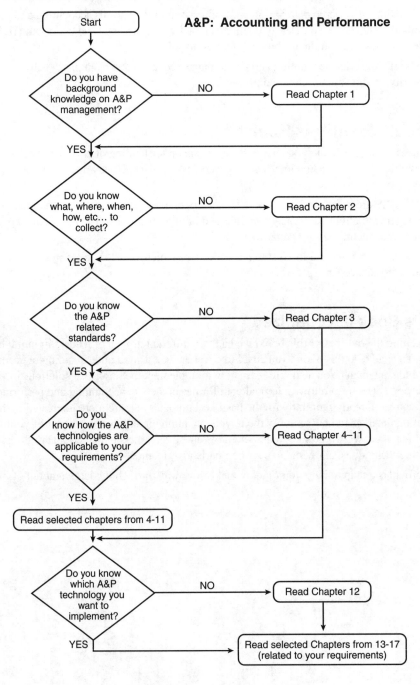

This book's overall structure is as follows:

- **Part I, "Data Collection and Methodology Standards,"** addresses the generic concepts of data collection for accounting and performance purposes. It also describes some typical scenarios and discusses related standards.

  — **Chapter 1, "Understanding the Need for Accounting and Performance Management,"** discusses the basic concepts of accounting and performance management, distinguishes the two areas, and applies the relevant parts of both technologies to network design and applications.

  — **Chapter 2, "Data Collection Methodology,"** discusses relevant questions for any accounting or performance management project: What type of information should you collect? What level of detail is required in the data records? How should you meter, collect, and process the data records?

  — **Chapter 3, "Accounting and Performance Standards and Definitions,"** covers details about architectures, standards definitions, and protocols related to performance and accounting. It also provides an overview of the different standards bodies and architectures, along with the concepts and principles of each protocol.

- **Part II, "Implementations on the Cisco Devices,"** drills into the implementation specifics of accounting and performance features of Cisco network elements. Each chapter describes the principles first, followed by implementation details, and concludes with command-line examples, including MIB examples where appropriate.

  — **Chapter 4, "SNMP and MIBs,"** describes the capabilities of the different SNMP protocol versions on Cisco network elements. SNMP and MIB configuration examples as well as feature comparison tables help you understand and apply the information. The chapter also summarizes the most relevant accounting and performance MIBs.

  — **Chapter 5, "RMON,"** describes the capabilities of the Remote Monitoring (RMON) series of MIBs. A command-line reference plus SNMP MIB details and configuration examples make the chapter content quickly applicable.

  — **Chapter 6, "IP Accounting,"** describes IP accounting features in Cisco IOS. It covers the different IP accounting functions and includes a command-line reference as well as SNMP MIB details.

  — **Chapter 7, "NetFlow,"** describes NetFlow features in Cisco IOS. It covers the different NetFlow versions, the latest NetFlow features, and the natural NetFlow evolution toward IPFIX. Platform-specific details also are discussed, along with some command-line references, examples, and SNMP MIB details.

  — **Chapter 8, "BGP Policy Accounting,"** describes BGP Policy Accounting features in Cisco IOS. You'll see how to apply the features for a source- and destination-sensitive billing scheme, as well as the practical configuration details on the routers. Furthermore, you will understand the similarities between BGP Policy Accounting and the "Destination-Sensitive Billing" feature.

— **Chapter 9, "AAA Accounting,"** describes Authentication, Authorization, and Accounting (AAA), with an emphasis on accounting. The chapter starts with a general introduction to AAA, RADIUS, and Diameter. The various standards are discussed, and a dedicated section covers voice-specific extensions. You will be able to identify which AAA functions to use for which requirements and what Cisco has implemented.

— **Chapter 10, "NBAR,"** provides an overview of the Network-Based Application Recognition (NBAR) feature in Cisco IOS. This will enable you to decide in which situations NBAR is the appropriate mechanism for accounting and performance management. Based on concrete examples, you will be able to identify the appropriate CLI commands and MIB functions and quickly get NBAR setups operational.

— **Chapter 11, "IP SLA,"** describes Cisco IP SLA. This is an embedded feature set in Cisco IOS Software that allows you to analyze service-level agreements for protocols, applications, and services.

— **Chapter 12, "Summary of Data Collection Methodology,"** summarizes the high-level technical characteristics of the features covered in Chapters 1 through 11. It provides a way to structure, categorize, and compare the features. In addition, this chapter offers an entry point into the accounting and performance features. It can be used as an introduction to the features of interest.

- **Part III, "Assigning Technologies to Solutions,"** applies the details from Part II to real-world scenarios, such as monitoring, capacity planning, voice, security, and billing.

— **Chapter 13, "Monitoring Scenarios,"** is based on a series of questions that network operators ask themselves: "How should I check the device's health in the network?", "How do I evaluate the link capacity?", "When should links be upgraded?", "How should I verify network connectivity?", "How can I evaluate the response time between the locations?", "How can I ensure VoIP quality?", "How can I determine the application types in the network?", and "How do I discover the traffic sent to and received from the Internet?"

— **Chapter 14, "Capacity Planning Scenarios,"** covers link capacity planning and network-wide capacity planning. It describes the requirements and relationships with network performance monitoring, peering agreements, and traffic engineering.

— **Chapter 15, "Voice Scenarios,"** illustrates scenarios in the area of the Cisco voice accounting and performance measurement. It describes the technical background of voice accounting and performance management, which combines the device instrumentation features from Part II with management applications, such as Cisco CallManager and others.

— **Chapter 16, "Security Scenarios,"** provides a security scenario that is closely related to accounting and performance measurement. It describes how to leverage metering information to identify and block security attacks and to use performance management to proactively secure the network.

— **Chapter 17, "Billing Scenarios,"** highlights how accounting and performance management technologies can be used for billing. It applies technologies and products associated with accounting and performance management.

Data Collection and Methodology Standards

CHAPTER 1

Understanding the Need for Accounting and Performance Management

This chapter defines the foundation for this book and answers the following general questions:

- What is accounting management?
- What is performance management?
- What is the relationship between accounting and performance management?
- Why do networks require accounting and performance management?
- Why is accounting almost a stealth area within network management?
- Which problems do accounting and performance management solutions solve?
- How can the business use this information for network planning, redesign, and billing?
- What aspects make up accounting and performance monitoring (data collection, data analysis, reporting, billing, and so on)?

By the end of this chapter, you will be able to grasp the basic concepts of accounting and performance management, distinguish the two areas, and apply the relevant part of both technologies to network design and applications.

During the last decade, the Internet has changed our ways of communicating more than anything else. The Internet is almost ubiquitous today, and we take connectivity for granted until for some reason we cannot connect. At that point, we suddenly feel isolated. These days we expect Internet connectivity to be available anytime, anywhere. Most of us realize that this is impossible without intelligent systems managing the network. This leads us to technologies, processes, and applications in the area of Network Management and Network Management Systems and Operations Support Systems (NMS-OSS). NMS was a set of niche applications for quite some time, until businesses realized that their performance depended on the network. Then, suddenly, network downtime became a business issue instead of just a minor problem. Therefore, notions such as service level agreements (SLA) are imposed on the network to support specific business application requirements.

Nobody questions the need for fault and security management these days, and there is obviously a need for performance statistics, but still some questions are left open: "Do I really need accounting?" "Is accounting the same as billing?" "What can accounting do for me?" In this chapter, you will find answers to these questions and understand how accounting relates to performance management.

In a nutshell, accounting describes the process of gathering usage data records at network devices and exporting those records to a collection server, where processing takes place. Then the records are presented to the user or provided to another application, such as performance management, security management, or billing.

An example is collecting usage records to identify security attacks based on specific traffic patterns or measuring which applications consume the most bandwidth in the network.

This book focuses on accounting, but because accounting is so closely related to performance, this chapter also discusses performance aspects in detail and identifies how accounting and performance can be used together to support each other. Because many more networks have deployed performance management than accounting solutions, this chapter starts with a deeper inspection of accounting before addressing the performance area, where you will learn the relationship between performance management and service level agreements. The objective is to enable you to distinguish between accounting, performance management, service level monitoring, and fault management. This chapter briefly introduces management standards and concepts to help you understand common areas and demarcations between accounting and performance management. Chapter 3, "Accounting and Performance Standards and Definitions," describes these concepts in more detail and also describes the roles of the various standards bodies, along with their main objectives and directions.

Most network administrators ask themselves whether they need accounting when looking at the Fault, Configuration, Accounting, Performance, and Security (FCAPS) management model. The FCAPS model is an international standard defined by the International Telecommunication Union (ITU) that describes the various network management areas.

The FCAPS model was chosen as a structure even though other models exist, such as FAB and eTOM (which are introduced in Chapter 3). The advantage of the FCAPS model is that it clearly distinguishes between accounting and performance.

Table 1-1 describes the main objectives of each functional area in the FCAPS model.

Table 1-1   *ITU-T FCAPS Model*

Management Functional Area (MFA)	Management Function Set Groups
Fault	Alarm surveillance, fault localization and correlation, testing, trouble administration, network recovery
Configuration	Network planning, engineering, and installation; service planning and negotiation; discovery; provisioning; status and control
Accounting	Usage measurement, collection, aggregation, and mediation; tariffing and pricing
Performance	Performance monitoring and control, performance analysis and trending, quality assurance
Security	Access control and policy; customer profiling; attack detection, prevention, containment, and recovery; security administration

See ITU-T M.3400 and ISO/IEC 7498-4 (Open Systems Interconnection—Basic Reference Model, Part 4: Management Framework)

Fault management is compulsory for managing networks proactively. Unless you want to configure all devices sequentially via Telnet or Secure Shell (SSH), an application is required to configure multiple devices in parallel and automate actions such as backup, rollback, and inventory. A new virus hits the Internet almost every day, so the need for security management is critical. Measuring and monitoring network performance is required in today's complex networks; still, the importance of accounting is not as well understood.

One of the reasons the ITU was formed in 1865 was in recognition of the need to agree on a common method of dividing the revenues from international telegraph services between the originating and destination countries. According to the billing paradigm in those days, a network element either could account for data to be transmitted or would drop it. For example, phone calls were set up only if charging and billing could be achieved. Accounting was solely considered the task of collecting usage data, preprocessing it, and feeding it into a billing application. Service providers usually developed their own accounting and billing applications, and most enterprises were not interested in accounting information. With the introduction of data networks and the Internet Protocol (IP) becoming ubiquitous, the billing paradigm changed quickly. Internet access was only billed on access time, and services on the Internet were offered free of charge. Over time, accounting in the IP world was almost forgotten, even for network management experts. This was exacerbated by the roots of accounting, which was considered no more than a billing component. This also increased the isolation of accounting. Hence, this book's approach is to distinguish between accounting and billing, to identify areas where accounting can be used (billing is just one of them), and to discover how accounting and performance management relate to each other.

You should also consider accounting's potential levels of complexity. Although collecting interface counters is quite simple, mediation and correlation of large accounting records for a billing application can be difficult. It requires detailed knowledge of the underlying network architecture and technology, because collecting usage records from a legacy voice network is a completely different task than collecting usage records in data networks. Content switches generate a different set of records than an IP phone does. Likewise, there is not much similarity between an accounting record from an authentication server and the retrieval of a device interface counter, even though all of these are valid accounting sources. Figure 1-1 shows different networking devices and the various accounting records created. Do not be concerned by the figure's alphabet soup; it is used solely to represent the various accounting sources and different transport mechanisms. The following chapters describe each mechanism in detail, with emphasis on how they relate to each other.

Figure 1-1 *Accounting Sources/Usage Data Generation*

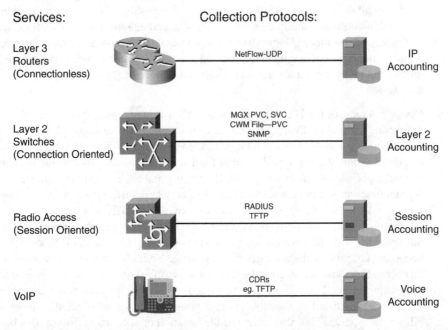

In addition, we distinguish between connectionless Layer 3 IP communications, connection-oriented Layer 2 services, session-oriented communication (for example, dialup) and legacy voice calls. All data records generated in these examples are different. For example, the Cisco IP device would export a Cisco NetFlow record. A Layer 2 Asynchronous Transfer Mode (ATM) switch stores connection details in a text log file and stores voice call results in a Signaling System 7 (SS7) record for legacy voice or call data records for voice over IP (VoIP). In a scenario of accounting for a phone call, each of the collected data sets describes a "phone call," but the technologies used are completely different. This causes the resulting records to be different in format and content; thus, they cannot simply be merged. Instead, understanding this data requires complex processing. Otherwise, instead of obtaining meaningful information, we end up with independent sets of unrelated data. No general accounting standard exists across the various technologies just described. Therefore, the network architect needs to understand the different accounting technologies, compare and relate them to each other, and design a solution that solves the business requests.

The trend toward IP as the unique communication protocol will certainly reduce the described complexity in the future, but this will take another couple of years. Therefore, it is important to understand the different accounting techniques and also identify the various sources in the network for generating usage data records.

Previously, the level of complexity combined with the close association of accounting and billing drew little attention from network administrators and operators. Although legacy telephony services are still charged on call duration, new broadband data services offer customers flat-rate billing. The advantage for the service provider is the simple business model. One price fits all, and it does not take a lot of additional equipment to collect usage data, because neither the user's total online time nor the transmitted volume is an input parameter for the monthly bill. Unfortunately, this model generates only limited and fixed revenue and provides no unique positioning or competitive advantage. Some providers have changed their billing model to be volume- or destination-sensitive, but these are still exceptions. A solid business model is required to justify the level of complexity and required investments, both for capital expenditures (CAPEX) and operational expenditures (OPEX) related to usage-based billing.

In the future, it is much more likely that providers will increase their focus on accounting. This is because competition is rapidly increasing, and providers need ways to differentiate their service offerings. Providing multiple offerings under a "one price fits all" model does not enable this to be accomplished.

To answer the question "What benefits do I get from accounting?", we have to expand our perspective. We should not limit the focus to service providers. We should consider the historically close linkage between accounting and billing. The outsourcing trend at the enterprises often results in independent IT groups, which are moving from a cost center to a profit center, offering services to internal customers. Other departments are using these services and either get a flat bill or are charged based on the usage of the service. The flat model is not different from the described service provider model and can be addressed in a similar manner. The usage-based model requires the collection of usage data, which means that suddenly accounting becomes relevant for enterprises, even though a full-blown billing application is not required. Instead, these enterprises only want to assign costs per department—for instance, having the ability to charge back the cost of Internet connectivity to the different departments that used the service. Challenged to reduce operational expenditures, IT departments are investigating accounting solutions from both a performance and billing perspective. Questions such as "How do I efficiently track network and application resource usage?" and "Which applications are active in the network?" and "Who is using the network, what is the traffic's destination, and when is the network utilized?" are becoming increasingly relevant. End users, on the other hand, are unwilling to pay the bill for other users and departments. Instead, they want to be charged for exactly the resources and services they have been using. Network planners ask, "How do I plan the allocation and deployment of resources and services most efficiently?"

Network operators realized that collected accounting data records are not limited to billing applications. In addition, they can also be used as input for other applications such as performance monitoring, checking that a configuration change fixed a problem, or even security analysis. This is in reality a paradigm change, because suddenly the "A" part of the FCAPS model can be used in conjunction with Fault, Performance, Security, and even Configuration. For example, if the administrator has configured the network so that business-critical data should go via one path and best-effort traffic should take another path, accounting can verify if this policy is applied and otherwise notify the fault and configuration tools. The previous "stealth area" of accounting now becomes a major building block for network and application design and deployment. This is the reason for the increasing interest in accounting technologies. Today, Cisco NetFlow records are becoming an extremely important source of security applications in detecting DoS attacks. Performance applications combine active and passive monitoring techniques to provide information that is more accurate. Traffic engineering applications rely on accurate usage data in real time to calculate the best routes through the network. The described flexibility is probably the biggest advantage of collecting accounting information. If a network architect designs the framework correctly, you can collect accounting data once and use it as input for various applications. Figure 1-2 illustrates a three-tier accounting architecture. Notice the clear separation between the different functions accomplished at each tier. This also relates to the FCAPS model that was chosen to structure the various network management areas. By identifying the possible usage scenarios, accounting becomes an integral part of the NMS.

Figure 1-2   *Accounting Infrastructure*

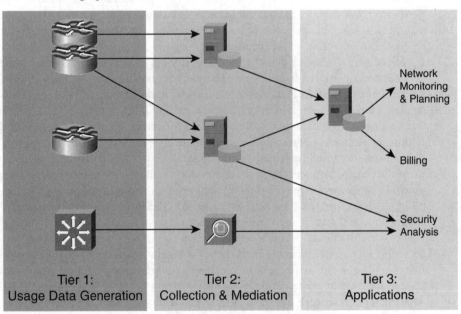

Although the paradigm of "accounting for billing only" terminates with the new approach, the level of complexity unfortunately remains. Not all accounting data records are useful for each application, and sometimes it is necessary to correlate the records with various external sources, adding an additional level of complexity. Therefore, accounting remains a challenging technology that we will uncover in the following chapters.

Definitions and the Relationship Between Accounting and Performance Management

To identify similarities and differences between accounting and performance management, we will first define both terms. Unfortunately, there is no exclusive definition of accounting, which sometimes results in different groups meaning different things. The following definitions are the most common ones used to describe accounting. Note that this section is purely theoretical; however, the objective of this book is to provide a comprehensive perspective on accounting and performance management, which makes this part relevant!

Defining Accounting Management

When searching for a common definition of accounting management, you will discover that several definitions exist. No one unique description is used for all applications. This might sound surprising, but because accounting received limited attention in the past, it is understandable. The authors decided to first present the various diverging definitions to help you understand the root of the problem. Then, the authors present their own definition of accounting management, which is used consistently throughout this book. This section investigates the definition of *accounting management* from the ITU (http://www.itu.int/home/index.html), the TeleManagement Forum (TMF, http://www.tmforum.com), and the Internet Engineering Task Force (IETF, http://www.ietf.org).

- ITU-T definition (M.3400 and X.700, *Definitions of the OSI Network Management Responsibilities*):

  "Accounting management enables charges to be established for the use of resources in the OSIE [Open Systems Interconnect Environment], and for costs to be identified for the use of those resources. Accounting management includes functions to:

  "inform users of costs incurred or resources consumed;

  "enable accounting limits to be set and tariff schedules to be associated with the use of resources;

  "enable costs to be combined where multiple resources are invoked to achieve a given communication objective."

- TMF definition:

  The TMF refers to the ITU-T accounting definition (M.3400) and provides additional details for billing in the enhanced Telecom Operations Map (eTOM), *The Business Process Framework*, Document GB921.

  The Fulfillment, Assurance, and Billing (FAB) model of TMF's eTOM positions the "Network Data Management" building block between assurance and billing. "Network Data Management: this process encompasses the collection of usage data and network and information technology events and data for the purpose of network performance and traffic analysis. This data may also be an input to Billing (Rating and Discounting) processes at the Service Management Layer, depending on the service and its architecture." Chapter 3 explains the FAB model in more detail.

NOTE   Most TMF documents are available free of charge to TMF members. Nonmembers can purchase them on the TMF's website at http://www.tmforum.org.

- IETF definition:

  The informational Request For Comment (RFC) 2975, *Introduction to Accounting Management*, gives the following definition of accounting: the collection of resource consumption data for the purposes of capacity and trend analysis, cost allocation, auditing, and billing. Accounting management requires that resource consumption be measured, rated, assigned, and communicated between appropriate parties."

As you can see from the preceding definitions, there is no universal definition of accounting management. The ITU-T addresses primarily the charging of resource usage, which is a major requirement for every service provider, but we think that this definition is too limited. Even if the IETF definition is not a standard but only an informational RFC, it mostly suits our view of "accounting management." To overcome the numerous definitions and the limitations of some of them, we decided to develop our own definition.

In this book, we use the term *accounting management* to describe the following processes:

- Collecting usage data records at network devices
- Optionally preprocessing data produced by the device (for example, filter, sample, aggregate)
- Exporting the data from the device toward a collection server
- Processing the data at the collection server (for example, filter, sample, aggregate, de-duplicate)
- Converting usage records into a common format to be used by higher-layer applications (for example, performance, SLA, fault, security, billing, planning, and so on): the mediation procedure

Figure 1-3 illustrates the use of accounting management for multiple applications. Notice the functions of the different layers and the distinction between record generation and processing (such as data collection, exporting, and aggregation) and the applications that will use the records.

Figure 1-3   *Accounting Management Architecture*

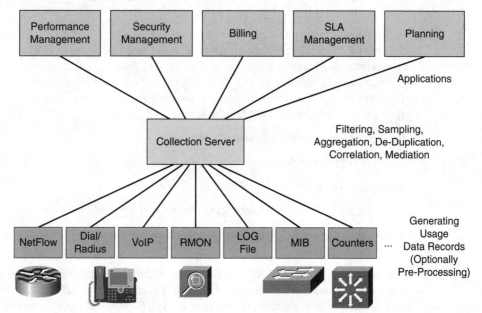

The temptation is great to relate accounting exclusively to billing, because the dictionary (*Merriam-Webster's*) characterizes accounting as follows:

"The system of recording and summarizing business and financial transactions and analyzing, verifying, and reporting the results."

This definition does not even mention the term "billing," but it indirectly relates accounting to billing. Nevertheless, in our mind, accounting is different from billing, because billing is just one of the applications that leverage accounting.

Defining Performance Management

Although there is no unique definition of accounting management, as just described, performance management at least has more parts that are common across the various definitions. The authors decided to take the same approach as for accounting and investigate the definitions from the ITU-T and TMF. Note that none of the IETF RFCs cover the definition of performance management. Finally, the authors decided to create their own definition, which is used throughout this book.

ITU-T definition (M.3400 and X.700, *Definitions of the OSI Network Management Responsibilities*):

> "Performance Management provides functions to evaluate and report upon the behavior of telecommunication equipment and the effectiveness of the network or network element. Its role is to gather and analyze statistical data for the purpose of monitoring and correcting the behavior and effectiveness of the network, network elements, or other equipment and to aid in planning, provisioning, maintenance and the measurement of quality.

> "Performance management includes functions to:

> "a) gather statistical information

> "b) maintain and examine logs of system state histories

> "c) determine system performance under natural and artificial conditions

> "d) alter system modes of operation for conducting performance management activities"

- TMF definition: The TMF defines performance and SLA management in the context of assurance. The assurance process is responsible for the execution of proactive and reactive maintenance activities to ensure that services provided to customers are continuously available and to SLA or quality of service (QoS) performance levels. It performs continuous resource status and performance monitoring to detect possible failures proactively, and it collects performance data and analyzes it to identify potential problems to resolve them without affecting the customer. This process manages the SLAs and reports service performance to the customer. Related documents are TMF 701, *Performance Reporting Concepts & Definitions*; TMF GB917, *SLA Management Handbook*, which also refers to ITU M.3010; and the FAB model of the eTOM. Performance collection is part of the network data management process, according to the TMF:

  > "This process encompasses the collection of usage data and network and information technology events and data for the purpose of network performance and traffic analysis."

As you see from these definitions, performance management does not have a unique classification. ITU-T's definition addresses primarily the behavior and effectiveness of the telecommunication equipment and network, but we feel that this definition is too limited, because it does not address the supervision of the services running on the top of the network. The TMF definition describes the notion of service-level management in detail but only briefly mentions the need for network element monitoring. To overcome the numerous slightly different definitions, we decided to develop our own definition.

At this point, we can distinguish between performance *monitoring* and performance *management*.

Performance *monitoring* collects device-, network-, and service-related parameters and reports them via a graphical user interface, log files, and so on. Performance *management* builds on these data collections but goes one step further by actively notifying the administrator and reconfiguring the devices if necessary. An example is the data collection for SLAs. Performance monitoring and accounting would only collect the data and store it at a collection point. Performance management would analyze the data and compare it against predefined thresholds and service definitions. In the case of a service level violation, it then would generate a trouble ticket to a fault application or reconfigure the device. For example, it would filter best-effort traffic or increase the committed access rate, and so on.

This book uses the term *performance management* to describe the following processes:

1 **Performance monitoring**—Collecting network activities at the device level for the sake of

— Device-related performance monitoring

— Network performance monitoring

— Service performance monitoring

Monitoring subtasks include

— Availability monitoring

— Response time reporting

— Monitoring utilization (link, device, CPU, network, service, and so on)

— Ensuring accuracy of the collected data

— Verification of quality-of-service parameters

— Data aggregation

2 **Data analysis**—Baselining and reporting

Data analysis subtasks include

— Network and device traffic characterization and analysis functions

— Performance

— Exceptions

— Capacity analysis

— Baselining

— Traffic forecasting

3 **Performance management**—Whereas monitoring only observes activities in the network, management modifies device configurations. In the case of performance management, this means adjusting configurations to improve the network's performance and traffic handling (threshold definitions, capacity planning, and so on).

Management subtasks include

— Ensuring compliance of SLAs and class-of-service (CoS) policies and guarantees

— Defining thresholds

— Sending notifications to higher-level applications

— Adjusting configurations

— Quality assurance

Figure 1-4 shows the performance management architecture. When comparing it to the accounting architecture, you can see several similarities, but also differences. The next section discusses both. Whereas accounting focuses on passive collection methods only, performance management can also apply active measurements. In this case, we inject synthetic traffic into the network and monitor how the network treats it.

Figure 1-4 *Performance Management Architecture*

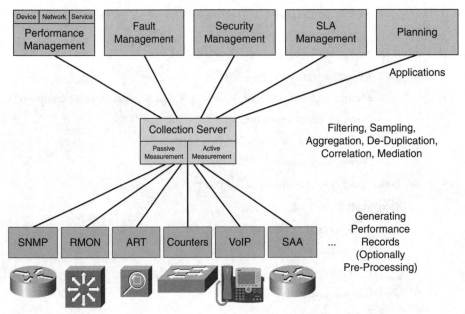

The definitions of performance management just described partly mingled the management of devices and services. A further refinement of performance management identifies three subcategories:

● Device-specific performance management

● Network-centric operations management

● Service management

Device-specific performance management considers the device in an isolated mode. The device status is almost binary: it operates correctly, or a fault occurred. Performance monitoring at the network element level can also be considered binary, after the thresholds definition. For example, if CPU utilization in the range of 5 to 80 percent is considered normal, link utilization should be below 90 percent, and interface errors should not exceed 1 percent. Therefore, depending on whether the established threshold is exceeded, those situations are either normal or abnormal.

Network-centric performance management extends the focus to a network edge-to-edge perspective. Even though all devices might appear OK from a device perspective, the overall network performance might be affected by duplex mismatches, spanning-tree errors, routing loops, and so on.

Service management addresses the level above network connectivity. A service can be relatively simple, such as the Domain Name Server (DNS), or complex, such as a transactional database system. In both cases, the user expects the service to be available and have a predictable response time. Performance monitoring at the service level needs to include service monitoring as well as management functions to modify components of the service in case of failures.

The Relationship Between Accounting and Performance

This section covers both the similarities and differences between accounting management and performance management. We see a strong relationship between performance and accounting, which is reflected by some of the standard definitions. Even though a few have different descriptions (for example, the FCAPS model), the concepts are closely related. As an interesting observation, the TMF combines these two areas.

Both parts collect usage information, which can be applied to similar applications afterward, such as monitoring, baselining, security analysis, and so on. Some technologies, such as Simple Network Management Protocol (SNMP) counters, can be assigned to both performance and accounting and could lead to long theoretical discussions concerning which area they belong to.

Accounting and performance monitoring are important sources not only for performance management, but also for security management—this is another common area. A security management application can import the collected traffic information and analyze the different types of protocols, traffic patterns between source and destination, and so on. A comparison of current data sets versus a defined baseline can identify abnormal situations or new traffic patterns. In addition, the same application can collect device performance monitoring details, such as high CPU utilization. The combination of the two areas can be a strong instrument to identify security attacks almost in real time. The security example is perfectly suited to explaining the benefits of performance monitoring and accounting. Each symptom by itself (abnormal traffic or high CPU utilization) might not be critical per se, but the amalgamation of them could indicate a critical situation in the network.

From a network perspective, performance takes into account details such as network load, device load, throughput, link capacity, different traffic classes, dropped packets, congestion, and accounting addresses usage data collection.

The collection interval can be considered a separation factor between accounting and performance monitoring. A data collection process for performance analysis should notify the administrator immediately if thresholds are exceeded; therefore, we need (almost) real-time collection in this case. Accounting data collection for billing does not have real-time collection requirements, except for scenarios such as prepaid billing.

History is certainly a differentiator. An accounting collection for billing purposes does not need to keep historical data sets, because the billing application does this. Performance management, on the other hand, needs history data to analyze deviation from normal as well as trending functions.

Monitoring device utilization is another difference between the two areas. Device health monitoring is a crucial component of performance monitoring, whereas accounting management is interested in usage records. We will examine this in the following example. Imagine a normal network situation with average traffic load. Now think of a user installing "interesting" software without notifying the administrator. For example, suppose someone installs a monitoring tool and starts discovering devices in the network. Even though it is strongly recommended to secure device access and use cryptic values for SNMP communities instead of the default values "public" and "private," sometimes these suggestions are not followed. If at the same time security restrictions (such as access control lists [ACL]) are not in place, the user discovers network- and device-related details. The situation becomes critical when the user's monitoring tool collects the routing table of an Internet edge router. For example, retrieving the complete routing table of a Cisco 2600 router with 64 MB of RAM and 4000 routes takes about 25 minutes and utilizes about 30 percent of the CPU. An accounting application would not be able to identify this scenario, because the issue is not the amount of traffic transferred, but device utilization. A performance-monitoring application would identify this situation immediately and could report it to a fault application. Even this simple example illustrates the close relationship between performance and fault management as well as the fact that neither accounting nor performance management alone is a sufficient solution for network management.

Another situation would be a misconfigured link. Imagine that a logical connection between two routers was configured as a trunk of three parallel links. For troubleshooting, the administrator shut down two of the links and then solved the issue. However, imagine if he put only one link back to operational, providing only two-thirds of the required bandwidth. Traffic would still go through, and accounting records would be generated, but the increased utilization of the two active links could only be identified by a performance monitoring tool.

This leads to the observation that "fault" is another differentiator between accounting and performance management. In the first example, a performance management application could send a notification to a fault application and configure an ACL at the device to stop the unauthorized SNMP information gathering. In the second example, the performance management tool could automatically activate the third link and notify the administrator. Accounting management applications do not collect device health information, such as CPU utilization, and therefore would not have identified these issues. The close relationship between performance management and fault management is the subject of other publications. For more details, refer to *Performance and Fault Management* (Cisco Press, 2000).

A fundamental difference between monitoring approaches is active and passive monitoring. Accounting management is always passive, and performance monitoring can be passive or active.

Passive monitoring gathers performance data by implementing meters. Examples range from simple interface counters to dedicated appliances such as a Remote Monitoring (RMON) probe. Passive measurement needs to monitor some or all packets that are destined for a device. It is called *sampling* if only a subset of packets is inspected versus a full collection. In some scenarios, such as measuring response time for bidirectional communications, implementing passive measurement can become complex, because the request and response packets need to be correlated. An example is the Application Response Time (ART) Management Information Base (MIB), which extends the RMON 2 standard. ART measures delays between request/response sequences in application flows, such as HTTP and FTP, but it can monitor only applications that use well-known TCP ports. To provide end-to-end measurement, an ART probe is needed at both the client and the server end. Cisco implements the ART MIB at the Network Analysis Module (NAM).

The advantage of passive monitoring is that it does not interfere with the traffic in the network, so the measurement does not bias the results. This benefit can also be a limitation, because network activity is the prerequisite for passive measurement. For example, observed traffic can indicate that a phone is operational, but how do you distinguish between an operational phone that is not in use and a faulty one if neither one generates any traffic? In this case the better approach would be to send some test traffic to the phone and monitor the results or alternatively have the device send keepalives regularly. The active monitoring approach injects synthetic traffic into the network to measure performance metrics such as availability, response time, network round-trip time, latency, jitter, reordering, packet loss, and so on. The simplicity of active measurement increases scalability because only the generated traffic needs to be analyzed. The Cisco IP SLA is an example of active monitoring. See Chapter 11, "IP SLA," for details about IP SLA.

Best current practices suggest combining active and passive measurements because they complement each other.

As you can see from the preceding sections, there are common areas and differences, but in most cases, the combination of accounting and performance management provides benefits. Let us reflect on the following situation: a network operator has performance management and accounting management in place, which both collect usage information from the devices and store them at different collection servers. So far, the data sets have not been linked with to each other, but this can be useful. If you want to reduce the measurement's error rate, you can collect detailed usage records (accounting management) and basic SNMP counters (performance monitoring) and compare the results. This increases the confidence of the measurement.

Figure 1-5 illustrates the different network management building blocks.

Figure 1-5 *Network Management Building Blocks*

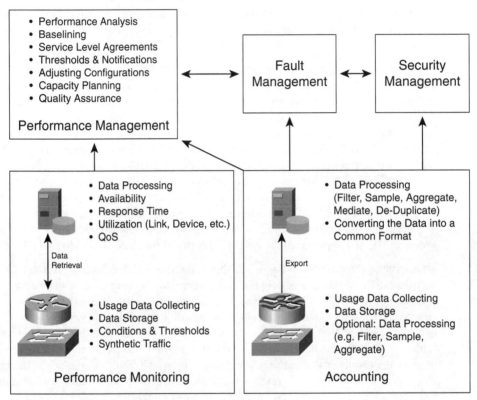

In summary, we suggest combining performance management and accounting, as well as fault and security management, to build a complete network management solution.

A Complementary Solution

These examples clearly point out that the right question is not "Why do I need accounting or performance management?" but instead "In which cases do I apply which method?" The first and most important question should always be "What is the purpose of collecting data?" When the administrator differentiates between security management, service-level management, billing, and so on by taking this top-down approach, it is straightforward to position accounting and performance management in the overall architecture.

To summarize, we want to emphasize that both performance monitoring and accounting management gather usage data used as input for various management applications. Performance management is one example of a management area that benefits from performance monitoring and accounting, but also actively modifies the network and its behavior. They are related, because without performance monitoring you operate the network blindfolded. Without accounting, you can hardly identify the cause of bottlenecks and outages identified by performance management. The intersection between the two areas is typically the network monitoring part (see the section "Network Monitoring"). This is a generic term for any data collection tasks that are common between accounting management and performance management. Figure 1-6 illustrates the overlap between the two areas.

Figure 1-6   *Complementary Solution*

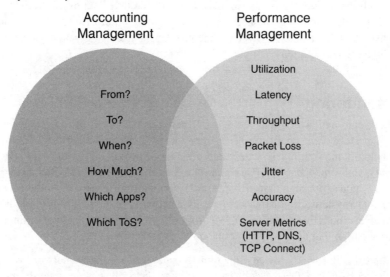

Now that we have clearly defined accounting management, performance monitoring, and performance management, we can take a closer look at the benefits network planners and administrators can achieve from each area.

The Purposes of Accounting

As defined previously, the focus of accounting is to track the usage of network resources and traffic characteristics. The following sections identify various accounting scenarios:

- Network monitoring
- User monitoring and profiling
- Application monitoring and profiling
- Capacity planning
- Traffic profiling and engineering
- Peering and transit agreements
- Billing
- Security analysis

This is certainly not an exhaustive list of the different accounting scenarios and categories. Nevertheless, it covers the needs of the majority of enterprise and service provider customers. Each section describes the problem space, examples of specific results, and some implementation examples.

Network Monitoring

Let's start by discussing some generic examples that are at the edge between accounting and performance monitoring. The fuzzy area of "network monitoring" fits in here. The term "network monitoring" is widely interpreted: one person might relate it to device utilization only, and someone else might think of end-to-end monitoring. In fact, network monitoring is a vague expression that includes multiple functions. Network monitoring applications enable a system administrator to monitor a network for the purposes of security, billing, and analysis (both live and offline). We propose to use the term "network monitoring" for any application that does not fit into the other categories.

Table 1-2 illustrates device utilization. Assume that we have a network with three service classes deployed. Class 0 delivers real-time traffic, such as voice over IP, and class 1 carries business-critical traffic, such as e-mail and financial transactions. Class 2 covers everything else; this is the "best-effort" traffic class. Table 1-2 illustrates the total amount of traffic collected per class, including the number of packets and number of bytes. This report provides relevant information to a network planner. The technology applied in this example is an SNMP data collection of the CISCO-CLASS-BASED-QOS-MIB (see Chapter 4, "SNMP and MIBs"), which describes all the CoS counters.

Table 1-2   *Example of a Daily Report with Three Servicee Classes*

	Class 0		Class 1		Class 2	
Time (Hour)	Packets	Bytes	Packets	Bytes	Packets	Bytes
0	38	2735	1300	59800	3	1002
1	55	3676	400	44700	61	9791
2	41	36661	400	16800	4	240
3	13	1660	200	8400	4	424
4	16	14456	400	44700	4	420
5	19	2721	400	44400	1	48
6	21	24725	600	35600	516	20648
7	19	3064	700	412200	15	677
8	5	925	1200	176000	1	48
9	4	457	1300	104100	1242	1489205
10	5	3004	1900	1091900	1	48
11	4	451	400	39800	545	22641
12	4	456	800	54200	1017	1089699
13	5	510	500	41600	36	3240
14	4	455	400	99300	15	3287
15	5	511	800	36800	685	27578
16	4	454	100	4000	3	144
17	4	457	500	309500	2	322
18	4	455	400	34100	4	192
19	5	3095	1300	104100	4	424
20	4	398	100	15200	4	424
21	5	1126	800	54200	12	936
22	7	782	1300	104100	4	835
23	9	7701	600	35600	1	235

Another scenario of network monitoring is the use of accounting usage resource records for performance monitoring. The accounting collection process at the device level gathers usage records of network resources. These records consist of information such as interface utilization, traffic details per application and user (for example, percentage of web traffic), real-time traffic, and network management traffic. They may include details such as the originator and recipient of a communication. Granularity differs according to the requirements. A service provider might collect individual user details for premium customers, whereas an enterprise might be interested in only a summary per department. This section's focus is on usage resource records, not on overall device details, such as CPU utilization and available memory.

A network monitoring solution can provide the following details for performance monitoring:

- Device performance monitoring:
  - Interface and subinterface utilization
  - Per class of service utilization
  - Traffic per application
- Network performance monitoring:
  - Communication patterns in the network
  - Path utilization between devices in the network
- Service performance monitoring:
  - Traffic per server
  - Traffic per service
  - Traffic per application

Applied technologies for performance monitoring include SNMP MIBs, RMON, Cisco IP SLA, and Cisco NetFlow services.

User Monitoring and Profiling

The trend of running mission-critical applications on the network is evident. Voice over IP (VoIP), virtual private networking (VPN), and videoconferencing are increasingly being run over the network. At the same time, people use (abuse?) the network to download movies, listen to music online, perform excessive surfing, and so on.

This information can be used to

- Monitor and profile users.
- Track network usage per user.
- Document usage trends by user, group, and department.
- Identify opportunities to sell additional value-added services to targeted customers.
- Build a traffic matrix per subdivision, group, or even user. A traffic matrix illustrates the patterns between the origin and destination of traffic in the network.

Accounting records can help answer the following questions:

- Which applications generate the most traffic of which type?
- Which users use these applications?
- What percentage of traffic do they represent?
- How many active users are on the network at any given time?
- How long do users stay on the network?
- Where do they come from?
- Where do they go?
- Do the users accept the policies on network usage?
- When will upgrades affect the fewest users?

There are also legal requirements related to monitoring users and collecting accounting records. For example, you could draw conclusions about an individual's performance on the job. In some countries, it is illegal to collect specific performance data about employees. One solution could be to collect no details about individuals. Although this is ideal from a legal perspective, it becomes a nightmare during a security attack. Consider a scenario in which a PC of an individual user has been infected by a virus and starts attacking the network, and the user is unaware of this. It would be impossible to identify this PC without collecting accounting records per user, so you need to collect this level of detail. The same applies to the victims of the attack: They will certainly complain about the bad network service, but the operator cannot help them without useful data sets. From a data analysis perspective, we need to store performance baseline information and apply statistical operations such as "deviation from normal" to spot abnormalities.

A compromise could be to gather all details initially and separate the storage mechanisms afterwards. You could keep all details for security analysis for a day (minimum) or a week (maximum) and aggregate the records at the department level for performance or billing purposes. This approach should be okay from a legal perspective if you ensure that there is no public access to the security collection.

NOTE   Check your country's legal requirements before applying per-user accounting techniques.

Applied technologies for user monitoring and profiling include RMON; Authentication, Authorization, and Accounting (AAA); and Cisco NetFlow services.

Application Monitoring and Profiling

With the increase in emerging technologies such as VoIP/IP telephony, video, data warehousing, sales force automation, customer relationship management, call centers, procurement, and human resources management, network management systems are required that allow you to identify traffic per application. Several years ago, this was a relatively easy task, because there were several different transmission protocols: TCP for UNIX communication, IPX for Novell file server sharing, SNA for mainframe sessions, and so on. The consolidation toward IP eliminated several of these protocols but introduced a new challenge for the network operator: how to distinguish between various applications if they all use IP. Collecting different interface counters was not good enough any more. From a monitoring point, it got worse. These days most server applications have a Web graphical user interface (GUI), and most traffic on the network is based on HTTP. In this case, traffic classification for deploying different service classes requires deep packet inspection, which some accounting techniques offer. Because of these changes, we need a new methodology to collect application-specific details, and accounting is the chosen technology. An example is Cisco Network-Based Application Recognition (NBAR), which is described in Chapter 10, "NBAR."

The collected accounting information can help you do the following:

- Monitor and profile applications:
  - In the entire network
  - Over specific expense links
- Monitor application usage per group or individual user
- Deploy QoS and assign applications to different classes of service
- Assemble a traffic matrix based on application usage

A collection of application-specific details is also very useful for network baselining. Running an audit for the first time sometimes leads to surprises, because more applications are active on the network than the administrator expected. Application monitoring is also a prerequisite for QoS deployment in the network. To classify applications in different classes, their specific requirements should be studied in advance, as well as the communication patterns and a traffic matrix per application. Real-time applications such as voice and video require tight SLA parameters, whereas e-mail and backup traffic would accept best-effort support without a serious impact.

The next question to address is how to identify a specific application on the network.

In most environments, applications fall into the following distinct categories:

- Applications that can be identified by TCP or UDP port number. These are either "well-known" (0 through 1023) or registered port numbers (1024 through 49151). They are assigned by the Internet Assigned Numbers Authority (IANA).

- Applications that use dynamic and/or private application port numbers (49152 through 65535), which are negotiated before connection establishment and sometimes are changed dynamically during the session.

- Applications that are identified via the type of service (ToS) bit. Examples such as voice and videoconferencing (IPVC) can be identified via the TOS value.

- Subport classification of the following:

  — HTTP: URLs, MIME (Multipurpose Internet Mail Extension) types or hostnames

  — Citrix applications: traffic based on published application name

- Classification based on the combination of packet inspection and multiple application-specific attributes. RTP Payload Classification is based on this algorithm, in which the packet is classified as RTP based on multiple attributes in the RTP header.

In some of these cases, deeper packet inspection is needed. This can be performed by Cisco NBAR, for example.

Figure 1-7 displays traffic details per application, aggregated over time.

Figure 1-7 *Characterizing Traffic by Application*

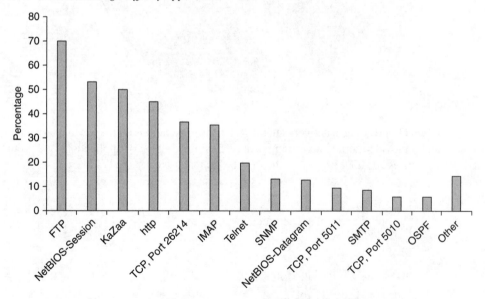

An alternative report would identify the various protocols on the network—for example, IPv4 traffic compared to IPv6 traffic or TCP versus UDP traffic. Figure 1-8 shows a protocol distribution.

Figure 1-8 *IP Protocol Distribution*

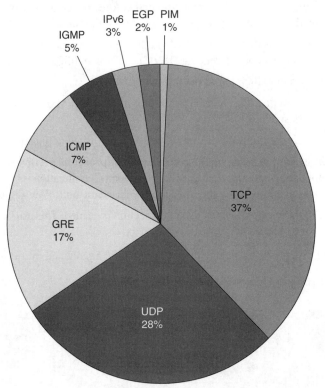

Cisco IT performed a network audit to track the applications on the Cisco internal network, and it provided some interesting results. The following list of applications and protocols comprises about 80 percent of the total traffic that traverses the WAN:

- HTTP
- E-mail
- IP telephony
- IP video
- Server and PC backups
- Video on demand (VoD)

- Multicast
- SNMP
- Antivirus updates
- Peer-to-peer traffic

Techniques to obtain the classification per application are RMON2, Cisco NetFlow, and Cisco NBAR. All three classify the observed traffic per application type. Chapter 5, "RMON," explains RMON; Chapter 7, "NetFlow," provides NetFlow details; and Chapter 10 covers NBAR.

A more advanced report could combine application-specific details and CoS information. A network planner can use such a report to isolate problems in a QoS-enabled environment (such as to detect when a certain class is almost fully utilized but the bandwidth cannot be increased). In this case, one or multiple applications could be moved to another class. For example, e-mail traffic could be reclassified from class 1 to class 2.

The next report, shown in Table 1-3, is based on Table 1-2, but it extends the level of detail by including some application-specific parts. For class 0, we are interested in the percentage of VoIP and non-VoIP traffic; in class 1 we distinguish between e-mail and SAP traffic (assuming that only these two applications get assigned to class 1). For the best-effort traffic in class 2 we distinguish between web traffic (HTTP), peer-to-peer-traffic, and the rest. This report cannot be compiled by retrieving SNMP data from the CISCO-CLASS-BASED-QOS-MIB, because it collects only counters per traffic class, not counters per application within a class. Hence, we leverage either NetFlow or RMON (*Remote Monitoring MIB Extensions for Differentiated Services*, RFC 3287) to gather the extra level of per-application details.

Best practice suggests monitoring the network before implementing new applications. Taking a proactive approach means that you analyze the network in advance to identify how it deals with new applications and whether it can handle the additional traffic appropriately. A good example is the IP telephony (IPT) deployment. You can run jitter probe operations with Cisco IP SLA, identify where the network needs modifications or upgrades, and start the IPT deployment after all tests indicate that the network is running well. After the deployment, accounting records deliver ongoing details about the newly deployed service. These can be used for general monitoring of the service as well as troubleshooting and SLA examination.

Table 1-3   *Example of Daily Report (Extended Version)*

	Class 0				Class 1				Class 2				
	Load		Application (Bytes)		Load		Application (Bytes)		Load		Application (Bytes)		
Time (Hour)	Packets	Bytes	Voice	Other	Packets	Bytes	E-mail	SAP	Packets	Bytes	HTTP	Peer-to-Peer	Other
0	38	2735	264	2471	1300	59800	38870	20930	13	1002	752	100	150
1	55	3676	128	3548	400	44700	29055	15645	61	9791	8812	979	0
2	41	56661	780	55881	400	16800	10920	5880	4	240	216	24	0
3	13	1660	328	1332	200	8400	5460	2940	4	424	382	42	0
4	16	14456	128	14328	400	44700	29055	15645	4	420	378	42	0
5	19	2721	1164	1557	400	44400	28860	15540	10	480	48	48	384
6	21	24725	9856	14869	600	35600	23140	12460	516	20648	18583	2065	0
7	19	3064	2048	1016	700	412200	267930	144270	15	677	609	68	0
8	5	925	512	413	1200	176000	114400	61600	12	960	48	96	816
9	4	457	256	201	1300	104100	67665	36435	1242	1489205	1340285	148921	0
10	5	3004	1684	1320	1900	1091900	709735	382165	3	256	230	26	0
11	4	451	96	355	400	39800	25870	13930	545	22641	20377	2264	0
12	4	456	64	392	800	54200	35230	18970	1017	1089699	980729	108970	0
13	5	510	128	382	500	41600	27040	14560	36	3240	2916	324	0
14	4	455	416	39	400	99300	64545	34755	15	3287	2958	329	0
15	5	511	496	15	800	36800	23920	12880	685	27578	24820	2758	0
16	4	454	128	326	100	4000	2600	1400	3	144	130	14	0
17	4	457	256	201	500	309500	201175	108325	2	322	290	32	0
18	4	455	196	259	400	34100	22165	11935	4	192	173	19	0
19	5	3095	2048	1047	1300	104100	67665	36435	4	424	382	42	0
20	4	398	286	112	100	15200	9880	5320	4	424	382	42	0
21	5	1126	956	170	800	54200	35230	18970	12	936	842	94	0
22	7	782	612	170	1300	104100	67665	36435	4	835	752	84	0
23	9	7701	2096	5605	600	35600	23140	12460	2	235	212	24	0

Capacity Planning

Internet traffic increases on a daily basis. Different studies produce different estimates of how long it takes traffic to double. This helps us predict that today's network designs will not be able to carry the traffic five years from now. Broadband adoption is one major driver, as well as the Internet's almost ubiquitous availability. Recently, Cisco internal IT department concluded that bandwidth consumption is doubling every 18 months.

This requires foresight and accurate planning of the network and future extensions. Enterprises and service providers should carefully plan how to extend the network in an economical way.

A service provider might consider the following:

- Which point of presence (PoP) generates the most revenue?
- Which access points are not profitable and should be consolidated?
- Should there be spare capacity for premium users?
- In which segment is the traffic decreasing? Did we lose customers to the competition? What might be the reason?

An enterprise IT department might consider the following:

- Which departments are growing the fastest? Which links will require an upgrade soon?
- For which department is network connectivity business-critical and therefore should have a high-availability design?

These questions cannot be answered without an accurate traffic analysis; it requires a network baseline and continuously collected trend reports. Service providers and professional IT departments should go one step further and offer service monitoring to their customers. This approach can identify potential bottlenecks in advance. It also lets the provider proactively notify customers and offer more bandwidth, different QoS, more high availability, and so on.

Capacity planning can be considered from the link point of view or from the network-wide point of view. Each view requires a completely different set of collection parameters and mechanisms.

Link Capacity Planning

For link capacity planning, the interface counters stored in the MIB are polled via SNMP, and the link utilization can be deduced. This simple rule of thumb is sometimes applied to capacity planning. If the average link utilization during business hours is above 50 percent, it is time to upgrade the link! The link utilization is calculated with the MIB variables from the interfaces group MIB (RFC 2863).

Apply the following equation to calculate utilization:

$$\text{input utilization} = [(\Delta(\text{ifInOctets})) * 8 * 100] / [(\text{number of seconds in } \Delta) * \text{ifSpeed}]$$
$$\text{output utilization} = [\Delta(\text{ifOutOctets})) * 8 * 100] / [(\text{number of seconds in } \Delta) * \text{ifSpeed}]$$

NOTE   On Cisco routers, the ifSpeed value is set by the **bandwidth** interface command. This bandwidth is a user-configurable value that can be set to any value for routing protocol metric purposes. You should set the bandwidth correctly and check the content of the BW (bandwidth) value in Kbps with the **show interface** command before doing any interface utilization calculations.

Some alarms, such as a trap or a syslog message, may be sent to the fault management application to detect a threshold violation. When we use accounting information for fault management, we enter the world of performance management, whose applications are described later in this chapter.

Network-Wide Capacity Planning

Link capacity planning might be enough in most cases when a network administrator knows about a bottleneck in the network. After a link's bandwidth is upgraded, the network administrator should identify the next bottleneck—this is a continuous process! In addition, most networks are designed with economical justifications, which means that very little overprovisioning is done. The term "network over-subscription" describes an abundance of bandwidth in the network, so that under normal circumstances, performance limitations are not caused by a lack of link capacity. Put another way, the only restriction that one application sees when communicating with another application is in the network's inherent physical limitations. In contrast, the term "network overprovisioning" describes a network design with more traffic than bandwidth. This means that, even under normal circumstances, not enough bandwidth is provided for all users to use the network to perform their tasks at the same time, using their maximum allocated bandwidth. The network over-subscription concept is obviously a more cost-effective approach than network overprovisioning, because it assumes that not all users will use their fully dedicated bandwidth at the same time. However, capacity planning is more complex in this case. The computation of what constitutes adequate provisioning, without gross overprovisioning, depends on accurate core capacity planning along with realistic assumptions about what group of users will use what applications and services at key time periods. Another approach is to do networkwide capacity planning by collecting the "core traffic matrix." The core traffic matrix is a table that provides the traffic volumes between the origin and destination in a network. To collect this for all the network's entry points, we need usage information (in number of bytes and/

or number of packets per unit of time) per exit point in the core network. Figure 1-9 shows the required bandwidth from Rome to all the other PoPs; Table 1-4 shows the results.

Figure 1-9   *Core Traffic Matrix Topology*

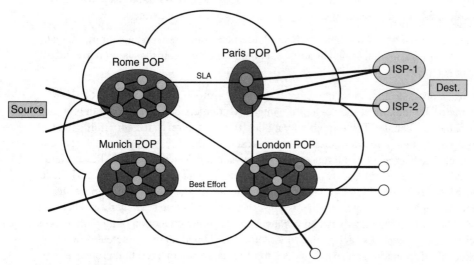

Table 1-4   *Core Traffic Matrix Results*

	Rome Exit Point	Paris Exit Point	London Exit Point	Munich Exit Point
Rome Entry Point	NA[*]	... Mbps	... Mbps	... Mbps
Paris Entry Point	... Mbps	NA[*]	... Mbps	... Mbps
London Exit Point	... Mbps	... Mbps	NA[*]	... Mbps
Munich Exit Point	... Mbps	... Mbps	... Mbps	NA[*]

[*]Not applicable. Traffic entering a specific entry point and leaving the same entry is not null. Each PoP contains more than a single interface and more than a single router, so the traffic local to the PoP is a reality. Nevertheless, this traffic is not taken into account for the capacity planning of the links inside the network.

The capacity planning can be done by mapping the core traffic matrix to the topology information. Because we know that the traffic from Rome to Paris usually takes the direct link(s) between Rome and Paris, the link dimensioning can be deduced easily in the case of simple design. Nevertheless, mapping the core traffic matrix to the routing information, typically the routing protocol's link state database, eases the process. A lookup in the routing table/link state database returns the path taken by the traffic from Rome to Paris. In addition, capacity planning can provide future projections, such as "What happens if the overall traffic grows 5 percent per month over the next year?" or "What happens if I expect the number of customers in Rome to double in the next six months?"

Which accounting mechanisms will help us create the core traffic matrix? First, we can try to deduce the core traffic matrix with the SNMP interface counters, but we see immediately that we have to solve an N^2-level problem with an N-level solution, where N is the number of entry points in the network. Consequently, this approach works in only a particularly well-structured and simple network design. Still, it is not very accurate.

A different approach is to combine the SNMP interface counters with another mechanism, such as the gravity model, which assumes that the traffic between sites is proportional to traffic at each site.

Some researchers even propose changing the routing protocol metrics to infer the core traffic matrix by looking at the delta of the interface counters before and after the routing protocol metrics change. The tomography model (the estimation of the core traffic matrix) is getting more and more attention from the research community nowadays, at events like the Internet Measurement Conference (http://www.acm.org/sigcomm/imc/), Passive and Active Measurement (http://www.pam2006.org/), and the INTIMATE workshops (Internet Traffic Matrices Estimation, http://adonis.lip6.fr/intimate2006/). In addition, more and more tomography white papers are being published on the Internet. Many researchers are trying to find a good balance between producing an accurate collection of all data records (which implies drawbacks such as network element CPU and memory increases, amount of collected information, and so on) and a simpler accounting method that produces an approximate traffic matrix. This book concentrates on a set of accounting features in Cisco routers and switches, including Cisco NetFlow services and BGP Policy Accounting (see Chapter 8, "BGP Policy Accounting"). Note that the core traffic matrix is interesting not only for capacity planning, but also for traffic engineering, as discussed in the next section.

Traffic Profiling and Engineering

A good analogy for understanding traffic engineering is examining vehicle traffic patterns. There are several highways in the area where I live, so I have several options to get to the airport or office. Based on the day of the week and time of day, I choose a different road to get to my destination. On a typical rainy Monday morning, I should avoid the freeway, because it is not free at all but jammed, so I take inner-city roads. The freeway on Tuesday night is usually perfectly suited for high speed. However, I might not want to pay tolls at a certain bridge or tunnel, so I choose an alternate route. In addition, I always check the radio for traffic announcements to avoid accidents, serious road construction, and so on. I could even go one step further and check the Internet for road traffic statistics before starting my journey. Most of us consider at least some of these options when driving. This analogy applies to network architects, modeling data traffic on the network for traffic engineering. Continuing the analogy, accounting data would be the traffic information, and an exceeded link utilization threshold would be the equivalent of a traffic report on the radio about a traffic jam.

The IETF Internet Traffic Engineering Working Group (TEWG) provides a very technical definition of traffic engineering:

"Internet Traffic Engineering is defined as that aspect of Internet network engineering concerned with the performance optimization of traffic handling in operational networks, with the main focus of the optimization being minimizing over-utilization of capacity when other capacity is available in the network. Traffic Engineering entails that aspect of network engineering, which is concerned with the design, provisioning, and tuning of operational Internet networks. It applies business goals, technology and scientific principles to the measurement, modeling, characterization, and control of Internet traffic, and the application of such knowledge and techniques to achieve specific service and performance objectives, including the reliable and expeditious movement of traffic through the network, the efficient utilization of network resources, and the planning of network capacity."

As soon as we have the core traffic matrix, we might start some network simulation, such as capacity planning. We want to go one step further and associate the notion of simulations (traffic profiling, service, network failure) with the core traffic matrix. If we assume that the network has been designed so that SLAs are respected under normal traffic conditions, what is important for a service provider? The service provider would like to know the consequences on the SLA (which is the direct impact for the customers) in cases of extra load in the network, a link failure, or a router reload—in other words, under abnormal conditions. This is called simulating what-if scenarios.

Networks have well-defined boundaries, set by the network administrator. From a traffic matrix perspective, it is relevant to know how much traffic stays within the boundaries of the core network and how much traffic is crossing them ("on-net" versus "off-net" traffic). More details might be of interest, such as identifying traffic from various sites or traffic destined for certain hosts or ingress and egress traffic per department. Traffic profiling is a prerequisite for network planning, device and link dimensioning, trend analysis, building specific business models, and so on. Traffic engineering has the objective of optimizing network resource utilization and traffic performance.

The core traffic matrix per CoS can be analyzed by an engineering tool. In this example, three classes of service are defined, each representing a specific service:

- CoS 1, VoIP traffic
- CoS 2, Business-critical traffic
- CoS 3, Best-effort traffic

By simulating the failure conditions just described, the service provider can answer questions such as the following: If this particular link fails, all traffic will be rerouted via a different route in the network, but will the VOIP traffic respect the SLA agreed to by the customers? Will it be the same for the business-critical traffic where SLAs are slightly lower? In addition, will the best-effort traffic still be able to go through the network, even though no SLA is assigned to it?

After answering those questions, we can accomplish capacity planning per class of service:

- "What happens if video traffic grows constantly by 5 percent per month over the next year?"
- "If voice traffic increases by 10 percent per year, where will the bottleneck be?"
- "Should I offer new services? Where should I start offering them?"

If the traffic is modeled correctly, simulation applications can benefit the network planner by analyzing network performance under different conditions.

The last step, after traffic measurement, classification, and simulation, is to assign traffic to interfaces and network links. Based on the simulations applied in the previous step, we can assign specific traffic to network links. Most network designs consist of redundant connections between sites and meshed links between the different locations to avoid single points of failure. We can leverage this additional connectivity to distinguish between different types of applications:

- Business-critical traffic is assigned to premium connections.
- Less-critical application data can be sent via the backup or cheaper links.
- Best-effort traffic gets transmitted on the links' remaining bandwidth.

In case of an outage, we might consider blocking the less-critical applications and reserve the bandwidth for the relevant applications. Figure 1-10 illustrates this design. Traffic from Rome to Paris is distinguished in a business-critical part, which is transmitted via the direct link, with SLAs in place. The best-effort fraction of the traffic is sent via Munich and London, where more bandwidth is available.

Figure 1-10 *Traffic Engineering and Capacity Planning*

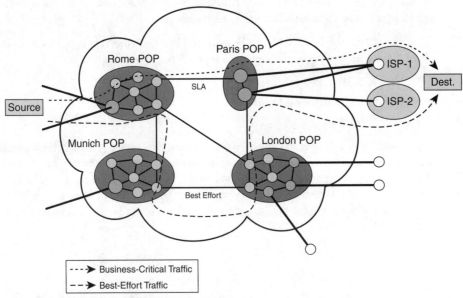

Several traffic engineering approaches exist:

- Increasing the links' bandwidth
- Changing the Interior Gateway Protocol (IGP) metrics
- Changing the Border Gateway Protocol (BGP) metrics
- Inserting traffic engineering tunnels for an MPLS core
- Introducing high-availability software features or hardware components

Traffic engineering is essential for service provider backbones. Such backbones offer high transmission capacity and require resilience so that they can withstand link or node failures. WAN connections are an expensive item in an Internet service provider's (ISP) budget. Traffic engineering enables the ISP to route network traffic so that it can offer the best service quality to its users in terms of throughput and delay. Traffic engineering accounts for link bandwidth and traffic flow size when determining explicit routes across the backbone.

For specific details about MPLS traffic engineering, refer to the informational RFC 2702, *Requirements for Traffic Engineering over MPLS*.

We will limit this book to collecting the core traffic matrix; we will not delve into the details of traffic engineering solutions.

Peering and Transit Agreements

Even the largest ISPs own only a fraction of the Internet routes and therefore need to cooperate with other ISPs. To ensure that all destinations of the Internet can be reached, ISPs enter into peering agreements with other ISPs (with other Autonomous Systems [AS] that can be reached using the Border Gateway Protocol [BGP]). BGP is one of the core routing protocols in the Internet. It works by maintaining a table of IP networks or prefixes that designate network reachability between autonomous systems. An AS is a collection of IP networks under control of a single entity—typically an ISP or a very large organization with redundant connections to the rest of the Internet.

The act of peering can be done as follows:

- **Private peering**—This is a relationship in which two ISPs equally provide access to each other's networks without charging. Usually the interconnection is constrained to the exchange of traffic between each other's customers or related companies. No traffic between other third-party networks is allowed to transit the interconnection.

- **Peering via an Internet Exchange Point (IXP)**—An IXP is a physical network infrastructure independent of any single provider that allows different ISPs to exchange Internet traffic between their AS by means of mutual peering agreements. IXPs are typically used by ISPs to reduce dependency on their respective upstream providers. Furthermore, they increase efficiency and fault tolerance.

- **Transit (or customer-provider relationship)**—This relates to traffic exchange between an ISP and another carrier. In contrast to private peering traffic, ISPs pay for the transit traffic to be successfully routed to its destination.

Tier 1 ISPs operate global backbone transit networks and together hold all the world's Internet routes. They tend to have private peering without charging each other to give each other access to all Internet routes. Tier 2 ISPs operate national wholesale transit networks and hence buy connectivity (upstream transit) to the worldwide Internet routes from one or more tier 1 ISPs. Thus, their IP network(s) becomes a subset of those tier 1 IP networks. This is described as a customer-provider relationship. Tier 2 ISPs also peer with each other to minimize the amount of traffic exchanged with tier 1 ISPs from whom they buy upstream transit. Tier 3 ISPs, such as local access ISPs, acquire upstream transit from tier 2 ISPs. The hierarchy model becomes increasingly vague at the tier 3 level, because a tier 3 ISP may buy upstream transit from both a tier 1 ISP and a tier 2 ISP, and may peer with tier 2 and tier 3 ISPs and occasionally with a tier 1 ISP.

Peering as a customer-provider relationship is most common at the bottom tiers of the Internet business. Note that this not a true peering relationship; rather, the customer pays for transit via his or her upstream ISP. Service providers with smaller traffic tend to converge at an IXP, which provides them with a commercially neutral venue for peering.

Figure 1-11 illustrates transit and peering agreements. To provide Internet access to all its customers, the tier 2 ISP-1 signs a transit agreement with the tier 2 ISP-B. Because ISP-B covers only a part of the whole Internet, it signs private peering agreements with other tier 1 ISPs—in this example, ISP-A and ISP-C. Similar to ISP-1, ISP-2 signs a transit agreement, but with the tier 1 ISP-A. According to the private peering agreement between ISP-A and ISP-B, ISP-B will transport all traffic from ISP-2 to ISP-1 free of charge, and ISP-A does the same for traffic from ISP-1 to ISP-2. Note that the private peering agreement between ISP-A and ISP-B does not include any traffic sent via ISP-C toward ISP-2 or ISP-1 by default, but the contract can be extended to incorporate this.

From a technical perspective, transit and peering agreements are controlled by exchanging routing table entries. A transit agreement covers the exchange of all routing table entries, and a private peering agreement includes only the routing table entries of related customers.

From an accounting perspective, an ISP is usually not interested in accounting for end systems outside of its administrative domain. The primary concern is accounting the level of traffic received from and destined for other adjacent (directly connected) administrative domains. In Figure 1-11, ISP-B sends an invoice to ISP-1 for the usage of its network. If ISP-1 wants to allocate the charges applied by ISP-B to end users or subsystems in its domain, it is the responsibility of ISP-1 to collect accounting records with more granularities. These can be used to charge individual users later. Because each provider cares about its direct neighbors, only the provider that charges the end customer needs to collect granular records per user. This accounting scheme is called recursive accounting. It can be applied within an administrative domain if this domain consists of several subdomains.

Figure 1-11 *Transit and Peering Agreements*

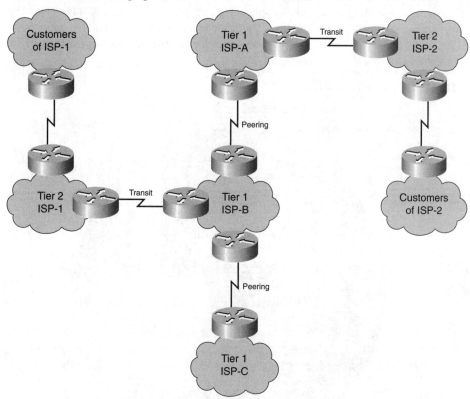

The private peering agreement should be fair and equitable. Private peering works best when two service providers pass a roughly equal amount of traffic between them, making the deal cost-efficient for both sides. So, even if no charging is involved, two ISPs bound by a private peering agreement would like to compare the volume of traffic sent versus the volume of traffic received. When optimizing peering exchange points with other autonomous systems, there is a need to determine where traffic is coming from, to make the appropriate routing policy changes, to plan, and in some cases to charge a service provider for excess traffic routed.

Transit traffic is related to a fee, so one of the downstream provider's primary tasks is to check the bill sent by the upstream provider. On the other hand, ISPs usually place a higher priority on revenue-generating traffic. Hence, the upstream ISPs want to monitor the traffic patterns to ensure that the transit traffic is indeed getting preferential quality of service without severely affecting the peering traffic.

From an ISP's accounting perspective, there is always a need to classify the traffic per BGP AS, as shown in Figure 1-12. This figure shows an ISP's BGP neighbors and the percentage of traffic exchanged. Determining additional peering partners is an important task. Existing service provider peering relationships may not provide the required Internet coverage. By understanding the destination and source demands of the traffic and the corresponding volume, you can make decisions about possible peering relationships with other service providers.

Figure 1-12 *Monitoring Peering Agreements*

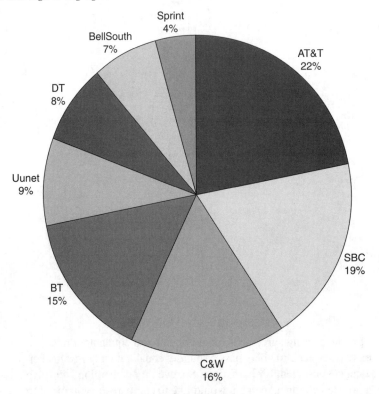

By analyzing the traffic matrix, an ISP might conclude that it is not peering with the right neighbor.

The sections "Capacity Planning" and "Traffic Profiling and Engineering" covered the advantages of the core traffic matrix. Let us make a further distinction between the *internal* core traffic matrix and the *external* core traffic matrix. The internal matrix was defined previously. It's a table providing the traffic volumes between origin and destination in a network, where origin and destination are the network's entry and exit points (typically a router in the PoP). The external core traffic matrix also offers the traffic volumes between origin and destination in a network, but in this case the origin and destination are not only the network's entry points and exit points to analyze, but also the source BGP AS and destination AS. On top of the internal traffic matrix, the external traffic matrix returns information about where the traffic comes from before entering the ISP network and where it goes after exiting.

What are the advantages of analyzing the external core traffic matrix?

First, an ISP might decide whether it is peering with the right neighbor AS. In Figure 1-13, the ISP-1 external core traffic matrix might identify that most of the traffic sent to ISP-B actually is determined at ISP-A, so ISP-1 can potentially negotiate a transit peering agreement directly with ISP-A. In-depth analysis might prove that a big percentage of the traffic sent to ISP-A is targeted for ISP-2, so ISP-1 could consider a private peering agreement with ISP-2. More specifically, statements such as "ISP-1 is receiving an equivalent amount of traffic from ISP-2" can quickly be proven or disproven by analyzing the external core traffic matrix.

Figure 1-13 *External Core Traffic Matrix: Topology*

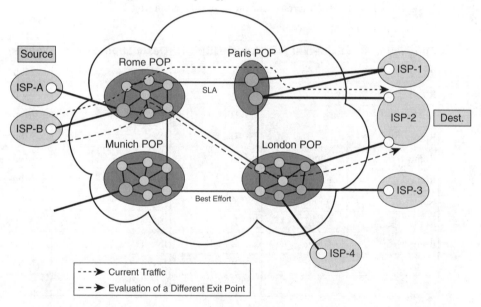

Second, the question "Is my network being used for transit or peering traffic?" will be resolved by the external core traffic matrix, because we can easily conclude whether the traffic is on-net or off-net. Normally, a priority is placed on keeping traffic within the network (on-net) to save money versus being sent to another service provider for a fee (off-net).

Third, when ISPs want to change either the peering agreements or the exit point for specific Internet routes, they first think about the implications of such changes on their network. Questions arise, such as "What about capacity planning? Will some links be overloaded as a consequence of the changes?", "What about customers' SLAs? Will they still be respected?", and "What about the traffic engineering setup? Should it be changed?" The combined inputs from the external core traffic matrix, the topology, and routing protocol information, along with an appropriate capacity planning and traffic-engineering application, offer valuable details in these situations.

Based on Figure 1-13, the external core traffic matrix for Rome is described in Table 1-5. Consider a practical example: The link between Rome and Paris is heavily loaded, so the ISP is evaluating the possibility of sending the traffic via London, because the link between Rome and London has available bandwidth. One way would be to forward all the traffic from Rome to ISP-2 via London, because the London PoP also has a direct link to ISP-2. Based on the external core traffic matrix, this traffic profile is identified. Next, we want to know the consequences of the core capacity planning. Again, the external core traffic matrix offers the right input for a traffic engineering tool, because it contains both the ISP exit point and the destination ISP. The tool will be able to quantify the load decrease for the Rome-Paris link and the increase for the Rome-London link.

Table 1-5   *External Core Traffic Matrix Results*

Entry Point	Exit Point	Source ISP	Destination ISP	Volume
Rome	Paris	ISP-A	ISP-1	… Mbps
Rome	Paris	ISP-A	ISP-2	… Mbps
Rome	Paris	ISP-B	ISP-1	… Mbps
Rome	Paris	ISP-B	ISP-2	… Mbps
Rome	London	ISP-A	ISP-2	… Mbps
Rome	London	ISP-A	ISP-3	… Mbps
Rome	London	ISP-A	ISP-4	… Mbps
Rome	London	ISP-B	ISP-2	… Mbps
Rome	London	ISP-B	ISP-3	… Mbps
Rome	London	ISP-B	ISP-4	… Mbps
…				

Finally, peering via an IXP entails a particular accounting requirement. An ISP connected to an IXP can exchange traffic with any other ISP that is connected to this IXP. An IXP infrastructure is usually based on switched Ethernet components (shared medium), where one switch port is dedicated per ISP. Because only a single physical connection to the IXP is required, this design solves the scalability problem of individual interconnections between all ISPs. However, an extra accounting requirement is to account the traffic per MAC address, because the MAC address identifies the entry point of the neighbor BGP AS.

Figure 1-14 displays two scenarios in which five ISPs interconnect. On the left side, for a full-mesh setup, each ISP needs four connections ($n - 1$). On the right side, only a single link to the IXP is necessary.

Figure 1-14 *One IXP Interconnecting Five ISPs*

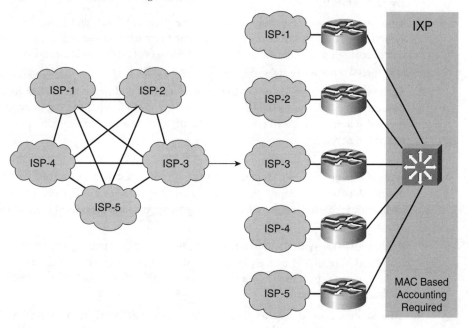

Which Cisco accounting features are useful for BGP peering agreement applications? Taking a NetFlow-based approach classifies and accounts traffic by source and destination BGP AS. On top of this, the BGP Policy Accounting feature supports regular expression manipulation on metrics involving the AS path, BGP community, and other attributes as additional classifications. For Layer 2 accounting per MAC address, the "IP accounting MAC-address" feature should be evaluated.

Billing

We've already mentioned the tight relationship between accounting and billing in the past, so we will now consider the differences between the two areas. Accounting describes the process of measuring and collecting network usage parameters from network devices or application servers, and billing is an application that makes use of these well-formatted usage records. A raw data collection cannot be sent to the user as an invoice. Because it contains technical details such as IP addresses instead of usernames or servers, usage data records occur multiple times without a relationship to each other, and so on. Instead, raw data needs aggregation, mediation, and de-duplication to be applied first to transform data into useful information for the customers. We will illustrate this through an example. If a user establishes a connection to an application server (for example, a database) at the start of the business day and works on the same server until the end of the business day, and if we collect these records at a device level, it would result in a collection of usage data records:

- Multiple records representing traffic from the client to the server, because no router or switch keeps statistics over several hours, due to memory resource limitations and the risk of losing records during an outage. Users expect a consolidated report, usually aggregated per hour of the day.

- Response traffic from the server to the client creates additional records, probably collected at a different network device or device interface. A user would expect a merged statement that still contains traffic per direction, but in a single statement instead of several.

- Device records contain IP addresses of the client and server; note that the client address especially might change over time. Users expect to be identified by names, not IP addresses, especially in a changing environment where IP addresses are assigned by a DHCP server. Hence, these raw records are processed to meet user needs.

- Records also consist of communication protocol and port details, but no user is interested in receiving a receipt that contains port 80 as resource usage element. Instead, users expect to see names of common applications, such as web traffic, VoIP traffic, and e-mail traffic.

- Time stamps at the device level can be the device's sysUpTime (an SNMP MIB variable that defines the time since the device booted), or the time since 1970 (Coordinated Universal Time [UTC], including the time zone), or the current date and time, as represented by the network time protocol (NTP). Users do not want the start and stop timer on the invoice displayed in a format such as "1079955900," but instead in a human-readable time-and-date format.

- Depending on the path the traffic traverses through the network, multiple records might be collected, containing the same user traffic information. De-duplication keeps the user from being charged twice for the same transmitted traffic.

An alternative to collecting usage records at the device is to collect usage records at the server level. If users need to authenticate at a server or using a service, before using applications, this authentication process could also collect billing information, such as

- Logon time
- Logoff time
- Number of transactions performed (for example, from a booking system)
- Number of database requests and responses
- CPU usage

In the preceding example, we only need to collect these usage records at the SAP server. The advantage of this approach is that no correlation of IP address and user needs to be performed. But the additional billing functionalities need to be implemented at each application server, which increases the overhead at the application level. A network consists of multiple applications and servers, so a server accounting function is required at every server in the network. This would be best implemented as a single sign-on solution, because users are usually very unhappy if they need to authenticate at every application individually. Figure 1-15 shows a scenario with server-based accounting.

Figure 1-15 *Per-Server Accounting*

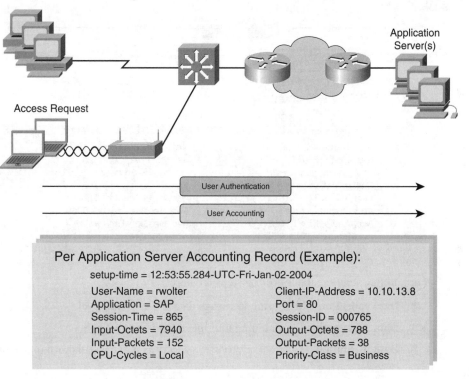

Per Application Server Accounting Record (Example):

setup-time = 12:53:55.284-UTC-Fri-Jan-02-2004

User-Name = rwolter	Client-IP-Address = 10.10.13.8
Application = SAP	Port = 80
Session-Time = 865	Session-ID = 000765
Input-Octets = 7940	Output-Octets = 788
Input-Packets = 152	Output-Packets = 38
CPU-Cycles = Local	Priority-Class = Business

Another method is to use a AAA server, where user authentication occurs once and total time and usage-based details are collected per user. However, the details collected with this approach are not as granular as the per-service accounting scenario just described, where service-specific accounting per server (for example, CPU, database requests, and so on) can be collected. A clear advantage of the AAA server is that all accounting records are centrally created and need not be collected from various servers or network devices. Figure 1-16 illustrates a Remote Authentication Dial-In User Service (RADIUS) accounting scenario.

Figure 1-16 *RADIUS Server Accounting*

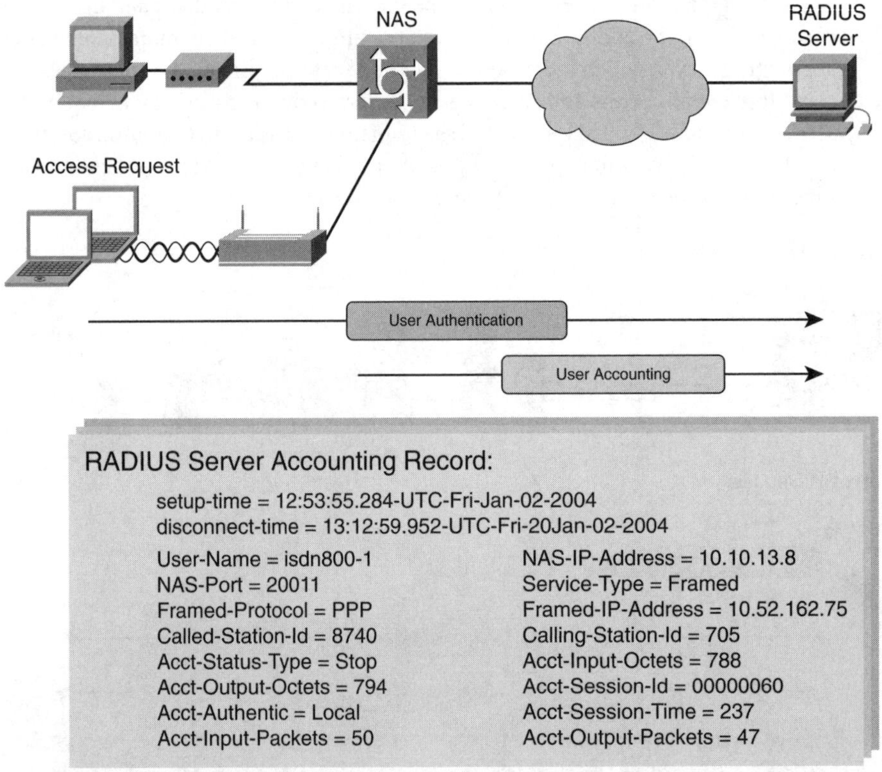
NAS
RADIUS
Server
Access Request
User Authentication
User Accounting
RADIUS Server Accounting Record:
setup-time = 12:53:55.284-UTC-Fri-Jan-02-2004
disconnect-time = 13:12:59.952-UTC-Fri-20Jan-02-2004
User-Name = isdn800-1
NAS-Port = 20011
Framed-Protocol = PPP
Called-Station-Id = 8740
Acct-Status-Type = Stop
Acct-Output-Octets = 794
Acct-Authentic = Local
Acct-Input-Packets = 50
NAS-IP-Address = 10.10.13.8
Service-Type = Framed
Framed-IP-Address = 10.52.162.75
Calling-Station-Id = 705
Acct-Input-Octets = 788
Acct-Session-Id = 00000060
Acct-Session-Time = 237
Acct-Output-Packets = 47

For a billing solution, the following steps are necessary:

- **Data collection**—Measuring the usage data at the device level.
- **Data aggregation**—Combining multiple records into a single one.
- **Data mediation**—Converting proprietary records into a well-known or standard format.
- **De-duplication**—Eliminating duplicate records.
- **Assigning usernames to IP addresses**—Performing a DNS and DHCP lookup and getting additional accounting records from AAA servers.
- **Calculating call duration**—Combining the data records from the devices with RADIUS session information and converting sysUpTime entries to time of day and date of month, related to the user's time zone.
- **Charging**—Assigning nonmonetary cost metrics to the accounting data based on call duration, transmitted data volume, traffic per class of service, and so on. Charging policies define tariffs and parameters to be applied.

- **Invoicing**—Translating charging information into monetary units and printing a final invoice for the customer. The form of invoicing is selected—whether it should be itemized or anonymized, electronically transmitted or sent by mail, or combine multiple users into a single overall bill (for example, for corporate customers). In addition, billing policies are applied, such as invoicing or charging a credit card.

Figure 1-17 shows the distinction between accounting and billing in the case of device-level accounting, such as Cisco NetFlow services.

Figure 1-17 *Network Device Accounting: Distinguishing Between Accounting and Billing*

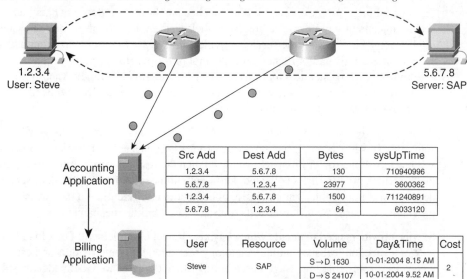

Src Add	Dest Add	Bytes	sysUpTime
1.2.3.4	5.6.7.8	130	710940996
5.6.7.8	1.2.3.4	23977	3600362
1.2.3.4	5.6.7.8	1500	711240891
5.6.7.8	1.2.3.4	64	6033120

User	Resource	Volume	Day&Time	Cost
Steve	SAP	S→D 1630	10-01-2004 8.15 AM	2
		D→S 24107	10-01-2004 9.52 AM	

In the current service provider market, usage-based billing in an IP network has a clear competitive advantage over a flat-rate billing model. Increasingly, service providers are creating revenue-generating services by offering flexible pricing models for differentiated value-added services and applications. Competitive pricing models can also be created with usage-based billing. Regardless of the enhanced services and their corresponding pricing model, billing records must be exact, and accuracy is mandatory. With the correct technologies, service providers can rapidly develop, price, and provision these new services. Because a flat-rate billing model is not always the provider's preferred choice, new services can be based on the following usage-based billing considerations:

- **Volume/bandwidth usage**—The more traffic that is sent, the greater the bill will be.

- **Distance-based**—If the customer traffic destination remains in the same city or region, sending the traffic can be cheaper than sending the traffic to a different country or continent. Depending on the service provider's network and design, customer traffic can be more expensive, depending on whether the traffic remains in the service provider's network (on-net) or whether it leaves it (off-net).

- **Application and/or per class of service**—Most customers will pay a higher price for the VoIP traffic *if* SLAs are linked to this specific traffic type. They would pay a medium price for the VPN traffic and a very cheap price for the best-effort traffic.

- **Time of day**—Traffic sent during the night is cheaper than traffic sent during working hours.

Complexity varies from flat-rate billing, where no accounting infrastructure is required, to volume-based billing per class of service. The next sections cover the different billing schemes in more detail.

Flat-rate billing is a very efficient billing mechanism, because it does not entail any accounting and billing infrastructure. Nevertheless, even the cost of the billing system implies some big gains for the service providers in the case of users who either use the service infrequently and/or do not generate a lot of traffic. However, this might not be the case for users who generate a lot of traffic. Hence, the providers might want to lower the access rate to attract more users who do not need sophisticated services, while having some sort of usage-based billing for users who do.

As an alternative, some providers collect SNMP interface counters for charge-back solutions. This is acceptable as long as a customer is connected by a dedicated interface or subinterface at the router or switch. But even then the result is very limited, because only the total amount of traffic is collected. Differentiation per application, class of service, or destination is impossible. The necessity of competitive differentiation has caused service providers to investigate different sorts of usage-based billing mechanisms.

Service providers need to decide which business model to implement. For a long time, the lack of an economical accounting technology prevented service providers and especially enterprises from deploying usage-based billing. Business cases were defined but resulted in enormous costs for infrastructure investments. Additionally, a complete end-to-end solution is often necessary. It is not enough to have only some of the network's elements being capable of tracking and exporting accounting information if you want to charge all customers for using their services.

Nowadays, Cisco features such as NetFlow services, BGP policy accounting, and destination-sensitive billing are adapted for the deployment of a usage-based billing system.

However, billing is not limited to service providers. In the past, enterprise IT expenditures were often pooled and distributed evenly between departments within an organization. Charges applied to those departments were usually based on head count or desktop equipment. As the environment is changing, these financial strategies become increasingly unacceptable. First, the amount of money spent on IT infrastructure by enterprises and service providers alike has steadily increased over the past decade, and those costs need to be recouped. Second, the degree of dependence on the network for any organization is increasing, but not equally across the various departments. Consider a simple example: an enterprise that would like to charge back the cost of its Internet link according the usage per department.

A suitable billing architecture enables a service provider or enterprise customer to do any of the following:

1 Allocate usage costs fairly between different organizations, departments, groups, and users

2 Show departments or enterprise customers how they are using the network

3 Strategically allocate network resources

4 Justify adding services and bandwidth

5 Offer new services to selected groups

Note that arguments 3, 4, and 5 are not the primary goal of a billing architecture; nevertheless, they can supply a service provider's Business Support System (BSS) with important information. Adding new services and bandwidth may not be applied to links of customers with best-effort services, even if the connections are highly utilized. For example, in a flat-rate environment, no additional revenue is related to more traffic. In contrast, premium customers might be offered additional bandwidth if they exceed the SLA limits, which gives the service provider a chance to propose upgrades proactively. Although this does not generate immediate revenue, it proposes a paradigm shift because service providers do not get anything extra for doing a good job but get penalized for violating the SLA. Even though a BSS takes this monetary information into account, accounting and performance management applications are unaware of it.

As soon as the decision for usage-based billing is made, several business models are possible, as discussed next.

Volume-Based Billing

In this case, you collect the transmitted raw bytes or packet volume per user, group, or department. This model is relatively easy to implement, especially when no application-specific data is required and only the total amount of traffic per group is relevant. Furthermore, a network design that connects one customer per interface or per subinterface can collect volume-based accounting information by polling the interface MIB counters. At first glance, this model sounds fair and intuitive, because bandwidth-intensive users or groups are charged more than others who generate less traffic. On the other hand, you could argue that bandwidth usage should be related to the time of day, because large transfers in the night use the network at a time when the majority of users are inactive. If QoS is deployed, you could also argue that, for instance, the few bytes of an IP phone call in the "gold" traffic class should be more expensive than a large file transfer, which is placed in the "best-effort" class.

For an enterprise customer, volume-based billing is an excellent alternative to a fixed assignment of IT costs, because the level of complexity is relatively low. In terms of destination, we only need to distinguish if the traffic stays within the perimeter (on-net) or if it is targeted at the Internet (off-net). In addition, departmental charge-back is applied. Figure 1-18 shows a typical enterprise scenario with various groups located on the central campus or distributed across wide-area links.

Figure 1-18 *Typical Enterprise Scenario*

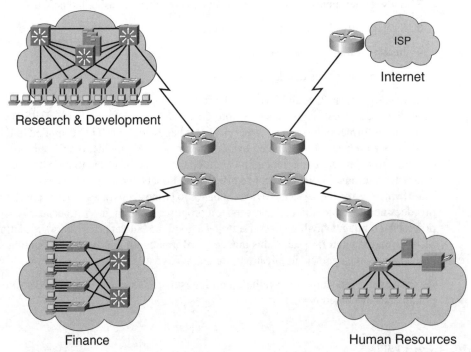

In summary, volume-based billing has the advantage of simplicity and, for service providers, the drawback of a lack of differentiation from the competition.

Destination-Sensitive Billing

This model takes into account the simple principle that the distance toward your traffic destination should classify your traffic according to one of a set of enumerated values (such as cheap, medium-priced, or expensive). Figure 1-19 illustrates this example. A customer in Germany might place a very cheap VoIP call to a destination in Germany. Accessing a web server in another country in Europe will cost more, and sending a huge video file to a friend in Sydney might prove to be very expensive.

Figure 1-19 *Case Study: Moving to Destination-Sensitive Billing*

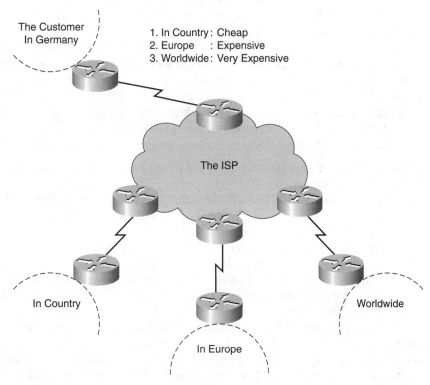

The drawbacks of this billing mechanism are twofold:

- The customer pays for only the traffic sent to the service provider. What would happen if the customer requested a very big file from a server in Sydney? The customer would pay for the very small file request, while the response contains a big file, which would be paid for by the server operator in Sydney! This model introduces a charge-back demand for an Application Service Provider (ASP)—in this case, the server operator in Sydney—to charge either individual users or the service provider to which the customer connects, which then adds this fee to the monthly invoice. This further complicates the billing mechanisms used.

- Destination-sensitive billing implies the collection of usage records on *all* ingress interfaces of the service provider's network. Like any ingress collection mechanism, the destination-sensitive billing feature needs to be enabled on *all* ingress interfaces in the network; otherwise, some traffic will not be accounted for! This is a challenge for ISPs, especially if multivendor equipment is used at the PoPs and not all access devices support the required features.

Destination and Source-Sensitive Billing

To circumvent the drawbacks of the destination-sensitive billing scheme, the destination and source-sensitive billing model takes into account the traffic's destination and source. Let's return to the example of the FTP request and FTP reply from a German customer to a server in Sydney. This customer would pay a high price for the traffic sent to and received from this server in Sydney, without introducing additional complexity, such as ASP charge-back. A major advantage of the destination and source-sensitive billing model is that it can be applied on a per-device and per-interface basis, because the usage records are captured in both directions. Remember that destination-sensitive billing, as described in the previous section, is applied at *all* interfaces in the network to avoid missing accounting records.

The combination of time and destination and source-sensitive billing is the classic Public Switched Telephone Network (PSTN) accounting model, which has been in place for more than 100 years. The political background of this model was to allow money to flow from developed countries to developing countries to subsidize the networking infrastructures of the developing countries. For billing in the Internet, this model mainly applies to VPN customers who have several sites around the globe connected to a single provider. It does not really apply to end customers for the simple reason that end customers have no indication where a server in the Internet is located, because network connectivity is transparent. However, a modified version of destination-sensitive billing already exists: on-net and off-net traffic. On-net is all traffic that the service provider can keep in its own network or in the network of peering partners. Off-net traffic requires peering agreements between ISPs. Some ISPs already offer on-net access free of charge—for instance, accessing the provider's Internet servers. Another example is free VoIP calls for all customers of the same service provider for all in-net VoIP traffic. Figure 1-20 and Table 1-6 illustrate various pricing categories.

Figure 1-20 *Typical Service Provider Scenario*

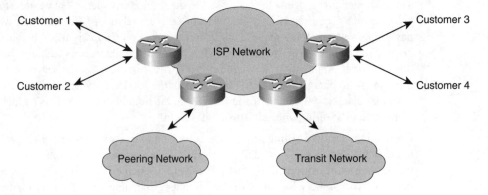

Table 1-6   *Usage-Based Billing (Different Pricing Can Be Applied for Each of the Six Categories of Traffic)*

Traffic Category	Description
Inbound on-net	Customer 1 receives traffic from Customer 3
Inbound off-net (peering)	Customer 1 receives traffic from someone in the peering network
Inbound off-net (transit)	Customer 1 receives traffic from someone in the transit network
Outbound on-net	Customer 1 sends traffic to Customer 3
Outbound off-net (peering)	Customer 1 sends traffic to someone in the peering network
Outbound off-net (transit)	Customer 1 sends traffic to someone in the transit network

Cisco features for destination- and/or source-sensitive billing are NetFlow services, BGP policy accounting, and destination-sensitive billing.

Quality-of-Service Billing

Another example is a class-dependent tariff in a Differentiated Services (DiffServ) network, where various applications can be charged differently. None of the billing models described so far consider application-specific design requirements for the network. Even though IP telephony application transfer only small amounts of data, they have very strict bandwidth and delay requirements compared to other applications, such as e-mail and web browsing. You could argue that the additional investments made for an appropriate VoIP infrastructure should be compensated by the voice application users only and not by every user. A QoS billing model can solve these requirements, because accounting records per class of service can be combined with destination- and/or source and destination-sensitive billing. We consider this the fairest model, because business-critical applications are charged more than less-relevant applications. Especially if the "best effort" class is free of charge, no user should complain about unfair treatment. Unfortunately, this model is not trivial to implement. Each network element not only needs to collect accounting data (which is already an issue for some components), but also needs to collect this data per class of service. For obvious reasons, this model is applicable only when a real business case justifies the investment. Extra care should be taken when the network elements collecting the accounting information are also modifying the traffic classification (such as by changing the value of the ToS or DSCP setting). For example, in a simple design, accounting information is collected on the ISP edge network element—specifically, at the interface facing the customer. However, what happens if this network element is the one classifying the customer traffic into bronze, silver, and gold classes of service? In this case, you collect the accounting information after the classification (after the ToS or DSCP rewrite) and don't report the accounting information as seen in the packets arriving on the interface. Otherwise, the QoS billing would be inaccurate, because it counts traffic as colored by the user and not as transported in the provider's network.

This also relates to concepts such as traffic flow through specific engineered paths, which is described in the section "Traffic Profiling and Engineering."

Figure 1-21 shows the different building blocks of the DiffServ architecture. To reduce the level of complexity, only the "gold" traffic is fully modeled. Packets entering the network are classified according to the traffic class definitions in three different classes. Gold could represent real-time protocols and applications, such as voice traffic. Business-relevant traffic that is not assigned to the gold class is moved to the silver class. All remaining traffic enters the bronze class and gets "best-effort" treatment.

Figure 1-21   *DiffServ Control Architecture*

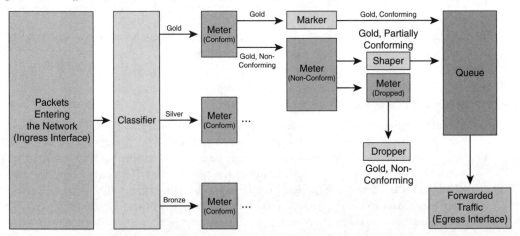

A meter for each class measures the total amount of traffic per class, checks the maximum defined transmission rate, and sends the amount of traffic that matches the class definition to the marker. Traffic exceeding the traffic profile definition is considered nonconforming and is treated differently—either shaped or dropped. Marked and shaped traffic is sent to the different output queues and is transmitted. From an accounting perspective, we are interested in the "meter" blocks. As you can see, we already need to implement three meters for the gold class, to account for

- Conforming traffic
- Partly conforming traffic
- Nonconforming traffic, which (in this example) is dropped

In our example, we therefore need to implement nine classes in total per device (three levels of conforming traffic times three classes of service).

The Cisco CLASS-BASED-QOS-MIB is the Cisco feature of choice in the deployment of QoS billing.

Application and Content-Based Billing

Content-based billing is already common on the Internet. Even though not everyone was happy about it, erotic pages were one of the first applications on the Internet that generated profit. Today we are offered knowledge-based services, translation services, training, children's games, product tests, and so on. We need to identify traffic per application to charge customers appropriately according to the application used. Both Application Service Providers (ASPs) and web-hosting companies charge customers for application access (this is called content-based billing). In many cases, the ASP works with the ISP to offer a solution to the customer. Who owns what part of the network differs with each scenario, but the need to guarantee QoS, network bandwidth, and response times does not change. Similarly, web-hosting firms can categorize access to their servers and networks into service classes based on SLAs. To build these business models, both SLA monitoring and usage-based billing are required from the technology deployed.

In summary, content-based billing can easily be linked to application-specific SLAs, which is an excellent approach for service differentiation. However, it is resource-intensive due to packet inspection. The Cisco NBAR device instrumentation feature and the Service Control Engine (SCE) offer the required functionality to implement application and content-based billing.

Time/Connection-Based Billing

Except for PSTN and GSM networks, time-based billing only applies to dial-in scenarios and pWLAN hotspots. Users get charged based on call duration and time of day. It is relatively simple to implement, because only a network access server (NAS) and a RADIUS server (or some other means of providing user AAA) are required. Accounting records are generated by the RADIUS server and are transferred to the billing application. We distinguish between prepaid and postpaid mode. Prepaid mode requires real-time connectivity between the billing server and the NAS to identify how much credit balance the subscriber has left. The advantage of prepaid billing is that the user can purchase ad hoc access without opening an account with the provider, and no credit check is required.

Voice over IP (VoIP) and IP Telephony (IPT) Billing

Because voice applications were the Postal, Telegraph, and Telephone (PTT) "cash cow" for decades, it is obvious that billing was not an afterthought when VoIP was invented. Nevertheless, VoIP-related billing presents many challenges, because different aspects of the overall solution should be considered:

- End-user billing (flat, per call, per call feature, per class of service, based on distance, or on-net/off-net)
- Billing for handing calls to or receiving calls from the PSTN (per call, total call volume)

- Billing for handing calls to other VoIP service providers (bandwidth, QoS, time)
- Voice-related traffic studies (type of calls, feature usage, and so on)

A typical VoIP call data record (CDR) consists of the following data fields:

- Call ID
- Call initiation time (the time when the user started dialing)
- Call connection time (the time when the destination phone was off-hook)
- Call disconnect time
- IP source address (call originator)
- Remote IP address (call receiver)
- Remote UDP port
- Calling number
- Called number
- Codec (G.711, G.722, G.723, G.726, G.728, G.729, others)
- Protocol (H.323, SIP, MGCP, others)
- Bytes transmitted
- Bytes received
- Packets transmitted
- Packets received
- Round-trip delay
- Delay variation (jitter)
- Erroneous packets (lost, late, early)

Where and what billing data to collect depends on the service provider's business model (flat-rate versus per-call, prepaid versus postpaid) as well as the details being charged for (time, bandwidth, QoS, feature usage). CDRs are generated and collected for the following scenarios:

- **End-user billing**—CDRs can provide the details needed to bill based on usage, bandwidth, or provided QoS. RADIUS provides the infrastructure for applying a prepaid billing model. Chapter 9, "AAA Accounting," offers more details on RADIUS.
- **Service provider or PSTN "peer" billing**—This information can be obtained through CDRs from call agents or SS7 gateways. For service provider-to-service provider peering, it is mainly an overall bandwidth view (and some traffic classification) rather than a per-call view.
- **Traffic studies**—CDRs can be used for a detailed analysis of the telephony studies (calling patterns, feature usage, and so on).

Due to the level of complexity and the small amount of data transferred, we assume that over time voice calls will be free of charge, at least for best-effort voice quality on-net. Alternatively, service providers can identify additional revenue opportunities by offering value-added services, such as business voice with guaranteed voice quality. Today, it is unclear if customers are willing to pay a premium fee for value-added services or if strong competition will result in increased quality for even best-effort services. The large success of skype for Internet-based telephony is a clear indicator.

Security Analysis

Operators of enterprise networks as well as service providers are increasingly confronted with network disruptions due to a wide variety of security threats and malicious service abuse. The originator of the attack could reside within the network or target it from the outside. Or—as a worst-case scenario—attacks could occur at the same time from the inside and outside of the network. Security attacks are becoming a scourge for companies as well as for individuals.

Fortunately, the same accounting technologies that are used to collect granular information on the packets traversing the network can also be used for security monitoring. When attacks are taking place, accounting technologies can be leveraged to detect unusual situations or suspicious flows and alarm a network operations center (NOC) as soon as traffic patterns from security attacks are detected, such as smurf, fraggle, or SYN floods. In a second step, the data records can be used for root cause analysis to reduce the risk of future attacks. Note that the root-cause analysis requires baselining, which is discussed in detail in the section "Purposes of Performance."

Chapter 16, "Security Scenarios," investigates in accounting for security purposes.

Due to business impact, operational costs, and lost revenue, there is an increasing emphasis on security detection and prevention. A design for security analysis should address the following requirements:

- End-to-end surveillance, to monitor the local network as well as WAN links connecting subsidiaries.

- 24/7 availability, because an outage of the security application means becoming vulnerable to attacks.

- Near-real-time data collection, because long transmission delays or aggregation intervals can hold up the identification of an attack. Most attacks last less than 15 minutes.

- Encrypted communication between the server and the client to avoid giving possible attackers valuable information and prevent some forms of attacks.

- Consolidate input from multiple sources and technologies to avoid false alarms. The more sources there are to confirm an assumption, the more likely it is to be true. Too many false alarms will cause the users to reject the tool, and this could cause an attack to be missed that could be business-critical.

A very efficient technology for traffic characterization and user profiling is the Cisco NetFlow accounting feature in the Cisco IOS software. At the NMS application layer, the previously described "deviation from normal" function is most useful in detecting anomalies related to security attacks.

Here's a list of possible checks to detect a security attack:

- Suddenly highly increased overall traffic in the network.

- Unexpectedly large amount of traffic generated by individual hosts.

- Increased number of accounting records generated.

- Multiple accounting records with abnormal content, such as one packet per flow record (for example, TCP SYN flood).

- A changed mix of traffic applications, such as a sudden increase in "unknown" applications.

- An increase in certain traffic types and messages, such as TCP resets or ICMP messages.

- A significantly modified mix of unicast, multicast, and broadcast traffic.

- An increasing number of ACL violations.

- A combination of large and small packets could mean a composed attack. The big packets block the network links, and the small packets are targeted at network components and servers.

All of these symptoms alone could still be considered normal behavior, but multiple related events could point to a security issue. Figure 1-22 illustrates the process of identifying a large number of flows at a device.

Figure 1-22 *Flowchart to Identify a High Number of Flows*

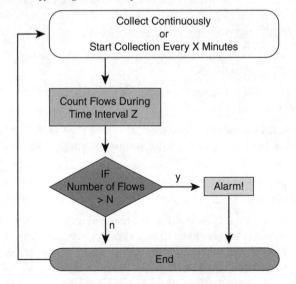

An intrusion detection system (IDS) takes these and additional considerations into account. It can also use stateful packet flow analysis to identify suspicious activities or unusual network activities. To understand this topic better, we describe the proposed steps to identify and block a potential DoS attack. An IDS compares the traffic with predefined patterns and either dumps all packets that do not fit these filter criteria or stores usage records for accounting purposes.

In the detection of security threads, a network baseline is compulsory, as described in the section "Fault Management." How can you deduce that something is wrong in the network without knowledge of the network during normal operating conditions? For example, how can you know if the router's CPU and memory utilization are currently low or high if you cannot compare them with the hourly, daily, or weekly values from the past? How can you figure out if an increased number of accounting records generated on Monday morning is a security threat without values defining the average number of records on a Monday morning? Accounting can answer these questions.

Here's a phased approach for identifying and blocking a security attack:

1 **Preparation**—Instrument the infrastructure to baseline and compare relevant security parameters:

   — Monitor network devices.

   — Identify key parameters.

   — Store statistics in a database.

   — Compare current data with stored values.

   — Generate an event if thresholds are exceeded or potential hostile deviations from normal are detected.

2 **Identification**—Spot involved devices:

   — Who is the victim? Check traffic flows for "top receivers" of traffic to identify compromised hosts, which is crucial in a distributed DoS attack.

   — Which network devices are involved? Monitor flows for irregularities.

3 **Classification**—Identify the attack's criticality:

   — A worm that "only" congests the network links might be considered the lesser evil, compared to a malicious virus that erases data on all PCs or extracts credit card details.

   — A DoS attack is initiated by a single client. A distributed DoS (DDoS) attack is started on a large number of compromised hosts in parallel, which increases the complexity of identifying the sources and also increases the attack's severity level.

4 **Track back**—Identify the source of the attack:

— Accounting records can help identify the subnet(s) or IP address where the attack was generated.

— Tracking a spoofed IP source address complicates the analysis; you can track the source by applying the following steps in the proposed sequence:

a. Start at the router next to the victim.

b. Track each upstream router, one at a time, identifying the specific interface where the attack arrived.

c. In shared media environments, a lookup by MAC address is the only way to identify the upstream device.

5 **Reaction**—Block the attack with an orchestrated approach of security, performance, fault, accounting, and configuration applications:

— Accounting applications provide the flow records to be monitored and analyzed.

— Performance and fault applications identify network outages or overload caused by the attack.

— Security applications consolidate the information and identify the attack.

— Configuration applications modify the device configurations to block the intruder by configuring mechanisms to block malicious traffic (such as by using access control lists).

— Accounting and performance monitoring applications identify when the attack is over.

6 **Postmortem**—Answer the following questions:

— What did we learn?

— Can we improve next time?

— Are modifications to the network architecture required?

— Do we need additional security functionality, procedures, applications, or personnel?

Phases 5 and 6 are very important in a complete security management strategy. However, the goal of this book is to collect the right accounting information for the determination and classification of the security threads, not to correct the fault. Therefore, proposed technology examples will address phases 1 through 4 only.

Specific MIB variables allow the polling of CPU utilization, memory utilization, interface utilization, and so on. A very efficient technology for traffic characterization and user profiling is the Cisco NetFlow services accounting feature in the Cisco IOS software, which allows classifying the network traffic per IP address, per application layer, and much more.

The RMON protocol could also be useful, because an RMON probe can analyze all the traffic on the link it is attached to, classify it, and report the results using MIB variables. Note also that some specific security devices, such as an Intrusion Detection System (IDS) or the Cisco PIX Firewall, simplify the detection of security threads. Because this topic goes beyond the scope of this book, we suggest further literature for readers who want to learn more about security concepts, such as *Network Security Architectures* by Sean Convery (Cisco Press, 2004).

Another area for security monitoring is detecting rogue wireless access points. Wireless LAN (WLAN) is becoming very popular these days, and the prices for WLAN cards as well as WLAN Access Points (AP) have dropped significantly. It is no surprise that users purchase their own APs and connect them to the corporate network, to increase access flexibility and maybe avoid "inconvenient" policies deployed by the corporate IT department. A rogue AP is not authorized for operation by the company's IT group. Operating rogue access points can generate serious security issues, such as opening an uncontrolled interface to the corporate network. An operator's nightmare is the combination of a rogue AP and a hacker identifying it. There are multiple approaches to identifying rogue APs; the most simple way is to scan all IP addresses in the network and check if a web server responds to a request on port 80, because most APs have an integrated web server. Unfortunately, this procedure would identify only rogue APs installed by novice users, because an experienced hacker would probably disable the AP's web server immediately.

How can accounting help in this case? Consider a scenario in which a user disconnects a notebook from the data outlet, plugs in an AP, and connects the notebook wireless instead of wired. Usage patterns would not change, and IP address-based accounting would not identify the new wireless Layer 2 connection. It would require MAC address accounting at the switch where the notebook was originally connected. The AP has a different MAC address than the PC, so the traffic source at this switch port suddenly has a new MAC address. Even though it is possible to apply accounting in this case, it is a complex approach. Easier options exist, such as allowing only a preconfigured MAC address per switch port (see the "Port Security" feature, for example).

However, if other users also start using the AP (on purpose or because the 802.11 client at their PCs identifies a stronger signal and connects through this AP instead of the corporate AP) and if a performance baseline is in place, you can identify changed traffic patterns at this specific port at the switch. This example illustrates how accounting in conjunction with network baselining can help identify network security issues based on altered traffic characteristics.

Purposes of Performance

This section is dedicated to performance management. It identifies various scenarios where performance data can help manage the network more effectively.

As mentioned before, the term "performance monitoring" can be interpreted widely. Our definition covers three aspects: the device, the network, and the service. In fact, device and network performance monitoring are closely related, as we will demonstrate. Therefore, we combine the two in a single section, while service monitoring is such a large domain that we address it separately. This chapter also covers the two key domains that require performance data collection: baselining and fault management.

Device Performance Monitoring

The most obvious area of performance monitoring is directly related to the overall network and individual devices within the network. Sometimes you have the feeling that the network is slow. This "feeling" is supported by the fact that users cannot distinguish between network and server performance. Whether it is the server or the connectivity between the client and the server, usually the network administrator is accused. Consequently, the first task is to monitor the network constantly to prove that the network is doing fine. This might sound strange, but it reflects the reality of many network operators, who are treated as guilty unless proven otherwise.

As the initial step, start monitoring the network for device and link availability. Availability is the measure of time for which the network is available to a user, so it represents the reliability of network components. Another description says availability is the probability that an item of the network is operational at any point in time.

A common formula is:

$$\text{Availability} = \text{MTBF} / (\text{MTBF} + \text{MTTR})$$

MTBF is the *mean time between failures* and describes the time between two consecutive failures. MTTR is the *mean time to repair* after a failure occurred and answers the question "How long did it take to fix the problem"? Availability is usually defined as a percentage, such as 99 percent or 99.99999 percent. You might think that 99 percent availability sounds like a good result, but considered over one year it means an outage of more than 3.5 days. We take a closer look at the meaning of these numbers in Table 1-7.

Table 1-7   *Defining High Availability*

Availability	Downtime Per Year
99.000 percent	3 days, 15 hours, 36 minutes
99.500 percent	1 day, 19 hours, 48 minutes
99.900 percent	8 hours, 46 minutes
99.950 percent	4 hours, 23 minutes
99.990 percent	53 minutes
99.999 percent	5 minutes
99.9999 percent	30 seconds

Most network operators try to achieve availability between 99.9 percent and 99.99 percent. From a technical perspective, it is possible to increase this even further, but the price is so high that a solid business case is required as a justification. Trading floors and banking applications are examples of high-availability requirements; the average e-mail server is certainly not. Because these are only general remarks about high availability, we will not cover these concepts in more detail, but instead suggest a book for further study. *High Availability Network Fundamentals* by Chris Oggerino (Cisco Press, 2001) is a perfect starting point.

Network Element Performance Monitoring

From a device perspective, we are mainly interested in device "health" data, such as overall throughput, per-(sub)interface utilization, response time, CPU load, memory consumption, errors, and so forth. Details about network element performance, such as interface utilization and errors, are provided by the various MIBs, such as MIB-II (RFC 1213), Interfaces-Group-MIB (RFC 2863), and TCP-MIB (RFC 2012).

Calculation of transmission efficiency is related to the number of invalid packets; it measures the error-free traffic on the network and compares the rate of erroneous packets to accurate packets. We measure only *ingress* transmission efficiency, because a router or switch does not send defect packets intentionally. The required parameters are provided by the Interface MIB (IF-MIB RFC 2863):

- **ifInErrors**—"For packet-oriented interfaces, the number of inbound packets that contained errors preventing them from being deliverable to a higher-layer protocol. For character-oriented or fixed-length interfaces, the number of inbound transmission units that contained errors preventing them from being deliverable to a higher-layer protocol."

- **ifInUcastPkts**—"The number of packets, delivered by this sub-layer to a higher (sub-) layer, which were not addressed to a multicast or broadcast address at this sublayer." These are the unicast packages.

- **ifInNUcastPkts**—"The number of packets, delivered by this sub-layer to a higher (sub-)layer, which were addressed to a multicast or broadcast address at this sub-layer." These are the nonunicast packages (the sum of multicast and broadcast traffic).

  transmission efficiency [%] = ΔifInErrors * 100 / (ΔifInErrors + ΔifInUcastPkts + ΔifInNUcastPkt)

The CISCO-IF-EXTENSION-MIB adds details such as cieIfInFramingErrs (misaligned or framing errors), cieIfInOverrunErrs (the receiver ran out of buffers), cieIfInRuntsErrs (too-small packets), and cieIfInGiantsErrs (too-large packets). These counters should be used for in-depth error analysis; if the ifInErrors counter is high, the root cause needs to be identified.

NOTE   A single SNMP polling cycle of the MIB counters is useless; the delta between two polling cycles provides relevant data!

More details related to device performance can be found in the Cisco Press book *Performance and Fault Management*.

System and Server Performance Monitoring

Most of the recommendations described for networking devices also apply to server monitoring. The low-level and operation systems functions need to be checked constantly to identify performance issues immediately. In addition to checking these details, you should also monitor the specific services running on the server. Consider a DNS service. It would not satisfy the users to know that the server response time to a ping request is okay if the logical service (DNS in this case) is very slow due to issues that might be caused by other applications running on the same physical hardware.

In the case of system and server monitoring, we make a distinction between low-level service monitoring and high-level service monitoring:

- Low-level service monitoring components:
  - System: hardware and operating system (OS)
  - Network card(s)
  - CPU: overall and per system process
  - Hard drive disks, disk clusters
  - Fan(s)
  - Power supply
  - Temperature
  - OS processes: check if running; restart if necessary
  - System uptime
- High-level service monitoring components:
  - Application processes: check if running; restart if necessary
  - Server response time per application
  - Optional: Quality of service per application: monitor resources (memory, CPU, network bandwidth) per CoS definition
  - Uptime per application

A practical approach is to measure the server performance with the Cisco IP SLA or Cisco NAM card for the Catalyst switch. The NAM leverages the ART MIB and provides a useful set of performance statistics if located in the switch that connects to the server farm. Figure 1-23 shows an ART MIB report. Chapter 5 includes details about the ART MIB.

Figure 1-23   *Catalyst 6500 NAM ART Measurement*

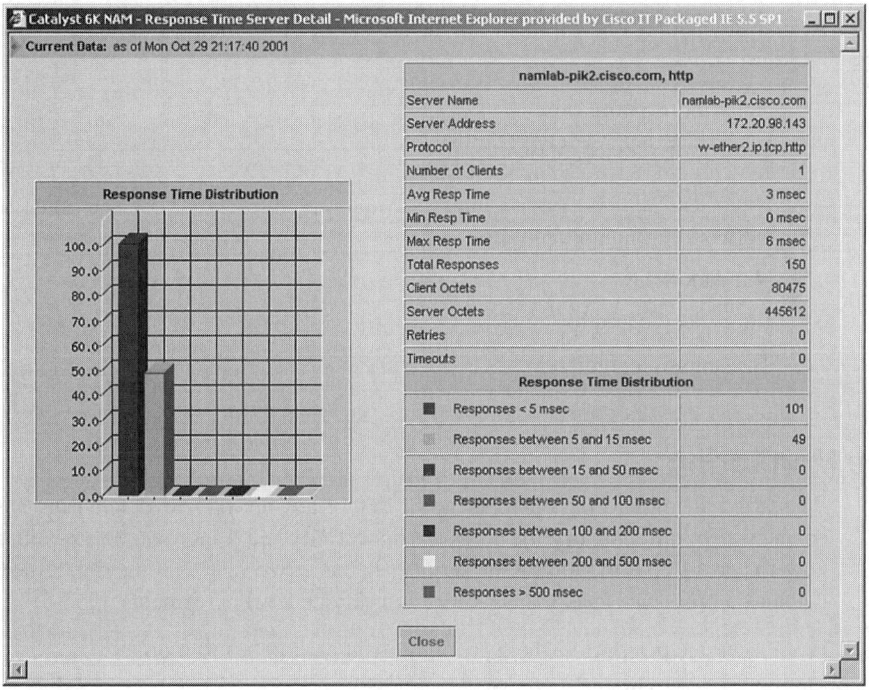

Network Performance Monitoring

Network connectivity and response time can be monitored with basic tools such as ping and traceroute or with more advanced tools such as Ping-MIB, Cisco IP SLA, external probes, or a monitoring application running at the PC or server. When measuring the network connectivity and response time, we recommended that the administrator monitor connectivity between the network devices and also to the servers. This can avoid finger-pointing between the networking and server departments.

In the context of network performance, we distinguish between the downtime measured by an application and the downtime experienced by a user. If you just monitor network and server availability and do not monitor the actual *service* (which runs on the physical server), we could measure 100 percent availability, even if this *service* has an availability of no more than 90 percent. Another example is related to the measurement interval. If the performance monitoring application pings the devices only every 5 minutes, the result could be 100 percent availability, even if there are short outages during the measurement interval. A user would experience these outages and argue that the measurement is inaccurate, even though in this case both parties are right. A similar situation could occur during the night. The user probably sleeps and does not care about the network, while the server is monitoring outages. You can already imagine the challenges of service level definitions and monitoring.

Availability is only one parameter in the area of network monitoring; others are also relevant:

- Network response time
- Utilization (device, network)
- Packet loss
- Network throughput/capacity
- Network delay
- Jitter (delay variation)
- Transmission efficiency

Service Monitoring

We started the monitoring approach at the device and network level to ensure basic connectivity. Assuming that the network connectivity and response time are well monitored now, the next step is to monitor the services in the network. This is the right time to discuss the notion of service level management and service level agreements.

From a service perspective, here are significant parameters to monitor:

- Service availability
- Service delay
- Packet loss
- Delay variation (jitter)
- Mean Opinion Score (MOS) in the case of voice
- Key Performance Indicators (KPI)
- Key Quality Indicators (KQI)

A good reference for service parameters such as KPI and KQI is the "SLA Management Handbook GB917" from the TeleManagement Forum (TMF).

Service availability measurements require explicit measurement devices or applications, because a clear distinction between server and service is necessary. Imagine a (physical) server operating without any problems, while the (logical) service running on the server has terminated without a notification. Client-based monitoring applications can generate application-specific requests (for example, SAP transactions) to identify if the service is operational and what the response time is.

We briefly discussed this issue in the "System and Server Performance Monitoring" section. We proposed using the Cisco NAM card in connection with the Response Time (ART) MIB, or Cisco IP SLA. IP SLA supports application-specific probe operations, like DNS/DHCP request or web server response time. In a voice over IP (VoIP) environment, IP SLA measures the delay variation (also known as jitter), which is a very important parameter to identify voice quality. Furthermore, it measures the MOS that is essential in Internet telephony, because it provides a numeric measure of the quality of human speech at the destination end of the circuit.

Because Chapter 3 describes the notion of a service, at this point we address this topic only briefly:

- **Service**—A generic definition by *Merriam-Webster* declares: "A facility supplying some public demand...." More specifically, related to IT, we define a service as a function providing network connectivity or network functionality, such as the Network File System, Network Information Service (NIS), Domain Name Server (DNS), DHCP, FTP, news, finger, NTP, and so on.

- **Service level**—The definition of a certain level of quality (related to specific metrics) in the network with the objective of making the network more predictable and reliable.

- **Service level agreement (SLA)**—A contract between the service provider and the customer that describes the guaranteed performance level of the network or service. Another way of expressing it is "An SLA is the formalization of the quality of the service in a contract between the Customer and the Service Provider."

- **Service level management**—The continuously running cycle of measuring traffic metrics, comparing those metrics to stated goals (such as for performance), and ensuring that the service level meets or exceeds the agreed-upon service levels.

Table 1-8 provides some generic SLA examples.

Table 1-8   *Generic SLAs*

Class	SLAs	Application
Premium	Availability: 99.98/99.998 percent Latency: 50 ms maximum Packet delivery: 100 percent Jitter: 2 ms maximum	Broadcast video Traditional voice
Optimized	Availability: 99.98/99.998 percent Latency: 50 ms maximum Packet delivery: 100 percent Jitter: 10 ms maximum	Compressed video Voice over IP Mixed application Virtual private network
Best effort	Availability: 99.98 percent Latency: 50 ms maximum Packet delivery: 99.95 percent	Internet data

Baselining

Baselining is the process of studying the network, collecting relevant information, storing it, and making the results available for later analysis. A general baseline includes all areas of the network, such as a connectivity diagram, inventory details, device configurations, software versions, device utilization, link bandwidth, and so on. The baselining task should be done on a regular basis, because it can be of great assistance in troubleshooting situations as well as providing supporting analysis for network planning and enhancements. It is also used as the starting point for threshold definitions, which can help identify current network problems and predict future bottlenecks. As a summary, the objective of baselining is to create a knowledge base of the network—and keep it up to date!

Baselining tasks include the following:

- Gather device inventory information (physical as well as logical). This can be collected via SNMP or directly from the command-line interface (CLI)—for example, **show version**, **show module**, **show run**, **show config all**, and others.
- Gather statistics (device-, network-, and service-related) at regular intervals.
- Document the physical and logical network, and create network maps.
- Identify the protocols on your network, including
  - — Ethernet, Token Ring, ATM
  - — Routing (RIP, OSPF, EIGRP, BGP, and so on)
  - — Legacy voice encapsulated in IP (VoIP)
  - — IP telephony

- — QoS (RSVP)
- — Multicast
- — MPLS/VPN
- — Frame Relay
- — DLSW
- Identify the applications on your network, including
  - — Web servers
  - — Mainframe-based applications (IBM SNA)
  - — Peer-to-peer applications (Kazaa, Morpheus, Grokster, Gnutella, Skype and so on)
  - — Backup programs
  - — Instant messaging
- Monitor statistics over time, and study traffic flows.

From a performance baselining perspective, we are primarily interested in performance-related subtasks:

- Collect network device-specific details:
  - — CPU utilization
  - — Memory details (free system memory, amount of flash memory, RAM, etc.)
  - — Link utilization (ingress and egress traffic)
  - — Traffic per class of service
  - — Dropped packets
  - — Erroneous packets
- Gather server- and (optionally) client-related details:
  - — CPU utilization
  - — Memory (main memory, virtual memory)
  - — Disk space
  - — Operation system process status
  - — Service and application process status
- Gather service-related information:
  - — Round-trip time
  - — Packet loss (delay variation—jitter)
  - — MOS (if applicable)

The collected baseline details are usually stored in a database so that relevant reports can be generated later. The next step is to define reporting requirements. Which level of detail do you need? Which level of granularity is required? These questions can be answered by looking at the specific types of applications that generated the traffic for the baseline. For example, you need a finer level of granularity for troubleshooting than for trending. If capacity planning includes QoS, the relevant QoS parameters need to be collected, which might not be required if the data is collected for computing the amount to charge back per department. Based on the demands of the particular use case, you can define polling intervals and the granularity of the data collection. Five-minute intervals are in most cases sufficient for baselining, so to start polling devices every 5 minutes. In a large network, this can create a nontrivial amount of overhead traffic. You can avoid this by creating different polling groups (that is, poll core devices every 5 minutes, distribution level devices every 10 minutes, and access devices every 15 minutes, for example).

Over time, you realize that the amount of collected data becomes huge, so you want to aggregate older data. This depicts the compromise between data granularity and storage capacity. For example, you could combine the original 5-minute interval collection into a 30- or 60-minute interval. The informational RFC 1857 proposes guidelines for the aggregation interval:

- Over a 24-hour period, aggregate data to 15-minute intervals. Aggregate three 5-minute raw data samples into one 15-minute interval, which results in a reduction of 33 percent.

- Over a 1-month period, aggregate data to 1-hour intervals. Aggregate four 15-minute data sets into a 1-hour period, thereby reducing the data by 25 percent.

- Over a 1-year period, aggregate data to 1-day intervals. Aggregate 24 1-hour data sets into one, resulting in a 4.2 percent reduction. Comparing the 5-minute raw data collections with the 1-year aggregation, a reduction by the factor $3 * 4 * 24 = 288$, or 0.35 percent takes place.

So far, you have collected performance statistics from the elements in the network and stored them in an archive or database. The next chapter shows that baselining is a foundation for effective fault management.

Fault Management

In addition to the close linkage between performance and accounting, we also recognize a strong association between performance and fault management. Figure 1-5 illustrated this, and we want to elaborate on its concepts. Remember that the objective of performance monitoring is collecting statistics from devices, networks, and services, and displaying them in various forms to the user. Performance management extends this approach and includes active modifications of the network to reconstitute the expected performance level. Note that an additional step should occur between the recognition of a deviation and the remedy—notifying the fault application of the abnormality. One could argue that a deviation is not a fault at all, but it is certainly an indicator of some form of abnormal behavior that should be examined further. This is the reason for sending a notification toward the fault application. At a high level, we can distinguish between two different fault events:

- State change (device, network, or service failure; outage; or restart)
- Performance deviation

Notifications about state changes are sent by devices proactively. As a result, a state change occurs at the application (for example, network map, event list, and so on). A state change from operational to nonoperational usually indicates an outage, while the opposite indicates either a recovery from a failure or the activation of a backup procedure. Therefore, events categorized under "state change (a)" require as much attention as events according to "performance deviation (b)." An example is the activation of an ISDN backup link when the primary DSL connection fails. Assuming the DSL connection has a flat rate, the ISDN link is probably charged per time interval and can result in a drastically increased monthly invoice. This would indicate a poorly designed fault management system, if only the invoice at the end of the month can indicate this situation.

Performance deviation events are much more closely linked to performance management than fault management. The challenge is to identify a deviation from "normal," because you need some history indicators to define what "normal" is for a specific network at a specific time. To achieve this, baselining is required, as explained in the preceding section. If the current measurement values exceed a predefined threshold above or below the expected value, a performance event is generated.

We will now analyze the performance baseline to understand the traffic flows in the network and to define appropriate thresholds for traffic or application guarantees. Thresholding is the process of specifying triggers on traffic patterns or situations and generating events when such situations occur.

We define two classes of thresholds:

- **Discrete thresholds**—Boolean objects with two values (yes/no, true/false, 0/1) that define the transition from one state to another.

    Examples: Link up/down, interface operational/failed, or service available/ unavailable. Boolean operators are either true or false and can easily be correlated; for instance:

    Symptoms: A specific service is unavailable *and* the physical link to the server that provides this service is down.

    Action: Check the link before checking the service.

- **Continuous thresholds**—Apply to continuous data sets and can optionally include time. In this case we need to define an absolute or relative threshold and generate an event whenever this value is exceeded.

Example: The number of erroneous packets as a percentage of total traffic.

The thresholding technique can be enhanced by adding a hysteresis function to reduce the volume of generated events. In this case, only one positive event is sent when the value exceeds the upper threshold, but no further events are sent until the lower threshold has been reached and one negative event is sent. This helps reduce the volume of events drastically without reducing the level of relevant information.

Figure 1-24 shows a response-time hysteresis function with a rising threshold of 100 ms and a falling threshold of 50 ms. In this example, a response time between 50 and 100 ms is considered normal, and a response time above 100 ms is critical and generates an alert. After the alert has occurred, the state remains critical until the response time drops to 50 ms. Alternatively, you could set both the upper and lower threshold to 100 ms to get immediate notification if the response time drops below 100 ms; however, this would remove the hysteresis function.

Figure 1-24 *Defining Reaction Conditions*

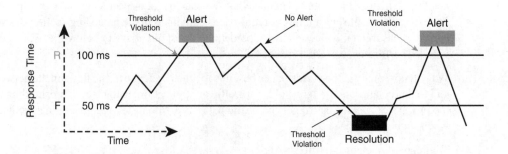

Statistical analysis can be visualized in a plot chart to identify normal and abnormal behavior. It is a good practice to start with a "soft" or lower threshold instead of too tight a value to avoid alert storms. Thresholds can be adjusted by taking a successive approach, which adjusts the values over time to closely match the normal behavior and identify abnormalities.

You can define thresholds at the NMS system by polling the device performance data and checking it against the thresholds. Alternatively, you can set thresholds directly at the device level and notify the NMS application proactively if a threshold has been exceeded. The first approach is the classic solution in which NMS frameworks such as HP OpenView, IBM Tivoli, CA Unicenter, and so on discover and poll all devices in the network. The second approach requires more intelligence at the device level and has additional resource requirements (memory and CPU). But it can help reduce network management traffic on the network, because only status polling and event notification between the NMS server and the device are required. The RMON-MIB, Event-MIB, and Cisco IP SLA (CISCO-RTTMON-MIB) can provide this functionality.

Which thresholds are relevant for your network? Almost every network administrator is searching for generic answers, only to discover that he or she has to find an individual answer to this question. Very few generic thresholds can be applied across all networks; thus, in most cases, defining thresholds is a task for the operator. For example, Cisco suggests that the average CPU load should not exceed 60 percent so that enough performance is available for sudden events such as routing protocol recalculations. However, you could argue that by purchasing a "full" CPU, you could expect a much higher utilization, and therefore define a threshold of 95 percent. Best practice suggests taking a more conservative approach to increase network availability.

Generic threshold recommendations for Cisco routers and switches are as follows:

- Total CPU utilization over 5 min $\geq$ 60 percent (CISCO-PROCESS-MIB)
- Free memory pool $\geq$ 25 percent (CISCO-MEMORY-POOL-MIB)
- Round-trip time between two devices $\geq$ 150 ms (CISCO-RTTMON-MIB)
- Jitter between two devices $\geq$ 10 ms (CISCO-RTTMON-MIB)
- DNS response time $\geq$ 2 sec (CISCO-RTTMON-MIB)
- DHCP request time $\geq$ 10 sec (CISCO-RTTMON-MIB)

With a performance baseline in place and threshold definitions applied, we will identify a more sophisticated feature called "deviation from normal." This function adds "intelligence" to the performance baseline collection by defining and analyzing network performance *metrics* over a timeline. For instance, if you identify link utilization above 90 percent as a critical situation, you can also ask at what time this is a particular problem. On a Monday morning, when every user downloads e-mails, updates virus definitions, or performs a backup, it can be acceptable to utilize the network almost completely, especially from an economical perspective. If the same situation occurs on a Saturday evening, you should think twice. The limitation of defining thresholds is that they are fixed and cannot be easily adjusted in a timely fashion. We can also avoid defining multiple simultaneous thresholds in a simple step. In this case, a performance management application should keep a baseline per hour and day and constantly compare the current data with the historical data. In a situation where the average CPU utilization of a specific device is expected to be about 30 percent, a "deviation from normal" function would generate an alarm if the current CPU utilization were far greater than 30 percent or far less than 30 percent, because both situations could indicate a serious issue. A high CPU utilization could indicate an attack on the network, and a very low CPU utilization could point to a misconfiguration in the network.

The following four steps summarize the necessary tasks for fault management:

Step 1   Define thresholds on core devices and services.

Step 2   Predict future network behavior, and identify potential problem areas and bottlenecks.

Step 3   Develop a what-if analysis methodology to speed up troubleshooting.

Step 4   Implement a change control process that specifies that network modifications need to be documented and planned in advance (maintenance window).

Notice that input from the sections on accounting and performance monitoring can provide relevant input to a fault application.

Applying the Information to the Business

After discussing the various aspects of accounting and performance management, now we want to relate the information to the business. How can the two areas help you design and operate a productive, reliable, and cost-efficient network? During the Internet hype, revenue generation and assurance were certainly not the center of attention, but this changed quickly when the global economic slowdown started. Today, if a network architect develops a new design or extends the existing design, a solid business case needs to be in place to rationalize the investment and calculate a quick return on investment, or the project might never kick off. Therefore, you need answers to the following questions:

- How can accounting and performance management increase revenue for a service provider?

- Can it help an enterprise to better utilize the network equipment and identify bottlenecks in the network, so that only these bottlenecks are resolved by an upgrade instead of upgrading the entire network?

- Can you justify an investment in accounting to increase revenue assurance?

- Will accounting and performance management help reduce the operational expenses?

- Can you classify the most- and least-profitable areas and access points of a service provider network?

The related costs of usage reporting are a major deterrent that might stop administrators from considering accounting a valuable solution for their network. Three main areas are related to these concerns:

- **Collection overhead**—Based on the selected technique, generating usage data records at the device level can create a significant resource impact on the device CPU utilization and can require additional memory and bandwidth utilization when exporting the data records to an external collector. This needs to be considered in the proposed accounting and performance management architecture.

- **Mediation, processing, and reporting overhead**—Additional resources are required to collect the records and aggregate and mediate them afterwards. At this point, the collection contains only *data* (collected usage records) and not processed *information*, such as end-to-end performance records, a list of security attacks during the last month, or a printable invoice for a customer. The next step is processing the data at a performance, security, planning, or billing application, which creates useful information for the NOC personnel. The costs of these applications cannot be neglected; even open-source software has related costs of server hardware and administration expenditures.

- **Security overhead**—A huge benefit of collecting accounting records is its inherent multipurpose functionality. As mentioned, multiple applications can benefit from data collection, which results in a "collect once and reuse multiple times" proposal. Imagine the disaster that happens when data sets have been manipulated. If multiple applications base their results on wrong data sets, the whole network operation is jeopardized. This is not limited to a customer's invoice, but also to network planning and especially security analysis. As soon as an attacker detects the corporate accounting architecture, he or she can manipulate data sets and bypass the traffic meters that were put in place to identify security threats. It is critical to implement mechanisms to protect accounting information from unauthorized access and manipulation.

A possible approach to address the collection overhead and security overhead issues just mentioned is to deploy a Data Communications Network (DCN). The DCN concept was developed in the service provider context, but it can also be useful in an enterprise environment, where it is usually referred to as out-of-band (OOB) management. What is a DCN? A DCN is a standalone out-of-band network providing connectivity between the network operations center (NOC) and the network elements, remotely and independently of the user traffic. The opposite approach is called in-band-management, where management traffic and user traffic share the same infrastructure. The DCN can be used for all network management operations, such as network surveillance, provisioning, testing, alarm monitoring, service enablement and restoration, and collecting accounting and performance details. Figure 1-25 illustrates a DCN.

The costs related to accounting solutions—both CAPEX (capital expenditures) and OPEX (operational expenditures)—can become an impediment that the network planner might not be able to eliminate. We propose building a strong business case before considering the technology and implementation details. The balance between costs and benefits can be harmonized by the granularity of the collected accounting records. Again, the level of required details is determined by the business case, not just the technical feasibility. If you can come up with good arguments to justify a short return on investment for the solution, we assume that the chances of getting project approval are much greater.

Figure 1-25 *Data Communications Network*

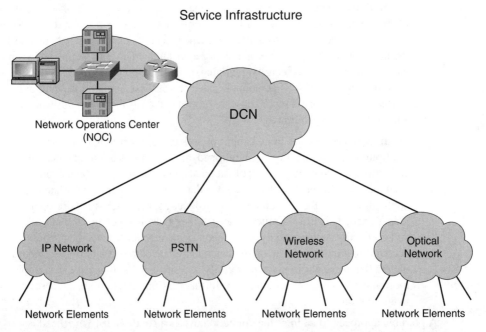

The following questions should be considered first:

- What is the benefit for the cooperation of collecting usage and performance data records?
- Which existing processes are impacted by the proposal?
- Can processes be optimized by leveraging results from an accounting and performance management application?
- Which new processes can be created that were not possible in the past?
- Does the proposal generate additional revenue? What is the ratio of investment (CAPEX) to revenue?
- Which additional operational costs (OPEX) are caused by the proposal?
- Can the solution achieve a competitive advantage?
- Does the project have an executive sponsor?
- Has outsourcing been considered?
- What are the low-cost alternatives? Which functions cannot be implemented by a low-cost design? Is the additional functionality worth the premium price?

- What is the price of not implementing anything? Keep in mind that not doing anything also has a related price, which can be monetary (such as losing potential revenue) or nonmonetary (such as decreased customer satisfaction or missing future opportunities).

Following these questions, we develop some suggestions that might apply to the situation of individual readers. This list is not complete, but it tries to give a comprehensive set of ideas that network operators can use for further consideration.

Nowadays, service providers are faced with increasing bandwidth demands from customers without a corresponding increase in revenue. All of us want flat-rate DSL or cable at home, while at the same time paying less than we did when using the dialup or ISDN network. This requires careful planning at the SP to ensure that only the necessary parts of the network are updated to meet customer needs. The days of a fully overprovisioned network are gone. Service providers need to find a balance between over- and underprovisioning the network. If the traffic that is placed on a link or circuit is greater than the bandwidth, it is underprovisioned (or over-subscribed). If less traffic is placed on the link than it can transport, it is overprovisioned. Making appropriate business decisions about network provisioning requires details that only network usage analysis (such as accounting and performance management) can facilitate.

We should take the time to define "service provider" in this context. Sometimes, people interpret service provider as an "incumbent" or PTT (Postal, Telegraph, and Telephone) company, which was the case several years ago. Due to the deregulation of the telecom market, there are incumbent (or telecom) providers (the classic ex-PTTs), challengers, Internet Service Providers (ISPs), Application Service Providers (ASP), and so on. Multiple large enterprises have outsourced their IT departments, and these have transitioned from cost centers to profit centers. National Research and Education Networks (NRN or NREN) provide networking services to the national universities but also have international agreements in place. All of these "service providers" have a common denominator— offering services to users. The user definition varies and so does the service, but thanks to competition, users have some level of freedom to select another provider, and that should be enough motivation to provide good quality.

So far, we have considered so-called "service provider"-specific benefits of accounting and performance management, but we don't stop at this point. Enterprises can benefit from the same functionality, except for billing. Instead, some use it for department charge-back and monitoring usage policies. Deploying accounting for charge-back per department might not reduce the network's operational costs, but it can lead to better assignment of the costs. Assuming you work in a group that requires high-speed networking access (for example, an automotive engineering team, spread across multiple sites and heavily using computer-aided design technology), it would probably be okay for you to get charged for an upgrade of the links you are using. On the other hand, if you lead the human resources department and have no high demands for the network, you would probably not be willing to support the complete corporate network upgrade just because of another department's request.

Accounting solutions can help assign the costs to the originator instead of an equal cost distribution; consequently, enterprises should consider accounting as a mechanism to enforce rational cost allocation and recovery.

Monitoring usage policies also falls in the same category. If the enterprise network was designed to meet the normal traffic demand during business hours, a policy could be established to run backup processes during the night to better utilize the network infrastructure. If some users decide to ignore the policy and run large backups during peak hours, all users would suffer and would have to pay the extra price for a network upgrade. Accounting and performance management can supply beneficial information.

Both enterprises and service providers use accounting and performance management to baseline and plan the network. We already explored several scenarios where a solid baseline is the foundation for higher-level services as well as planning. A service provider might offer baselining as a service to the enterprise, potentially without additional investments. If the provider already collects accounting data for billing purposes, these records could be used as input for a monitoring and planning application. Either the service provider offers the raw data collection to the customer, and he runs his own application, or the provider offers this service in addition and delivers the results as planning proposals to the customer.

Another common area is security management. Identifying and stopping security attacks in the network is one of a network operator's most critical tasks. Viruses and other malicious code attacks are growing in number, and so is the cost incurred by companies, government organizations, and private individuals to clean up systems and get them back in working order. Malicious code attacks include trojans, worms, and viruses.

Service providers can benefit by protecting their customers from DoS and worm attacks. Accounting techniques, such as Cisco NetFlow services, can be used to detect attacks, isolate attackers, and identify attack propagation. ISPs have the opportunity to offer security reporting and protection services to their customers and generate additional revenue. In the future, we expect that security parameters will be included in SLAs. Enterprise networks have had issues with the flood of worms, including SQL slammer, MS slammer, Nachi, and others. Security services that prevent attacks can significantly reduce enterprises' OPEX.

QoS and SLA management are two other areas for collecting performance and accounting usage records. The combination of QoS and SLA can provide a competitive advantage for an ISP, even though QoS deployment is not a necessary condition for offering SLAs. Some ISPs offer different service classes and SLAs already; unfortunately, no standardized SLA definitions and QoS settings are deployed *across* multiple ISPs today. Users notice this when using IP telephony in the Internet and the two parties are connected via different carriers. Unless SLAs between the ISPs themselves and toward the customer are defined, the traffic is treated as best-effort, with the result that quality of voice calls is not *predictable*.

The traditional models of carrier interconnection offered no end-to-end service level, which was a limiting factor for business-critical applications that require QoS. IP Telephony and video will most probably become the driving application for QoS in the Internet, and in contrast to current Internet applications, voice is the first real application that requires some level of service quality. Internet QoS might also become a revenue generator for ISPs, which is relevant when legacy telephony, which was the PTT's source of income for decades, will no longer be available. Of course, some users want IP telephony for free, but others are willing to pay for excellent voice quality, even though the price will still be drastically below the previous prices for long-distance legacy voice calls. SLAs across carriers will become available, and customers can select carriers based on SLA contracts and guarantees.

Finally, yet importantly, we want to address peering agreements and billing.

Peering agreements are mutual contracts of two providers to transfer each other's traffic free of charge. Transit agreements represent a service in which one provider charges the other for data transmission. In both cases, accurate collection of exchanged traffic is vital to both parties. Usually each of the two contractors measures both ingress and egress traffic, but obviously it would be more efficient to collect the data only once—which requires a level of trust between the two parties. Because there is not one, but multiple industry standards for collecting accounting information, the worst case happens if the parties use different accounting collection methods that are not interoperable. This leads to different measurements at the end of the month and can be a starting place for conflicts.

It gets even more complex when billing scenarios are addressed.

Managing large volumes of complex voice call-data-records and Internet usage-data-records is a challenge for most organizations. A list of challenges includes the following:

- There can be hundreds, or thousands, of accounts across the organization (depending on the granularity of the billing records).

- Different accounting records from various sources increase complexity and require mediation.

- Billing dates may not be aligned where more than one supplier is providing services.

- Some divisions may require electronic billing; others may prefer printed invoices.

In spite of these issues, billing can be a great source for identifying future growth opportunities and customer satisfaction (or dissatisfaction). A provider can identify profitable areas that show accelerated growth and increase bandwidth to maintain and increase customer satisfaction. Unprofitable areas could be examined to identify competitive strategies and launch marketing campaigns to gain new customers. Even though flat-rate billing sounds desirable to all customers, only heavy Internet users really benefit from it. An average individual user might not be able to generate the same volume of a family, where parents and kids use the Internet extensively. In this scenario, the low-volume users pay the bill for the high-volume users. This is exactly the situation we faced with enterprise networks in the past, where the costs were shared equally across all users. Nowadays, corporate users expect a fair distribution of costs and compliance with corporate policies instead of flat-rate distribution. The same might happen to commercial users when considering the cost of Internet access; thus, we expect usage-sensitive charges as a potential model for the future. Charging a fixed price per volume or connection time could be combined with a cost ceiling (such as a maximum fee per month) to avoid an incalculable price during peak periods.

In general, we believe service differentiation is imperative for service providers. The necessity of responding to competitive forces requires the ability to rapidly develop and implement new services, including the proper infrastructure to bill for them.

Summary

This book offers guidance for finding answers to one or more of the following questions:

- How do I efficiently track network and application resource usage?
- How do I know if my customers are adhering to usage policy agreements?
- How do I account and bill for resources being utilized?
- How do I effectively plan to allocate and deploy resources most efficiently?
- How do I track customers to enhance marketing customer service opportunities?

After discussing accounting and performance management concepts in some level of detail, we can summarize the essential points:

Accounting management means

- Collecting usage data records at network devices
- Optional preprocessing of the data records at the device (filter, sample, aggregate)
- Exporting the data records from the device toward a collection server
- Processing the data records at the collection server (filter, sample, aggregate, mediate, de-duplicate)
- Mediation: converting data records into a common format for higher-layer applications (performance, SLA, fault, security, billing, planning)

Performance management means

- Monitoring: collecting device, network, and services data records at the device level (availability, response time, device and link utilization)
- Data analysis: data record aggregation, QoS parameter verification, accuracy
- Transforming data records into information: baselining, reporting, performance analysis, capacity planning, SLA compliance tests, alarming, quality assurance

- Mediation: converting data records into a common format for higher-layer applications (baselining, reporting, performance analysis, capacity planning, SLA compliance tests, alarming, quality assurance)
- Configuration management: adjusting configurations to improve performance and traffic handling of the network (threshold definitions, capacity planning)

This book emphasizes the close relationship between accounting and performance management. We will prove that the two areas are indeed complementary and, by combining the best of both parts, we set the foundation for better network management.

We have discussed various areas of network management, which can benefit from accounting and performance management. Table 1-9 summarizes the applications and highlights the areas with the closest fit, where ✓ means a full match and ✓* means a partial match.

Table 1-9   *Accounting and Performance Management Applied*

Area	Accounting	Performance Management
Performance monitoring	✓	✓
User monitoring and profiling	✓	
Application monitoring and profiling	✓	✓
Capacity planning	✓	✓
Traffic profiling and engineering	✓	✓*
Peering and transit agreements	✓	
Usage-/volume-based billing	✓	✓*
Destination/source-sensitive billing	✓	
Quality-of-service billing	✓	✓*
Application- and content-based billing	✓	
Time/connection-based billing	✓	✓
Voice over IP (VoIP) and IP telephony (IPT) billing	✓	
Security analysis	✓	✓*
Baselining		✓
Fault management	✓	✓
Service monitoring		✓

We have also identified blocking factors for implementing accounting and performance management architecture; these are mainly cost and overhead concerns such as

- Collection
- Mediation, processing, and reporting

By now, you understand the rationale behind accounting and performance management and can develop an individual business case. Based on the business justification, you can derive the required technical parameters and develop an appropriate accounting and performance management architecture. This book addresses technology-specific details, standards, and implementation guidelines. Finally, we will assign technologies to solutions to give guidelines that you can apply in your network. Because the prime focus of this book is technology-related, we will not go into more details from a business and operational perspective. If you are interested in these areas, refer to *OSS Essentials* by Kornel Terplan (Wiley, 2001). A very good introductory book on network management is *Network Management Fundamentals* by Alexander Clemm (Cisco Press, 2006).

CHAPTER 2

Data Collection Methodology

This chapter defines the data collection methodology by asking those questions that are relevant for accounting or performance management projects:

- What type of information to collect?

- What level of detail is required in the data records?

- How to meter the data records (*metering* is the process of collecting and optionally preprocessing usage data records at devices)?

- Where to collect the data records?

- How to collect the data records?

- How to process the data records?

- How to ensure data authenticity and integrity?

This chapter addresses all the questions you should ask yourself throughout your project's evolution. The methodology explained in this chapter is well suited for both performance and accounting projects. More proof, if more is needed, is that the A and P in the acronym FCAPS (Fault, Configuration, Accounting, Performance, and Security) are closely related. Every accounting and/or performance project requires an answer to the what, who, how, and where questions. This chapter helps you answer all the questions, one by one, almost like a checklist.

Chapter 1, "Understanding the Need for Accounting and Performance Management," described the different applications in the accounting and performance management domains. Some distinguishers helped categorize accounting versus performance applications; however, a clear overlap exists between the two domains! Start classifying your project per application type: Are you solving a network monitoring issue, a capacity planning issue, a security issue, or a network performance issue? The answer is important, even if the questions in this chapter are almost identical for all applications types, because based on the application type you can already deduce a couple of answers.

This chapter sets up the theoretical foundations for the rest of the book. For the sake of clarity, a few references to the capabilities of the different Cisco accounting and performance features (SNMP, RMON, NetFlow, IP SLA, BGP Policy Accounting, and so on) illustrate the theory.

However, the goal of this chapter is not to delve into the technical specifications of the Cisco accounting and performance features. The next chapters cover each feature in detail.

When starting a project, the temptation is to try to solve all the problems at once. For example, while collecting some generic accounting records for capacity planning, why not try to reuse the information for security and billing purposes. Or why not try to augment the capacity planning records with some extra billing and security information? Although this is a legitimate goal, it is better to divide and conquer. The methodology, or list of questions described in this chapter, should be answered for each application type, at least with the first four questions:

- What to collect?
- Who is the user?
- How to meter?
- Where to collect?

As a second step, you analyze the common denominator(s) between the different application requirements. Can you meter the traffic so that the data records contain the types of data for all the application types? Can you centralize the collection for all the application types? After a trade-off analysis, a single accounting mechanism can potentially collect all the required information. However, at first glance, this is not obvious.

Finally, after you've answered the questions in the checklist, the answers will help you discover the required accounting and/or performance mechanisms adapted to your project. They will point you to one or two accounting features. The next chapters cover the technical details of these features. After a technical comparison, you can select and implement the most appropriate feature.

Data Collection Details: What to Collect

The Multi-Router Traffic Grapher (MRTG) and Round-Robin Database (RRDtool) are freely available tools under the terms of the GNU General Public License. MRTG, widely used throughout the industry, monitors and graphs the evolution of SNMP MIB variables and displays the traffic load on network links and devices. MRTG generates HTML pages containing graphical images that provide a near-real-time visual representation of this traffic. The RRDtool, considered a reimplementation of MRTG's graphing and logging features, stores the data in a very compact way and presents useful graphs after processing the data.

Figure 2-1 shows a typical monitoring graph generated with the RRDtool. This particular graph displays the bit rates received on and transmitted out of one interface, respectively using the ifInOctets and ifOutOctets MIB variables from the interfaces group MIB (RFC 2863).

Figure 2-1   *Interface Counter Collection with MRTG*

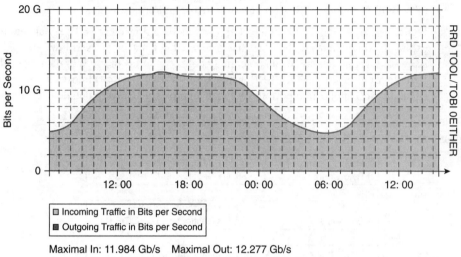

Maximal In: 11.984 Gb/s   Maximal Out: 12.277 Gb/s
Average In: 9.007 Gb/s   Average Out: 9.237 Gb/s
Current In: 11.852 Gb/s   Current Out: 12.197 Gb/s

The most basic function of performance management is the collection of the interface utilization. Even if the interpretation of the results is useful for some link capacity planning, and if the graph visualization helps during troubleshooting, the usability is still limited. No traffic classification is possible, the link view limitation applies as opposed to a network-wide view, the image is updated every 5 minutes, and so on.

At the other extreme of the accounting granularity, the Cisco NetFlow solution analyzes the packets received on an interface to classify them into flows and then exports the flow records to a NetFlow collector. Flows consist of packets related to each other—for example, because they belong to an exclusive data session between a client and a server.

NetFlow version 9 defines a flow in RFC 3954, *Cisco Systems NetFlow Services Export Version 9*:

"An IP Flow, also called a Flow, is defined as a set of IP packets passing an Observation Point in the network during a certain time interval. All packets that belong to a particular Flow have a set of common properties derived from the data contained in the packet and from the packet treatment at the Observation Point."

Packet accounting, as opposed to flow accounting, refers to individual packets, without identifying a relationship between each other. An aggregation is a whole-part relationship, where individual components form a larger whole. A flow is always an aggregation, even though you can define an almost unlimited number of aggregation schemes. Aggregation scheme examples are the combination of all packets with the same criteria:

- IP address (source and/or destination)
- Layer 4 port number (source or destination)

- Type of service field (ToS, DSCP)

- BGP Autonomous System number (source and/or destination)

Figure 2-2 shows the details of the NetFlow version 5 flow records. The goal here is not to explain NetFlow in depth, because that is covered in Chapter 7, "NetFlow." Instead, you'll see what level of detail you can potentially collect in terms of types of data. Note that the Remote Monitoring (RMON) MIB, which offers a level of detail almost similar to NetFlow (IP addresses, application port number, and so on), is also a very detailed accounting feature.

Figure 2-2 *NetFlow Version 5 Flow Export Format*

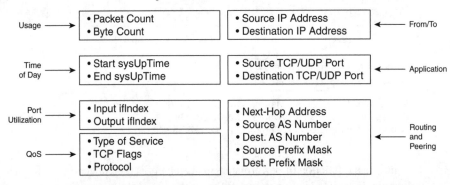

The question of what to collect? finally translates into "Which types of data are required for my project?" Do you need only some MIB interface counters? Alternatively, do you need to export NetFlow records for very detailed accounting reports? In most cases, the answer is between these two extremes. After you understand the principles of accounting and performance management (see Chapter 1), what to collect? is the next question. This question is not as simple as it seems! The answer depends on the translation from the problem space into a detailed technical analysis of the problem. The best way to proceed is to take an empty sheet of paper and draw the report you want. The column titles of your report are the most important information. Assume that your report requires the notions of user, application, volume, and time. For now, keep the generic names. In this chapter you will discover which types of data are required. For example, the user can be represented by a MAC address, an IP address, a subnet, a virtual private network (VPN), an interface index, and so on.

While sketching your report, you will quickly conclude that you need to break down the task into several subquestions about what to collect:

- What are the keys?

- What are the values?

- What are the required versus nice-to-have types of data?

What Are the Keys?

The key is a data field that creates a unique entry in the report. The keys define the granularity of the classification: the more keys, the better the level of detail. For example, if you want to monitor the volume per interface, the report needs to contain the interface as a key. On top of that, if you want to monitor the application types in the network, the report also needs to contain the application's destination port as a key. Furthermore, if you want to monitor the top talkers in the network, you require two extra keys: one for the source and one for the destination address. However, ensure that the addition of flow keys does not come at the cost of resource consumption, as discussed in the section "What Are the Required Versus Nice-to-Have Types of Data?"

Cisco NetFlow services use a combination of different types of data as keys to define a flow:

- IP source address
- IP destination address
- Source port
- Destination port
- Protocol field
- ToS field
- Input or output (sub)interface
- Multiprotocol Label Switching (MPLS) label
- Other criteria

NOTE   The first seven data types in the list are the default key for NetFlow.

What Are the Values?

The value does not create a unique entry in the report, as a key would do. Instead, it augments the record with extra information. Volume is a typical example, expressed in number of bytes and/or number of packets. Other potential useful values are the observed time of the record, round-trip time (RTT), jitter, and so on.

The distinction between values and keys is comprehensible for some types of data, such as volume, which is always a value. However, for some types of data, the key or value selection depends on whether the type of data content is constant in the predefined report. If you collect a certain type of data as a key, does the content remain the same across all entries? It also depends on whether you want the flexibility to report on those different instances, assuming that the type of data content differs in the predefined classification.

The following sections provide some examples for distiguishing keys and values.

Value Versus Key Example: DiffServ Code Point

In this example, the question is "Should the DiffServ Code Point (DSCP) type of data be classified as a value or a key?"

If all incoming traffic contains the same DSCP, or if the incoming traffic contains different DSCPs but you want to report only one value of it (for example, the DSCP's first observed value), you need a report like the one shown in Table 2-1.

Table 2-1 *DSCP Report 1*

Number of Packets (Value)	Ingress DSCP (Value)
100	1

Alternatively, if you want to monitor the different ingress DSCPs of the packets arriving at the network element, define the ingress DSCP as a key. Table 2-2 shows an example with two DSCP values: 1 and 2.

Table 2-2 *DSCP Report 2*

Number of Packets (Value)	Ingress DSCP (Key)
50	1
50	2

If the network element executes recoloring—that is, if the network element rewrites the egress DSCP—you would potentially want to report the egress DSCP. Whether the egress DSCP is a key or a value in that case depends on the context.

If there is one-to-one matching between the ingress DSCP traffic and the egress DSCP traffic, and if the ingress DSCP value is already a key, you might report the egress DSCP as a value. Table 2-3 shows an example of all ingress traffic with a DSCP value of 1 recolored to 2 and all ingress traffic with a DSCP value of 2 recolored to 3 at the egress interface.

Table 2-3 *DSCP Report 3*

Number of Packets (Value)	Ingress DSCP (Key)	Egress DSCP (Value)
50	1	2
50	2	3

If you want to monitor all data records with the different instances of ingress and egress DSCPs, specify both the ingress and egress DSCP as keys. Table 2-4 shows the type of report to expect in case of two DSCP instances.

Table 2-4   *DSCP Report 4*

Number of Packets (Value)	Ingress DSCP (Key)	Egress DSCP (Key)
25	1	1
25	1	2
25	2	1
25	2	2

If you want to distinguish your data records per application, you need the application as a type of data in your report. Should you request the application type to be a key or a value in this case? Again, it depends. If DSCP characterizes the application type, the application is a value. Table 2-5 shows an example of a report in which all VPN traffic has an ingress DSCP setting of 2, and all FTP traffic has an ingress DSCP setting of 1.

Table 2-5   *DSCP Report 5*

Number of Packets (Value)	Ingress DSCP (Key)	Application Type (Value)
50	1	FTP
50	2	VPN

Alternatively, if different Classes of Service (CoS) are defined in the network, even for the same application type, reporting the DSCP as a key allows the breakdown of application per CoS.

Table 2-6 shows the example of a report in which VPN traffic contains an ingress DSCP setting of 2 or 3 and FTP traffic contains an ingress DSCP setting of 1 or 2.

Table 2-6   *DSCP Report 6*

Number of Packets (Value)	Ingress DSCP (Key)	Application (Key)
25	1	FTP
25	2	FTP
25	2	VPN
25	3	VPN

Value Versus Key Example: BGP Autonomous System Path

If you want to report the BGP autonomous systems (AS) to which your network traffic is destined, you define the BGP destination AS as a key. On top of that, you might want to add the BGP AS path taken to reach the final destination. In that case, you define the AS path as a value in your record. For a dual-homed network, which connects to two different service providers, you can distinguish the traffic sent via one ISP versus the traffic sent to the other: the solution is to specify the AS path as a key. In that case, two distinct data records are created if the AS path is different, even if all the other parameters of the data record are similar.

The network shown in Figure 2-3 serves as the basis of the examples. The traffic goes from AS1 to AS2 and AS3, and the router in AS1 is the point of observation. Table 2-7 displays the different data record possibilities when the AS path is a value, and Table 2-8 reports the AS path as a key. Note that two different AS paths are possible when the AS path is a value (see Table 2-7). The selection depends on the metering process. The AS path reported is the value of either the first or last metered traffic. In both cases, the metering process reports only one value.

Figure 2-3   *BGP Autonomous System Path*

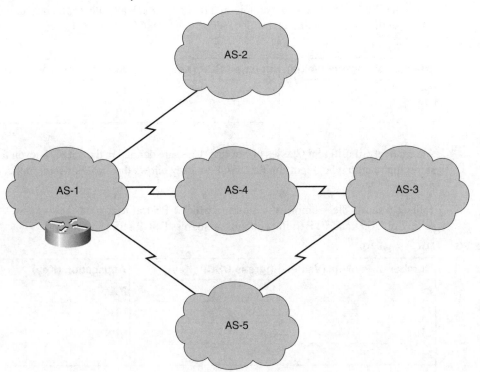

Table 2-7   *AS Path as a Value*

Destination AS DSCP (Key)	AS Path (Value)	Volume (Value)
AS2	AS1-AS2	100
AS3	AS1-AS4-AS3 or AS1-AS5-AS3	100

Table 2-8 *AS Path as a Key*

Destination AS DSCP (Key)	AS Path (Key)	Volume (Value)
AS2	AS1-AS2	100
AS3	AS1-AS4-AS3	50
AS3	AS1-AS5-AS3	50

What Are the Required Versus Nice-to-Have Types of Data?

The accounting application types described and classified in Chapter 1 require some volume estimation, such as number of bytes or number of packets. However, only one type of data is sufficient in most cases—either packets or bytes. For example, most billing applications express the volume in terms of bytes, not packets. It might be nice for a billing application to report the number of packets, which is the point of this section. You need to clearly draw the line between "required" and "nice-to-have" types of data. In the billing example, the volume in bytes is required, because the user pays proportionally to the volume, whereas the number of packets is a nice-to-have parameter. On the other hand, a security application requires the volume in both bytes and packets. The ratio of packets to bytes gives useful hints about types of attacks: an attack composed of many small packets to block a server (typically a SYN flood attack), or an attack composed of huge packets to saturate a link.

Within the nice-to-have types of data, you should clearly differentiate the values and the keys, because the implications are different. Maintaining a value such as the number of packets in a flow, on top of the number of bytes, is an easy task for the network element as well as for the network management systems. However, if an additional nice-to-have key is added, the consequences might be significant:

- Increased CPU on the network element as more data records are classified and processed

- Memory impact on the network element as more data records are maintained

- Higher bandwidth requirements between the network element and the management system to transfer the data records

- More data records processed and maintained by the network management system

Keys define the granularity of the collection: the more keys, the greater the level of detail, at the price of additional resource consumption.

Data Types List

All types of data relate to the notion of device, network, or service. The types of data are any keys that classify the traffic in a report, or any values that augment the data record.

Therefore, there is not a complete list of types of data. However, several categories of types of data exist:

- **Packet header fields**—The types of data, as defined in NetFlow services: source IP address, destination IP address, source TCP/UDP port, destination TCP/UDP port, DSCP, input interface, and so on. You can extend this definition to any additional header parameters of other protocols. For example, a monitoring application might want to observe the traffic per Frame Relay Data Link Connection Identifier (DLCI), per ATM Permanent Virtual Circuit (PVC), or per Data Link Switching (DLSw) circuit, and so on.

- **Characteristics of the packet itself**—For example, the number of MPLS labels in the stack, the interpacket delay in case of active measurement, the packet length, the number of unicast IP addresses versus multicast IP addresses versus broadcast IP addresses, and so on.

- **Fields derived from packet treatment at the device**—For example, the Interior Gateway Protocol (IGP) or BGP next hop, the output interface, the one-way delay, the round-trip delay, the flow packet loss, the flow jitter, and so on.

As a final note on the types of data, you see that these three categories combine fields from both passive monitoring and active probing. The answer to what to collect does not require this distinction! The section "Metering Methods: How to Collect Data Records" compares the arguments in favor of active probing and passive monitoring.

Example: Application Monitoring

Considering what to collect requires a fresh start on an empty sheet of paper. Your next task is to fill in the columns of what to report. The generic term "application type" will certainly be a column title, along with "volume of traffic." Even though "what to collect for application monitoring" is the right question, a different formulation of the same question will help. That is, "How are the application types differentiated in the network?"

The Internet Assigned Numbers Authority (IANA) provides the answer to the question about the IP protocol number, as shown in Table 2-9.

Table 2-9   *IANA Assigned Protocol Numbers*

Protocol #	Keyword	Protocol	Reference
1	ICMP	Internet Control Message Protocol	RFC 792
2	IGMP	Internet Group Management Protocol	RFC 1112
6	TCP	Transmission Control Protocol	RFC 793
17	UDP	User Datagram Protocol	RFC 768
...			

However, it is not enough to classify the traffic by the protocol type, because the application port numbers also differentiate the application types: the well-known port numbers (0 to 1023), the IANA registered port numbers (1024 to 49151), or the dynamic and/or private ports (49152 to 65535). In addition to the IP protocol, another flow key is required: the application port number.

The *well-known* ports, shown in Table 2-10, are assigned by the IANA. On most systems, they can be used only by system (or root) processes or by programs executed by privileged users. The *registered* ports are listed by the IANA. On most systems they can be used by ordinary user processes or programs executed by ordinary users. The IANA registers these ports as a convenience to the community.

Table 2-10   *IANA Well-Known Ports*

Port # Transport Protocol	Keyword	Protocol	Reference
20/tcp	FTP-data	File transfer	RFC 414
20/udp	FTP-data	File transfer	RFC 414
21/tcp	FTP-control	File transfer	RFC 414
21/udp	FTP-control	File transfer	RFC 414
23/tcp	telnet	Telnet	RFC 854
23/udp	telnet	Telnet	RFC 854
80/tcp	http	World Wide Web	RFC 2616
80/udp	http	World Wide Web	RFC 2616
...			

Some applications use dynamic and/or private port numbers, negotiated during connection establishment. Stateful inspection is required for classification of such applications. Stateful inspection, also known as dynamic packet filtering, is the ability to discover data connections and examine the header information plus the packet's contents up to the application layer. A simple approach to identifying such applications can be applied if there is a finite number of associated source or destination addresses in the network. The Cisco Unified Messaging application (Unity) is an example in this case. It uses dynamic ports, but as there are usually only a few Unity servers on the network—in this special case—they can be identified by their IP address.

In another situation it can be sufficient to just use the CoS classification as a flow key. If applications are identified by CoS, you can use the 3 precedence bits (from P0 to P2 in Figure 2-4), the 6 DSCP bits (from D0 to D5 in Figure 2-4), or the 4 ToS bits (from T0 to T3 in Figure 2-4), depending on your CoS configuration in the network. Examples such as voice and videoconferencing (IPVC) are identifiable via the ToS value. Figure 2-4 shows the relationship between the three types of data, and Figure 2-5 shows the conversion mechanism between the three types of data.

Figure 2-4 *Relationship Between the Precedence, ToS, and DSCP Bits*

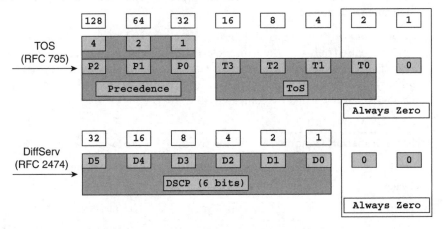

Figure 2-5 *Conversion Mechanism Between the ToS, Precedence, and DSCP Bits*

Multiply by 4 Divide by 8

Binary	ToS	DSCP	Precedence
101 000	160 (0xA0)	40	5
101 100	176 (0xB0)	44	5
001 110	56 (0x1C)	14	1

The destination IP address, used as a key, may classify additional application types. For example, by looking at the traffic with a multicast IP address, you classify the video traffic in your network (assuming that the only multicast traffic in your network is video). Another example is to monitor all traffic destined for the Domain Name System (DNS) server, which lets you quantify the volume of DNS traffic.

In some cases where you cannot distinguish the application by any of the keys already discussed, you might need deeper packet inspection. The subport classification is also a potential flow key for application type distinction. For example:

- **HTTP**—Uniform Resource Locator (URL) with a specific file.

- **Multipurpose Internet Mail Extension (MIME)**—MIME extends the format of Internet mail to allow non-US-ASCII text messages, nontext messages, multipart message bodies, and non-US-ASCII information in message headers. Note that MIME types are also used in HTTP to mark different types of web documents.

- **Citrix applications**—Traffic based on published application names.

The Cisco Network-Based Application Recognition (NBAR) feature provides deeper packet inspection capabilities.

As a summary of the different flow keys available to distinguish the application type, Table 2-11 shows some typical applications and describes the ways to identify them.

Table 2-11   *Typical Application Characteristics*

Application/Protocol	Identification
VoIP	UDP TOS = 5
IP Video Conferencing	TOS = 4
H323	TCP port = 1719, 1720 and TOS = 3
Multicast	Class D address

For the traffic volume, you need to decide which type of data is most appropriate, unless you choose to keep both the number of bytes and the number of packets.

The notion of volume implies the notion of time granularity. Do you require a report every half hour or every hour? As a result, the collection server has records with a 30-minute or 60-minute granularity, and the volume of identical flow records is cumulated over the selected time interval. An alternate option is for each data record to contain time information, which implies that each data record must contain the absolute time of its metering. Note that, depending on the metering procedure, a data record may contain two absolute timestamps: one for the data record start, and one for the data record end.

As the conclusion of this example, you have to determine the generic terms of your defined report (such as application, volume, time), and the specific types of data required. Throughout this example, you have answered the question "How can you classify the different applications in your network?"

Example: Traffic Matrix

You learned in Chapter 1 introduced the core traffic matrix, a table that provides the traffic volumes between origin and destination in a network, which is useful for network-wide capacity planning and traffic engineering.

What are the keys and values to generate a core traffic matrix similar to Table 1-5? The report contains the entry point, the exit point, and the volume in bytes. The entry and exit points are keys, and the bytes number is a value, as shown in Table 2-12.

Table 2-12 *Core Traffic Matrix*

Entry Point (Key)	Exit Point (Key)	Bytes Number (Value)
Rome	Paris	X
Rome	Munich	Y
London	Munich	Z
...		

You can classify the entry point by

- **A router**—The key is then the router from which the data records are retrieved.
- **A Point of Presence (PoP)**—The key is a group of routers from which the data records are retrieved, because a PoP is composed of several routers.
- **A router's interface**—The key is the interface index (ifIndex).

The exit point classification depends on the routing protocol running in the network:

- If the core network runs MPLS, the Forwarding Equivalent Class (FEC) associated with the top label classifies the core's exit point.
- If the core network is a pure IP network, the BGP next hop classifies the core's exit point.

Chapter 1 also explained that the external traffic matrix is useful to look at the influence of the BGP peering selection for your network-wide capacity planning.

The external traffic matrix, such as the core traffic matrix, offers the traffic volumes between the source and destination in the network. However, the external traffic matrix contains more details, because it augments the core traffic matrix with the source and destination ISPs information.

To generate an external traffic matrix similar to Table 1-5, you declare the entry and exit points as keys, the source and destination ISPs as other keys, and the volume in bytes as a value, as shown in Table 2-13.

Table 2-13 *External Traffic Matrix*

Entry Point (Key)	Exit Point (Key)	Source ISP (Key)	Destination ISP (Key)	Bytes Number (Value)
Rome	Paris	ISP-A	ISP-1	X
Rome	Paris	ISP-A	ISP-2	Y
Rome	Paris	ISP-B	ISP-1	Z
...				

You can classify the destination ISPs by

- **The AS of your BGP next hop**—The next AS in the AS path, or, in other words, the BGP AS of your neighbor
- **The destination BGP AS**—The last item of the AS path.

Equivalent logic would apply to the source ISP.

Example: SLA Monitoring

A typical ISP Service Level Agreement (SLA) contains the maximum values of the round-trip time, the packet loss, and the jitter across the network, as shown in Table 1-8. Those maximum values depend on the level of services. The three characteristics of the traffic are defined as values. What is/are the key(s), then? The measurement points in the network define the keys. Even if a table such as Table 1-8 will never show the measurement points, the ISP has to define the report shown in Table 2-14. The key will then be a specific router in a PoP, a dedicated router to perform the IP SLA operations in a PoP (also called a shadow router), customer premises equipment, and so on. Curiously, the measurement points are often "forgotten" in SLA marketing messages; however, they are essential to determine how the ISP meters its SLAs.

Table 2-14 *ISP SLA Monitoring*

Measurement Point (Key)	Round-Trip Time (Value)	Packet Loss (Value)	Jitter (Value)
router-1	50 ms	0	1 ms
...	...	...	...

From a conceptual point of view, reporting the ISP's possible SLAs or reporting the VoIP call quality via active probing are two scenarios that would need exactly the same keys and values. The only difference is in the definition of the measurement point, where VoIP monitoring would impose the measurement point to be an IP phone, the network element (potentially the one to which the IP phone is connected), a passive measurement device in the network, or the VoIP telephony server.

Defining the User

Many application types require the notion of the user: user monitoring and profiling, billing, security analysis, and so on. From the question of what to collect, you saw that various types of data can represent the same notion; for example, the application can be classified by many types of data. This is especially true for the notion of the user; hence, this section is dedicated to the topic. Throughout this section, billing examples illustrate the points.

Table 2-15 shows an example for a user called Mister Joe. He is the customer of an ISP and receives a monthly invoice with detailed records from his provider.

Table 2-15   *Mister Joe's Bill Produced by the ISP*

User	Date	Traffic Transferred	Cost
Mister Joe	Monday	122 MB	$12
Mister Joe	Tuesday	98 MB	$10
Mister Joe	...	...	...

Who is Mister Joe? From the ISP's networking perspective, he is a subscriber to a service, but this label does not distinguish between a user, a group of users, a customer, an organization, and so forth. Even if Mister Joe is a human being, the ISP has to find a clear way to identify him from a networking point of view. Mister Joe can be a single interface if the ISP dedicates an access link to him. In that case, the key is the interface index (ifIndex in RFC 2863).

If several customers share the same access link, the ISP needs a different key. It could be the source IP address if the ISP assigns a static IP address to each customer. In case of dynamic IP address assignment, the IP address allocation could change. In that case, the MAC address, which is always unique because it is bound to a Network Interface Card (NIC), could be the new key. However, using the MAC address as a key entails that Mister Joe always uses the same NIC to access the network resource—that is, the same PC, the same cable modem, or the same DSL modem.

Instead of classifying the user with a networking characteristic (such as the access interface index, source IP address, or MAC address), another approach is user authentication. The Remote Authentication Dial-In User Service (RADIUS) is used for general login purposes: dial-in, Telnet, Secure Shell (SSH), Point-to-Point Protocol (PPP), and so on. The user first authenticates at a Network Access Server (NAS). The next phase is authorization, and the last one is accounting. Whereas RADIUS is a standard protocol defined by the IETF (RFC 2865), the Terminal Access Controller Access Control System + protocol (TACACS+) is a Cisco-specific protocol with similar capabilities. The advantage of both RADIUS and TACACS is that the username is automatically linked to the accounting record. Consequently, in case of RADIUS or TACACS, Mister Joe automatically appears in the data records.

The opposite situation occurs if no authentication takes place and a username is not part of the accounting record. In this case, translation is required to deduce Mister Joe from networking characteristics such as an IP address, a MAC address, an interface, a VPN, or a PVC. For a mediation device in charge of translating a networking characteristic into a user as Mister Joe, getting the real username can be a major challenge:

- How accurate is the database linking the translation to the customer?

- In case of changes in the networking characteristic allocation (IP address, MAC address, VPN, PVC, or the equivalent), what is the process to update the database?

- In case of changes in the networking characteristic allocation, how long does the update take before the database is up-to-date?

- Do multiple users in one location (such as a home network) use the same networking characteristics?

The notion of the user does not always concern individuals. For example, an enterprise may want to charge back the cost of its Internet link to the different departments. In this scenario, the department represents a user in a billing report. In some network designs, where each department is assigned a specific (sub)interface, the ifIndex is again a useful key. In other networks, the key could be the network prefix if the IP address allocation is planned by department. If the user is a prefix, the prefix is deduced from the IP address with the associated subnet mask. This entails that either the metering process takes place at a routing device, or the prefix and subnet mask are also exported as part of the data record and the aggregation is applied at a server. As a practical example, the user cannot be the prefix in case of an RMON collection, because RMON gathers no routing capabilities and traffic-forwarding information.

Furthermore, the user could be an entire company. If an ISP delivers Internet connections to enterprise companies, the ISP bills those companies individually, so the users are the companies. This leads to the same question: How can you distinguish the different users? The answer is: per interface, per IP address range, per ATM PVC, per Frame Relay DLCI, per VPN, and so on.

An ISP can offer different billing reports with different users, according to the level of services offered to customers. In other words, the ISP could offer the user billing-level granularity as a level of service:

- **Basic level of service**—The report contains the billing for the entire company (for example, if the key is the interface index or the VPN).

- **Medium level of service**—The report contains the billing per department within the company. This makes it easy for the department to charge back (for example, if the key is the network prefix).

- **Top level of service**—The report contains the top talkers within the department and company (for example, if the key is the IP address).

Figure 2-6 shows the relationships between the different levels of users.

Figure 2-6 *Relationship Between the Different Levels of Users*

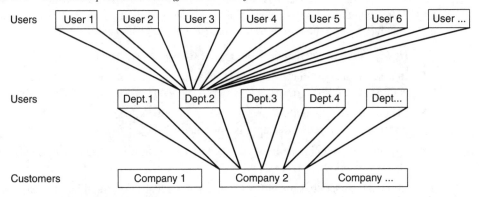

In this section, you learned that the generic notion of the user can be translated into many different types of data, depending on the network design and infrastructure, the network protocol in place, and the level of detail associated with your service.

Metering Methods: How to Collect Data Records

With a clear definition of what to collect and who the user is, the question of how to collect data records becomes relevant. Common terms are *meter* and *metering*. The term meter describes a measuring process, even though a more precise definition is required for accounting purposes. The definition of meter used in this book describes the measurement function in the network element or in a dedicated measurement device. Metering is the process of collecting and optionally preprocessing usage data records at devices in the network. These devices can be either network elements with integrated metering functionality or a dedicated measurement device ("black box") that is specifically designed as a meter.

The following details need to be considered for metering:

- Meter placement, at the device interface or the central processor
- Unidirectional or bidirectional collection
- Collection accuracy
- Granularity, which means aggregating packets into flows or aggregating multiple meters into a single value
- Collection algorithm, which means inspecting every packet with a full collection, or only some packets with sampling
- Inspecting the packet content for selection with filtering
- Adding details to the collected data sets, such as time stamps and checksums
- Export details, such as protocols, frequency, compression, and security

Active Versus Passive Monitoring

You can distinguish between two major monitoring concepts:

- **Passive monitoring**—Also referred to as "collecting observed traffic," this form of monitoring does not affect the user traffic, because it listens to only the packets that pass the meter. Examples of passive monitoring functions are SNMP, RMON, Application Response Time (ART) MIB, packet-capturing devices (sniffer), and Cisco NetFlow Services.

- **Active monitoring**—Introduces the concept of generating synthetic traffic, which is performed by a meter that consists of two instances. The first part creates monitoring traffic, and the second part collects these packets on arrival and measures them.

Note that both instances can be implemented in the same device or at two different devices.

A simple example of an active test is to set up a phone call to check if the destination's phone bell is operational. The Cisco IP SLA feature is an instantiation of active measurement. The main argument for passive monitoring is the bias-free measurement, while active monitoring always influences the measurement results. On the other hand, active measure-ments are easily implemented, whereas some passive measurements, such as the ART MIB, increase the implementation complexity. Table 2-16 summarizes the pros and cons of both approaches. Best practice suggests combining active and passive measurements to get the best of both worlds.

Table 2-16 *Comparison of Active and Passive Monitoring*

	Active Monitoring	**Passive Monitoring**
Advantages	Identifies issues and bottlenecks in the network before users experience a service degradation, or even before a service is in place. Measures application-specific parameters and per traffic class (DSCP). Easy to implement and deploy.	Directly monitors the user traffic. No interference with live traffic. Most accurate for application traffic on a specific link.
Disadvantages	It is difficult to define the right parameters to simulate realistic traffic. The result is only an approximation of the real traffic. Increases the network load. Influences the results by injecting traffic into the measured traffic.	Continuous measurement is required to avoid missing traffic types that are not present on the network during a short measurement interval. Full collection can lead to overload situations; therefore, sampling is a requirement.

Passive Monitoring Concepts

Passive monitoring concepts are categorized into two groups:

- **Full collection**—Accounts all packets and performs various operations afterwards.
- **Partial collection**—Applies sampling or filtering to select only some packets for inspection.

In both cases, you can store either packets or flows, which leads to the definition of the two terms. Packets refer to individual instances, without identifying a relationship between them. Flows consist of packets related to each other—for example, because they belong to an exclusive data session between a client and a server.

A major distinguisher between different passive monitoring techniques is the unidirectional versus bidirectional type of collection. Unidirectional concepts, such as Cisco NetFlow, collect traffic in one direction only, resulting in multiple collection records (for example: record 1 is source → destination; record 2 is destination → source). These have to be consolidated afterwards. Other technologies, such as RMON and the ART MIB, measure traffic in both directions and directly aggregate the results at the meter. At first glance, the bidirectional method seems more practical. Unfortunately, it cannot be applied in networks with asymmetric routing (which means that the return traffic takes a different route) or load sharing across multiple devices.

Full Collection

Full collection processes every packet and therefore guarantees that the output of the metering process is always exactly equal to the data passing the network element. Accuracy is *the* main advantage of a full collection! Major disadvantages are the large number of generated data records and the performance overhead caused by the collection. Full collection concepts are implemented for packet collection as well as flow collection. Various collection technologies have different performance impacts. For example, updating the device's SNMP interface counters consumes fewer resources than collecting NetFlow records. A clear distinguisher between various collection methods is the ability to differentiate applications in the data records. For example, SNMP interface counters collect only the total number of packets. They do not identify a relationship between packets of a type of application, which is also called stateful collection. Stateful collection identifies the associations between packets that belong to the same session (such as **ftp file transfer**) and does it bidirectionally: from source to destination and destination to source. In the case of TCP sessions, NetFlow implements a partly stateful flow collection, because flows are identified by start (SYN) and stop (FIN or RST) flags. It is not completely stateful, because no bidirectional correlation exists. Another full collection technique is the ART MIB, which is an extension of RMON and proposes a transactional method. Instead of the stateless collecting approach taken by RMON, ART identifies the start of a session, creates an entry for this transaction, and monitors the network for the associated return packet. The elapsed time between the initial packet and the response is measured and stored in the MIB. ART can identify all TCP applications as well as two protocols on top of UDP: NFS and SNMP.

Partial Collection

The increasing speed of interface technologies forced the development of alternative technologies to a full collection—for example, filtering and sampling. Today, Fast Ethernet is the default interface speed for a PC, whereas workgroup switches have multigigabit uplinks and optical WAN links that drastically increase transmission capabilities. To avoid CPU and memory resource exhaustion in the network elements and to avoid overloading the collection infrastructure, new sampling concepts are required. In the future, full collection methods such as NetFlow will not be scalable for high classification techniques; instead, they will require dedicated devices. For network elements, the proposed solution is to focus on sampling techniques, which is the reason for the in-depth analysis of sampling techniques in this book. Using sampling techniques for billing introduces a paradigm change, compared to the legacy world of SS7. Instead of applying "Don't forward traffic if you can't bill it," the new paradigm can be described as "First, forward traffic as fast as possible and apply billing as the second instance."

The definition of sampling used in this book is as follows:

Sampling is the technology of selecting a subset (the samples) of the total data set in the network, typically for accounting purposes, with the aim that the subset reflects most accurately the characteristics of the original traffic.

Another analogy would be a puzzle. How many pieces do you need until you can identify the full picture that the puzzle depicts? You have probably done this, so you know that not all pieces are required. Sampling in this case means assembling just enough puzzle pieces to envision the big picture. Therefore, the idea is to select only "important" packets and ignore "unimportant" packets. If you want to relate this to the puzzle analogy, you need to collect only those puzzle pieces that shape the object enough so that you can recognize the full picture.

Filtering Versus Sampling

An alternative technique to sampling is filtering, which applies deterministic operations based on the packet content. Whereas sampling can depend on the packet's position in time, space, or a random function, filtering is always a deterministic operation.

The definition of filtering used in this book is as follows:

Filtering is a deterministic operation that differentiates packets <u>with</u> specific characteristics from packets <u>without</u> these properties.

To follow the puzzle example, you apply a filter when you select all border pieces first. The filter criterion in this case would be "Select pieces only if one side has a straight line." After building the frame, you would probably select significant middle pieces with contrast and pictures, not pieces that are completely blue, such as those from the sky or the ocean. Figure 2-7 demonstrates the results of sampling and filtering.

Figure 2-7   *Parent and Child Populations*

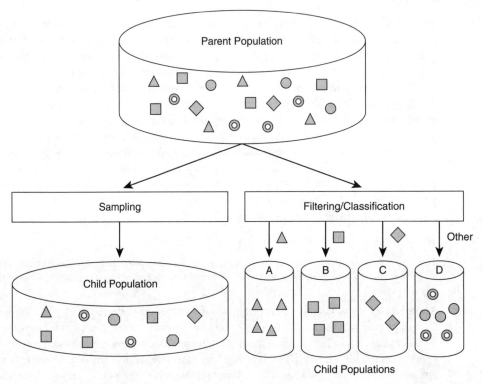

Two terms are commonly used in the area of sampling and filtering:

- **Parent population** describes the original data set from which samples are taken.
- **Child population** describes the remaining data set after sampling, which is the sample.

The objective of sampling is to have the child population represent the parent population characteristics as exactly as possible; otherwise, the collection is biased and most likely of less use.

Sampling Methods

Shifting the focus back to the networking environment, it is advantageous to leverage sampling, especially on high-speed interfaces of the networking devices. The sampling process selects a subset of packets by either applying deterministic functions to the packet position in time or space or applying a random process. Deterministic sampling selects every nth packet or packets every n seconds, for example. An example of random sampling is selecting one out of 100 packets based on a random algorithm or a packet every 5 ms. Figure 2-8 illustrates random and deterministic packet sampling.

Figure 2-8   *Deterministic and Random Sampling*

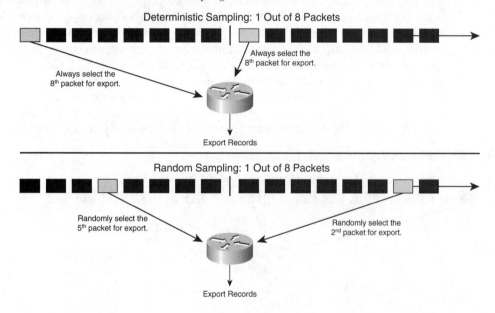

Sampling compared to a full collection provides advantages for the metering device, the network that transports the data sets, and the application that processes the data afterwards:

- **Meter**—Sampling increases the scalability to collect traffic at high-speed interfaces. Processing all packets becomes increasingly difficult.

- **Transport network**—Sampling can reduce the data export from the meter to the collection server.

- **Application**—A smaller data set reduces the required processing power at the mediation and application server.

After deciding to sample traffic, consider the sampling rate and the required accuracy, which is also called the confidence interval. If the sampling rate is too low (which means undersampling), the child population is less accurate as required by the confidence interval and does not correctly represent the parent population traffic received at the device. If the sampling rate is too high (oversampling), you consume more resources than necessary to get the required accuracy. For a better understanding of the different sampling techniques, the following structure applies in this chapter.

A relevant concept is the sampling strategy, such as deterministic (or *systematic*) and random (or *pseudo-random, probabilistic*) sampling. Deterministic sampling involves the risk of biasing the results if a periodic repetition occurs in the traffic that exactly matches the sampling rate or a multiple of it, as illustrated in Figure 2-9. Biasing reduces the match of the child and parent population and is counterproductive to the objective of an accurate matching between the two. Unfortunately, a periodic repetition of events in the observed traffic might not be known in advance, so a criterion for a "good" sampling algorithm is to have a good mixture of packets, and that is the starting point to consider random sampling. In other words, the deterministic sampling model is sufficient when the observed traffic does not contain any repetitions, which typically applies at high-speed interfaces. Random sampling is slightly more complex than deterministic sampling, because it implies the generation of the random numbers. However, random sampling increases the probability for the child population to be closer to the parent population, specifically in case of repetitions in the observed traffic. Best practice recommends using random sampling.

Figure 2-9 *Examples of Deterministic and Random Packet Sampling*

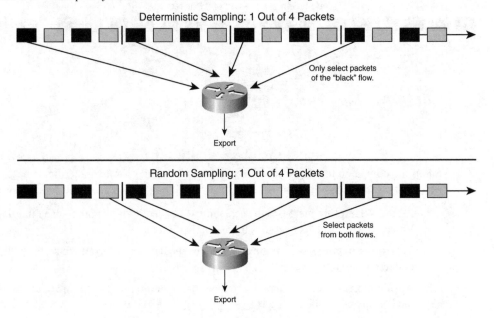

A number of research publications address this topic; consequently, it is sufficient to have just a simple example, as illustrated in Figure 2-9. In this case, traffic consists of two flows, and packets from each flow arrive in round-robin order. In the case of deterministic sampling 1-in-4, packets from only one flow are selected for processing, and random sampling "catches" packets from both flows. The reason is that the inverse of the sampling rate (4) is a multiple of the traffic repetition (2).

Another concept is packet sampling versus flow sampling, which applies for both random and systematic sampling:

- Packet sampling selects packets according to an algorithm and may combine multiple packets into a flow. In this case, flows are created based on the subset of packets that were collected from the sampling instance. In other words, packet sampling occurs first and is optionally followed by flow aggregation.

- Flow sampling takes a different approach. It starts with a selection of all packets and applies algorithms to merge them into flows, which results in a full collection of the original traffic (or parent population). Afterwards, flow entries in the cache are sampled either randomly or systematically, based on criteria such as largest flows, shortest flows, flow duration, and so on. In other words, aggregating packets into flows happens first, followed by flow sampling.

Even though packet and flow sampling are described separately, both techniques can be applied in conjunction. For example, you could sample packets first and then sample the aggregated flows afterwards to export only a subset of the total number of flows.

Deterministic Sampling

The first algorithm to examine is deterministic sampling, also known as periodic or systematic sampling. This sampling algorithm can be systematic count-based (for example, sample every 100th packet), systematic time-based (such as sample every 10 ms), or systematic size-based (select only packets whose length meets a certain criterion, such as 100 bytes).

These schemes are easy to implement and sufficient for applications such as performance management that require less accuracy than applications such as billing, which have high accuracy requirements. A valid concern related to the systematic approach is the dynamic nature of the traffic, which for a given confidence interval may result in inaccurate undersampling or excessive oversampling under changing traffic conditions. In general, the higher you sample, the better the results are, but there is no need for overachieving the confidence interval that you defined originally. Unfortunately, no mathematical model exists to describe deterministic sampling, which means that there is no mathematical proof that deterministic sampling is not biased. Empirical observations have shown that in high-speed network environments, the traffic is sufficiently mixed so that no repetitions of any kind exist. Consequently, there is no risk of biasing by always selecting the same type of traffic in the parent population, if by chance the sampling rate is a multiple of the traffic repetition rate. However, to be on the safe side, you should not select random sampling techniques for applications such as usage-based billing.

Deterministic Packet Sampling: 1 in *N* Also known as periodic fix-interval sampling, it is a relatively simple count-based algorithm that allows the selection of one packet out of every *N* packets. You configure a value for *N* in the meter. Then you multiply the volume of the accounting records at the collection server by the same factor, *N*, to get the estimated total traffic volume. This is useful for network baselining and traffic analysis, even though the accuracy cannot be determined exactly and the results might be biased.

Example: $N = 100$
Result: sample packets 100, 200, 300, 400, 500, ...
Effective sampling rate: 1 percent

Note that NetFlow supports deterministic packet sampling, but it calls the feature "systematic packet sampling."

NOTE For more details on Sampled NetFlow, refer to http://www.cisco.com/univercd/cc/td/doc/product/software/ios120/120newft/120limit/120s/120s11/12s_sanf.htm. xxx

---

The 1 in *N* packet sampling scheme can be extended to collect multiple adjacent packets at each collection interval. In this case, the interval length defines the total number of packets sampled per interval, while the trigger for the operation is still counter-based. Collecting a number of contiguous packets increases the probability of collecting more than one packet of a given flow. Two parameters define the operation:

- The packet-interval parameter is the denominator of the ratio (1/*N*) of packets sampled. For instance, setting a packet interval of 100, one packet out of every 100 will be sampled.

- The interval-length statement defines the number of samples following the initial trigger event, such as collecting the following three packets.

    Example: packet-interval = 100, interval-length = 3
    Result: sample packets 100, 101, 102, 200, 201, 202, 300, 301, 302, ...
    Effective sampling rate: 3 percent

Deterministic Time-Based Packet Sampling The schemes described so far use the packet position (also known as "spatial") as the trigger to start the sampling process. Alternatively, a trigger can be a clock or timer, which initiates the selection in time intervals, such as every 100 ms. The stop trigger can also be a timer function, such as one that collects all traffic during an interval of 5 ms. Because you cannot determine in advance how much traffic occurs at the meter during the measurement time interval, three situations are possible:

- The accuracy of the child population matches the defined confidence interval; in this case, the sampling rate is correct.

- The accuracy of the child population is lower than required, which means that additional samples would be necessary to match the confidence interval. Undersampling describes the situation in which not enough samples are available to offer the required accuracy.

- The accuracy of the child population is higher than required, which means that more samples are selected than needed to match the confidence interval. Oversampling describes the situation in which a smaller number of samples still provides a correct result.

Figure 2-10 illustrates this effect. The solid bars represent required sampling, and the open bars show oversampling. Undersampling is illustrated by the encircled arrows.

Figure 2-10 *Time-Based Packet Sampling: Oversampling Compared to Undersampling*

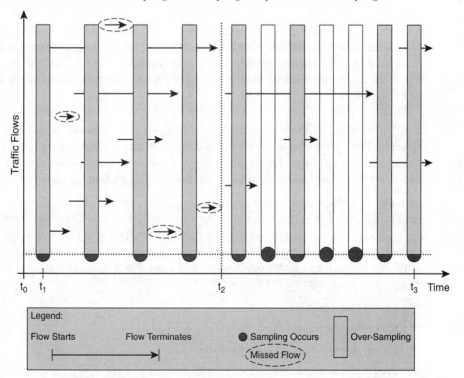

In the specific example of Figure 2-10, traffic is considered as flows or unidirectional conversations, which have a define start and stop time, and the goal is to identify the occurrence of each individual flow. Packets are collected at fixed time intervals, indicated by the bullets and vertical bar. Note that the figure explains a conceptual sampling scenario;

it does not describe how packet sampling is implemented. For example, do not assume that four flows are captured in parallel.

During interval $t_1 - t_2$, undersampling occurs because not all flows are collected. The missed ones are encircled by the dotted lines. To solve this problem, you need to increase the sampling interval. In interval $t_2 - t_3$, oversampling takes place, and more traffic is collected than required to gather all flows (redundant sampling points marked with a pattern). In this case, you could decrease the sampling interval without loosing a flow. Best practice suggests that the selected sampling rate should be a compromise between these two extremes. To avoid empty collections and to gather at least a minimum number of samples, an alternative approach is to combine the time-based start trigger with a packet counter (N) or a content-based function. In that case, you start the collection every n ms but do not stop unless N packets are collected. Afterwards the meter idles for n seconds and starts again. Instead of collecting N packets in a row when the trigger starts, the meter can select those N packets by applying some random selection, or even by applying a filter to match certain traffic criteria.

In the example in Figure 2-10, it is possible to identify over- and undersampling and therefore define the "right" sampling interval. In reality, there is no perfect answer for how to derive an appropriate sampling rate from a given confidence interval, or how to compute an appropriate confidence interval for a given application. This makes it hard to identify the "right" sampling rate.

Deterministic Size-Based Sampling

A different deterministic approach is to collect packets or flows based on their size. From a monitoring perspective, you can be interested in analyzing the traffic's packet size to draw conclusions from the packet size for specific applications, such as security monitoring, or for general planning purposes.

Instead of reporting the exact size per packet, a simple aggregation approach is to define buckets of packet size at the device and aggregate packets into these buckets. This aggregation provides statistics about the packet size distribution but does not supply additional traffic details, such as source or destination. A benefit of this method is the simplicity, because only three collection buckets need to be implemented. Here's an example of the different packet size buckets:

- Packet size < 64 bytes
- Packet size between 64 and 200 bytes
- Packet size between 201 and 500 bytes
- Packet size between 501 and 1000 bytes
- Packet size > 1000 bytes

The size-based sampling concept can also be applied to the size of a flow, which can be the total number of packets for a flow or the total number of bytes for a flow.

Previously, we defined a flow as an aggregation of packets with common key fields, such as source or destination IP address. The flow size is indeed a relevant indicator of communication characteristics in the network, as you will see in the following examples. A huge number of very small packets can indicate a security attack. Instant-messaging communication usually generates a constant number of small packets; the same applies for IP telephony. File transfer sessions use the maximum packet size and transmit a large volume in a short time period.

NOTE   An interesting article on the subject of Internet traffic is "Understanding Internet Traffic Streams: Dragonflies and Tortoises" by N. Brownlee and KC Claffy (http://www.caida.org/outreach/papers/2002/Dragonflies/cnit.pdf).

Size-based flow sampling works as follows: during time interval *T*, all packets are aggregated into flows. At the end of interval *T*, size-based flow sampling selects only flow records with a large volume for export, either in number of packets or in number of bytes. This method reduces the number of data sets exported from the meter to the collection server and trims the required processing cycles at the meter, because only a subset of entries from the cache are exported. Tables 2-17 and 2-18 describe size-based flow sampling. Both tables contain flow entries; the major difference is the sequence of the flow entries. Table 2-17 shows a flow table, where flows are added based on their creation time. Table 2-18 displays the same entries, but this time sorted by the flow size (number of packets). Consider a function that lets you select the Top-*N* entries, where you define a packet size threshold (such as number of packets) and export only those flows above the threshold. For Table 2-18, a threshold of 10,000 packets would result in exporting flow entry numbers 995 and 4.

Table 2-17   *Unsorted Flow Table*

Flow Entry	IP Source Address	IP Destination Address	Packets	TOS	Source AS	Destination AS
1	10.1.1.1	10.2.2.2	5327	160	13123	5617
2	1.2.3.4	1.1.1.1	294	176	13123	3320
3	10.61.96.101	171.69.2.78	15	0	0	5617
4	171.69.2.78	10.61.96.101	10382	0	13123	3215
5	144.254.71.181	10.1.1.3	816		13123	1668
...						
995	10.2.1.5	10.64.30.123	290675	176	13123	7018
996	144.210.17.180	171.71.180.91	8410	0	21344	5617
997	10.1.1.1	10.2.2.2	481	160	13123	22909
...						

Table 2-18   *Flow Table Sorted by Flow Size*

Flow Entry	IP Source Address	IP Destination Address	Packets	TOS	Source AS	Destination AS
995	10.2.1.5	10.64.30.123	290675	176	13123	7018
4	171.69.2.78	10.61.96.101	10382	0	13123	3215
996	144.210.17.180	171.71.180.91	8410	0	21344	5617
1	10.1.1.1	10.2.2.2	5327	160	13123	5617
5	144.254.71.181	10.1.1.3	816		13123	1668
997	10.1.1.1	10.2.2.2	481	160	13123	22909
2	1.2.3.4	1.1.1.1	294	176	13123	3320
3	10.61.96.101	171.69.2.78	15	0	0	5617

Random Sampling

A valid concern of deterministic sampling is the potential biasing of the collection results. Related to sampling, the objective for the child population is to represent the parent population accurately. The term "random sampling" implies that for a finite quantity each member has the same chance of being selected. The random samples should be representative of the entire parent population. Algorithms that meet this requirement are also called pseudo-random-number generators. From a mathematical perspective, random sampling can be represented in a model, whereas deterministic sampling can only be investigated in an empirical manner. This is the main reason for the selection of random sampling versus deterministic sampling in all situations where determination of the accuracy is relevant.

Random Packet Sampling   In this sampling mode, an average of 1-out-of-N sequential packets are randomly selected for processing (where N is a user-configurable integer parameter), ultimately providing information on $100/N$ percent(s) of total traffic. The notation $1:N$ is used to describe sampling of 1-out-of-N packets. For example, if a random sampling of 1:100 is configured, the algorithm randomly selects one packet out of each 100 sequential packets, providing information on 1 percent of the total traffic. Figure 2-11 illustrates 1-out-of-N sampling with a sampling interval of $N = 5$, so a random selection of one packet within a set of five packets takes place. Cisco NetFlow implements random sampling; it is called *Random Sampled NetFlow*.

NOTE	For more details on Random Sampled NetFlow, check http://www.cisco.com/en/US/ products/sw/iosswrel/ps5207/products_feature_guide09186a00801a7618.html.

Figure 2-11 *Random Packet Sampling: 1-out-of-N Sampling*

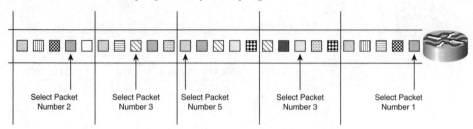

A modified version of the 1-out-of-N sampling is n-out-of-N mode. It is similar to random 1-out-of-N sampling just described, except this time, not just a single packet gets collected, but several packets. If you configure $n = 100$ and $N = 10,000$, you randomly sample 100 nonconsecutive packets at random positions within the 10,000 packets.

Random Flow Sampling   In contrast to random packet sampling, where the random factor applies to the packet selection, random flow sampling takes a different approach. The meter aggregates the observed traffic into flows, based on the defined key aggregation fields, such as source or destination address, port number, or device interface. This aggregation step can be applied to all packets, in case of a full collection, or can be applied after packet sampling. Random flow sampling is accomplished afterwards, where not all flows are exported, but only a subset of flows, based on the random factor. Instead of defining a random factor for packets, you define a factor for 1-out-of-N flows. Figure 2-12 illustrates the four steps of random flow sampling:

1 Collect every packet or alternatively sample packets first.

2 Aggregate packets into flows, and create entries in the flow table.

3 Randomly select a number of flow entries from the table.

4 Export only the selected flow entries, and clear the table.

Figure 2-12 *Random Flow Sampling*

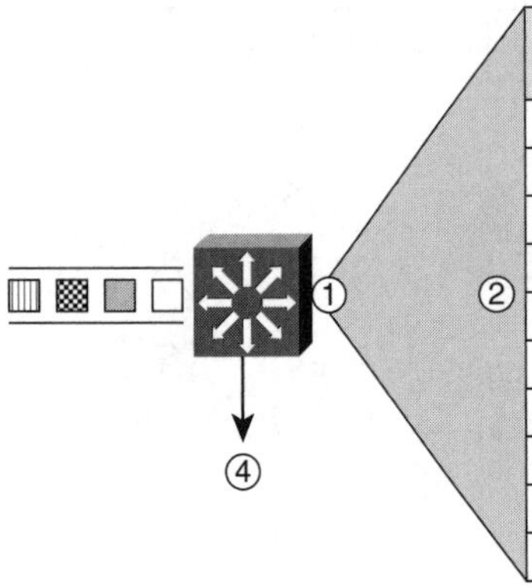

Flow Entry	IP SA	IP DA	Packets	TOS	Source AS	Dest AS	Other Details
#1	10.1.1.1	10.2.2.2	5327	160	13123	5617	
#2	1.2.3.4	1.1.1.1	294	176	13123	3320	
#3	10.61.96.101	171.69.2.78	15	0	0	5617	
#4	171.69.2.78	10.61.96.101	10382	0	13123	3215	
#5	144.254.71.181	10.1.1.3	816		13123	1668	
...							
#995	10.2.1.5	10.64.30.123	290675	176	13123	7018	
#996	144.210.17.180	171.71.180.91	8410	0	21344	5617	
#997	10.1.1.1	10.2.2.2	481	160	13123	22909	
...							

Flow Entry	IP SA	IP DA	Packets	TOS	Source AS	Dest AS	Other Details
#1	10.1.1.1	10.2.2.2	5327	160	13123	5617	
#2	1.2.3.4	1.1.1.1	294	176	13123	3320	
#3	10.61.96.101	171.69.2.78	15	0	0	5617	
#4	171.69.2.78	10.61.96.101	10382	0	13123	3215	
#5	144.254.71.181	10.1.1.3	816		13123	1668	
...							
#995	10.2.1.5	10.64.30.123	290675	176	13123	7018	
#996	144.210.17.180	171.71.180.91	8410	0	21344	5617	
#997	10.1.1.1	10.2.2.2	481	160	13123	22909	
...							

⟶ Entries Selected for Export

Probabilistic Packet Sampling   Probabilistic sampling describes a method in which the likelihood of an element's selection is defined in advance. For example, if you toss a coin and select a packet if only the coin shows heads, the selection chance is 1 out of 2. If you cast a die and select a packet if one dot is displayed, chances are 1 out of 6 that a packet will get chosen. Probabilistic sampling can be further divided into a uniform and non-uniform version.

Uniform probabilistic sampling uses a random selection process, as described with the coin and dice examples, and is independent of the packet's content. An example of uniform probabilistic sampling addresses flow sampling: Most of the time you want to export the flows with a high volume because these are the most important ones. The solution is to export all large flow records with a high probability, while the small flow records are exported with a low probability, such as proportional to the flow record volume.

Nonuniform probabilistic sampling does not use a random function for packet selection; instead, it uses function based on the packet position or packet content. The idea behind it is to weight the sampling probabilities to increase the likelihood of collecting rare but relevant packets. Imagine that you want to select routing protocol updates to identify changes to the paths in your network. Compared to user traffic, these packets represent a minority of the total traffic but are important to meet your objective.

Stratified Sampling

For the sake of completeness, the theoretical aspects of stratified sampling are highlighted next. Stratified sampling takes the variations of the parent population into account and applies a grouping function before applying sampling. Stratification is the method of grouping members from the parent population with common criteria into homogeneous subgroups first; these groups are called strata. The benefit is that a lower sampling rate per strata is sufficient to achieve the same level of accuracy. For example, if a sampling rate of 1 out 10 is required to achieve a certain confidence interval, after grouping by strata, the same goal could be achieved by a sampling rate of 1 out of 20. The key to successful stratification is to find a criterion that will return a stratification gain.

Two requirements are relevant for the selection process:

- **Comprehensiveness**—Every element gets selected; none can be excluded.
- **Mutual exclusiveness**—Every element has to be assigned to exactly one group (stratum).

Referring to Figure 2-7, child populations A, B, C, and D are taken from the parent population and are grouped according to their characteristics. After the packets are grouped, sampling techniques are performed on each stratum individually, which means that different sampling algorithms can be applied in parallel. Stratification also achieves the same confidence interval with a lower sampling rate.

A practical illustration is first to classify traffic per application (such as HTTP, FTP, Telnet, peer-to-peer, and management traffic) and then sample per group (stratum). This method is useful to correct the allocation of variances in the parent population.

For example, the volume of web-based traffic on a link is 10 times the amount of Telnet traffic. Assuming that you want to sample packets, the child population should contain the same volume of HTTP and Telnet packets, possibly for packet content analysis. If you apply sampling across the mixed traffic, a higher sampling rate is required to select enough Telnet packets, due to their small occurrence, while a lower sampling rate would be sufficient for HTTP. If you group (stratify) the traffic first into a stratum of HTTP packets and then into a stratum of Telnet packets, the same sampling rate can be applied to both groups.

Filtering at the Network Element

Filtering is another method to reduce the number of collection records at the meter. Filters are deterministic operations performed on the packet content, such as match/mask to identify packets for collection. This implies that the packet selection is never based on a criterion such as packet position (time or sequence) or a random process in the first place.

Three steps are applied for filtering. As the first step, you define "interesting" packets, which are the selection criterion for the collection process. One example is to filter packets based on selected IP or MPLS fields; another example is filtering based on the packet's QoS parameters. A final example is the matching of IPv4 and IPv6 header types that provide the operator with adequate information during the transition phase from IPv4 to IPv6. A practical implementation for selecting packets is the use of Access Control List (ACL) match statements. Step 2 selects either full packet collection or sampling operations. Step 3 exports packets immediately or aggregates them into flows before exporting. Figure 2-13 shows the various alternatives and combinations of filtering and sampling.

Figure 2-13 *Packet Selection Options*

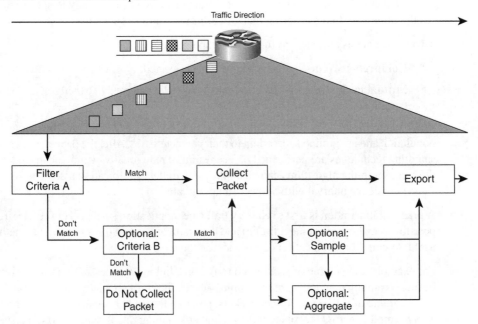

The combination of filtering and sampling is a very efficient approach to dealing with the increasing traffic volume in the networks. Instead of choosing between full collection and sampling, you can apply the preferred methodology based on traffic types. If a network already has service classes defined, these classes can act as the traffic distinguisher for collecting accounting and performance data records. Figure 2-14 shows three different traffic classes:

- **Priority traffic**—A network operator requires detailed accounting records from the priority traffic for billing purposes, so a full collection is configured.

- **Business traffic**—Business traffic needs to be monitored closely to validate SLAs, but it is not charged, so a sampling rate of 100 is acceptable.

- **Best-effort traffic**—The best-effort traffic class is provided without any SLA; therefore, a basic collection with a sampling rate of 1000 is adequate.

These requirements can be fulfilled by deploying a combination of filtering and sampling.

Figure 2-14 *Combining Filtering and Sampling*

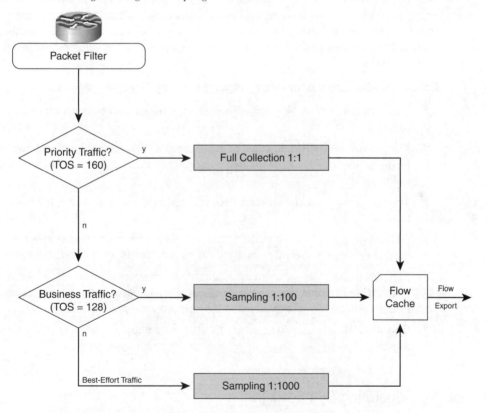

A sophisticated design is to continuously collect all packets under normal circumstances and apply sampling and filtering during "special" situations, such as very high utilization or security attacks. During a DoS attack, it is critical to collect detailed traces of the specific portion of the traffic that is related to the attack, such as if a significant fraction of the traffic has the same destination address.

Note that NetFlow supports input filtering mechanisms, under the name "input filters."

Filters described so far take actions on the packet content. An alternative are filters based on the router's state. For instance, a violated ACL can trigger a collection of flows for a security analysis. Alternatively, traffic that matches a certain BGP AS number or range of AS numbers can be metered, while traffic from other AS numbers is not metered.

Active Monitoring Concepts

Whereas passive collection methods are based on the concept of not affecting the live traffic on the network, active monitoring applies the exact opposite paradigm. Specific synthetic traffic is generated and the results are collected to *indirectly* measure the performance of a device, the network, or a service. This section describes how to generate and meter synthetic traffic.

Certain conditions are to be met when actively measuring the network and creating test traffic:

- The characteristics of the user traffic must be represented, such as packet size and QoS parameters.

- The ratio of test traffic compared to the total capacity is required to be relatively low. Best practices suggest a maximum of 1 percent test traffic compared to production traffic.

- Test traffic must not be blocked by security instances, such as ACLs, firewalls, or proxies.

- Devices must treat the test traffic exactly like any other traffic (for example, a router must not process test traffic in software if other traffic is processed in hardware).

- The start time of the operations should provide a random component to avoid biased results. (For example you can define an operation to occur every 30 seconds, but a Poisson process would actually start the operation at intervals of ±5 percent.)

- Operations should support excessive short-term operations to support troubleshooting as well as low-impact long-term operations for trending purposes.

Concepts for Generating Synthetic Traffic

There are various ways to generate synthetic traffic, but before we investigate them, a fundamental decision is required: Where should availability be measured?

- At the device?
- At the network?
- At the service?

You can start at the device level to ensure that the device still exists and responds to requests. Monitoring a device in an isolated approach has limited value, so the measurements are extended to include the network level by checking end-to-end availability. Sometimes this might not be sufficient, so the service is monitored in addition to devices and the network. There is no single answer to the question of where to monitor availability, because it depends on the purpose of the measurements. If you want to generate service-level reports, the right level to focus on is the service availability, including mean time to restore (MTTR). For troubleshooting purposes, network and device availability statistics are very beneficial.

The following statements outline the fundamentals of synthetic measurement:

- The measurement is performed indirectly by inserting test traffic. This means that records are not collected from the live traffic on the network and there is *no direct relationship* between the live traffic and the test traffic, except that network elements should treat both traffic types the same and they should traverse the same paths.

- Injecting additional test traffic can cause a dilemma. Imagine a situation in which the production traffic is just below the defined threshold and the extra traffic hits the utilization threshold and raises an alarm, even though the network was performing well before. Although this is a valid argument against synthetic measurement traffic, the same could happen with user traffic, when just one additional session creates enough traffic to start an alarm.

- There is a performance impact on the measured devices, such as routers, switches, probes, or agents running on the client or server, that should not be neglected. Best practice suggests continuous monitoring of the device CPU utilization.

Device Availability

The simplest approach to test device availability is to send a test packet to the device and watch the result. Even though this sounds almost primitive, it is exactly what the most-used network management tool does: ping (the correct name is ICMP echo) tests a device's availability. Ping provides a set of useful statistics about a device and the network layer that connects the device to the network. Besides the limitations, such as testing only the network interface and related drivers plus parts of the operating system, the outcome can contribute valuable information, especially when these tests are performed continuously, resulting in general device availability reports and statistics. More advanced tests, such as Cisco IP SLA, also measure the device processing time by adding time stamps. Best practice suggests monitoring device availability continuously, preferably not only with a ping test, but with more advanced functions, such as SNMP monitoring of the sysUptime MIB parameter. This reports information on how long the device was operational since the last reboot.

Network Availability

Network availability takes a holistic approach to monitor the network as a system and not just check individual components. Proactive measurement operations include generating synthetic traffic from one end of the network to the other end—but first the term "end" must be defined. For a server operator it would probably mean the client on one side of the network and the server on the other end. A network administrator considers the test between two network edge devices end-to-end.

Ping can help measure network availability. If a ping test reports slow response time, it indicates a general network problem, which usually affects other applications as well. Unfortunately, the reverse assumption is not always correct: Even if ping test results are OK, there might be a severe problem in the network. Consider another case: Just because a server can ping router 1 and router 2, this does not imply that router 1 and router 2 can communicate. This scenario confirms that active probing between the network elements is required, such as by utilizing the PING-MIB or Cisco IP SLA.

Ping is an example of a round-trip measurement. The sender generates a test traffic packet and sends it to the receiver, which marks the packet as read and returns it to the sender. The sender has a timer to measure the total traveling time of the packet, while the receiver only echoes the packets to the sender. Another tool, traceroute, also builds on top of ICMP. It provides more detailed results than ping, such as the round-trip time (RTT) for every hop in the path. This helps identify the slowest link in the path. See the section "Active Monitoring Technologies and Tools: ping, traceroute, and IP SLA" later in this chapter for an in-depth explanation. The general assumption behind round-trip measurement is that the forward and return traffic uses the same paths through the network.

In case of load balancing, where two paths operate in parallel, you need to measure all possible paths. There are multiple types: load balancing per packet, load balancing per destination, load balancing based on the combination of source and destination IP addresses, etc. The load-sharing configuration of all routers along the path is important. In case of per-destination load sharing, all packets for the same destination take the same path. In case of load balancing based on the combination of source and destination IP addresses, all packets from the same flow (defined by IP addresses) take the same path. In case of per-packet load sharing, all possible paths are taken and are measured separately as a consequence. The latter case might cause peaks of RTT: one per path. The described actions apply for ping, IP SLA, and traceroute. Best practice suggests avoiding per-packet load balancing when time measurement is involved.

One-way measurement is an appropriate measuring method for asymmetric routing, load balancing, and increased report granularity. Figure 2-15 shows three different scenarios:

- A is the symmetric design. In this case, round-trip measurements are fine, but one-way operation provides the time measurement per direction.

- B illustrates the symmetric design with load balancing. A round-trip operation is still OK. However, as explained in the case of load balancing based on a combination of source and destination IP addresses (which is the most deployed load-balancing scheme), only one path is measured by the flow if the IP addresses of the generated packets don't change.

- C exemplifies an asymmetric design with a distinct path from source to destination and a different path for the return traffic. Under normal circumstances, an RTT measurement provides sufficient details, because RTT returns the asymmetric path a normal packet would take (R1→R2→R3→R4→R1). If the RTT results exceed a threshold and the operator wants to identify on which path the bottleneck occurs, two one-way measurement operations are required: R1→R2→R3 for the forwarding path and R3→R4→R1 for the return path.

Figure 2-15 *Network Design Implications for Active Measurement*

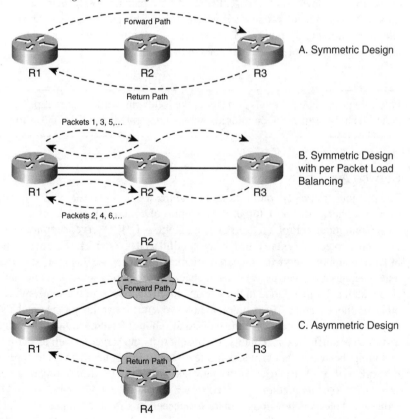

One-way measurement increases the measurement's level of detail, because it provides separate statistics for the forward and return traffic. In the symmetric design (A) in Figure 2-15, assume that you have defined an SLA with an RTT of 20 ms between R1 and R3. suddenly RTT values are above 50 ms, caused by someone who configured one interface of the middle router (R2) with wrong QoS parameters, resulting in delayed forwarding of packets. Round-trip measurement cannot determine where the delay occurs, but a one-way measurement would identify in which direction the delay occurs. For advanced trouble-shooting, the operator can configure additional one-way measurements between R1→R2 and R2→R3 to get a detailed picture per hop.

For round-trip measurements, the same device sends and receives the generated traffic; therefore, the absolute time is not relevant for the results. For one-way operations, two different devices need to cooperate, because one device generates the test packets, and a different device receives them and calculates the result. This requires synchronized system clocks on both devices; otherwise, the results are meaningless! Accurate timing is an important requirement in one-way measurement. This can be achieved by connecting Global Positioning System (GPS) receivers to the network elements or by configuring the network time protocol (NTP) in the network.

NOTE   For more information about NTP, refer to the following white paper: http://www.cisco.com/en/US/tech/tk869/tk769/technologies_white_paper09186a0080117070.shtml.

Service Availability

The previous traffic generation examples addressed the network. Now the focus shifts toward services offered on top of it. Examples of common network services are Dynamic Host Configuration Protocol (DHCP) and DNS. A DHCP server supplies IP addresses to the clients, so you meter the time it takes to fulfill a DHCP request. To monitor the availability of an IP telephony service, you can implement test software that emulates a virtual phone that generates and receives test calls to check the telephony server. An alternative approach is to install a dummy phone in the wiring closet, connect it to the same switch that serves other IP phones, and perform automated test operations at this phone (such as registering the phone at the server and sending calls to the phone). You see immediately that the second approach is much closer to reality, because it tests the server as well as the infrastructure, including the switch that provides inline power to IP phones. The same applies for testing network services. You can perform a ping test to monitor the availability of your central web server. But to be assured that the web server is operational, you need to send an HTTP request and measure how long it takes to succeed. A similar example is the DNS service: a simple ping would prove that the server is operational and connected to the network. It does not tell you anything about the DNS service, so a DNS query and response is necessary to prove the DNS service operation.

Besides DNS and DHCP, examples of synthetic service operations are

- HTTP website download
- TCP connect (how long it takes to establish a TCP connection)
- FTP/TFTP download
- Database operations (insert a record, retrieve it, delete it)
- IP telephony tests (register and unregister a phone, generate a call)

The demarcation line between the network and server components can be achieved by implementing time stamps. The first time stamp is applied immediately after arrival at the device input interface. Another one can be applied before sending the packet to the device output queue, and the final one immediately before putting the packet on the wire.

Figure 2-16 illustrates the time stamp concept:

- **TS^0 (time stamp 0)** is the initial time stamp, created when the packet is sent at the source router.
- **TS^1** is the time stamp when the packet arrives at the destination router's ingress interface.
- **TS^2** is the time stamp when the packet is returned at the destination router's egress interface.
- **TS^3** is the time stamp when the packet is received at the source router's ingress interface.
- **TS^4** is the final time stamp when the packet is received at the source measurement function.

The following results can be analyzed afterwards:

- **$T_{Network\,(S \to D)}$** is the time it took the packet to travel through the network from source (S) to destination .
- **$T_{Network\,(D \to S)}$** is the time it took the packet to travel through the network from destination to source.
- **$TS^2 - TS^1$** is the processing time at the destination device.
- **$TS^4 - TS^3$** is the processing time at the source device.

Figure 2-16 *Increasing Accuracy with Time Stamps*

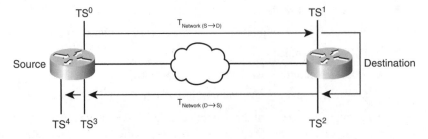

A service availability report is more complex than a device availability report. A service can be operational and handle requests, but if the response time suddenly increases drastically, users will certainly declare the service to be unavailable. This leaves the network planner in the situation of predefining response time thresholds per service to identify when they are considered unavailable due to performance issues. At this point, the concept of baselining, introduced in Chapter 1, becomes relevant for service management. To estimate the current quality of a specific service, relating it to the overall long-term performance of this service, as well as to other services and the network quality, is more meaningful than considering isolated statements. Service measurement from the user's perspective should be included in the baselining process.

Active Monitoring Technologies and Tools: ping, traceroute, and IP SLA

Multiple functions exist to generate synthetic traffic. The best-known and most widely used active measurement tool is certainly the ping test. The correct name is ICMP operation. It consists of a sender and receiver component that interact in the transaction. The sender generates an *ICMP echo request* packet toward the destination and starts a timer. The receiver reverses the source and destination address in the ICMP header and returns the packet to the sender. As soon as the sender receives the response, the timer is stopped, and the elapsed time is displayed. Options exist to run multiple or continuous operations. At the end some statistics are reported. Ping can be directed to take a specific path through the network, because it supports Loose Source Routing (LSR); however, LSR is disabled most of the time in today's networks. Note that the accuracy of the ping results is limited, because they combine network response time and the processing time at the sender and receiver in one record. Depending on the implementation specifics of the operating system (OS), significant delay can be added if the OS treats ping requests with low priority. Nevertheless, ping is a very useful diagnostic and troubleshooting tool. Results can be displayed at the command-line interface or through MIBs (CISCO-PING-MIB or the IETF pingMIB [RFC 2925]).

A sample ping report is as follows:

```
C:\WINNT>ping www.cisco.com

Pinging www.cisco.com [198.133.219.25] with 32 bytes of data:

Reply from 198.133.219.25: bytes=32 time=240ms TTL=235
Reply from 198.133.219.25: bytes=32 time=340ms TTL=235
Reply from 198.133.219.25: bytes=32 time=601ms TTL=235
Reply from 198.133.219.25: bytes=32 time=231ms TTL=235

Ping statistics for 198.133.219.25:
    Packets: Sent = 4, Received = 4, Lost = 0 (0% loss),
Approximate round trip times in milli-seconds:
    Minimum = 231ms, Maximum = 601ms, Average = 353ms
```

Traceroute is probably the second-best-known network management tool; it is also based on the ICMP protocol and can be considered an advanced ping. Ping measures only the total round-trip time between source and destination, but traceroute displays the full path and provides statistics such as delay and packet loss on a per-hop basis. This can easily spot a performance bottleneck in the network as well as routing loops or failed devices. Traceroute leverages the time-to-live (TTL) field in the IP header, which is normally used to avoid packets circling forever during a routing loop. When forwarding packets, each Layer 3 device decreases the TTL counter. If it is 0, an ICMP *time exceeded* message is sent to the originator. Traceroute uses this function, generates a series of ping tests, each with an increased TTL value (starting from 1), and starts a separate timer for each packet. The timer stops when the corresponding ICMP time-exceeded message arrives.

Here's an example of a traceroute report:

```
C:\>tracert -d www.cisco.com
Tracing route to www.cisco.com [198.133.219.25] over a maximum of 30 hops:
  1    <10 ms    <10 ms    <10 ms   10.61.96.201
  2     80 ms     80 ms     81 ms   144.254.221.45
  3     80 ms     80 ms     80 ms   144.254.221.35
  4     80 ms     80 ms     80 ms   144.254.220.57
  5    251 ms     80 ms     80 ms   10.112.2.21
  6    411 ms    180 ms    180 ms   10.112.2.25
  7    231 ms    170 ms    180 ms   10.112.3.74
  8    231 ms    170 ms    180 ms   10.112.3.1
  9    240 ms    190 ms    190 ms   10.112.3.109
 10    220 ms    190 ms    190 ms   10.112.3.117
 11    210 ms    190 ms    190 ms   10.112.3.130
 12    230 ms    210 ms    201 ms   10.112.3.114
 13    200 ms    210 ms    201 ms   10.112.3.94
 14    200 ms    200 ms    211 ms   10.112.3.105
 15    240 ms    230 ms    231 ms   10.112.3.82
 16    250 ms    241 ms    250 ms   10.112.3.65
 17    230 ms    241 ms    230 ms   171.69.7.229
 18    230 ms    241 ms    230 ms   171.69.7.174
 19    231 ms    240 ms    240 ms   128.107.240.193
 20    231 ms    240 ms    240 ms   128.107.239.106
 21    230 ms    240 ms    591 ms   198.133.219.25

Trace complete.
```

A sophisticated tool for generating synthetic traffic is the Cisco IP SLA feature (described in more detail in Chapter 11, "IP SLA"). IP SLA is an active performance-monitoring agent embedded in Cisco IOS software. The agent measures performance by sending synthetic packets to a generic IP device or Cisco device. The packets are echoed to the sender, similar to the functionality of ping. IP SLA uses the time-stamp information to calculate performance metrics (such as jitter, latency, response time, and packet loss).

A target router that is running Cisco IOS software can act as an "IP SLA responder" that processes the IP SLA measurement packets and adds time-stamps. IP SLA can monitor per-class traffic in different traffic classes by setting the Differentiated Service Code Point (DSCP) bits. IP SLA operations can be scheduled to run once or continuously. To support proactive notification, thresholds are defined, and SNMP notifications are generated when these are exceeded. This feature can monitor the actual performance against defined SLAs by notifying the administrator of potential service-level violations. To expedite problem resolution, IP SLA can start an additional operation when a threshold is crossed, which allows for immediate real-time problem analysis. Measurement results can be retrieved with SNMP or from the Cisco IOS command-line interface (CLI).

Table 2-19 summarizes the different characteristics of the three active probing technologies described in this section.

Table 2-19 *Probing Technologies*

	ping	**traceroute**	**IP SLA**
Metric	RTT	RTT	OWD or RTT
Metric Target	From source to destination	From source to destination, including each hop in the path	From source to destination. Note that the processing time at the destination is subtracted.
Management	CLI or PING-MIB	CLI	CLI or RTTMON-MIB

Best Practice: How to Position Active and Passive Monitoring

When comparing active and passive measurement concepts, both have benefits and limitations, which leads to the question of how to position both in the best way. Passive measurement offers benefits for network monitoring in general, for application identification, and for troubleshooting, but it assumes that the traffic of interest is already present on the network. To maintain up-to-date statistics and trend reports about network performance, utilization, and the protocol and application mix on the network, you should apply passive measurement concepts. Active measurement extends this by proactively probing if the current performance metrics of the network and the services are within the defined range. As soon as service level agreements are deployed, you should implement proactive collection techniques and link them to a fault management system. As the network administrator, you need tools to identify and solve issues, such as slow service response times. Active monitoring helps identify the problem ideally even before the users call the help desk, but in most cases, it cannot point to the root cause of the issue ("Why is it slow?"). Passive collection helps you identify the root cause, because it meters the live traffic, from which conclusions can be drawn.

Take a situation in which a user calls the network operator and complains about slow network access. Active monitoring could have warned the operator that the RTT between a remote location and a server farm has increased, but it does not explain why it happened. By looking at live network traffic (passive monitoring), the operator found that a user who downloads large video files from the Internet was the cause of the delay. Now the operator can take appropriate action to solve the problem.

Outlook: Passive Monitoring for One-Way Delay Analysis

In the past, one-way delay (OWD) measurements were implemented as either simple active operations, such as Cisco IP SLA, or complex passive operations, such as the ART MIB. A new approach in the research community considers using packet collection technologies, such as NetFlow, for passive OWD calculation. The basic architecture requires two measurement instances—one on each side of the monitored network. Instead of aggregating packets into flows, raw packets are exported by the meter. The packet selection process is deterministic, and a set of classification rules are required:

- Packets must not be modified in any way
- Packet recognition must be based on existing packet fields and attributes
- Select attributes that do not change across hops (such as IP source/destination address, port number, DSCP/TOS)
- Generate an ID for each selected packet by using a hash function
- Export the packet ID to the collector and apply a time stamp
- Network Time Protocol (NTP) is a prerequisite

By implementing the concept of a unique ID for each selected packet, you also can identify a packet's path through the network and measure OWD on a per-hop basis. Compared to ART, this new approach does not require the network element to identify and measure transaction details. Instead, packets are selected based on different criteria, and the processing is offloaded to a collection station.

NOTE   For more information, refer to "Passive One-way Delay Measurements and Data Export" at http://www.fokus.gmd.de/research/cc/meteor/employees/carsten.schmoll/powd-netflow9.pdf.

Metering Positions: Where to Collect Data Records

After deciding how to meter, the next item on the checklist is defining where to position metering devices in the network. Consider the following options for meter positions:

- Meter at the edge opposed to the core.
- Meter at the network element or end user device.
- Leverage integrated agents at network elements or deploy dedicated probes.
- Ingress compared to egress collection.

Network Element Versus End Device Collection

Most customers organize their IT operations into different groups. One team is responsible for designing and operating the networking infrastructure, such as routers and switches. A second group takes care of the servers and applications. Yet another group is in charge of security, such as firewalls, intrusion detection systems, and antivirus agents. There are good arguments for running like this, but one limitation is the isolation, which can lead to finger-pointing between the groups during troubleshooting an organization. The proposed solution to overcome these situations is to meter both at the network elements and at the end devices and servers. In most corporations, the network is considered *the* cause of an outage, unless the network administrator can prove that the network runs fine. You might not like it, but for many network operators this is the usual situation. How can you make the best of it? Become proactive by collecting and publishing *network* statistics, which documents the availability of your network, overall as well as per network element. Put a system in place that updates these reports regularly. Afterwards, make sure that the other groups become aware of those reports, and educate them to check your website before calling you. You might see miracles happen! A good way to collect these reports is network-centric metering. Identify relevant locations, ideally close to the data center and client locations. If you can proactively monitor the end-to-end connections between the switch at the client location and the central switches in the data center, you reduce the time to troubleshoot during an outage.

NOTE   If traffic is encrypted before it is transmitted on the network, the network elements can no longer identify details such as applications. This special case requires metering before the encryption device (such as a VPN concentrator or router) or directly at the server or user PC if end-to-end tunnels are established.

The alternative approach to metering at the network element is including end devices in the monitoring process. These can be PCs, servers, organizers, IP phones, and so on. From a user's perspective, including end devices is a direct measurement because it meters exactly the users' experiences, whereas measurement at the network element is indirect. A drawback of installing management agents at PCs and servers, especially in large environments, is the operational burden it creates for the administrator. In addition to the technical challenges, such as dealing with various operating systems, this requires client software distribution programs and the collection of accounting records from the PCs. Do not underestimate the psychological aspect of monitoring user devices; some users feel like Big Brother is watching. An optimized design combines device- and network-centric collection methods by installing special metering software at the servers (instead of the end-user PC) and enabling metering features at the network elements. Table 2-20 summarizes the pros and cons of both approaches. Best practice suggests combining measurements at network elements and the end device to get the best of both worlds.

Table 2-20   *Comparison of Network Element and End Device Collection Methods*

	Network Element Collection	**End Device Collection**
Advantages	Identifies network performance issues. Measures network-specific parameters, such as per traffic class (DSCP) or path-specific. Can be deployed without modifying end devices.	Accurately measures the end user experience. Most realistic for application-specific monitoring.
Disadvantages	Indirectly measures the user experience. Performance impact at the network element.	End-to-end results are provided without network-specific measurements. Introduces end-device challenges, such as dealing with different operating systems, inconsistent configurations, and scalability. Intrusive on the desktop.

Another approach is technology-specific collection, which can directly limit the number of choices. For example, if you need the classification by specific routing information, it can be collected only at the network edge. Alternatively, if you plan VoIP measurement, you need to shift the focus to the end device. These arguments are addressed in the "Technology-Dependent Special Constraints" section.

Edge Versus Core Collection

For measurements where meters are best suited in the network, as opposed to the end devices, it is suggested that you consider the specific location in the network. This leads immediately to the discussion of what types of data are required, because it limits the choices. For instance, if you need the classification per customer, collect at the edge. The same applies if two customers connect at the same PoP and the traffic between the two should be monitored. For core traffic engineering, the best collection place is the core network. When comparing edge and core metering positions, technology dependence is one factor, but business requirements and applications also need to be considered. If you have a choice between edge and core collection, a good starting point is the business requirements, because they provide solid justification for selecting the appropriate technology afterwards. Here are two examples:

- If you want to deploy a usage-based billing system for a large, distributed network, chances are high that a collection only at the core devices might not be sufficient. If adjacent remote locations can communicate directly without passing through the core, edge collection is required.

- Best practice suggests performing traffic analysis, policing, and metering at edge devices so that core devices can focus on fast forwarding. Sometimes this rule cannot be applied: in case of a traffic engineering application for the core network, the core is the *only* place to meter.

From a technology perspective, you need to distinguish between active and passive measurements, as defined in the section "Metering Methods: How to Collect Data Records."

Passive measurement records, such as basic SNMP polling of device interface counters and global status information, such as CPU load, can be collected both at the edge and at the core of the network without significant effort, as long as moderate polling rates are configured. Activating NetFlow at the core and edge at the same time is usually not recommended, because it has higher resource consumption than basic SNMP operations and exports a larger set of data records to the collector. Instead of putting an extra burden on network elements, links, and collection servers, the better approach is to identify relevant metering positions and limit the collection to these. If you need NetFlow statistics for core monitoring, collect them at the core devices. If you want to monitor SLA agreements with your service provider, measure at the edge devices toward the provider. Also, note that collecting the same data sets at the core and at the edge results in duplicated records, which need to be correlated and de-duplicated afterwards.

RMON and ART MIB also require specific considerations in terms of where to meter. RMON provides general network utilization details, such as traffic patterns, top talkers, and applications in the network. RMON information can be collected both at the core and at the edge. ART MIB separately measures the "flight time" of datagrams through the network and the server processing time and reports both values. This mandates the meter to be as close to the end devices as possible; therefore, place one ART MIB meter close to the server and the other one close to the users. Never place an ART MIB meter in the middle of the network, between the client and the server. You lose the benefit of distinguishing between network delay and device processing time, because in this case the results are a mixture of network and server response times. Figure 2-17 identifies strategic locations for various metering techniques. In this scenario, SNMP and NetFlow are used in conjunction. Data sent from the data center or clients toward the core can be metered with SNMP interface counters as well as NetFlow services. Even though SNMP collects only an aggregated view of the NetFlow data records, if you want to measure the total traffic from the edge to the core, both techniques are valid options. For collecting edge traffic, SNMP was selected to meter the total volume of user traffic, and NetFlow was chosen at the core to identify traffic patterns, such as traffic source and destination, which cannot be identified by SNMP counters.

Figure 2-17 *Passive Measurement Deployment*

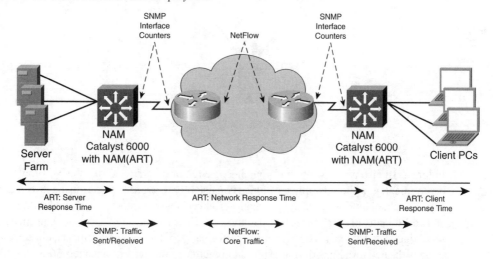

Especially in case of NetFlow deployments, additional factors need to be considered; these are related to Figure 2-18:

- **Billing**—Enable full NetFlow on the aggregation routers to avoid overloading the core network.

- **Capacity planning**—Configure sampled NetFlow on the aggregation or core routers.

- **BGP**—Collect full or sampled NetFlow on the BGP peering routers (usually at the edge of the network).

- **MPLS VPN**—Deploy full or sampled NetFlow for monitoring the MPLS PE-CE links.

Figure 2-18 *Passive Measurement Deployment*

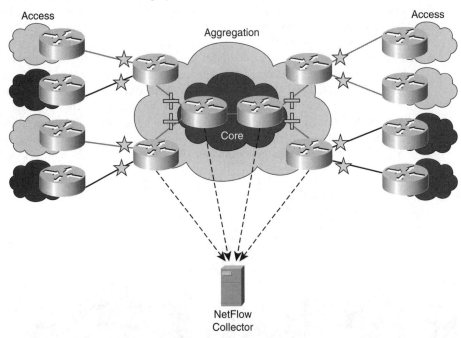

Figure 2-18 also expresses that if you choose edge or core devices for the NetFlow deployment, you should apply the choice consistently to avoid duplicating the flow records. If you enable NetFlow at each aggregation router's ingress interface (marked with a star) and additionally at each core router's ingress interface (marked with a +), it results in a large set of duplicated records. This affects the performance of the network elements, unnecessarily utilizes the network links during export, and increases the performance requirements of the collection server without adding details to the overall collection.

For selecting passive measurement technologies, a business case is also a good starting point, as demonstrated by the following two examples:

- A service provider offers different service levels to its customers and wants to measure and publish the results. In this case, the SP meters between different PoPs or from the central network operations center (NOC) to each PoP.

- An enterprise wants to check if the existing network is capable of supporting VoIP traffic. The administrator sets up meters close to the user in the central and remote locations and measures the relevant voice metrics, such as jitter.

Figure 2-19 provides examples of active metering locations, using the Cisco IP SLA feature. The shadow router in the PoP is deployed by the provider; it measures SLA parameters between the different PoPs. The edge router at the client locations A and A' measures the SLA parameters and verifies the results. Note that the shadow router in the PoP can also perform tests toward the customer locations, as illustrated for networks C and C'.

Figure 2-19 *Active Measurement Deployment*

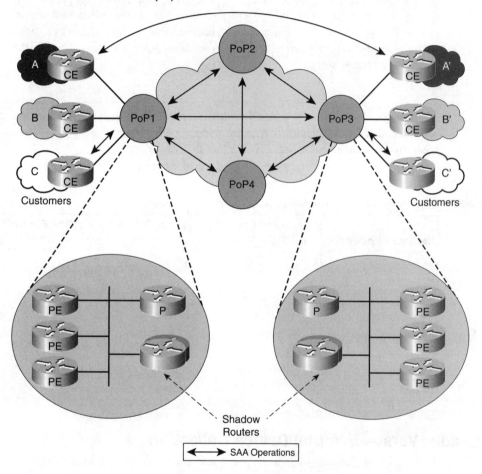

In cases of both active and passive measurement, scalability can become an issue when the networks grow. For passive measurement, the number of data records is a concern. If a single server cannot handle the total number of data records any longer, or if too much collection traffic is transmitted over the network to the central collector, a distributed design becomes necessary. Remote collectors can filter and aggregate the data records and transmit them to the central collector in a compressed format. For active measurement in large environments, the number of operations rises above scalability, especially if you want to measure response time between all locations (CE) in a full-mesh design. The number of operations for a full-mesh collection increases exponentially, as explained in Table 2-21. Because CE-to-CE measurement does not scale, best practice suggests PoP-to-PoP (PE-to-PE) monitoring; in this case, scalability can be improved by deploying IP SLA "shadow" routers in each PoP. As the name implies, the router is almost invisible to the network, because it exists only for measurement purposes. A shadow router is deployed only for IP SLA measurement, and it can be very efficient. In addition to the PoP-to-PoP measurement, PoP-to-CE operations can be defined for all remote locations. This doesn't provide a direct measurement between remote sites but is a good starting point to identify critical performance situations on the network.

NOTE	Measuring all PoPs from one central instance is a single-point-of-failure scenario and is not recommended. Instead, deploy two central metering devices and share the workload among them. In this case, an outage affects only half the network.

Table 2-21   *Required Measurement Operations in a Full-Mesh Environment*

Number of Nodes	Number of Probe Operations, Determined by the Formula $n(n-1)/2$
2	1
3	3
4	6
5	10
6	15
...	...
100	4950

Embedded Versus External Device Collection

When selecting between integrated agents and dedicated metering devices, you notice that there are good arguments for both approaches. It is not simply a question of which one is better, but of what is the right approach for a certain situation. Some scenarios are described in more detail.

A network operator needs to collect usage information for performance trend analysis, troubleshooting, and long-term planning. By leveraging integrated meters at network elements, the operator can deploy the metering quickly, without a massive rollout of dedicated metering devices and making use of existing NMS applications for configuration, software image management, and inventory management. All of those functions are additional requirements when deploying dedicated metering devices. The advantages of a fast and easy deployment vote for integrated agents. But there are also good arguments against them, such as additional resource consumption, plus the fact that network elements are not designed to collect a large number of accounting and performance records.

Technology sometimes reduces the flexibility to choose between integrated network element functionality and external devices. If the application requires "BGP next hop" as a data type, this can be metered only by an internal agent at the network element.

Another scenario is the metering of details, such as application response time, volume of traffic per application, and capturing packets for troubleshooting. In this case, the operator could use integrated RMON groups at network elements. To balance resource consumption, Cisco routers implement only the RMON *alarm* and *event* groups (a group in this sense can be considered a subset of a MIB), whereas Cisco switches support the *statistics* and *history* groups in addition to the *alarm* and *event* groups. Due to the performance requirements of RMON and the ART MIB, a full deployment of both technologies is exclusive to dedicated RMON probes, which can be standalone devices or integrated blades such as the Cisco Network Analysis Module (NAM). The penalty for analyzing the RMON2 data would be such for a router that the traffic throughput would suffer. The NAM can be considered a hybrid device, because it has its own processing power, memory, and communication interfaces but is deployed in a slot of a modular switch or router. Dedicated devices are designed solely for network monitoring and can do so very efficiently, without other simultaneous processes interrupting the metering, such as routing, packet forwarding, and others. External devices offer troubleshooting flexibility of being connected to different devices at different locations, which is a cost-efficient way of troubleshooting. External devices can be connected directly to the network by using a splitter or TAP to insert the device into the active link. Alternatively, they can connect to a mirror port (also called a SPAN port) of a switch, which builds on port copy functionality at the switch. Limitations on external devices are the deployment overhead, if ubiquitous monitoring is required and the price of a large number of high-speed interfaces is metered, such as in a WAN environment where all links should be monitored directly and not through mirroring. Note that a mirroring port can support only half-duplex connections, because the measured traffic flows unidirectionally from the switch to the probe. This can cause the dropping of monitoring packets in a full-duplex environment if the utilization is higher than half-duplex speed. If possible, the mirroring port should have a higher interface speed than mirrored ports. As discussed earlier, dedicated metering devices cannot analyze traffic in encrypted tunnels or network-based VPNs. In those scenarios, traffic needs to be metered at or behind the VPN concentrator.

Mirroring traffic to a probe requires fault management to identify situations of service disruption. When metering at an integrated agent, the network element identifies a disconnected link or other connectivity issues. A collection device behind a mirroring port does not receive any traffic during an outage. As long as the mirroring network element is operational, the meter connected to it cannot distinguish between a situation where nothing is mirrored due to no live traffic or due to an outage behind or at the network element.

A special case of a dedicated device for active monitoring is the Cisco IP SLA shadow router. Synthetic IP SLA probe operations can be configured by SNMP with the CISCO-RTTMON-MIB. Any SNMP-based performance application can collect the results from the same MIB. The shadow router concept increases flexibility, because it can run the latest and even experimental images to support the newest probe operations without affecting the stability of the production network. Because it is a "real" Cisco router, it can be managed by the existing management applications, such as CiscoWorks, which offer configuration management, IOS software image upgrades, inventory, and so on.

Table 2-22 summarizes the pros and cons of embedded collection versus external device collection.

Table 2-22   *Comparison of Embedded and External Collection Methods*

	Embedded Collection	**External Device Collection**
Advantages	Leverages the existing infrastructure, including the management. Measures network element-specific parameters, such as BGP next hop. Includes the routing state in the metering, such as ACLs. Measures encrypted traffic if it terminates at the meter.	Network element-independent deployment. Efficient collection, because the device was designed specifically for metering. Offloads management functionality from the network element.
Disadvantages	Performance impact at the network element. The architecture of the network element was not designed for metering purposes.	Deployment and management costs and effort. Cannot monitor encrypted traffic.

Ingress Versus Egress Collection

Ingress metering accounts for all incoming traffic before any packet operations are performed by the network element, such as ACLs, QoS marking, and policing. In a service provider environment, ingress traffic at the provider edge (PE) router is metered to identify the traffic volume a customer sends toward the carrier. These data records can be taken into account to check the allowed traffic peak and sustain rate toward the SP as well as for usage-based billing. Egress metering collects traffic that a device forwards after performing operations such as queuing, policing, and dropping; this can be used for traffic analysis and usage-based billing. The contract between the customer and the provider defines where the policing and shaping take place.

From an end-to-end network perspective, the choice between ingress and egress collection is not too relevant, because the egress interface of one router is connected via a WAN or LAN link to the ingress interface of the next router. If you want to collect details at the egress interface of one router, and if a specific accounting feature is implemented as ingress only, you can usually collect it at the subsequent router's ingress interface. This does not apply to all situations; therefore, the focus of this section is on the exceptions. Also, note that the concept of ingress or egress metering applies to only some technologies, such as SNMP interface counters (for incoming and outgoing traffic) and Cisco NetFlow (ingress and egress interface), but not to RMON, which meters the traffic per segment. Integrated agents at the device can distinguish between ingress and egress. For an external device that receives traffic via a mirroring port, it does not make sense to distinguish between the two.

Figure 2-20 depicts an enterprise network with a central router that connects users to the Internet. Note that the "Traffic Flow" arrow identifies the direction from source to destination, which is relevant to define ingress and egress interfaces at the router.

Figure 2-20 *Ingress and Egress Metering*

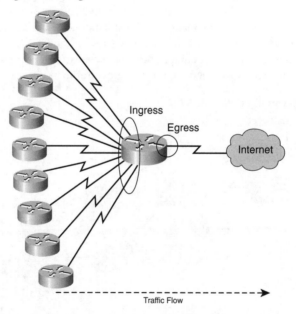

For the returning traffic, egress becomes ingress and ingress becomes egress. If you only need to measure the traffic that is exchanged externally but do not want any local traffic collected, you would meter at the egress interface only. Alternatively, you can also collect traffic from all nine ingress interfaces, but it is very likely that they also carry local traffic, which needs to be filtered afterwards. In case of NetFlow, this filtering can be applied at the mediation server, while it is impossible to filter SNMP interface counters.

NOTE   To avoid duplication of records, do not select ingress and egress collection at the same device unless no alternative solution exists.

Flow Destination or Source Lookup

Another relevant concept, closely linked to ingress versus egress collection, is the flow lookup direction. In case of destination-sensitive billing, the user pays according to the distance between source and destination. If the traffic remains local, such as a local VoIP call, the cost of transferring the packet could be neglected; consequently, the service can potentially be offered free of charge. However, if a service is accessed across an expensive WAN link, this traffic should be charged adequately to the user.

If you consider the destination-sensitive billing model in more detail, you can ask yourself if it is a fair billing scheme. In Figure 2-21, the customer requests a 10-MB file from a remote server. In the case of destination-sensitive billing, he gets charged for only the FTP request (very small). The server's directly connected client (in this case, the ISP) pays to send the 10-MB file. A combination of a destination and source-sensitive billing scheme would be a fair model, because the user now pays for the FTP-REQUEST and the 10-MB file. Consequently, the meters in the ISP network must support destination lookup for the ingress traffic and a source lookup for the egress traffic.

Figure 2-21 *Destination-Sensitive Billing Model*

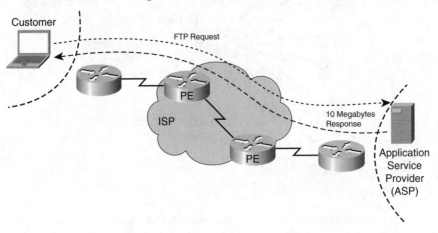

Combining the different options results in Table 2-23.

Table 2-23   *Traffic Direction Lookup*

PE Router	Source Lookup	Destination Lookup
Ingress interface	Traffic received from an ISP	Traffic received from a customer
Egress interface	Traffic sent to a customer	Traffic sent to an ISP

A common practice in the ISP community is the notion of "hot-potato routing." This basically means that the traffic is routed to the nearest exit point of the ISP network to save bandwidth (and, as a consequence, money) in the ISP core network. However, from an accounting point of view, the traffic's asymmetry characteristic can lead to unexpected results in case of flow source lookup.

As a follow-up to the core traffic matrix example, Figure 2-22 analyzes the source BGP AS.

Figure 2-22   *Asymmetric Traffic Constraint*

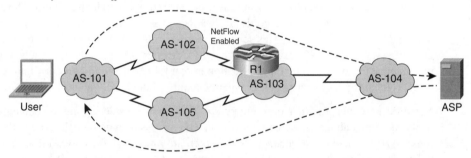

The traffic is initiated in BGP AS 101 and is routed to a destination in BGP AS 104 via BGP AS 102. The return path is different: the alternative path containing AS 105 is used. If router R1 in AS 103 analyzes the neighbor source BGP AS, it executes a lookup in the BGP table with the source IP address of the metered packets. The asymmetric nature of the traffic causes a problem, because the lookup at R1 does not provide the BGP AS from which the packets arrive, but instead the BGP AS that the router would take to reach the packet's source IP address. In the specific situation of Figure 2-22, router R1 assumes that the traffic comes from AS 105 (because R1 would choose this path to get to AS 101), while the user traffic actually comes from AS 102. A possible solution in this case is to meter at multiple points in the network and perform a sanity check afterwards.

Technology-Dependent Special Constraints

In some scenarios, the deployed technology demands where to collect performance and accounting records. In a dial-up environment, the NAS accepts the user authentication and verifies the credentials against the user records at the AAA server. The NAS also generates a RADIUS accounting start record after successful user authentication and a RADIUS stop record when the user terminates the session. As the AAA server identifies the user during the authentication phase, the services accessed during the session can be directly linked to the user's account and turned into an invoice by the billing application. In this case, the meter position is in the NAS.

Consider a different approach. Accounting records are required but no user authentication takes place, which is the case in many enterprise campus networks. If static IP addresses are used, the administrator can create a lookup table that correlates the individual username to the IP address. The billing application can afterwards aggregate accounting records per IP address and substitute the username for the address. Although this method worked well in the past, it does not fit into today's mobile network environments. As an alternative to static address assignment, DHCP assigns IP addresses dynamically to users. In this case, the lookup table approach would not be useful; alternatively, a link between the DHCP server and a DNS server can be established. Now the DNS server creates a dynamic DNS entry per user, based on the computer name (for example, foo) and the domain (research.cisco.com), resulting in a unique user entry (foo.research.cisco.com). The billing application can leverage these records afterwards and assign the utilized network resources to an individual user account. This scenario requires multiple meter placements: at the DHCP server, at the DNS server, and at network devices. The records from these various meters must be correlated by the application in real time to avoid incorrect assignments of users to IP addresses because of the dynamic nature of the DHCP environments.

Network protocols provide a different perspective when considering ingress and egress metering. Think about the edge router between the access network and the core network; it runs the IP protocol in the access part and potentially MPLS in the core. Traffic sent from the user toward the core can be collected as ingress IP records or egress MPLS records. The return traffic therefore is MPLS on the ingress interface from the core network and IP on the egress side toward the user. If the accounting application can handle only IP records and not MPLS records, you need to collect ingress traffic from the source toward the core and egress traffic from the destination to the source, all at the same PE device.

Figure 2-23 demonstrates ingress and egress metering from a network element perspective. It represents an MPLS core with multiple VPNs, and accounting per VPN is needed. In this case, accounting records need to be collected at the provider edge (PE) router, where the individual customers are identified by the logical or physical interface that they connect. Ingress accounting in this example provides the traffic generated by the user; a more complex approach is to aggregate per destination address, in case of destination-sensitive billing. At the destination location, egress accounting collects the traffic volume transported through the network. The accounting application can aggregate the PE-PE traffic, consolidate it per customer, and calculate the traffic volume transmitted over the MPLS cloud. Total traffic sent from the source PE minus traffic received at the destination PE equals packet loss in the core network. Figure 2-23 illustrates the different meter positions for this example. The "Traffic Flow" arrow indicates the traffic direction, where location 1 is the source and location 2 the destination. In this scenario, you can meter various details at the different devices and interfaces, as summarized in Table 2-23.

Figure 2-23 *Ingress and Egress Metering: Technology-Specific*

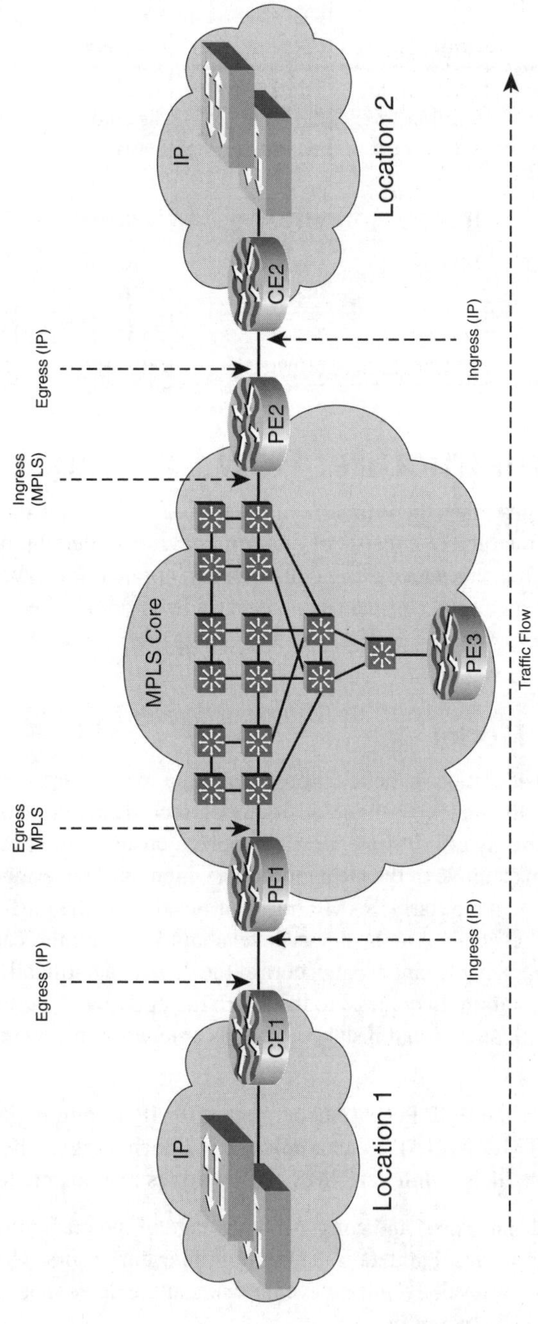

Table 2-24   *Results of Ingress and Egress Metering*

Device (Interface)	CE1 (Egress)	PE1 (Ingress)	PE1 (Egress)	PE2 (Ingress)	PE2 (Egress)	CE2 (Ingress)
Meter	Traffic from location 1 to the core	Traffic from location 1 to the core	Traffic toward the core network	Traffic from the core network	Traffic from the core to location 2	Traffic from the core to location 2
Protocol	IP	IP	MPLS	MPLS	IP	IP
Application	Monitoring	Billing	Core traffic matrix	Core traffic matrix	Billing	Monitoring
Applied by	Customer (location 1)	Service provider	Service provider	Service provider	Service provider	Customer (location 2)

Collection Infrastructure: How to Collect Data Records

This section describes the infrastructure required to collect accounting and performance data. The infrastructure consists of metering devices collecting data records, collection and mediation devices mediating data sets, and application servers generating business information, such as performance and service level reports, security analysis, and usage-based billing.

Pull Versus Push Model

The first consideration is the location where data records are stored immediately after generation at the meter. With the push model, records are not stored at the devices or are kept there for only a short time, until the device pushes them toward a collection server. NetFlow is an example of the push model, in which the device aggregates packets into flows and exports them regularly. SNMP notifications deploy the push model, based on the assumption that changes at the device level should be communicated in a proactive manner. Therefore, when a relevant event occurs at the device, a notification is generated toward the management station. In contrast to this, with the pull model, collection details are stored at the device until an external instance, such as a network management server, requests that they be sent.

MIBs, such as the BGP Policy Accounting MIB, IP accounting MIB, and IP SLA MIB (CISCO-RTTMON-MIB), are examples of pull technology, where the device constantly updates the counters while the NMS application is responsible for regular collection.

Both methods have pros and cons. An advantage of the push model is the event-driven aspect, which means that data is sent only if an event occurs. The pull model requires constant data retrieval, even if no event occurs at the device, because the device status can be identified only by polling.

Figure 2-24 provides a schematic view of the collection infrastructure, starting at the device level and continuing from the mediation layer up to the application layer. It illustrates that the push and pull models are not limited to the meter, but apply at the upper layers as well. At the element level, multiple metering instances can work in parallel, and aggregation is optional. The aggregation and exporting processes can be applied per instance or can be combined, for the pull model as well as the push model.

Figure 2-24 *Collection Infrastructure*

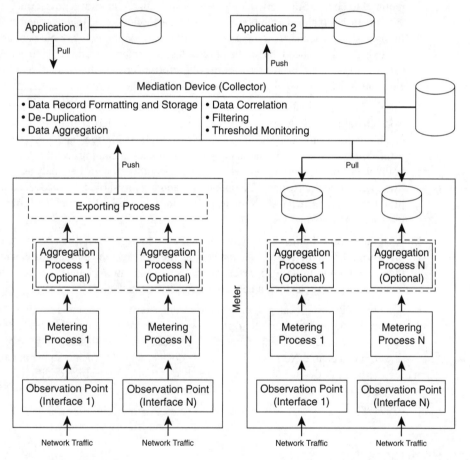

Event-Based Model

Instead of selecting between pull and push, a more practical approach is to create a solution in which the two models come together. The event-based model is the most effective combination of the push and pull model. It builds on the advanced metering functionalities of the network element and combines them with the intelligence of the network management application. Here are some examples:

- By defining SNMP MIB thresholds for CPU utilization, interface utilization, link errors, and more, the network element monitors its status continuously. If a threshold is exceeded, a notification is pushed to the NMS application, which can start pulling for more details from the various MIB objects at the network element. After resolving the issue, the process returns to the initial state. Note that some server polling is required to check if the network element is alive. In the case of a power outage or system crash, no alarms can be pushed from the device to the management system. In the described scenario, management traffic between the network element and the server is greatly reduced, but at the price of less information received the management station. A good compromise is to retrieve performance statistics from the network elements at least once per hour for baselining and other purposes.

- The Cisco IP SLA feature implements an event-based model as a trigger for operations. You can define IP SLA operations that are performed under normal circumstances, configure thresholds, and specify an additional probe operation that is performed only if the threshold is exceed. The management application can retrieve the results from both the normal operation and the additional operation for further analysis. For example, a router performs RTT operations, and if a threshold is exceeded, additional jitter probes are initiated. As soon as RTT values are back to normal, no further jitter tests are performed.

- A configuration change at the network element can trigger a notification to the provisioning system (push). When receiving the message, the application can retrieve the new configuration (pull), determine if the configuration changes are accepted, or overwrite them by pushing a new configuration to the device.

- A monitoring system can pull information from a network element's NetFlow MIB to inspect the summary of current traffic flows, such as total number of flows, top talkers, average flow size, and others. If any of these values passes a threshold at the application server, it can enable NetFlow export at the device, which then starts pushing all flow records to the collection server for further inspection. After traffic conditions return to normal, NetFlow export can be disabled, and the monitoring of the NetFlow MIB continues.

Export Protocols

For the description of the export protocols, Table 2-25 documents the structure that has been applied.

Table 2-25   *This Chapter's Export Protocol Structure*

Overview	Description
Connection mode, congestion handling, reliability	Discussion about the connection mode (connection-oriented versus connectionless) and its built-in congestion and reliability mechanisms
Send and retrieve frequency	Description of send and receive frequency depending on the protocol characteristics (push versus pull mode)

When setting up a connection-oriented session, the status of the session is known to both parties at any time during the conversation. This is achieved by implementing status messages (keepalives), acknowledgments, and potentially retries if datagrams got lost. When the connection is disrupted, the sender and receiver notify it and can reestablish it. The Transmission Control Protocol (TCP) is an example of a connection-oriented protocol with mechanisms to identify congestion in the network and react accordingly.

Connectionless sessions avoid the overhead of keepalives, acknowledgments, and retries, and consequently have a higher throughput rate, at the price of less reliability. When the connection is lost, data is sent into "the dark," without the sender's being aware of it. This can become an issue for the network infrastructure if a sender keeps transmitting large traffic sets, even if the network cannot transport the traffic any longer, resulting in dropped traffic or congested networks. User Datagram Protocol (UDP) is an example of a connectionless protocol without congestion handling.

A solution in between the two extremes is using congestion-aware protocols, which avoid the overhead of TCP but add mechanisms to identify network congestion situations and adopt the sending rate accordingly. Stream Control Transmission Protocol (SCTP) is an example in this category.

The reporting frequency depends on the mode: push or pull.

For push mode, the sending frequency depends on the technology as well. SNMP notifications are sent immediately upon occurrence of an event, while NetFlow uses a combination of triggers.

The retrieval frequency of the pull mode is configured at the management server; it determines how often data is retrieved from the network elements. The memory strategy at the network element for pull mode can be implemented in three ways:

- In case of detailed accounting records, overwrite the oldest records when the maximum number of entries is reached.

- Wrap the counters when they reach the maximum value (for example, SNMP interface counters).

- Stop adding new entries before the existing ones have been retrieved or erased.

SNMP

SNMP illustrates how to combine the pull and push models effectively. Most MIBs consider the majority of information gathered relevant but not critical—for example, interface counters, system up time, the routing table, and so on. These data sets are stored in the device memory and can be retrieved from a network management application by SNMP polling; this is a pull approach. A subset of the information gathered by the device is classified as critical information. This is sent to the management station without waiting for a request to send; in SNMP terminology, this is called a notification, which applies to the push model. Note that the SNMP notification can be sent in an unacknowledged way (the trap) or in an acknowledged way (the inform). Examples of default notifications are device warm-start or cold-start and interface up or down. A subset of MIB data exists that can be considered critical, but it has no default notifications assigned—for example, CPU monitoring or a change in the device configuration. For increased flexibility, the operator can define thresholds for MIB variables, and a specific notification is generated after a threshold is exceeded.

Connection Mode, Congestion Handling, and Reliability

SNMP datagrams are transported over UDP, which is a connectionless and unreliable transport protocol. Timers and retries are implemented to reduce the effects, but a valid concern is not losing relevant information in notifications on the way from the device to the management station. By default, the notifications are sent as a trap, which is an unacknowledged message. This reliability concern is addressed by SNMP "informs," which were introduced in SNMP version 2c. Instead of a "fire and forget" approach, the device sends a notification to the NMS server and requires an acknowledgment. If the acknowledgment is not received within a certain amount of time, the message gets sent again—three times by default. SNMP has no concept of congestion handling.

Send and Retrieve Frequency

The retrieval frequency depends very much on the traffic volume that is processed by the network element. In the past, SNMP MIB counters were implemented as 32-bit integers only. 64-bit counters are required in today's high-speed environments to avoid rapid counter rollover. RFC 2863, *Evolution of the Interfaces Group of MIB-II*, defines the relationship between interface speed and counter size:

- ifSpeed ≥ 20 Mbps: 32-bit byte and packet counters
- ifSpeed > 20 Mbps and ifSpeed < 650 Mbps: 32-bit packet counters and 64-bit byte counters
- ifSpeed ≥ 650 Mbps: 64-bit byte and packet counters

RFC 2863 also provides an example:

"A 10-Mbps stream of back-to-back, full-size packets causes ifInOctets to wrap in just over 57 minutes; at 100 Mbps, the minimum wrap time is 5.7 minutes, and at 1 Gbps, the minimum is 34 seconds."

The sending frequency is not relevant, because the occurrence of critical events cannot be determined in advance, and SNMP notifications are sent immediately after an event occurs.

A disadvantage of SNMP is the time scale of information. Depending on the implementation, counters are updated in intervals of seconds or tens of seconds. In general, polling faster than every 30 seconds implies that the results might be inaccurate.

NetFlow

Historically, Cisco NetFlow has incorporated the push model, in which the devices send records periodically to the collection server, up to multiple times per second at fully utilized high-end devices. The alternative of storing all accounting records at the device would require a large amount of memory; therefore, the push model was chosen.

An alternative is the NetFlow MIB, which does not collect individual flow records. Instead, it keeps summary details, such as Top-N active flows, flows with the largest number of packets, and some flow-specific details, such as AS numbers. The MIB is based on the pull model, so an application has to request the data export explicitly.

These two cases of NetFlow make it clear that one accounting technology can implement both the push and pull models in parallel, based on different requirements.

Connection Mode, Congestion Handling, and Reliability

Histprically, he NetFlow export was based on the UDP protocols and as a result is connectionless. Performance was the main reason for choosing UDP, because a NetFlow-enabled high-end network element can fully utilize an OC-3 link with NetFlow data records. UDP has no mechanism for congestion handling. This results in the best practice of placing a collection server close to the NetFlow devices and assigns a dedicated interface for the export if possible. The only reliability function is a sequence number in the export datagrams: collection applications can interpret the number, calculate the number of lost flows, and notify the administrator.

NetFlow version 9 offers the flexibility to choose another protocol than UDP: SCTP-PR (Partially Reliable SCTP). Historically, reliability has been directly related to the connection approach. For example, TCP implements a fully reliable mode, and UDP chooses the unreliable mode. SCTP introduces a paradigm shift and offers three different modes of reliability: fully reliable, partially reliable, and unreliable. Applications can choose which model fits best, potentially changing the modes dynamically under different circumstances, but still using the same transport protocol.

Note that reliability can also be increased by exporting to two different collection servers, which is a feature that NetFlow supports.

Send and Retrieve Frequency

For NetFlow, the send frequency is actually the exporting frequency of the push model that NetFlow deploys. Two timers and two extra conditions determine when flow entries are exported from the cache:

- Active flows timeout (the default is 30 minutes)
- Inactive flows timeout (the default is 15 seconds)
- Transport is completed (TCP FIN or RST)
- The flow cache has become full

This means that long-lasting flows are terminated after 30 minutes, the flow records get pushed to the collector, and new cache entries are created. "Transport completed" applies only to TCP flows, where the session termination can be identified by checking either the finish (FIN) or reset (RST) bit in the TCP header. Alternatively, inactive UDP flows are terminated almost immediately, after 15 seconds by default. If the flow cache is almost full and not enough memory is available for new entries, the network element starts exporting flows more aggressively to free up memory resources.

FTP

Another illustration of the pull model is to store data in the device flash memory and retrieve it using File Transfer Protocol (FTP) afterwards. An example is system-logging messages, which provide error and debug messages generated by the router. These messages can be stored in a router's memory buffer instead of being sent to an NMS station via syslog or SNMP, which could lead to lost messages due to the unreliable nature of UDP. The drawbacks of this mechanism are that older messages are overwritten by new messages when the buffer is full and that all logging messages are erased when the router reboots. An alternative is to write messages to the router's flash card, which provides persistent data storage when the router reboots. An example is the "syslog writing to flash feature" in Cisco IOS, which enables system logging messages to be saved on the router's flash disk. A server retrieves these messages by executing a **copy** command on the router, which then pushes the log files through FTP to the server. Potentially, this method could be implemented for all MIB variables to store data persistently.

Connection Mode, Congestion Handling, and Reliability

FTP uses TCP as the transport protocol. TCP was covered earlier in this chapter.

Authentication, Authorization, and Accounting (AAA) Architecture

Accounting is a relevant part of the AAA architecture, as defined by the IETF in RFCs 2905, 3127, and 3539. Authentication, Authorization, and Accounting (AAA) was developed to identify users who connect to the network or administrators who perform operations on network elements. The AAA architecture requires at least one NAS, which can be a router with dial-in interfaces to authenticate external users' access to the network. Or it can be any core router or switch with AAA client functionality to authenticate network operators' access to devices. To increase scalability and manageability, the user profiles should be defined at a central AAA server (RADIUS, TACACS+, Diameter) and not on each NAS.

Connection Mode, Congestion Handling, and Reliability

AAA builds on three protocols: RADIUS, TACACS+, and Diameter. Diameter is the next generation of AAA, specified by the IETF (RFC 3588, *Diameter Based Protocol*). It is based on RADIUS, but it offers additional functions and extensibility, such as reliable data transfer over TCP and SCTP, failover, extended error handling, and improved security features such as IPsec and TLS. Although RADIUS and TACACS+ were developed to address dialup and terminal server access, Diameter also supports new access technologies, such as DSL and roaming support for mobile wireless environments.

Send and Retrieve Frequency

AAA deploys a push model, in which messages from the NAS get sent to the AAA server based on events such as user connects or disconnects. Accounting records are sent at the end of the user session but can optionally be sent regularly. The IOS command **aaa accounting update** causes an interim accounting record to be sent to the accounting server whenever there is new accounting information to report.

NOTE   Configuring the NAS to send periodic accounting updates can cause heavy congestion when many users are logged into the network.

Network Design for the Collection Infrastructure

With a good understanding of the push and pull concepts, the next step is to identify how to transfer the collected data sets from the network elements to the collection server. One approach is to leverage the existing infrastructure that transports the users' traffic. This is also referred to as in-band management; it's certainly the easiest and cheapest option. You should be aware of the limitations, such as consuming user bandwidth for administrative purposes, and the vulnerability of the management traffic to attacks or modifications from the user community. An alternative is to set up a dedicated infrastructure for management purposes; this is also called the Data Communication Network (DCN). A good analogy for this is a dedicated traffic lane for buses, taxis, and emergency vehicles, which offers "bandwidth" independently of the normal traffic. Related to networks, this concept is known as out-of-band (OOB) management; it uses either a dedicated network infrastructure (DCN) or a logical network on top of the shared infrastructure. The dedicated infrastructure can be a simple dial connection to a terminal server in a remote location, which connects to the terminal ports of the equipment, or the Cadillac solution with separate LAN and WAN connections. Benefits are the reliable bandwidth and throughput under all circumstances and the security enhancements of shielding the management traffic from users. Best practices recommend the use of OOB infrastructure whenever possible.

A compromise is to set up a dedicated VLAN or VPN for management purposes. In this case, the common infrastructure is leveraged for user traffic and network management operations, but the traffic types cannot interfere with each other. In this case, defining quality-of-service classes is strongly recommended, to keep management traffic from being delayed or dropped under congestion situations.

Communication Concepts

After defining the transport infrastructure, communication concepts between the metering device and the receiver of the performance and accounting records need to be identified. The following communication concepts exist:

- Unicast (one to one)
- Multicast (one to many)
- Broadcast (one to all)
- Communication bus (a combination of unicast, multicast, and broadcast)

Unicast communication is applied in case of a central NMS server scenario, in which network elements communicate with a central server. Because a single server is also a single point of failure, a backup server concept should be implemented. Although this increases availability, it also requires the device to send the records to both servers—either continuously or by checking the availability of the primary server and by sending traffic to the backup server only if the primary server is unavailable. An alternative to exporting data twice is to send it to a multicast address so that the export device does not need to inspect to which server the records need to be sent. For completeness, it should be mentioned that broadcasting the messages to every device in the network is not recommended!

A relatively new concept introduces a communication bus for data exchange, also referred to as the publish and subscribe bus. All communication partners are connected to the bus and have a special listener component installed that monitors messages on the bus. Messages are classified into specific categories and are broadcast on the bus. To receive a message, you subscribe to one or multiple categories. The benefit of this approach is that the sender does not need to know anything about the receiver, which makes the integration of new applications easier. Imagine you have a communication bus in place, and you plan to deploy a billing application. Without a bus concept in place, you have to configure all devices and some of the existing management applications to send information to the new billing application. Now you only need to enable the collection of accounting records at the device level and have the billing application register for accounting records. Note that the broadcast concept of a bus architecture is not designed for bulk data transfer, because the bus interconnects multiple senders and receivers. In most cases the large number of accounting records only needs to be transferred between the collection device and the collection application. For example, exchanging RADIUS records over the bus is acceptable, while exchanging all NetFlow records from multiple devices over the bus is not appropriate. The bus communication is limited to a LAN environment (broadcast domain) and can be extended across WAN connections by point-to-point software adapters.

Figure 2-25 illustrates the one-to-one, one-to-many, and many-to-many communication methods. Collection server 1 has a one-to-one relationship with mediation device 1, and collection server 2 has a one-to-many relationship with mediation device 1 and the backup meditation server. Both mediation devices and all application servers use the publish and subscribe bus for many-to-many communication.

Figure 2-25 *Communication Concepts*

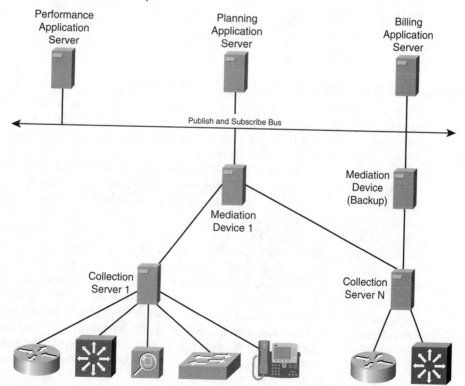

Collection Server Concepts

The next instance to consider is the collection server. Distinguishing the various processing steps provides a better understanding of the overall collection. After metering at the device level, data records are either *sent* to a collection server (push model) or *retrieved* by the server (pull model). Collecting device MIB information via SNMP is an example of the pull model. Waiting for a device to push NetFlow records to the collecting server is an illustration of the push model. In both cases, post-processing is required to transform data sets into useful business information. Collection also includes monitoring the received packets for completeness. For example, NetFlow includes a flow counter that helps the collection server identify lost datagrams. The post-processing functions are described in the next chapter. For now, the focus is on the collection part only. In summary, the collection server performs the following tasks:

- Data retrieval (pull or push)

- Monitoring the retrieved records and identifying lost data record loss between the device and the collection server (if the protocol supports it)

- Basic filtering functions (for example, filter all network management traffic) (optional)

- Threshold monitoring (optional)

- Data record formatting

- Data record storage

Placing the Collection Server (Centralized, Distributed)

A significant task is identifying how many collection servers are required and where in the network to place them. In a small or medium network, it can be sufficient to have one or two central servers and collect all accounting and performance records at these central instances. This eases the administration but increases the network load, because all records are transferred from the devices to the servers. Alternatively, distributing servers in the network reduces the transmitted traffic, because it gets sent after processing. Best practice suggests a central design if only a small number of (central) network elements collect data records and the traffic overhead is low to medium. In case of a NetFlow deployment at multiple network elements with high-speed interfaces, a distributed model is appropriate. You should calculate the estimated amount of generated accounting and performance data before selecting the central or distributed concept. If you want to monitor the traffic flows through the core of your network, it is sufficient to export the data records from the core devices to a central server. In case of usage-based billing, distributed collectors at the main remote locations are probably a better solution than deploying a central server. Figure 2-26 shows the collection server placement for these examples. In this case, the CEs export to the local collector in each PoP, and the PEs export to the central collector. The billing application collects data records from the three local collectors, and the core planning application server connects to only the central server.

Figure 2-26 *Central and Local Collection Servers*

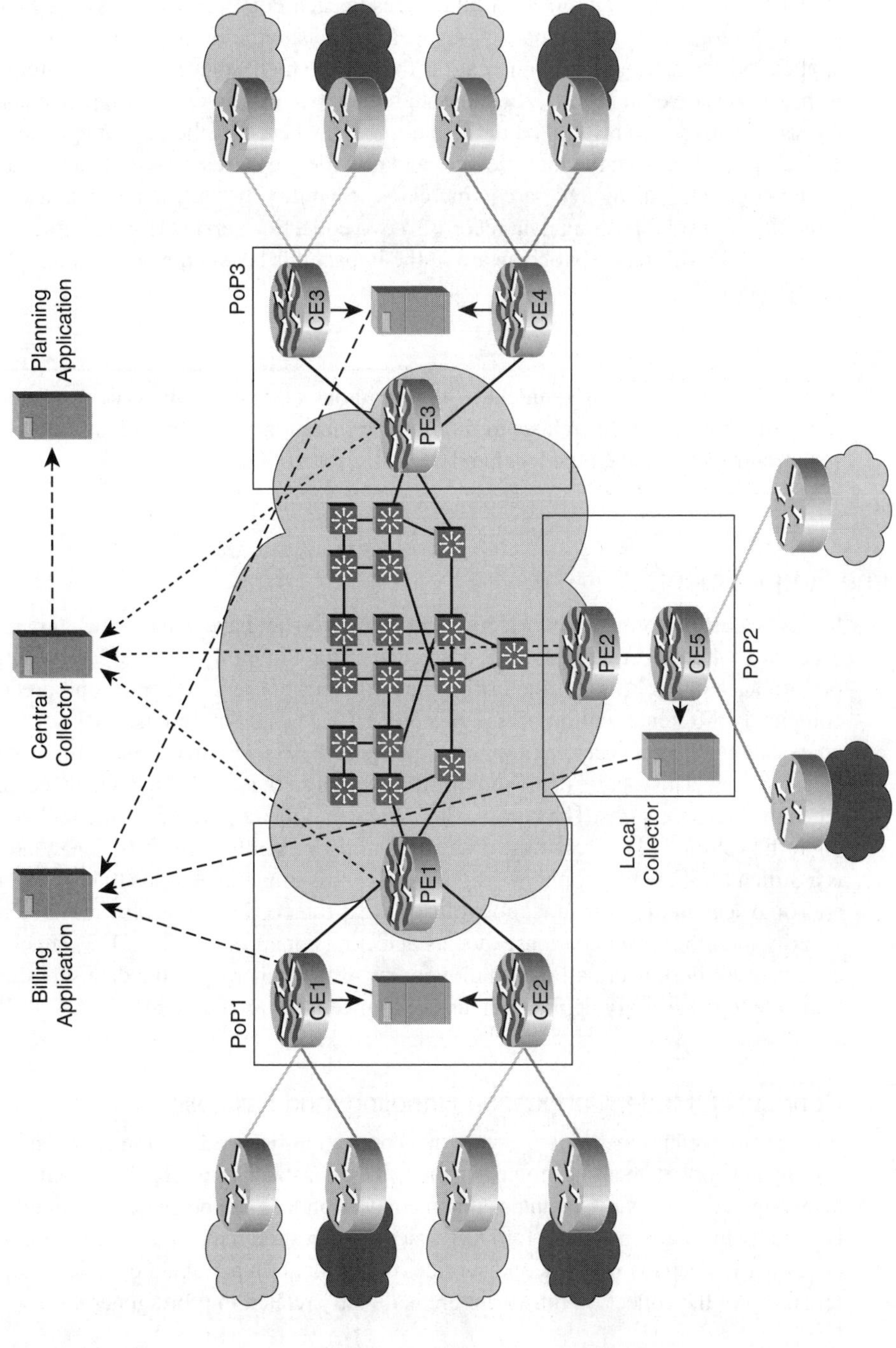

In a distributed environment, as illustrated in Figure 2-26, the hierarchy concept becomes relevant. A different scenario is for all devices in each PoP (CEs and PEs) to export to the local collector, which then sends aggregated data sets to the central collection server. An application server would communicate with only the highest level in the hierarchy, which is the central server in Figure 2-26. Although these two examples describe the push model, the same concept can be applied to the pull model, where distributed management servers collect (pull) data from the local devices and provide preprocessed data sets for the central application. Introducing a hierarchy increases scalability. If you want to increase the reliability, consider pushing data records to two collection servers (for example, NetFlow records or SNMP traps), but be aware of the impact this has on the network and device performance.

NOTE   In a distributed server environment, with or without a hierarchy, the synchronization of servers is important. This relates to time synchronization (NTP) as well as data set synchronization between the local and central servers.

Real-Time Requirements

In most cases, performance and accounting records do not have to be collected in real time, especially when accounting records are gathered for a monthly invoice. Identifying performance peaks is more time-critical but still does not require per-second precision. A completely different scenario occurs in a prepaid environment. If a user pays upfront for a voice call or Internet access at a wireless hotspot, these scenarios demand real-time measurement. This can be deployed on a time basis so that the NAS disconnects the user when the budget expires. The complexity increases if the requirements are deployed based on traffic volume, where real-time processing of packets or flow records is mandatory. This is a difficult task, which explains why most business implementations today only apply real-time accounting over time, not volume. Real-time collection is also required by security monitoring applications, such as detecting denial-of-service (DoS) attacks. Most attacks occur during a relatively small window of time; therefore, the data sets should be available to the security application almost immediately after generation.

Connection Mode, Congestion Handling, and Reliability

For real-time requirements, some form of a connection-oriented session between the server and the network element has to be established. A constant status check (keepalive) might be enough, as long as it guarantees that a connection loss can be detected immediately. Especially in case of metering for DoS attacks, congestion management and reliability are necessary to keep the network and services operational. In a prepaid environment, the reliability of the collection infrastructure is directly related to profit generation—or profit loss.

Send and Retrieve Frequency

The send frequency in real-time environments mostly depends on the business case. If the requirements demand 1-minute exactness, the retrieval frequency needs to be less than 1 minute. This might also call for a modification of the timers in the different technologies. The default active timer in NetFlow is 30 minutes; it would have to be reduced. The same applies for polling of SNMP counters from the management application, which occurs more frequently in real-time environments.

Mediation Device Functionality: How to Process Data Records

Now that you understand collection concepts, this section covers data processing strategies and mediation device features. As the name indicates, the mediation device is located between two instances—either between the network element (meter) and the application server, or between the collection server(s) and the application server(s). Mediation functionality does not implicitly require a separate physical entity; it can be a (software) subfunction of the collection or application server. Alternatively, multiple collection servers can be consolidated at one mediation device, which then provides a central interface for all application servers to retrieve accounting and performance records. As discussed in the preceding section, selecting the right location for the collection server is an important task. In case of the mediation device, the functionality is more relevant than the location. As shown earlier in Figure 2-24, the main functions of the mediation device are as follows:

- Filtering
- Estimation from sampling (if sampling applies)
- Threshold monitoring (optional)
- Data aggregation:
  - Based on common criteria (key fields)
  - Aggregation over time
- Data record correlation (from different sources) and enrichment data record formatting and storage
- Flow de-duplication
- Data record formatting and storage

Filtering

Two main areas of filtering exist at the mediation device:

- Filtering to reduce the volume of the data collection
- Filtering for application purposes

Complex filtering for volume reduction is a mediation device task, because the implementation of process-intensive filters at the network element has a performance impact. Ideally, the collection granularity and filtering functions at the device would allow for configuring exactly the data set that is required. Although some accounting and performance technologies, such as NetFlow, support filters at the network element, others, such as SNMP interface counters and RMON, do not offer a filter concept at the meter. To reduce the performance impact of metering to a minimum, simple filters are implemented at the device, ideally in hardware instead of software operations. Complex and CPU-intensive operations are realized at the mediation device.

Filtering for application purposes is based on the "divide and conquer" paradigm: collect data records once, but use them as input for multiple applications, such as capacity planning, billing, and security monitoring. In this case, different aggregations with different filters are required. Table 2-26 lists examples of filters provided by the Cisco NetFlow Collector (NFC).

Table 2-26   *NetFlow Collector Filter Keys*

Type	Value	Description
srcaddr	Source IP address	Filters the input data based on the source IP address
dstaddr	Destination IP address	Filters the input data based on the destination IP address
srcport	Source port number	Filters the input data based on the source port number
dstport	Destination port number	Filters the input data based on the destination port number
srcinterface	Source interface number	Filters the input data based on the source interface number
dstinterface	Destination interface number	Filters the input data based on the destination interface number
nexthop	Next-hop IP address	Filters the input data based on the next-hop IP address
Protocol	Protocol name	Filters the input data based on the protocol definitions
prot	Protocol number	Filters the input data based on the protocol number in the flow record
ToS	Type of service	Filters the input data based on the type of service (ToS)
srcas	Source AS	Filters the input data based on the autonomous system number of the source, either origin or peer
dstas	Destination AS	Filters the input data based on the autonomous system number of the destination, either origin or peer

Table 2-26 is sourced from http://www.cisco.com/univercd/cc/td/doc/product/rtrmgmt/nfc/nfc_3_6/iug/tuning.htm#1035085

Filtering can also be required because of a lack of configuration granularity at the meter. For example, in the past, NetFlow could be configured only on a physical interface level, not on a logical (or subinterface) level. Fortunately, the subinterface details were reported in the accounting record, so it was possible to filter everything except for the required subinterface information. Because this is not a very efficient way to collect accounting records, Cisco introduced a new feature to configure data collection on a subinterface level. Even though the feature is in place now, it might still be useful to collect data from all subinterfaces and filter some afterwards.

Estimation from Sampling

This section is specific to NetFlow and applies only if NetFlow sampling is configured at the device. However, it is an important task, because the child population gathered by sampling must be adjusted for the estimation of the parent population and to deduce an approximation of the volume based on the sampling rate.

A NetFlow mediation device estimates the absolute traffic volumes by renormalizing the volume of sampled traffic through multiplication with the meter's sampling frequency. If sampling is applied with a sampling rate of 1:100, the data records need to be multiplied by a factor of 100. Now you see why metering accuracy is so important. If the child population, which is gathered by sampling techniques, is biased or inaccurate, the multiplication increases it even more. Estimation from sampling must be performed per metering instance, because multiple meters with different sampling rates can be configured per device and even per interface if filtering and sampling apply in conjunction.

The example in the section "Filtering at the Network Device" defined three traffic classes: priority, business, and best effort. Priority traffic was fully collected and needs no adjustment. Business traffic was sampled with a rate of 1:100 and therefore needs to be multiplied by a factor of 100. Best-effort traffic had a sampling rate of 1:1000 and needs to be multiplied by 1000. This scenario makes it clear why the sampling factor must be included in the exported data record, because otherwise the estimation from sampling is incorrect.

Threshold Monitoring

Threshold monitoring is an optional task for the mediation device; it can be implemented at both the mediation device and the application server level. It is not so relevant where the function is located, but which purpose it serves. A metering device for a traffic planning application might leave the monitoring of the threshold up to the application server, because they are not critical for planning purposes. On the other hand, if metering is applied for security monitoring, a relevant feature is to set thresholds for the received traffic and monitor them in real time, because a reaction to an attack must occur quickly. Exceeded thresholds can identify security issues, such as a denial-of-service (DoS) attack, in which a huge number of very small datagrams flood a network and eventually stop the services in the network. In case of a NetFlow collection during a DoS attack, the mediation device monitors a sudden increase of the number of flows; at the same time, the average flow size decreases. This does not have to be an attack per se, but it certainly indicates a change in the traffic patterns, which should be brought to the administrator's attention immediately. Again, a prerequisite for monitoring thresholds is a baseline of the network performance under normal circumstances.

Data Aggregation

Although filtering reduces the volume of collected data, a further reduction is required to keep the total data volume manageable. The concept of aggregation describes the task of reducing the granularity by identifying common criteria (key fields) and combining information from multiple records into a single record. Two different aggregation concepts exist:

- Aggregation of key fields
- Aggregation over time

Aggregation of common criteria is related specifically to accounting records, whereas aggregation over time can be applied to both accounting and performance records. For example, a service provider might be interested in NetFlow records per BGP autonomous system (AS) instead of a full NetFlow collection. In this case, all records with the same source or destination AS are consolidated into a single record. An enterprise IT department might not want detailed records for each user, but rather aggregate all records belonging to the same department. Note that you have a smaller number of records after aggregation, but also reduce the granularity. Another method of aggregation is to define buckets and maintain only the summary per bucket instead of single transactions. The Cisco IP SLA feature and the ART MIB implement this concept of aggregation at the device level; a summary is displayed in Table 2-27. The first column represents the metered values, such as the delay of a round-trip time operation. The meter calculates the square sum and adds both values as a matrix in the defined buckets. At the end of the aggregation interval, only the bottom three rows are maintained per bucket: the total number of entries, the sum of the values, and the sum of the squares of each value.

Table 2-27 *Aggregating Values into Buckets*

Probe Value	Square Value	Buckets			
[ms]	[ms^2]	< 10 ms	10 to 30 ms	30 to 100 ms	> 100 ms
30	900		(30, 900)		
97	9409			(97, 9409)	
167	27889				(167, 27889)

Table 2-27 *Aggregating Values into Buckets (Continued)*

Probe Value	Square Value	Buckets			
[ms]	[ms^2]	< 10 ms	10 to 30 ms	30 to 100 ms	> 100 ms
74	5476			(74, 5476)	
29	841		(29, 841)		
84	7056			(84, 7056)	
7	49	(7, 49)			
73	5329			(73, 5329)	
12	144		(12, 144)		
21	441		(21, 441)		
Number of entries		1	4	4	1
Sum		7	92	328	167
Sum of squares		49	2326	27270	27889

Aggregation of key fields can be combined with aggregation over time. One approach is for the mediation device to store all received flow records immediately to disk. Alternatively, the server can aggregate packets in memory first and write the aggregated records to the disk when the aggregation interval expires. Table 2-28 shows accounting records before aggregation.

Table 2-28 *Accounting Records (Before Aggregation)*

Entry Number	Source IP Address	Destination IP Address	Interface Number (Ingress)	Destination Port Number (Application)	BGP Autonomous System (AS) Number (Source)	Number of Bytes
1	10.1.1.1	144.1.1.1	1	23 (Telnet)	0	450
2	10.14.2.3	144.1.1.5	5	80 (HTTP)	0	2753
3	20.61.96.101	171.69.96.78	3	20 (FTP)	13123	158765
4	10.14.2.3	171.69.96.78	5	20 (FTP)	0	234515
5	20.61.96.23	144.1.1.5	3	80 (HTTP)	13123	8630
6	10.1.1.54	10.71.30.123	1	23 (Telnet)	0	652

Table 2-26 shows several aggregation examples (the entry numbers where aggregation applies are in parentheses):

- Aggregate per ingress interface (1 and 6, 2 and 4, 3 and 5)

- Application aggregation (1 and 6, 2 and 5, 3 and 4)

- BGP AS (1, 2, 4 and 6, 3 and 5)

- IP source address range, depending on the net mask (1 and 6, 2 and 4, 3 and 5)

- IP destination address range, depending on the net mask (1, 2, and 5, 3 and 4, 6)

As you can see, there is not one "best aggregation" scheme; the application's requirements determine how granular the data set needs to be, to determine the appropriate aggregation scheme. If the objective of metering is to collect data sets for multiple aggregations, individual records need to be stored and must be aggregated individually per application. In case of three applications (capacity planning, billing, and security), you aggregate three times from the same set of records.

The following are some generic examples of the Cisco NetFlow Collector's aggregation schemes, separating key fields and value fields:

- HostMatrix

  Description: A HostMatrix aggregation scheme creates one record for each unique source and destination IP address pair during the collection period.

  Key fields: IP source address, IP destination address, potentially the QoS (ToS or DSCP)

  Value fields: packet count, byte count, flow count

- CallRecord

  Description: The output of a CallRecord aggregation scheme consists of one record for each unique combination of source IP address, destination IP address, source port, destination port, protocol type, and type of service during the collection period.

  Key fields: IP source address, IP destination address, source port number, destination port number, protocol byte, the QoS (ToS or DSCP)

  Value fields: packet count, byte count, flow count, first time stamp, last time stamp, total active time

- DetailASMatrix

  Description: The output of a DetailASMatrix aggregation scheme consists of one record for each unique combination of source IP address, destination IP address, source port, destination port, protocol, input interface, output interface, source autonomous system number, and destination autonomous system number during the collection period.

Key fields: IP source address, IP destination address, source port number, destination port number, protocol, input interface, output interface, source AS number, destination AS number

Value fields: packet count, byte count, flow count

Aggregating records based on key fields is very useful for the mediation device, because it merges multiple data sets into one, which reduces the required storage capacity for the records. If data should be stored for longer periods, such as months or years, an additional data reduction mechanism is required to condense the total volume of stored records. Performance management applications analyze and identify traffic trends in the network, which requires data records from the last several months or, ideally, years. Keeping all the details from a daily record set for years is neither necessary nor economical; therefore, time-based aggregation is applied to older data sets. By aggregating hourly collection records into a daily set, 24 detailed records are aggregated into one summary record for the day. Aggregation over time should be applied to all data collections that are stored for trend reporting and other applications. As a rule of thumb, keep detailed records for the maximum time that is useful for troubleshooting (for example, one month), and aggregate to longer periods afterwards.

Time-based aggregation can be applied to all collected data sets, independent of the technology, because the collection or aggregation occurs during a fixed time interval, usually between 5 and 30 minutes. These intervals can be increased to reduce the total number of records. RFC 1857 suggests the following aggregation periods:

- Over a 24-hour period, aggregate to 15 minutes
- Over a 1-month period, aggregate to 1 hour
- Over a 1-year period, aggregate to 1 day

Tables 2-29 and 2-30 exemplify aggregation over time. Table 2-29 consists of 12 entries; each represents a 5-minute interval of an SNMP interface counter. These records should be aggregated from the 5-minute interval into a 1-hour interval; therefore, 12 records are consolidated into one, as shown in Table 2-30.

Table 2-29 *Individual Interface Counters*

Entry Number	Interface Number (Ingress)	Number of Bytes	Interface Number (Egress)	Number of Bytes
1	1	450	2	8876
2	1	2753	2	33456
3	1	158765	2	3321
4	1	234515	2	778
5	1	8630	2	223456
6	1	652	2	777
7	1	1756	2	344566
8	1	2667890	2	55679892
9	1	23345	2	4456
10	1	66791	2	22345
11	1	98	2	990
12	1	3221	2	2341

Table 2-30 *Aggregated Records*

Entry Number	Interface Number (Ingress)	Number of Bytes	Interface Number (Egress)	Number of Bytes
1	1	3168866	2	56325254

An advanced function of time-based aggregation is the definition of aggregation thresholds, which means that time-based aggregation applies to only data sets in which the data values are within a defined normal range. Records that pass thresholds are not aggregated, which provides the operator with additional information about abnormal situations even after aggregating the data sets.

Data Record Correlation and Enrichment

Another task at the mediation layer is correlating information from different metering sources to enrich the data records. Here are some examples:

- Augmenting the NetFlow records with logical VPN information, to assign the records to a customer
- Gathering the call data record from multiple sources (call leg correlation)
- Modifying a data record by correlating the record details with DNS information to replace an IP address with a username

Grouping information from different sources into a common data records is a clear benefit of upper-layer applications, such as billing, which can retrieve enriched data sets instead of very basic sets, which need correlation afterwards.

Flow De-Duplication

The next mediation task is flow de-duplication, which is specific to flow-based technologies such as NetFlow. If NetFlow records are collected at several locations in the network, chances are great that one flow will be collected multiple times at different metering locations. Duplicate records lead to inaccurate results at the application level; therefore, these duplications need to be eliminated. The de-duplication algorithm identifies a flow's constant parameters. Parameters that change per hop, such as ingress and egress interface and next-hop address, are not considered. The time stamp per accounting record is very relevant, because duplicate flows occur within a short time interval. If multiple flows have the same constant parameters and were received from multiple devices within a defined time window, they can be considered duplicates, and all flows except one are eliminated. The following steps are performed:

- Identify common flow parameters, such as source and destination address, port numbers, AS number, ToS/DHCP fields, and others
- Check the time-stamps
- Associate the information and eliminate duplicate flows

Data Record Formatting and Storage

Finally, yet importantly, the processed data records are stored in a database and made available to other applications. Records have to describe usage type details, such as keys and values, where a key links to an index in a database table. A common data format definition protects the NMS and OSS applications from the variety of accounting formats that are implemented at the device level. Because these device formats change regularly, applications would need to adapt to all of these changes; instead, the mediation device shields them by providing consistent formats. The location where the records are stored can be a simple flat file system, where a new folder is created for each device and subfolder per interface, with separate text files for each aggregation scheme and interval. Alternatively, the data store can be a complex relational database system that provides sophisticated operations for local and remote access. In both cases, the format in which data records are stored should be consistent among various vendors. Consistency requires either a standard defined by a standards organization or a "de facto" standard, which is a commonly used method across the industry. Today, several different standards describe in detail the format in which the data sets are saved, as discussed in Chapter 3, "Accounting and Performance Standards and Definitions." A summary of the record specification "Network Data Management Usage (NDM-U)" from the IPDR organization serves as a useful example.

The records are implemented as XML schemas with self-defining field attributes, including five major attributes: who, what, where, when, and why. Here's a brief summary of NDM-U:

- **Who?**—Responsible user ID
- **When?**—Time when the usage took place
- **What?**—Service description and consumed resources
- **Where?**—Source and destination ID
- **Why?**—Reason for reporting the event

Figure 2-27 summarizes all mediation device functions in a flow chart. As mentioned, some tasks, such as threshold monitoring and aggregation over time, can be applied at the upper-layer application level instead of the mediation device.

Figure 2-27 *Mediation Tasks*

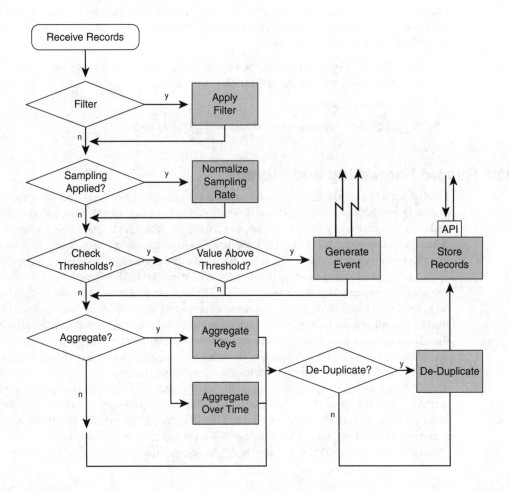

Security Considerations: How to Ensure Data Authenticity and Integrity

Two terms are significant for metering and processing data records:

- **Data authenticity**—Another term for the genuineness of data. In the case of metering accounting and performance records, this means that the data received at the collection server is original and was received exactly as it was sent by the meter's export process.

- **Data integrity**—The data records are real and were not faked or modified.

Accounting and performance management strongly depend on the integrity of the collected data records. Accounting management provides the foundation for billing services and is directly related to revenue. Performance management supplies business-critical information for network monitoring and planning, which is indirectly related to revenue as well.

Therefore, accounting and performance management are potential subjects for fraud in the areas of device configuration and transmission of data records. If an unauthorized person has access to the meter, he can easily modify the meter configuration. Enterprises as well as service providers may suffer financially and lose reputation if intruders modify accounting and performance data records. Distorted accounting records can result in erroneous customer invoices and potentially legal implications. Even if the devices are protected against unauthorized access and the data transfer is encrypted, network elements and servers are targets for denial-of-service attacks. Although an attack does not modify the collected data records, it has an impact on the service quality, which in the end helps the attackers achieve their goals. The objective for each operator is to protect the accounting and performance management infrastructure from security threats.

Source Authentication

In contrast to network element discovery, in which new devices show up after a discovery run, new meters should not pop up by surprise. Instead, the operator needs to identify the right location in the network for placing meters and then enable the required functionality. From this perspective, new or unknown meters can be considered suspicious. The real authentication challenge relates to device authentication. Does the mediation device receive data records generated by the original device or a faked device? Digital signature solutions offer authentication of the sender.

Another security aspect is the connection mode between the source and destination: connection-oriented or connectionless. Connectionless sessions introduce potential risk, because no authentication is executed before data is transmitted. Connection-oriented sessions are established between the two parties before any data records are sent, so there is usually no authentication problem. Examples are the security add-ons of SNMPv3, which provide three security modes:

- **noAuthNoPriv**—No security model is used besides the community string.
- **authNoPriv**—Provides authentication based on the HMAC-MD5 or HMAC-SHA algorithms.
- **authPriv**—Adds Data Encryption Standard (DES) 56-bit encryption in addition to authentication based on DES-56, and the Advanced Encryption Standard (AES) 128-bit encryption.

Another example of sender authentication is the Cisco IP SLA feature. Optionally, IP SLA uses a control message protocol to secure communication between two Cisco routers, executing IP SLA operations, by providing Message Digest 5 (MD5) authentication. This authentication requires MD5 key definitions on the source and target IP SLA routers.

Ensuring Data and Device Integrity

Assuming that the device identity has been authenticated, the next step is to inspect the content of the data records. Is the data genuine? Was it modified during the transmission from the device to the management station? To prepare for these questions, you should first secure the access to the device. Configure access control lists (ACL) that restrict management traffic to the NMS stations, but do not forget to include an entry for your backup servers at each network element! Instead of authenticating users at the device level, deploy a central AAA server and change administrative passwords regularly, at least if NOC staff leave your company. Disable all device services that you do not need, such as open ports. Then verify the results by running a network security scanner, which reports potential vulnerabilities that you should deal with immediately.

Next, secure the communication between a meter and a collection server. Unauthorized people or devices must not be able to read or modify data records. While read access (eavesdropping) does not have an immediate impact on the performance or billing applications, the information provided by data records can be an excellent source for an intruder to learn many details about the network infrastructure and prepare an attack against sensitive areas. Forgery of flow records is another concern. With the push model (such as NetFlow), someone might send spurious data records that contain negative values. Even though no instance between the meter and the application should expect negative values, and therefore process only positive integer fields, without a clear verification, this idea remains possible. Certainly, a hacker could send horribly oversized volume values in the data records (for example, a total volume that is above the available link bandwidth). This would prove that the ISP's billing system works incorrectly and therefore that the invoice is incorrect.

The best solution for transmission confidentiality is to use IPsec encryption between the meter and the collection server. Unfortunately, this can have a severe performance impact on the device. Here is an example: Activating NetFlow services introduces a performance impact at the device, which becomes even bigger if all exported flow records need to be encrypted. This might lead to situations in which the performance impact of metering is higher than the benefit. An alternative to data encryption is out-of-band communication, as provided by a DCN. Even when using a DCN, digital signatures should be applied to ensure that data was not modified on the way from the sender to the receiver.

A compromise between IPsec encryption and a separate network (DCN) would be to use a VPN for management traffic. The VPN concept is to transport data from different user groups over the same physical network infrastructure with a strict separation of the groups. In this case, a management VPN would be set up, consisting of all devices that should be managed.

In addition to data and device integrity, the privacy of users needs to be protected. Meters collect live user traffic, but the details of how individual customers use the network is part of their privacy and cannot be used for inspection, except for legal intercept circumstances. The proposed solution is to anonymize data records whenever possible. Except for billing systems, most applications can get as much value from anonymized data sets as from the original ones.

Denial-of-Service (DoS) Attacks

After securing device access and data transmission, the remaining task is protecting the collection infrastructure from attacks from inside and outside your network. A hacked AAA server cannot provide proper authentication and authorization and might open access to all devices in the network. A successful attack against the performance management server can seem like a well running network to the operator while the attacker invisibly modifies the infrastructure. A hacked billing system results in lost revenue. Forgery of data records for a security analysis application can trick the application by generating false alarms, with the result that security personnel consider the system untrustworthy and do not accept alarms, even when they are correct.

Dealing with these challenges is a general task for every network operator and is not limited to accounting and performance management. However, these two areas can help significantly increase network security. As described in Chapter 1, accounting and performance records can help identify traffic abnormalities, such as DoS attacks. Combining billing and security analysis is a good example of collecting network usage records once and leveraging it for multiple applications. Another approach to identifying attacks is implementing a firewall between the network and the central servers, such as the AAA server, collection server, mediation device, and application servers. An easy but often forgotten method is monitoring the violation of ACL statements with the Cisco accounting feature called IP Accounting for Access-List. Additionally, deploy intrusion detection servers or virus scanners, or even hire a hacker to identify vulnerabilities in the network.

Summary

The focus of this chapter was data collection. Starting at the device level, collection details were discussed to help you recognize the required type of information and level of detail. A methodology was developed that distinguished between key and value fields, and a checklist was provided that identified which fields to select and if they are treated as a key or value. Next, the chapter discussed how to translate the concept of a user into information that can be collected.

Then you identified at which devices metering should be enabled and learned about collection methods and intervals. This was followed by a discussion about active versus passive monitoring.

The next discussion point was the collection infrastructure, including different models for collecting data and characteristics of protocols and communication concepts. Then the chapter discussed the transport from the device to the collection server and distinguishing between the collection server and the mediation device.

There, tasks such as filtering, aggregation, and mediation are executed and then are stored for the sake of higher-layer applications, such as performance, billing, and security management. Finally, security considerations were addressed and solutions proposed.

CHAPTER 3

Accounting and Performance Standards and Definitions

This chapter describes architectures, standards definitions, and protocols related to performance and accounting. Starting with the big picture, this chapter drills down into definitions and specifications for data collection, data representation, and service notions. This chapter is also an overview of the different standards bodies and architectures, along with the concepts and principles of each protocol. This chapter also includes references for further investigation.

Understanding Standards and Standards Organizations

Instead of following the "classic" book structure of defining all standards in an introductory chapter, we decided to start by defining the requirements, followed by the collection methodology. With the use cases in mind, this is the right moment to introduce standards. The question "Why are standards required?" leads toward two answers:

- If you operate a single-vendor equipment environment, you might not see a big need for standards, because products are expected to interoperate as long as you stay with the same vendor. Interoperability between different products or versions from one vendor (such as a Cisco IOS version) is still an important requirement.

- In a multivendor environment, you expect vendors to agree on at least a minimum common denominator for functionality, which is what standards provide.

Which approach is better? Probably both have their pros and cons; the answer mainly depends on your business requirements. If you change your perspective slightly, the need for standards becomes evident. For example, suppose you travel abroad and rent a car. You expect the traffic rules to be similar to those in your home country. Cars might drive on the "wrong" side of the road, but you expect a red traffic light to mean "stop" and a green one to mean "go." If you stay in a hotel on your trip, you expect warm water to be associated with a red symbol, while blue stands for cold water. What is the conclusion? Standards are helpful to provide a kind of "lingua franca" to ensure that participants talk about the same subject.

Data normalization is another benefit of a standard. Suppose you ask two people what the temperature is. One says 68, and the other says 20. Who is right? Both are correct if the first person means Fahrenheit and the second person means Celsius. The same applies to metering data from network elements. Unless all devices apply the same measurement and report the same information with the same unit, normalization is required to turn raw data into information. For example, in a networking scenario, an ISP offers SLAs to an enterprise customer, and both parties measure the service with different tools. In the worst case, the results are completely different, leading to finger-pointing and misapprehension. As another example, two service providers collect accounting data for a peering agreement but use accounting measurement techniques that collect records with different data units. At the end of the month, different collection results lead to misapprehension. Data normalization can help address these issues.

For this book, the authors applied the following definition of a standard: "Obtaining common information across multiple network elements by using common terminology, protocols, and measurement units rather than each network element using its own syntax and reporting scheme."

Bridging the gap to network management, one person might interpret "management" to mean device monitoring, and someone else might consider "management" to mean the active part of modifying device configuration. When selecting the required Network Management System (NMS) applications, operators are sometimes overwhelmed by the functionality offered by applications. When asked what they are looking for, the answer might be "Just something to manage my complete network." In these cases, a helpful approach is to step back and ask, "Which functionality is required?", "Which devices need to be managed?", "Which services are planned?", and more. Afterwards, the answers can be mapped to a standard model, such as Fault, Configuration, Accounting, Performance, and Security (FCAPS)—as introduced in Chapter 1, "Understanding the Need for Accounting and Performance Management"—to categorize and prioritize the required functionality. As a last step, potential NMS applications are also mapped against the selected model, such as the Telecommunications Management Network (TMN) FCAPS model or the TMF eTOM model, to identify which product addresses which requirements.

Two types of standards need to be clearly distinguished:

- A de facto industry standard
- A formally committed standard from an official standards organization

When the majority of users or vendors accept and implement the same technical specification defined outside a standards body, it becomes a de facto standard. An example is IBM's Systems Networking Architecture (SNA), which originally defined networking only for IBM devices but was also implemented by other vendors. Formal standards are defined by global, regional, or national standards bodies. The International Telecommunications Union (ITU) is an international organization within the United Nations System where governments and the private sector coordinate global telecom networks and services. The ITU Telecommunication Standardization Sector (ITU-T) was created on March 1, 1993, replacing the former International Telegraph and Telephone Consultative Committee (CCITT), which originated in 1865.

In addition to the formal standard definitions and vendor de facto standards, specifications are defined by consortia. If a consortium's proposal is widely accepted, it becomes a de facto standard. These consortia are groups where different vendors (and sometimes also large customers, service providers, system integrators, and others) agree on a common definition and implement it afterwards. Examples are the TeleManagement Forum (TMF), the World Wide Web Consortium (W3C), Internet Protocol Detail Record (IPDR), Distributed Management Task Force (DMTF), and others. In all these cases, interoperability is gained if different vendors implement the same specification.

If you investigate a little further into standards organizations, you will realize the variety of standards organizations, some of which have overlapping focus areas and competing standards definitions. Why are there so many standards? This is not a simple question to answer; multiple answers are possible. One reason for the existence of different standards organizations is history. After the CCITT defined interoperability standards for Post, Telephone, and Telegraph (PTT) organizations, a need for Internet standards evolved, and the Internet Engineering Task Force (IETF) was founded. To meet the need for enterprise management standards, the DMTF was founded. The emerging web technologies required common standards, so the W3C was set up. Another reason for diversity is political discussions and disagreements within groups. Sometimes it is easier to define a new standard than to come to an agreement across the industry. Introducing competition by founding a new standards group can also increase the pace of another group.

With several different standards groups and organizations in place and a multitude of standards, the next question is how to identify the "right" standard. This requires defining the perspective first: a customer's request, a system integrator's offering, or a vendor's implementation? From an end-user perspective, a simple approach is to select the standard that you like the most; however, there might be better selection criteria.

Best practice suggests starting with the requirements. Why are you looking for standards that provide interoperability in a multivendor environment? Do you want investment protection to replace one vendor's network element with another vendor's? In this case, your management software also needs to support multiple vendors' equipment. Are you looking for operational transparency, which means you want the same management and reporting functionalities across vendors? This requires device instrumentation to be standardized. How do you integrate different management applications? If they use standard application programming interfaces (API), integration takes less effort than different APIs for each application. In summary, selecting the "right" standard depends on various criteria:

- Business requirements
- Single-vendor or multivendor strategy
- Device instrumentation

- Application interoperability
- Technical feasibility—identifying if implementing a function is technically achievable
- Common sense—requesting a standard just for the heck of it is not a wise decision

Taking a top-down approach to accounting and performance management, mainly two specifications are relevant to the big picture: the ITU-T TMN/FCAPS model and the TMF eTOM definition.

Information modeling also has two groups: the DMTF and TMF with their information model definitions of the Common Information Model (CIM; DMTF) and Shared Information/Data (SID; TMF). From a protocol perspective the two relevant standards bodies are the IETF (SNMP, AAA, IPFIX, PSAMP, and others) and the ITU (CMIP/CMISE and GDMO). These protocols are discussed later.

A top-down approach to accounting and performance management includes three components, which are discussed in detail in subsequent chapters:

- Framework/architecture:
    — The ITU with the TMN/FCAPS model.
    — The TMF with the definition of eTOM. Note that ITU-T M.3050 recommends eTOM as well.
- Information modeling:
    — The DMTF with CIM.
    — The TMF with SID.
- Protocols:
    — The IETF with SNMP, AAA, IPFIX, PSAMP, and others.
    — The ITU with CMIP/CMISE and GDMO.

Architectural and Framework Standards: The TMN/ FCAPS Model (ITU-T)

The ITU-T introduced the term Telecommunications Management Network (TMN) to describe a separate network that has interfaces to the telecommunication network (or production network). TMN defines interconnection points between the two networks and specifies management functionalities. The best description of how to operate a TMN is defined by the ITU-T recommendations M.3010, M.3400, and X.700.

The purpose of a framework is to describe the big picture, illustrate different functional areas, and identify how they interoperate. The focus of ITU-T M.3400 and X.700 is the specification and classification of management functionalities only. For example, it does not define whether syslog or trap messages are mandatory for event notifications. Neither does it define specific formats for storing accounting records. These details are defined in the lower-level specifications standards. In addition to the framework of M.3400, another recommendation (M.3010) defines the principles for a TMN. It includes details of a Data Communications Network (DCN) as a transport vehicle between the management applications and network elements. A DCN is also known as out-of-band-management, which separates user traffic from management traffic. Figure 3-1 illustrates the relationship between the telecommunications network, also called the service infrastructure, and the TMN.

Figure 3-1   *TMN and Telecommunications Networks*

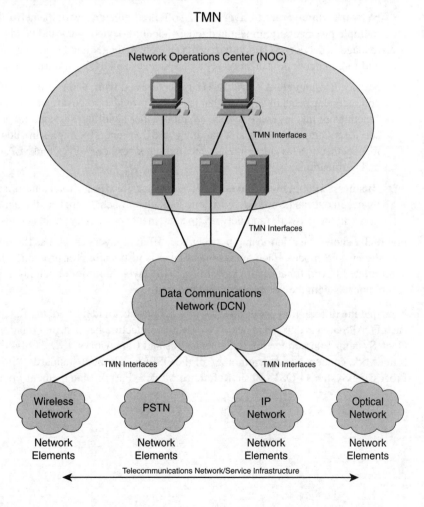

Another relevant aspect of M.3010 is the concept of layers. Network management tasks are grouped into functional areas such as FCAPS. In addition, a logical layered architecture (LLA) consists of five management layers:

- **Network Element Layer (NEL)** defines interfaces for the network elements, instantiating functions for device instrumentation, ideally covering all FCAPS areas.

- **Element Management Layer (EML)** provides management functions for network elements on an individual or group basis. It also supports an abstraction of the functions provided by the network element layer. Examples include determining equipment errors, measuring device temperatures, collecting statistical data for accounting purposes, and logging event notifications and performance statistics.

- **Network Management Layer (NML)** offers a holistic view of the network, between multiple pieces of equipment and independent of device types and vendors. It manages a network as supported by the element management layer. Examples include end-to-end network utilization reports, root cause analysis, and traffic engineering.

- **Service Management Layer (SML)** is concerned with, and responsible for, the contractual aspects of services that are being provided to customers. The main functions of this layer are service creation, order handling, service implementation, service monitoring, complaint handling, and invoicing. Examples include QoS management (delay, loss, jitter), accounting per service (VPN), and SLA monitoring and notification.

- **Business Management Layer (BML)** is responsible for the total enterprise. Business management can be considered a goal-setting approach: "What are the objectives, and how can the network (and network management specifically) help achieve them?"

Figure 3-2 shows the relationship between the different layers as well as the relationship with the FCAPS model. Each management layer is responsible for providing the appropriate FCAPS functionality according to the layer definition. Each layer communicates with the layers above and below it.

Now that the different layers of the TMN model have been identified, the functionality of each FCAPS area is described next. The TMN architecture has a strong relationship to Open Systems Interconnection (OSI) standards and frameworks. ISO 7498-4 defines the framework, concepts, and terminology of the OSI Management standards: "Information Processing Systems - OSI - Basic Reference Model - Part 4: Management Framework."

Figure 3-2   *ITU-T M.3010: TMN Logical Layer Architecture*

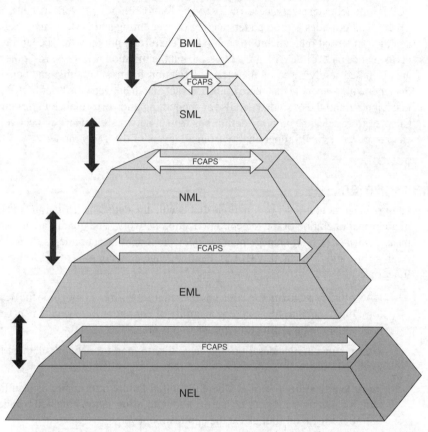

The ITU-T M.3400 recommendation is one document within the M series. It specifies five management functional areas (FCAPS):

- **Fault management**—Detect, isolate, notify, and correct faults encountered in the network.

- **Configuration management**—Configure aspects of network devices, such as configuration file management, inventory management, and software management.

- **Accounting management**—Collect usage information of network resources.

- **Performance management**—Monitor and measure various aspects of performance so that overall performance can be maintained at a defined level.

- **Security management**—Secure access to network devices, network resources, and services to authorized individuals.

The following section provides more details about each area. This chapter covers the FCAPS model extensively, because it sets the foundation for network management in general and provides a good understanding of accounting and performance management and their potential relationship to each other. Therefore, not only the accounting and performance parts of FCAPS are addressed, but the full model. Afterwards, other standards are discussed solely based on their specific relationship to accounting and performance management. Also, note that there is not an exact match between the brief FCAPS summary in Chapter 1 and the extended details for accounting and performance in this chapter. Chapter 1 provides the authors' definitions from a network element perspective, and this chapter covers FCAPS functionality from all layers of the TMN model.

Fault Management

Fault management is a set of functions that enable the detection, isolation, and correction of abnormal operation of the telecommunication network. The quality assurance measurements for fault management include component measurements for Reliability, Availability, and Survivability (RAS). Fault management consists of the following functions:

- **RAS quality assurance** establishes the reliability criteria that guide the design policy for redundant equipment (a responsibility of configuration management) and the policies of the other function groups in this area.

- **Alarm surveillance** describes the capability to monitor network element failures in near-real time.

- **Fault localization** describes where the initial failure information is insufficient for fault localization. It has to be augmented with information obtained by additional failure localization routines at the application level.

- **Fault correction** transfers data concerning the repair of a fault and the control of procedures that use redundant resources to replace equipment or facilities that have failed.

- **Testing** can be carried out in two ways. In one case, a network element analyzes equipment functions, where processing is executed entirely within the network element. Another method is active testing of external device components, such as circuits, links, and neighbor devices.

- **Trouble administration** transfers trouble reports originated by customers and trouble tickets originated by proactive failure-detection checks. It supports action to investigate and clear the problem and provides access to the status of services and the progress in clearing each problem.

Configuration Management

Configuration management provides functions to identify, collect configuration data from, exercise control over, and provide configuration data to network elements. Configuration management supports the following functions:

- Installing the physical equipment and logical configurations.

- Service planning and negotiation, which addresses planning for the introduction of new services, changing deployed service features, and disconnecting existing services.

- Provisioning, which consists of necessary procedures to bring equipment into service but does not include installation. As soon as the unit is ready for service, the supporting programs are initialized via the TMN. The state of the unit (in service, out of service, standby, or reserved) and selected parameters may also be controlled by provisioning functions.

- Status and control where the TMN provides the capability to monitor and control certain aspects of the network element (NE) on demand. Examples include checking or changing an NE's service state (in service, out of service, or standby) or the state of one of its subparts and initiating diagnostic tests within the NE. Normally, a status check is provided in conjunction with each control function to verify that the resulting action has taken place. When associated with failure conditions, these functions are corrective in nature (such as service restoration).

- Network planning and engineering deals with functions associated with determining the need for growth in capacity and the introduction of new technologies. Planning and engineering are examples of functions across multiple areas, because they relate to the performance section from a monitoring perspective and to the configuration section from an enforcement perspective.

Accounting Management

Accounting management lets you measure the use of network services and determine costs to the service provider and charges to the customer for such use. It also supports the determination of charges for services. Accounting management includes the following functions:

- **Usage measurement**—Consists of the following subfunctions:
    - Planning and management of the usage measurement process
    - Network and service usage aggregation, correlation, and validation
    - Usage distribution
    - Usage surveillance
    - Usage testing and error correction

- — Measurement rules identification
- — Usage short-term and long-term storage
- — Usage accumulation and validation
- — Administration of usage data collection
- — Usage generation

- **Tariffing and pricing**—A tariff is used to determine the amount of payment for services usage.

- **Collections and finance**—Functionality for administering customer accounts, informing customers of balances and payment dates, and receiving payments.

- **Enterprise control**—This group supports the enterprise's financial responsibilities, such as budgeting, auditing, and profitability analysis.

Performance Management

Performance management provides functions to evaluate and report on the behavior of telecommunication equipment and the effectiveness of the network or network element. Its role is to gather and analyze statistical data for the purpose of monitoring and correcting the behavior and effectiveness of the network, network elements, or other equipment, and to aid in planning, provisioning, maintenance, and quality measurement. Performance management includes the following functions:

- **Performance quality assurance**—Includes quality measurements, such as performance goals and assessment functions.

- **Performance monitoring**—This component involves the continuous collection of data concerning the performance of the network element. Acute fault conditions are detected by alarm surveillance methods. Very low rate or intermittent error conditions in multiple equipment units may interact, resulting in poor service quality, and may not be detected by alarm surveillance. Performance monitoring is designed to measure the overall quality, using monitored parameters to detect such degradation. It may also be designed to detect characteristic patterns of impairment before the quality has dropped below an acceptable level. Performance monitoring includes the following functions:

  - — Performance monitoring policy
  - — Network performance monitoring event correlation and filtering
  - — Data aggregation and trending
  - — Circuit-specific data collection
  - — Traffic status
  - — Threshold crossing alert processing

— Trend analysis

— Performance monitoring data accumulation

— Detection, counting, storage, and reporting

- **Performance management control**—This group includes the setting of thresholds and data analysis algorithms and the collection of performance data. It has no direct effect on the managed network. For network traffic management and engineering, this includes functions that affect the routing and processing of traffic.

- **Performance analysis**—The collected performance records may require additional processing and analysis to evaluate the entity's performance level. Therefore, performance analysis includes the following functions:

  — Recommendations for performance improvement

  — Exception threshold policy

  — Traffic forecasting (trending)

  — Performance summaries (per network and service, and traffic-specific)

  — Exception analysis (per network and service, and traffic-specific)

  — Capacity analysis (per network and service, and traffic-specific)

  — Performance characterization

Security Management

Security is required for all functional areas. Security management consists of two main functions:

- Security services for communications provide authentication, access control, data confidentiality, data integrity, and nonrepudiation. These may be exercised in the course of any communications between systems and between users or customers and systems. In addition, a set of pervasive security mechanisms are defined that are applicable to any communication, such as event detection, security audit-trail management, and security recovery.

- Security event detection and reporting reports activities that may be construed as a security violation (unauthorized user, physical tampering with equipment) on higher layers of security applications.

Security management includes the following functions:

- Prevention
- Detection
- Containment and recovery
- Security administration

The TMN Framework

The framework shown in Figure 3-3 brings it all together. The different logical layers sit on top of each other; each layer is responsible for implementing the FCAPS functionality and passes the collected information to the next layer. From a customer's applicability perspective, after identifying and prioritizing the requirements, you can map various network management products to this matrix and identify what is required to meet your needs.

Figure 3-3   *TMN Management Layers and FCAPS*

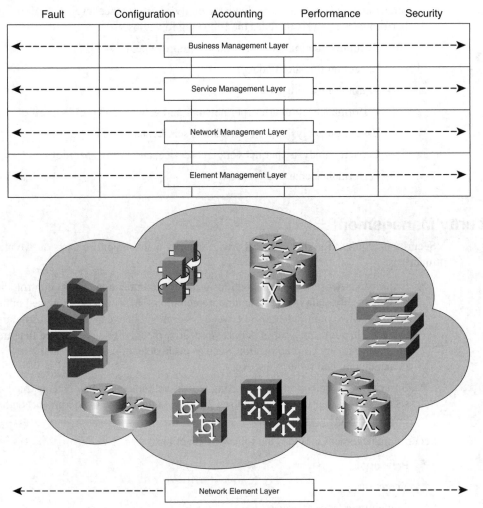

From the perspective of this book, relevant layers of the TMN architecture are the Network Element Layer (NEL); the Element Management Layer (EML), related to similar device types; the Network Management Layer (NML), related to mediation; and the Service Management Layer (SML), related to service monitoring and accounting. The Business Management Layer (BML) is outside the scope of this book. If you're interested, you're encouraged to study the ITU-T M series for more details.

Note that the FCAPS model describes the conceptual model of functional areas; it does not define accounting and performance standards for data collection. Therefore, a second level of standards is required for data collection. At the network element layer, it can be SNMP or IPFIX. IPDR is appropriate at the Element Management Layer.

Architectural and Framework Standards: the eTOM Model (TMF)

The TeleManagement Forum (TMF) is a nonprofit global consortium that works on telecommunications management and the development of management systems and standards. It was established in 1988 as the OSI/Network Management Forum under the sponsorship of the ITU. Later the name was changed to TeleManagement Forum. The strategic goal of the TMF is to create or identify standard interfaces that allow a network to be managed consistently across various network element suppliers.

A major deliverable of the TMF was the TOM (Telecom Operations Map, GB910) model, a framework for telecom and Information Services business processes.

It was developed to drive a consensus around the processes, inputs, outputs, and activities required for service provider operations management. Its focus and scope were operations and operations management. TOM was extended and superseded by the eTOM (enhanced Telecom Operations Map, GB921 v6) model.

eTOM is a reference framework that categorizes the business processes that a service provider will use. It broadens the TOM model to a complete enterprise framework and addresses the impact of e-business environments and business drivers. eTOM can be considered a blueprint for standardizing business processes as well as operations support systems (OSS) and business support systems (BSS). Another area of improvement is process-modeling methodology, which provides the linkage necessary for Next-Generation Operations Support Systems (NGOSS). NGOSS programs implement a common system infrastructure framework, in which components that adhere to the specifications can interoperate in a flexible application infrastructure.

The eTOM model serves as a reference framework for categorizing all the business activities of a service provider. It categorizes them into different levels of detail according to their significance and priority for the business. The eTOM structure establishes the business language and foundation for the development and integration of BSS and OSS, respectively. eTOM provides a reference point and common language for service providers' internal process (re)engineering needs, partnerships, alliances, and general working agreements with other providers. For suppliers, the eTOM framework outlines potential boundaries of software components, and the required functions, inputs, and outputs that need to be supported by products using the common language of the service providers.

The ITU-T TMN models define management layers and focuses on general network management functionality. The eTOM focuses on managing operations, services, and interactions between the various components and building blocks. eTOM defines three major building blocks:

- Operations (OPS)
- Strategy, Infrastructure, and Product (SIP)
- Enterprise Management (EM)

Related to this book's perspective, the OPS area is most relevant, because SIP and EM describe different functions such as marketing, supply chain, and financial management.

The core of the operations area is the Fulfillment, Assurance, and Billing (FAB) model. The Operations Support and Readiness (OSR) part was added to the original TOM FAB model (GB910). FAB operations are directly related to customer services, whereas OSR ensures that the operational environment is in place for FAB to be successful.

Therefore, the two definitions do not overlap, but complement each other. The TMN model lays the foundation for managing the infrastructure. eTOM adds service functions and processes, such as service definition and quality management, as well as customer management functionality, such as sales, order handling, and customer relationship management. eTOM can be used to analyze existing processes in organizations as well as for defining new processes. Note that the eTOM model introduces both vertical functions (OSR, fulfillment, assurance, billing) and functional process grouping in horizontal layers:

- Customer Relationship Management (CRM)
- Service Management and Operations (SM&O)
- Resource Management and Operations (RM&O)
- Supplier/Partner Relationship Management (S/PRM)

Figure 3-4 is an overview of the eTOM operations areas. In August 2004, the ITU completed the ratification of eTOM as an official ITU standard. eTOM is published in the ITU M.3050 recommendation; however, it is based on a previous version of eTOM, GB921 v4.0. This book references eTOM GB921 v6.0 and v6.1.

Figure 3-4   *TMF eTOM: Operations Area*

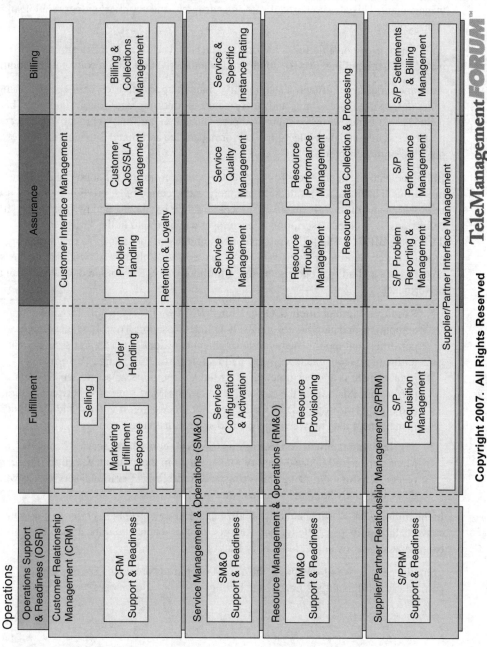

Operations includes processes that support customers, network operations, and management. This also consists of sales management and supplier/partner relationships management.

Fulfillment is responsible for delivering products and services to the customer. This includes order handling, service configuration and activation, and resource provisioning.

Assurance consists of proactive and reactive maintenance activities, service monitoring (SLA or QoS), resource status and performance monitoring, and troubleshooting. This includes continuous resource status and performance monitoring to proactively detect possible failures, and the collection of performance data and analysis to identify and resolve potential or real problems.

Billing collects usage data records (accounting), various rating functions, and billing operations. This includes production of timely and accurate bills, providing pre-bill use information and billing to customers, processing their payments, and performing payment collections. A detailed description of each layer can be found in the TMF's eTOM document (GB921). The following is a brief summary of the two areas that are most relevant for accounting and performance management. Within these two, the emphasis is on assurance and billing, because neither fulfillment nor OSR is related to accounting and performance:

- **Resource Management & Operations (RM&O)** is responsible for application, computing, and network resources. It includes Resource Trouble Management, which performs fault monitoring and management functions, such as processing device notifications, root cause analysis, and fault reporting. Resource Performance Management is another function of RM&O. It monitors, analyzes, and reports performance data from the devices. A common RM&O function between assurance and billing is Resource Data Collection and Processing. It gathers and distributes management data between devices and service instances.

- **Service Management & Operations (SM&O)** consists of Service Problem Management and Service Quality Management in the assurance section. These are responsible for monitoring, analyzing, and controlling operational services, as well as detecting, analyzing, and localizing service problems.

In the billing area, Service and Specific Instance Rating correlates service events and converts them into a specific format. Reports for chargeable and noncacheable events can be generated—for example, to identify fraud.

From the perspective of this book, the eTOM operations processes are relevant—particularly fulfillment, assurance, and billing.

Informational IETF Standards

Informational RFCs are not official IETF standard track documents. RFC 2026 defines the details. An informational RFC specification is published for the general information of the Internet community and does not represent an Internet community consensus or recommendation. The informational designation is intended to provide for the timely publication of a very broad range of responsible informational documents from many sources, subject only to editorial considerations and to verification that there has been adequate coordination with the standards process.

Because informational RFCs are valuable sources of information, the following sections describe RFCs 2924 and 2975.

IETF RFC 2924, *Accounting Attributes and Record Formats*

This informational RFC summarizes relevant documents related to accounting from both the IETF and ITU-T. A very basic architecture model is introduced that consists of a service consumer accessing a service element. The service element collects accounting records and sends usage events to an accounting server. The following protocols are examined in terms of providing accounting attributes:

- RADIUS
- Diameter
- ROAMOPS (The Accounting Data Interchange Format [ADIF])
- RTFM (traffic flow measurement)
- ISDN
- AToM MIB
- QoS: RSVP and DiffServ
- ITU-T Q.825: Call Detail Recording
- Telecommunications and Internet Protocol Harmonization Over Networks (TIPHON): ETSI TS 101 321

This RFC can be used in a cookbook approach: After selecting your protocol and technology of choice, check for the provided accounting details. Note that RFC 2924 is an informational standard defining the terminology rather than a protocol that can be implemented. Therefore, it is a good starting point for an introduction to accounting.

IETF RFC 2975, *Introduction to Accounting Management*

This informational RFC provides an overview of accounting and billing terms and concepts and develops a more advanced architecture than RFC 2924 does. A protocol section discusses the use of UDP and TCP as a transport protocol and proposes SCTP as an alternative. The pros and cons of different data collection approaches (such as polling and event-driven models) are addressed, followed by an analysis of various accounting protocols:

- RADIUS
- TACACS+
- SNMP
- FTP
- HTTP

This document can be used as an extended introduction to accounting because it addresses all accounting areas, such as collection methods at the device level, considerations of exporting and storing data records, and a review of accounting protocols.

Information Modeling

Information modeling is one aspect of describing a managed environment, because it explains concepts from a high-level perspective up to specific details, and it does this in a neutral way without defining implementation details. It provides common definitions and terminology that help structure information. This can be applied for designing processes, applications, interfaces between software components, and other business areas.

In addition, information models help operators and users understand the general concepts. Therefore, information models are also called abstract models or conceptual models. They are protocol- and implementation-neutral. We use the following definition of the information model from RFC 3198:

"An abstraction and representation of the entities in a managed environment—their properties, operations, and relationships. It is independent of any specific repository, application, protocol, or platform."

A data model instantiates the information model by specifying the implementation details. Again, we use the definition from RFC 3198:

"A data model is basically the rendering of an information model according to a specific set of mechanisms for representing, organizing, storing and handling data."

Information models can be defined in an informal way using natural languages such as English, but because a natural language can always be interpreted in different ways, a formal language is preferred, to be as specific as possible. An example of a formal language is the Unified Modeling Language (UML), which is standardized by the Object Management Group (OMG). Two groups are most active in developing standard information models in the IT world: the DMTF with the Common Information Model (CIM), and the TMF with the Shared Information and Data (SID) model. Distinguishing the two approaches is not a simple task. In most cases customers either are not concerned about the models, or they select a model based on the group's history and association. The DMTF has a strong enterprise background as well as a relationship to the storage industry, and the TMF has a strong telecommunications and service provider background.

A liaison has been set up between the TMF and DMTF. The objective is to achieve technology and business model convergence and coordination between SID and CIM.

NOTE   For more information, consult the following sources:

- RFC 3444, *On the Difference between Information Models and Data Models*

- *Directory Enabled Networks* by John Strassner (Macmillan Technical Publishing, 1999)

- *Policy-Based Network Management: Solutions for the Next Generation* by John Strassner (Morgan Kaufmann, 2003)

Data Collection Protocols: SNMP, SMI, and MIB

There are so many valuable references, books, and tutorials dedicated to the technical aspects of Simple Network Management Protocol (SNMP), Structure of Management Information (SMI), and Management Information Base (MIB) that there is no point in covering everything in detail in this book. However, this section describes in a few pages the necessary concepts, theory, and terminology. Chapter 4, "SNMP and MIBs," details some useful accounting and performance MIB modules. Furthermore, this chapter provides the complete list of RFCs for further reference.

Internet Management Model and Terminology

SNMP is an Internet protocol developed by the IETF. It is designed to facilitate the exchange of management information between network elements. By transporting information over the SNMP protocol (such as packets per second and network error rates), network administrators can easily manage network performance and accounting, find and solve network problems, and plan for network growth.

The most basic elements of the Internet management model are shown in Figure 3-5.

Figure 3-5   *Internet Management Model*

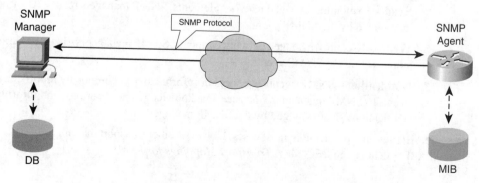

As specified in IETF RFCs and other documents, a managed device is composed of the following:

- **SNMP agent**—A software module that resides in network elements; it collects and stores management information specified in the supported MIB modules. The SNMP agent responds to SNMP requests from an NMS station for information and actions. The SNMP agent can send fault notifications proactively to the SNMP manager.

- **Managed object**—A representation of something that can be managed. For example, a list of currently active TCP circuits in a particular computer is a managed object. Managed objects differ from variables, which are particular object instances. Using our example, an object instance is a single active TCP circuit in a particular network element. Managed objects can be scalar (defining a single object instance) or tabular (defining multiple related instances).

- **Management Information Base (MIB)**—A collection of managed objects residing in a virtual information store. A collection of related managed objects is defined in a specific MIB module. A MIB can be considered a local data store at the network element.

- **Syntax notation**—A language used to describe managed objects in a machine-independent format. Consistent use of a syntax notation allows different types of computers to share information. SNMP-based management systems use a subset of the International Organization for Standardization's (ISO) Open System Interconnection (OSI) Abstract Syntax Notation 1 (ASN.1, International Telecommunication Union Recommendation X.208) to define both the packets exchanged by the management protocol and the objects that are to be managed.

- **Structure of Management Information (SMI)**—Defines the rules for describing management information (the MIB). The SMI is defined using ASN.1.

The NMS, which contains an SNMP manager, executes management applications that monitor and control network elements. At least one NMS is required in each managed environment.

Interactions between the SNMP manager and managed network elements (SNMP agents) can be any of three different types of commands:

- **Read**—To monitor managed network elements, SNMP managers read MIB variables maintained by the SNMP agents.

- **Write**—To control managed network elements, SNMP managers write MIB variables stored within the SNMP agents.

- **Notification**—SNMP agents use traps or informs to asynchronously report certain events to SNMP managers. Traps are unacknowledged notifications, and informs are notifications acknowledged by the SNMP manager.

SNMP runs on top of UDP in most cases. However, other transport mappings exist, such as IPX. For details, see RFC 3417, *Transport Mappings for SNMP*.

MIB Modules and Object Identifiers

An SNMP MIB module is a specification of management information on a device. The SMI represents the MIB database structure in a tree form with conceptual tables, where each managed resource is represented by an object. The SNMP agent on a device has access to this local repository. A management application may read and modify this repository via SNMP operations.

Relative to this tree structure, the term MIB is used in two senses. In one sense it is actually a MIB branch, usually containing information for a single aspect of technology, such as a transmission medium or a routing protocol. A MIB used in this sense is more accurately called a MIB module and is usually defined in a single document. In the other sense, a MIB is a collection of such branches. Such a collection might comprise, for example, all the MIB modules implemented by a given SNMP agent, or the entire collection of managed objects.

A MIB module is an abstract tree with an unnamed root. Individual data items, the MIB variables, make up the leaves of the tree. The MIB variables are identified by specifying a "path" through the tree; Object Identifiers (OIDs) uniquely identify or name MIB variables in the tree. An OID is an ordered sequence of nonnegative integers written left to right, containing at least two elements. For easier human interaction, string-valued names also identify the OIDs. They are like telephone numbers, organized hierarchically with specific digits assigned by different organizations.

The OID top structure of the SNMP MIB tree defines three main branches:

*   Consultative Committee for International Telegraph and Telephone (CCITT)
*   International Organization for Standardization (ISO)
*   Joint ISO/CCITT

Much of the current MIB module activity occurs in the portion of the ISO branch defined by object identifier .1.3.6.1, dedicated to the Internet community. After a MIB module is published, OIDs are bound for all time to the objects defined. OIDs cannot be deleted and can only be made obsolete; even minor changes to an object are discouraged.

The MIB tree is extensible with new standard MIB modules or by experimental and private branches. Vendors can define their own private branches to include instances of their own products. For example, the Cisco private MIB is represented by the object identifier .1.3.6.1.4.1.9. It includes objects such as rttMonLatestHTTPOperRTT, which is identified by object ID 1.3.6.1.4.1.9.9.42.1.5.1.1.1, and specifies the round-trip time taken to perform a configured HTTP operation.

For example, the Internet prototypical standard MIB module is MIB-II (RFC 1213), which contains 171 objects. MIB-II contained branches for the basic areas of instrumentation, such as the system, its network interfaces, and protocols such as IP, TCP, SNMP, and others. Note, for completeness, that all these branches started out in a single MIB module, but as SNMPv2 evolved, they were split into separate modules. The basic MIB structure, including MIB-II (object ID 1.3.6.1.2.1) and the Cisco private MIB (object ID 1.3.6.1.4.1.9), is shown in Figure 3-6.

Figure 3-6 *Basic MIB Structure*

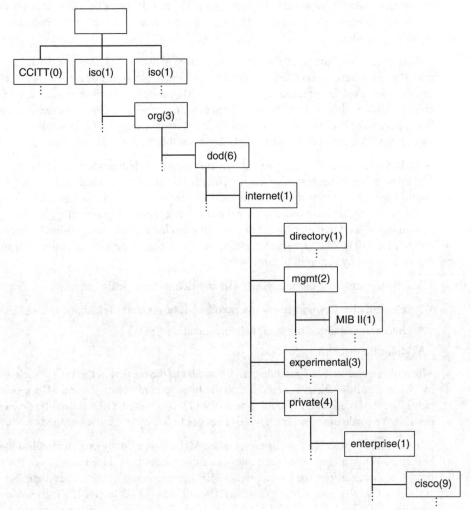

SMI Definitions

The SMI defines the framework in which a MIB module can be defined or constructed. In other words, it defines the components of a MIB module and the formal language for describing the managed objects. The SMI specifies that all managed objects should have a name, syntax, and encoding. The name is characterized by the OID. The syntax defines the managed object's data type (for example, integer or string). A subset of ASN.1 definitions are used for the SMI syntax. The encoding describes how the information associated with the managed object is formatted as a series of data items for transmission on the network.

The two versions of SMI are SMIv1 (RFC 1155) and SMIv2 (RFC 2578). SMIv2 offers richer, more precise syntax for defining MIB modules.

SMI data types are divided into three categories: *simple types, application-wide types*, and *simply constructed types*.

Simple types include four primitive ASN.1 types:

- **Integer**—A unique value that is a positive or negative whole number (including 0).
- **OctetString**—A unique value that is an ordered sequence of zero or more octets, more commonly called bytes.
- **ObjectID**—A unique value from the set of all object identifiers allocated according to the rules specified in ASN.1.
- **Bits**—New in SMIv2, these are zero or more named bits that specify a value.

Application-wide data types refer to special data types defined by the SMI:

- **Network address**—Represents an address from a particular protocol family. Examples are InetAddressType and InetAddress.
- **Counter**—A nonnegative integer that increments by +1 until it reaches a maximum value, when it is reset to 0. The total number of bytes received on an interface is an example of a counter. In SMIv1, counter size was not specified (it was 32-bit by default). In SMIv2, 32-bit and 64-bit counters are defined.
- **Gauge**—A nonnegative integer that can increase or decrease but that latches at a maximum value. The interface load is an example of a gauge. SMIv2 redefined the gauge as gauge32.
- **Timetick**—Hundredths of a second since an event. The time since an interface entered its current state is an example of a tick.
- **INTEGER**—Represents signed, integer-valued information. This data type redefines the ASN.1 integer simple data type, which has arbitrary precision in ASN.1 but bounded precision in the SMI. Although SMIv1 specifies only integer, SMIv2 redefines INTEGER as Integer32.
- **Unsigned integer**—Represents unsigned integer-valued information. It is useful when values are always nonnegative. This data type redefines the ASN.1 integer simple data type, which has arbitrary precision in ASN.1 but bounded precision in the SMI. SMIv2 defines UInteger32 (where U stands for unsigned).

Simply constructed types include two ASN.1 types that define multiple objects in tables and lists:

- **Row**—References a row in a table. Each element of the row can be a simple type or an application-wide type.

- **Table**—References a table of zero or more rows. Each row has the same number of columns.

The IETF mandates that all IETF-produced MIB modules use the SMIv2 specifications. However, SMIv2, which is the data structure, does not require SNMPv2 as the "transport protocol." Therefore, SNMPv1 could still be used. SNMPv2 is required only in case the MIB module defined with SMIv2 contains a Counter64 data type, because SNMPv1 does not support this data type. If the MIB module does not contain any Counter64 data type, MIB compilers can translate MIB modules from SMIv2 to SMIv1.

Another ISO specification, called the *Basic Encoding Rule* (BER, International Telecommunication Union Recommendation X.209), details SMI encodings. The BER allows dissimilar machines to exchange management information by specifying both the position of each bit within the transmitted octets and the structure of the bits. Bit structure is conveyed by describing the data type, length, and value.

SNMP Versions

SNMP version 1 (SNMPv1) is the original version of SNMP. SNMPv1 uses a clear-text community string for context selection. Although sometimes used for security-like purposes, this community string offers only limited security, because it is transmitted in clear text over the wire. Therefore, eavesdropping must be avoided, such as deploying an out-of-band management infrastructure. The community string is defined as an OCTET STRING that can contain any value: spaces, any character, or hex values. However, it is suggested that you avoid $, #, &, /, !, and so on, because those characters might be misinterpreted by NMS applications and scripts. According to the specifications, there is no limitation in terms of length; Cisco IOS limits the length to 128 bytes, though.

SNMPv1 is a simple request/response protocol that specifies five SNMP operations, also called Protocol Data Unit (PDU):

- **Get**—Allows the SNMP manager to retrieve an object instance from the agent.

- **Get-Next**—Allows the SNMP manager to retrieve the next object instance from a table or list within an SNMP agent. In SNMPv1, when an SNMP manager wants to retrieve all elements of a table from an agent, it initiates a Get-Next operation to the base OID of the table/column, which returns the first instance (row). Then it continues sending Get-Next requests until a return value is outside of the table, indicating that all elements have been retrieved.

- **Set**—Allows the SNMP manager to set values for object instances within an SNMP agent.

- **Trap**—Used by the SNMP agent to asynchronously notify the SNMP manager of some event.

- **Response**—Used as a response for the Get and Set.

SNMPv2, specified in RFC 1445 through RFC 1447, specified a new party-based security model. However, SNMPv2 never caught on and was finally moved to historic. Hence, SNMPv2c, where the "c" stands for "community," was specified in RFC 1901. This community-based SNMP version 2 (SNMPv2c) is an experimental SNMP framework that supplements the SNMPv2 framework (RFC 3416). Indeed, it uses the SNMPv2 PDUs specified in the SNMPv2 Framework within a community-based message wrapper. Note that SNMPv2c is still widely used throughout the industry.

Even though SNMPv2c has no improved security compared to SNMPv1, it offers some advantages, thanks to the SNMPv2 Framework:

- Richer error handling (error-status: wrongType, wrongLength, wrongEncoding, etc.)

- New data types (for example, 64-bit counters)

- New PDUs:

  - **GetBulk**—The GetBulk operation was added to make it easier to acquire large amounts of related information without initiating repeated get-next operations. GetBulk was designed to virtually eliminate the need for GetNext operations. As an example, retrieving a routing table of 100 entries from a network element requires one GetBulk operation in SNMPv2 compared to 101 GetNext PDUs in SNMPv1 (the 101st operation indicates the end of the row). This assumes that all entries fit into a single packet. However, a total of 83 Integer32s values are the maximum to fit into a 1500-byte packet.

  - **Inform**—The Inform operation was added to allow the acknowledgment of notification, because one of the drawbacks of the trap is its unreliability due to the UDP transport protocol. The Inform is retransmitted until it is acknowledged (with a maximum retry count) and thus is more reliable than traps. Note that full reliability would require an infinite number of retries, hence infinite queue on the SNMP agent.

  - **Trap**—The trap operation has been redesigned in SNMPv2. The Trap PDU is now similar to the other PDUs, which ease the processing at the SNMP manager. Furthermore, the first two variable bindings in the variable binding list of an SNMPv2-Trap-PDU are always sysUpTime.0 and snmpTrapOID.0, respectively (both of them are defined in RFC 3418).

Figure 3-7 illustrates the SNMPv2 operations, along with the respective direction: from the SNMP manager to the SNMP agent or vice versa.

Figure 3-7 *SNMP Operations*

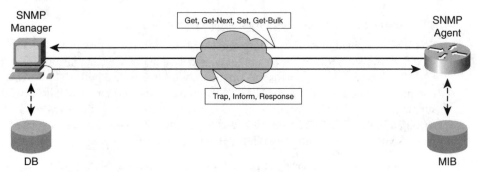

The SNMP version 3 (SNMPv3) Management Framework addresses the deficiencies in SNMPv2 related to security and administration. Although the concept of a view was defined in SNMPv1, SNMPv3 redefined it and gave a structure to security that included the *View-based Access Control Model (VACM) for the Simple Network Management Protocol* (RFC 3415). VACM defines the controlling elements for accessing the management information.

SNMPv3 provides secure access to network elements through a combination of authenticating and encrypting packets over the network. Here are the security features provided in SNMPv3:

- **Message integrity**—Ensuring that a packet has not been tampered with in transit.

- **Authentication**—Determining that the message is from a valid source.

- **Encryption**—Encrypting the content of a packet prevents eavesdropping on the exchanges between the SNMP manager and agent.

- **Message stream modification**—Avoids malicious reordering, delay, or replay of messages.

Therefore, data can be collected securely from SNMP agents without fear that it was tampered with or corrupted. Also, confidential information, such as SNMPSet PDU packets that change a router's configuration, can be encrypted to prevent their contents from being exposed on the network.

SNMPv3 provides for both security models and security levels. A security model is an authentication strategy that is set up for a user; it specifies the user's permitted level of security within a security model. RFC 3414, *User-based Security Model (USM) for version 3 of the Simple Network Management Protocol (SNMPv3)*, defines the details of SNMP message-level security. A combination of a security model and a security level determines which security mechanism is employed when handling an SNMP packet. Three security models are available: SNMPv1, SNMPv2c, and SNMPv3. Table 3-1 identifies what the combinations of security models and levels mean.

Table 3-1   *SNMP Security Models and Levels*

Model	Level	Authentication	Encryption	What Happens
v1	noAuthNoPriv	Community String	No	Uses a community string match for authentication.
v2c	noAuthNoPriv	Community String	No	Uses a community string match for authentication.
v3	noAuthNoPriv	Username	No	Uses a username match for authentication.
v3	authNoPriv	MD5 or SHA	No	Provides authentication based on the HMAC-MD5 or HMAC-SHA algorithm.
v3	authPriv	MD5 or SHA	DES or AES	Provides authentication based on the HMAC-MD5 or HMAC-SHA algorithms. Provides DES 56-bit or CFB128-AES-128 encryption in addition to authentication based on the CBC-DES (DES-56) standard.

While the SNMPv3 architecture adoption takes time throughout the industry, discussions are occurring about the efficiency and suitability of SNMP as a configuration protocol. However, SNMP is a sufficient protocol for retrieving performance and accounting data.

References for SMIv1 and SMIv2

For the sake of completeness and for further reading, Tables 3-2 and 3-3 list the IETF references for the two SMI versions and three different SNMP versions. Note that SNMPv1 attained historic status. The Status column differentiates informational versus standard-track RFCs, along with the standard-track maturity level (Proposed Standard, Draft Standard, Internet Standard) as specified in the Internet Standards Process (RFC 2026). The list following the tables references relevant books.

Table 3-2   *References for SMIv1 and SMIv2*

RFC	Status	Title	Description
1155	Standard	*Structure of Management Information*	The elements that make up SNMP
1212	Standard	*Concise MIB Definitions*	Conventions for defining a Management Information Base
1215	Informational	*Concise Trap Definitions*	Conventions for defining traps
2578	Standard	*Structure of Management Information Version 2*	The elements that make up SNMPv2
2579	Standard	*Textual Conventions for SMIv2*	Additional data types without extending the SMI
2580	Standard	*Conformance Statements for SMIv2*	Techniques for indicating conformance

Table 3-3   *References for SNMPv1, SNMPv2, and SNMPv3*

RFC	Status	Title	Description
1157	Historic	*Simple Network Management Protocol*	SNMPv1: the protocol specification
1215	Informational	*Concise Trap Definitions*	Conventions for defining traps
1901	Historic	*Introduction to Community-based SNMPv2*	SNMPv2c: the protocol specification
3410	Informational	*Introduction and Applicability Statements for Internet Standard Management Framework*	An overview of the third version of the Internet-Standard Management Framework, termed the SNMP version 3 Framework
3411	Standard	*An Architecture for Describing Simple Network Management Protocol*	Overall architecture with special emphasis on security and administration
3412	Standard	*Message Processing and Dispatching for the Simple Network Management Protocol*	Multiple message processing models and dispatcher portion, part of an SNMP protocol engine
3413	Standard	*Simple Network Management Protocol Applications*	Five types of applications associated with an SNMPv3 engine and their elements of procedure
3414	Standard	*User-based Security Model (USM) for version 3 of the Simple Network Management Protocol*	Threats, mechanisms, protocols, and supporting data used to provide SNMP message-level security

Table 3-3   *References for SNMPv1, SNMPv2, and SNMPv3 (Continued)*

RFC	Status	Title	Description
3415	Standard	*View-based Access Control Model (VACM) for the Simple Network Management Protocol*	VACM for use in the SNMP architecture
3416	Standard	*Version 2 of the Protocol Operations for SNMP*	SNMPv2 specifications for the PDUs and operations
3417	Standard	*Transport Mappings for the Simple Network Management Protocol*	Operation over various lower-level protocols
3584	Best Current Practice	*Coexistence between Version 1, Version 2, and Version 3 of the Internet-standard Network Management Framework*	Coexistence guidelines and MIB module conversion from SMIv1 format to SMIv2 format
3826	Proposed Standard	*The Advanced Encryption Standard (AES) Cipher Algorithm in the SNMP User-based Security Model*	Symmetric encryption protocol that supplements the protocols described in the User-based Security Model

Books for further reference:

- *SNMP, SNMPv2, SNMPv3, and RMON 1 and 2*, 3rd Edition by William Stallings (Addison-Wesley Professional, 1998)

- *A Practical Guide to SNMPv3 and Network Management* by David Zeltserman (Prentice-Hall, 1999)

- *Understanding SNMP MIBs* by David Perkins (Prentice-Hall, 1997)

Data Collection Protocols: NetFlow Version 9 and IPFIX Export Protocols

Cisco IOS NetFlow services give network administrators access to information about IP flows within their networks. In the context of Cisco NetFlow, an IP flow is defined as a unidirectional sequence of packets between given source and destination endpoints. IP flows are highly granular; flow endpoints are identified by IP address and by transport layer application port numbers. NetFlow Services also uses the IP protocol type, type of service (ToS), and the input interface identifier to uniquely identify flows.

NetFlow flow records are exported to an external device, a NetFlow collector, and can be used for a variety of purposes, including network management and planning, enterprise accounting, departmental chargeback, ISP billing, data warehousing, user monitoring and profiling, combating denial of service (DoS) attacks, and data mining for marketing purposes.

NetFlow services, deliberately a generic term, refers to two completely different components: the NetFlow metering process and the NetFlow export protocol. Chapter 7, "NetFlow," analyzes in detail different aspects of the metering process: metering process concepts and features, configurations examples, deployment guidelines. This section covers the export protocol (NetFlow version 9 and the IPFIX protocol).

The IETF IPFIX charter is not intended to "fix" IP, nor does it define a fixed solution, as its name might imply. IPFIX, which stands for "IP Flow Information eXport," is an IETF effort to standardize an export protocol similar to NetFlow—specifically, a protocol that exports flow-related information. Actually, the IPFIX protocol specifications are largely based on the NetFlow version 9 export protocol. With the NetFlow version 9 export protocol in mind, the IPFIX section covers the NetFlow version 9 export protocol improvements added to the IPFIX protocol to make it a more robust protocol.

NOTE	IPFIX addresses only data export, while the term NetFlow includes the collection of records and the export process. So far, NetFlow records can be exported only with Cisco NetFlow export protocols (versions 1, 5, 7, 8, and 9). IPFIX defines the standard export protocol, which will eventually succeed the various Cisco NetFlow export protocols. The NetFlow metering process is independent of the IPFIX export protocol.

NetFlow Version 9 Export Protocol

A few years ago, NetFlow became the de facto IP accounting standard throughout the industry. By publishing the protocol details, Cisco encouraged third-party companies to develop their own NetFlow collectors. Therefore, many vendors have implemented the NetFlow export protocol at network elements or specific NetFlow collectors. Examples of open-source implementations of NetFlow collectors are nfdump/NetFlow sensor (http://nfdump.sourceforge.net/), Flow-Tools (http://www.splintered.net/sw/flow-tools/), and ntop (http://www.ntop.org/netflow.html).

The Template Mechanism

The basic output of NetFlow is a *flow record* exported from an exporter—a device (such as a router) with the NetFlow services enabled. An exporter monitors packets entering an observation point (such as a network interface) and creates flow records from these packets. The term "exporter" is introduced in the NetFlow version 9 and IPFIX RFCs and is used in this chapter for consistency with the RFCs. Several different formats for *flow* records have evolved as NetFlow has matured. The most recent evolution of the NetFlow flow record format is known as version 9. The distinguishing feature of the NetFlow version 9 format compared to the previous version is its *template-based feature*. Templates, which define collections of fields with corresponding descriptions of structure and semantics, provide a flexible design for the record format.

The important principle of the NetFlow version 9 flow export protocol is that it first exports the templates from the network elements to a NetFlow collector and then the flow records. As soon as a NetFlow collector receives the template(s), it can decode the subsequent flow records. The templates are composed of the field types, the field lengths, and a generated unique template ID. The flow records are composed of the unique template ID and the field values.

Using templates provides several key benefits:

- Because the template mechanism is flexible, it allows the definition and export of only the required flow fields to a NetFlow collector. This helps reduce the exported flow data volume and provides potential memory savings for the exporter and NetFlow collector.

- New field types can be added to NetFlow version 9 flow records without changing the structure of the export record format. With previous NetFlow versions (1, 5, 7, and 8), adding a new field in the flow record implied a new version of the export protocol format and a new version of the NetFlow collector that supported the parsing of the new export protocol format. The template mechanism in NetFlow version 9 provides an extensible design to the record format. It allows future enhancements to NetFlow services without requiring changes to the export format. Indeed, as the NetFlow metering process now can classify new traffic types such as IPv6 and MPLS, no changes are required to the NetFlow export protocol (just new templates). The only requirement is an update of the information model with the definitions of the new information elements.

- Templates sent to a NetFlow collector contain the structural information about the exported flow record fields. Therefore, even if the NetFlow collector does not understand the semantics of new data types, it can still decode the entire flow record. After the collector updates the information model with new data types, it can interpret the meaning of the flow record information elements.

To summarize, the NetFlow version 9 export protocol is a result of the previously fixed NetFlow export formats. Whenever an additional export field was required, a new export format was specified. NetFlow export version 9 overcame this limitation. Note that the IPFIX protocol is based on the NetFlow version 9 export protocol.

The Export Protocol

Without explaining all the details from the specification terminology section (RFC 3954, *Cisco Systems NetFlow Services Export Version 9*), let's review the most useful terms and concepts.

Cisco NetFlow incorporates the push model, in which the exporter sends flow records periodically to a NetFlow collector. The export frequency depends on the active and inactive flow timeouts, the flow expiration detection, and the flow cache full condition.

Some terms are capitalized in the NetFlow specification (RFC 3954) because they have a formal definition. Those terms keep their capitalizations in this section (see Table 3-4).

Table 3-4   *NetFlow Version 9 Terminology Summary*

FlowSet	Contents	
	Template Record	**Data Record**
Data FlowSet	/	Flow Data Record(s) or Options Data Record(s)
Template FlowSet	Template Record(s)	/
Options Template FlowSet	Options Template Record(s)	/

The NetFlow version 9 record format consists of a packet header followed by one or more Template FlowSets or Data FlowSets. A FlowSet is a generic term for a collection of flow records that have a similar structure. There are three different types of FlowSets:

- A Data FlowSet is composed of Options Data Record(s) or Flow Data Record(s). No Template Record is included.

- A Template FlowSet is composed of Template Record(s). No Flow or Options Data Record is included.

- An Options Template FlowSet is composed of Options Template Record(s). No Flow or Options Data Record is included.

The Template Record, sent in a Template FlowSet, specifies the type and length of the flow record-specific fields. Those flow records are called Flow Data Records and are present in Data FlowSets. In other words, the flow record template is defined in a Template Record, which is sent in a Template FlowSet, and the associated instances of flow records are sent as Flow Data Records in the Data FlowSet.

An additional record type is very important within the NetFlow version 9 specification: the Options Template FlowSet (and its corresponding Options Data Record). Rather than supplying information about IP flows, Options Template Records are used to define information about the NetFlow metering process configuration or NetFlow metering process-specific data. The information is supplied by the Option Data Records. For example, the Options Template FlowSet can report the sample rate of a specific interface, along with the sampling method used (if sampling is supported). Those sampling parameters are defined in an Options Template Record sent in a Template FlowSet, and the associated instances of records are sent in Options Data Records in subsequent Data FlowSets.

The Options Template Set lets the exporter provide additional information to the collector that would not be possible with Flow Records only. The scope, which is provided in the Options Template Set, gives the context of the reported Information Elements. One Options Template Set example is the "Metering Process statistics," which reports the statistics for the Observation Domain, defined as the scope. Another example is the "Template configuration," which reports the sampling configuration parameter(s) for the template, defined as the scope.

A Data FlowSet consists of one or more records of the same type, which are grouped in an Export Packet. Each record is either a Flow Data Record or an Options Data Record previously defined by a Template Record or an Options Template Record, respectively.

To achieve efficiency in terms of processing at the network elements when handling high volumes of Export Packets, the NetFlow FlowSets are encapsulated into UDP (RFC 768) datagrams for export to a NetFlow collector. UDP is a non-congestion-aware protocol. Therefore, when deploying NetFlow version 9 in a congestion-sensitive environment, best practice suggests setting up a connection between the network element and the NetFlow collector through a dedicated link. This ensures that any burstiness in the NetFlow traffic affects only this dedicated link. In a network where the NetFlow collector cannot be placed within one hop of the Exporter, or when the export path from the Exporter to the NetFlow collector cannot be exclusively used for the NetFlow export packets, the export path should be designed so that it can always sustain the maximum burstiness of NetFlow traffic from the network element. However, the NetFlow version 9 export protocol has been designed to be transport protocol-independent. Therefore, it supports the Stream Control Transmission Protocol–Partial Reliability Extension (SCTP-PR, RFC 3758) as an alternative to UDP. SCTP-PR establishes an association between a network element and a NetFlow collector. Within this association, SCTP-PR offers the possibility of having multiple streams, and potentially multiple streams with different levels of reliability: a fully reliable stream, a partially reliable stream, and an unreliable stream. Depending on the importance of the data to export, a different stream type could be used. Typically, the Template Records use the fully reliable stream. Within the same SCTP-PR association, the billing records might use the fully reliable stream, whereas some sampled capacity planning records might use the partially reliable stream. As a final remark, note that the exporter can export to multiple collectors using independent transport protocols.

Regarding template management, the NetFlow version 9 export protocol follows a few basic rules, due to the unreliable property of UDP:

- A newly created Template Record is assigned an unused Template ID from the NetFlow metering process. If the template configuration is changed, the current Template ID is abandoned and should not be reused until the NetFlow metering process restarts. A template ID must be unique per network element.

- After a NetFlow process restarts, the exporter should not send any Data FlowSet without sending the corresponding Template FlowSet and the required Options Template FlowSet in a previous packet or including it in the same Export Packet.

- In the event of configuration changes, the exporter should send the new template definitions at an accelerated rate.

- The exporter must send the Template Records and Options Template Records on regular basis to refresh the collector's database.

- In the event of a clock configuration change on the Exporter, the exporter should send the template definitions at an accelerated rate.

Table 3-5 describes a few field type definitions that an exporter may support, as examples. The complete series of field types is a selection of packet header fields, lookup results (for example, the BGP Autonomous System numbers or the IP subnet masks), and packet properties (for example, the packet length). The list should represent all useful flow related field types. However, for extensibility, the new field types are added to the existing list. These new field types have to be updated on the exporter and NetFlow collector field type lists while the NetFlow export format remains unchanged.

Table 3-5   *NetFlow Version 9 Information Model (Extract)*

Field Type	Value	Length (in Bytes)	Description
IN_BYTES	1	N	Incoming counter with length $N * 8$ bits for the number of bytes associated with an IP Flow. By default, N is 4.
IN_PKTS	2	N	Incoming counter with length $N * 8$ bits for the number of packets associated with an IP Flow. By default, N is 4.
FLOWS	3	N	The number of flows that were aggregated. By default, N is 4.
PROTOCOL	4	1	IP protocol byte.
...	...	...	...

In some cases, the size of a field type is fixed by definition—for example, PROTOCOL or IPV4_SRC_ADDR. However, in other cases, they are defined as a variant type. This improves the memory efficiency in the collector and reduces the network bandwidth requirements between the exporter and the NetFlow collector. As an example, in the case of IN_BYTES, on an access router it might be sufficient to use a 32-bit counter ($N = 4$), while on a core router a 64-bit counter ($N = 8$) would be required.

NetFlow Version 9 Export Protocol Example

In this example, the exporter must send Flow Data Records composed of the protocol, number of bytes received, and number of packets received. Three Flow Data Records with the values shown in Table 3-6 are registered by the metering process and consequently must be exported.

Table 3-6   *Flow Data Record Values*

PROTOCOL (Field Type Value 4)	IN_BYTES (Field Type Value 1)	IN_PACKETS (Field Type Value 2)
6	1000	10
17	2000	25
1	100	3

The exporter first sends a Template Record (in a Template FlowSet) specifying the new template ID (256), the length of the FlowSet, the number of field types in the Template Record (three in this case), and each field type value and length, as shown in Figure 3-8.

Figure 3-8   *NetFlow Version 9 Template Record*

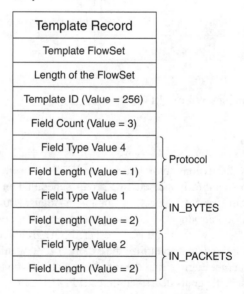

Then the exporter sends the Data FlowSet specifying the associated Template ID (256), the length of the FlowSet, and the Flow Data Records, as shown in Figure 3-9. Each Flow Data Record contains the three values of the associated Template Records field type.

Figure 3-9 *Data FlowSet*

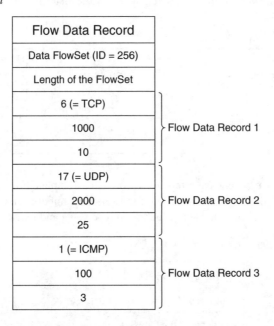

For further examples, refer to RFC 3954.

IPFIX

The first IPFIX discussions started during the IETF 51 meeting with a BOF (Birds of a Feather) session (an informal discussion group, scheduled on a conference program to consider a specific issue or subject) in London in August 2001. With some early IP flow requirements as an introduction, and with the presentation of different IP flow solutions (among them, NetFlow version 9 was presented), the group considered it worthwhile to create a working group to standardize the export of IP flow information. For the next IETF meeting, the Internet Engineering Steering Group (IESG) created the working group, with the following specific goals described in the IPFIX charter:

- Define the notion of a "standard IP flow." The flow definition will be a practical one, similar to those currently in use by existing nonstandard flow information export protocols that have attempted to achieve similar goals but have not documented their flow definition.

- Devise data encodings that support analysis of IPv4 and IPv6 unicast and multicast flows traversing a network element at packet header level and other levels of aggregation.

- Consider the notion of IP flow information export based on packet sampling.

- Identify and address any security privacy concerns affecting flow data. Determine technology for securing the flow information export data, such as Transport Layer Security (TLS, RFC 2246).

- Specify the transport mapping for carrying IP flow information—one that is amenable to router and instrumentation implementers and deployment.

- Ensure that the flow export system is reliable in that it will minimize the likelihood of flow data being lost due to resource constraints in the exporter or receiver and to accurately report such a loss if it occurs.

The IPFIX working group went through the process of evaluating the current existing candidate protocols to determine which protocol would serve best as the foundation for the IPFIX protocol specifications. The evaluation process required the formalized IPFIX requirements; RFC 3917, *Requirements for IP Flow Information Export*, fulfilled that need. The working group evaluated the following five protocols:

- Common Reliable Accounting for Network Element (CRANE), RFC 3423

- Diameter (RFC 3588)

- Lightweight Flow Accounting Protocol (LFAP), developed by Riverstone Networks

- Streaming Internet Protocol Detail Records (IPDR), developed by the IPDR open consortium (http://www.ipdr.org)

- NetFlow version 9 export protocol (RFC 3954)

After the process of determining the relative weight of the different requirements, the working group finally decided in RFC 3955, *Evaluation of Candidate Protocols for IP Flow Information Export*, to select the NetFlow version 9 export protocol as the IPFIX protocol basis. However, some improvements were needed: first, to address the specific goals of the IPFIX charter; second, to make the protocol more robust; and third, for the IESG to approve it.

The IPFIX Export Protocol

The IPFIX protocol maintains the same principles of separate templates and records as NetFlow version 9. It even preserves the same terminology as NetFlow version 9 (see Table 3-4), with one exception: the FlowSets are now called Sets in IPFIX. The IPFIX improvements over NetFlow version 9 are significant. They address transport protocol, security, IETF, and vendor-specific information elements, new information elements registration with the Internet Assigned Numbers Authority (IANA), time synchronization, etc. The rest of this section describes the improvements.

The biggest change in IPFIX compared to the first NetFlow version 9 is certainly that the data transfer must be a congestion-aware protocol. Therefore, the IPFIX protocol specifies that the Stream Control Transport Protocol (SCTP, RFC 2960) and that the Stream Control Transport Protocol–Partially Reliable (SCTP-PR, RFC 3758) must be implemented by all compliant implementations, and that UDP and TCP may also be implemented. SCTP-PR *should* be used in deployments in which Exporters and Collectors are communicating over links that are susceptible to congestion, because SCTP-PR can provide any required degree of reliability: full reliability, partial reliability, or unreliability. The IPFIX specification also mentions that "TCP *may* be used in deployments where Exporters and Collectors communicate over links that are susceptible to congestion, but SCTP-PR is preferred, due to its ability to limit back pressure on Exporters and its message versus stream orientation." Finally, a door is left open to use UDP as a transport protocol, but only under certain circumstances: "UDP *may* be used although it is not a congestion-aware protocol. However, the IPFIX traffic between Exporter and Collector *must* run in an environment where IPFIX traffic has been provisioned for or is contained through some other means."

There are several scenarios in which increased security is needed compared to NetFlow version 9—more specifically, in situations where the IPFIX protocol is run across the Internet:

- **Disclosure of flow information data**—The IPFIX messages themselves may contain valuable information for an attacker, such as active flow in the network, communications endpoints, and traffic patterns. Thus, care should be taken to confine their visibility to authorized users.

- **Forgery of flow records**—If flow records are used in billing and/or security applications, there are potentially strong incentives to forge exported flow records (for example, to save money, prevent the detection of an attack, or simply confuse the collector). This can be done either by altering flow records on the path or by injecting forged flow records that pretend to be originated by the original exporter.

Regarding the security of the IPFIX records transferred from the exporter to the collector, the confidentiality, integrity, and authenticity must be ensured. The IPFIX protocol specification does not mandate that all three functions be enabled at all times. However, any IPFIX-compliant implementation must support confidentiality, integrity, and authenticity with Datagram Transport Layer Security (RFC R4347).

Now that the IANA administers all the IPFIX exported information elements, the IPFIX Sets formats have been adapted so that a combination of IANA administered information element(s) and private information element(s) could coexist in the same records. The private information elements are vendor-proprietary elements—either on their way to be registered by IANA, under experimental testing, or maintained confidentially for business-related reasons.

Regarding time synchronization, the IPFIX protocol supports by default the microsecond precision of the flow start and flow stop times.

However, specific mechanisms exist in case the millisecond time precision is enough or in case the nanosecond time precision is required.

Work in Progress

In June 2006, the IPFIX charter was revised to incorporate the new documents of interest to the IPFIX working group. The new objectives of the charter are as follows:

- Develop guidelines for implementers based on experiences gained individually by implementers and jointly at interoperability testing events. The outcome should be "IPFIX implementation guidelines" and "IPFIX testing" documents.

- Develop methods and means for an efficient use of the IPFIX protocol by reducing redundancy in flow reports.

- Create an IPFIX MIB for reporting information and statistics of IPFIX metering, exporting, and collecting processes.

- Develop an effective method for exporting information about bidirectional flows (biflows), requested by the IP security community.

IPFIX References

Table 3-7 lists RFCs that cover IPFIX.

Table 3-7   *IPFIX References*

RFC	Status	Title	Description
3917	Informational	*Requirements for IP Flow Information Export*	List of requirements for the IPFIX protocol
(*)	Informational	*Architecture Model for IP Flow Information Export*	The IPFIX architecture
3955	Informational	*Evaluation of Candidate Protocols for IP Flow Information Export (IPFIX)*	The five existing flow information protocol evaluation results
(*)	Standard	*IPFIX Protocol Specifications*	The protocol itself
(*)	Standard	*Information Model for IP Flow Information Export*	The information elements exported by the protocol
(*)	Informational	*IPFIX Applicability*	Which applications can use IPFIX, and how?

(*) IETF draft, work in progress that will be published as RFC.

Data Collection Protocols: PSAMP

The Packet Sampling (PSAMP) working group history started soon after the IPFIX working group creation: the IETF 53 meeting in March 2002 held the first BOF. There was a clear need to define a standard set of capabilities for network elements to sample subsets of packets by statistical and other methods—specifically, on the high-end routers where monitoring every packet was practically impossible. The focus of the working group was to

- Specify a set of selection operations by which packets are sampled.
- Specify the information that is to be made available for reporting on sampled packets.
- Describe protocols by which information on sampled packets is reported to applications.
- Describe protocols by which packet selection and reporting are configured.

The PSAMP working group was created but did not limit the selection operations to packet sampling, as its name may imply; it also covered the filtering and hashing functions. PSAMP addressed the standardization of the metering process, one component that was not addressed by the IPFIX working group.

The RFC draft *Sampling and Filtering Techniques for IP Packet Selection* covers all sampling and filtering techniques described in Chapter 2, plus some additional ones:

- Systematic sampling (also known as deterministic sampling)
- Random *n*-out-of-*N* sampling, random probabilistic sampling
- Uniform probabilistic sampling, nonuniform probabilistic sampling
- Nonuniform flow state-dependent sampling
- Mask/match filtering and hash-based selection
- Stratified sampling

PSAMP Protocol Specifications

For export of PSAMP packet information, the IPFIX protocol is used. The IPFIX protocol is well suited for this purpose, because the IPFIX architecture matches the PSAMP architecture very well, and the means provided by the IPFIX protocol are sufficient.

Concerning the protocol, the major difference between IPFIX and PSAMP is that the IPFIX protocol exports flow records while the PSAMP protocol exports packet records because there is no notion of a flow in PSAMP. The exported packet records, called "packet reports" in the PSAMP terminology, must contain the following:

- The input sequence number.
- Some number of contiguous bytes from the start of the packet, including the packet header (which includes link layer, network layer, and other encapsulation headers), plus some subsequent bytes of the packet payload.

Optionally, the packet reports may contain the following:

- A field related to the observed protocols (IPv4, IPV6, transport protocols, MPLS)
- A field related to the packet treatment
- A field associated with the packet (for example, timestamps)

From a pure export point of view, the IPFIX protocol does not distinguish a flow record composed of several aggregated packets from a flow record composed of a single packet (a PSAMP packet report). So the PSAMP export is a special IPFIX Flow Record containing information about a single packet. Even if the IPFIX export protocol was developed with the notion of a flow record in mind, it is a generic export protocol and is well suited for PSAMP.

Because the developments of the IPFIX and PSAMP drafts were carried out in parallel, all PSAMP requirements regarding the IPFIX protocol were introduced directly in the IPFIX protocol specification. Extensions of the IPFIX protocol needed by PSAMP are rather limited. A basic requirement is the need for a data type for protocol fields that have a flexible length, such as an octet array. This is needed by the PSAMP protocol for reporting content of captured packets because the hash-based selection for trajectory sampling requires the first few bytes of payload. Because the different encapsulation headers might modify the total packet length, IPFIX specifies the notion of flexible length field type, referred to as the "Variable-Length Information Element" in the IPFIX protocol specifications.

From an information model point of view, the overlap of both protocols is still quite large. Most of the field types in the IPFIX protocol also apply to PSAMP—for example, all the packet header field types. Because the IPFIX information model is rather limited concerning sampling, and because specific field types are required to fully describe the different PSAMP techniques, a set of several additional field types specific to PSAMP will be published as an RFC (currently work in progress, <draft-ietf-psamp-info-05.txt>) *PSAMP Information Model*, exploiting the extensibility of the IPFIX information model.

The authors think that over time, boundaries will fade between PSAMP and IPFIX from an export and information element point of view and that the IPFIX information elements well beyond flow records and packet sampling-related information will be registered. In other words, the IFPIX and PSAMP efforts will probably merge over time.

PSAMP References

Table 3-8 lists the RFCs that describe PSAMP.

Table 3-8   *PSAMP References*

RFC	Status	Title	Description
(*)	Informational	*A Framework for Packet Selection and Reporting*	Framework, components of the architecture, and requirements
(*)	Informational	*Sampling and Filtering Techniques for IP Packet Selection*	Sampling and filtering techniques, with the required parameters
(*)	Standard	*Packet Sampling (PSAMP) Protocol Specifications*	The protocol itself
(*)	Standard	*Definitions of Managed Objects for Packet Sampling*	MIB managed objects for the PSAMP protocol
(*)	Standard	*Information Model for Packet Sampling Exports*	The information elements exported by the protocol

(*) IETF draft, work in progress: will be published as RFC.

Data Collection Protocols: AAA (RADIUS, Diameter, and TACACS+)

RADIUS, Diameter, and TACACS+ are three protocols for carrying Authentication, Authorization, and Accounting (AAA) information between a Network Access Server (NAS) that wants to authenticate its links or end users and a shared authentication server. The end user connects to the NAS, which in turn becomes a AAA client trying to authenticate the end user to the AAA server.

This section concentrates on the last "A" of AAA (even though most of the time AAA is not primarily used for billing, but for authentication and authorization). However, when binding the accounting information with the authentication informs, the AAA protocols offer an interesting advantage for billing: the authenticated username.

RADIUS

Remote Authentication Dial-In User Service (RADIUS) is a client/server protocol developed by the IETF. The RADIUS client is typically a NAS, and the RADIUS server is usually a daemon process running on a UNIX or Windows server.

The RADIUS client (that is, the NAS) passes user information to designated RADIUS servers and acts on the returned response. RADIUS servers receive user connection requests via the NAS, authenticate the user, and then provide the NAS with configuration information necessary for it to deliver a specific service to the user.

Transactions between the RADIUS client and RADIUS server are authenticated with a shared secret key, which is never sent over the network. In addition, user passwords are sent encrypted between the RADIUS client and RADIUS server to eliminate the possibility that someone snooping on an insecure network could determine a user's password.

The accounting features of the RADIUS protocol can be used independently of RADIUS authentication or authorization. The NAS, which provides a service to the dial-in user (such as PPP or Telnet) is responsible for passing user accounting information to a designated RADIUS accounting server. At the start of service delivery, the NAS generates an "Accounting Start" packet describing the type of service being delivered and the user accessing the service. This packet is sent to the RADIUS accounting server, which returns an acknowledgment (the Accounting-Response) to the NAS, acknowledging that the "Accounting Start" packet has been received. At the end of the service delivery, the NAS client generates an "Accounting Stop" packet, describing the type of service that was delivered and session statistics such as elapsed time, input and output octets, and input and output packets. Here is the complete list of RADIUS accounting attributes, as described in RFC 2866: Acct-Status-Type, Acct-Delay-Time, Acct-Input-Octets, Acct-Output-Octets, Acct-Session-Id, Acct-Authentic, Acct-Session-Time, Acct-Input-Packets, Acct-Output-Packets, Acct-Terminate-Cause, Acct-Multi-Session-Id, and Acct-Link-Count. If the RADIUS server returns no response to the RADIUS client within a defined timeout, the request is resent a number of times. The RADIUS client can also forward requests to an alternate RADIUS server or servers in case the primary server is down or unreachable.

The UDP transport is a major issue in RADIUS accounting, where packet loss may translate directly into revenue loss.

For further references on RADIUS, refer to Table 3-9, which mainly focuses on the RADIUS accounting references. Note, for completeness, that other RADIUS RFCs are available: 2548, 2618, 2619, 2809, 2882, 3162, 3575, 3576, 3579, and 3580.

Table 3-9   *RADIUS References*

RFC	Status	Title	Description
2620	Informational	*RADIUS Accounting Client MIB*	Managed objects used to manage RADIUS accounting clients
2621	Informational	*RADIUS Accounting Server MIB*	Managed objects used to manage RADIUS accounting servers
2865	Standard	*Remote Authentication Dial-In User Service (RADIUS)*	Protocol specifications for authentication, authorization, and configuration information
2866	Standard	*RADIUS Accounting*	Specifies the RADIUS Accounting protocol
2867	Informational	*RADIUS Accounting Modifications for Tunnel Protocol Support*	Defines new RADIUS Accounting attributes and new values for tunneling in dialup networks

continues

Table 3-9 *RADIUS References (Continued)*

RFC	Status	Title	Description
2868	Informational	*RADIUS Attributes for Tunnel Protocol Support*	RADIUS attributes designed to support the provision of compulsory tunneling in dialup networks
2869	Informational	*RADIUS Extensions*	Attributes for carrying authentication, authorization, and accounting information

Note that the IETF RADIUS Extensions Working Group currently is focusing on extensions to the RADIUS protocol required to enable its use in applications such as IP telephony and local-area network AAA. To keep backward compatibility, the working group decided not to define new transports (such as TCP and SCTP).

TACACS+

Terminal Access Controller Access Control System Plus (TACACS+) is a Cisco-proprietary AAA protocol. Even though it's proprietary, TACACS+ is well-known across the industry. It is recommended for rich feature support because it allows command authorization and accounting. The biggest difference compared to RADIUS is that TACACS+ runs on the top of TCP and encrypts the full packet, not just the password section.

Diameter

The Diameter protocol, standardized by the IETF Authentication, Authorization and Accounting working group, is the successor to the RADIUS protocol and was developed to overcome several limitations of RADIUS.

AAA protocols such as TACACS+ and RADIUS were initially deployed to provide dialup Point-to-Point Protocol (PPP) and terminal server access. Over time, with the growth of the Internet and the introduction of new access technologies, including wireless, DSL, Mobile IP, and Ethernet, routers and network access servers (NAS) have increased in complexity and density, putting new demands on AAA protocols.

Diameter introduced a couple of improvements compared to RADIUS:

- Application-layer acknowledgments and failover algorithms
- Mandatory IPsec and optional TLS supports
- Reliable transport mechanisms (TCP, SCTP)
- Support for server-initiated messages

- Data object security is supported but not mandatory
- Capability negotiation between clients and servers
- Peer discovery and configuration

Table 3-10 lists the Diameter references.

Table 3-10 *Diameter References*

RFC	Status	Title	Description
3588	Standard	Diameter Base Protocol	Protocol description
3589	Informational	Diameter Command Codes for Third Generation Partnership Project	Managed objects used to manage RADIUS accounting clients

For completeness, RFC 3589 also deals with Diameter, but not with accounting. Note also that several Diameter IETF drafts currently are in progress.

Data Collection Protocols: IPDR

IPDR.org, founded in 1999, is an open consortium of service providers, equipment vendors, system integrators, and billing and mediation vendors. They collaborate to facilitate the exchange of usage and service measurement between network and hosting elements and operations and business support systems by deploying IPDR the de facto standard. IPDR.org, a nonprofit organization, is facilitating service measurement and exchange for emerging services. It targets emerging services such as voice over IP, CableLabs DOCSIS, WLAN access service, streaming media service, and more.

IPDR stands for Internet Protocol Detail Record; the name comes from the traditional telecom term CDR (Call Detail Record), used to record information about usage activity within the telecom infrastructure, such as call completion.

IPDR promotes the use of IPDR Network Data Management–Usage (NDM-U), which lays a framework for a standard mechanism to exchange usage data between systems. NDM-U defines a mechanism to create and transport either files or streams of network usage information that follow the IPDR format. IPDR uses an information modeling technique based on the use of a subset of the XML Schema specification language, in conjunction with a well-defined mapping to a binary format based on the eXtensible Data Record (XDR, RFC 1832). XDR is a standard for the description and encoding of data: it forms the basis of Sun's Remote Procedure Call and Network File System protocols and has proven to be both space- and processing-efficient. The XML record structure and service definitions provide a means to begin representing service usage information in a self-describing human-readable or machine-readable format. IPDR uses a subset of the XML-Schema language for extensibility, thus allowing for vendor- and application-specific extensions of the data model.

IPDR.org released the IPDR Streaming Protocol (IPDR/SP) specification in 2004; it provides an advanced streaming protocol for accounting information exchange. The IPDR Streaming Protocol is a real-time reporting protocol that works with templates, negotiated between the collector and the exporter. Possible transport protocols may be TCP or SCTP, or even BEEP (RFC 3080). The IPDR streaming protocol offers reliability with the transport protocol itself and with IPDR streaming protocol-level acknowledgments. Note that the IPDR streaming protocol is largely based on the CRANE protocol. For further information, refer to http://www.ipdr.org.

The authors' view is that the NDM-U and IPDR streaming protocols focus on the exchange of usage information between collecting mediation systems and Business Support Systems (BSS), always with the notion of service consumer perspective in mind. Therefore, the areas of applicability of the NDM-U and IPDR streaming protocols are the higher layers of the TMN, as opposed to the TMN Network Elements Layer.

Data Collection Protocols: CMISE/CMIP and GDMO

The fundamental function of the Common Management Information Service Element (CMISE) is the exchange of management information between manager and agent entities.

CMISE is specified in two parts:

- The Common Management Information Service (CMIS) is a user interface specifying the services provided (ISO 9595).
- The Common Management Information Protocol (CMIP) specifies the Protocol Data Unit (PDU) format and associated procedures (IOS 9596).

CMIP was proposed as a replacement for SNMP as part of the ITU-T Telecommunications Management Network (TMN). The major advantages of CMIP over SNMP are as follows:

- CMIP variables contain information similar to SNMP and can also define actions and perform tasks.
- CMIP has built-in security mechanisms for authorization, access control, and security logs.
- CMIP provides flexible reporting of unusual network conditions.
- The CMIP information model is object-oriented compared to the object-based model from SNMP.

Guideline for Definition of Managed Objects (GDMO) provides a language for defining managed objects within TMN-based systems. GDMO is a structured description language for specifying object classes and the objects' behaviors, attributes, and class ancestry. While there is an analogy to the SNMP Structures of Managed Information (SMI), the GDMO format is not derived from Abstract Syntax Notation 1 (ASN.1).

Although the "S" for Simple in the SNMP acronym reflects the philosophy behind the SNMP protocol design, CMIP/CMIS was designed to be much more powerful and therefore is more complex and resource-intensive to implement. This, along with some performance issues, explains why CMIP/CMIS were not widely adopted throughout the industry. In the competition between the IETF SNMP and the OSI CMIP, the industry clearly selected SNMP as the winner because of quick developments and freely accessible standards. Although this section is interesting from a reference and quick overview point of view, the authors advise you not to investigate CMISE, CMIP, and GDMO further.

NOTE   CMIP/CMIS are defined in ISO (http://www.iso.org) documents 9595 and 9596 and ITU (http://www.itu.org) X.700 and X.711.

GDMO is specified in ISO/IEC 10165/ITU-T X.722.

Service Notions

Performance management deals with the notion of services, among other things, as discussed in Chapter 1, "Understanding the Need for Accounting and Performance Management." The term service implies the concept of a Service Level Agreement (SLA). This is an agreement whereby a service provider agrees to provide certain SLA parameters for a specific service: uptime, guaranteed bandwidth, minimum response time, minimum jitter, minimum packet loss, and so on.

SLAs offer service providers the ability to provide additional services, implement competitive pricing schemes, and gain a competitive edge. For example, a premium price can be defined for a faster (either faster than or just fast) VPN connection so that the users can take advantage of real-time applications. After defining the SLA parameters, the service provider is supposed to verify the delivered level of service. Note that the customers also should monitor the delivered service quality.

We distinguish between two categories of SLA parameters, also called metrics: intrinsic and operational. Intrinsic parameters are essential to the service itself, and operational factors depend on the procedures to deliver and maintain a service:

- **Intrinsic**—These metrics are related to the service quality and can consist of some or all of the following components:

  — **Latency or network delay**—The time it takes a packet to traverse from one endpoint to another.

    Network delay = propagation delay + serialization delay + queuing delay (at the device)

— **Jitter or latency variance**—The variation of the delay due to queuing, load balancing, etc., which is an issue especially for voice and real-time applications.

— Availability of the network or a specific service

Availability = (uptime) / (total time)

Throughput / available bandwidth

CPU utilization

Buffer and memory allocation (size, misses, hit ratio)

— **Packet loss**—This feature requires the counting of packets between the outbound interface of the source device and the inbound interface of the destination device. Reasons for packet loss can be CRC errors, queue dropping, route changes, device outages, misconfigured access control lists, and others.

— **Out of sequence/packet reordering**—This can be caused by queuing or load balancing.

— **Errors**—Include failed components, devices, links, and others.

• **Operational**—These metrics relate to a service's functional factors:

— Mean Time to Provision

— Mean Time to Restore

— Mean Time to Repair

— Mean Time Between Failures

Figure 3-10 summarizes the service level parameters.

Figure 3-10 *Service-Level Parameters*

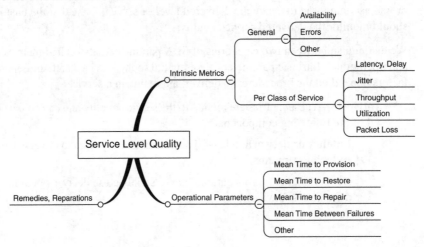

Even though the TMN and eTOM framework building blocks describe the concepts of service level management and TMF's GB917 specifies SLA management, service providers often offer similar services with different SLA parameters.

Most of the time, the SLA implies monetary penalties under certain circumstances—for example, no connectivity for a period of time, a too-high percentage of packet loss, or exceeding delay or jitter results in a refund to the customer. Therefore, the implications are important. Yet TMN and eTOM leave some details open. How should you measure the intrinsic SLA parameters? Should you use active probing or passive measurement for delay measurement? If active probing is the solution, which interval, frequency, or packet size should you use? In case of passive measurement, which packet sampling parameters should be applied? How should you deduce the statistics of the real traffic?

The ITU-T defined a set of objectives for performance service parameters in specification Y.1541, *Network Performance Objectives for IP-Based Services*:

"The objectives apply to public IP Networks. The objectives are believed to be achievable on common IP network implementations. The network providers' commitment to the user is to attempt to deliver packets in a way that achieves each of the applicable objectives. The vast majority of IP paths advertising conformance with Recommendation Y.1541 should meet those objectives. For some parameters, performance on shorter and/or less complex paths may be significantly better."

In summary, Y.1541 suggests these parameters, and they can be considered current best-practice definition.

The IETF IP Performance Metric (IPPM) working group developed a set of standard metrics that can be applied to the quality, performance, and reliability of Internet data delivery services. The metrics, as defined by IPPM, do not represent a value judgment (they don't define "good" and "bad") but rather provide guidelines for unbiased quantitative measures of performance.

For voice quality, there is a specific parameter: the Mean Opinion Score (MOS). However, the MOS is subjective. It ranges from 5 (excellent) to 0 (unacceptable). A typical desirable range for a voice over IP network is from 3.5 to 4.2. MOS is defined by ITU-T Recommendation G.107 (E-Model). Chapter 15, "Voice Scenarios," describes voice management in detail.

Most of the time, you have to rely on best practices, and these rely on some (basic) statistics.

Measuring SLAs requires some basic understanding of statistical knowledge to analyze and understand performance data and predict future network performance:

- **Average or mean**—The sum of the collected values divided by the number of values.
- **Mode**—The most common occurrence of a value in a distribution.
- **Median**—The middle value in the distribution.
- **Variance**—A measure of how spread out a distribution is.

- **Standard deviation**—The square root of the variance. It measures the spread of the data around the mean value, where a smaller standard deviation is better than a larger value.

- ***n*th percentile**—A score in the *n*th percentile is a score that is greater than *n* percent of the scores attained within a given set. For example, a response time SLA is defined as the 90th percentile of 100 ms for latency values. This implies that 90 percent of the network traffic has latency less than or equal to 100 ms. This excludes "extreme" values caused by abnormal situations or collection errors.

Table 3-11 lists some IPPM standard-track RFCs.

Table 3-11 *IPPM References*

RFC	Status	Title	Description
2678	Standard	*IPPM Metrics for Measuring Connectivity*	Defines a series of metrics for connectivity between a pair of Internet hosts
2679	Standard	*A One-way Delay Metric for IPPM*	Defines a metric for one-way delay of packets across Internet paths
2680	Standard	*A One-way Packet Loss Metric for IPPM*	Defines a metric for one-way packet loss across Internet paths
2681	Standard	*A Round-trip Delay Metric for IPPM*	Defines a metric for round-trip delay of packets across Internet paths
3393	Standard	*IP Packet Delay Variation Metric for IPPM*	Refers to a metric for variation in delay of packets across Internet paths
3432	Standard	*Network Performance Measurement with Periodic Streams*	Describes a periodic sampling method and relevant metrics for assessing the performance of IP networks

For more information on statistics, refer to *Probability and Statistics* by Spiegel, Schiller, and Srinivasan (McGraw-Hill Professional, 2001) or other statistical books.

Summary

The focus of this chapter was to provide relevant details on general architectures, standard definitions, and protocols and their relationship to performance and accounting management. Because of the variety of standards, you might feel overwhelmed when selecting a standard. Therefore, keep in mind that the variety of user requirements was one reason for multiple standards definitions. The first step should always be to determine your requirements and objectives precisely and then to identify the standard that matches all or most of your requirements. Best practice suggests starting with the TMN layered architecture and FCAPS, which can help with mapping requirements to operational areas and product functionalities. From a device perspective, SNMP is necessary in most cases; the challenge is to identify the right version (2c or 3). For consistent results with accounting and performance measurement, applying IPFIX and PSAMP is suggested: IPFIX for the exporting protocol, and PSAMP for the metering process if sampling, filtering, or hashing is required. However, while waiting for IPFIX and PSAMP to become widely available in the Internet, the network administrator should focus on NetFlow as a metering and exporting process. (NetFlow version 9 offers a wide range of information elements.) IPDR is applicable if multiple collection or mediation applications should cooperate. Specifically, for service providers, TMF's eTOM model can be very helpful to define and implement customer-oriented processes. However, even though all these standards organizations are valuable, there might still be situations in which you need a specific feature that only one vendor offers and no standard covers yet. If this specific feature helps you gain additional revenues or reduce costs, there is no need to wait for a standard; select this innovative vendor. Except for these situations, it is always the right decision to build your network based on standards!

Table 3-12 summarizes the different standards covered in this chapter.

Table 3-12   *Standards Summary*

Standard	Where to Apply It
ITU-T (FCAPS)	Defining specific areas of network management functionality. Providing a matrix to map requirements and products.
TMF (eTOM, FAB, GB917)	Operational and business procedures in a service provider environment.
SNMP	Basic network management functionality.
CMIP/CMISE	Complex and advanced network management functionality.
IETF (IPFIX)	Export protocol for flow metering at network elements.
IETF (PSAMP)	Definition of sampling technologies for network elements.
IETF (AAA)	Accounting standard in dial-in and wireless environments.
IPDR	Standard for interoperability between mediation and accounting applications.

Implementations on the Cisco Devices

CHAPTER 4

SNMP and MIBs

After studying this chapter, you should have a good understanding of the capabilities of the different SNMP protocol versions on Cisco network elements. Simple Network Management Protocol (SNMP) and Management Information Base (MIB) configuration examples and feature comparison tables help you understand and apply the information. This chapter also summarizes the most relevant accounting and performance MIBs.

Chapter 3, "Accounting and Performance Standards and Definitions," analyzes SNMP from a theoretical point of view. It describes the Internet management model and terminology, comparing the different SNMP versions, explaining the Structure of Management Information (SMI), and considering the SNMP operations.

This chapter explains how to configure SNMP on Cisco devices and how to use tools such as snmpget and snmpwalk to retrieve the managed objects content. However, the remote SNMP configuration of the accounting and performance MIB modules is a pure configuration task (remember the Configuration part of the FCAPS model). Therefore, the examples in this chapter do not explain the use of the snmpset utility.

The three different versions of SNMP (1, 2, and 3) clearly indicate the evolution of SNMP since the initial version, RFC 1067, in 1988. SNMPv1 is not used as much anymore. More and more MIB modules need the high-capacity counters (64-bit, counter64) specified in SMIv2, which in turn requires the SNMPv2c encodings. Furthermore, the SNMPv1 protocol has the status of historical, as designated by the IETF. Therefore, this chapter does not contain a specific SNMPv1 configuration example. Instead, the configuration of the SNMPv2c agent on the router implicitly enables SNMPv1.

After long discussions without a clear consensus, the IETF abandoned the SNMPv2 standard because of a flawed security portion in the initial design. As a result, the community-based approach of SNMPv2c was chosen. This chapter contains an example of SNMPv2c because it is still widely deployed in the current networks. SNMPv3 became the successor of SNMPv2 and is an IETF standard (RFC 3411).

This chapter also contains two SNMPv3 examples explained in detail. They cover authentication only (AuthNoPriv) and authentication combined with encryption (AuthPriv).

Every network element that can be managed by SNMP contains a Management Information Base (MIB), which is a conceptual data store for management information. The SMI defines the framework for constructing MIBs. RFC 1155, which specifies SMI version 1, was extended by RFC 2578 to SMI version 2. The basic elements are described by the Abstract Syntax Notation 1 (ASN.1) notation. The Basic Encoding Rule (BER) defines the elements coding. MIB managed objects are specified by a series of numbers called object identifiers (OID). The managed objects are arranged in a hierarchical tree.

For example, if you want to identify the ifPhysAddress, representing an interface's physical or MAC address, the OID is 1.3.6.1.2.1.2.2.1.6:

iso-1
org-3
dod-6
internet-1
mgmt-2
mib-21
interfaces-2
ifTable-2
ifEntry-1
ifPhysAddress-6

A specific instance of such a managed object is called a MIB variable or managed object instance (ifPhysAddress in the preceding example). The two different object types are scalar and column. A scalar object has only one instance, and a columnar object has multiple instances.

MIBs

The focus of the MIBs described in this chapter is on accounting and performance management. The following books offer an in-depth description of SNMP and MIBs:

- *SNMP, SNMPv2, SNMPv3, and RMON 1 and 2*, Third Edition, William Stallings, Addison-Wesley Professional, 1998.

- *A Practical Guide to SNMPv3 and Network Management*, David Zeltserman, Prentice-Hall, 1999.

- *Understanding SNMP MIBs*, David Perkins, Prentice-Hall, 1997.

MIB objects need to be polled by a Network Management System. Remember that the first priority of a router or switch is to forward packets. Therefore, depending on the platforms, the SNMP counters might not be updated in real time. Distributed platform systems such as line cards and Versatile Interface Processors (VIP) do not update the counters in real time, because this would overload the internal bus with counter update messages. Polling the counters less frequently than every 30 seconds is a good deployment guideline.

IOS Support for SNMP Versions

Summarized by IOS trains, Table 4-1 shows the support of the different SNMP versions. You can see that, as SNMPv2 evolved, SNMPv2c replaced SNMPv2. Also note that even if SNMPv1 status is historical, the latest IOS trains still support it.

Table 4-1   *SNMP Version Support Per IOS Train*

SNMP Version	IOS Support
SNMPv1 and SNMPv2	10.3, 11.0, 11.1, 11.2
SNMPv1 and SNMPv2c	11.3, 12.0
SNMPv1, SNMPv2c, SNMPv3	12.0(3)T and higher 12.0(6)S and higher 12.1, 12.2, 12.3

net-snmp Utilities

This book uses the well-known **net-snmp** tools, which can be downloaded from the Internet for free, to illustrate the examples. From the long list of **net-snmp** utilities, this book describes **snmpget** and **snmpwalk**, the most useful utilities for accounting and performance data retrieval. For further information—specifically, on the different command-line options—refer to the documentation at http://www.net-snmp.org/. The examples in this book use **net-snmp** version 5.1.2. The different options for **snmpget** and **snmpwalk** are explained in the following sections.

Most of the **snmpget**, **snmpwalk**, and **snmpbulkwalk** examples in this book always have the same arguments:

- **-v 1 | 2c | 3** specifies the SNMP version to use.
- **-c COMMUNITY** sets the community string. It is SNMP version 1- or 2c-specific.
- **-a PROTOCOL** sets the authentication protocol (**MD5 | SHA**). It is SNMP version 3-specific.
- **-l LEVEL** sets the security level (**noAuthNoPriv | authNoPriv | authPriv**). It is SNMP version 3-specific.
- **-u USER-NAME** sets the security name (such as **bert**). It is SNMP version 3-specific.
- **-x PROTOCOL** sets the privacy protocol (**DES | AES**). It is SNMP version 3-specific.
- **-X PASSPHRASE** sets the privacy protocol passphrase. It is SNMP version 3-specific.

The syntax for the **net-snmp** utilities is always the same:

```
snmpget optional-arguments router managed-object
```

```
snmpwalk optional-arguments router managed-object
snmpbulkwalk optional-arguments router managed-object
```

CLI Operations and Configuration Example for SNMPv2c

The commands to configure SNMPv2c are as follows:

- **snmp-server community** *string* [**view** *view-name*] [**ro** | **rw**] [*access-list number*]
  sets up the community access string to permit access to Simple Network Management Protocol (SNMP) via SNMPv1 and SNMPv2c. The *view-name* restricts the available objects to the community string. **ro** stands for read-only, and **rw** stands for read-write. Finally, an access list uses the community string to restrict access to the SNMP agent.

- **snmp-server enable traps** [*notification-type*]
  enables the SNMP notifications (traps or informs) available on your system.

- **snmp-server host** *host-address* [**traps** | **informs**] [**version** {**1** | **2c** | **3** [**auth** | **noauth** | **priv**]}] *community-string* [**udp-port** *port*] [*notification-type*] [**vrf** *vrf-name*]
  specifies the recipient of the SNMP notification operations, defines how to send them (trap or inform), sets the SNMP version, and specifies the community string to be placed in the notification. Optional arguments include the specific UDP port on the management station where the notification is exported, the notification type for this specific host, and the Virtual Routing and Forwarding (VRF) in which the notification is sent.

SNMPv2c Configuration Example

Here is an example of the SNMPv2c configuration:

```
router(config)# snmp-server community not_public RO
router(config)# snmp-server community not_private RW
router(config)# snmp-server enable traps
router(config)# snmp-server host 10.10.10.10 version 2c trap_community
```

NOTE   Even if most of the SNMP examples in the literature use the community strings **public** for read-only and **private** for read-write, using different community strings in real configurations is strongly recommended. Too many devices in the Internet still use the **public** and **private** community strings, which implies serious security holes.

As already described, the first two commands enable both the SNMPv1 agent and the SNMPv2c agent on the router.

SNMPv2c Data Retrieval

To retrieve SNMPv2c data using the **snmpget** utility, enter the following:

```
SERVER % snmpget -v 1 -c not_public router sysObjectID.0
sysObjectID.0 = OID: CISCO-PRODUCTS-MIB::cisco2611
SERVER % snmpget -v 2c -c not_public router sysObjectID.0
sysObjectID.0 = OID: CISCO-PRODUCTS-MIB::cisco2611
```

Displaying SNMPv2c Statistics

The **show snmp** command displays all the SNMP statistics: number of input and output SNMP packets, number of community string violations (unknown community name), number of requested variables (with the SNMP get, getnext, or getbulk operations), number of altered variables (with the SNMP set operation). Here's an example:

```
Router# show snmp
Chassis: JAD0352065J (891283838)
637082 SNMP packets input
    0 Bad SNMP version errors
    465 Unknown community name
    0 Illegal operation for community name supplied
    0 Encoding errors
    6859663 Number of requested variables
    442 Number of altered variables
    537965 Get-request PDUs
    93444 Get-next PDUs
    257 Set-request PDUs
636841 SNMP packets output
    0 Too big errors (Maximum packet size 1500)
    640 No such name errors
    162 Bad values errors
    0 General errors
    636625 Response PDUs
    204 Trap PDUs
SNMP logging: enabled
    Logging to 10.10.10.10.162, 0/10, 0 sent, 0 dropped. The show snmp
```

CLI Operations and Configuration Examples for SNMPv3

The first task in configuring SNMPv3 is to configure the SNMP engineID. This engineID is an unambiguous identifier of an SNMP engine in the administrative domain. Consequently, it is a unique identifier of the SNMP entity, because there is a one-to-one association between SNMP engines and SNMP entities.

View-Based Access Control (RFC 3415) defines five elements:

- **MIB views**—Identifies a set of managed objects defined in terms of a collection of subtrees, with each subtree being included in or excluded from the view.

- **Groups**—Identifies the set of users, defined by securityModel and securityName. The access rights are the same inside the group. A user, also called a *principal*, belongs to only one group.

- **Security level**—Identifies the level of security when checking access rights. The possible choices are noAuthPriv, authNoPriv, and authPriv. SNMP entities maintain authentication and privacy keys, which are generated from a user's password and the SNMP engineID. Note that noAuthPriv is not a valid level of security because the privacy key defined in SNMPv3 is linked to a user. In other words, authentication is a prerequisite for privacy to be present.

- **Contexts**—Specified by the contextEngineID and contextName, this identifies the collection of management information accessible by an SNMP entity. Note that the default contextName is an empty string. A typical context example is a customer accessing the specific information on a provider edge router in an MPLS/VPN network. In this case, the SNMP context is attached to the customer VRF. Consequently, only SNMP operations on the VRF managed objects of the user's network are allowed.

- **Access policy**—Access to a managed object depends on the principal (user) and the characteristics of the group it belongs to, such as the securityLevel, the securityModel, the context (if configured), the object instance, and the type of access (read, read-write).

After the SNMP engineID is configured, the order of an SNMPv3 configuration task list is groups, users, optional view(s), and optionally the host(s) where the notifications will be sent.

To enable SNMPv3 on a router, you use the following commands:

- **snmp-server engineID local** *engineID-string* specifies the SNMP engine ID (a character string of up to 24 characters) on the local device. If the SNMP engine ID value is not specifically configured with this command, the SNMP entity automatically allocates a value. Because the user's authentication and privacy keys are generated from the SNMP engineID and the user itself, reconfiguring a new SNMP engineID implies that the already-configured users will not be granted access anymore. In this case, all SNMP users have to be reconfigured.

- **snmp-server group** *group-name* {**v1** | **v2c** | **v3** {**auth** | **noauth** | **priv**}} [**read** *read-view*] [**write** *write-view*] [**notify** *notify-view*] [**access** *access-list*] configures an SNMP group that maps SNMP users to three SNMP views—read access, write access, and notifications.

- **snmp-server user** *username group-name* [**remote** *host* [**udp-port** *port*]] {**v1** | **v2c** | **v3** [**encrypted**] [**auth** {**md5** | **sha**} *auth-password*]} [**access** *access-list*] [**priv** {**des** | **3des** | **aes** {**128** | **192** | **256**}} privpassword] configures a new user to an SNMP group. This user can use SNMPv1, SNMPv2c, or SNMPv3. If SNMPv3 is selected, the password, which can optionally be encrypted, has to be specified for the

MD5 or SHA authentication. Furthermore, SNMPv3 requires that you specify the privacy algorithm to be used (DES, 3-DES, AES, AES-192, or AES-256) and the password to be associated with this privacy protocol.

* **snmp-server view** *view-name oid-tree* {**included** | **excluded**} creates or updates a view entry. The *oid-tree* is the object identifier of the ASN.1 subtree to be included in or excluded from the view. The *oid-tree* is composed of numbers such as 1.3.6.2.4 or a word such as system.

authNoPriv SNMP Example

The SNMP IOS configuration with user authentication and no encryption is straightforward:

```
router(config)# snmp-server engineID local 1234567890
router(config)# snmp-server group benoitgroup v3 auth
router(config)# snmp-server user benoit benoitgroup v3 auth md5 benoitpassword
router(config)# exit
```

In this example, the user benoit belongs to benoitgroup, which is defined with SNMPv3 authentication. The user benoit is specified with the password benoitpassword, using the MD5 authentication algorithm.

The running configuration does not show the SNMP user-related command:

```
Router # show running-config | include snmp
Router # snmp-server engineID local 1234567890
Router # snmp-server group benoitgroup v3 auth
```

This behavior is explained in RFC 3414, which describes SNMPv3: "A user's password or non-localized key MUST NOT be stored on a managed device/node." Because the configuration file is not useful in this case, you check for configured users as follows:

```
Router # show snmp user
User name: benoit
Engine ID: 1234567890
storage-type: nonvolatile          active
```

The **show snmp group** command displays the names of configured SNMP groups, the security model being used, the status of the different views, and the storage type of each group:

```
Router # show snmp group
groupname: ILMI                          security model:v1
readview : *ilmi                         writeview: *ilmi
notifyview: <no notifyview specified>
row status: active

groupname: ILMI                          security model:v2c
readview : *ilmi                         writeview: *ilmi
notifyview: <no notifyview specified>
row status: active

groupname: benoitgroup                   security model:v3 auth
```

```
readview : v1default                              writeview: <no writeview specified>
notifyview: <no notifyview specified>
row status: active
```

The first two groups, one in SNMPv1 and the second for SNMPv2c, are defined specifically for the Interim Local Management Interface (ILMI). ILMI is an ATM Forum protocol for managing ATM links. It uses SNMP to negotiate and exchange parameters across ATM links through the ATM-FORUM-MIB. The "ilmi" community string is created by default automatically and can be used for ILMI purposes only. Note that this community is for valid ILMI packets only—the ones that come in on the ILMI reserved ATM virtual circuit (0,16).

The last entry shows benoitgroup with SNMPv3 authentication configured. This group does not contain any write and notify views, and the readview is v1default. No view specified means that no access is granted. In this case, user benoit cannot set any managed objects, because the write view is not specified.

```
Router # show snmp view
*ilmi system - included permanent active
*ilmi atmForumUni - included permanent active
v1default iso - included volatile active
v1default internet.6.3.15 - excluded volatile active
v1default internet.6.3.16 - excluded volatile active
v1default internet.6.3.18 - excluded volatile active
v1default ciscoMgmt.252 - excluded volatile active
```

From the command **show snmp view**, you see that v1default contains every managed object below iso but excludes the SNMP User Security Model MIB (SNMP-USM-MIB, internet.6.3.15), the SNMP View-Based Access Control Model MIB (SNMP-VACM-MIB, internet.6.3.16), and the SNMP community MIB (SNMP-COMMUNITY-MIB, internet.6.3.18). Without this default read-view access, all SNMPv3 parameters could be polled—users, groups, community, etc. Access to the MIB variables describing those SNMPv3 parameters means full SNMP control over the entire network element, because the read-write community is available. Note that this default view also is applied to SNMPv1 or SNMPv2c if they are configured. Finally, the v1default view refuses access to the CISCO-TAP-MIB (ciscoMgmt.252), which is used for the cable modem intercept feature. In this case, Cisco Architecture for Lawful Intercept in IP Networks (RFC 3924) can monitor and intercept traffic from network elements. It offers service providers Lawful Intercept capabilities.

To specify a read-view access, you would enter the following:

```
Router(config) # snmp-server group benoitgroup v3 auth read myview
Router(config) # snmp-server view myview mib-2 included
Router(config) # snmp-server view myview cisco excluded
```

The **show snmp view** command now displays a new entry:

```
myview mib-2 - included nonvolatile active
myview cisco - excluded nonvolatile active
```

To conclude, an additional SNMPv3 **show** command returns the SNMP engineID:

```
Router # show snmp engineID
```

```
Local SNMP engineID: 1234567890
Remote Engine ID          IP-addr      Port
```

According to the preceding configuration, the arguments for the net-snmp utility **snmpget** are as follows:

```
SERVER % snmpget -v 3 -u benoit -l authNoPriv -a MD5 -A benoitpassword router
   sysUpTime.0
sysUpTime = Timeticks: (840889259) 97 days, 7:48:12.59
```

authPriv SNMP Example

The SNMPv3 IOS configuration with user authentication and encryption is as follows:

```
Router(config) # snmp-server group benoitgroup v3 auth
Router(config) # snmp-server user benoit benoitgroup v3 auth md5
   authenticationpassword md5 authenticationpassword priv des privacypassword
router(config)# exit
```

The configuration line with the SNMPv3 user specification does not appear in the running-config. The **show snmp-server user** and **show snmp-server group** commands return exactly the same output as in the authNoPriv example. Note, however, that the SNMP engineID is not specified from the command-line interface (CLI). Instead, it is generated from the SNMP entity:

```
Router # show running-config | include snmp
snmp-server group benoitgroup v3 auth
Router # show snmp user
User name: benoit
Engine ID: 80000009030000B0647AE7E0
storage-type: nonvolatile            active
```

According to this configuration, the arguments for the net-snmp utility **snmpget** are as follows:

```
SERVER % snmpget -v 3 -u benoit -l authPriv -a MD5 -A authenticationpassword -X
   privacypassword router sysUpTime.0
sysUpTime = Timeticks: (61485) 0:10:14.85
```

MIB Table Retrieval Example

In all previous SNMPv2c and SNMPv3 examples, a simple SNMP Get operation illustrated how to query a managed object. This section covers the other SNMP operations, such as SNMP Get-Next and Get-Bulk, and explains how the indexing works in an SNMP table. Even if in reality the ifTable contains more managed objects, the sample ifTable shown in Table 4-2 serves for illustration purposes. To simplify the examples, SNMPv2c is used.

Table 4-2   *Table Representation of the ifTable*

ifTable (ifEntry)	ifDescr	ifType	ifSpeed	ifAdminStatus
ifIndex.1	Ethernet0/0	6 (ethercsmacd)	10 Mbps	Up
ifIndex.2	Serial0/0	22 (propPointToPointSerial)	128 kbps	Up

Figure 4-1 shows a hierarchical representation of the ifTable.

Figure 4-1 *Hierarchical Representation of the ifTable*

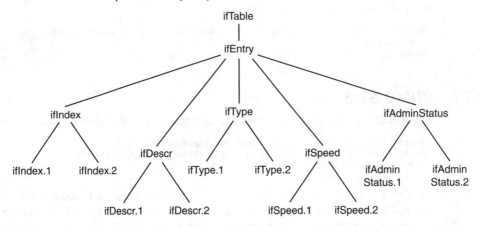

As required by the SNMP Get operation, the **snmpget** utility always needs to specify a leaf managed object:

```
SERVER % snmpget -c public -v 2c <router> ifDescr.1
RFC1213-MIB::ifDescr.1 = STRING: "Ethernet0/0"
```

However, the SNMP specifications do not impose a single SNMP request for each managed object to be polled; instead, multiple managed objects can be polled with a single request. For example, to poll all managed objects related to Serial0/0 in this table, a single SNMP Get operation is sufficient:

```
SERVER % snmpget -c public -v 2c router ifDescr.2 ifType.2 ifSpeed.2 ifAdminStatus.2
RFC1213-MIB::ifIndex.2 = INTEGER: Serial0/0
RFC1213-MIB::ifType.2 = INTEGER: 22
RFC1213-MIB::ifSpeed.2 = Gauge32: 10000000
RFC1213-MIB::ifAdminStatus.2 = INTEGER: up(1)
```

The SNMP Get-Next operation polls the next managed object. If you specify **ifDescr.1** as the argument, Figure 4-1 shows that the next managed object is **ifDescr.2**:

```
SERVER % snmpgetnext -c public -v 2c router ifDescr.1
RFC1213-MIB::ifDescr.2 = STRING: "Serial0/0"
```

Following the same logic, a SNMP GetNext operation on ifDescr.2 returns the next object, which is **ifType.1**:

```
SERVER % snmpgetnext -c public -v 2c router ifDescr.2
RFC1213-MIB::ifType.1 = INTEGER: ehernetCsmacd(6)
```

The **snmpwalk** utility initiates a series of SNMP GetNext operations, one per polled managed object:

```
SERVER % snmpwalk -c public -v 2c router ifTable
RFC1213-MIB::ifIndex.1 = INTEGER: Ethernet0/0
```

```
RFC1213-MIB::ifIndex.2 = INTEGER: Serial0/0
RFC1213-MIB::ifDescr.1 = DISPLAY STRING-(ascii): Ethernet0/0
RFC1213-MIB::ifDescr.2 = DISPLAY STRING-(ascii): Serial0/0
RFC1213-MIB::ifType.1 = INTEGER: 6
RFC1213-MIB::ifType.2 = INTEGER: 22
RFC1213-MIB::ifSpeed.1 = Gauge32: 10000000
RFC1213-MIB::ifSpeed.2 = Gauge32: 128000
RFC1213-MIB::ifAdminStatus.1 = INTEGER: up(1)
RFC1213-MIB::ifAdminStatus.2 = INTEGER: up(1)
```

Executing the **snmpbulkwalk -c public -v 2c** *router* **ifTable** command returns exactly the same output as the **snmpwalk -c public -v 2c** *router* **ifTable** command. However, the SNMP Get-Bulk operation is used! Fewer SNMP packets are exchanged, which improves performance and reduces the bandwidth requirements to exchange management traffic.

Note that the **snmptable** utility repeatedly uses the SNMP GETNEXT or GETBULK requests to query for information on a MIB table and formats the output into a readable format. Especially interesting are the **-Cb** parameter, which displays only a brief heading (any common prefixes of the table field names are deleted), and the **-Ci** parameter, which prepends the entry's index to all printed lines. The following output displays the output of Table 4-2 with the **snmptable** utility:

```
SERVER % snmptable -c public -v 2c -Cb -Ci router ifTable
               SNMP table: IF-MIB::ifTable
 index Index  Descr                      Type      Speed AdminStatus
     1     1  Ethernet0/0          ethercsmacd  10000000          up
     2     2  Serial0/0  propPointToPointSerial    128000          up
```

MIB Functional Area Comparison Table

Table 4-3 compares the MIBs covered in this chapter. It provides an overview of the MIBs by assigning them to the different functional areas of accounting and performance management, as described in Chapter 1, "Understanding the Need for Accounting and Performance Management." The selected MIBs can be placed in two groups: general-purpose MIBs and transport technology-specific MIBs. The general-purpose MIBs have been selected based on general availability (for example, MIB-II is supported on almost every vendor's network equipment) or special feature support (PING-MIB is very valuable in a remote monitoring environment). The technology MIBs cover Frame Relay and MPLS, because most of today's networks are based on one of these two transport protocols. CISCO-CAR-MIB and CISCO-CLASS-BASED-QOS-MIB are applicable in a quality-of-service (QoS) environment. CISCO-DATA-COLLECTION-MIB is a special solution for accounting solutions, because it makes it easy to collect large sets of data in a single operation. The voice accounting information is provided by multiple MIBs, depending on the technology (dialup, ISDN, or VoIP).

Table 4-3 does not compare the MIBs' features, because they are covered in detail in specific chapters (RMON MIBs, NetFlow-MIB, RADIUS MIBs, BGP Policy Accounting MIB, etc.). Chapter 12, "Summary of Data Collection Methodology," compares them.

Table 4-3 *MIB Functional Area Comparison*

Area/MIB	MIB-II, IF-MIB	PING-MIB	PROCESS-MIB	ENVMON-MIB, MEMORY-POOL-MIB, HEALTH-MONITOR	CAR-MIB	CB-QOS-MIB	FRAME-RELAY-DTE-MIB	MLS-TE-MIB	VOICE-DIAL-CONTROL-MIB	CISCO-CALL-HISTORY-MIB
Device Performance Monitoring	✓	✓	✓	✓	✓		✓			
Network Performance Monitoring	✓	✓				✓	✓	✓		
Service Monitoring		✓				✓			✓	
User Monitoring and Profiling	✓					✓	✓		✓	✓
Application Performance Monitoring and Profiling										
Link Capacity Planning	✓				✓	✓	✓	✓		
Network-Wide Capacity Planning								✓		
Traffic Profiling and Engineering					✓	✓		✓		
Peering and Transit Agreements										
Destination-Sensitive Billing									✓	✓
Destination-and Source-Sensitive Billing									✓	✓
Quality-of-Service Billing						✓		✓	✓	
Application-and Content-Based Billing										

Table 4-3   *MIB Functional Area Comparison (Continued)*

Area/MIB	MIB-II, IF-MIB	PING-MIB	PROCESS-MIB	ENVMON-MIB, MEMORY-POOL-MIB, HEALTH-MONITOR	CAR-MIB	CB-QOS-MIB	FRAME-RELAY-DTE-MIB	MLS-TE-MIB	VOICE-DIAL-CONTROL-MIB	CISCO-CALL-HISTORY-MIB
Time- or Connection-Based Billing									✓	✓
Security Analysis	✓		✓		✓					

The Cisco DATA-COLLECTION MIB is a special MIB that allows a management application to select a set of MIB object instances whose values need to be collected periodically. This applies for any area of Table 4-3 as long as other MIBs deliver the required measurements. The top flows variable (cnsTopFlows) from the NetFlow-MIB provides a mechanism that allows the Top-*N* flows in the NetFlow cache to be viewed in real time. It is another function related to the areas described in Table 4-3. Indeed, associated with criteria that can limit the feature to particular flows of interest, monitoring some of the top flows provides relevant details for capacity planning, security analysis, etc.

General-Purpose MIBs for Accounting and Performance

The MIBs discussed in the following sections are a collection of general-purpose information sources for accounting and performance management. They are not related to a specific technology, which means that they can be used in any type of network. There is a close relationship between performance and fault management, which especially the health-related MIBs clearly illustrate.

These MIBs do not provide direct performance counters. They indirectly monitor device and network performance by sending proactive notifications for potential fault sources, such as temperature indicators or failed system fans. For more details on fault and performance management, refer to *Performance and Fault Management* (Cisco Press, 2000). The following sections describe relevant accounting and performance management MIB details.

MIB-II (RFC 1213), IF-MIB (RFC 2863), and CISCO-IF-EXTENSION-MIB

RFC 1213 provides the latest MIB-II definition, after multiple RFC iterations (the initial definition was RFC 1066, MIB-I). The concept is simple and effective: an interface is explained as ifEntry, which has a table structure (ifTable) that contains a sequence of objects. Some of these are listed here:

- **ifIndex** is a unique value for each interface.
- **ifSpeed** is an estimate of the interface's current bandwidth in bits per second.
- **ifInOctets** is the total number of octets received on the interface, including framing characters.
- **ifInUcastPkts** is the number of (subnet) unicast packets delivered to a higher-layer protocol.
- **ifInNUcastPkts** is the number of nonunicast (subnet broadcast or subnet multicast) packets.
- **ifInErrors** is the number of inbound packets that contained errors preventing them from being delivered to a higher-layer protocol.
- **ifInDiscards** is the number of inbound packets that were discarded, even though no errors were detected, to prevent their being delivered to a higher-layer protocol. One possible reason for discarding such a packet could be that the existing buffer was occupied.
- **ifOutOctets, ifOutUcastPkts, ifOutNUcastPkts, ifOutErrors, ifOutDiscards** are the same as the ifInDiscards object, except that they are for outgoing traffic instead. However, the reasons for errors and discards are probably different.

The Interface-MIB (RFC 2863) extends the distinction between unicast and nonunicast by introducing two new objects and deprecating the former nonunicast objects (ifInNUcastPkts, ifOutNUcastPkts):

- **ifInMulticastPkts** is the number of packets, delivered by this sublayer to a higher (sub)layer, that were addressed to a multicast address at this sublayer.
- **ifInBroadcastPkts** is the number of packets, delivered by this sublayer to a higher (sub)layer, that were addressed to a broadcast address at this sublayer.

In addition, RFC 2863, based on SMIv2, introduces the concept of 64-bit high-capacity counters to avoid quick counter wrap. Indeed, as the speed of network media increases, the minimum time in which a 32-bit counter wraps decreases. For example, a 10-Mbps stream of back-to-back, full-size packets causes ifInOctets to wrap in just over 57 minutes. At 100 Mbps, the minimum wrap time is 5.7 minutes, and at 1 Gbps, the minimum is 34 seconds. Requiring interfaces to be polled frequently to avoid missing a counter wrap becomes increasingly problematic.

ifTable is augmented with new counters, reflected by an extended syntax including HC (high capacity counter):

- ifHCInOctets, ifHCOutOctets
- ifHCInUcastPkts, ifHCOutUcastPkts
- ifHCInMulticastPkts, ifHCOutMulticastPkts
- ifHCInBroadcastPkts, ifHCOutBroadcastPkts

The Cisco private CISCO-IF-EXTENSION-MIB extends the IF-MIB even further by providing additional objects that are essential for identifying abnormal packets and conditions:

- **cieIfInRuntsErrs** is the number of packets input on a particular physical interface that were dropped because they were smaller than the minimum allowable physical media limit.

- **cieIfInGiantsErrs** is the number of input packets on a particular physical interface that were dropped because they were larger than the ifMtu (largest permitted size of a packet that can be sent/received on an interface).

- **cieIfInFramingErrs** is the number of input packets on a physical interface that were misaligned or had framing errors.

- **cieIfInputQueueDrops, cieIfOutputQueueDrops** indicate the number of packets dropped by the interface, even though no error was detected.

CISCO-PING-MIB

The CISCO-PING-MIB enables a Cisco network element to ping remote devices. This can be useful in distributed environments to reduce the overhead of central polling. A possible scenario would be a provider edge router (PE) in a PoP that polls unmanaged customer edge (CE) routers for availability in their respective VRFs. After completing the number of configured ping operations, the PE can optionally generate an event toward a central fault management application, which draws conclusions from the results of the ping operation.

Relevant MIB Objects (Read-Write)

The ciscoPingTable table offers the following read-write parameters (among others) for each entry:

- **ciscoPingAddress** is the address of the device to be pinged.

- **ciscoPingPacketCount** specifies the number of ping packets to send to the target in this sequence.

- **ciscoPingPacketTimeout** specifies how long to wait for a response to a transmitted packet before declaring the packet dropped.

- **ciscoPingDelay** specifies the minimum amount of time to wait before sending the next packet in a sequence after receiving a response or declaring a timeout for a previous packet.
- **ciscoPingTrapOnCompletion** specifies whether a trap (ciscoPingCompleted) should be issued on completion of the sequence of pings.

If a management station wants to create an entry in the ciscoPingTable table, it should first generate a pseudo-random serial number to be used as the index to this sparse table.

Relevant MIB Objects (Read-Only)

The ciscoPingTable table offers the following read-only parameters (among others) for each entry:

- **ciscoPingMinRtt** is the minimum round-trip time (RTT) of all the packets that have been sent in this sequence.
- **ciscoPingAvgRtt** is the average RTT of all the packets that have been sent in this sequence.
- **ciscoPingMaxRtt** is the maximum RTT of all the packets that have been sent in this sequence.
- **ciscoPingCompleted** is set to true when all the packets in this sequence either have been responded to or have timed out.

A trap **ciscoPingCompleted** can be generated after a completed operation. It contains the following details: ciscoPingCompleted, ciscoPingSentPackets, ciscoPingReceivedPackets, ciscoPingMinRtt, ciscoPingAvgRtt, ciscoPingMaxRtt, and ciscoPingVrfName. The latter object has a valid value only if the ping was sent to a VPN address.

NOTE If enabled, the ciscoPingCompleted trap is sent after the operation completes, independent of the results (succeed or failed). There is no option to issue a trap only if the operations failed!

CISCO-PROCESS-MIB

The CISCO-PROCESS-MIB collects statistics on the network element's CPU utilization, both globally for the device and additionally per process. The MIB provides a great level of detail for each process, such as allocated memory, the number of times the process has been invoked, and so on. From a device performance perspective, the following global device parameters are applicable. This MIB has no read-write objects. The relevant read-only MIB objects are as follows:

- **cpmCPUTotal5secRev** is the overall CPU busy percentage in the last 5-second period.
- **cpmCPUTotal1minRev** is the overall CPU busy percentage in the last 1-minute period.
- **cpmCPUTotal5minRev** is the overall CPU busy percentage in the last 5-minute period.
- **cpmProcessPID** contains the process ID.
- **cpmProcessName** is the name associated with this process.
- **cpmProcessTimeCreated** is the time when the process was created.
- **cpmProcExtRuntimeRev** is the amount of CPU time the process has used, in microseconds.
- **cpmProcExtInvokedRev** is the number of times that the process has been invoked since cpmProcessTimeCreated.
- **cpmProcExtUtil5SecRev** provides a general idea of how busy a process caused the processor to be over a 5-second period. Similar objects exist for the process utilization over 1 and 5 minutes.
- **cpmProcExtPriorityRev** is the priority level at which the process is running (critical, high, normal, low, not assigned).

The same results that the MIB offers can be retrieved at the CLI using the **show process cpu** command, as shown in Table 4-4.

Table 4-4   *CPU Utilization for 5 Seconds, 1 Minute, and 5 Minutes*

PID	Runtime (ms)	Invoked	uSecs	5 Seconds	1 Minute	5 Minute	TTY	Process
1	0	4	0	0.00%	0.00%	0.00%	0	Chunk Manager
2	6352	2886952	2	0.00%	0.00%	0.00%	0	Load Meter
3	10976	14228937	0	0.00%	0.00%	0.00%	0	NTP
4	29497900	2200650	13404	1.51%	0.27%	0.19%	0	Check heaps
5	8	7	1142	0.00%	0.00%	0.00%	0	Pool Manager
6	0	2	0	0.00%	0.00%	0.00%	0	Timers
7	0	2	0	0.00%	0.00%	0.00%	0	Serial background
8	0	1	0	0.00%	0.00%	0.00%	0	AAA_SERVER_DEADT
9	0	2	0	0.00%	0.00%	0.00%	0	AAA high-capacity
10	22800	6730089	107	0.00%	0.00%	0.00%	0	EnvMon

Note that because of the indexing mechanism defined in the ENTITY-MIB (cpmCPUTotalPhysicalIndex specified in the CISCO-PROCESS-MIB points to entPhysicalEntry in the ENTITY-MIB), the CISCO-PROCESS-MIB can monitor the CPU of the processes running on the distributed system. A typical example is the CPU monitoring on line cards or VIP cards.

CISCO-ENVMON-MIB and CISCO-HEALTH-MONITOR-MIB

The CISCO-ENVMON-MIB collects environmental details, such as temperature, voltage conditions, and fan status. It contains various predefined thresholds and notifications to warn an operator about potential issues. Because these objects are not directly relevant for accounting and performance management, no further MIB objects are described here. However, it is advisable to enable the notifications and point them toward a fault management system. An automatic shutdown of a network element—such as one caused by overheating, less voltage, or malfunctioning fans—certainly has an impact on the network's overall performance.

The CISCO-HEALTH-MONITOR-MIB is similar to the CISCO-ENVMON-MIB; however, the health status is represented by a metric that consists of a set of predefined rules. An advantage of the CISCO-HEALTH-MONITOR-MIB is the configurable thresholds that can be adjusted by the operator in units of 0.01 percent.

CISCO-MEMORY-POOL-MIB

The CISCO-MEMORY-POOL-MIB collects statistics on the memory utilization, such as used memory, amount of free memory, largest free blocks, and memory pool utilization over the last 1, 5, and 10 minutes. Similar to the health monitoring, memory monitoring should be enabled for proactive identification of critical situations. Because this MIB does not provide accounting and performance managed objects, no further details are presented here.

CISCO-DATA-COLLECTION-MIB

The CISCO-DATA-COLLECTION-MIB is a new approach to overcome the issue of SNMP for performance and accounting management. A Network Management System (NMS) needs to poll the network elements frequently—sometimes every 30 seconds—to get up-to-date information, get (close to) real-time information, and avoid counter wrapping.

This causes additional network utilization as well as CPU resource consumption at the NMS. During network connectivity issues, the NMS might not retrieve any information from the network element. As an alternative to regular MIB object polling from the NMS, the network element can collect its own MIB data and store it in a local file. This is the concept of the CISCO-DATA-COLLECTION-MIB. Locally storing bulk statistics also helps minimize data loss during temporary network outages, because network elements can store the collected data in volatile memory.

Another aspect is the CPU consumption at the network element concerning local versus remote polling. Having devices poll their own (locally) managed variables might reduce the CPU impact, because internal communication could be implemented more efficiently than handling SNMP requests from the NMS server.

Introduced in Cisco IOS 12.0(24)S and 12.3(2)T, this MIB module allows a management application to select a set of MIB object instances whose values need to be collected periodically. The configuration tasks consist of the following:

- Specifying a set of instances (of the MIB objects in a data group) whose values need to be collected—that is, the grouping of MIB objects into data groups. All the objects in an object list have to share the same MIB index. However, the objects do not need to be in the same MIB and do not need to belong to the same MIB table. For example, it is possible to group ifInOctets and an Ethernet MIB object in the same schema, because the containing tables for both objects are indexed by the ifIndex.

- Data selection for the Periodic MIB Data Collection and Transfer Mechanism requires the definition of a schema with the following information: name of an object list, instance (specific or wildcarded) that needs to be retrieved for objects in the object list, and how often the specified instances need to be sampled (polling interval). Wildcarding is an important benefit, because all indexed entries in a table can be retrieved by selecting the main object identifier (OID) with the wildcard function.

- Collecting the required object values into local virtual files, either periodically or on demand. The collection period is configurable.

- Reporting statistics and errors during the collection interval by generating an SNMP trap (cdcVFileCollectionError).

- After the collection period ends (the default is 30 minutes), the virtual file is frozen, and a new virtual file is created for storing data. The frozen virtual file is then transferred to a specified destination. The network management application can choose to retain such frozen virtual files on the network element for a certain period, called the retention period.

- Transferring the virtual files to specified locations in the network (such as to the Network Management System) by using FTP, TFTP, or RCP. The transfer status can be reported to the NMS by generating an SNMP trap (cdcFileXferComplete, which is either true or false) and logging a syslog error message locally at the network element. You can also configure a secondary destination for the file to be used if the file cannot be transferred to the primary destination.

- Deleting virtual files periodically or on demand. The default setting is to delete the file after a successful transfer.

CISCO-DATA-COLLECTION-MIB introduces a number of new terms:

- **Base objects** are MIB objects whose values an application wants to collect.

- **Data group** is a group of base objects that can be of two types—object or table. An object type data group can consist of only one fully instantiated base object. A table type data group can consist of more than one base object, where each is a columnar object in a conceptual table. In addition, a table type data group can specify the instances of the base objects whose values need to be collected into the VFiles.

- **Virtual file (VFile)** is a file-like entity used to collect data. A network element can implement a VFile as a simple buffer in the main memory, or it might use a file in the local file system. The file is called virtual because a network management application does not need to know the location of the VFile, because the MIB provides mechanisms to transfer the VFile to a location specified by the NMS application.

- **Current VFile** points to the VFile into which MIB object data is currently being collected.

- **Frozen VFile** refers to a VFile that is no longer used to collect data. Only frozen VFiles can be transferred to specified destinations.

- **Collection interval** is associated with a VFile and specifies the interval at which the VFile is used to collect data. However, there are conditions under which a collection interval can be shorter than the specified time. For example, a collection interval is prematurely terminated when the maximum size of a VFile is exceeded or when an error condition occurs.

- **Polling period** is associated with a data group. It determines the frequency at which the base MIB objects of a data group should be fetched and stored in a VFile.

A produced VFile looks like this:

```
Schema-def ATM2/0-IFMIB "%u, %s, %u, %u, %u, %u"
epochtime ifDescr instanceoid ifInOctets ifOutOctets ifInUcastPkts ifInDiscards
ATM2/0-IFMIB: 954417080, ATM2/0, 2, 95678, 23456, 234, 345
ATM2/0-IFMIB: 954417080, ATM2/0.1, 8, 95458, 54356, 245, 454
ATM2/0-IFMIB: 954417080, ATM2/0.2, 9, 45678, 8756, 934, 36756
```

The CISCO-DATA-COLLECTION-MIB is mainly targeted for medium to high-end platforms that have sufficient local storage (volatile or permanent) to store the VFiles.

A legacy alternative to the CISCO-DATA-COLLECTION-MIB is the CISCO-BULK-FILE-MIB. It provides similar functionality as the CISCO-DATA-COLLECTION-MIB, but it offers only a manual mode and has no timers for scheduled operations. Because this MIB has multiple advantages over the CISCO-BULK-FILE-MIB (such as more powerful and flexible data selection features and grouping of MIB objects from different tables into data groups), it will replace the CISCO-BULK-FILE-MIB in the future. It is suggested that you use the CISCO-DATA-COLLECTION-MIB instead of the CISCO-BULK-FILE-MIB if applicable.

Advanced Device Instrumentation

Cisco network elements contain a rich set of device instrumentation features, such as NetFlow, IP SLA (formerly known as Service Assurance Agent), Network-Based Application Recognition (NBAR), Application Response Time (ART), Remote Monitoring (RMON), and others. The related MIBs are described in the following chapters:

- RMON (RFC 2819 and RFC 3577), SMON (SMON-MIB), Application Performance Measurement (APM) MIB (RFC 3729)—Chapter 5, "RMON"

- IP accounting (CISCO-IP-STAT-MIB)—Chapter 6, "IP Accounting"

- NetFlow (CISCO-NETFLOW-MIB)—Chapter 7, "NetFlow"

- BGP policy accounting (CISCO-BGP-POLICY-ACCOUNTING-MIB)—Chapter 8, "BGP Policy Accounting"

- NBAR (CISCO-NBAR-PROTOCOL-DISCOVERY-MIB)—Chapter 10, "NBAR"

- IP SLA (CISCO-RTTMON-MIB)—Chapter 11, "IP SLA"

Technology-Specific MIBs for Accounting and Performance

So far, this chapter has discussed MIB objects for generic performance monitoring, which can be applied across any network. For a detailed analysis or for troubleshooting help, you should also consider technology-specific monitoring variables. A classic example is Spanning Tree Protocol (STP) in a LAN environment. A misconfigured spanning-tree environment can result in drastically reduced performance even though all basic monitoring parameters (such as CPU and link utilization) indicate a normal situation. In contrast to the preceding section, this section offers pointers on how to retrieve accounting and performance management information associated with technology-specific environments, such as Frame Relay, MPLS, QoS, IPv6, VLAN, and others.

Because most data networks are based on Frame Relay or MPLS, only these two transport technologies are discussed in detail. To focus on accounting and performance management, the MIB selection criteria were based on the question "Does the MIB contain relevant counters?" For example, at least four MPLS MIBs exist. The MPLS LSR MIB (RFC 3813) and MPLS Traffic Engineering MIB (RFC 3812) offer the most details.

Frame Relay

Frame Relay is a mature technology. Adequate monitoring functionality is provided by the IETF Frame Relay MIB (RFC 2115), which is supplemented by the CISCO-FRAME-RELAY-MIB. To gain the most benefit from using these MIBs, an understanding of Frame Relay concepts is helpful.

Relevant objects from the FRAME-RELAY-DTE-MIB (RFC 2115) are as follows:

- **frCircuitReceivedFrames** is the number of frames received over this Frame Relay virtual circuit since it was created.

- **frCircuitReceivedOctets** is the number of octets received over this Frame Relay virtual circuit since it was created.

- **frCircuitSentFrames** is the number of frames sent from this Frame Relay virtual circuit since it was created.

- **frCircuitSentOctets** is the number of octets sent from this frame-relay virtual circuit since it was created.

- **frCircuitThroughput** is the average number of 'Frame Relay Information Field' bits transferred per second across a user network interface in one direction.

- **frCircuitReceivedFECNs** is the number of frames received from the network indicating forward congestion since the virtual circuit was created. The FECN mechanism, Forward Explicit Congestion Notification, is a means to notify network congestion to the destination station (receiver).

- **frCircuitReceivedBECNs** is the number of frames received from the network indicating backward congestion since the virtual circuit was created. Backward Explicit Congestion Notification (BECN) is a means to notify the sending station about network congestion. Closely monitoring these two variables is advisable, because it helps identify link overload situations early on.

- **frCircuitCommittedBurst** is a read/write variable that describes the maximum amount of data, in bits, that the network agrees to transfer under normal conditions.

NOTE   The variables frCircuitCommittedBurst and frCircuitThroughput are configurable operational parameters related to outgoing traffic. They cannot be used to monitor the incoming burst and throughput traffic rate. The CISCO-FRAME-RELAY-MIB provides additional monitoring parameters.

Relevant objects from the CISCO-FRAME-RELAY-MIB (read-only) are as follows:

- **cfrCircuitTable** is a table of descriptive and statistics information that are generic to Frame Relay virtual circuits:

    — **cfrCircuitDEins** is the number of packets received with the Discard Eligibility indicator (the DE bit) set. This indicates that the committed interface rate (the maximum transmission rate in bits per second per virtual circuit) for a specific virtual circuit is being exceeded.

— **cfrCircuitDEouts** is the number of packets transmitted with the DE bit set.

— **cfrCircuitDropPktsOuts** is the number of discarded packets.

- **cfrSvcTable** is a table of Frame Relay switched virtual circuits (SVC) of specific statistics:

  — **cfrSvcThroughputIn** is the circuit's incoming throughput. This is the ingress *monitoring*_variable that is related to the egress *configuration* parameter frCircuitThroughput from RFC 2115.

  — **cfrSvcCommitBurstIn** is the circuit's incoming Committed Burst Rate. This is the ingress *monitoring* variable that is related to the egress *configuration* parameter frCircuitCommittedBurst from RFC 2115.

MPLS

MPLS is a standardized and widely deployed technology today, for both service provider networks and large enterprises. Several MIBs are available, standardized by the IETF, with extensions for Operation, Administration, and Maintenance (OAM) capabilities. From an accounting and performance perspective, these MIBs help an operator increase the availability of the MPLS network, carry out traffic engineering and network redesign, build the core traffic matrix, and feed the data into a billing system.

The following sections detail the MIBs that are relevant to an MPLS environment.

MPLS Label Switch Router (LSR) MIB (RFC 3813)

This MIB can be used for configuration and monitoring purposes. Ingress and egress MPLS statistics are available for accounting and performance management. A global table for each interface gathers the total amount of traffic, and two tables per segment collect LSR-specific information. RFC 3813 contains 32- and 64-bit counters. Three tables are of main interest:

- **mplsInterfacePerfTable** provides MPLS performance information on a per-interface basis. This table aggregates details across different MPLS labels on the physical interface:

  — **mplsInterfaceInPackets** is the number of labeled packets received on this interface (ingress traffic).

  — **mplsInterfaceInDiscards** is the number of inbound labeled packets that were discarded even though no errors were detected.

  — **mplsInterfaceOutPackets** is the number of labeled packets transmitted on this interface (egress traffic).

  — **mplsInterfaceOutDiscards** is the number of outbound labeled packets that were chosen to be discarded even though no errors were detected.

- **mplsInSegmentPerfTable** contains statistical information for incoming MPLS segments to an LSR:

  — **mplsInSegmentPerfOctets, mplsInSegmentPerfHCOctets** is the total number of octets received by this segment (32- and 64-bit).

  — **mplsInSegmentPerfPackets** is the total number of packets received by this segment.

  — **mplsInSegmentPerfErrors** is the number of erroneous packets received on this segment.

  — **mplsInSegmentPerfDiscards** is the number of labeled packets received on this segment that were chosen to be discarded even though no errors have been detected.

- **mplsOutSegmentPerfTable** is a similar table for outgoing segments from an LSR.

MPLS Traffic Engineering MIB (RFC 3812)

These MIB modules include managed object definitions for MPLS Traffic Engineering (TE). Traffic engineering is the process of identifying and selecting paths through the MPLS network. This enables load balancing on parallel links and choosing paths based on performance metrics such as delay, bandwidth, and utilization. The ultimate goal is to increase availability and reliability while optimizing utilization and traffic performance. TE is a complex task, and the details are outside the scope of this book. However, remarkable accounting and performance statistics can be polled from the MPLS-TE-MIB. The mplsTunnelTable is the configuration part, which creates and modifies MPLS tunnels between an originating LSR and a remote endpoint, the terminating LSR:

- **mplsTunnelPerfTable** provides per-tunnel MPLS performance information:

  — **mplsTunnelPerfPackets, mplsTunnelPerfHCPackets** is the number of packets forwarded by the tunnel (32- and 64-bit counters).

  — **mplsTunnelPerfErrors** is the number of erroneous packets.

  — **mplsTunnelPerfBytes, mplsTunnelPerfHCBytes** are the number of bytes forwarded by the tunnel (32- and 64-bit counters).

- **mplsTunnelTrapEnable** is a read-write object that enables the generation of mplsTunnelUp and mplsTunnelDown traps, which are very important from a fault and performance standpoint.

NOTE   More details can be found in *MPLS Network Management: MIBs, Tools, and Techniques* by Thomas Nadeau (Morgan Kaufmann, 2002).

IPv6

IP version 6 is a the IP protocol designed to become the successor of IP version 4, the Internet protocol that is predominantly deployed and extensively used throughout the world. In 1990, the IETF identified the potential issue of a lack of IPv4 addresses and started the IPNG working group. In 1995, RFC 1883 defined the IPv6 specification. RFC 2460 obsoletes RFC 1883 and is the present standard for IPv6. The first MIBs for IPv6 were standardized in 1998 as RFC 2465 and RFC 2466. At that time, the approach was to have separate tables for IPv4 and IPv6 addresses. However, this approach turned out to be unsuccessful, with only a limited number of implementations. Starting in 2001, the new approach was to extend the existing MIBs to manage IPv4 and IPv6 in combined tables. This applies particularly for RFC 2011 (SNMPv2 MIB for IP using SMIv2), RFC 2012 (SNMPv2 MIB for TCP using SMIv2), RFC 2013 (SNMPv2 MIB for UDP using SMIv2), and RFC 2096 (IP Forwarding Table MIB).

RFC 4293 is the IETF's proposed standard and defines the MIB for IP, unified for IPv4 and IPv6. RFC 4022 is the MIB counterpart for TCP, and RFC 4113 is the MIB for UDP. The new MIBs obsolete RFCs 2011, 2012, 2013, 2465, and 2466. Implementations at the obsolete MIB are no longer suggested by the IETF.

From an accounting and performance perspective, these MIBs offer basic interface counters, which are useful to distinguish between IPv4 and IPv6 traffic. From an operator's perspective, this is one of the most relevant monitoring tasks during the network's IPv4-to-IPv6 transition, because it answers the question "How much traffic has already been migrated to IPv6 and which percentage remains on IPv4?"

The following extract from RFC 4293 is a representative example of the other MIBs:

"The IP statistics tables (ipSystemStatsTable and ipIfStatsTable) contain objects to count the number of datagrams and octets that a given entity has processed. Unlike the previous attempt, this document uses a single table for multiple address types. Typically, the only two types of interest are IPv4 and IPv6; however, the table can support other types if necessary. The first table, ipSystemStatsTable, conveys system-wide information. (That is, the various counters are for all interfaces and not a specific set of interfaces.) Its index is formed from a single sub-id that represents the address type for which the statistics were counted. The second table, ipIfStatsTable, conveys interface-specific information. Its index is formed from two sub-ids. The first represents the address type (IPv4 and IPv6), and the interface within that address type is represented by the second sub-id."

Cisco never implemented the deprecated IPv6 MIBs (RFC 2465 and RFC 2466). Instead, the early drafts of the updated MIBs are partly supported; however, the interface statistics to differentiate IPv4 and IPv6 traffic at the interface level are not implemented:

- **CISCO-IETF-IP-MIB**—This MIB is based on draft-ietf-ipngwg-rfc2011-update-00.txt.

- **CISCO-IETF-IP-FORWARD-MIB**—This MIB was extracted from draft-ietf-ipngwg-rfc2096-update-00.txt.

- **IPv6-MIB**—This MIB was extracted from RFC 2465.

You can find the latest status updates for Cisco IPv6 MIB implementation at http://www.cisco.com/go/ipv6.

SNMP can be configured over IPv6 transport so that an IPv6 host can perform SNMP queries and receive SNMP notifications from a device running Cisco IOS with IPv6 enabled. The following MIBs can be configured with SNMP over IPv6:

- CISCO-DATA-COLLECTION-MIB
- CISCO-CONFIG-COPY-MIB
- CISCO-FLASH-MIB
- ENTITY-MIB
- NOTIFICATION-LOG-MIB
- SNMP-TARGET-MIB

NOTE   CISCO-CONFIG-COPY-MIB and CISCO-FLASH-MIB support IPv6 addressing if FTP, TFTP, or Remote Copy Protocol (RCP) is used.

SNMP over IPv6 transport is initially supported in IOS 12.0(27)S; more features are added to IOS 12.0(30)S and 12.3(14)T.

NetFlow also supports the collection of IPv6-related flows since IOS 12.3(7)T; however, the flow export is still based on IPv4.

Multicast

In general, network conversations can be distinguished as one-to-one traffic (unicast), one-to-many conversations (multicast), or one-to-all transmissions (broadcast). This separation is relevant for the network design as well as accounting and performance monitoring, because it is relevant to have accounting and performance statistics per unicast, multicast, and broadcast traffic. Historically, monitoring of multicast traffic was an issue, because there was no separation between multicast and broadcast traffic. The ifTable from RFC 1213 gathers only unicast (ifInUcastPkts) and nonunicast (ifInNUcastPkts) traffic.

Today, at least three different measurement approaches exist for monitoring multicast traffic: the interface group MIB (RFC 2863), the RMON-MIB (RFC 1757), and the Multicast Routing MIB for IPv4 (RFC 2932):

Interface Group MIB (RFC 2863)

The interface group MIB IF-MIB distinguishes between unicast, multicast, and broadcast packets and adds 64-bit high-capacity counters:

- ifHCInUcastPkts, ifHCOutUcastPkts
- ifHCInMulticastPkts, ifHCOutMulticastPkts
- ifHCInBroadcastPkts, ifHCOutBroadcastPkts

RMON-MIB (RFC 1757)

The RMON-MIB also separates multicast and broadcast packets (etherStatsBroadcastPkts, etherStatsMulticastPkts). Implementations of RFC 1757 can gather multicast packets per interface; however, no statement about the packets belonging to a specific multicast group can be made. This might be sufficient from a performance perspective; however, a billing application would require identifying the multicast group details.

Multicast Routing MIB for IPv4 (RFC 2932)

This MIB assigns packets to the related multicast groups (ipMRouteGroup). It gathers multicast routing status information plus traffic statistics. A table (ipMRouterInterfaceTable) offers per-interface octet counters for ingress and egress multicast traffic. The MIB contains high-capacity (64-bit) counters and has three performance and accounting MIB tables:

- The IP Multicast Route Table holds multicast routing information for IP datagrams sent by particular sources to the IP multicast groups known to a router.
- The IP Multicast Routing Next Hop Table includes information on the next hops for the routing IP multicast datagrams. The list contains entries of next hops on outgoing interfaces for sources sending to a multicast group address.
- The IP Multicast Routing Interface Table has multicast routing information specific to interfaces.

VLAN

No specific VLAN performance MIB exists, so you need to leverage the existing MIBs (such as MIB-II RFC 1213, interfaces group MIB RFC 2863, TCP-MIB RFC 2012) to collect performance details in a VLAN environment. For example, STP can become an issue if it is configured incorrectly or if link-up/link-down causes time-consuming STP operations. Therefore, it is suggested that you poll MIB objects from the CISCO-STACK-MIB and the BRIDGE-MIB (RFC 1493). For example, if a 10-Mbps link and a 1-Gbps link are parallel connections between two switches, under normal circumstances the 1-Gbps link should be in forwarding mode, and the 10-Mbps link should be in blocking mode. From a monitoring perspective, monitor the LAN. For each VLAN, identify which ports of a network element are in forwarding or blocking spanning tree mode. Afterwards, ensure that backup links with less capacity (10 Mbps in the preceding example) are not used during normal operations. The cvbStpForwardingMap object from the CISCO-VLAN-BRIDGING-MIB returns this information (1 = forwarding; 0 = disabled, blocking, listening, learning, broken, or nonexistent). Network management tools such as CiscoWorks can draw a nice map that illustrates the spanning tree in the LAN.

Community String Indexing

Retrieving the content of the BRIDGE-MIB returns the MAC addresses associated with all VLANs, because there is no notion of the VLANS indexing in the MIB specification. However, a special feature called community string indexing lets you retrieve a particular instance of the MIB. In these cases, community string indexing is provided to access each instance of the MIB. The syntax is *community string@instance number*. For example, the Catalyst switch includes one instance of the BRIDGE-MIB for each VLAN. If the read-only community string is public and the read-write community string is private, you could use public@25 to read the BRIDGE-MIB for VLAN 25 and use private@33 to read and write the BRIDGE-MIB for VLAN 33.

NOTE   Community string indexing does not affect access to MIBs that have only one instance. Thus, public@25 can be used to access RFC1213-MIB at the same time that the BRIDGE-MIB for VLAN 25 is accessed.

Community string indexing was created before the introduction of SNMPv3. SNMPv3 offers the notion of context instead of the community string index. The VLAN number is replaced by the VLAN name (vlan-25, vlan-33); the names are displayed with the **show snmp context** CLI command.

NOTE   Note that community string indexing also applies to a number of other MIBs.

Additional Monitoring Parameters

The following checklist helps you identify configuration errors in a VLAN environment:

- Check for link configuration mismatch (full- or half-duplex, different interface speed, trunking or nontrunking).

- Check if the uplink fast parameter is enabled on connection ports between switches.
- Check if the port fast parameter is enabled on ports toward end devices.
- Check if Cisco Discovery Protocol (CDP) is enabled only between Cisco devices and disabled toward end-user ports (this is a potential security issue) and is also disabled on WAN interfaces (for performance and security reasons, because knowing device details can be attractive for hackers). CDP does not supply accounting and performance details; however, it offers relevant indirect information about network connectivity, which relates to performance monitoring.

More details on VLAN monitoring can be found in Chapter 5.

Traffic Management and Control

Two different approaches for traffic management and control are briefly described in this section: rate limiting and service classes. Even though both methods use different technologies, related parts from an accounting and performance perspective are the traffic counters. Statistics such as the number of forwarded and dropped packets are collected, optionally per class of service.

CISCO-CAR-MIB

Cisco weighted rate limit, also known as Committed Access Rate (CAR), is a method for traffic control. It lets you regulate traffic at the network element level by configuring sets of rate limits to packets flowing into and out of an interface. Each rate limit has a configurable action associated with specific traffic conditions. The CISCO-CAR-MIB provides weighted rate-limit packet-filtering information. Rate-limit actions are defined per interface and traffic direction (ingress or egress) separately. Whereas the MIB also provides a set of read-write objects for configuration purposes, the described MIB objects gather traffic statistics related to accounting and performance management. The CISCO-CAR-MIB has 32-bit counters and 64-bit (high-capacity [HC]) counters.

Relevant MIB objects (read-only) are as follows:

- **ccarStatHCSwitchedPkts, ccarStatHCSwitchedBytes** are the counters of packets or bytes permitted by the rate limit.
- **ccarStatHCFilteredPkts, ccarStatHCFilteredBytes** are the counters of packets or bytes that exceeded the rate limit.
- **ccarStatCurBurst** is the current received burst size.

These objects are specifically defined in a table (ccarStatTable) with separate entries (ccarStatEntry) for each interface (ifIndex) and for each direction (ingress/egress).

CISCO-CLASS-BASED-QOS-MIB

This MIB supplies QoS information for Cisco network elements that support the modular quality of service command-line interface (MQC). It provides configuration capabilities as well as monitoring statistics, including summary counts and rates by traffic class before and after the enforcement of QoS policies. In addition, detailed feature-specific statistics are available for select PolicyMap features. Policy actions are defined per interface and traffic direction (ingress or egress). The CISCO-CLASS-BASED-QOS-MIB supports 32-bit counters as well as 64-bit (HC) counters. From an accounting and performance management perspective, the following tables are significant. This MIB is structurally very similar to the IETF DIFFSERV-MIB (RFC 3289).

The following relevant MIB tables for QoS contain statistical information only; no configuration information is associated with them. They are indexed by the instance indexes, such as cbQosPolicyIndex and cbQosObjectsIndex:

- **cbQosClassMapStats**—Each entry in this table describes statistical information about *class maps*, such as pre/post-policy packet/byte counts, bit rates, drop packet/ bytes, and no-buffer drops.

- **cbQosMatchStmtStats**—Each entry in this table describes statistical information about *match statement-*specific information, such as prepolicy packet/byte counters and bit rates.

- **cbQosPoliceStats**—Each entry in this table describes statistical information about *police actions*, such as conformed or exceeded packet/byte counters and bit rates.

- **cbQosQueueingStats**—Each entry in this table describes statistical information about *queuing actions*, such as various queue depth and discard packet/byte counters.

- **cbQosTSStats**—Each entry in this table describes statistical information about *traffic-shaping actions*, such as various delay and drop packet/byte counters, state of feature, and queue size.

- **cbQosREDClassStats**—Each entry in this table describes statistical information about *per-precedence Weighted Random Early Detection (WRED) actions*, such as random packet/byte counters and tail drop packet/byte counters.

- **cbQosPoliceActionCfg**—Required objects to display class-based QoS objects' *configuration information.*

This MIB is quite comprehensive and complex; a good understanding of the QoS mechanisms is a suggested prerequisite before you get started. Reading this MIB is recommended, because it is well structured and presents additional details and examples.

NOTE   *Cisco DQOS Exam Certification Guide* by Wendell Odom and Michael Cavanaugh (Cisco Press, 2003) is an excellent resource for information on QoS. Although this book is geared toward the Cisco DQOS exam #9E0-601 and QOS exam #642-641, it is considered the definitive Cisco Press book on QoS, going far beyond what is covered on the specific QOS and DQOS exams.

Telephony

Telephony is a term that covers a wide range of topics, including legacy telephony networks with dedicated infrastructure over dial-in connections, ISDN links, and legacy voice encapsulated in IP-to-IP telephony. This section covers MIB-related telephony details. Chapter 17, "Billing Scenarios," discusses how to gather telephony statistics from multiple sources.

Performance and accounting statistics can be retrieved from the various Cisco voice gateways that are implemented in Cisco IOS. The following terminology provides guidance for understanding accounting and performance collection in a VoIP environment. The ITU-T H.323 standard specifies four VoIP components:

- **Gateway**—An H.323 gateway is an endpoint on a LAN that provides real-time, two-way communication between H.323 terminals on the LAN and other International Telecommunication Union Telecommunication Standardization Sector (ITU-T) terminals in the WAN. Gateways are the translation mechanism for call signaling, data transmission, and audio and video transcoding. An H.323 gateway can also communicate with another H.323 gateway. Gateways allow H.323 terminals to communicate with non-H.323 terminals by converting protocols. The gateway is the point at which a circuit-switched call is encoded and repackaged into IP packets. Because gateways function as H.323 endpoints, they provide admission control, address lookup and translation, and accounting services.

- **Gatekeeper**—A gatekeeper is an H.323 entity that provides services such as address translation and network access control for H.323 terminals, gateways, and Multipoint Control Units (MCU). Gatekeepers are used to group H.323 gateways into logical zones and perform call routing between them. They are also responsible for edge routing decisions between the Public Switched Telephone Network (PSTN) and the H.323 network. In addition, they can provide other services, such as bandwidth management, accounting, and dial plans, that can be centralized to provide scalability. Gatekeepers are logically separated from H.323 endpoints such as terminals and gateways. They are optional in an H.323 network, but if a gatekeeper is present, endpoints have to use the services provided. In an environment in which both gatekeepers and gateways are used, only gateways are configured to send VoIP data. Cisco offers a VoIP gatekeeper called the Multimedia Conference Manager, which is an H.323-compliant program implemented as part of Cisco IOS Software. It is supported by the Cisco 2500, 2600, 3600, 3700, 7200, and MC3810 Multiservice Access Concentrators.

- **Multipoint Control Unit (MCU)**—An MCU is an endpoint on the LAN that enables three or more terminals and gateways to participate in a multipoint conference. It controls and mixes video, audio, and data from terminals to create a robust videoconference. An MCU can also connect two terminals in a point-to-point conference that can later develop into a multipoint conference.

- **Terminal**—This is a LAN client endpoint that provides real-time two-way communication. According to H.323, terminals must support voice communications, whereas video and data support is optional.

Table 4-5 compares the different relevant MIBs and assigns them to the related voice technology.

Table 4-5   *Voice MIB Technology Comparison*

	Dial	ISDN	VoIP
CISCO-CALL-HISTORY-MIB	✓		
DIAL-CONTROL-MIB (RFC 2128)	✓	✓	
CISCO-DIAL-CONTROL-MIB	✓	✓	
CISCO-VOICE-DIAL-CONTROL-MIB	✓	✓	✓
CISCO-VOICE-COMMON-DIAL-CONTROL-MIB	✓	✓	✓
CISCO-CAS-IF-MIB	✓		
CISCO-CALL-APPLICATION-MIB			✓
CISCO-DSP-MGMT-MIB			✓
CISCO-VOICE-ANALOG-IF-MIB	✓		
CISCO-VOICE-IF-MIB	✓	✓	
CISCO-GATEKEEPER-MIB			✓
CISCO-POP-MGMT-MIB	✓	✓	

The following MIBs supply general information on the gateways or gatekeepers:

- **Cisco Channel Associated Signal Interface MIB (CISCO-CAS-IF-MIB)**—Configures and monitors the generic Channel Associated Signaling (CAS) or DS0 clear-channel interfaces in the router.

- **CISCO-VOICE-DIAL-CONTROL-MIB and the CISCO-DIAL-CONTROL-MIB**—Enhances the IETF Dial Control MIB (RFC 2128) by providing configuration and monitoring of voice telephony peers on both a circuit-switched telephony network and an IP data network.

- **CISCO-VOICE-COMMON-DIAL-CONTROL-MIB**—Contains voice-related parameters that are common across more than one network encapsulation—voice over IP (VoIP), voice over Asynchronous Transfer Mode (VoATM), and voice over Frame Relay (VoFR).

- **CISCO-CALL-APPLICATION-MIB**—Allows configuration and monitoring of call applications on a network device. A call application is a software module that processes calls, such as data, voice, video, or fax calls.

- **Digital Signal Processing MIB (CISCO-DSP-MGMT-MIB)**—Monitors the DSP resource and status.

- **CISCO-VOICE-ANALOG-IF-MIB**—Supports multiple different voice interfaces in a gateway, such as the analog interface general group, the E&M (receive and transmit) interface group, the Foreign Exchange Office (FXO) interface group, and the Foreign Exchange Station (FXS) interface group.

- **CISCO-VOICE-IF-MIB**—Manages the common voice-related parameters for both voice analog and ISDN interfaces.

- **CISCO-GATEKEEPER-MIB**—Supports the functions of an H.323 gatekeeper. The gatekeeper is a function of the H.323 Packet-Based Multimedia Communications Systems, a standard of ITU-T. The gatekeeper provides address translation and controls access to the network for H.323 terminals.

The following MIBs grant reporting explicitly for performance and accounting details, for both completed calls and calls in progress:

- **Dial Control Management MIB (RFC 2128)** provides configuration details as well as statistics about active calls and call history in a circuit-switched telephony network.

- **CISCO-VOICE-DIAL-CONTROL-MIB** manages voice telephony peers on both a circuit-switched telephony network and an IP data network.

- **CISCO-CALL-HISTORY-MIB** reports accounting statistics on completed calls. Note that this MIB monitors only a dial environment!

- **Point of Presence (PoP) Management MIB (CISCO-POP-MGMT-MIB)** reports on DSX0 and DSX1 facilities management and call summaries for analog and ISDN.

The following sections offer more details on the CISCO-CALL-HISTORY-MIB and CISCO-VOICE-DIAL-CONTROL-MIB, because these are the two main MIBs for accounting and performance management.

Dial Control Management MIB (RFC 2128)

RFC 2128 provides statistics for circuit-switched telephony networks (ISDN) and dial-in networks. For accounting purposes, these two groups should be monitored:

- The callActive group is used to store active call information.

- The callHistory group is used to store call history information. The calls could be circuit-switched, or they could be virtual circuits. Call history is stored for successful and unsuccessful or rejected calls. An entry is created when a call is cleared.

The CISCO-VOICE-DIAL-CONTROL-MIB and CISCO-VOICE-COMMON-DIAL-CONTROL-MIB are extensions to RFC 2128.

CISCO-VOICE-DIAL-CONTROL-MIB

This MIB consists of four groups and a trap definition:

- **cvGatewayCallActive**—This group contains two tables—one for the telephony interfaces and one for the VoIP interfaces:

  - **cvCallActiveTable**—The voice extension to the call active table of the IETF Dial Control MIB (RFC 2128). It contains call leg information for voice encapsulation, which is derived from the statistics of the lower-layer telephony interface. Each call has a cvCallActiveEntry with information on the voice encapsulation call leg.

  - **cvVoIPCallActiveTable**—Contains the VoIP call leg information about specific VoIP call destinations and the selected QoS value for the call leg. cvVoIPCallActiveEntry is instantiated for a single call in progress. It offers IP-specific call details, such as the remote IP address and UDP port (cvVoIPCallActiveRemoteIPAddress, cvVoIPCallActiveRemoteUDPPort), round-trip delay (cvVoIPCallActiveRoundTripDelay), QoS (cvVoIPCallActiveSelectedQoS), and lost, early, and late packets.

- **cvGatewayCallHistory**—This group also has one table for the telephony interface and one for the VoIP interface:

  - **cvCallHistoryTable**—Stores information for each nonactive voice encapsulation call in cvCallHistoryEntry. It includes the call duration details (cvCallHistoryTxDuration, cvCallHistoryVoiceTxDuration, cvCallHistoryFaxTxDuration).

  - **cvVoIPCallHistoryTable**—Stores similar information, but VoIP-related. cvVoIPCallHistoryEntry holds the remote system details (cvVoIPCallHistoryRemoteIPAddress, cvVoIPCallHistoryRemoteUDPPort) and performance statistics (cvVoIPCallHistoryRoundTripDelay, cvVoIPCallHistorySelectedQoS, cvVoIPCallHistoryIcpif).

- **cvPeer**—The objects in this group are responsible for voice-related peer configuration, which controls the dial string and the interface or session target for the call establishment to a peer on the telephony network or on the IP backbone.

- **cvGeneralConfiguration**—This group contains one object (cvGeneralPoorQoVNotificationEnable), which indicates whether a trap (cvdcPoorQoVNotification) should be generated for poor-quality-of-voice calls.

CISCO-VOICE-COMMON-DIAL-CONTROL-MIB

This MIB also extends RFC 2128 by offering voice-related objects that are common across more than one network encapsulation (such as VoIP, VoATM, and VoFR). These objects are structured into two MIB groups:

- **cvCommonDcCallActive**—This group has one table (cvCommonDcCallActiveTable) with an instance of cvCommonDcCallActiveEntry for each call in progress. Information such as the global call identifier (cvCommonDcCallActiveConnectionId) and call-specific details are stored.

- **cvCommonDcCallHistory**—This group also has one table (cvCommonDcCallHistoryTable) that stores the details from the active table (cvCommonDcCallActiveTable) after call completion.

CISCO-CALL-HISTORY-MIB

The Call History MIB includes ciscoCallHistoryTable, which contains information about specific calls. Here is a selection of relevant table elements:

- **ciscoCallHistoryEntry**—Information on a single connection. The following MIB objects are instantiated for each call. They are indexed by ciscoCallHistoryStartTime and ciscoCallHistoryIndex:

    ciscoCallHistoryStartTime is the value of sysUpTime when this call history entry was created. This is useful for an NMS to retrieve all calls after a specific time.

    ciscoCallHistoryCallingNumber is the calling number for this call. This variable is instantiated if this is an incoming call.

    ciscoCallHistoryCalledNumber is the number this call is connected to. This variable is instantiated if this is an outgoing call.

    ciscoCallHistoryCallConnectionTime is the value of sysUpTime when the call was connected.

    ciscoCallHistoryCallDisconnectTime is the value of sysUpTime when the call was last disconnected.

    ciscoCallHistoryConnectTimeOfDay is the time of day at the time of call connect.

ciscoCallHistoryDisonnectTimeOfDay is the time of day when the call disconnected.

ciscoCallHistoryTransmitPackets is the number of packets transmitted when this call was up.

ciscoCallHistoryTransmitBytes is the number of bytes transmitted when this call was up.

ciscoCallHistoryReceiveBytes is the number of packets received when this call was up.

ciscoCallHistoryReceivePackets is the number of bytes received when this call was up.

ciscoCallHistoryCurrency, ciscoCallHistoryCurrencyAmount, ciscoCallHistoryMultiplier are call billing details.

SIP MIB

The MIBs just described were created for legacy telephony services. Currently the IT industry is strongly moving toward Session Initiation Protocol (SIP)-based services, such as IP Multimedia Subsystem (IMS). SIP is an application-layer signaling protocol for creating, modifying, and terminating multimedia sessions, such as Internet telephone calls and multimedia conferences. SIP is defined in RFC 3261. Whereas the earlier voice architectures were built on central voice control, SIP is designed as a peer-to-peer protocol. The MIB for SIP is in a late draft status (draft-ietf-sip-mib-12.txt), close to completion, but it has not been implemented yet.

The SIP MIB describes a set of managed objects that are used to manage SIP entities, which include User Agents, Proxy, Redirect, and Registrar servers. The goal is to provide a basic set of management functions for SIP devices. (Managing SIP applications and services is out of the scope of this discussion.) These include basic device configuration operations, which also means that the MIB has both read-only and read-write objects. Although this book is not a SIP reference, the major SIP entities are as follows:

- **User Agent Client (UAC)** is a logical entity that creates new requests, such as a phone call. The UAC role lasts for only the duration of that transaction, which means that a SIP-based application that initiates a request acts as a UAC for the duration of that transaction. If it receives a request later, it assumes the role of a User Agent Server (UAS) for the processing of that transaction.

- **User Agent Server (UAS)** is the counterpart to the UAC because it responds to SIP requests. The request can be accepted, rejected, or redirected. The UAS role lasts for only the duration of a transaction. From a voice application perspective, both the UAC and UAS should be implemented for calls to be initiated and received.

- **Proxy server** is an intermediary entity that acts as both a server and a client for the purpose of making requests on behalf of other clients. A proxy server primarily plays the role of routing by ensuring that a request is sent to an entity that is "closer" to the targeted user. Proxies are also useful for enforcing policy, because they can rewrite specific parts of a request message before forwarding it.

  Proxy servers can have three different flavors: stateless, transaction stateful, or call stateful:

  — A stateless proxy does not maintain the client or server transaction state machines. It forwards every request it receives downstream and every response it receives upstream.

  — A transaction stateful proxy, also called a stateful proxy, maintains the client and server transaction state during the processing of a request.

  — A call stateful proxy retains the state for a dialog from the initiating message to the terminating request. A call stateful proxy is always transaction stateful, but the converse is not necessarily true.

- **Redirect server** is a user agent server that accepts requests from clients and directs the client to contact an alternative set of Uniform Resource Identifiers (URI).

- **Registrar** is a server that accepts register requests and places the request information into the location service for the domain it handles.

Figure 4-2 illustrates the different SIP components.

Figure 4-2 *SIP Architecture*

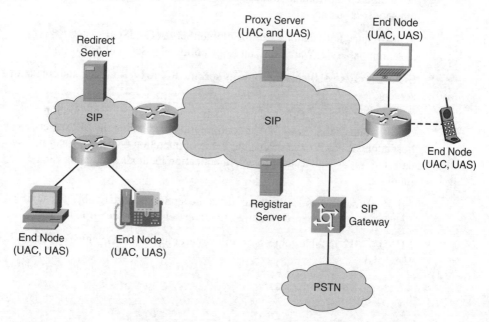

Four modules are specified in the SIP MIB:

- **SIP-TC-MIB** defines the textual conventions used throughout MIB modules.
- **SIP-COMMON-MIB** defines management objects common to all SIP entities, as just described. Different groups and tables exist for configuration, monitoring, and notifications.

  The sipCommonCfgBase object includes the SIP protocol version, the type of SIP entity (UA, Proxy, Redirect, or Registrar server), the operational and administrative status, the SIP organization name, the maximum number of SIP transactions an entity can manage, etc. The sipCommonCfgTimer object group defines timer configuration objects applicable to SIP user agent and stateful SIP proxy entities.

  Various statistics tables are defined for monitoring purposes, such as the summary of all requests and responses (sipCommonSummaryStats), the number of in and out SIP responses on a per-method basis (sipCommonStatusCode), a gauge reflecting the number of transactions currently awaiting definitive responses (sipCommonStatsTrans), a counter for retransmissions (sipCommonStatsRetry), and other statistics (sipCommonOtherStats).

  SNMP notification objects are defined by the sipCommonNotifObjects object group. The monitoring indicator sipCommonStatusCodeNotif shows that a specific status code was sent or received. Threshold notifications can be configured. sipCommonStatusCodeThreshExceededNotif indicates that a threshold was breached.

  Status-related notifications are sipCommonServiceColdStart, sipCommonServiceWarmStart, and sipCommonCfgServiceLastChange.

- **SIP-SERVER-MIB** contains objects specific to Proxy, Redirect, and Registrar servers.

  The server (sipServerCfg) and proxy (sipServerProxyCfg) configuration object groups define basic server configurations, including the SIP server host address. For Proxy servers, the mode of operation (stateless, stateful, call stateful) as well as the proxy authentication methods and realm, can be modified.

  SIP Registrar servers are configured via the sipServerRegCfg object group. Statistics can be obtained from the sipServerRegStats object group.

- **SIP-UA-MIB** includes objects specific to user agents (UA), which can act as both a UAC and a UAS.

The sipUACfgServer object group specifies SIP server configuration objects applicable to SIP user agents, including the IP address of the SIP server to register, proxy, or redirect calls.

Creating New MIB Objects: EXPRESSION-MIB

Even though the previous sections on generic accounting and performance MIBs and the technology-specific MIBs were comprehensive, you might experience situations in which the required managed object does not exist. As initially described in RFC 1213, a common MIB design principle is to minimize the number of managed objects:

"To avoid redundant variables, it was required that no object be included that can be derived from others in the MIB."

A typical example is link utilization. To graph a real-time view of a link's utilization, the NMS needs to poll three variables (ifInOctets, ifOutOctets, and ifSpeed) on a regular basis, insert the values in a formula, calculate the results, and graph the utilization. Rather than filling more MIBs with standardized objects, the EXPRESSION-MIB supports externally defined expressions of existing MIB objects. The EXPRESSION-MIB is a way to create and customize MIB objects for monitoring purposes.

Although new objects can reduce network traffic and overhead on network management systems, this is not the main reason to create new variables. The real benefit of the Expression-MIB is that using the new MIB variables in conjunction with the thresholding capabilities from the RMON-MIB (event and alarm group, as discussed in Chapter 5) or the EVENT-MIB (discussed in a moment) enables self-monitoring for network elements. Instead of a network management application regularly polling devices for potential faults, the network element monitors itself and sends a notification if a threshold violation occurs. Wildcarding is an interesting feature of the Expression-MIB, because a single expression can be applied to multiple instances of the same MIB object. A similar expression is applied to all a router's interfaces, and only a single entry is required in the EXPRESSION-MIB. For example, the link utilization for all interfaces can be monitored with a single entry.

Initially sketched by Cisco engineers, the idea of the EXPRESSION-MIB was proposed to the IETF DISMAN (Distributed Management) working group. It was accepted as a working group item, improved, and published as the standard track RFC 2982. Currently Cisco IOS implements only an earlier draft version of RFC 2982. The differences between the draft version and RFC 2982 are minor from a technical standpoint. The biggest change is that the draft implements the managed OID in the Cisco namespace, as opposed to the IANA standard namespace.

EXPRESSION-MIB Examples

The EXPRESSION-MIB can be configured only via SNMP. The IOS CLI commands are limited to **show** commands and debugging operations. The main example described in this section enables the network element to monitor the utilization of its links. When combined with the EVENT-MIB (described in the next section), this example permits a simple link capacity monitoring and planning tool. If the link utilization rises above 50 percent during one hour, a notification is sent to the network management station, indicating that it might be time to upgrade the link capacity.

In this example, you create a new MIB variable, *e1exp*, which is refreshed every 60 seconds, for the link utilization of the half-duplex interface with ifIndex = 6:

$$\text{e1exp} = \frac{(\text{delta (ifInOctets.6)} + \text{delta (ifOutOctets.6)}) * 8 * 100}{\text{delta (sysUpTime)} * \text{ifSpeed.6}}$$

The router is accessed with SNMP2c (SNMP version 2c), the read-write community string is private, and the SNMP tool net-snmp is used. In this example, managed objects are set to integer, unsigned, string, and object identifier, respectively represented by i, u, s, and o in the net-snmp syntax.

To avoid confusion with an existing entry, the expNameStatus managed object entry must be destroyed (delete = integer 6) before the new entry is set up (createAndWait = integer 5). See the RowStatus SNMPv2 textual convention for more details. The entry index is 101.49.101.120.112, which is the ASCII form of e1exp:

```
SERVER % snmpset -v 2c -c private router expNameStatus.101.49.101.120.112 i 6
SERVER % snmpset -v 2c -c private router expNameStatus.101.49.101.120.112 i 5
```

As a unique numeric identification for the object entry, expExpressionIndex is set to 1:

```
SERVER % snmpset -v 2c -c private router expExpressionIndex.101.49.101.120.112 u 1
```

A comment is added for the object entry—expExpressionComment.1. .1 is the chosen expExpressionIndex:

```
SERVER % snmpset -v 2c -c private router expExpressionComment.1 s "e1 expression"
```

The refresh time for the generation of this object entry is defined by expExpressionDeltaInterval. In this case, the chosen interval is 60 seconds:

```
SERVER % snmpset -v 2c -c private router expExpressionDeltaInterval.1 i 60
```

This expression calculates the utilization, with the parameters $1, $2, $3, and $4, as defined later. This expression type is an integer32 (expExpressionValueType = 4):

```
SERVER % snmpset -v 2c -c private router expExpression.1 s '($1+$2)*800/($3*$4)'
SERVER % snmpset -v 2c -c private router expExpressionValueType.1 i 4
```

Now you create (createAndWait = integer 5) the formula's four parameters. As mentioned, a good practice is to delete all existing entries (delete = integer 6) to avoid any preset values.

See the RowStatus SNMPv2 textual convention for more details. These are the executed operations:

```
SERVER % snmpset -v 2c -c private router expObjectStatus.1.1 i 6
SERVER % snmpset -v 2c -c private router expObjectStatus.1.2 i 6
SERVER % snmpset -v 2c -c private router expObjectStatus.1.3 i 6
SERVER % snmpset -v 2c -c private router expObjectStatus.1.4 i 6
SERVER % snmpset -v 2c -c private router expObjectStatus.1.1 i 5
SERVER % snmpset -v 2c -c private router expObjectStatus.1.2 i 5
SERVER % snmpset -v 2c -c private router expObjectStatus.1.3 i 5
SERVER % snmpset -v 2c -c private router expObjectStatus.1.4 i 5
```

The formula's four parameters are configured next, as $1 = ifInOctets.6, $2 = ifOutOctets.6, $3 = SysUpTime.0, and $4 = ifSpeed.6:

```
SERVER % snmpset -v 2c -c private router expObjectID.1.1 o .1.3.6.1.2.1.2.2.1.10.6
SERVER % snmpset -v 2c -c private router expObjectID.1.2 o .1.3.6.1.2.1.2.2.1.16.6
SERVER % snmpset -v 2c -c private router expObjectID.1.3 o .1.3.6.1.2.1.1.3.0
SERVER % snmpset -v 2c -c private router expObjectID.1.4 o .1.3.6.1.2.1.2.2.1.5.6
```

The expObjectSampleType object specifies whether the parameters are absolute (integer 1) or delta (integer 2) values:

```
SERVER % snmpset -v 2c -c private router expObjectSampleType.1.1 i 2
SERVER % snmpset -v 2c -c private router expObjectSampleType.1.2 i 2
SERVER % snmpset -v 2c -c private router expObjectSampleType.1.3 i 2
SERVER % snmpset -v 2c -c private router expObjectSampleType.1.4 i 1
```

The expObjectIDWildcard object indicates whether the parameters use wildcards; true = integer 1, and false = integer 2:

```
SERVER % snmpset -v 2c -c private router expObjectIDWildcard.1.1 i 2
SERVER % snmpset -v 2c -c private router expObjectIDWildcard.1.2 i 2
SERVER % snmpset -v 2c -c private router expObjectIDWildcard.1.3 i 2
SERVER % snmpset -v 2c -c private router expObjectIDWildcard.1.4 i 2
```

Finally, the four object entries and the e1exp expression entries are activated (active = integer 1):

```
SERVER % snmpset -v 2c -c private router expObjectStatus.1.1 i 1
SERVER % snmpset -v 2c -c private router expObjectStatus.1.2 i 1
SERVER % snmpset -v 2c -c private router expObjectStatus.1.3 i 1
SERVER % snmpset -v 2c -c private router expObjectStatus.1.4 i 1
SERVER % snmpset -v 2c -c private router expNameStatus.101.49.101.120.112 i 1
```

At this point, the configuration and activation of the new MIB variable are completed, and the network element starts the self-monitoring of the link utilization of a specific interface. The new MIB variable e1exp contains the link utilization; it is calculated every 60 seconds. Wildcard operations could be the next step to multiply this setup to match all interfaces of a network element.

The possibilities for the EXPRESSION-MIB are numerous:

- When there is no counter for the sum of entries in a MIB table, the EXPRESSION-MIB can create an expression (such as numEntries) that matches the number of entries in this table. A second expression (such as sumEntries) can then sum up the total number of entries in the first expression.

- For an access router to send a fault notification for only high-speed interfaces above 100 kbps, the EXPRESSION-MIB creates a wildcard expression (such as ifSpeedHigh), which contains the results of the expression: ifSpeed > 100000 and ifOperStatus = 2. The EVENT-MIB generates a notification when the expression ifSpeedHigh is true (integer 1).

The main use of the EXPRESSION-MIB is to offer customized objects for the EVENT-MIB. The collaboration between the two MIBs is described in the next section.

EVENT-MIB Associated with EXPRESSION-MIB

In 2000, Cisco engineers proposed the idea of the EVENT-MIB to the IETF DISMAN working group. It was accepted as a working group item, improved, and published as the standard track RFC 2981. It provides the ability to monitor MIB objects on a network element by using SNMP and to initiate simple actions whenever a trigger condition is met. Actions can be SNMP notifications or SNMP set operations of MIB objects. When notifications are triggered by events, the NMS no longer needs to poll the network elements constantly to identify changes. A simple "status poll" is enough to monitor that the network element is still alive.

Following the EXPRESSION-MIB example regarding link utilization, the EVENT-MIB can poll the newly created managed object e1exp on a regular basis, set a threshold violation policy, and send a notification if the threshold is exceeded.

Without going into detail, the EVENT-MIB offers many advantages and superior flexibility compared to the RMON events and alarms:

- **Managed object existence** can be used to test the existence of a managed object. A typical example is to test if a second power supply is present or missing.

- **Boolean tests** provide operations such as greater than, greater than or equal to, equal to, not equal to, less than, and less than or equal to.

- **Wildcarding** speeds up the configuration, because a single EVENT-MIB entry can monitor indexed managed objects. For example, an entry polling ifOperStatus.* checks the operational status of all interfaces on the network element.

- **Options to customize SNMP notifications** increase the operator's flexibility. Following the example of monitoring ifOperStatus.*, customized linkUp/linkDown notifications can be sent. A useful example is to use the sysContact object, which contains the administrator contact information for a particular network element.

Without the EXPRESSION-MIB capabilities, the EVENT-MIB monitoring would be limited to the existing objects in other MIBs, which explains why the combination of both MIBs provides the best results.

Obtaining MIBs

You might be wondering where you can find MIBs. The suggested starting point for Cisco MIBs is http://www.cisco.com/go/mibs. It offers a set a powerful tools, such as the MIB Locator, SNMP Object Navigator, MIBs for Cisco IOS and non-IOS products, and various technical tips about MIBs in general and how to load them onto the NMS.

If you are looking for IETF RFCs, you can check http://www.rfc-editor.org/ or http://www.faqs.org/rfcs/; these are IETF archives. If instead you want to find "work-in-progress documents" (drafts), a good search engine is the Draft Tracker, at https://datatracker.ietf.org/. You can find new tools at http://tools.ietf.org/.

Here are some simple examples. Note that the tool also allows queries that are more complex.

Find out which devices support the EXPRESSION-MIB:

1 Go to http://www.cisco.com/go/mibs and start the MIB Locator.

2 Select the EXPRESSION-MIB from the list of MIBs.

   Result: 75304 entries found.

3 Narrow the search by IOS release, platform family, or feature set.

   By selecting IOS 12.1(3), you reduce the number of results to 197. Next, you can select the desired platform or feature set or just browse through the results. If you select the IP PLUS image, 13 results remain.

Translate the OID into an object name or the object name into an OID to receive object details:

1 Go to http://www.cisco.com/go/mibs and start the SNMP Object Navigator.

2 Enter the MIB object name, such as ifHCInMulticastPkts.

   Click Translate, which displays the following results:

   Object: ifHCInMulticastPkts
   OID: 1.3.6.1.2.1.31.1.1.1.8
   Type: Counter64
   Permission: read-only
   Status: current
   MIB: IF-MIB

3 Click View Supporting Images, which results in a long list of all supported IOS images.

Display all MIBs that are supported by a particular IOS release:

1 Go to http://www.cisco.com/go/mibs and start the MIB Locator.

2 Select the following:

IOS release: 12.2(16)
Device: 3660
Image: IP PLUS

You see the following results:

Image information: c3660-is-mz.12.2-16
MIBs supported in this image: A list of 132 MIBs is displayed.

Identify the MIB dependencies for the EXPRESSION-MIB, list the compilation sequence, and download the MIB(s):

1 Go to http://www.cisco.com/go/mibs and start the SNMP Object Navigator.

2 Click MIB Support in Software.

3 Click View and Download MIBs.

   a You can choose a MIB or browse through the list.

   b You can view the MIB content or MIB dependencies and download the MIB. This step provides useful help.

The result for the EXPRESSION-MIB is the following MIB sequence:

— SNMPv2-SMI

— SNMPv2-TC

— SNMPv2-CONF

— SNMPv2-MIB

— CISCO-SMI

— IANAifType-MIB

— RFC1155-SMI

— RFC-1212

— RFC1213-MIB

— IF-MIB

— CISCO-TC

— SNMPv2-SMI-v1

— SNMPv2-TC-v1

— EXPRESSION-MIB

In addition to a specific MIB file, another relevant file is CAPABILITY. It describes the implementation details—specifically, per platform. Capability statements are used when describing functionality of agents with respect to object and event notification definitions. RFC 2580 defines the AGENT-CAPABILITIES construct, which is used to concisely convey such capabilities. Here is an example:

Identify the MIB capabilities of the CISCO-PING-MIB:

1 Go to http://www.cisco.com/go/mibs and start the SNMP Object Navigator.

2 Click MIB Support in Software.

3 Click View and Download MIBs.

4 Choose the CISCO-PING-MIB:

In the section More Downloads you see Capability File: CISCO-PING-CAPABILITY.

This links to the capability file, CISCO-PING-CAPABILITY.

Alternatively, you can download the file from ftp://ftp.cisco.com/pub/mibs/v2/CISCO-PING-CAPABILITY.my.

Afterwards, you can extract the details:

```
ciscoPingCapabilityV10R02 AGENT-CAPABILITIES
    PRODUCT-RELEASE    "Cisco IOS 10.2"
    STATUS             current
    DESCRIPTION        "Cisco Ping MIB capabilities."
    SUPPORTS           CISCO-PING-MIB
        INCLUDES       { ciscoPingMIBGroup }
    ::= { ciscoPingCapability 1 }
```

The preceding seven lines explain that ciscoPingMIBGroup has been supported since IOS release 10.2.

The file contains more details:

```
ciscoPingCapabilityCatOSV08R0301 AGENT-CAPABILITIES
    PRODUCT-RELEASE    "Cisco CatOS 8.3(1)."
    STATUS             current
    DESCRIPTION        "CISCO-PING-MIB capabilities."
    SUPPORTS           CISCO-PING-MIB
        INCLUDES       { ciscoPingMIBGroupVpn }
        VARIATION      ciscoPingVrfName
            ACCESS     not-implemented
            DESCRIPTION
                       "Information not available on CatOS."
```

These ten lines explain that ciscoPingMIBGroupVpn has been supported since Cisco CatOS 8.3 (1); however, ciscoPingVrfName is not implemented.

If you are interested in a specific MIB, but you do not like reading MIBs in plain text, http://www.mibdepot.com/ graphically represents the MIB context. After searching for the MIB, you can display a summary view, a tree view, and a detailed view.

CHAPTER 5

RMON

After studying this chapter, you have a good understanding of the capabilities of the Remote Monitoring (RMON) series of MIBs. A command-line reference plus SNMP MIB details and configuration examples makes this chapter content quickly applicable.

RMON is a set of standardized MIB variables that monitor networks. All previously defined MIBs monitored only nodes. Even if RMON initially referred to only the RMON MIB, the term RMON now is often used to refer to the concept of remote monitoring and to the entire series of RMON MIB extensions. The standardization of RMON took place at the IETF RMON working group (now concluded), where many activities occurred over the last couple of years. This chapter covers the main RMON achievements in more detail. Four main IETF standard MIBs are mentioned:

- **RMON 1 and RMON 2 MIBs**—Remote Monitoring MIB versions 1 and 2
- **DSMON MIB**—Remote Monitoring MIB Extensions for Differentiated Services
- **SMON MIB**—Remote Network Monitoring MIB Extensions for Switched Networks
- **APM MIB**—Application Performance Measurement MIB

It is important to understand that these are separate MIBs with the purpose of providing in-depth statistics for monitoring certain network environments. They are not special *protocols*, but MIB *extensions* that are accessed with SNMP (as described in Chapter 4, "SNMP and MIBs"). Each MIB is explained in detail, followed by Cisco IOS command-line examples in conjunction with SNMP commands (where applicable) to illustrate the two approaches to configuring and monitoring these MIBs.

RMON 1 and RMON 2 MIBs

The initial goal of RMON was to monitor network traffic in a local-area network (LAN) environment and to provide comprehensive information for network fault diagnosis, planning, and performance tuning to network administrators. RMON implements a passive collection approach that measures specific aspects of the traffic without interfering by adding monitoring traffic. RMON can be implemented in network elements, such as Cisco routers and switches, or it can be deployed using dedicated RMON probes. The RMON specifications are quite mature. The first RMON MIB for Ethernet was issued as RFC 1271 in 1991. Later, this specification was superseded by RFC 1757 for SMIv1 and by RFC 2819 for SMIv2. In parallel, the RMON MIB for Token Ring environments was specified in RFC 1513.

Although RMON became successful, implementations made it clear that monitoring on OSI Layer 2 was limited when monitoring wide-area network (WAN) traffic (OSI Layer 3 and above), which led to further extensions, defined by RFC 2021, *Remote Network Monitoring Management Information Base Version 2 using SMIv2*. RMON version 2 (RMON 2) is an extension to RMON version 1 (RMON 1), which refers to the initial RMON specifications monitoring on OSI Layer 2. RMON 2 focuses on the layers of traffic above the Media Access Control (MAC) layer; the main enhancement of RMON 2 is the capability to measure Layer 3 network traffic and application statistics.

RMON 1 and 2 provide a comprehensive set of monitoring details that requires more resources from the SNMP agent than typical MIBs. To balance monitoring capabilities and resource consumption, the implementation of the groups in this MIB is optional, which means that vendors can select which groups to implement. However, chosen groups must be implemented completely, including all objects of the group. Cisco implements the Alarms and Events groups on all routers and Catalyst switches, which additionally support the Statistics and History groups; the support of these four groups is called "Mini-RMON." Figure 5-1 illustrates the RMON tree, where groups 1 through 10 represent RMON 1 (groups 1 to 9 are for Ethernet, and group 10 is specific to Token Ring) and groups 11 through 20 correspond to RMON 2.

Figure 5-1 *RMON MIB Tree*

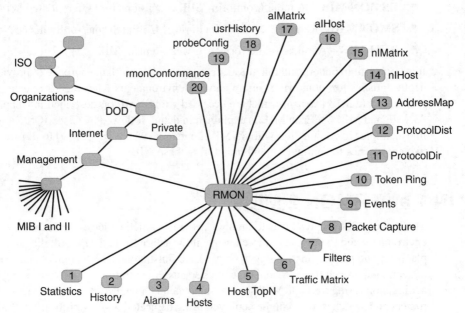

Table 5-1 offers details about RMON 1 groups. Table 5-2 provides additional information about RMON 2 groups, where the extensions mostly concentrate on the higher layers of the protocol stack. More details on Table 5-2 can be found in RFC 3577.

Table 5-1   *RMON 1 Groups*

RMON 1 Group	Function	Elements
Statistics	Contains statistics measured by the RMON probe for each monitored interface on this device.	Packets dropped, packets sent, bytes sent (octets), broadcast packets, multicast packets, CRC errors, runts, giants, fragments, jabbers, collisions, and counters for packets ranging from 64 to 128, 128 to 256, 256 to 512, 512 to 1024, and 1024 to 1518 bytes.
History	Records periodic statistical samples from a network and stores them for later retrieval.	Sample period, number of samples, items sampled.
Alarms	Periodically takes statistical samples from variables in the probe and compares them with previously configured thresholds. If the monitored variable crosses a threshold, an event is generated.	Includes the alarm table: alarm type, interval, starting threshold, stop threshold. Note: The Alarms group requires the implementation of the Events group.
Hosts	Contains statistics associated with each host discovered on the LAN.	Host MAC address, packets, and bytes received and transmitted, as well as number of broadcast, multicast, and error packets.
HostTopN	Prepares tables that describe the hosts that top a list ordered by one of their base statistics over an interval specified by the management station. Thus, these statistics are rate-based.	Statistics, host(s), sample start and stop periods, rate base, and duration.
Traffic Matrix	Stores statistics for conversations between sets of two MAC addresses. As the device detects a new conversation, it creates a new entry in its table.	Source and destination MAC address pairs and packets, bytes, and errors for each conversation.
Filters	Enables packets to be matched by a filter equation. These matched packets form a data stream that might be captured or that might generate events.	Bit-filter type (mask or not mask), filter expression (bit level), conditional expression (and, or, not) to other filters.
Packet Capture	Enables packets to be captured.	Size of buffer for captured packets, full status (alarm), and number of captured packets.
Events	Controls the generation and notification of events from this device.	Event type, description, the last time the event was sent.
Token Ring	Provides additional statistics for Token Ring networks.	MAC layer statistics, promiscuous statistics, MAC layer history, promiscuous history, ring station order table, alarms, events.

Table 5-2 *RMON 2 Groups*

RMON 2 Group	Function
protocolDir	Lists the protocols supported by the RMON probe. Allows the addition, deletion, and configuration of entries in this list.
protocolDist	Shows statistics (number of octets and packets) on a per-protocol basis.
addressMap	Lists MAC address to network address bindings and the interface they were last seen on.
nlHost	Network Layer Host group. Counts the amount of traffic sent from and to each discovered network address.
nlMatrix	Network Layer Matrix group. Counts the amount of traffic sent between each pair of discovered network addresses.
alHost	Application Layer Host group. Counts the amount of traffic, per protocol, sent from and to each discovered network address.
alMatrix	Application Layer Matrix group. Counts the amount of traffic, per protocol, sent between each pair of discovered network addresses.
usrHistory	User History group. Combines mechanisms from the Alarms and History groups to provide history collection based on user-defined criteria.
probeConfig	Controls the configuration of RMON features.
rmonConformance	Describes conformance requirements.

From an Accounting and Performance Management perspective, not all 20 groups are equally important. The Alarms and Events groups are mainly used for fault management purposes by defining triggers for rising and falling alarm thresholds. The Statistics and History groups provide valuable input for Performance Management. The application and network layer Host and Matrix groups are relevant for Accounting purposes, because they can identify individual host addresses.

RMON 1 and 2, as defined by RFC 2819 and RFC 2021, respectively, define only 32-bit counters, which is an issue for 100-Mbps and Gigabit ports. RFC 3273, *Remote Network Monitoring Management Information Base for High Capacity Networks*, also referred to as "HC-RMON," has been updated by RFC 4502, *Remote Network Monitoring Management Information Base Version 2*. It offers 64-bit counters for each of the tables in the RMON 1, RMON 2, and Token Ring extension MIBs, except for the mediaIndependentTable. RFC 3434, *Remote Monitoring MIB Extensions for High Capacity Alarms*, specifies managed objects for extending the alarm thresholding capabilities found in RFC 2819 to provide similar threshold monitoring of objects based on the Counter64 data type.

The rmonConformance group was added in RMON 2. Subgroups provide details about the support of RMON 1, RMON 2, SMON, HCMON, etc. This group is very helpful for identifying which specific RMON group is supported by the network elements, because polling it from an NMS station returns the provided functions.

RMON Principles

The principles of RMON are as follows:

- It is a set of standardized MIB variables monitoring networks.

- It offers information that lets administrators analyze network utilization, including data and error statistics.

- RMON 1 includes only data link layer (Layer 2) details.

- RMON 2 offers network layer to application layer details (Layer 3 and up).

- Collection data is accessible via SNMP, and the initial configuration can be done by CLI or SNMP. To retrieve the collection results via SNMP, you need to enable SNMP on the network element first. When configuring SNMP, distinguish between read-only access and read-write access. For more details about SNMP configuration, see Chapter 4.

- The RMON MIBs contain only 32-bit SNMP counters, unless RFC 3273 or RFC 4502 is used.

- The MIB objects are intended as an interface between a network agent and a management application; they are not intended for direct manipulation by humans. These functions should be handled by the network management application. This suggestion is generally applicable to all MIB variables mentioned!

Supported Devices and IOS Versions

The following list defines the devices and Cisco IOS Software Releases that support RMON:

- RMON was introduced in IOS 11.1.

- Polling the probeCapabilities MIB object identifier (OID) (from the probeConfig group) indicates which RMON 1 and 2 groups are supported on at least one interface by this RMON probe.

- Full RMON 1 and 2 functionality is supported by external probes, such as the Network Analysis Module (NAM) for the Cisco Catalyst switches, and the branch router series NAM.

- Cisco routers support the Alarms and Events groups.

- Cisco Catalyst switches support the Alarms, Events, Statistics, and History groups.

- A special IOS image is offered for the Cisco 2500 and AS5200 routers to support nine RMON 1 groups for Ethernet interfaces. In IOS 12.0(5)T, the RMON agent for these platforms has been rewritten to improve performance and add new features.

- Polling hcRMONCapabilities indicates which High Capacity RMON MIB groups (RFC 3273) are supported on at least one interface by this probe. For example, high-capacity counter extensions for the Ethernet and History groups are included in the Cisco 6000 and 7600.

- Cisco routers and switches currently do not support RFC 3434; however, CISCO-HC-ALARM-MIB, which is based on an interim Internet draft, is supported on the MDS 9000.

For up-to-date information, check the Cisco Feature Navigator home page at http://www.cisco.com/go/fn.

Cisco NAM Modules

Because of the extensive CPU and resource impact of full RMON 1 and 2 implementations, Cisco invented a separate monitoring module—the NAM—for the Cisco Catalyst 6500 and 7600 router series. It gives network managers visibility into all layers of network traffic by providing RMON 1 and 2 functions as well as support for SMON, DSMON, HC-RMON, and ART. The NAM adds to the built-in "mini-RMON" features (which support the Alarms, Events, Statistics, and History groups) in Cisco Catalyst 6500 series switches and Cisco 7600 series routers that provide port-level traffic statistics at the MAC or data link layer. The NAM provides functions to analyze traffic flows for applications, hosts, conversations, and network-based services such as quality of service (QoS) and voice over IP (VoIP).

Related to the NAM, Cisco Catalyst switches provide a relevant concept to better leverage the RMON probes and NAM modules, which is the Switched Port Analyzer (SPAN) and Remote SPAN (RSPAN) port concept. The operator can configure any interface to act as a copy port, where selected traffic is transmitted. An external RMON probe can be connected to the SPAN port and therefore receive traffic for in-depth analysis. The source can be any of the following:

- A single physical port
- Multiple physical ports
- A single VLAN
- Multiple VLANs

The operator can also define the traffic direction for the copy function:

- Received traffic only
- Transmitted traffic only
- Received and transmitted traffic

An extension to the initial SPAN concept is the RSPAN function at the Catalyst 6500, which enables remote copy functions among different switches to better leverage deployed

NAMs. This concept was adopted by the SMON standard in the portCopy function. A later feature is Encapsulated Remote SPAN (ERSPAN), which overcomes the Layer 2 link limitation of RSPAN. ERSPAN can send captured packets with Generic Route Encapsulation (GRE) via a routed network.

Supported MIB groups in NAM software version 3.5 are as follows:

- **MIB-II (RFC 1213)**—All groups except Exterior Gateway Protocol (EGP) and transmission
- **RMON (RFC 2819)**—All groups
- **RMON 2 (RFC 2021)**—All groups
- **SMON (RFC2613)**—DataSourceCaps and smonStats
- **DSMON (RFC 3287)**—All groups
- **HC-RMON (RFC 3273)**—All groups except medialIndependentGroup
- **Application Response Time (ART)**—All groups

To address the need for traffic monitoring in enterprise branch offices, Cisco developed the branch router series NAM for the Cisco 2600XM, Cisco 2691, Cisco 2800, Cisco 3660, Cisco 3700, and Cisco 3800 series access routers. It can be considered a small version of the 6500 NAM, with similar functionality and fewer performance and storage capabilities.

CLI Operations

From an accounting and performance perspective, RMON support at the Cisco routers is of limited use, because they support only the Alarms and Events groups, which mainly address fault management requirements. In addition to the Alarms and Events groups, the Catalyst switches also support the Statistics and History groups, which are relevant for performance management. Therefore, this configuration section covers only the statistics and history RMON functions of a Catalyst switch. Notable commands are as follows:

- Switch(config-if)# **rmon collection stats** *index* [**owner** *ownername*]
  enables the RMON 1 Statistics group. The index is any arbitrary number that has not yet been used.

- Switch(config-if)# **rmon collection history** *index* [**buckets** *bucket-number*] [**interval** *seconds*] [**owner** *ownername*]
  enables history collection for the specified number of buckets and time period. The index is any arbitrary number that has not yet been used. Because this index is different from the **rmon collection stats** index (they come from two different MIB tables), it does not have to contain the same value. However, you should use the same value for both indexes, because it makes troubleshooting easier.

- Switch(config-if)# **rmon** {**native** | **promiscuous**}
  In native mode, RMON monitors only the packets targeted toward the interface. In promiscuous mode, RMON monitors all packets on the LAN segment.

Note that the syntax is similar for the routers. For more information, refer to the IOS commands **rmon collection host** and **rmon collection matrix**.

SNMP Operations

The RMON 1 and 2 MIBs are large and comprehensive, so only the main concepts are described in this section. For further information, refer to *SNMP, SNMPv2, SNMPv3, and RMON 1 and 2*, Third Edition, by William Stallings (Addison-Wesley Professional, 1998).

RMON Row Concept

Because of the complex nature of the available features in the RMON MIB, most functions need initial parameter configuration before the RMON agent (router, switch, probe, NAM blade) can activate the data collection operation.

Many functional groups in this MIB have one or more control tables to set up control parameters and one or more data tables where the results of the operation are stored. The control tables are typically read-write, and the data tables are typically read-only. Because the parameters in the control table often describe results in the associated data table, many of the parameters can be modified only when the control entry is inactive. Thus, the method for modifying these parameters is first to invalidate the control entry, causing its deletion and the deletion of any associated data entries, and then to create a new control entry with the modified parameters. Deleting the control entry also is a convenient way to reclaim the resources used by the associated data. A similar approach is taken for row creation, suspension, and deletion, as explained in more details next.

In the initial RMON MIB, the EntryStatus textual convention was introduced to provide table entry creation, validation, and deletion. This function then was added to the SNMP framework as the RowStatus textual convention (RFC 2579, *Textual Conventions for SMIv2*). The RowStatus textual convention is used to define all new tables. The old RMON 1 MIB (RFC 2819) uses EntryStatus, and the new RMON 2 MIB (RFC 2021) uses RowStatus. However, the principles of EntryStatus and RowStatus are exactly the same. The following example from RFC 2579 explains the row concept in detail (see the RFC for the full description in the last line):

```
RowStatus::= TEXTUAL-CONVENTION
STATUS current
DESCRIPTION
"The status of a table entry..."
```

The status column has six defined values:

- **active** indicates that the conceptual row is available for use by the managed device.
- **notInService** indicates that the conceptual row exists in the agent but is unavailable for use by the managed device.

- **notReady** indicates that the conceptual row exists in the agent but is missing information it needs to be available for use by the managed device (i.e., one or more required columns in the conceptual row have not been instantiated).

- **createAndGo** is used by a management station that wants to create a new instance of a conceptual row and to have its status automatically set to active, making it available for use by the managed device.

- **createAndWait** is used by a management station that wants to create a new instance of a conceptual row without making it available for use by the managed device.

- **destroy** is used by a management station that wants to delete all the instances associated with an existing conceptual row.

active and notInService are states; values may be read or written.

notReady is also a state that can only be read, not written.

createAndGo, createAndWait, and destroy are actions, which can be written but are never read.

Rows can be created, suspended, and deleted:

- Conceptual row creation

    There are four potential interactions when creating a conceptual row:

    — Selecting an instance identifier that is not in use

    — Creating the conceptual row

    — Initializing any objects for which the agent does not supply a default

    — Making the conceptual row available for use by the managed device

- Conceptual row suspension

    When a conceptual row is "active," the management station may issue a management protocol set operation that sets the instance of the status column to notInService. If the agent is unwilling to do so, the set operation fails, with an error of wrongValue or inconsistentValue. Otherwise, the conceptual row is taken out of service, and a noError response is returned. It is the responsibility of the DESCRIPTION clause of the status column to indicate under what circumstances the status column should be taken out of service (in order for the value of some other column of the same conceptual row to be modified).

- Conceptual row deletion

    For deletion of conceptual rows, a management protocol set operation is issued that sets the instance of the status column to destroy. This request may be made regardless of the current value of the status column. It is possible to delete conceptual rows that are either notReady, notInService, or active. If the operation succeeds, all instances associated with the conceptual row are immediately removed.

Operations to Activate the Network Layer Host Group from the RMON 2 MIB

The RMON nlhost group (14) consists of an hlHostControlTable, which is responsible for creating the data table nlhostTable for collection operations afterwards. After the entry in the hostControlTable has been created with createAndGo (or createAndWait followed by "active"), the following parameters need to be set up:

- hlHostControlDataSource (source interface)
- hlHostControlNlMaxDesiredEntries (number of network layer entries)
- hlHostControlAlMaxDesiredEntries (number of application layer entries)
- hlHostControlOwner
- hlHostControlStatus

After they are set up, the entry can be activated with valid (1). From that point on, the RMON agent starts collecting the statistics in the nlhostTable.

Examples

The following example provides a systematic introduction to configuring and monitoring mini-RMON in the Cisco Catalyst switch. It displays the results for both CLI and SNMP. Because RMON 2 is required for a full collection of all RMON 2 parameters, an additional NAM example is provided afterwards.

Initial Configuration

The following example shows how to configure and monitor the RMON 1 Statistics and History groups on a switch:

```
switch(config)#int fastethernet 3/41
switch(config-if)#rmon promiscuous
switch(config-if)#rmon collection stats 333 owner me
switch(config-if)#rmon collection history 333 buckets 100 interval 3600 owner me
```

For configuration details on the Cisco NAM, refer to the online documentation at http://www.cisco.com/go/nam.

Collection Monitoring

```
switch#show rmon statistics
  Collection 333 on FastEthernet3/41 is active, and owned by me,
  Monitors ifEntry.1.67 which has
```

```
Received 3348827 octets, 41749 packets,
34673 broadcast and 6468 multicast packets,
0 undersized and 0 oversized packets,
0 fragments and 0 jabbers,
0 CRC alignment errors and 0 collisions.
# of dropped packet events (due to lack of resources): 0
# of packets received of length (in octets):
 64: 28441, 65-127: 11278, 128-255: 675,
 256-511: 1294, 512-1023: 61, 1024-1518:0
```

The router is accessed with SNMP2c (SNMP version 2c), the read community string is public, and the SNMP tool net-snmp is used. The snmpwalk for the Statistics group configuration is as follows:

```
SERVER % snmpwalk -c public -v 2c <switch> etherStatsTable
etherStatsIndex.333 = INTEGER: 333
etherStatsDataSource.333 = OID: RFC1213-MIB::ifIndex.67
etherStatsDropEvents.333 = Counter32: 0
etherStatsOctets.333 = Counter32: 3348827
etherStatsPkts.333 = Counter32: 41749
etherStatsBroadcastPkts.333 = Counter32: 34673
etherStatsMulticastPkts.333 = Counter32: 6468
etherStatsCRCAlignErrors.333 = Counter32: 0
etherStatsUndersizePkts.333 = Counter32: 0
etherStatsOversizePkts.333 = Counter32: 0
etherStatsFragments.333 = Counter32: 0
etherStatsJabbers.333 = Counter32: 0
etherStatsCollisions.333 = Counter32: 0
etherStatsPkts64Octets.333 = Counter32: 28441
etherStatsPkts65to127Octets.333 = Counter32: 11278
etherStatsPkts128to255Octets.333 = Counter32: 675
etherStatsPkts256to511Octets.333 = Counter32: 1294
etherStatsPkts512to1023Octets.333 = Counter32: 61
etherStatsPkts1024to1518Octets.333 = Counter32: 0
etherStatsOwner.333 = STRING: "me"
etherStatsStatus.333 = INTEGER: valid(1)
```

The snmpwalk of the etherHistoryTable MIB OID returns the same content as **show rmon history**:

```
switch#show rmon history
Entry 333 is active, and owned by me
 Monitors ifEntry.1.67 every 3600 second(s)
 Requested # of time intervals, ie buckets, is 100,
  Sample # 2554 began measuring at 6w6d
   Received 642 octets, 6 packets,
   0 broadcast and 6 multicast packets,
   0 undersized and 0 oversized packets,
   0 fragments and 0 jabbers,
   0 CRC alignment errors and 0 collisions.
   # of dropped packet events is 0
   Network utilization is estimated at 0
  Sample # 2555 began measuring at 6w6d
   Received 642 octets, 6 packets,
   0 broadcast and 6 multicast packets,
   0 undersized and 0 oversized packets,
   0 fragments and 0 jabbers,
   0 CRC alignment errors and 0 collisions.
   # of dropped packet events is 0
   Network utilization is estimated at 0
```

Figure 5-2 graphically illustrates **show rmon stats** with a report from the NAM.

Figure 5-2 *NAM RMON Statistics Example*

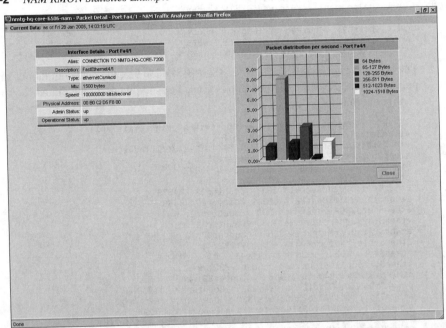

Figure 5-3 is an RMON 2 collection example. You see the RMON probe details in the top left corner. The bottom left part lists the discovered protocols and usage percentage per protocol. The upper right diagram provides received conversation details, separated by hosts, applications, and volume. The lower right covers the same details for traffic generated from this specific host.

DSMON MIB

Differentiated Services (DiffServ) monitoring, also called DSMON, is designed to monitor the network traffic usage of Differentiated Services Code Point (DSCP) values (0 to 63) as defined by RFC 2474. The DSMON MIB (Remote Monitoring MIB Extensions for Differentiated Services, specified by RFC 3287) extends the RMON mechanisms to support additional packet classification, based on DSCP values observed in monitored packets. By polling DSCP counters, a network management application can determine performance details, such as network throughput for traffic associated with different DSCPs.

Figure 5-3   *NAM RMON Host Conversation Example*

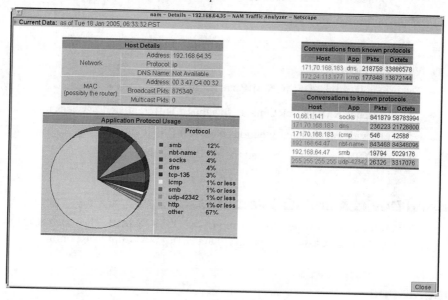

The DSMON MIB is intended to be implemented in RMON probes that support the RMON-2 MIB (RFC 2021). The DSMON functions should be implemented in conjunction with the associated RMON functions, but the MIB is independent of all other RMON data tables. Several concepts and even MIB objects from the RMON MIBs are used in the DSMON MIB. The RMON-2 MIB defines the protocolDirTable, which is a directory of all the protocols that the RMON-2 agent can decode and count. The DSMON MIB uses this directory to identify the protocols detected in monitored packets. The protocolDirLocalIndex MIB object is used to identify protocol encapsulations in all DSMON data tables, which classify and aggregate by protocol type in some manner. The DSMON MIB uses the "SNMPv1 coexistence" strategy adopted by the RMON working group. That is, where a 64-bit counter is provided, a 32-bit version of the counter and a 32-bit overflow counter are also provided. The DSMON MIB uses the same Top-*N* reporting MIB structure as the RMON-2 MIB. Top-*N* reporting can greatly reduce the polling overhead required to analyze DSCP usage patterns.

The DSMON MIB uses the following statistics:

- Full Duplex Interface Statistics
- Protocol Statistics
- Protocol Top-*N* Statistics
- Network Host Statistics
- Network Host Top-*N* Distribution

- Application Matrix Statistics
- Application Matrix Top-N Distribution

DSMON MIB Principles

The principles of the DSMON MIB are as follows:

- It extends RMON functionality to support Differentiated Services monitoring.
- It provides aggregated functions based on DSCP values.
- The MIB contains 32-bit and 64-bit SNMP counters.

Supported Devices and IOS Versions

Cisco routers and switches do not support the DSMON MIB. The Cisco NAM for the Catalyst 6500 series and the Branch Router Series NAM fully support it.

CLI Operations

Cisco routers and switches do not support DSMON. For configuration details on the Cisco NAM, refer to the online documentation at http://www.cisco.com/go/nam.

SNMP Operations

The DSMON MIB contains six groups of MIB objects:

- **dsmonAggregateControl group** controls the configuration of counter aggregation groups for the purpose of reducing the total number of counters maintained by the agent.
- **dsmonStatsObjects group** reports a distribution statistics per counter aggregation group for a particular RMON dataSource.
- **dsmonPdistObjects group** reports per-counter aggregation group distribution statistics for each application protocol detected on a particular RMON dataSource.
- **dsmonHostObjects group** reports host address distribution statistics for each counter aggregation group detected on a particular RMON dataSource.
- **dsmonCapsObjects group** reports the static DSMON MIB functional capabilities of the agent implementation.
- **dsmonMatrixObjects group** exports host address pair distribution statistics for each counter aggregation group detected on a particular RMON dataSource.

Examples

Cisco routers and switches do not support DSMON. For configuration details on the Cisco NAM, refer to the online documentation at http://www.cisco.com/go/nam.

Figure 5-4 shows the result of a DSCP monitoring run by the NAM. The various DSCP values are measured by traffic rate over time.

Figure 5-4 *NAM DSCP Monitoring Example*

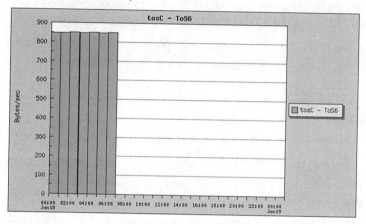

SMON MIB

When the RMON specification was developed, LANs were mainly shared Ethernet or Token Ring networks, and the virtual LAN (VLAN) concept did not exist. A monitoring device such as an RMON probe was connected to an Ethernet hub or Token Ring and it could see all the traffic from all the devices in this segment. With the advent of switches and VLANs, this concept was no longer operational, so extensions were required. Initially, Cisco supported VLAN monitoring by offering probes with an implementation of the Cisco VLAN Trunk Protocol (VTP). The standardization of VLANs and VLAN monitoring evolved in parallel, resulting in the IEEE 802.1Q standard for VLANs and SMON for network monitoring purposes. The SMON MIB, as specified by RFC 2613, extends the RMON MIB by providing remote monitoring device implementations specifically for switched network environments, supporting 802.1Q VLAN definitions. SMON supports a port copy feature to copy traffic from one switched port to a monitoring port on the same switch. Although a portCopy function already exists in RMON 1, SMON extends this concept to copy complete VLAN information. This eases the operators' task, because only the desired VLAN needs to be selected, not individual ports. The copy can be done as port-to-port, multiport-to-port, or multiport-to-multiport.

The principles behind SMON are as follows:

- SMON extends RMON by adding support for standard VLAN monitoring.
- The MIB contains 32-bit and 64-bit SNMP counters.

Supported Devices and IOS Versions

Polling the smonCapabilities MIB OID (from the probeConfig group) indicates which SMON MIB capabilities this RMON probe supports. For example:

- The 6500/7600 devices support the portCopy and VLAN statistics functionalities.
- The Cisco NAM for the Catalyst 6500 supports SMON.

CLI Operations

The Catalyst 6500 supports the smonVlanStats; however, the functionality can be configured only by SNMP, not via the CLI.

SNMP Operations

The SMON MIB contains four different groups:

- **smonVlanStats** configures and monitors the VLAN statistics tables. The statistics collected represent a distribution based on the IEEE 802.1Q VLAN ID (VID) for each good frame attributed to the data source for the collection. Counters include the number of packets and bytes (32-bit and 64-bit), nonunicast packets, the number of counter overflows, and a time stamp to identify the last update.
- **smonPrioStats** allows configuration and monitoring of collections based on the value of the 3-bit user priority field encoded in the Tag Control Information (TCI) field. This table merely reports the priority encoded in the VLAN headers, not the priority (if any) given to the frame for switching purposes. Counters include the number of packets and bytes (32-bit and 64-bit), as well as the number of counter overflows.
- **dataSource** describes data sources and port copy capabilities, which an NMS can use to discover the identity and attributes on a given agent implementation. A description exists for each port to describe functions, such as counting error frames, acting as an SMON or RMON collection source, and express port copy functions. This table is populated by the SMON agent, with one entry for each supported data source.
- **portCopy** provides the ability to copy all frames from a specified source to a specified destination within a switch. One-to-one, one-to-many, many-to-one, and many-to-many source-to-destination relationships may be configured. Source and destination are described by ifIndex parameters. The packet direction at the source port is provided as copyRxOnly (copy only the received packets), copyTxOnly (copy only the

transmitted packets), or copyBoth (copy received and transmitted packets). Because it is possible to oversubscribe a destination port, the portCopyDestDropEvents counter should be monitored, because it counts the total number of events in which the switch dropped port copy packets at the destination port because of lack of resources. Note that this number is not necessarily the number of packets dropped; it is just the number of times this condition has been detected.

Examples

For configuration details on the Cisco NAM, refer to the online documentation at http://www.cisco.com/go/nam.

Collection Monitoring

Instead of including a long **snmpwalk** summary, Figure 5-5 illustrates the VLAN monitoring via SMON-MIB.

Figure 5-5   *NAM VLAN Monitoring Example*

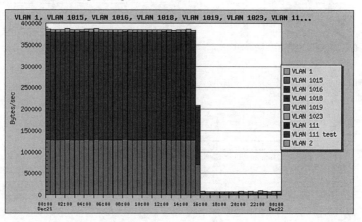

APM MIB and ART MIB

Several extensions to the original RMON specification have been described. However, all of them focused on the inspection of packets per interface or VLAN. None of them considered an end-to-end approach. This is the value-add that the Application Performance Measurement (APM) MIB offers, because it measures the delay between request-response sequences in application flows for protocols such as HTTP and FTP. The original proposal was defined by Netscout as the Application Response Time (ART) MIB; it was proposed to the IETF RMON working groups and standardized as RFC 3729. Cisco currently implements the ART MIB at the NAM. The ART MIB can be customized to support any application that uses well-known TCP ports. If multiple agents are placed in the network, ART can distinguish between the response time of the network component (packet flight time) and the client or server response time (processing time). The results are aggregated into six different response time buckets, which the user can configure via an NMS application. Because ART takes a passive approach to collecting user traffic in the network, concerns exists about the scalability of resources at the probe as well as the number of required probes in the network. ART provides the most useful results when a probe is deployed close to a connection's source and destination. Figure 5-6 illustrates the placement of the Cisco NAM to collect application response time and distinguish between network response time and client and server response time.

Figure 5-6   *NAM Placements for Collecting Application Response Time Details*

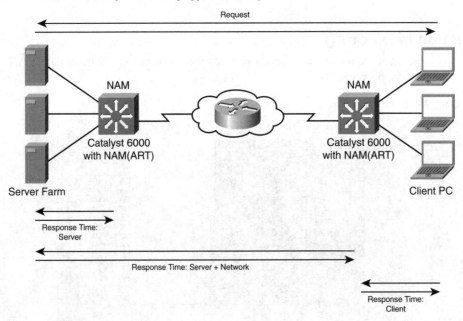

The ART MIB principles are as follows:

- It collects application response times in the network.
- It supports only well-known TCP ports.
- It aggregates collection details in six different buckets.
- It contains 32-bit and 64-bit SNMP counters.

Supported Devices and IOS Versions

Cisco routers and switches do not support the ART MIB. However, it is fully supported by the Cisco NAM for the Catalyst 6500 series as well as the Branch Router Series NAM.

CLI Operations

Cisco routers and switches do not support ART. For configuration details on the Cisco NAM, refer to the online documentation at http://www.cisco.com/go/nam.

SNMP Operations

The ART MIB augments the RMON 2 protocol directory by adding a column to the protocolDirTable. The protocolDir2ArtConfig object describes the probe's capabilities and configures the artControlTable. This table consists of six response time objects (artControlRspTime {1...6} in milliseconds), with collection and report details for each corresponding data source.

Suggested default values for the response time ranges are as follows:

- artControlRspTime1: 25 milliseconds
- artControlRspTime2: 50 milliseconds
- artControlRspTime3: 100 milliseconds
- artControlRspTime4: 200 milliseconds
- artControlRspTime5: 400 milliseconds
- artControlRspTime6: 800 milliseconds

Additional MIB details include the collection start time, the sampling period, the maximum number of collection entries for the associated data source, and the number of dropped frames. The ART report table contains details for each client/server connection. The ART summary report table reports the arithmetic mean of the individual response times observed during the collection interval.

Examples

Cisco routers and switches do not support ART. For configuration details on the Cisco NAM, refer to the online documentation at http://www.cisco.com.

Collection Monitoring

Figure 5-7 shows a summary report of the ART MIB, collected by the Cisco NAM module. The chart on the left is a graphical representation of the response time distribution. The right side provides the server details in the upper part and the table for response time distribution in the lower part.

Figure 5-7   *ART MIB Measurement Example of a Catalyst 6500 NAM Details*

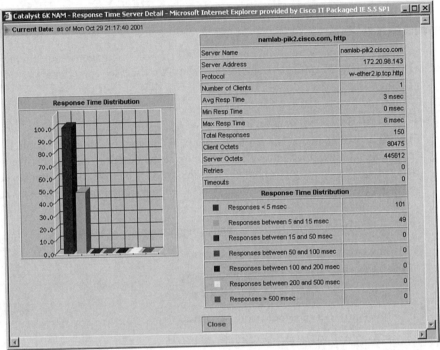

Applicability

Table 5-3 compares RMON, DSMON, SMON, and ART and relates them to the fundamental questions discussed in Chapter 2, "Data Collection Methodology."

Table 5-3   *Comparison of RMON, DSMON, SMON, and ART*

Criterion	RMON	DSMON	SMON	ART
What to collect (data collection details)?	RMON 1: Network traffic at Layer 2 (MAC), including host details, alarms, statistics, and top talkers RMON 2: Network traffic at Layer 3 and at the application layer	Monitor QoS-specific network traffic and application layer details for DSCP values (0 to 63)	Network Layer 2 (MAC) details in switched networks. Supports the 802.1Q VLAN standard.	End-to-end traffic response time statistics for well-known TCP ports

continues

Table 5-3 *Comparison of RMON, DSMON, SMON, and ART (Continued)*

Criterion	RMON	DSMON	SMON	ART
Where to collect?	Edge or core, limited functionality at network elements. Dedicated RMON probes required for all details.	Edge or core, LAN or WAN. Implemented only at dedicated probes/Cisco NAM module.	Layer 2 and 3 switches	On the NAM module, close to source and destination of monitored areas in the network
How to configure?	CLI (scripts), SNMP	NAM CLI (scripts), SNMP	CLI (scripts), SNMP	NAM CLI (scripts), SNMP
How to collect?	Pull model: CLI (scripts) SNMP	Pull model: CLI (scripts) SNMP	Pull model: CLI (scripts) SNMP	Pull model: CLI (scripts) SNMP
How to identify the user?	RMON 1: MAC address RMON 2: IP address or application port	IP address	MAC address	Per application
Use case example	Network monitoring and planning, user monitoring, usage-based billing	Network QoS monitoring and planning	Network monitoring and planning in switched networks	Application-specific response time reporting
Counter support	Supports only 32-bit SNMP counters, unless RFC 3273 (HC-RMON) is used	32-bit and 64-bit SNMP counters	32-bit and 64-bit SNMP counters	32-bit and 64-bit SNMP counters
Support and initial IOS version	IOS 11.2(1) for RMON1; 12.0(5)T for HC-RMON; RMON2 is exclusively supported in the NAM module	Only in the NAM module	IOS 12.0(5)T (available only for the switches)	Only in the NAM module

Further Reading

The focus of this chapter was on the main RMON functions and extensions. However, other RFCs produced by the IETF RMON working group are worth mentioning, either for reference or for further investigation:

- RFC 3919, *Remote Network Monitoring (RMON) Protocol Identifiers for IPv6 and Multi Protocol Label Switching (MPLS)*

  This informational RFC defines basic protocol identifiers for IP version 6 and MPLS protocols. RFC 2896, *Remote Network Monitoring MIB Protocol Identifier Macros*, defines various protocol identifiers, and RFC 2895 defines the syntax of the protocol identifier descriptors. The intent of this document is not to adapt each protocol identifier defined in RFC 2895 and in RFC 2896 for IP version 6, but to define protocol identifiers for IP version 6 protocols and for MPLS protocol. Note that this RFC is informational only, which means that it is not a standard definition.

- RFC 3577, *Introduction to the Remote Monitoring (RMON) Family of MIB Modules*

  This informational RFC provides a very useful tutorial about RMON objectives, foundations, architecture, various extensions, and relationship information to other MIBs.

- RFC 4149, *Definition of Managed Objects for Synthetic Sources for Performance Monitoring Algorithms*

  This RFC defines a method of describing Synthetic Sources for Performance Monitoring (SSPM). This is useful within the RMON framework for performance monitoring in cases where it is desirable to inject packets into the network for monitoring their performance with the other MIBs in that framework.

- RFC 4150, *Transport Performance Metrics MIB*

  This RFC continues the architecture created in the RMON 2-MIB (RFC 2021) by providing a major feature upgrade. It primarily provides new metrics and studies to help analyze performance for subapplication transactions in the network, in direct relationship to the transporting of application layer protocols. The monitoring covers both passive and active traffic generation sources.

- RFC 4710, *Real-time Application Quality-of-Service Monitoring (RAQMON) Framework*

  RAQMON allows end devices and applications to report QoS statistics in real time. There is a need to monitor end devices such as IP phones, pagers, instant messaging clients, mobile phones, and various other handheld computing devices. This RFC extends the RMON family of specifications to allow real-time QoS monitoring of various applications that run on these devices. It also allows this information to be integrated with the RMON family using Simple Network Management Protocol (SNMP). The companion RFCs are RFC 4711, *Real-time Application Quality-of-Service Monitoring (RAQMON) MIB*, and RFC 4712, *Transport Mappings for Real-time Application Quality-of-Service Monitoring (RAQMON) Protocol Data Unit (PDU)*.

CHAPTER 6

IP Accounting

This chapter describes the IP Accounting features in Cisco IOS and enables you to distinguish the different IP Accounting functions and understand SNMP MIB details. This chapter also provides a command-line reference.

IP Accounting is a very useful accounting feature in Cisco IOS, but it's not as well known as other features, such as NetFlow. The fact that Cisco has considered replacing IP Accounting by adding new features to NetFlow potentially turns IP Accounting into a corner case solution. However, compared to NetFlow, IP Accounting offers some advantages that make it an interesting feature to investigate: easy results retrieval via a MIB and limited resource consumption. Furthermore, access-list accounting currently cannot be solved with the NetFlow implementation. Note that NetFlow recently added the export of the MAC address as a new information element. Refer to coverage of NetFlow Layer 2 and the Security Monitoring Exports feature in Chapter 7, "NetFlow."

IP Accounting comes in four variations:

- Basic IP Accounting, which this book calls "IP Accounting (Layer 3)"
- IP Accounting Access Control List (ACL)
- IP Accounting MAC Address
- IP Accounting Precedence

Note that Cisco documentation is not always consistent for the different IP Accounting features. Therefore, this book uses the command-line interface (CLI) commands as titles, except for "IP Accounting Access Control List," where the related CLI command is **ip accounting access-violations**.

This chapter discusses in detail each flavor of IP Accounting, using a basic structure. First, the fundamentals are explained, followed by an overview of CLI operations, and then SNMP operations. It concludes by comparing the IP Accounting features to the questions raised in Chapter 2, "Data Collection Methodology":

- What to collect?
- Where and how to collect?
- How to configure?

- Who is the user?
- Potential scenarios.

IP Accounting (Layer 3)

IP Accounting (Layer 3) collects the number of bytes and packets processed by the network element on a source and destination IP address basis. Only transit traffic that enters and leaves the router is measured, and only on an outbound basis. Traffic generated by the router or traffic terminating in the router is not included in the accounting statistics. IP Accounting (Layer 3) collects individual IP address details, so it can be used to identify specific users for usage-based billing. To provide the operator with the opportunity of "snapshot" collections in the network, IP Accounting (Layer 3) maintains two accounting databases: an active database and a checkpoint database. The active collection process always updates the active database and therefore constantly increments the counters while packets pass the router. To get a snapshot of the traffic statistics, a CLI command or SNMP request can be executed to copy the current status from the active database to the checkpoint database. This copy request can be automated across the network to be executed at the same time, and a Network Management application can later retrieve the accounting details from the checkpoint database to present consistent accounting data to the operator. The checkpoint database offers a "frozen" snapshot of the complete network. Trying to achieve the same result by synchronously polling entire MIB tables across multiple network elements would introduce some inaccuracies, and hence no real "frozen" snapshots. The collected data can be used for performance and trending applications that require collections at regular intervals. The snapshot function is unique to IP Accounting.

IP Accounting (Layer 3) Principles

The principles of IP Accounting (Layer 3) can be summarized as follows:

- IP Layer 3 outbound (egress) traffic is collected.
- Only transit traffic that enters and leaves the router is collected; traffic that is generated by the router or terminated in the router is not included.
- IP Accounting (Layer 3) also collects IPX traffic. In this case, IPX source and destination addresses are reported instead of IP addresses.
- Egress MPLS core traffic collection is a new feature.
- Active and checkpoint databases enable "snapshot" collections.

- Collection data is accessible via CLI and SNMP; however, the initial configuration must be done via CLI. To retrieve the collection results via SNMP, you need to enable SNMP first. When configuring SNMP, distinguish between read-only access and read-write access. For more details about SNMP configuration, see Chapter 4, "SNMP and MIBs."

- The MIB contains only 32-bit SNMP counters.

Supported Devices and IOS Versions

The following list defines the devices and Cisco IOS Software releases that support IP Accounting (Layer 3):

- IP Accounting (Layer 3) was introduced in IOS 10.0.

- It is supported on all routers, including Route Switch Module (RSM) and Multilayer Service Feature Card (MSFC), except for the Cisco 12000. Note that IP Accounting cannot account for MLS-switched traffic on the Catalyst 6500/7600, so it collects only a subset of traffic on these platforms.

- It is supported on all physical interfaces and logical subinterfaces.

- IP Accounting (Layer 3) runs on the top of all switching paths, except for autonomous switching, silicon switching engine (SSE) switching, and distributed switching (dCEF) on the interface. On the Cisco 7500 router, IP Accounting (Layer 3) causes packets to be switched on the Route Switch Processor (RSP) instead of the Versatile Interface Processor (VIP), which can cause additional performance degradation.

CLI Operations

Notable commands for configuring, verifying, and troubleshooting IP Accounting (Layer 3) are as follows:

- router(config-if)# **ip accounting output-packets**
  enables IP Accounting (Layer 3) for output traffic on the interface.

- router(config)# **ip accounting-list [ip address] [ip address mask]**
  defines filters to control the hosts for which IP Accounting (Layer 3) information is kept. The filters are similar to an aggregation scheme and can be used to reduce the number of collected records. If filters are applied, details such as number of packets and bytes are kept only for the traffic that matches the filters, while all others are aggregated into "transit records."

- router(config)# **ip accounting-transits** *count*
  controls the number of transit records that are stored in the IP Accounting (Layer 3)
  database. Transit entries are those that do not match any of the filters specified by the
  global configuration command **ip accounting-list**. If no filters are defined, no transit
  entries are possible. The default number of transit records that are stored in the IP
  Accounting (Layer 3) database is 0.

  Note that the term "transit" in this case refers to packets that are not matched by
  the filter statements. In the IP Accounting (Layer 3) definition, "transit" refers to
  packets that traverse the router, compared to traffic that is generated at the router
  or destined for the router.

- router(config)# **ip accounting-threshold** *count*
  sets the maximum number of accounting entries to be created. The accounting
  threshold defines the maximum number of entries (source and destination address
  pairs) that are accumulated. The default accounting threshold is 512 entries, which
  results in a maximum table size of 12,928 bytes. The threshold counter applies to both
  the active and checkpoint tables.

  The threshold value depends on the traffic mix, because different traffic types create
  different records for the source and destination address pairs. Whenever the table is
  full, the new entries (overflows) are not accounted. However, **show ip accounting**
  displays the overflows: "Accounting threshold exceeded for X packets and Y bytes."
  Alternatively, these values are available in the MIB: actLostPkts (lost IP packets
  due to memory limitations) and actLostByts (total bytes of lost IP packets). You
  should monitor the overflows number, at least during the deployment phase, to find
  the right balance between the number of entries and memory consumption.

- router# **show ip accounting [checkpoint] output-packets**
  displays the active accounting or checkpoint database.

- router# **clear ip accounting**
  copies the content of the active database to the checkpoint database and clears the
  active database afterward.

- router# **clear ip accounting checkpoint**
  clears the checkpoint database.

NOTE	The IP Accounting (Layer 3) and IP Accounting Access Control List entries share the same databases. Consequently, there is no explicit command to erase the IP Accounting (Layer 3) entries independently of the IP Accounting ACL entries.

SNMP Operations

The OLD-CISCO-IP-MIB has two tables:

- lipAccountingTable, the active database
- lipCkAccountingTable, the checkpoint database

The MIB variable actCheckPoint must be read first and then set to the same value that was read to copy the active database into the checkpoint database. After a successful SNMP set request, actCheckPoint is incremented by 1. Setting actCheckPoint is the equivalent of the **clear ip accounting** CLI command. A Network Management application can retrieve the MIB variable lipCkAccountingTable to analyze stable data in the checkpoint database. There is no SNMP variable to erase the content of the checkpoint database; however, setting actCheckPoint again flushes the checkpoint database and copies the content of the active database.

Details of the IP Accounting MIB (OLD-CISCO-IP-MIB) are as follows:

- **Active database**—The lipAccountingTable table contains four relevant components:
  - actSrc is the active database source.
  - actDst is the active database destination.
  - actPkts is the active database packets.
  - actByts is the active database bytes.

  The table indexes are actSrc and actDst.

- **Checkpoint database**—The lipCkAccountingTable table contains four relevant components:
  - ckactSrc is the checkpoint database source.
  - ckactdDst is the checkpoint database destination.
  - ckactPkts is the checkpoint database packets.
  - ckactByts is the checkpoint database bytes.

  The table indexes are ckactSrc and ckactDst.

- actCheckPoint MIB variable

NOTE	The active and checkpoint MIB tables contain an ACL violations entry. Because it is relevant only to the IP Accounting Access Control List, it is not discussed in this section.

Examples (CLI and SNMP)

The following example provides a systematic introduction for configuring and monitoring IP Accounting (Layer 3) and displays the results for both CLI and SNMP.

Initial Configuration

Initially, both the active database (lipAccountingTable) and checkpoint database (lipCkAccountingTable) are empty, as shown from the router CLI and from the SNMP tables.

```
router#show ip accounting output-packets
    Source        Destination              Packets          Bytes
    Accounting data age is 0
router#show ip accounting checkpoint output-packet
    Source        Destination              Packets          Bytes
    Accounting data age is 0
```

The router is accessed with SNMP2c (SNMP version 2c), the read community string is public, and the SNMP tool net-snmp is used.

```
SERVER % snmpwalk -c public -v 2c <router> lipAccountingTable
    actDst.0.0.0.0.0.0.0.0 = IpAddress: 0.0.0.0
    actByts.0.0.0.0.0.0.0.0 = INTEGER: 0
SERVER % snmpwalk -c public -v 2c <router> lipCkAccountingTable
    ckactDst.0.0.0.0.0.0.0.0 = IpAddress: 0.0.0.0
    ckactByts.0.0.0.0.0.0.0.0 = INTEGER: 0
```

The IP Accounting (Layer 3) configuration is straightforward:

```
router(config)#int serial 0/0
router(config-if)#ip accounting output-packets
router(config-if)#exit
```

Collection Monitoring

After configuring IP Accounting (Layer 3), the active database populates:

```
router#show ip accounting output-packet
    Source        Destination              Packets          Bytes
    192.1.1.110   192.1.1.97                  5              500
    192.1.1.110   192.1.1.26                  5              500
```

The corresponding MIB table shows the identical entries:

```
SERVER % snmptable -Ci -Cb -c public -v 2c <router> lipAccountingTable
                       index              Src           Dst  Pkts  Byts
            192.1.1.110.192.1.1.26 192.1.1.110 192.1.1.26    5     500
            192.1.1.110.192.1.1.97 192.1.1.110 192.1.1.97    5     500
```

At this point, the checkpoint database is still empty. The active database content is cleared by copying its content to the checkpoint database:

```
router#clear ip accounting
```

As an alternative, the **clear ip accounting** mechanism can be mimicked by using the actCheckPoint MIB variable procedure. That means reading the content of the MIB variable and setting it again to the same value that was read:

```
SERVER % snmpget -c public -v 2c <router> actCheckPoint.0
        actCheckPoint.0 = INTEGER: 0
SERVER % snmpset -c private -v 2c <router> actCheckPoint.0 i 0
        actCheckPoint.0 = INTEGER: 0
        SERVER % snmpget -c public -v 2c <router> actCheckPoint.0
        actCheckPoint.0 = INTEGER: 1
```

The two entries just discussed are now in the checkpoint database, but the active database is empty:

```
router#show ip accounting output-packets
   Source          Destination          Packets              Bytes
   Accounting data age is 0
router#show ip accounting output-packets checkpoint output-packets
   Source          Destination          Packets              Bytes
   192.1.1.110     192.1.1.97              5                   500
   192.1.1.110     192.1.1.26              5                   500
SERVER % snmptable -Ci -Cb -c public -v 2c <router> lipCkAccountingTable
                   index          Src          Dst   Pkts   Byts
      192.1.1.110.192.1.1.26 192.1.1.110 192.1.1.26    5     500
      192.1.1.110.192.1.1.97 192.1.1.110 192.1.1.97    5     500
```

IP Accounting Access Control List (ACL)

The IP Accounting ACL identifies IP traffic that *fails* an IP access control list. This is a relevant security feature, because a sudden increase in traffic being blocked by an ACL can indicate a security attack in the network. Identifying IP source addresses that violate IP access control lists can help track down attackers. Alternatively, this mechanism can be used to identify when an attack is over, because an ACL is usually applied to block the attack. The data might also indicate that you should verify the network element configurations of the IP access control list. It is important to understand that the IP Accounting ACL does not account the amount of traffic that passes an individual ACL; therefore, it cannot be used for ACL optimization. However, the IP Accounting ACL can be used in conjunction with IP Accounting (Layer 3). For example, if ACLs are configured at a router, packets passing all ACLs are accounted by the IP Accounting (Layer 3) feature, and blocked traffic is collected via the IP Accounting ACL.

IP Accounting ACL is supported on ingress and egress traffic. There is no explicit command to recognize if the *incoming* traffic was blocked (the **ip access-group** *ACL-number* **IN** command, called ACL IN for simplicity) or the *outgoing* traffic was blocked (the **ip access-group** *ACL-number* **OUT** command, called ACL OUT). Nevertheless, because the blocking access list number is reported by the IP Accounting ACL, the direction can be identified in most cases.

NOTE   There are rare exceptions where the network element modifies ACL-related parts of a packet and these packet changes relate to ACLs. An example is if an ACL blocks certain precedence values and Policy Routing or Committed Access Rate (CAR) is active (where the precedence could be changed). In a case where the ACL IN statement passes the original packet, but the ACL OUT statement blocks the modified packet, you cannot measure if ACL IN or ACL OUT has blocked the packet.

IP Accounting ACL Principles

The principles of IP Accounting ACL can be summarized as follows:

- It provides information for identifying IP traffic that fails IP ACLs.

- It supports standard and extended ACLs, but not named ACLS.

- It supports ACLs applied as both ingress and egress.

- It has the same database concept as IP Accounting (Layer 3): active and checkpoint databases.

- If the packet is blocked by an ACL, only the IP Accounting ACL database is updated, not the IP Accounting (Layer 3) database.

- Collection data is accessible via CLI and SNMP; however, the initial configuration is required via CLI. To retrieve the collection results via SNMP, you need to enable SNMP on the router first. When configuring SNMP, distinguish between read-only access and read-write access. For more details about SNMP configuration, see Chapter 4.

- The MIB contains only 32-bit SNMP counters.

Supported Devices and IOS Versions

The following list defines the devices and Cisco IOS Software releases that support IP Accounting ACL:

- IP Accounting ACL was introduced in IOS 10.3.

- It is supported on all routers, including the RSM and MSFC, except for the Cisco 12000.

- It is supported on all physical interfaces and logical subinterfaces.

- It is supported on all switching paths, except for autonomous switching, SSE switching, and dCEF. On the Cisco 7500 router, the IP Accounting ACL causes packets to be switched on the RSP instead of the VIP, which can cause performance degradation.

CLI Operations

Notable commands for configuring, verifying, and troubleshooting IP Accounting ACL are as follows:

- router(config-if)# **ip accounting access-violations**
  allows IP Accounting ACL to identify IP traffic that fails IP ACLs.

- router(config)# **ip accounting-threshold** *count*
  sets the maximum number of accounting entries to be created. The accounting threshold defines the maximum number of entries (source and destination address pairs) that are accumulated, with a default of 512 entries.

- router# **show ip accounting [checkpoint] access-violations**
  displays the active accounting or checkpoint database for ACL violations.
- router# **clear ip accounting**
  copies the content of the active database to the checkpoint database and afterwards clears the active database for both IP Accounting (Layer 3) and IP Accounting ACL.
- router# **clear ip accounting checkpoint**
  clears the checkpoint database.

NOTE   The IP Accounting ACL and IP Accounting (Layer 3) entries share the same databases. Consequently, there is no explicit command to erase the IP Accounting ACL entries independently of the IP Accounting (Layer 3) entries.

SNMP Operations

IP Accounting ACL uses the same MIB (OLD-CISCO-IP-MIB) as IP Accounting (Layer 3), which was described previously. IP Accounting ACL cannot be configured via SNMP, but a copy function from the active database to the checkpoint database is provided. First, you should copy the active database to the checkpoint database. Afterward, retrieve the data from the checkpoint database if you want to collect consistent accounting data across multiple network elements at the same time. IP Accounting ACL uses the same MIB tables as IP Accounting (Layer 3) but augments the information with the ACL Identifier—the ACL number that was violated by packets from source to destination. The ACL identifier is represented by actViolation in the lipAccountingTable table (the active database) and ckactViolation in the lipCkAccountingTable table (the checkpoint database). actCheckPoint copies the active database into the checkpoint database. For details about the MIB configuration, see the section "SNMP Operations" under "IP Accounting (Layer 3)."

Examples (CLI and SNMP)

The following example for IP Accounting ACL provides CLI and SNMP commands and extends them to display the entries of the IP Accounting (Layer 3) database as well. This helps you understand the close relationship between IP Accounting (Layer 3) and IP Accounting ACL.

Initial Configuration

Initially, the active and checkpoint databases are empty for both IP Accounting (Layer 3) and IP Accounting ACL. An SNMP query to the lipAccountingTable MIB table (active) and to the lipAcCkAccountingTable MIB table (checkpoint) confirms this:

```
router#show ip accounting output-packets
   Source          Destination        Packets          Bytes
   Accounting data age is 0
```

```
router#show ip accounting access-violations
   Source       Destination       Packets       Bytes       ACL
   Accounting data age is 0

router#show ip accounting checkpoint output-packets
   Source       Destination       Packets       Bytes
   Accounting data age is 0

router#show ip accounting checkpoint access-violations
   Source       Destination       Packets       Bytes       ACL
   Accounting data age is 0
```

For this example, IP Accounting ACL is configured in addition to IP Accounting (Layer 3); however, it can be configured independently of IP Accounting (Layer 3). An access list is inserted, which blocks the traffic coming from the source IP address 192.1.1.110 and going to the destination IP address 192.1.1.97:

```
router(config)#access-list 107 deny ip host 192.1.1.110 host 192.1.1.97
router(config)#access-list 107 permit ip any any
router(config)#int serial 0/0
router(config-if)#ip accounting output-packets
router(config-if)#ip accounting access-violations
router(config-if)#ip access-group 107 out
router(config-if)#exit
```

Collection Monitoring

Afterwards, the following results can be retrieved from the router:

```
router#show ip accounting access-violations
   Source       Destination       Packets       Bytes     ACL
   192.1.1.110    192.1.1.97          3            300     107
   Accounting data age is 3
router#show ip accounting output-packets
   Source       Destination       Packets       Bytes
   192.1.1.110    192.1.1.26          5            500
   Accounting data age is 3
```

Three packets from the traffic (192.1.1.110, 192.1.1.97) are blocked by access list 107 and therefore are accounted by the IP Accounting ACL. The traffic (192.1.1.110, 192.1.1.26) is accounted by IP Accounting (Layer 3).

For the SNMP example, the router is accessed with SNMP2c, a read community string public, and the net-snmp SNMP utility. The entries from both IP Accounting (Layer 3) and the IP Accounting ACL appear in the same MIB lipAccountingTable table. The only difference is that the entries from the IP Accounting ACL will have a non-null value in the actViolation MIB variable:

```
SERVER % snmpwalk -c public -v 2c <router> lipAccountingTable
actSrc.192.1.1.110.192.1.1.26 = IpAddress: 192.1.1.110
actSrc.192.1.1.110.192.1.1.97 = IpAddress: 192.1.1.110
actDst.192.1.1.110.192.1.1.26 = IpAddress: 192.1.1.26
actDst.192.1.1.110.192.1.1.97 = IpAddress: 192.1.1.97
actPkts.192.1.1.110.192.1.1.26 = INTEGER: 5
actPkts.192.1.1.110.192.1.1.97 = INTEGER: 3
actByts.192.1.1.110.192.1.1.26 = INTEGER: 500
```

```
actByts.192.1.1.110.192.1.1.97 = INTEGER: 300
actViolation.192.1.1.110.192.1.1.26 = INTEGER: 0
actViolation.192.1.1.110.192.1.1.97 = INTEGER: 107
```

Formatting the result in a different way, the distinction between **show ip accounting output-packets** and **show ip accounting access-violations** is clear.

The first entry (**show ip accounting output-packets**) is

```
actSrc.192.1.1.110.192.1.1.26 = IpAddress: 192.1.1.110
actDst.192.1.1.110.192.1.1.26 = IpAddress: 192.1.1.26
actPkts.192.1.1.110.192.1.1.26 = INTEGER: 5
actByts.192.1.1.110.192.1.1.26 = INTEGER: 500
actViolation.192.1.1.110.192.1.1.26 = INTEGER: 0
```

The second entry (**show ip accounting access-violations**) is

```
actSrc.192.1.1.110.192.1.1.97 = IpAddress: 192.1.1.110
actDst.192.1.1.110.192.1.1.97 = IpAddress: 192.1.1.97
actPkts.192.1.1.110.192.1.1.97 = INTEGER: 3
actByts.192.1.1.110.192.1.1.97 = INTEGER: 300
actViolation.192.1.1.110.192.1.1.97 = INTEGER: 107
```

NOTE	In this example, the first entry corresponds to **show ip accounting output-packets** and the second to **show ip accounting access-violations**. This correspondence is a coincidence in this case.

At this point, the checkpoint database is still empty. The **clear ip accounting** CLI command or the actCheckPoint MIB variable procedure copies the active database content to the checkpoint database. The two entries just discussed are now in the checkpoint database, and the active database is empty.

```
router#show ip accounting checkpoint access-violations
   Source        Destination         Packets          Bytes    ACL
 192.1.1.110     192.1.1.97             3               300    107
   Accounting data age is 10

router#show ip accounting checkpoint output-packets
   Source        Destination         Packets          Bytes
 192.1.1.110     192.1.1.26             5               500
   Accounting data age is 10

router#show ip accounting access-violations
   Source        Destination         Packets          Bytes    ACL
   Accounting data age is 11

router#show ip accounting output-packets
   Source        Destination         Packets          Bytes
   Accounting data age is 11

SERVER % snmpwalk -c public -v 2c <router> lipcKAccountingTable
ckactSrc.192.1.1.110.192.1.1.26 = IpAddress: 192.1.1.110
ckactSrc.192.1.1.110.192.1.1.97 = IpAddress: 192.1.1.110
ckactDst.192.1.1.110.192.1.1.26 = IpAddress: 192.1.1.26
ckactDst.192.1.1.110.192.1.1.97 = IpAddress: 192.1.1.97
```

```
ckactPkts.192.1.1.110.192.1.1.26 = INTEGER: 5
ckactPkts.192.1.1.110.192.1.1.97 = INTEGER: 3
ckactByts.192.1.1.110.192.1.1.26 = INTEGER: 500
ckactByts.192.1.1.110.192.1.1.97 = INTEGER: 300
ckactViolation.192.1.1.110.192.1.1.26 = INTEGER: 0
ckactViolation.192.1.1.110.192.1.1.97 = INTEGER: 107
```

IP Accounting MAC Address

IP Accounting MAC Address is comparable to the IP Accounting (Layer 3) feature. However, MAC addresses are collected instead of IP addresses, and there is no concept of a checkpoint database. IP Accounting MAC Address calculates the total number of packets and bytes for IP traffic on LAN interfaces, based on the source and destination MAC addresses. It also records a time stamp for the last packet received or sent. This feature helps the operator determine how much traffic is exchanged with various peers at Layer 2 exchange points, such as an Internet peering point. IP Accounting MAC Address collects individual MAC addresses, so it can be used to identify a specific user for usage-based billing. It also helps security administrators identify a sender's MAC address in case of an attack with faked IP addresses.

The maximum number of MAC addresses that can be stored at the network element for each physical interface is 512 entries for input and an additional 512 MAC addresses for output traffic. After the maximum is reached, subsequent MAC addresses are ignored. To keep addresses from not being taken into account, you should constantly check the number of available entries in the network element's local database and clear entries if it's getting close to 512.

IP Accounting MAC Address Principles

The principles of IP Accounting MAC Address can be summarized as follows:

- Inbound and outbound traffic statistics are collected per MAC address.

- Only LAN interfaces and subinterfaces (Ethernet, FastEthernet, FDDI, and VLAN) are supported.

- A time stamp is recorded (or updated) when the last packet is sent or received.

- When IP Accounting MAC Address is enabled, header compression is turned off so that the MAC information can be extracted from the header. When IP Accounting MAC Address is turned off, header compression is enabled.

- There is no concept of a checkpoint database.

- The maximum number of entries per physical interface and per direction (incoming or outgoing) is 512.

- Collection data is accessible via CLI and SNMP. However, all configuration changes must be done via CLI, because the CISCO-IP-STAT-MIB has no read-write parameters. To retrieve the collection results via SNMP, you need to enable SNMP on the network element first. For more details about SNMP configuration, see Chapter 4.

- The MIB contains 32-bit and 64-bit SNMP counters.

Supported Devices and IOS Versions

The following devices and Cisco IOS Software releases support IP Accounting MAC Address:

- IP Accounting MAC Address was introduced in IOS 11.1CC.

- It is supported on Ethernet, FastEthernet, FDDI, and VLAN interfaces. It works in conjunction with Cisco Express Forwarding (CEF), distributed Cisco Express Forwarding (dCEF), flow, and optimum switching.

- It is supported on all routers, including the MSFC, but not the RSM.

- On the Cisco 12000 router, it is supported only by the 3-port Gigabit Ethernet line cards.

CLI Operations

Notable commands for configuring, verifying, and troubleshooting IP Accounting MAC Address are as follows:

- router(config-if)# **ip accounting mac-address** {**input** | **output**}, where:

  — **input** performs accounting based on the source MAC address on received packets.

  — **output** performs accounting based on the destination MAC address on transmitted packets.

- router# **show interface** [*type number*] **mac-accounting**
  displays information for all interfaces configured for MAC accounting. To display information for a single interface, use the appropriate information for the *type number* arguments.

- router# **clear counters** [*interface-type interface-number*]
  clears all the interface counters. Because the IP Accounting MAC Address entries are stored per interface, the **clear counters** command clears the number of bytes and packets for each IP Accounting MAC Address entry in the output of **show interface** [*type number*] **mac-accounting**. However, the **clear counters** command does not remove any IP Accounting MAC Address entries. In the output from **show interface** [*type number*] **mac-accounting**, **clear counters** keeps the value of the time stamp for the last packet sent or received for that entry. The **clear counters** command does not clear the MIB counters, because SNMP counters can never be cleared, and it does not remove any IP Accounting MAC Address entries in the MIB table. An analogy is the **clear counters** command that clears the number of bytes and packets in the output of

show interface while the SNMP counters in the ifTable are not cleared. Note also that the **clear counters** command is applicable globally for all interfaces or for a single interface.

SNMP Operations

IP Accounting MAC Address uses the Cisco IP Statistics MIB to collect incoming and outgoing packets and bytes per MAC address. There is a maximum of 512 entries per physical interface per direction (ingress or egress). You have to use the CLI to enable and disable IP Accounting MAC Address. Entries can be read but not deleted via SNMP. They can be deleted using the CLI command **clear counters** instead. The CISCO-IP-STAT-MIB (Cisco IP Statistics MIB) was updated to support 32-bit and 64-bit counters. For high-speed interfaces, 64-bit counters are relevant, because on a 1-Gigabit interface, a 32-bit counter wraps after 34 seconds.

The IP Accounting MAC Address part of the MIB consists of two tables with separate 32-bit counters and 64-bit counters, plus an extra table for the number of free entries in the database:

- **cipMacTable** is the MAC table for 32-bit counters, where an entry is created for each unique MAC address that sends or receives IP packets. It contains four variables:
  - **cipMacDirection** is the object's data source.
  - **cipMacAddress** is the MAC address.
  - **cipMacSwitchedPkts** is the counter in packets with respect to cipMacAddress.
  - **cipMacSwitchedBytes** is the counter in bytes with respect to cipMacAddress.

  The table indexes are ifIndex, cipMacDirection, and cipMacAddress.

- **cipMacXTable** is the extended MAC table for 64-bit counters, which contains only two entries.
  - **cipMacHCSwitchedPkts** is the high-capacity counter in packets with respect to cipMacAddress. This object is the 64-bit version of cipMacSwitchedPkts.
  - **cipMacHCSwitchedBytes** is the high-capacity counter in bytes with respect to cipMacAddress. This object is the 64-bit version of cipMacSwitchedBytes.

  The table indexes are ifIndex, cipMacDirection, and cipMacAddress.

- **cipMacFreeTable** specifies the number of available entries in the database.
- **cipMacFreeCount** is the number of items in the MAC free space.

The table indexes are ifIndex and cipMacFreeDirection.

Examples (CLI and SNMP)

The following example provides a systematic introduction to configuring and monitoring IP Accounting MAC Address and displays the results for both CLI and SNMP.

Initial Configuration

Initially, there are no IP Accounting MAC Address entries.

In this configuration, both IP Accounting MAC Address input and output are enabled:

```
router(config-if)#interface fastethernet 0/0
router(config-if)#ip accounting mac-address input
router(config-if)#ip accounting mac-address output
router(config-if)#exit
```

Collection Monitoring

The entries populate:

```
Router#show interface mac-accounting
FastEthernet1/0 Eth -> Nms-bb-1: Port 4/20
    Input (504 free)
0010.8305.c421(115): 7 packets, 590 bytes, last: 95924ms ago.
    .
    .
    .

                Total:  111 packets, 10290 bytes
      Output   (504 free)
0800.2087.66c1(8 ): 2 packets, 375 bytes, last: 8520ms ago
    .
    .
    .

                Total:  39 packets, 5536 bytes
```

For clarity, only the first input and output entries are displayed. The corresponding MIB table shows the identical entries, only one of which is displayed:

```
SERVER % snmpwalk -c public -v 2c martel cipMacTable
cipMacSwitchedPkts.9.input.0.16.131.5.196.33 : Counter: 7
cipMacSwitchedBytes.9.input.0.16.131.5.196.33 : Counter: 590
```

The table indexes are as follows:

* ifIndex is 9 in this case, which represents fastethernet 1/0:

```
Router #show snmp mib ifmib ifIndex fastethernet 1/0
   Interface = fastethernet 1/0, ifIndex =9
```

* cipMacDirection is input or output.

* cipMacAddress, where 0.16.131.5.196.33 is the MAC address, such as 0010.8305.c421.

This SNMP entry corresponds to the following entry in the **show** command:

```
0010.8305.c421(115): 7 packets, 590 bytes, last: 95924ms ago.
```

NOTE   The information about the last time a packet was observed from/to the specific MAC
address is not available in the MIB—only from the **show** command.

The SNMP request confirms that 504 entries are available:

```
SERVER % snmpwalk -c public -v 2c <router> cipMacFreeTable
CISCO-IP-STAT-MIB::cipMacFreeCount.9.input = Gauge32: 504
CISCO-IP-STAT-MIB::cipMacFreeCount.9.output = Gauge32: 504
```

In a situation where the counters are small, polling cipMacXTable, which contains the high-
capacity counter counter64, would return the same results as polling cipMacTable.

Finally, the IP MAC address counters can be cleared, either specifically for the interface or
globally for all interfaces, but no entries are deleted:

```
Router(config)#clear counters [fastethernet 1/0]
Router#show interface mac-accounting
FastEthernet1/0 Eth -> Nms-bb-1: Port 4/20
      Input   (504 free)
0010.8305.c421(115): 0 packets, 0 bytes, last: 125876ms ago
```

In the preceding example, the counters for packets and bytes are reset to 0. All other entries,
along with the content of the "last" field, are preserved. The **clear counters** CLI command
has no effect on the MIB's content.

NOTE   The **clear counters** command affects both the IP Accounting Precedence and IP
Accounting MAC Address counters. This could be considered a limitation when enabled
on the same interface.

IP Accounting Precedence

The IP Accounting Precedence feature provides IP precedence-related traffic accounting
information. The collection per interface consists of the total number of packets and bytes
for each of the eight IP Precedence values, separately per direction (send and receive).

IP Accounting Precedence does not collect individual IP or MAC addresses, so it cannot
be used to identify a specific user for usage-based billing, except in cases where the
(sub)interface can serve as user identifier. There is no concept of a checkpoint database.
Regarding QoS operations, it is important to distinguish between ingress and egress traffic
on an interface:

- For incoming packets on the interface, the accounting statistics are gathered before input CAR/Distributed CAR (DCAR) is performed on the packet. Therefore, if CAR/DCAR changes the precedence on the packet, it is counted based on the old precedence setting with the **show interface precedence** command.

- For outgoing packets on the interface, the accounting statistics are gathered after output features such as DCAR, Distributed Weighted Random Early Detection (DWRED), and Distributed Weighted Fair Queuing (DWFQ) are performed on the packet.

IP Accounting Precedence Principles

The principles of IP Accounting Precedence can be summarized as follows:

- Both inbound and outbound traffic is collected for eight IP precedence classes.

- IP Accounting Precedence is supported on physical interfaces and subinterfaces.

- There is no concept of a checkpoint database.

- Individual IP or MAC addresses are not collected.

- Collection data is accessible via CLI and SNMP. However, all configuration changes need to be done via CLI, because the CISCO-IP-STAT-MIB has no read-write parameters.

- The MIB contains 32-bit and 64-bit SNMP counters.

- To retrieve the collection results via SNMP, you have to enable SNMP on the network element first. When configuring SNMP, distinguish between read-only access and read-write access. For more details about SNMP configuration, see Chapter 4.

Supported Devices and IOS Versions

The following list defines the devices and Cisco IOS Software releases that support IP Accounting Precedence:

- IP Accounting Precedence was introduced in IOS 11.1CC.

- It is supported on CEF, dCEF, and optimum switching.

- It supports Virtual Routing and Forwarding (VRF) interfaces but does not support tunnel interfaces.

- It is supported on all routers, including the RSM and MSFC, except for the Cisco 12000.

CLI Operations

Notable commands for configuring, verifying, and troubleshooting IP Accounting Precedence are as follows:

- router(config-if)# **ip accounting precedence** {**input** | **output**}, where:
  - **input** performs accounting based on IP precedence on received packets.
  - **output** performs accounting based on IP precedence on transmitted packets.

- router# **show interface** [*type number*] **precedence**
  displays information for all interfaces configured for IP Accounting Precedence. To display information for a single interface, enter the appropriate values for the *type number* arguments.

- router# **clear counters** [*interface-type interface-number*]
  clears interface counters. Because the IP Accounting Precedence entries are stored per interface, the **clear counters** command clears all IP Accounting Precedence entries. Note that this function is different from the IP Accounting MAC Address feature. The **clear counters** command does not delete the content of the cipPrecedenceTable MIB table. An analogy would be the **clear counters** command that clears the number of bytes and packets in the output of **show interface** while the SNMP counters in the ifTable are not cleared. Note also that the **clear counters** command is applicable globally for all interfaces or for a single interface.

SNMP Operations

IP Accounting Precedence can be configured only by using the CLI. Collection data can be read but not deleted via SNMP. It can be deleted using the CLI command **clear counters**. CISCO-IP-STAT-MIB supports 32-bit and 64-bit counters.

The IP Accounting Precedence part of the MIB consists of two tables with separate 32-bit counters and 64-bit counters:

- **cipPrecedenceTable**—The 32-bit counter table for IP Accounting Precedence contains four variables:
  - **cipPrecedenceDirection** is the object's data source (incoming or outgoing traffic).
  - **cipPrecedenceIpPrecedence** is the IP precedence value this object is collected on, with a total of eight different precedence values (0 to 7).
  - **cipPrecedenceSwitchedPkts** is the number of packets per IP precedence value (cipPrecedenceIpPrecedence).
  - **cipPrecedenceSwitchedBytes** is the number of bytes per IP precedence value (cipPrecedenceIpPrecedence).

The indexes of the three tables are ifIndex, cipPrecedenceDirection, and cipPrecedenceIpPrecedence

- **cipPrecedenceXTable**—The 64-bit counter extension table for IP Accounting Precedence contains two variables:

  — **cipPrecedenceHCSwitchedPkts** is the number of packets per IP precedence value (cipPrecedenceIpPrecedence). This object is the 64-bit version of cipPrecedenceSwitchedPkts.

  — **cipPrecedenceHCSwitchedBytes** is the number of bytes per IP precedence value (cipPrecedenceIpPrecedence). This object is the 64-bit version of cipPrecedenceSwitchedBytes.

The three table indexes are ifIndex, cipPrecedenceDirection, and cipPrecedenceIpPrecedence.

Examples (CLI and SNMP)

The following example provides a systematic introduction to configuring and monitoring IP Accounting Precedence and displays the results for both CLI and SNMP.

Initial Configuration

Initially, there are no IP Accounting Precedence entries.

In this configuration, both IP Accounting Precedence input and output are enabled:

```
router(config-if)#interface serial 0/0
router(config-if)#ip accounting precedence input
router(config-if)#ip accounting precedence output
router(config-if)#exit
```

Collection Monitoring

The entries populate:

```
router#show interfaces precedence
Serial0/0
  Input
            Precedence 6:  8 packets, 467 bytes
  Output
            Precedence 0:  6 packets, 504 bytes
            Precedence 6:  11 packets, 863 bytes
```

The corresponding MIB table shows the identical entries.

The router is accessed with SNMP2c (SNMP version 2c), the read community string is public, and the SNMP tool **net-snmp** is used:

```
SERVER % snmpwalk -c public -v 2c <router> cipPrecedenceTable
cipPrecedenceSwitchedPkts.1.input.0 = Counter32: 0
cipPrecedenceSwitchedPkts.1.input.1 = Counter32: 0
cipPrecedenceSwitchedPkts.1.input.2 = Counter32: 0
```

```
cipPrecedenceSwitchedPkts.1.input.3 = Counter32: 0
cipPrecedenceSwitchedPkts.1.input.4 = Counter32: 0
cipPrecedenceSwitchedPkts.1.input.5 = Counter32: 0
cipPrecedenceSwitchedPkts.1.input.6 = Counter32: 8
cipPrecedenceSwitchedPkts.1.input.7 = Counter32: 0
cipPrecedenceSwitchedPkts.1.output.0 = Counter32: 6
cipPrecedenceSwitchedPkts.1.output.1 = Counter32: 0
cipPrecedenceSwitchedPkts.1.output.2 = Counter32: 0
cipPrecedenceSwitchedPkts.1.output.3 = Counter32: 0
cipPrecedenceSwitchedPkts.1.output.4 = Counter32: 0
cipPrecedenceSwitchedPkts.1.output.5 = Counter32: 0
cipPrecedenceSwitchedPkts.1.output.6 = Counter32: 11
cipPrecedenceSwitchedPkts.1.output.7 = Counter32: 0
cipPrecedenceSwitchedBytes.1.input.0 = Counter32: 0
cipPrecedenceSwitchedBytes.1.input.1 = Counter32: 0
cipPrecedenceSwitchedBytes.1.input.2 = Counter32: 0
cipPrecedenceSwitchedBytes.1.input.3 = Counter32: 0
cipPrecedenceSwitchedBytes.1.input.4 = Counter32: 0
cipPrecedenceSwitchedBytes.1.input.5 = Counter32: 0
cipPrecedenceSwitchedBytes.1.input.6 = Counter32: 467
cipPrecedenceSwitchedBytes.1.input.7 = Counter32: 0
cipPrecedenceSwitchedBytes.1.output.0 = Counter32: 504
cipPrecedenceSwitchedBytes.1.output.1 = Counter32: 0
cipPrecedenceSwitchedBytes.1.output.2 = Counter32: 0
cipPrecedenceSwitchedBytes.1.output.3 = Counter32: 0
cipPrecedenceSwitchedBytes.1.output.4 = Counter32: 0
cipPrecedenceSwitchedBytes.1.output.5 = Counter32: 0
cipPrecedenceSwitchedBytes.1.output.6 = Counter32: 863
cipPrecedenceSwitchedBytes.1.output.7 = Counter32: 0
```

The table indexes are as follows:

- ifIndex

  In this case it is 1, which represents serial 0/0:

  ```
  Router #show snmp mib ifmib ifIndex serial 0/0
              Interface = Serial0/0, ifIndex = 1
  ```

- cipPrecedenceDirection: input or output

- cipPrecedenceIpPrecedence: a value from 0 to 7

For example, the entry (Input, Precedence 6, 8 packets, 467 bytes) is represented in the SNMP table by

```
cipPrecedenceSwitchedBytes.1.input.6 = Counter32: 467
```

In a situation where the counters are small, polling cipPrecedenceXTable, which contains the high-capacity counter counter64, returns the same results as polling cipPrecedenceTable.

Finally, the IP Accounting Precedence counters can be cleared, either specifically for the interface or globally for all interfaces:

```
router(config)#clear counters [serial 0/0]
router#show interfaces precedence
Serial0/0
  Input
            none
         Output
            none
```

NOTE   The **clear counters** affects the IP Accounting Precedence counters and the IP Accounting MAC Address counters. This could be considered a limitation when enabled on the same interface.

Applicability

Table 6-1 compares the four different variations of IP Accounting and relates them to the fundamental questions that were discussed in Chapter 2.

Table 6-1   *Comparison of the Different IP Accounting Features*

Criterion	IP Accounting (Layer 3)	IP Accounting ACL	IP Accounting MAC Address	IP Accounting Precedence
What to collect (data collection details)?	Total traffic (packets and bytes) per: IP source address IP destination address	Total traffic (packets and bytes) per failed ACL: IP source address IP destination address ACL identifier	Total traffic (packets and bytes) per: Source MAC address Destination MAC address	Total traffic (packets and bytes) per: Eight different IP precedence values
Where to collect?	Edge or core, LAN or WAN (any interface type)	Edge or core, LAN or WAN (any interface type)	Edge: LAN interface types only	Edge or core, LAN or WAN (any interface type)
How to configure?	CLI (scripts)	CLI (scripts)	CLI (scripts)	CLI (scripts)
How to collect?	Pull model: CLI (scripts) SNMP	Pull model: CLI (scripts) SNMP	Pull model: CLI (scripts) SNMP	Pull model: CLI (scripts) SNMP
How to identify the user?	IP address	IP address	MAC address	Not available
Use case example	Network monitoring and planning, user monitoring, usage-based billing	Security analysis	Security analysis, network monitoring and planning, user monitoring, usage-based billing, peering agreements	Network QoS monitoring and planning
Additional details	Only 32-bit SNMP counters Two different databases provide a global "snapshot" of the network	Only 32-bit SNMP counters Two different databases provide a global "snapshot" of the network	32-bit and 64-bit SNMP counters	32-bit and 64-bit SNMP counters

CHAPTER 7

NetFlow

This chapter describes the NetFlow features in Cisco IOS. It enables you to distinguish the different NetFlow versions, recognize the latest NetFlow features, and understand the natural NetFlow evolution toward IPFIX. Platform-specific details are discussed, along with command-line references, examples, and SNMP MIB details.

Cisco IOS NetFlow technology is an integral part of Cisco IOS software that collects packets, classifies packets into flows, and measures flow statistics as the packets enter or exit the network element's interface.

By analyzing NetFlow data, a network engineer can identify the cause of congestion, determine the Class of Service (CoS) for users and applications, identify the source and destination network, and so on. NetFlow allows granular and accurate traffic measurements as well as high-level aggregated traffic collection. Because it is part of Cisco IOS software, NetFlow enables networks to perform IP traffic flow analysis without deploying external probes, making traffic analysis economical even on large IP networks.

The key components of NetFlow are the NetFlow cache that stores IP flow information and the NetFlow export mechanism that sends NetFlow data to a collector, such as the NetFlow Collector. These two key components, the metering process and the exporting process, sometimes lead to confusion, because the term "NetFlow" refers to both of them. NetFlow operates by creating a NetFlow cache entry (also called flow record) for each active flow. NetFlow maintains a flow record within the cache for active flows. Each flow record contains multiple data fields, which are exported to a NetFlow collector. The Cisco NetFlow Collection Engine (NFC) is a device that provides flow filtering and aggregation capabilities. Afterwards, Network Management applications, such as performance monitoring, security analysis, and billing solutions, can access the aggregated NetFlow records for further processing. As illustrated in Figure 7-1, the Network Analysis Module (NAM) on the Catalyst 6500/Cisco 7600 can also collect flow records.

Figure 7-1 *Hierarchical Representation of the NetFlow Collection*

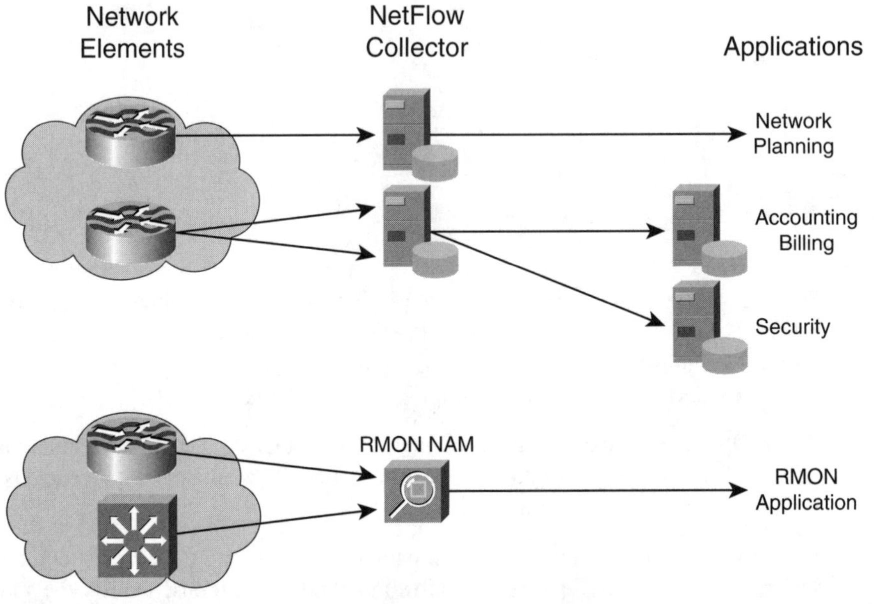

NetFlow is by far the most granular and complete accounting mechanism in the Cisco devices. This is reflected by the size of this chapter as well as the number of deployed NetFlow solutions in customer networks and the large number of partner applications that support NetFlow. The latest NetFlow developments position NetFlow as a superset of several existing accounting features. Therefore, NetFlow enables several key customer applications:

- **Network monitoring**—NetFlow enables extensive near-real-time network monitoring capabilities. Flow-based analysis techniques may be used to visualize traffic patterns associated with individual network elements. Traffic patterns can also be analyzed on a network-wide basis, providing aggregate traffic- or application-based views and offering proactive problem detection, efficient troubleshooting, and rapid problem resolution.

- **Application monitoring and profiling**—NetFlow gives network managers a detailed and time-based view of bandwidth usage per application in the network. You use this information to plan and understand the requirements of new services and allocate network and application resources (such as Web server sizing and VoIP deployment) to meet customer demands.

- **User monitoring and profiling**—NetFlow enables network engineers to gain a detailed understanding of how users consume network resources. This information may then be used to efficiently plan and allocate access, backbone, and application resources, as well as detect and resolve potential security and policy violations.

- **Network planning**—NetFlow can be used to capture data over a long period, producing the opportunity to track and anticipate network growth and plan upgrades. NetFlow services data optimizes network planning, including peering, backbone upgrade planning, and routing policy planning. NetFlow helps minimize the total cost of network operations while maximizing network performance, capacity, and reliability. NetFlow detects unwanted traffic, validates bandwidth and quality of service (QoS), and lets you analyze new network applications. NetFlow offers valuable information to reduce your network's operational expenses (OPEX).

- **Security analysis**—NetFlow identifies and classifies distributed denial-of-service (DDOS) attacks, viruses, and worms in near-real time. NetFlow data can point out changes in network traffic and indicate potential anomalies. The data is also a valuable forensic tool to understand and analyze the sequence of past security incidents.

- **Accounting/billing**—NetFlow records provide fine-grained metering (flow data includes details such as IP addresses, packet and byte counts, timestamps, type of service, and application ports) for flexible and detailed resource utilization accounting. Service providers may use the information for billing based on time of day, bandwidth usage, application usage, quality of service, etc. Enterprise customers may use the information for departmental chargeback or cost allocation for resource utilization.

- **NetFlow data warehousing and data mining**—NetFlow records can be warehoused for further marketing and customer service programs (such as to figure out which applications and services are being used by users and to target them for improved services, advertising, etc.). In addition, NetFlow data gives market researchers access to the who, what, where, when, and how long traffic details.

As you will see later in this chapter, new information is exported by leveraging the NetFlow version 9 export format, including Layer 2 information, new security detection and identification information, IPv6, Multicast, MPLS, BGP information, and more. NetFlow version 9 has the advantage of being flexible and extensible. Furthermore, it is the basis protocol for the IP Flow Information eXport (IPFIX) working group, developed as an IETF standards track protocol. IPFIX was designed to transport any accounting and performance information from network elements to a collection device.

Fundamentals of NetFlow

NetFlow identifies packet flows for IP packets, where a flow is identified by a number of fields in the data packet. NetFlow does not involve any connection-setup protocol between routers, networking devices, or end stations. NetFlow does not change the IP packets and is transparent to the existing network infrastructure.

NetFlow operates by creating a NetFlow cache entry that contains the information for each active flow. Unless sampling has been configured, the NetFlow process inspects every packet and creates a new flow record in the cache or updates the usage parameters (such as the number of packets and bytes) of existing flow records. Each flow record is created by identifying packets with same flow characteristics and counting or tracking the packets and bytes per flow. The cache entries are exported to a collector periodically based on the flow timers. The NetFlow Collector stores the flow records that were exported by the network elements.

It is important to note that NetFlow is not a switching path, as it was originally. In fact, NetFlow is an accounting feature on top of existing switching paths, such as Cisco Express Forwarding (CEF) or Distributed CEF. NetFlow is very efficient; the typical amount of export data is about 1.5 percent of the switched traffic in the network element. On most Cisco platforms, NetFlow accounts for every packet and provides a highly condensed and detailed view of all network traffic that passed the device. Some high-end platforms, such as the Cisco 12000 router, prefer sampled NetFlow, which meters ("samples") only a subset of all packets entering the interface.

Next to the monitoring of IPv4 flows, NetFlow supports the monitoring of IPv6 environments. NetFlow captures data from ingress (incoming) and egress (outgoing) packets. NetFlow gathers data for the following *ingress* IP packets:

- IP-to-IP packets
- IP-to-Multiprotocol Label Switching (MPLS) packets
- Frame Relay-terminated packets
- ATM-terminated packets

NetFlow captures data for *egress* packets through the following features:

- Egress NetFlow Accounting gathers data for egress packets for IP traffic only
- NetFlow MPLS Egress gathers data for egress MPLS-to-IP packets

Flow Definition

A *flow* is defined as a set of packets having common properties: one or more packet header fields (e.g. destination IP address, transport header field), one or more characteristics of the packet itself (e.g. number of MPLS labels), one or more fields derived from packet treatment (e.g. the BGP next hop). A packet belongs to a flow record if it completely matches all defined flow properties.

NetFlow defines a flow by a combination of key-fields in the packet. In the documentation they are also called "flow keys" because they define a flow. Usually additional information is reported in a flow, such as number of packets and bytes, start and stop time, and so on. These reporting fields do not define a flow; therefore, they are called "flow values" or "non-key-fields". For consistency, we use only the terms "key-field" and "non-key-field."

Initially, NetFlow defines a flow as the combination of the following seven key-fields:

- Source IP address.
- Destination IP address.
- Source port number.
- Destination port number.
- Layer 3 protocol type.
- ToS byte.
- Logical interface (ifIndex), which is the input ifIndex in case of ingress NetFlow, or the output ifIndex with egress NetFlow. Note also that the command **ip flow-egress input-interface** lets you use the input ifIndex as a key-field even if NetFlow egress is configured. This means that the input ifIndex is an additional key-field.

Key-fields are a set of values that determine how a flow is identified. The seven key-fields define a unique flow that represents a unidirectional stream of packets. If a flow has a different field than another flow, it is considered a new flow. A flow contains other accounting fields (such as the AS number in the NetFlow version 5 flow format) that depend on the version record format that you configure for export. Next to the key-fields, the non-key-fields complete the flow records with extra information such as number of packets, number of bytes, and BGP AS numbers.

Specific to the router, the "router-based aggregation feature" aggregates the flow records further. It works by reducing or modifying the initial set of seven key-fields. For example, as described later, in Table 7-3, the Protocol Port-TOS aggregation type applies the source and destination application ports as key-fields. Alternatively, the destination IP address key-field can be modified to the destination prefix key-field, entailing flow records aggregation. Various aggregation types imply different key-field selection. More details are described in the section "NetFlow Version 8: Router-Based Aggregation."

Additionally, the Catalyst 6500/Cisco 7600 offers extra flexibility in the key-field configuration. The flow mask is used for data aggregation in the NetFlow cache. You can select (configure) the flow mask from a predefined set of values. For example, if you are interested in the traffic accounting per source and destination IP address, the destination-source (see Figure 7-2) is the best flow mask option, because it uses only the source and destination IP addresses as key-fields to classify the observed packets.

Figure 7-2 *Catalyst 6500/Cisco 7600 Flow Masks*

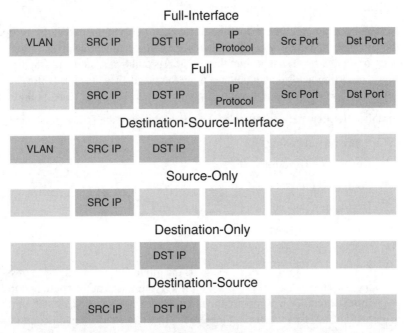

This "flow mask" concept is different from the router-based aggregation scheme. Router-based aggregation uses multiple caches; data aggregation is performed by processing flow entries as they expire from the main cache. Flow mask aggregates the flow information directly into the main NetFlow cache on the Catalyst 6000/Cisco 7600. Enhanced scalability is the main reason for the flow mask concept, which also decreases the amount of flow export. While the flow mask increases the NetFlow cache efficiency, it also decreases the level of information. Figure 7-2 shows the Catalyst 6500/Cisco 7600 flow masks' possible options.

Originally, the key-fields on the routers were defined by a fixed seven tuples of packet fields or were determined by the selected router-based aggregation. However, Flexible NetFlow overcomes those limitations by letting you define aggregation schemes. This extra flexibility for the metering process allows administrators to specify their own set of key-fields and non-key-fields. On one hand, this optimizes the metering process, because only the flows of interest are looked at. On the other hand, it optimizes the exporting process, because only the information of interest is exported. Each aggregation specified with Flexible NetFlow produces its own cache on the router and allows real-time diagnosis without exporting the flow records to the collector. In addition to the available key-fields defined in NetFlow versions 5, 8, and 9, Flexible NetFlow introduces a series of new information elements available as key-fields or non-key-fields. A full section is dedicated to Flexible NetFlow later in this chapter.

Cache Concept

The characteristics of active flows can be analyzed by displaying the cache, which makes NetFlow a powerful troubleshooting tool, even without exporting the flow records to a collector. For a better understanding, look at the following output from the NetFlow command **show ip cache flow**:

```
7200-netflow#show ip cache flow
1. IP packet size distribution (1693 total packets):
2. 1-32 64    96    128   160   192   224   256   288   320   352   384   416   448   480
3. .000 .190  .190  .615  .000  .000  .000  .000  .000  .000  .000  .000  .000  .000
.000
4. 512    544   576   1024  1536  2048  2560  3072  3584  4096  4608
5. .000  .000  .003  .000  .000  .000  .000  .000  .000  .000  .000
6. IP Flow Switching Cache, 4456704 bytes
7. 2 active, 65534 inactive, 7 added
8. 120 ager polls, 0 flow alloc failures
9. Active flows timeout in 30 minutes
10. Inactive flows timeout in 15 seconds
11. last clearing of statistics 00:03:18
12. Protocol  Total  Flows  Packets  Bytes  Packets  Active (Sec)  Idle (Sec)
13. -----     Flows  /Sec   /Flow    /Pkt   /Sec     /Flow         /Flow
14. TCP-Telnet 3     0.0    12       106    0.1      4.2           15.8
15. ICMP       2     0.0    500      100    5.2      2.6           15.4
16. Total:     5     0.0    207      100    5.4      3.6           15.6
17. SrcIf      SrcIPaddress  DstIf   DstIPaddress  Pr  SrcP  DstP  Pkts
18. Et0/0      10.10.10.34   Et0/0   10.10.10.255  11  0208  0208  1
19. Se3/0.16   10.1.10.1     Fa4/0   192.168.10.1  06  0017  2AFF  6
```

The first portion of the output, in lines 1 through 5, is the packet size distribution. Several questions that operators ask are answered here, such as "What percentage of packets of each size have passed through this router?" This information can be very useful for network troubleshooting, traffic engineering, and capacity planning.

Lines 6 through 8 describe the parameters assigned to the NetFlow cache. The default maximum number of cached flows is 65,536. In this example, two cache entries are in use, and 65,534 are available for new flows. Furthermore, the "added" parameter on line 7 displays the total number of flows examined in the cache.

Lines 9 through 11 show how long a particular flow will stay in the cache. In this example, if there were no activity on the flow for 15 seconds, the entry would have been exported and purged from the cache. If an active entry is in the cache for 30 minutes, it is expired, even if traffic still exists. A new cache entry is built on the receipt of the next packet for that particular flow. Connection-oriented flows, such as Telnet and FTP, are purged as soon as the session is closed, which is identified by TCP-FIN (finish) or TCP-RST (reset) packets.

Lines 12 through 16 break down the flows by protocol. Again, this is an ideal source of information for the network administrator, because it lists traffic distribution by type of applications.

Lines 17 through 19 show the actual NetFlow cache entries. The **show ip cache verbose flow** command shows extra information about all the information elements contained in the flow record. Actually, every information element that will be exported to a NetFlow collector is visible in the cache. The following example offers the output of flow records displayed by the **show ip cache verbose flow** command.

```
7200-netflow#show ip cache verbose flow
12. SrcIf      SrcIPaddress  DstIf  DstIPaddress   Pr  TOS  Flgs                 Pkts
13. Port       Msk           AS     Port           Msk AS   NextHop           B/pk  Active
14. Et0/0      10.10.10.34   Et1    10.10.10.255   11  00   10                   1
15. 0208       /0            0      0208           /0  0    10.48.71.1       52    0.0
16. Se3/0.16   10.1.10.1     Fa4/0  192.168.10.1   06  00   10                   3
17. 0017       /24           0      2AFF           /24 0    10.1.20.1        78    1.5
```

Compared to the output of **show ip cache flow**, only the flow records section is different (starting at line 12), because it now contains extra information elements for the flow. The first flow records are displayed in lines 14 and 15, and the second flow records are displayed in lines 16 and 17. The information element type is shown in lines 12 and 13.

The NetFlow cache size can vary from 1024 to 524,288 entries and is configurable for software-based platforms (such as the Cisco 7200 and 7500 routers). Each cache entry consumes a minimum of 64 bytes of memory. Some features such as BGP Next-Hop and MPLS-Aware NetFlow require extra bytes for additional information elements. The amount of memory on a Cisco 12000 line card denotes how many flows are possible in the cache. The maximum number of entries is directly related to the physical memory. For example, if an engine 3 line card has 256 MB of memory, NetFlow allocates 256 K entries (where K equals 1024). The Cisco Catalyst 6500/Cisco 7600 has different hardware cache sizes, based on the supervisor card and Policy Feature Card (PFC).

Table 7-1 displays the number of effective flow entries of the different supervisor engines on the Catalyst 6500/Cisco 7600.

The hash efficiency and the effective number of flow entries improved dramatically from the very first to the latest supervisor types. This was achieved by using more bits in the hash key size and algorithm enhancements. Combined with the table size of 256 K, the maximum effective size is 230-K entries on the latest SUP720-3BXL.

Table 7-1 *Effective Size of Flow Entries on the Catalyst 6500 and Cisco 7600*

	Table Size	Hash Efficiency	Effective Size	Hash Key Size
Sup2	128 KB	25 percent	32 K	17 bits
Sup720	128 KB	50 percent	64 K	36 bits
Sup720-3B	128 KB	90 percent	115 K	36 bits
Sup720-3BXL	256 KB	90 percent	230 K	36 bits

Aging Flows on a Router

On the router, the rules for expiring flow records from the cache entries include the following:

- Inactive timer. Flows that have been idle for a specified time are expired and removed from the cache for export. The inactive timer has a default setting of 15 seconds of traffic inactivity. The user can configure the inactive timer between 10 and 600 seconds.

- Active timer. Long-lived flows are expired and removed from the cache. By default, flows are not allowed to live longer than 30 minutes, even if the underlying packet conversation remains active. The user can configure the active timer between 1 and 60 minutes.

- If the cache reaches its maximum size, a number of heuristic expiry functions are applied to export flows faster to free up space for new entries. Note that in this case, the "free-up" function has a higher priority than the active and passive timers do!

- TCP connections that have reached the end of byte stream (FIN) or that have been reset (RST).

Figure 7-3 illustrates the life of a non-TCP flow. The active timer 1 (AT1) starts when the first packet arrives and a flow entry is created in the cache. In this example, we assume that packets flow constantly, with 18 packets in total. AT1 expires when it exceeds the default value of 30 minutes. At this time, the flow record, which contains the accounting details for the first 30 minutes, is exported. Because packets for this flow definition continue to arrive, the metering process creates a new flow entry in the cache that is identical to the previous one. This triggers the start of a new active timer (AT2). The inactive timer immediately starts after every packet and is cleared if new packets arrive before it expires. When no more packets for this flow arrive, the inactive timer (IT1) continues to count and expires after the default value of 15 minutes. At this point, the flow is considered inactive and is expired from the cache and exported. (Note that in Figure 7-3, IT1 actually starts 18 times and is cleared 17 times, but for simplicity this is shown only once.)

Figure 7-3   *NetFlow Flow Aging Mechanism on Routers*

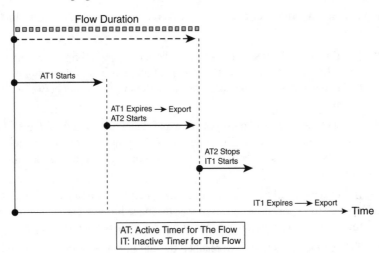

Figure 7-4 shows the flow aging mechanism for the export of flow records from the main cache.

Figure 7-4   *NetFlow Flow Aging Mechanism from the Router's Main Cache*

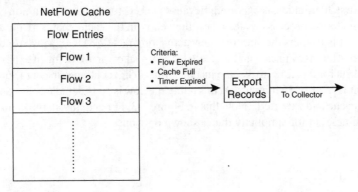

Aging Flows on a Catalyst

Flows on Catalyst switches use different flow aging timers than the ones associated with the NetFlow cache on routers. However, the flow records aging mechanisms are almost similar to the ones on the router. On a Catalyst switch, the following three timers influence the flow aging:

- **Aging timer**—Flows that have been idle for a specified time are expired and removed from the cache. The inactive timer exports a packet with a default setting of 256 seconds of traffic inactivity. The user can configure the time interval for the inactive timer between 32 and 4092 seconds. The configuration statement is **mls aging normal**.

- **Fast aging timer**—Expires flows that have not received X number of packets during the last Y seconds since the flow creation. The user can configure the values X and Y. By default, this timer is disabled. The configuration command is **mls aging fast**, where both X and Y range from 1 to 128.

- **Long aging timer**—Flows are not allowed to live more than 32 minutes (1920 seconds) by default, even if the underlying packet conversation remains undisturbed. The user can configure the time interval for the active timer between 64 and 1920 seconds in increments of 64. The configuration statement is **mls aging long**.

The aging of a flow entry occurs when no more packets are switched for that flow (inactive timer). Fast aging reduces the number of entries in the cache for short-duration connections. For example, the fast aging timer can be configured to 128 seconds. That would ensure that short-lived flows or very slow flows would be purged more frequently. This setting can help limit the growth of the NetFlow table if the number of flows is still below the recommended upper bound and the growth trend is low. Much faster aging is required when the NetFlow table utilization gets closer to its limit. You can configure a minimum fast aging time as the most aggressive way of purging active entries to free up space for new flows. However, this drastic approach has an increasing impact on the CPU utilization as more flows are exported. A good example of fast-aging timers is to quickly clean out the many single-packet flows, such as DNS, NTP, and port scans, that consume valuable space in the flow table and offer little value in the reports.

Export Version and Related Information Elements

Expired flows are grouped into NetFlow export packets to transport them from the network element to a collector. NetFlow export packets may consist of up to 30 flow records, depending on the NetFlow protocol version.

A NetFlow export packet consists of a header and a sequence of flow records. The header contains information such as sequence number, record count, sysUpTime, and universal time (UTC). The flow record provides flow information elements such as IP addresses, ports, and routing information.

The next sections cover NetFlow versions 1, 5, 7, 8, 9 and IPFIX in detail. Versions 2, 3, and 4 were never released, and version 6 was developed for one specific customer and is no longer supported.

NetFlow Version 1: The Beginning

NetFlow version 1 is the original export protocol format and has been supported since IOS version 11.0. It is rarely used today and should not be used unless a legacy collection system requires it. Preferably, use version 5 or 9 instead.

NetFlow Version 5: The Foundation

The NetFlow protocol version 5 format adds Border Gateway Protocol (BGP) Autonomous System information and flow sequence numbers.

Figure 7-5 shows the information elements available in the NetFlow version 5 export format. The **show ip route cache verbose flow** command visualizes the content of all these information element values. Remember the seven key-fields: input ifIndex, type of service, protocol, IP source and destination addresses, and TCP/UDP source and destination port numbers.

Figure 7-5   *NetFlow Version 5*

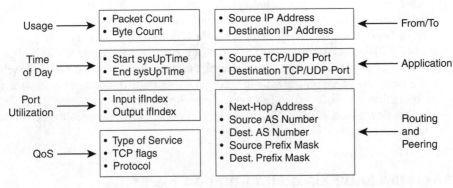

The export of flow records with NetFlow version 5 offers answers to many questions, such as "Who are the users?", "Which applications are they using?", "In what quantities?", "At what times?", and "For how long?".

NetFlow Version 7: Catalyst-Specific

The Catalyst is the only platform that supports NetFlow version 7. From an architectural perspective, the Catalyst 6500/Cisco 7600 are composed of a supervisor, called the Policy Feature Card (PFC), and an optional Multilayer Switch Feature Card (MSFC), which performs the routing function. To grasp the NetFlow version 7 concepts on the Catalyst, you must understand the Multilayer Switching (MLS) architecture in conjunction with PFC version 1. MLS is an excellent method of accelerating routing performance with dedicated

Application-Specific Integrated Circuits (ASIC). MLS offloads a significant portion of the routing function (packet rewrite) to hardware; thus, it is also called switching. Hence, MLS and Layer 3 switching are equivalent terms. MLS identifies flows on the PFC after the first packet is routed by the MSFC. By creating an entry on the PFC for routed flows, MLS transfers the process of traffic forwarding for these flows to the PFC. This mechanism bypasses the MSFC for subsequent packets of the same flow, which reduces the load on the MSFC. The **flow mask** command specifies the properties of these entries on the PFC.

In practical terms, if five related ping packets traverse a Catalyst 6500/Cisco 7600 with a PFC1, only the first one is routed through the MSFC. The four remaining packets are switched on the PFC. However, the five ping packets are considered a single flow because the characteristics of the packets (such as source address, destination address, and source port number) do not change. At the end of the flow, the Catalyst generates two NetFlow records. Record 1 is composed of the first packet accounted on and exported by the MSFC. Record 2 is composed of the subsequent packets of the same flow accounted on and exported by the PFC. Both records are exported to a NetFlow collector, which can aggregate them into a single flow record. To enable an easy way to merge flow records that are exported by two separate components with two different source IP addresses, the PFC provides the MLS traffic statistics in a NetFlow version 7 flow record. The only difference between NetFlow version 5 and version 7 is an extra information element in version 7: the shortcut IP address, which is the IP address of the MSFC. Because the IP address of the MSFC is also included in the MSFC's flow record, a NetFlow collector can combine the two records into a single flow entry.

With the introduction of PFC version 2, Cisco Express Forwarding (CEF) was introduced. CEF works with a Forwarding Information Base (FIB), which maintains next-hop address information based on the information in the IP routing table. When the Catalyst contains an MSFC card, it runs Distributed CEF (DCEF), which maintains a FIB on the PFC and the MSFC. As a special feature of DCEF, the FIB on the PFC synchronizes routing entries with the FIB on the MSFC, and vice versa. If a packet arrives on the Catalyst and there is no entry for the destination in the FIB on the PFC, the first packet of the flow is sent to the MFSC. Next, the MFSC performs the Address Resolution Protocol (ARP) request to map the destination IP network addresses to the MAC addresses and identify the destination port. Then the MSFC FIB creates the new entry and updates the PFC FIB. Therefore, the MSFC accounts for the first packet for this specific destination, and the PFC accounts for all the subsequent packets of a flow. Although this principle is similar to MLS, the big difference in case of DCEF is that only the first packet to a new adjacency (next hop) is accounted and collected by the MSFC. Note that the first packet to use a new adjacency is incomplete (no output interface, no IGP next hop, no destination prefix) because the ARP reply has not arrived yet. After the initial packet to a new adjacency creates an entry in the PFC's FIBs, all subsequent packets toward this destination are switched by the PFC. MLS, in contrast to DCEF, sends every initial packet of a routed flow to the MSFC. As a consequence, fewer flow records are gathered by the MSFC with DCEF, compared to MLS.

Before PFC version 2, the PFC and MSFC were treated as separate devices and used different source IP addresses, which were reported as different flows at a NetFlow collector and needed to be aggregated there. Starting with PFC version 2, the flow records from the PFC and the MSFC use the same source IP address. This means that even if the collector receives flow records from two different entities, the flow records appear as being exported by the same network element. Consequently, there was no longer a need to export the shortcut IP address. Starting with PFC version 2, flow records are exported with NetFlow version 5, which is the preferred solution.

To summarize NetFlow version 7 at the Catalyst:

- NetFlow version 7 adds NetFlow support for Catalyst switches with PFC1. It adds the shortcut IP address to NetFlow version 5. The shortcut IP address is the IP address of the MSFC, bypassed by the Layer 3 switched flows.

- Catalyst 6500/Cisco 7600 series switches provide Layer 3 switching with Cisco Express Forwarding (CEF) for Supervisor Engine 2 with Policy Feature Card 2 (CEF for PFC2) and Supervisor Engine 720 with PFC3 (CEF for PFC3). When the Catalyst 6500/Cisco 7600 contains an MSFC, DCEF is automatically enabled.

- On the PFC2, NetFlow version 5 is the preferred version (as opposed to NetFlow version 7) starting with IOS version 12.1(13)E.

- The NetFlow cache on the MSFC captures statistics for flows routed in software. Typically, in the case of PFC2 and PFC3, the first packet to a new adjacency or in certain situations where packets are "punted" to the MSFC (NAT, for example).

- The NetFlow cache on the PFC captures statistics for flows routed in hardware.

NetFlow Version 8: Router-Based Aggregation

Enabling NetFlow on multiple interfaces on high-end routers (such as the Cisco 12000) usually results in a large volume of NetFlow records. Aggregation of export data is typically performed by NetFlow collection tools on management workstations. Router-based aggregation allows first-level aggregation of NetFlow records on the router. The NetFlow router-based aggregation feature enables on-board aggregation by maintaining one or more extra NetFlow caches with different combinations of fields that determine which flows from the main cache are grouped. This mechanism offers benefits such as reduced bandwidth requirements between the router and the collector, and a reduced number of collection workstations.

Router-based NetFlow aggregation introduces extra aggregation schemes with separate caches in addition to the main NetFlow cache. As flows expire in the main cache, depending on the selected aggregation scheme, relevant fields are extracted from the expired flows, and the corresponding flow entry in the aggregation cache is updated. As illustrated in Figure 7-6, the same flow aging mechanisms are applied for both the main cache and the router-based aggregation caches. The exception is terminated TCP connections, because TCP flags are not present in any of the aggregation caches.

Figure 7-6   *NetFlow Versions 5 and 8*

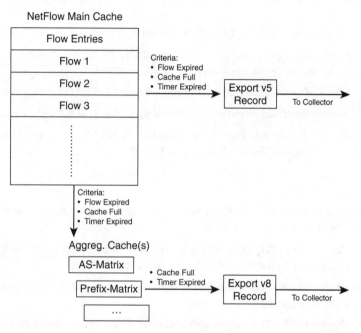

Router-based aggregation flow records are exported with NetFlow version 8. Note that some router-based aggregations introduce new information elements and therefore require exclusive export with NetFlow version 9. The BGP Next-Hop ToS aggregation scheme is an example of this. For more details, see the next section about NetFlow version 9. For completeness and comparison purposes, Figure 7-6 shows the export of both NetFlow version 5 and 8 flow records. However, when router-based aggregation is enabled, there is no need to export from the main cache with NetFlow version 5, because the router would send redundant information. An exception to this rule is a scenario in which the content of the main cache is exported to the first collector (such as for security monitoring) while the content of the aggregation cache(s) is exported to the second collector (for example, for billing purposes). Indeed, each aggregation cache scheme allows configuration of its individual cache size, its flow aging timeout parameters, its export destination IP address, and its export destination UDP port number. The default size for the secondary NetFlow aggregation cache is 4096 entries.

Selecting a NetFlow Aggregation Scheme

The following are the five non-TOS-based aggregation schemes:

- **AS aggregation scheme**—Aggregates for both source and destination BGP AS number.
- **Destination-prefix aggregation scheme**—Aggregates on the destination prefix.
- **Prefix aggregation scheme**—Aggregates on source and destination prefixes, along with the source and destination BGP AS numbers.
- **Protocol-port aggregation scheme**—Aggregates on the protocol and port number.
- **Source prefix aggregation scheme**—Aggregates on the source prefix.

The NetFlow ToS-based router aggregation feature introduces seven additional aggregation schemes that include the ToS byte as a key-field:

- **AS-ToS aggregation scheme**—Aggregates on both source and destination AS number and ToS field.
- **Destination-prefix-ToS aggregation scheme**—Aggregates on the destination prefix and ToS field.
- **Prefix-ToS aggregation scheme**—Aggregates on source and destination prefixes, the source and destination BGP AS numbers, and the ToS.
- **Protocol-port-ToS aggregation scheme**—Aggregates on the protocol and ToS field plus source and destination ports.
- **Source prefix-ToS aggregation scheme**—Aggregates on the prefix and ToS field.
- **Prefix-port-ToS aggregation scheme**—Aggregates on the prefix, port number, and ToS field.
- **BGP next-hop ToS aggregation scheme**—Aggregates on the BGP next-hop address and ToS field.

Note that the BGP next ToS aggregation scheme is special because the BGP next hop is a new information element introduced with NetFlow version 9. Therefore, this aggregation exports its flow records exclusively with NetFlow version 9. The section "BGP Next-Hop Information Element" in this chapter covers this new aggregation scheme, along with an example.

Tables 7-2 and 7-3 outline the router-based aggregation scheme information, with the exception of the BGP Next Hop ToS aggregation scheme. Table 7-2 shows the flow information elements used in non-ToS-based aggregation schemes; Table 7-3 lists the ones used in ToS-based aggregation schemes.

Table 7-2   *Non-ToS-Based Aggregation Schemes*

	AS	Protocol Port	Source Prefix	Destination Prefix	Prefix
Source Prefix			✓		✓
Source Prefix Mask			✓		✓
Destination Prefix				✓	✓
Destination Prefix Mask				✓	✓
Source Application Port		✓			
Destination Application Port		✓			
Input Interface	✓		✓		✓
Output Interface	✓			✓	✓
IP Protocol		✓			
Source AS	✓		✓		✓
Destination AS	✓			✓	✓
First Timestamp	✓	✓	✓	✓	✓
Last Timestamp	✓	✓	✓	✓	✓
Number of Flows	✓	✓	✓	✓	✓
Number of Packets	✓	✓	✓	✓	✓
Number of Bytes	✓	✓	✓	✓	✓

The Catalyst 6500 and Cisco 7600 platforms also support NetFlow version 8, with all the aggregation schemes described in Table 7-3. NetFlow aggregation is configured automatically on the PFC and Daughter Feature Cards (DFC) when configured on the MSFC. On the PFC, aggregation is implemented in software and therefore consumes additional CPU cycles.

Table 7-3   *ToS-Based Aggregation Schemes*

	AS-TOS	Protocol Port-TOS	Source Prefix-TOS	Destination Prefix-TOS	Prefix-TOS	Prefix-Port
Source Prefix			✓		✓	✓
Source Prefix Mask			✓		✓	✓
Destination Prefix				✓	✓	✓
Destination Prefix Mask				✓	✓	✓

continues

Table 7-3 *ToS-Based Aggregation Schemes (Continued)*

	AS-TOS	Protocol Port-TOS	Source Prefix-TOS	Destination Prefix-TOS	Prefix-TOS	Prefix-Port
Source Application Port		✓				✓
Destination Application Port		✓				✓
Input Interface	✓	✓	✓		✓	✓
Output Interface	✓	✓		✓	✓	✓
IP Protocol		✓				✓
Source AS	✓		✓		✓	
Destination AS	✓			✓	✓	
TOS	✓	✓	✓	✓	✓	✓
First Timestamp	✓	✓	✓	✓		✓
Last Timestamp	✓	✓	✓	✓		✓
Number of Flows	✓	✓	✓	✓		✓
Number of Packets	✓	✓	✓	✓		✓
Number of Bytes	✓	✓	✓	✓		✓

After taking a glance at these comprehensive tables, you probably are wondering which aggregation scheme to choose. The first step is to determine the information elements required by the application, as explained in the section "Data Collection Details: What to Collect" in Chapter 2, "Data Collection Methodology." Next, from the preceding lists you select the best-suited aggregation scheme that maintains the required information elements. Note that the following non-key-fields are present in all aggregation schemes: the timestamps of the first and last packet of the flow, the number of flows summarized by the aggregated flow record, the number of packets in the aggregated flow record, and the number of bytes in the aggregated flow record.

NetFlow Version 9: Flexible and Extensible

NetFlow version 9 is a flexible and extensible export protocol that provides the versatility needed to support new fields and record types. The distinguishing feature of version 9 is the template-based approach. A template describes the record format and field attributes (such as type and length) within the record. In other words, it defines a collection of fields, with corresponding descriptions of the structure and semantics. NetFlow version 9 accommodates NetFlow support for new technologies or features such as multicast, MPLS, and BGP next hop. NetFlow version 9 is required for these and future information elements and can also be used to export information elements that were previously exported by NetFlow version 5. This entails that the main cache flow records can be exported with version 5 or version 9. Similarly, the router-based aggregation flow records can be exported with version 8 or version 9, with the exception of the BGP next-hop ToS aggregation scheme, which requires NetFlow version 9. Indeed, the BGP next hop was the first information element that was supported by only version 9. Nowadays, NetFlow meters multiple new technologies and information elements specified for NetFlow version 9 only. The Cisco command-line interface displays the available export versions. The following example enables both the BGP AS and BGP next-hop ToS aggregation schemes. You can see that the first scheme offers two export protocol versions and the second scheme restricts the usage to NetFlow version 9:

```
Router(config)# ip flow-aggregation cache as
Router(config-flow-cache)# export version ?
  8  Version 8 export format
  9  Version 9 export format
Router(config)# ip flow-aggregation cache bgp-nexthop-tos
Router(config-flow-cache)# export version ?
  9  Version 9 export format
```

The section "Data Collection Protocols: NetFlow Version 9 and IPFIX Export Protocols" in Chapter 3, "Accounting and Performance Standards and Definitions," describes the advantages of using templates, the protocol itself, and some examples. For more details, refer to the protocol specifications in the informational RFC 3954, *Cisco Systems NetFlow Services Export Version 9*. RFC 3954 specifies the list of information elements supported by the protocol. The Cisco website is regularly updated with the new additions at http:// www.cisco.com/go/netflow.

NetFlow Version 10: IPFIX

The IETF IPFIX (IP Flow Information eXport) working group has chosen NetFlow version 9 as the basis for a standard IP Flow Export Protocol. After some improvements, the IPFIX protocol specification was born. To make it clear that this new protocol is an evolution of NetFlow version 9, the version number in the IPFIX header is 10.

The IPFIX section in Chapter 3 describes the history and goals of the IETF IPFIX working group; the reasons for selecting NetFlow version 9 as the basis protocol; the IPFIX protocol specification, including the enhancements compared to NetFlow version 9; and the referenced RFCs. Currently the *Specification of the IPFIX Protocol for the Exchange of IP Traffic Flow Information* draft is in the RFC-editor queue, waiting for publication. A major advantage for current NetFlow users is the fact that the already-specified NetFlow information elements keep their unique IDs with IPFIX. This eases the smooth transition from NetFlow version 9 to the IPFIX protocol.

NOTE	The IETF PSAMP (packet sampling) working group selected IPFIX as the export protocol. Refer to the section "Data Collection Protocols: PSAMP" in Chapter 3 for more details.

Comparison of Information Elements and NetFlow Version

Tables 7-2 and 7-3 analyzed the content of the flow records for the different router-based aggregation schemes. Table 7-4 compares the most common information elements with the different export protocol versions. The NetFlow metering process is executed in hardware on the Catalyst 6500/Cisco 7600. Therefore, this platform imposes some extra conditions on the classification of some information elements. Note that the latest hardware and/or software version might be required to support these new features! Finally, do not forget to select the right flow mask for the Catalyst 6500/Cisco 7600.

Table 7-4   *NetFlow Flow Record Contents*

Field	Version 5	Version 5 Catalyst 6500/ Cisco 7600[*]	Version 9	Version 7 Catalyst 6500 /Cisco 7600[*]
Source IP address	Yes	Yes	Yes	Yes
Destination IP address	Yes	Yes	Yes	Yes
Source TCP/UDP application port	Yes	Yes	Yes	Yes
Destination TCP/UDP application port	Yes	Yes	Yes	Yes
Next-hop router IP address	Yes	Yes; 12.1(13)E[*****]	Yes	Yes[*****]
Input physical interface index	Yes	Yes[****]	Yes	Yes[****]
Output physical interface index	Yes	Yes; 12.1(13)E	Yes	Yes
Packet count for this flow	Yes	Yes	Yes	Yes
Byte count for this flow	Yes	Yes	Yes	Yes
Start of flow timestamp	Yes	Yes	Yes	Yes
End of flow timestamp	Yes	Yes	Yes	Yes
IP Protocol (for example, TCP = 6; UDP = 17)	Yes	Yes	Yes	Yes
Type of service (ToS) byte	Yes	PFC3B and PFC3BXL only[**]	Yes	PFC3B and PFC3BXL only[**]
TCP flags (cumulative OR of TCP flags)	Yes	No	Yes	No
Source AS number	Yes	Yes; 12.1(13)E	Yes	Yes; 12.1(13)E
Destination AS number	Yes	Yes; 12.1(13)E	Yes	Yes; 12.1(13)E

Table 7-4   *NetFlow Flow Record Contents (Continued)*

Field	Version 5	Version 5 Catalyst 6500/ Cisco 7600[*]	Version 9	Version 7 Catalyst 6500/Cisco 7600[*]
Source subnet mask	Yes	Yes	Yes	Yes
Destination subnet mask	Yes	Yes	Yes	Yes
Flags (indicates, among other things, which flows are invalid)	Yes	Yes	Yes	Yes
Shortcut router IP address[***]	No	No	No	Yes
Other flow fields[***]	No	No	Yes	No

[*]Assumes configuration of the Full-Interface flow mask.

[**]TOS is based on the first packet in the flow.

[***]Refer to NetFlow version 9 for a complete list of other flow information elements available.

[****]The flow mask Full-Interface or Destination-Source-Interface is required for correct input interface export.

[*****]Always 0 when Policy-Based Routing (PBR), Web Cache Control Protocol (WCCP), or Server Load Balancing (SLB) is configured.

From Table 7-4, you can see that a major difference between NetFlow versions 5 and 7 is the shortcut router IP address. This is the IP address of the Layer 3 device that provides the initial Layer 3 connection, which is shortcut by the Catalyst afterwards. This field has historical reasons from the Catalyst 5000, where originally an external router was required for the Layer 3 shortcut. For the Catalyst 6500/Cisco 7600 it contains the IP address of the MSFC.

Supported Interfaces

NetFlow supports IP and IP encapsulated traffic over a wide range of interface types and encapsulations. This includes Frame Relay, Asynchronous Transfer Mode, Interswitch Link, 802.1q, Multilink Point-to-Point Protocol, General Routing Encapsulation, Layer 2 Tunneling Protocol, MPLS VPNs, and IPsec tunnels.

To account for traffic entering a tunnel, configure ingress NetFlow on the router. To account for tunnel and post tunnel flows, enable ingress NetFlow at the tunnel endpoint.

Each interface is identified by a unique value of the ifIndex object, as defined in the SNMP MIBs (RFC 2863). NetFlow is also supported per subinterface and reports the ifIndex value related to the specific subinterface. If NetFlow is configured on the physical interface, all logical subinterfaces are monitored. Alternatively, NetFlow can be enabled per subinterface with the **ip flow ingress** or **ip flow egress** CLI command.

Export Protocol: UDP or SCTP

Historically, UDP has been the protocol of choice to export the NetFlow records to minimize the impact on the network elements. However, the simplicity of UDP comes with some drawbacks. As a nonacknowledged transport protocol, UDP faces the risk of losing packets in case of network congestion, because UDP has no retransmission function. Cisco routers and switches offer the option to export simultaneously to two different collectors, which offers increased reliability at the expense of correlating the missing flow records at the collector level.

With the emergence of router-based aggregation, leading to better aggregation and a reduced export rate, plus the definition of Flexible NetFlow, offering an optimal aggregation, losing NetFlow export packets becomes an important issue. To address the higher reliability demands from billing applications, NetFlow offers the option to export flow records over the Stream Control Transport Protocol (SCTP) instead of UDP.

SCTP (RFC 2960), along with its partially reliable extension (PR-SCTP, RFC 3758), is a reliable message-oriented transport layer protocol. It allows data to be transmitted between two endpoints in a fully reliable, partially reliable, or unreliable manner. An SCTP session consists of an association between two endpoints, which may contain one or more logical channels called streams. SCTP's stream-based transmission model facilitates the export of a mix of different data types, such as NetFlow templates and NetFlow data, over the same connection. The maximum number of inbound and outbound streams supported by an endpoint is negotiated during the SCTP association initialization process.

When configuring the NetFlow version 9 export, NetFlow creates a minimum of two streams:

- Stream 0, used for sending templates, options templates, and option records, configured as fully reliable

- One or more streams for carrying data, configured as fully reliable, partially reliable, or unreliable

Compared to UDP, stream 0 offers the advantage that the NetFlow version 9 templates are sent only once, with guaranteed delivery.

When more than one cache (main cache and one or more aggregation caches) is exporting data, each cache creates its own streams with their own configured reliability levels. For example, configuring the main cache to use SCTP in full reliability mode and the NetFlow prefix aggregation cache to use partial reliability mode sends messages to the same collector over the same SCTP port.

NOTE

When using SCTP as the transport protocol for exporting NetFlow traffic, the traffic is usually referred to as messages instead of datagrams because SCTP is a message-oriented protocol. When using UDP as the transport protocol for exporting NetFlow traffic, the traffic is usually referred to as datagrams because UDP is a datagram-oriented protocol.

When SCTP is operating in full reliability mode, it uses a selective acknowledgment scheme to guarantee the ordered delivery of messages. The SCTP protocol stack buffers messages until their receipt is acknowledged by the receiving endpoint, which is the NetFlow collector. SCTP has a congestion control mechanism that can be used to limit how much memory is consumed by SCTP for buffering packets.

If a stream is specified as unreliable, the packet is simply sent once and not buffered on the exporter. If the packet is lost on the way to the receiver, the exporter cannot retransmit it. This mode is equal to UDP transport.

When a stream is specified as partially reliable, a limit is placed on how much memory is dedicated to storing unacknowledged packets. This limit can be configured using the **buffer-limit** command. If the limit is exceeded and the router attempts to buffer another packet, the oldest unacknowledged packet is discarded, and a message called forward-tsn (transmit sequence number) is sent to the collector to indicate that this packet will not be acknowledged. This mechanism prevents NetFlow from consuming all the free memory on a router in a situation that requires buffering many packets—for example, if SCTP is experiencing long response times from a collector.

Because SCTP is a connection-oriented protocol, a backup collector can be used as a message destination in the event that the primary collector becomes unavailable. When connectivity with the primary collector has been lost, and a backup collector is configured, SCTP uses the backup collector. The default time that SCTP waits until it starts using the backup collector is 25 seconds. You can configure a different value for this interval with the **fail-over time** command. The router sends periodic SCTP heartbeat messages to the SCTP collectors configured and uses the heartbeat function to monitor the status of each collector. This notifies the NetFlow exporting process quickly if connectivity to a collector is lost.

Two SCTP backup options exist:

- **Failover mode**—When the router is configured in failover mode, it does not activate the association with the backup collector until the timeout for the SCTP heartbeat messages from the primary collector occurs.

- **Redundant mode**—When the router is configured in redundant mode, it activates the association with the backup collector immediately. The router does not start sending SCTP messages to a backup collector in redundant mode until the timeout for the SCTP heartbeat messages from the primary collector occurs.

Failover mode is the preferred method when the backup collector is on the end of an expensive lower-bandwidth link such as ISDN. During the time that SCTP is using the backup collector, it tries to restore the association with the primary collector. This continues until connectivity is restored or the primary SCTP collector is removed from the configuration.

Under either failover mode, any records that have been queued between losing connectivity with the primary destination and establishing the association with the backup collector might be lost. A counter tracks how many records are lost, which you can view with the **show ip flow export sctp verbose** command.

To avoid a flapping SCTP association with a collector where the connection goes up and down in quick succession, the period configured with the **restore-time** command should be greater than the period of a typical connectivity problem. Consider a scenario in which a router is configured to use IP fast convergence for its routing table. Suddenly a LAN interface starts flapping, causing the IP route to the primary collector to be added and removed from the routing table every 2000 msec. In this case, the restore time should have a value greater than 2000 msec.

NetFlow Device-Level Architecture: Combining the Elements

NetFlow services at the device level can be categorized as follows:

- Preprocessing features allow you to collect subsets of the network traffic instead of metering all packets. This includes fine-tuning the collection of NetFlow data. Examples in this category are packet sampling and packet filtering.

- Advanced features and services based on the flexible NetFlow version 9 export format make it possible to collect different types of traffic. For example, you might want to meter BGP next hop, multicast, MPLS, IPv6, NetFlow Layer 2, etc.

- Post-processing features enable you to control how flow records are exported. For example, you could configure aggregation schemes, export records over UDP or SCTP, export to multiple destinations, filter some flow records before the export (Catalyst 6500/Cisco 7600 specific), sample flow records (Catalyst 6500/Cisco 7600 specific), etc.

Figure 7-7 illustrates these three categories.

Figure 7-8 assembles all elements at the device level. The first step is the creation and classification of flows in the main cache. The expiration of flows from the main cache is the second step. Step 3 checks if an aggregation scheme is enabled. If this is the case, step 4 is executed, and the flow records are further combined in the aggregation cache. If no aggregation is configured, nonaggregated flow records are exported. Finally, when the flow records are ready for export, step 5 takes place and selects the NetFlow version (5, 8, 9), along with the choice of the transport protocol (UDP or SCTP).

Figure 7-7 *NetFlow Services Categories*

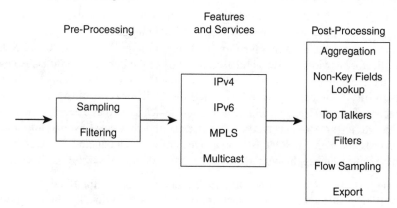

Figure 7-8 *NetFlow Device-Level Architecture*

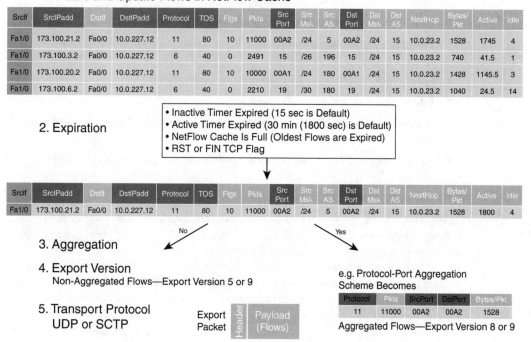

Cisco NetFlow Collector

The Cisco NetFlow Collection Engine offers fast and scalable data collection, filtering, and aggregation of exported NetFlow records. Even though the official Cisco documentation uses the name "Cisco CNS NetFlow Collection Engine," the term "Cisco NetFlow Collector" is widely known and used throughout the industry, and it is also used in this book. Note that the Network Analysis Module (NAM) for the Catalyst 6500/Cisco 7600 performs a similar role as the Cisco NetFlow Collector. The NAM receives NetFlow records from the Catalyst 6500/Cisco 7600 device as well as external routers and switches. Records are not stored in NetFlow format; instead, they are converted into standard RMON records and stored in RMON format. This introduces a benefit for customers who already have an RMON application and do not want to deploy a NetFlow Collector.

One part of the NetFlow network element configuration is the IP address that identifies a NetFlow Collector as the recipient of flow records. Additionally, the transport protocol (UDP or SCTP) is selected, along with the port number (a logical port designator) in case of UDP. The NetFlow Collector listens for exported flow records from the network elements and performs the following functions:

- NetFlow data collection from multiple export devices
- Data volume reduction through filtering and aggregation
- Flow records data augmentation, by adding additional details such as BGP path, DNS name, etc.
- Hierarchical data storage for classification and retrieval
- File system disk space management
- A simple monitoring, analysis, and troubleshooting tool with a web-based user interface and reporting engine
- An interface to a Tibco messaging bus, where status messages can be sent and received
- An XML interface for programmatic configuration

The NetFlow Collector aggregates flow records into data files based on user-defined criteria, which are called *aggregators*. An aggregator defines a set of user-configurable attributes that specify how a NetFlow Collector summarizes the flow records. Two important aggregator functions are the aggregation schemes and the filters. The aggregation schemes define which subset of data in flow records are relevant, and they state which statistics are gathered. The filters define the criteria for accepting or rejecting flow records for aggregation afterwards. For example, an aggregation scheme might impose the aggregation of all flow records based on the same source and/or destination IP addresses, and a filter might exclude all flow records whose destination is the network 10.0.0.0. As a special feature, the Cisco NetFlow Collector offers to augment the flow records with extra information. For example, the BGP passive peer client at the collector can add BGP-related information, which can be used for an aggregator, as either non-key-fields or key-fields. The key-fields and non-key-fields have exactly the same meaning at the NetFlow Collector as they have at the network element. Another example is the DNS name resolution, in which the DNS name replaces the source and destination IP addresses. In an MPLS environment, a NetFlow Collector can match the flow record interface with the Virtual Routing and Forwarding (VRF) by querying MPLS topology-aware applications such as Cisco IP Solution Center (ISC).

CLI Operations

This section includes the most important configuration commands to enable NetFlow on Cisco routers. Subsequent sections of this chapter cover specific NetFlow versions and more advanced features and describe the respective commands. Because the NetFlow configuration on the Catalysts is slightly different, it is covered in a separate section.

- router(config)# **ip flow-export** {**destination** {*ip-address* ι *hostname*} *udp-port* ι **source** {*interface-name*} ι **version** {**1** ι [{**5** ι **9**} [**origin-as** ι **peer-as**] [**bgp-nexthop**]]} ι **template** {**refresh-rate** *packets* ι **timeout-rate** *minutes*} [**options** {**export-stats** ι **refresh-rate** *packets* ι **sampler** ι **timeout-rate** *minutes*}]}
  enables the export of information in NetFlow cache entries. The minimum to specify is the IP address or hostname for exporting the flow records, the UDP port where the collector is listening, and the NetFlow version. Optionally, the configuration allows the collection and reporting of the BGP Autonomous System numbers and the BGP next-hop address.

  The **source** {*interface-name*} keyword is very useful to configure in the **ip flow-export** command, because it overrides the default behavior for the source IP address of the UDP NetFlow export packets (using the IP address of the interface that the datagram is transmitted over as the source IP address for the NetFlow export packets). The source IP address of the NetFlow export packets is used by the collector to determine from which router the NetFlow records arrive. In a situation where the primary link from the router to the collector is not operational, the router might send the flow records via a different interface, and the collector receives the records from the same router with a different source IP addresses if **source** {*interface-name*} is not set.

- router(config-if)# **ip flow ingress**
  configures NetFlow on an interface or subinterface.

- router(config-if)# **ip flow egress**
  configures egress support for NetFlow on an interface or subinterface.

- router(config)# **ip flow-cache timeout** [**active** *minutes* ι **inactive** *seconds*]
  specifies the main flow cache active and inactive parameters for flow expiration. The default values are 30 minutes for the active timeout (with a configurable range from 1 to 60) and 15 seconds for the inactive timeout (with a configurable range from 10 to 600).

- router(config)# **ip flow-cache entries**
  changes the number of entries maintained in the main NetFlow cache. The valid range
  is from 1024 to 524288 entries. The number of entries should be changed only if the
  main cache capacity reaches its limit and if the router has additional free memory
  available.

SNMP Operations with the NETFLOW-MIB

The CISCO-NETFLOW-MIB MIB, supported on the Cisco routers, provides real-time
access to a limited number of fields in the flow cache. Exporting the entire cache via SNMP
is not technically feasible in many cases, because a flow cache may fill up to 64 MB.
Therefore, the MIB does not allow the retrieval from the entire cache content.

The NetFlow MIB defines managed objects that enable a network administrator to do the
following:

- Configure the number of cache entries, both on the main cache and on the aggregation
  caches
- Configure the cache timeout values, both on the main cache and on the aggregation
  caches
- Configure NetFlow export parameters on the main and aggregation caches: NetFlow
  version, NetFlow Collector IP address and port number, export protocol, BGP
  Autonomous System, BGP next hop, etc.
- Configure NetFlow on physical and logical (sub)interfaces
- Configure the source and destination minimum mask for the aggregation caches
- Configure NetFlow version 9 specific details, such as template options, etc.
- Monitor the NetFlow cache statistics per protocol and port
- Monitor the NetFlow export statistics

Also included with the NetFlow MIB is the Top Talkers feature to display the Top-N flows
in the NetFlow cache. The NetFlow MIB and Top Talkers feature provide information about
traffic patterns and application usage in the network. The Top Talkers feature can be
configured for the Top-N flows to appear sorted in a dedicated new cache. The NetFlow
MIB allows the retrieval of the information elements for the Top-N flows. The CISCO-
SWITCH-ENGINE-MIB, which is specific for the Catalyst 6500/Cisco 7600, offers a
couple of interesting MIB variables to monitor the MLS table:

- cseCacheUtilization monitors the flow utilization level in percent.
- cseL3ActiveFlows monitors the number of active flows in the Layer 3 flow table.
- cseL3FlowLearnFailures monitors the number of flows that failed to be learned
  because the Layer 3 flow table was full.

Example: NetFlow Version 5 on a Router

In the following example, the configuration shows the three ways to enable the NetFlow metering process on an interface. The command **ip route-cache flow**, which is valid only on the main interface, is the old way. This command was superseded by the **ip flow ingress** and **ip flow egress** commands, which can be enabled on the main interface or a subinterface:

```
Router(config)# interface serial 0/0
Router(config-if)# ip route-cache flow
Router(config)# interface serial 0/1
Router(config-if)# ip flow ingress
Router(config)# interface FastEthernet 1/0
Router(config-if)# ip flow ingress

Router# show ip flow interface
Serial0/0
  ip route-cache flow
Serial0/2
  ip flow ingress
FastEthernet1/0
  ip flow egress
```

The following lines configure the NetFlow version 5 exports to a collector with IP address 10.48.71.219 and UDP port 1234, with the loopback 0 IP address as the source IP address of the UDP packets. Finally, the autonomous system fields are populated with information about the adjacent peers and are exported in the flow records:

```
Router(config)# ip flow-export source Loopback0
Router(config)# ip flow-export version 5 peer-as
Router(config)# ip flow-export destination 10.48.71.219 1234

Router# show ip flow export
Flow export v5 is enabled for main cache
  Exporting flows to 10.48.71.219 (1234)
  Exporting using source interface Loopback0
  Version 5 flow records, peer-as
  679912 flows exported in 123007 udp datagrams
  0 flows failed due to lack of export packet
  30 export packets were sent up to process level
  0 export packets were dropped due to no fib
  0 export packets were dropped due to adjacency issues
  0 export packets were dropped due to fragmentation failures
  0 export packets were dropped due to encapsulation fixup failures
  0 export packets were dropped enqueuing for the RP
  0 export packets were dropped due to IPC rate limiting
```

The **show ip flow export** command displays the NetFlow version 5 configuration and some interesting statistics, such as the number of flow records exported, the number of export packets, the number of packets that were not exported, and the reason for failures. To increase reliability in case of network failure, optionally configure a second collector that duplicates the flow records to two destinations.

To change the default active and inactive timeouts (respectively, 30 minutes and 15 seconds), enter the following:

```
Router(config)# ip flow-cache timeout active 60
Router(config)# ip flow-cache timeout inactive 20
```

The confirmation of these new timeouts is displayed in the output of the **show ip cache flow** command.

Example: NetFlow Configuration on the Catalyst

The following example shows the configuration of NetFlow on a Cisco 7600. The flow records from both the PFC and the MSFC are exported to the collector with the IP address 10.48.71.129 and UDP port 9991. NetFlow is configured with the interface-full flow mask, to export the flow records with NetFlow version 5, and to exclude the flow records whose destination IP address is part of the 10.10.10.0/24 network. The command **mls nde sender version 5** is specific to the flow records accounted on the PFC, and the command **ip flow-export version 5** is specific to the flow records accounted on the MSFC.

```
7600(config)# mls flow ip interface-full
7600(config)# mls netflow
7600(config)# mls nde sender version 5
7600(config)# mls nde flow exclude destination 10.10.10.0 255.255.255.0

7600(config)# interface GigabitEthernet1/8
7600(config-if)# ip flow ingress

7600(config)# interface Vlan1
7600(config-if)# ip flow ingress

7600(config)# ip flow-export version 5
7600(config)# ip flow-export destination 10.48.71.129 9991
```

The NetFlow cache contains the flow records, PFC, and MSFC, with a clear separation in the output. This happens because the flows are monitored at two different logical entities and because the flows are classified according to two different sets of key-fields. Note also the Null interface for the flow records monitored by the MSFC.

```
7600# show ip cache flow
- - - - - - - - - - - - - - - - - - - - - - - - - - - - - - - - - - - - - - - - - -
MSFC:
IP packet size distribution (58 total packets):
  1-32   64   96  128  160  192  224  256  288  320  352  384  416  448  480
  .000 .982 .000 .000 .000 .000 .000 .000 .000 .000 .017 .000 .000 .000 .000

  512  544  576 1024 1536 2048 2560 3072 3584 4096 4608
  .000 .000 .000 .000 .000 .000 .000 .000 .000 .000 .000

IP Flow Switching Cache, 4456704 bytes
  11 active, 65525 inactive, 11 added
  193 ager polls, 0 flow alloc failures
  Active flows timeout in 30 minutes
  Inactive flows timeout in 15 seconds
IP Sub Flow Cache, 270664 bytes
  11 active, 16373 inactive, 11 added, 11 added to flow
  0 alloc failures, 0 force free
  1 chunk, 1 chunk added
  last clearing of statistics never
Protocol          Total    Flows   Packets Bytes   Packets Active(Sec) Idle(Sec)
--------          Flows    /Sec    /Flow  /Pkt     /Sec    /Flow       /Flow

SrcIf          SrcIPaddress    DstIf        DstIPaddress    Pr SrcP DstP Pkts
```

```
Vl1              0.0.0.0           Null          255.255.255.255 11 0044 0043  1
SrcIf           SrcIPaddress      DstIf            DstIPaddress   Pr SrcP DstP  Pkts
07C1     7 Vl1           10.48.77.118  Null          224.0.0.2       11 07C1
07C1     8 Vl1           10.48.73.58   Null          224.0.0.10      58 0000
0000     5
-------------------------------------------------------------------
PFC:

Displaying Hardware entries in Module 5
SrcIf            SrcIPaddress          DstIPaddress     Pr       SrcP
DstP     Pkts
Vl1             10.48.71.129          10.48.72.208     tcp      62816
telnet   0              --            0.0.0.0                  0.0.0.0
0        0              0       6
```

The **show mls nde** and **show ip flow export** commands display the NetFlow export
information for the PFC and MSFC, respectively. The fact that the two exports use the same
source IP address (10.48.72.208) allows the export from NetFlow version 5 from both the
PFC and the MSFC.

```
7600# show mls nde
 Netflow Data Export enabled
 Exporting flows to 10.48.71.129 (9992)
 Exporting flows from 10.48.72.208 (56986)
 Version: 5
 Include Filter not configured
 Exclude Filter is:
   destination:  ip address 10.10.10.0, mask 255.255.255.0
 Total Netflow Data Export Packets are:
    0 packets, 0 no packets, 0 records
 Total Netflow Data Export Send Errors:
        IPWRITE_NO_FIB = 0
        IPWRITE_ADJ_FAILED = 0
        IPWRITE_PROCESS = 0
        IPWRITE_ENQUEUE_FAILED = 0
        IPWRITE_IPC_FAILED = 0
        IPWRITE_OUTPUT_FAILED = 0
        IPWRITE_MTU_FAILED = 0
        IPWRITE_ENCAPFIX_FAILED = 0
 Netflow Aggregation Disabled

7600# show ip flow export
Flow export v5 is enabled for main cache
  Exporting flows to 10.48.71.129 (9992)
  Exporting using source IP address 10.48.72.208
  Version 5 flow records
  50826 flows exported in 23589 udp datagrams
  0 flows failed due to lack of export packet
  0 export packets were sent up to process level
  0 export packets were dropped due to no fib
  0 export packets were dropped due to adjacency issues
  0 export packets were dropped due to fragmentation failures
  0 export packets were dropped due to encapsulation fixup failures
  0 export packets were dropped enqueuing for the RP
  0 export packets were dropped due to IPC rate limiting
```

Example: NetFlow Version 8

The following example shows how to configure a destination prefix aggregation cache with a size of 2046, an inactive timeout of 200 seconds, an active timeout of 45 minutes, an export destination IP address of 10.42.42.1, and a destination port of 9992:

```
Router(config)# ip flow-aggregation cache destination-prefix
Router(config-flow-cache)# cache entries 2046
Router(config-flow-cache)# cache timeout inactive 200
Router(config-flow-cache)# cache timeout active 45
Router(config-flow-cache)# export destination 10.42.42.1 9992
Router(config-flow-cache)# enabled
```

As opposed to the main cache, the export of the flow records from an aggregation cache must be enabled specifically.

The output of **show ip flow export** displays the router-based aggregation configuration:

```
Router# show ip flow export
 ...
  Cache for destination-prefix aggregation:
    Exporting flows to 10.42.42.1 (9992)
    Exporting using source IP address 192.2.1.5
 ...
```

The **show ip cache verbose flow aggregation** *aggregation-scheme* command, which is quite similar to **show ip cache verbose flow** for the main cache, displays the content of the aggregation scheme. Furthermore, it shows the number of active flows, the configured timeout, and so on:

```
Router# show ip cache verbose flow aggregation destination-prefix
IP Flow Switching Cache, 135048 bytes
  2 active, 2044 inactive, 4 added
  924 ager polls, 0 flow alloc failures
  Active flows timeout in 45 minutes
  Inactive flows timeout in 200 seconds
IP Sub Flow Cache, 8968 bytes
  4 active, 507 inactive, 4 added, 4 added to flow
  0 alloc failures, 0 force free
  1 chunk, 1 chunk added

Dst If      Dst Prefix    Msk AS   Flows  Pkts B/Pk  Active
Se0/2       10.48.71.0    /24 0       24   849   68   327.5
Fa0/1       192.1.1.104   /30 0        1     5  100     0.1
```

Example: NetFlow Version 9

The following example shows how to configure NetFlow version 9 on a router. NetFlow version 9 sends the templates and options templates every 20 packets or every 30 minutes per default. This example shows how to modify these default values. Finally, the last two commands enable two specific options templates:

- The export-stats template includes the number of packets sent and the number of flows exported.

- The sampler template contains the random-sampler configuration, including the sampler ID, sampling mode, and sampling interval for each configured random sampler.

```
Router(config)# ip flow-export version 9
Router(config)# ip flow-export destination 10.48.71.219 1234
Router(config)# ip flow-export source Loopback0
Router(config)# ip flow-export template refresh-rate 40
Router(config)# ip flow-export template timeout-rate 60
Router(config)# ip flow-export template options refresh-rate 40
Router(config)# ip flow-export template options timeout-rate 60
Router(config)# ip flow-export template options export-stats
Router(config)# ip flow-export template options sampler
```

Along with the **show ip flow export** command, already described, the **show ip flow export template** command is specific to NetFlow version 9. It shows the number of (option) templates, the number of active (option) templates, the configured timeout for the (option) templates, and so on:

```
Router# show ip flow export template
   Template Options Flag = 3
   Total number of Templates added = 4
   Total active Templates = 4
   Flow Templates active = 2
   Flow Templates added = 2
   Option Templates active = 2
   Option Templates added = 2
   Template ager polls = 1629
   Option Template ager polls = 1420
Main cache version 9 export is enabled
 Template export information
   Template timeout = 60
   Template refresh rate = 40
 Option export information
   Option timeout = 60
   Option refresh rate = 40
```

New Features Supported with NetFlow Version 9

The flexibility and extensibility of the NetFlow version 9 protocol offers new possibilities for the metering process. This section lists a series of features enabled on top of NetFlow version 9.

SCTP Export

In the following example, shown in Figure 7-9, the router exports flow records for two different applications:

- Flow records from the *main cache* for security purposes. The flow records are exported to 10.10.10.10 with partial reliability with a backup in failover mode to the host 11.11.11.11.

- Flow records from the *aggregation cache* for billing purposes, which implies that flow records cannot be lost. They are exported with full reliability to 12.12.12.12, while the backup to 13.13.13.13 is configured in redundant mode.

Figure 7-9   *Scenario: SCTP Export*

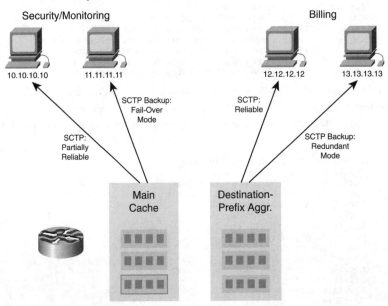

The following CLI configures the scenario shown in Figure 7-9. The backup restore time for the billing scenario has been set to a minimum value. As a result, a smaller number of flow records are transferred to the primary collector in case of backup and restore. This is less critical for the monitoring case.

```
Router(config)# ip flow-export destination 10.10.10.10 9999 sctp
Router(config-flow-export-sctp)# reliability partial buffer-limit 100
Router(config-flow-export-sctp)# backup destination 11.11.11.11 9999
Router(config-flow-export-sctp)# backup fail-over 1000
Router(config-flow-export-sctp)# backup mode fail-over

Router(config)# ip flow-aggregation cache destination-prefix
Router(config-flow-cache)# export destination 12.12.12.12 9999 sctp
Router(config-flow-export-sctp)# backup destination 13.13.13.13 9999
Router(config-flow-export-sctp)# backup mode redundant
Router(config-flow-export-sctp)# backup restore-time 1
Router(config-flow-export-sctp)# exit
Router(config-flow-cache)# enabled
```

In the following **show** command, you see that the backup association to 11.11.11.11 is not connected (backup mode failover), while the backup association to 13.13.13.13 is connected because the selected mode is redundant:

```
Router# show ip flow export sctp verbose
```

```
IPv4 main cache exporting to 10.10.10.10, port 9999, partial
status: connected
backup mode: fail-over
104 flows exported in 84 sctp messages.
0 packets dropped due to lack of SCTP resources
fail-over time: 1000 milli-seconds
restore time:   25 seconds
backup: 11.11.11.11, port 9999
   status: not connected
   fail-overs: 0
   0 flows exported in 0 sctp messages.
   0 packets dropped due to lack of SCTP resources
destination-prefix cache exporting to 12.12.12.12, port 9999, full
status: connected
backup mode: redundant
57 flows exported in 42 sctp messages.
0 packets dropped due to lack of SCTP resources
fail-over time: 25 milli-seconds
restore time:    1 seconds
backup: 13.13.13.13, port 9999
   status: connected
   fail-overs: 0
   0 flows exported in 0 sctp messages.
   0 packets dropped due to lack of SCTP resources
```

Sampled NetFlow

Due to the increasing interface speed and the higher density of ports on network elements, sampling becomes a very relevant feature in NetFlow. Without sampling, network elements gather so many flow records that these flows consumes a significant part of the total CPU utilization. In addition, the bandwidth requirements for the export link to the collector increase, and the collector requires extensive resources to process all exported flow records.

Sampled NetFlow significantly decreases CPU utilization. On average, at a Cisco 7500, sampling 1:1000 packets reduces the CPU utilization by 82 percent, and sampling 1:100 packets reduces the CPU utilization by 75 percent. The conclusion is that sampled NetFlow is a significant factor in reducing CPU utilization.

Even with NetFlow implementations in hardware ASIC on Cisco platforms such as the Catalyst 4500, 6500, 7600, 10000, and 12000 routers, sampled NetFlow offers advantages. Exporting flow records has a major impact on the CPU utilization on hardware-based NetFlow implementations.

Chapter 2 describes the different types of sampling in detail. Random packet sampling is statistically more accurate than deterministic packet sampling because it avoids any bias due to potential traffic repetitions and patterns.

Packet-Based Sampling on the Routers

NetFlow's ability to sample packets was first implemented as a feature called Sampled NetFlow. It uses *deterministic* sampling, which selects every *n*-th packet for NetFlow processing on a per-interface basis. For example, if you set the sampling rate to 1 out of 100 packets, Sampled NetFlow samples packets 1, 101, 201, 301, and so on. The Sampled NetFlow feature does not support random sampling and thus can result in inaccurate statistics when traffic arrives with fixed patterns.

Even though the Cisco 12000 router still offers Sampled NetFlow, the majority of the Cisco platforms offer Random Sampled NetFlow. Random Sampled NetFlow selects incoming packets based on a random selection algorithm so that *on average* one out of *n* sequential packets is selected for NetFlow processing. For example, if you set the sampling rate to 1 out of 100 packets, NetFlow might sample packets 5, 120, 199, 302, and so on. The sample configuration 1:100 provides NetFlow data on 1 percent of the total traffic. The *n* value is a configurable parameter, ranging from 1 to 65,535.

The Modular QoS Command-Line Interface (MQC) consists of three components:

- The class map defines the traffic for inspection.
- The policy map defines action on the classified traffic.
- The service policy enables a policy at an interface.

This section offers a typical configuration example on a router, with three configuration steps.

Step 1: Defining a NetFlow Sampler Map

A NetFlow sampler map defines a set of properties (such as the sampling rate and the NetFlow sampler name) for NetFlow sampling. Each NetFlow sampler map can be applied to one or many subinterfaces, as well as physical interfaces. For example, you can create a NetFlow sampler map named mysampler1 with the following properties: random sampling mode and a sampling rate of 1 out of 100 packets. This NetFlow sampler map can be applied to any number of subinterfaces, each of which would refer to mysampler1 to perform NetFlow sampling. In this case, traffic from these multiple subinterfaces is merged into flows, which introduces even more randomness than sampling per single subinterface does.

```
router(config)# flow-sampler-map mysampler1
router(config-sampler)# mode random one-out-of 100
```

Step 2: Applying a NetFlow Sampler Map to an Interface

The following example shows how to apply a NetFlow sampler map called mysampler1 to Ethernet interface 1:

```
router(config)# interface ethernet 1/0
router(config-if)# flow-sampler mysampler1
```

Enabling Random Sampled NetFlow on a physical interface does not automatically enable it on all its subinterfaces. In addition, disabling Random Sampled NetFlow on a physical interface or subinterface does not enable full NetFlow. This restriction prevents the unwanted transition from sampling to full NetFlow. Instead, full NetFlow must be configured explicitly.

```
Router# show flow-sampler
Sampler : mysampler1, id : 1, packets matched : 10, mode : random sampling mode
  sampling interval is : 100
```

Step 3: Checking the NetFlow Cache

The following example displays the NetFlow output of the **show ip cache verbose flow** command, in which the sampler, class-id, and general flags are set:

```
Router# show ip cache verbose flow
...
SrcIf           SrcIPaddress    DstIf           DstIPaddress    Pr TOS Flgs  Pkts
Port Msk AS                     Port Msk AS     NextHop            B/Pk  Active
BGP: BGP NextHop

Et1/0           8.8.8.8         Et0/0*          9.9.9.9         01 00  10      3
0000 /8  302                    0800 /8  300    3.3.3.3                100   0.1
BGP: 2.2.2.2         Sampler: 1  Class: 1  FFlags: 01
```

The ID of the class that matches a packet is stored in the flow. The class ID is exported with version 9. A mapping of the class ID to the class name is sent to the collector using the options templates in NetFlow data export version 9. The collector maintains a mapping table from the class ID to the class name, and the table associates a class name with a flow at the collector so that you can determine which flow is filtered by a specific class.

For information, NetFlow flags (FFlags) that might appear in the **show ip cache verbose flow** command output are as follows:

- FFlags: 01 (#**define FLOW_FLAGS_OUTPUT 0x0001**)—Egress flow
- FFlags: 02 (#**define FLOW_FLAGS_DROP 0x0002**)—Dropped flow (for example, dropped by an ACL)
- FFlags: 04 (#**define FLOW_FLAGS_MPLS 0x0004**)—MPLS flow
- FFlags: 08 (#**define FLOW_FLAGS_IPV6 0x0008**)—IPv6 flow
- FFlags: 10 (#**define FLOW_FLAGS_RSVD 0x0010**)—Reserved

Sending the Flow-Sampler Information

When the collector receives sampled flow records, a correlation between the sampled traffic and actual traffic that passed the device is required. An approximation is to multiply the sampled number of packet and bytes with the sampling rate. This implies that for each sampler ID the sampling rate is known to the collector. NetFlow version 9 exports the sampling rate in an option template field that matches the sampler ID of the exported flow records.

```
router(config)# ip flow-export version 9 options sampler
```

The previous CLI entry enables the export of an option containing random-sampler configuration, including the sampler ID, the sampling mode, and the sampling interval for each configured random sampler. In our example, the collector receives a flow record with the sampler ID equal to 1, along with an option template record containing sampler ID = 1, mode = random sampled NetFlow, and sampling rate = 100.

Flow-Based Sampled NetFlow on the Catalyst

On the Catalyst 6500/Cisco 7600, the NetFlow cache on the Policy Feature Card (PFC) captures statistics for flows routed in hardware. These platforms do not support packet sampling, because the collection process is implemented in ASICs and does not have any impact on the CPU utilization. Although the metering process is implemented in hardware, the flow export still requires software processing, which has a CPU impact. To reduce this, the PFC supports flow-based sampling, which decreases the CPU utilization, because only a subset of flow records is exported. As opposed to packet-based sampling, flow-based sampling is a post-processing feature, which means a sampling mechanism selects a subset of the existing flow entries for export to a collector.

With a Supervisor Engine 720, sampled NetFlow *always* uses the full-interface flow mask. With a Supervisor Engine 2, sampled NetFlow uses the full-interface *or* destination-source-interface flow masks. Sampled NetFlow per LAN port is supported with the full-interface flow mask or the destination-source-interface flow mask. This is a major enhancement compared to Supervisor Engine 2 functions and the other flow masks, where sampled NetFlow can be applied only at the device level instead of the interface level.

Two different flavors of flow-based sampling exist: time-based sampling and packet-based sampling.

Time-based sampling exports a snapshot of the NetFlow cache at certain intervals. The time-based sampling rate is specified in Table 7-5, which displays the corresponding sampling time and export interval for a given sampling rate.

Table 7-5   *Time-Based Sampling Rate and Export Interval*

Sampling Rate (R)	Sampling Interval P (ms)	Sampling Time ΔT (ms)	Idle Time I (ms)
64	8192	128	8064
128	8192	64	8128
256	8192	32	8160
512	8192	16	8176
1024	8192	8	8184

Table 7-5   *Time-Based Sampling Rate and Export Interval (Continued)*

Sampling Rate (R)	Sampling Interval P (ms)	Sampling Time ΔT (ms)	Idle Time I (ms)
2048	8192	4	8188
4096	16384	4	16380
8192	32768	4	32762

The sampling interval (P) is the time between two purging events of the NetFlow cache, where ΔT is the length of the sampling window in which a snapshot of all flows traversing the device is taken. The idle time (I) is the sampling interval minus the active sampling time (I = P − ΔT). At time 0, the table is cleared, and flow entries are added. At time 0 + ΔT, all flows are exported, the table is flushed again, and the idle time starts. At time 0 + P the cache is cleared without exporting any data, and all previous steps are repeated cyclically.

For time-based sampled NetFlow, the export interval cannot be configured; the sampling time is calculated as ΔT = P/R. Note that the sampling rate is globally defined for the entire Catalyst chassis.

For example, if you configure a rate of 64, flow-based sampled NetFlow meters traffic for the first 128 ms of a total interval of 4096 ms. If the rate is 2048, sampled NetFlow accounts traffic from the first 4 ms of a 8192-ms interval.

The following configuration enables time-based sampling on the fastethernet 5/12 interface, with a sampling rate of 1 in 64:

```
Catalyst(config)# mls sampling time-based 64
Catalyst(config)# interface fastethernet 5/12
Catalyst(config-if)# mls netflow sampling
```

Packet-based sampling allows the post-processing of flow records based on the number of packets observed in the flow. At each sampling interval (configured in milliseconds), NetFlow exports the flow records for which the number of packets is greater than the configured packet-based sampling rate. The user-configurable parameters are the packet rate and the sampling interval. If no sampling interval is specified, 8192 is used as a default.

Packet-based sampling uses the following formula to sample a flow: the number of times sampled is approximately the length divided by the rate (*packets_in_flow/sampling_rate*). For example, if the flow is 32768 packets long and the sampling rate is 1024, the flow is sampled approximately 32 times (32768/1024).

```
Catalyst(config)# mls sampling packet-based rate [interval]
```

- *rate* is the packet-based sampling rate. Valid values are 64, 128, 256, 512, 1024, 2046, 4096, and 8192.

- *interval* (optional) is the sampling interval. Valid values are from 8000 to 16000 milliseconds.

NetFlow Input Filters

NetFlow Input Filters provide traffic metering on a specific subset of traffic by creating input filters. For example, you can select traffic from a specific group of hosts. NetFlow Input Filters is another NetFlow preprocessing feature, similar to packet-based Random Sampled NetFlow.

For the NetFlow Input Filters feature, classification of packets can be based on any of the following: IP source and destination addresses, Layer 4 protocol and port numbers, incoming interface, MAC address, IP Precedence, DSCP value, Layer 2 information (such as Frame Relay DE bits or Ethernet 802.1p bits), and Network-Based Application Recognition (NBAR). First, the packets are classified (filtered) on these criteria, and then they are grouped into NetFlow flows.

The filtering mechanism uses the MQC to classify flows. You can create multiple filters with matching samplers per subinterface. You can also configure different sampling rates by defining higher sampling rates for high-priority traffic classes and lower sampling rates for low-priority traffic. Figure 7-10 shows a typical example. You probably have a tight SLA linked with the VoIP traffic; therefore, full packet monitoring is executed on this traffic class, while a sampling rate of 1:100 checks the SLA on the VPN traffic. Finally, for monitoring purposes, sampled NetFlow classifies the best-effort traffic with a 1:1000 sampling rate.

Figure 7-10 *NetFlow Input Filters Example*

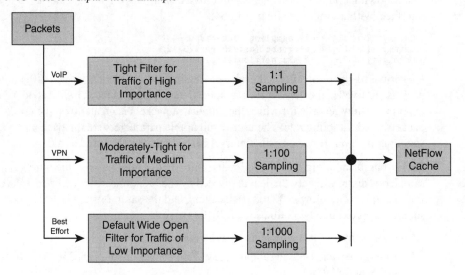

MQC offers multiple policy actions, such as limiting bandwidth rates and queuing management. These policies are applied only if a packet matches a criterion in a class map that is applied to the subinterface. A class map contains a set of match clauses and instructions on how to evaluate the clauses and acts as a filter for the policies. The NetFlow Input Filters feature combines NetFlow accounting with the MQC infrastructure. This implies that flow accounting is done on a packet *format* if it satisfies the match clauses.

NetFlow Input Filters require no additional memory. When comparing native NetFlow with NetFlow Input Filters, it enables a smaller number of NetFlow cache entries, because it can significantly reduce the number of flows. Accounting of classified traffic saves router resources by reducing the number of flows being processed and exported.

NetFlow Input Filters is supported in versions 5 and 9. The following four steps describe a configuration example combined with different sampling rates for different classifications:

Step 1 Creating a class map for a policy map:

Referring to Figure 7-10, the VoIP traffic is classified with access list 101 and a precedence of 5 (DSCP value of 40), and the VPN traffic is classified with access list 102:

```
router(config)# class-map my_high_importance_class
router(config-cmap)# match access-group 101
router(config-cmap)# match dscp cs5
router(config)# class-map my_medium_importance_class
router(config-cmap)# match access-group 102
```

Step 2 Creating a sampler map for a policy map:

In the following example, three sampler maps called my_high_sampling, my_medium sampling, and my_low_sampling are created for use with a policy map:

```
router(config)# flow-sampler-map my_high_sampling
router(config-sampler)# mode random one-out-of 1
router(config)# flow-sampler-map my_medium_sampling
router(config-sampler)# mode random one-out-of 100
router(config)# flow-sampler-map my_low_sampling
router(config-sampler)# mode random one-out-of 1000
```

Step 3 Creating a policy containing NetFlow sampling actions:

The following example shows how to create a class-based policy containing three NetFlow sampling actions. In this example, a sampling action named my_high_sampling is applied to a class named my_high_importance_class, a sampling action named my_medium_sampling is applied to a class named my_medium_importance_class, and a sampling action named my_low_sampling is applied to the default class:

```
router(config)# policy-map mypolicymap
router(config-pmap)# class my_high_importance_class
router(config-pmap-c)# netflow-sampler my_high_sampling
```

```
router(config-pmap)# class my_medium_importance_class
router(config-pmap-c)# netflow-sampler my_medium_sampling
router(config-pmap)# class class-default
router(config-pmap-c)# netflow-sampler my_low_sampling
```

Step 4 Applying a policy to an interface:

The following example shows how to apply a policy containing NetFlow sampling actions to an interface. In this example, a policy named mypolicymap is attached to interface POS1/0:

```
router(config)# interface POS1/0
router(config-if)# service-policy input mypolicymap
```

MPLS-Aware NetFlow

NetFlow can be used effectively in an MPLS network for VPN accounting and capacity planning. Ingress NetFlow can be used to account for traffic entering an MPLS VPN network from the customer site. The customer name can be linked to the associated VRF with the particular customer site by correlating it with the ifIndex value. MPLS-Aware NetFlow is a feature dedicated to the monitoring of MPLS flows, because it aggregates traffic per MPLS label within the MPLS core. This feature meters how much traffic is destined for a specific Provider Edge (PE) router in the network, allowing an operator to calculate a traffic matrix between PE routers in the MPLS network.

An MPLS flow contains up to three incoming MPLS labels of interest, with experimental bits (EXP) and the end-of-stack (S) bit in the same positions in the packet label stack. MPLS-Aware NetFlow captures MPLS traffic that contains Layer 3 IP and Layer 2 non-IP packets and uses the NetFlow version 9 export format.

When MPLS traffic is observed, MPLS-Aware NetFlow captures and reports up to three labels of interest and the label type and associated IP address of the top label, along with the normal NetFlow version 5 data record. Unlike NetFlow, MPLS-Aware NetFlow reports a 0 value for IP next hop, source and destination BGP Autonomous System numbers, or source and destination prefix masks for MPLS packets. A Label Switch Router (LSR) does not have routing information about the IP addresses in the MPLS packets payload. Other fields, such as source IP address, destination IP address, transport layer protocol, source application port number, destination application port number, IP type of service (ToS), TCP flags, input interface, and output interface, may be utilized as key-fields.

When you configure the MPLS-Aware NetFlow feature, you can select MPLS label positions in the incoming label stack that are of interest. You can capture up to three labels from positions 1 to 6 in the MPLS label stack. Label positions are counted from the top of the stack. For example, the position of the top label is 1, the position of the next label is 2, and so on. You enter the stack location value as an argument to the following command:

```
router(config)# ip flow-cache mpls label-positions [label-position-1 [label-
position-2
  [label-position-3]]] [no-ip-fields] [mpls-length]
```

The *label-position-n* argument represents the position of the label on the incoming label stack. For example, the **ip flow-cache mpls label-positions 1 3 4** command configures MPLS-Aware NetFlow to capture and export the first (top), third, and fourth labels. **mpls-length** reports the length of the MPLS packets, as opposed to the included IP packet length. If the **no-ip-fields** option is specified, the IP-related fields are reported with null values. With the introduction of Flexible NetFlow supporting MPLS fields, a more convenient solution would be the definition of a new template without those fields containing null values.

In Figure 7-11, some VPN traffic comes from the Customer Edge router 1 (CE1), enters the MPLS core via the Provider Edge router 1 (PE1), is metered with MPLS-Aware NetFlow at Provider router 1 (P1), and exits on PE2, PE3, or PE4.

Figure 7-11 *NetFlow Input Filters Example*

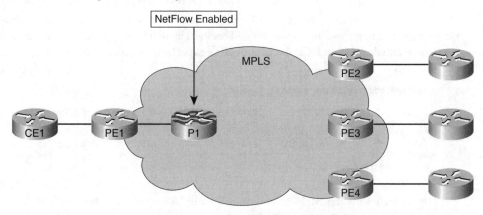

The following configuration enables MPLS-Aware NetFlow on the PE1-facing interface of P1. It uses the top MPLS label as the key-field (along with the 3 EXP bits and the bottom of the stack bit [S bit]). The bytes reported by NetFlow include the full MPLS packet lengths.

```
Router(config)#ip flow-cache mpls label-positions 1 no-ip-fields mpls-length
```

The following show command illustrates that NetFlow cache contains this flow, with a top label of 486, with the 3 EXP bits value of 4, with a bottom-of-the-stack S bit value of 0, and, most importantly, with the Forwarding Equivalent Class (FEC) value of 10.10.10.3. The FEC value points to the loopback of the exit PE router, which is the exit point of the core network.

```
P1# show ip flow verbose cache
...
SrcIf  SrcIPaddress DstIf  DstIPaddress  Pr  TOS Flgs  Pkts
Port  Msk  AS  Port  Msk  AS  NextHop  B/Pk  Active
PO2/0  0.0.0.0       PO3/0  0.0.0.0        00   00   10    1729
```

```
0000  /0   0   0000  /0   0   0.0.0.0   792  14.6
Pos:Lbl-Exp-S 1:486-4-0 (LDP/10.10.10.3)
```

Enabling MPLS-Aware NetFlow on all PE-facing interfaces of the P routers produces flow records that provide input to capacity planning tools to draw the core traffic matrix.

BGP Next-Hop Information Element

The BGP next hop is an important key-field in network-wide capacity planning where the core traffic is required, because the BGP next hop characterizes the network's exit point.

NetFlow adds the BGP next-hop information to the flow records to the main cache and—if aggregation is enabled—to the BGP Next-Hop ToS aggregation cache. The router performs a lookup on the destination IP address in the BGP table and adds the BGP next-hop information to each NetFlow flow record. This action adds an extra 16 bytes to the flow entry, resulting in a total of 80 bytes per entry.

```
Router(config)# ip flow-export version 9 [origin-as | peer-as] bgp-nexthop
```

This command enables the export of origin or peer AS information as well as BGP next-hop information from the NetFlow main cache. The **origin-as** option exports the flow's source and destination BGP AS, and **peer-as** exports the adjacent source and destination BGP AS.

```
Router# show ip cache verbose flow
...
SrcIf           SrcIPaddress    DstIf           DstIPaddress    Pr TOS Flgs Pkts
Port Msk AS                     Port Msk AS     NextHop            B/Pk  Active
BGP:BGP_NextHop
Et0/0/2         10.10.10.100    Et0/0/4         10.20.10.10     01 00  10   20
0000 /8  10                     0800 /8  20     10.10.10.6         100   0.0
BGP:10.10.10.1
```

The following command enables the BGP Next-Hop ToS aggregation. It reports the BGP origin and destination BGP Autonomous System (AS) value, the input and output interfaces, the DSCP, and the BGP next hop. In addition, the following information elements are present in all aggregations: number of flows, number of packets, number of bytes, and the sysUpTime of the flow start and end time. Note that for ingress NetFlow, the DSCP information element value is the one contained in the observed packet, before any QoS operations are applied on the packet.

```
Router(config)# ip flow-aggregation cache bgp-nexthop-tos
Router(config-flow-cache)# enabled

Router# show ip cache flow aggregation bgp-nexthop-tos
...
Src If          Src AS  Dst If          Dst AS  TOS Flows   Pkts  B/Pk Active
BGP NextHop
Et0/0/2         10      Et0/0/4         20      00   9      36    40 8.2
BGP:10.10.10.1
```

Enabling the BGP Next-Hop ToS feature on all the CE-facing interface of the PE routers would produce flow records that, when combined, would produce the core traffic matrix as input to any capacity planning tools. The principles are similar to MPLS-Aware NetFlow.

The differences are that NetFlow is enabled at different routers, that MPLS-Aware NetFlow might produce fewer flow records due to the MPLS top-label aggregation, and that the BGP Next-Hop ToS aggregation monitors only IP traffic.

NetFlow Multicast

NetFlow Multicast provides usage information about network traffic for a complete multicast traffic monitoring solution, because it allows metering multicast-specific data for multicast flows, along with the traditional NetFlow data records.

NetFlow Multicast offers three configuration choices:

- **Multicast ingress accounting**—Multicast packets are counted as unicast packets with two additional fields: the number of replicated packets and the byte count. With multicast ingress accounting, the destination interface field and the IP next-hop field are set to 0 for multicast flows.

    The number of replicated packets (egress) divided by the number of observed packets (ingress) delivers the multicast replication factor. The total number of flows is limited in the case of multicast ingress accounting, because a new flow entry is generated for the senders only.

- **Multicast egress accounting**—All outgoing multicast streams are counted as separate flows. Note that this option generates a higher number of flow entries as a separate flow for each IP Multicast receiver.

- **Multicast ingress and multicast egress accounting**—Care should be taken not to duplicate the flow records by enabling ingress and egress accounting at the same device.

The following example shows how to configure multicast egress NetFlow accounting on the Ethernet 0/0 interface:

```
Router(config)# interface ethernet 0/0
Router(config-if)# ip multicast netflow egress
```

The following example shows how to configure multicast ingress NetFlow accounting on the ingress Ethernet 1/0 interface:

```
Router(config)# interface serial 2/1/1.16
Router(config-if)# ip multicast netflow ingress
Router# show ip cache verbose flow
...
SrcIf          SrcIPaddress    DstIf         DstIPaddress    Pr TOS Flgs  Pkts
Port Msk AS                    Port Msk AS   NextHop            B/Pk  Active
IPM:OPkts      OBytes
Et1/1/1        11.0.0.1        Null          227.1.1.1       01 55  10    100
0000 /8  0                     0000 /0  0    0.0.0.0            28    0.0
IPM:  200      5600
Et1/1/1        11.0.0.1        Se2/1/1.16    227.1.1.1       01 55  10    100

0000 /8  0                     0000 /0  0    0.0.0.0            28    0.0
```

The IPM:OPkts column displays the number of IP multicast output packets, the IPM:OBytes column displays the number of IPM output bytes, and the DstIPaddress column displays the destination IP address for the IP Multicast output packets.

In this example, the first flow is monitored with Multicast NetFlow ingress. The replication factor is 2, as you can deduce from the 200 multicast output packets and the 100 observed packets. Note that the destination interface reports Null, because in this case, NetFlow does not have an information element suitable for reporting a set of multiple interfaces. The second flow in the cache reports the same multicast flow metered by Multicast NetFlow egress: the destination interface is correct, and the number of packets is 100, as observed on the outgoing interface. This flow does not report the IPM:OPkts and IPM:OBytes because unicast and multicast flows cannot be distinguished at the egress interface.

Figure 7-12 illustrates a typical multicast flow, coming from the source 10.0.0.2 and multicast to 224.10.10.100.

Figure 7-12 *NetFlow Multicast Configuration Scenarios, Part 1*

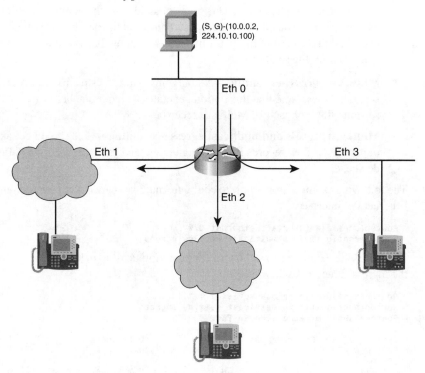

Figure 7-13 displays relevant IP Multicast information elements of the flow records, with the three possible configuration scenarios.

Figure 7-13 *NetFlow Multicast Configuration Scenarios, Part 2*

Scenario 1: Traditional NetFlow

Srclf	SrcIPadd	Dstlf	DstIPadd	NextHop	Bytes	Packets
Eth 0	10.0.0.2	Null	224.10.10.100	Null	23100	21

Scenario 2: Multicast NetFlow Ingress

Srclf	SrcIPadd	Dstlf	DstIPadd	NextHop	Bytes	Packets	IPM Bytes	IPM Packets
Eth 0	10.0.0.2	Null	224.10.10.100	Null	23100	21	69300	63

Scenario 3: Multicast NetFlow Egress

Srclf	SrcIPadd	Dstlf	DstIPadd	NextHop	Bytes	Packets
Eth 0	10.0.0.2	Eth 1	224.10.10.100	10.10.1.1	23100	21
Eth 0	10.0.0.2	Eth 2	224.10.10.100	10.10.2.1	23100	21
Eth 0	10.0.0.2	Eth 3	224.10.10.100	10.10.3.1	23100	21

Another interesting feature of NetFlow Multicast is the accounting for multicast packets that fail the Reverse Path Forwarding (RPF) check:

```
Router(config)# ip multicast netflow rpf-failure
```

In multicast, the primary purpose of the RPF check is to prevent loops, which could lead to multicast storms. NetFlow Multicast accounts the dropped packets and supplies relevant information for multicast routing debugging.

NetFlow Layer 2 and Security Monitoring Exports

The NetFlow Layer 2 and Security Monitoring Exports feature adds the ability for NetFlow to capture the values from several extra fields in Layer 3 IP traffic and Layer 2 LAN traffic to identify network attacks and their origin.

The following fields are reported:

- Time-to-Live (TTL) field, extracted from the IP packet header. The TTL field is used to prevent the indefinite forwarding of IP datagrams. It contains a counter (1 to 255) set by the source host. Each router that processes this datagram decreases the TTL value by 1. When the TTL value reaches 0, the datagram is discarded.

- Identification (ID) field, extracted from the IP packet header. All fragments of an IP datagram have the same value in the ID field. Subsequent IP datagrams from the same sender have different values in the ID field.

- Packet length field, extracted from the IP packet header.

- ICMP type and code, extracted from ICMP data.
- Source MAC address field from received frames.
- Destination MAC address field from transmitted frames.
- VLAN ID field from received frames.
- VLAN ID field from transmitted frames.

NetFlow reports the minimum and maximum values of TTL and packet length in a flow; note that these two attributes are non-key-fields. Reporting only the value of a specific packet in the flow (such as the first or the last) would not offer relevant information for security analysis.

To enable NetFlow version 9 to report the described functions, the following additional configuration command is required:

```
Router(config)# ip flow-capture {icmp | ip-id | mac-addresses | packet-length |
    ttl | vlan-id}
```

A typical flow in the NetFlow cache looks like this:

```
Router# show ip cache verbose flow
...
SrcIf           SrcIPaddress     DstIf          DstIPaddress      Pr TOS Flgs  Pkts
Port Msk AS                      Port Msk AS    NextHop              B/Pk  Active
Et0/0.1         10.251.138.218   Et1/0.1        172.16.10.2       06 80  00      65
0015 /0  0                       0015 /0  0     0.0.0.0              840    10.8
MAC: (VLAN id)  aaaa.bbbb.cc03   (005)           aaaa.bbbb.cc06   (006)
Min plen:       840                             Max plen:         840
Min TTL:        59                              Max TTL:          59
IP id:              0
```

Top Talkers

The NetFlow Top Talkers feature can be useful for analyzing network traffic in any of the following ways:

- **Security**—List the top talkers to see if traffic patterns consistent with a denial of service (DoS) attack are present in your network.
- **Load balancing**—Identify the heavily used network elements and paths in the network, and move network traffic to less-used routes in the network.
- **Traffic analysis**—Consult the data retrieved from the NetFlow MIB and Top Talkers feature to assist in general traffic study and planning for your network. Because the top flow records can be retrieved via SNMP, this feature offers new possibilities in network baselining.

The Top Talkers feature allows the top flows to be sorted for easier monitoring, trouble-shooting, and retrieval at the CLI level. Top talkers can be sorted by the following criteria:

- Total number of packets in each top talker
- Total number of bytes in each top talker

In addition to sorting top talkers, specific criteria provide a structured output. The **match** command, which acts as a filter, is used to specify the criteria, such as source IP address, destination IP address, application port, and many more.

The **match** command has the following syntax:

```
match {[byte-range [max-byte-number min-byte-number | max max-byte-number | min min-
byte-number] | class-map map-name | destination [address ip-address [mask | /nn] | as
as-number | port [max-port-number min-port-number | max max-port-number | min min-
port-number] | direction [ingress | egress] | flow-sampler flow-sampler-name | input-
interface interface-type interface-number | nexthop-address ip-address [mask | /nn] |
output-interface interface-type interface-number | packet-range [max-packets min-
packets | max max-packets | min min-packets] | protocol [protocol-number | udp | tcp] |
source [address ip-address [mask | /nn] | as as-number | port max-port-number min-
port-number | max max-port-number | min min-port-number] | tos [tos-byte | dscp dscp |
precedence precedence]
```

Table 7-6 lists the different **match** statement options for the NetFlow Top Talkers feature.

Table 7-6   **match** *Statement Options for the NetFlow Top Talkers Feature*

Option	Description
source address	Specifies that the match criterion is based on the source IP address.
destination address	Specifies that the match criterion is based on the destination IP address.
nexthop address	Specifies that the match criterion is based on the next-hop IP address.
ip-address	IP address of the source, destination, or next-hop address to be matched.
Mask	Address mask in dotted-decimal format.
/nn	Address mask as entered in Classless Interdomain Routing (CIDR) format. An address mask of 255.255.255.0 is equivalent to a /24 mask in CIDR format.
source port	Specifies that the match criterion is based on the source port.
destination port	Specifies that the match criterion is based on the destination port.
port-number	Specifies that the match criterion is based on the port number.
min *port*	The minimum port number to be matched. Any port number equal to or greater than this number constitutes a match. Range: 0 to 65535.
max *port*	The maximum port number to be matched. Any port number equal to or less than this number constitutes a match. Range: 0 to 65535.
min *port* **max** *port*	A range of port numbers to be matched. Range: 0 to 65535.
source as	Specifies that the match criterion is based on the source autonomous system.
destination as	Specifies that the match criterion is based on the destination autonomous system.
as-number	The autonomous system number to be matched.
input-interface	Specifies that the match criterion is based on the input interface.

continues

Table 7-6   **match** *Statement Options for the NetFlow Top Talkers Feature (Continued)*

Option	Description
output-interface	Specifies that the match criterion is based on the output interface.
interface	The interface to be matched.
tos	Specifies that the match criterion is based on the type of service (ToS).
tos-value	The ToS to be matched.
dscp *dscp-value*	Differentiated Services Code Point (DSCP) value to be matched.
precedence *precedence-value*	Precedence value to be matched.
Protocol	Specifies that the match criterion is based on the protocol.
Protocol-number	The protocol number to be matched. Range: 0 to 255.
tcp	The protocol number to be matched as TCP.
udp	The protocol number to be matched as UDP.
flow-sampler	The match criterion is based on top talker sampling.
flow-sampler-name	Name of the top talker sampler to be matched.
class-map	Specifies that the match criterion be based on a class map.
Class	Name of the class map to be matched.
packet-range	The match criterion is based on the number of IP datagrams in the flows.
byte-range	The match criterion is based on the size in bytes of the IP datagrams in the flows.
min-range-number max-range-number	Range of bytes or packets to be matched. Range 1 to 4,294,967,295.
min *minimum-range*	Minimum number of bytes or packets to be matched. Range: 1 to 4,294,967,295.
max *maximum-range*	Maximum number of bytes or packets to be matched. Range: 1 to 4,294,967,295.
min *minimum-range* **max** *maximum-range*	Range of bytes or packets to be matched. Range: 1 to 4,294,967,295.

Here is a simple example of configuration for the Top Talkers NetFlow feature:

```
Router(config)# ip flow-top-talkers
Router(config-flow-top-talkers)# top 50
Router(config-flow-top-talkers)# sort-by bytes
Router(config-flow-top-talkers)# cache-timeout 2000
```

This example specifies a collection of the top 50 flows, sorted by bytes. The top talker list is processed only once in a configurable interval (timeout period), because constant processing of large numbers of flow records would be too CPU-intensive. The cache-timeout specifies the length of time, in seconds, for which the list of top talkers is retained. A long timeout period limits the impact on system resources. If a request is made more than once during the timeout period, the same results are displayed, and the list of top talkers is not recalculated until the timeout period expires. A short timeout period ensures that the latest list of top talkers is retrieved; however, the list of top talkers is lost when the timeout period expires. It is advised that you configure the timeout period to be equal to or greater than the time it takes the network management system (NMS) to retrieve the top talkers list. The following example completes the preceding example by adding two **match** statements. Only flows that fit these criteria are taken into account for the top talkers list.

```
Router(config)# ip flow-top-talkers
Router(config-flow-top-talkers)# top 50
Router(config-flow-top-talkers)# sort-by bytes
Router(config-flow-top-talkers)# cache-timeout 2000
Router(config-flow-top-talkers)# match destination port min 80 max 80
Router(config-flow-top-talkers)# match destination address 10.10.10.0/24
```

The **match** statements are used to filter the number of entries in the cache. A range of information element values, such as application port range, is also a valid option.

The NetFlow MIB and Top Talkers feature can be configured for a router either by entering command-line interface (CLI) commands or by using the SNMP interface that is available in the CISCO-NETFLOW-MIB. As well as allowing the configuration of the NetFlow Top Talkers feature, the cnfTopFlows group in the CISCO-NETFLOW-MIB permits the retrieval of the top flow records.

Another simple but very interesting feature allows the user to sort and aggregate flows in the NetFlow cache in various ways. With the "dynamic top talkers" feature (note that the "dynamic" keyword is added compared to the "top talkers" previously described), the user can specify how to sort and aggregate the flow records. The main advantage compared to the NetFlow Top Talkers is that the user does not have to configure the search criteria before generating the top talkers list. Therefore, the **show** command is executed ad hoc, with specific arguments, to delve into the data of interest.

For example, consider the possible output from the **show ip flow top 5 aggregate source-address** command:

- If no match criterion is specified, the aggregated statistics for the top five source IP addresses from the flows on a router are displayed.

- If no match criterion is specified, the aggregated statistics for the top five source IP addresses that meet the match criteria that you specified are displayed. The following example looks for up to five top talkers, aggregates them on the source IP address, sorts them in descending order by the number of bytes in the flow, matches on the port range of 20 to 21 (FTP data and control ports, respectively), and displays the output in descending order:

```
Router# show ip flow top 5 aggregate source-address sorted-by bytes descending
   match destination-port min 20 max 21
```

```
There are 5 top talkers:

IPV4 SRC-ADDR        bytes          pkts         flows
================    ==========    ==========   ==========
10.231.185.254         920            23            2
10.10.12.1             480            12            2
10.251.138.218         400            10            2
10.132.221.111         400            10            2
10.71.200.138          280             7            1

9 of 34 flows matched.
```

NOTE   IPV4 SRC-ADDR is shown in uppercase (capital) letters because it is the field that the display is aggregated on.

The **sorted-by** option, which specifies which field to sort by, offers the following arguments:

— **aggregate**—Sorts by the aggregated field in the display data.

— **bytes**—Sorts by the number of bytes in the display data.

— **flows**—Sorts by the number of flows in the display data.

— **packets**—Sorts by the number of packets in the display data.

The **match** option, which specifies the filtering criteria, offers the possibility to select any fields from the cache. This means that the full content of Table 7-8 and some morefields, such as ICMP type, ICMP code, incoming MAC address, outgoing MAC address, TTL, and so on.

Flexible NetFlow

As mentioned earlier, Flexible NetFlow allows the network administrator to configure key-fields and non-key-fields for a flow record, effectively customizing the data collection for an application-specific set of requirements. The key-fields determine how traffic is attributed to a flow, and the non-key-fields provide additional information about the traffic in the flow record. A change in the value of a non-key-field does not create a new flow. Values for the majority of non-key-fields are taken only from the first packet in the flow. There are a few exceptions to this rule. For example, the minimum and maximum packet length fields are monitored and potentially updated for each packet in a flow.

The benefits of Flexible NetFlow include the following:

- Flow records can be specified with a minimum set of information elements (key-fields and non-key-fields), resulting in export of flow records of a minimum *size*. This is a significant gain in export bandwidth. For example, there is no need to export the timestamp fields in every flow record if this information is not required for a particular application.

- Flow records can be defined with a minimum set of key-fields, which results in a minimum number of flow records being generated. Compared to the historical seven key-fields, which may not always be required, this significantly reduces the number of flow records. This leads to a lower cache size and export bandwidth, as well as lower CPU consumption for flow classification and export (depending on the NetFlow implementation in hardware or software). Finally, filtering and aggregation overhead at a NetFlow collector are reduced if only the required information elements are exported. For example, it is not necessary to specify the source IP address as a key-field if the monitoring application is only interested in the flows' destination.

- Because Flexible NetFlow offers new information elements for key-fields and non-key-fields (for example, Layer 2 payload size, ICMP type and code), an entirely new set of monitoring applications and particular services are now possible.

- The Flexible NetFlow infrastructure offers the possibility of creating multiple caches with different flow definitions from the same monitored packets.

Flexible NetFlow is a great innovation that has the potential to change how accounting is done in networks. With the latest extensions, such as MAC address reporting and BGP traffic index, Flexible NetFlow is now ready to replace legacy accounting features such as Cisco IP accounting and BGP Policy Accounting. The permanent cache can even mimic the running counters of a MIB table with the advantage of defining the table columns with Flexible NetFlow key-fields and non-key-fields.

Figure 7-14 shows the major components of Flexible NetFlow.

Figure 7-14 *Flexible NetFlow Components*

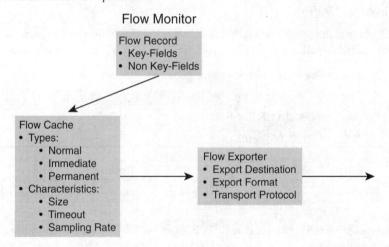

Flow Monitors are the Flexible NetFlow components that are applied to interfaces for traffic monitoring. Flow Monitors consist of a Flow Cache definition, which is the data structure whose content is specified by the Flow Record definition attached to the Flow Monitor. The Flow Cache is automatically created when a Flow Monitor is applied to an interface. Flow Records are collected based on the definitions of key-fields and non-key-fields and are stored in the Flow Cache.

Based on the Flow Exporter characteristics (such as export format, export destination, and transport protocol), flow records are sent to a remote NetFlow collector. Flow Exporters are created as separate entities in the configuration and are assigned to Flow Monitors.

The term "flexible" in Flexible NetFlow is applicable to both the flow record definition and the infrastructure. Indeed, several Flow Monitors can monitor the same packets for different purposes and therefore create multiple Flow Caches. Note that it is possible with traditional NetFlow under the condition that multiple router-based aggregations are enabled, aggregating the flow records from the main cache.

The new Flexible NetFlow CLI specifies a series of predefined records to allow a phased approach to Flexible NetFlow: you can start using the new CLI while exporting the same information as in NetFlow version 5 and then tune the flow monitor with the user-defined records. Flexible NetFlow includes several predefined records. Two of them (**netflow-original** and **netflow ipv4 original-output**) emulate original (ingress) NetFlow and the egress NetFlow Accounting feature, respectively.

The Flexible NetFlow feature is available with Cisco IOS Software Releases 12.4(9)T and 12.0(33)S.

Fields in Flexible NetFlow

Looking at the list of new key-fields shown in Table 7-7, the number increased considerably compared to traditional NetFlow. Here are just a few of the fields that were added:

- The payload size field
- The traffic index coming from the BGP Policy Accounting field
- Any individual TCP flag field

Table 7-7 *Flexible Flow Record: Key-Fields*

IPv4		Transport		Routing	Flow	Interface
IP (Source or Destination)	Payload Size	Destination Port	TCP Flag: ACK	Source AS	Sampler ID	Input
Prefix (Source or Destination)	Packet Section (Header)	Source Port	TCP Flag: CWR	Destination AS	Direction	Output
Mask (Source or Destination)	Packet Section (Payload)	ICMP Code	TCP Flag: ECE	Peer AS		

Table 7-7   *Flexible Flow Record: Key-Fields (Continued)*

IPv4		Transport		Routing	Flow	Interface
Minimum-Mask (Source or Destination)	TTL	ICMP Type	TCP Flag: FIN	Traffic Index (BGP PA)		
Protocol	Options Bitmap	IGMP Type	TCP Flag: PSH	Forwarding Status		
Fragmentation Flags	Version	TCP ACK Number	TCP Flag: RST	IS-Multicast		
Fragmentation Offset	Precedence	TCP Header Length	TCP Flag: SYN	IGP Next Hop		
ID	DSCP	TCP Sequence Number	TCP Flag: URG	BGP Next Hop		
Header Length	TOS	TCP Window-Size	UDP Message Length			
Total Length		TCP Source Port	UDP Source Port			

The list of non-key-fields also has been extended, as shown in Table 7-8. The number of bytes and packets can be selected between the counters 32-bit and 64-bit (with the **long** keyword). The minimum and maximum total length of the packets of the flow, and the minimum and maximum TTL, are among the non-key-fields.

Table 7-8   *Flexible Flow Record: Non-Key-Fields*

Counter	IPv4	Timestamp
Bytes	Total Length Minimum	sysUpTime First Packet
Bytes Long	Total Length Maximum	sysUpTime First Packet
Bytes Square Sum	TTL Minimum	
Bytes Square Sum Long	TTL Maximum	
Packets		
Packets Long		

Furthermore, any of the key-fields specified in Table 7-7 can be reported as non-key-fields. In this case, its content is the value of the first packet observed in the flow. The only exceptions are the TCP flags and the fragment offset.

The answer to the question of when to select a key-field versus a non-key-field depends on the application using the flow records. For example, should the output interface be a key-field or a non-key-field? Think about a scenario of a load-balancing network design, where you want flow records for each path. The output interface must be a key-field. Otherwise, if reported as a non-key-field, its value is the output interface of the first packet observed in the flow, which is the path the first packet took.

Packet Sections

Flexible NetFlow records let you monitor a contiguous section of a packet of a user-configurable size. This can be exported in a flow record as a key-field or a non-key-field, along with other fields and attributes of the packet. The section may also include Layers 3 and 4 and some payload data from the packet.

The packet section fields let you monitor any packet fields that are not covered by the predefined key-fields. The packet sections feature provides more detailed monitoring, facilitates the investigation of distributed denial of service (DDoS) attacks, and lets you implement other security applications such as URL monitoring.

Flexible NetFlow has the following predefined types of packet sections of a user-configurable size:

- **ipv4 section header size** *header-size* starts capturing the number of bytes specified by the *header-size* argument from the beginning of a packet's IPv4 header.

- **ipv4 section payload size** *payload-size* starts capturing bytes immediately after the IPv4 header from each packet. The number of bytes captured is specified by the *payload-size* argument.

Flexible NetFlow Cache Types

There are three types of Flow Caches: normal, immediate, and permanent.

The default Flow Cache type is normal. In this mode, the entries in the cache are aged out according to the timeout active and timeout inactive settings. When a cache entry is aged out, it is removed from the cache and exported via any exporters configured.

A Flow Cache of type immediate ages out every record as soon as it is created. As a result, every flow contains just one packet. This mode is desirable when only very small flows are expected or when a minimum amount of latency is required between seeing a packet and exporting a flow. A typical example is attack detection in security monitoring—specifically if the packet section is used as a key-field.

NOTE	In case of an immediate cache, there is no difference between key and non-key-fields.

Note that the immediate cache type may result in a large number of export flow records, which can overload low-speed links and overwhelm a NetFlow collector. Therefore, using sampling in conjunction with the immediate cache is strongly recommended.

A Flow Cache of type permanent never ages out any flows. This behavior is useful when you expect to see a small number of flows and there is a need to keep long-term statistics on the router. For example, when monitoring IP ToS as a key-field, there are only 256 values, resulting in a maximum of 256 flow entries in the cache. Permanent caches are also useful for billing applications and for an edge-to-edge traffic matrix where a fixed set of flows are being tracked. Update messages are sent periodically to flow exporters. The export interval can be configured with the **timeout update** command. Note that when a permanent cache becomes full, new flows are not added and a "Packets not added" counter in the cache statistics (**show flow monitor** *monitor-name* **cache**) reflects the number of unaccounted packets.

Comparison of Original NetFlow and Flexible NetFlow

Some features from the original NetFlow versions (1, 5, 7, 8) are not supported yet with Flexible NetFlow. The objective of Flexible NetFlow is to support all features over time; however, some of the unsupported features can be mimicked easily. Table 7-9 provides a feature-by-feature comparison of original NetFlow and Flexible NetFlow and describes how to emulate a feature.

Table 7-9 *NetFlow Feature Comparison*

Feature	Original NetFlow	Flexible NetFlow	Comments
NetFlow Data Capture	Supported	Supported	Data capture is available with the predefined[*] and user-defined records in Flexible NetFlow.
NetFlow Data Export	Supported	Supported	Flow exporters export data from the Flexible NetFlow flow monitor caches to remote systems.
NetFlow for IPv6	Supported in version 9	Should be available by the time this book is published.	IP version 6 monitoring.
MPLS-Aware NetFlow	Supported in version 9	Not supported	MPLS core monitoring.
MPLS Egress NetFlow	Supported in version 9	Not supported	MPLS edge monitoring.

continues

Table 7-9 *NetFlow Feature Comparison (Continued)*

Feature	Original NetFlow	Flexible NetFlow	Comments
NetFlow BGP Next Hop	Supported in version 9	Supported	Available in the predefined and user-defined keys in Flexible NetFlow records.
Random Packet Sampled NetFlow	Supported	Supported	Available with Flexible NetFlow sampling.
NetFlow version 9 Export Format	Supported in version 9	Supported	Available with Flexible NetFlow exporters.
NetFlow subinterface	Supported	Supported	Flexible NetFlow monitors can be assigned to subinterfaces.
Multiple Export Destinations	Supported	Supported	Available with Flexible NetFlow exporters.
NetFlow ToS-Based Router Aggregation	Supported	Supported	Available in the predefined and user-defined records in Flexible NetFlow records.
NetFlow Minimum Prefix Mask for Router-Based Aggregation	Supported	Supported	Available in the predefined and user-defined records.
NetFlow Input Filters	Supported in version 9	Not supported	MQC filters.
NetFlow MIB	Supported	Not supported	NetFlow statistics via MIB.
NetFlow MIB and Top Talkers	Supported	Not supported	Top Talkers statistics in the NetFlow MIB.
NetFlow Dynamic Top Talkers CLI	Supported in version 9	Not supported	Top Talker statistics via CLI.
NetFlow Multicast	Supported	Not supported	Flexible NetFlow collects statistics for multicast flows. However, specific additional fields such as replication counts for bytes (OBYTES) and packets (OPACKETS) are not supported by Flexible NetFlow in Cisco IOS Software Release 12.4(9)T.
NetFlow Layer 2 and Security Monitoring Exports	Supported in version 9	Not supported	Monitoring of Layer 2 details.

Table 7-9   *NetFlow Feature Comparison (Continued)*

Feature	Original NetFlow	Flexible NetFlow	Comments
Egress NetFlow Accounting	Supported	Supported	Flexible NetFlow monitors can be used to monitor egress traffic on interfaces and subinterfaces.
NetFlow Reliable Export with SCTP	Supported in version 9	Not supported	

*Flexible NetFlow has several predefined keys that emulate data analysis with original NetFlow.

CLI Operations

This section describes the most important configuration commands to enable Flexible NetFlow on Cisco routers. Figure 7-15 displays, using a very simple example, the different configuration steps:

  1 Exporter configuration

  2 Flow Record configuration

  3 Flow Monitor configuration

  4 Interface configuration

Figure 7-15 *Flexible NetFlow: High-Level View of the Configuration*

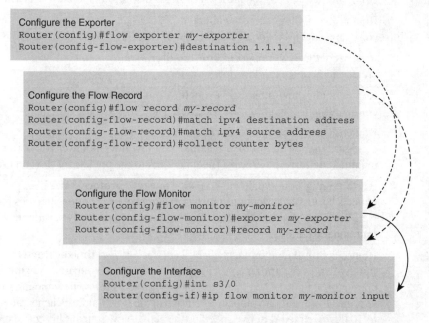

Configure the Exporter
```
Router(config)#flow exporter my-exporter
Router(config-flow-exporter)#destination 1.1.1.1
```

Configure the Flow Record
```
Router(config)#flow record my-record
Router(config-flow-record)#match ipv4 destination address
Router(config-flow-record)#match ipv4 source address
Router(config-flow-record)#collect counter bytes
```

Configure the Flow Monitor
```
Router(config)#flow monitor my-monitor
Router(config-flow-monitor)#exporter my-exporter
Router(config-flow-monitor)#record my-record
```

Configure the Interface
```
Router(config)#int s3/0
Router(config-if)#ip flow monitor my-monitor input
```

Note that the CLI configuration of Flexible NetFlow for predefined records, which is considered an intermediate step toward flexible records configuration, is not described in this book.

The most important configuration commands to enable Flexible NetFlow on Cisco routers are as follows:

- Router(config)# **flow exporter** *exporter-name*
  creates a Flexible NetFlow flow exporter.

- Router(config-flow-exporter)# **destination** {{*ip-address* ⏐ *hostname*} ⏐ **vrf** *vrf-name*}
  configures an export destination for a Flexible NetFlow flow exporter, optionally in a VRF.

- Router(config-flow-exporter)# **dscp** *dscp-number*
  configures a DSCP value for Flexible NetFlow flow exporter datagrams.

- Router(config-flow-exporter)# **source** *source-interface*
  configures the source IP address interface for flow exporters.

- Router(config-flow-exporter)# **ttl** *tt*
  configures the TTL value for a Flexible NetFlow flow exporter.

- Router(config-flow-exporter)# **transport udp** *udp-port*
  configures the UDP transport protocol and the UDP destination port for a Flexible NetFlow flow exporter.

- Router(config)# **flow record** *record-name*
  creates a Flexible NetFlow flow record.

- Router(config-flow-record)# **match ...**
  configures a key-field. The full list of fields displayed in Table 7-7 is available.

- Router(config-flow-record)# **collect ...**
  configures a non-key-field. The full list of fields displayed in Table 7-8 is available.

- Router(config-flow-monitor)# **flow monitor** *monitor-name*
  creates a Flexible NetFlow flow monitor.

- Router(config-flow-monitor)# **exporter** *exporter-name*
  configures a flow exporter for a Flexible NetFlow flow monitor.

- Router(config-flow-monitor)# **record** *record-name*
  configures a flow record for a Flexible NetFlow flow monitor. The option (**netflow-original** ⏐ **netflow ipv4** *record* [**peer**]}) refers to the predefined flow records.

- Router(config-flow-monitor)# **statistics packet** {**protocol** ⏐ **size**}
  collects protocol distribution statistics and/or size distribution statistics for a Flexible NetFlow flow Monitor. Note that those statistics were always available with traditional NetFlow.

- Router(config-flow-monitor)# **cache** {**entries** *entries* ⏐ **timeout** {**active** *active* ⏐ **inactive** *inactive* ⏐ **update** *update*} ⏐ **type** {**immediate** ⏐ **normal** ⏐ **permanent**}}
  configures a flow cache parameter for a Flexible NetFlow flow monitor. **entries** specifies the maximum number of entries in the flow monitor cache, ranging from 16 to 1048576. **timeout active** specifies the active flow timeout in seconds. **timeout**

inactive specifies the inactive flow timeout in seconds. **update** specifies the update timeout for a permanent flow cache in seconds. **type** specifies the type of the Flow Cache, where **type immediate** means immediate flow removal from the flow cache, **type normal** means normal flow removal from the flow cache, and **type permanent** means disable flow removal from the flow cache.

- Router(config-if)# **ip flow monitor** {*monitor-name* [**sampler** *sampler-name*] {**input** ⏐ **output**}}

  enables a Flexible NetFlow flow monitor for traffic that the router is receiving (**input**) or forwarding (**output**). Sampling is optionally configured with **sampler** argument. (Note that the sampler should be configured before it's referenced here.)

Flexible NetFlow Examples

The following examples are just two of many possible scenarios of how Flexible NetFlow can be used. The associated CLI configuration and **show** commands are illustrated for the first scenario only.

By targeting specific information, you can reduce the amount of collected data and the number of exported flows, allowing enhanced scalability and aggregation. If you are interested in TCP application analysis, with Flexible NetFlow you configure the tracking of the source and destination IP addresses, protocol, TCP source, and destination ports. The collected flow records provide traffic statistics for each application port number. For the same scenario in original NetFlow, you would collect more data records based on the seven tuples flow definition and aggregate them afterwards. In Flexible NetFlow, the aggregation is provided with the key-field definition, avoiding collection of unnecessary fields (four fields compared to seven).

Here's the configuration for the preceding scenario:

```
flow exporter my-exporter
 destination 10.10.10.10
 source FastEthernet0/0
 ttl 2

flow record my-record
 match ipv4 source address
 match ipv4 destination address
 match transport tcp source-port
 match transport tcp destination-port
 collect counter packets
 collect counter bytes

flow monitor my-monitor
 record my-record
 exporter my-exporter
 statistics packet size

interface fastethernet0/0
 ip flow monitor my-monitor input
```

In this case, the NetFlow Collector 10.10.10.10 is situated two hops away from the router. The router's fastethernet0/0 IP address identifies the exporting router. Instead of browsing the full configuration for Flexible NetFlow-related commands, the following set of **show** commands has been added:

```
show running flow exporter
show running flow monitor
show running flow record
```

These **show** commands allow the configuration to be verified. For example:

```
Router#show flow exporter my-exporter
Flow Exporter my-exporter:
  Description:             User defined
  Tranport Configuration:
    Destination IP address: 10.10.10.10
    Source IP address:      10.48.71.24
    Source Interface:       FastEthernet0/0
    Transport Protocol:     UDP
    Destination Port:       9995
    Source Port:            50232
    DSCP:                   0x0
    TTL:                    2

Router#show flow record my-record
flow record my-record:
  Description:            User defined
  No. of users:          1
  Total field space:  22 bytes
  Fields:
    match ipv4 source address
    match ipv4 destination address
    match transport tcp source-port
    match transport tcp destination-port
    collect counter packets
    collect counter bytes
```

The following **show** command, which describes the newly created NetFlow version 9 template, is of great help when troubleshooting:

```
Router#show flow exporter templates

Flow Exporter my-exporter:
  Client: Flow Monitor my-monitor
  Exporter Format: NetFlow Version 9
  Template ID   : 258
  Record Size   : 20
  Template layout
```

Field	Type	Offset	Size
ipv4 source address	8	0	4
ipv4 destination address	12	4	4
transport tcp source-port	182	8	2
transport tcp destination-port	183	10	2
counter packets	2	12	4
counter bytes	1	16	4

```
Router#show flow interface fastethernet0/0
Interface FastEthernet0/0
  FNF:  monitor:            my-monitor
```

```
                    direction:        Input
                    traffic(ip):      on
```

The next three commands display the content of the cache, with three different options: record, table, and csv:

```
Router#show flow monitor my-monitor cache format record
    Cache type:                         Normal
    Cache size:                         4096
    Current entries:                      45
    High Watermark:                       45

    Flows added:                          45
    Flows aged:                            0
      - Active timeout   (  1800 secs)    0
      - Inactive timeout (    15 secs)    0
      - Event aged                        0
      - Watermark aged                    0
      - Emergency aged                    0
IPV4 SOURCE ADDRESS:            10.48.71.17
IPV4 DESTINATION ADDRESS:       10.48.71.24
TCP SOURCE PORT:                0
TCP DESTINATION PORT:           0
counter packets:                6
counter bytes:                  456

IPV4 SOURCE ADDRESS:            10.48.71.129
IPV4 DESTINATION ADDRESS:       10.48.71.24
TCP SOURCE PORT:                0
TCP DESTINATION PORT:           0
counter packets:                28
counter bytes:                  3136

IPV4 SOURCE ADDRESS:            10.48.71.199
IPV4 DESTINATION ADDRESS:       10.48.71.24
TCP SOURCE PORT:                11011
TCP DESTINATION PORT:           18710
counter packets:                15
counter bytes:                  702
. . .


Router#show flow monitor my-monitor cache format table
    Cache type:                         Normal
    Cache size:                         4096
    Current entries:                      45
    High Watermark:                       45

    Flows added:                          45
    Flows aged:                            0
      - Active timeout   (  1800 secs)    0
      - Inactive timeout (    15 secs)    0
      - Event aged                        0
      - Watermark aged                    0
      - Emergency aged                    0

IPV4 SRC ADDR    IPV4 DST ADDR   TCP SRC PORT   TCP DST PORT   pkts   bytes
=============    =============   ============   ============   ====   =====
10.48.71.17      10.48.71.24               0              0      7     532
10.48.71.129     10.48.71.24               0              0     30    3360
10.48.71.199     10.48.71.24           11011          18710     15     702
. . .

Router#show flow monitor my-monitor cache format csv
    Cache type:                         Normal
```

```
Cache size:                               4096
Current entries:                            45
High Watermark:                             45

Flows added:                                45
Flows aged:                                  0
  - Active timeout    (  1800 secs)         0
  - Inactive timeout  (    15 secs)         0
  - Event aged                              0
  - Watermark aged                          0
  - Emergency aged                          0
IPV4 SRC ADDR,IPV4 DST ADDR,TCP SRC PORT,TCP DST PORT,pkts,bytes
10.48.71.17,10.48.71.24,0,0,7,532
10.48.71.129,10.48.71.24,0,0,29,3248
10.48.71.199,10.48.71.24,11011,18710,15,702
```

Some of the flow records in the cache, and therefore in the NetFlow Collector, have a value of 0 for the source and destination TCP ports. However, the IANA port assignment lists the value 0 as reserved for both TCP and UDP. Although the configuration has defined the TCP source and destination ports as key-fields, this TCP flow key does not work as a filter. In other words, this does not imply that only TCP flows are monitored. If a UDP flow is monitored, the values of the source and destination ports are 0. So the NetFlow Collector must filter out the flow records with the source and destination value of 0. Note that flexible filtering will be implemented in the future.

NOTE   If a field is not available for a packet, Flexible NetFlow reports this field with a value of 0.

For troubleshooting purposes, statistics such as the current number of entries and the high watermark are available:

```
Router#show flow monitor my-monitor statistics
  Cache type:                             Normal
  Cache size:                               4096
  Current entries:                            51
  High Watermark:                             51

  Flows added:                                51
  Flows aged:                                  0
    - Active timeout    (  1800 secs)         0
    - Inactive timeout  (    15 secs)         0
    - Event aged                              0
    - Watermark aged                          0
    - Emergency aged                          0

Packet size distribution (2350 total packets):
   1-32    64    96   128   160   192   224   256   288   320   352   384   416
   .000  .127  .500  .126  .013  .016  .002  .035  .036  .004  .037  .028  .042

    448   480   512   544   576  1024  1536  2048  2560  3072  3584  4096  4608
   .000  .014  .000  .004  .004  .005  .000  .000  .000  .000  .000  .000  .000
```

In the exporter statistics output, which reports the export failures, most of the counters must be 0 (except potentially for the first export packets if ARP is required).

```
Router#show flow exporter my-exporter statistics
Flow Exporter my-exporter:
  Packet send statistics:
    Ok 0
    No FIB 0
    Adjacency failure 0
    Enqueued to process level 2
    Enqueueing failed 0
    IPC failed 0
    Output failed 0
    Fragmentation failed 0
    Encap fixup failed 0
    No destination address 0
  Client send statistics:
    Client: Flow Monitor my-monitor
      Records added 0
      Packets sent 0 (0 bytes)
      Packets dropped 0 (0 bytes)
      No Packet available errors 0
```

Finally, the following command displays NetFlow version 9 export IDs for all fields that are supported by Flexible NetFlow. This facilitates the lookup within the NetFlow version 9 RFC (RFC 3954), the IPFIX Information Model RFC, and the IPFIX IANA registry:

```
Router#show flow exporter export-ids netflow-v9
Export IDs used by fields in NetFlow-common export format:
  ip version                           :    60
  ip tos                               :   194
  ip dscp                              :   195
  ip precedence                        :   196
  ip protocol                          :     4
  ip ttl                               :   192
  ip ttl minimum                       :    52
  ip ttl maximum                       :    53
  ip length header                     :   189
  ip length payload                    :   204
  ip section header                    :   313
  ip section payload                   :   314
  routing source as                    :    16
  routing destination as               :    17
  routing source as peer               :   129
  routing destination as peer          :   128
  routing source traffic-index         :    92
  routing destination traffic-index    :    93
  routing forwarding-status            :    89
  routing is-multicast                 :   206
  routing next-hop address ipv4        :    15
  routing next-hop address ipv4 bgp    :    18
  routing next-hop address ipv6 bgp    :    63
  ipv4 header-length                   :   207
  ipv4 tos                             :     5
  ipv4 total-length                    :   190
  ipv4 total-length minimum            :    25
  ipv4 total-length maximum            :    26
  ipv4 id                              :    54
  ipv4 fragmentation flags             :   197
  ipv4 fragmentation offset            :    88
  ipv4 source address                  :     8
  ipv4 source prefix                   :    44
  ipv4 source mask                     :     9
  ipv4 destination address             :    12
  ipv4 destination prefix              :    45
  ipv4 destination mask                :    13
```

```
ipv4 option map                               :     208
transport source-port                         :       7
transport destination-port                    :      11
transport icmp ipv4 type                      :     176
transport icmp ipv4 code                      :     177
transport igmp type                           :      33
transport tcp source-port                     :     182
transport tcp destination-port                :     183
transport tcp sequence-number                 :     184
transport tcp acknowledgement-number          :     185
transport tcp header-length                   :     188
transport tcp window-size                     :     186
transport tcp urgent-pointer                  :     187
transport tcp flags                           :       6
transport udp source-port                     :     180
transport udp destination-port                :     181
transport udp message-length                  :     205
interface input snmp                          :      10
interface output snmp                         :      14
interface name                                :      82
interface description                         :      83
flow direction                                :      61
flow exporter                                 :     144
flow sampler                                  :      48
flow sampler algorithm export                 :      49
flow sampler interval                         :      50
flow sampler name                             :      84
flow class                                    :      51
v9-scope system                               :       1
v9-scope interface                            :       2
v9-scope linecard                             :       3
v9-scope cache                                :       4
v9-scope template                             :       5
counter flows                                 :       3
counter bytes                                 :       1
counter bytes long                            :       1
counter packets                               :       2
counter packets long                          :       2
counter bytes squared long                    :     198
counter bytes permanent                       :      85
counter packets permanent                     :      86
counter bytes squared permanent               :     199
counter bytes exported                        :      40
counter packets exported                      :      41
counter flows exported                        :      42
timestamp sys-uptime first                    :      22
timestamp sys-uptime last                     :      21
```

The second scenario deals with security. Flexible NetFlow is an excellent attack detection feature. It can track all parts of the IPv4 header and even packet sections, and can aggregate the data into flows. It is expected that security detection systems will listen to NetFlow data and, upon finding an issue in the network, create a cache that will be configured to track specific information and pinpoint details about the attack pattern or worm propagation. The capability to create caches ad hoc positions Flexible NetFlow as an enhanced security detection feature, compared to current flow technologies. It is anticipated that Flexible NetFlow will track common attacks such as port scans for worm target discovery and worm propagation. The TCP SYN flood attack is a simpler approach in which TCP flags are used to send a large number of connection requests to a server. The attacking device sends a stream of TCP SYN packets to a given destination address but never sends an ACK in response to the destination's SYN-ACK as part of the TCP three-way handshake. This results in a large number of open TCP requests, finally consuming all the victim's resources. The flow information needed for this security monitoring requires the tracking of three key-fields: destination address or subnet, TCP flags, and packet count. The network element may monitor some general NetFlow information initially, and this data may trigger the setup of an additional Flow Monitor, providing a more detailed view of this particular attack. If the security application identifies the attack's root cause, it might then configure an additional Flow Monitor to gather payload information or sections of packets to take a deeper look at a signature within the packet. Because the configuration for this example can be easily derived from the previous example (TCP application monitoring), the CLI and **show** commands are not displayed. An interesting example of how to use the permanent cache type of Flexible NetFlow for capacity planning is included in Chapter 14, "Capacity Planning Scenarios."

Deployment Guidelines

Historically, NetFlow has been an ingress measurement technology. With the introduction of new features such as Egress NetFlow, careful planning of NetFlow deployment is required to monitor all the flows of interest and avoid duplicate flow collection by enabling NetFlow at each ingress and egress interface. Indeed, duplicated flow records are difficult to track and eliminate.

Before enabling NetFlow on a network element, the CPU utilization is the first parameter to monitor. Enabling NetFlow and exporting the flow records with NetFlow version 5 increases the CPU utilization by about 15 percent on average, up to a maximum of 25 percent on some platforms. The additional CPU utilization on software platforms (as opposed to platforms where the NetFlow classification is done in hardware ASIC) due to NetFlow varies based on the number of flows, as described in Table 7-10. Note that the number of flows relates both to the rate at which flows are created and exported and to the occupation of the NetFlow table. The first is more relevant to CPU utilization, and the second relates to memory requirements. Even on platforms such as the Cisco 12000 and 7600 and Catalyst 6500, where NetFlow collection is implemented in ASIC, the export of flows requires CPU cycles.

Table 7-10   *Approximate CPU Utilization for a Given Number of Active Flows*

Number of Active Flows in Cache	Additional CPU Utilization
10,000	< 4 percent
45,000	< 12 percent
65,000	< 16 percent

Enabling an extra aggregation scheme on a router increases the CPU utilization by 2 to 5 percent, depending on the number of aggregations enabled, with a maximum of 6 percent for multiple aggregation schemes.

Exporting flows with NetFlow version 5 or 9 has the same impact on CPU utilization. Furthermore, dual export of flows has no significant CPU impact.

If the CPU utilization is a problem or monitoring of all flows is not required, sampled NetFlow offers an alternative solution that is less CPU-intensive. Another alternative is to increase the flow expiration timeout. Finally, configuring the minimum required set of key-fields (in the case of Flexible NetFlow) or the minimum required flow mask (in the case of the Catalyst 6500/Cisco 7600) is essential in lowering the export bandwidth requirements. Figure 7-16 shows the CPU impact decrease by enabling sampled NetFlow as opposed to full NetFlow for a Cisco 7505 router.

Figure 7-16 *NetFlow CPU Utilization*

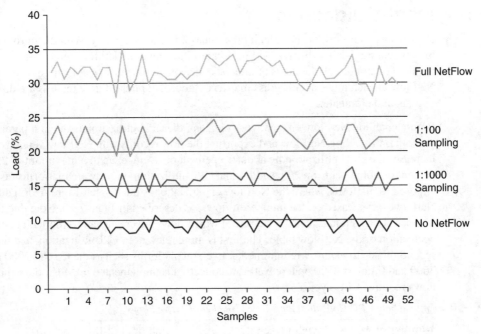

Supported Devices and IOS Versions

As described in this chapter, NetFlow is not just a single feature, but a set of different features. It has features related to the NetFlow metering process part, such as Router-Based Aggregation, MPLS-Aware NetFlow, NetFlow Input Filters, and Sampled NetFlow. Additionally, other features address the NetFlow protocol (such as versions 5, 8, and 9). Therefore, listing all the different features along with the IOS releases, platforms, and line cards would be extensive and still offer limited information. Furthermore, due to the growing adoption of NetFlow features on the Cisco platforms, line cards, and IOS versions, there is a risk of presenting obsolete information. The suggested approach to get the latest NetFlow information is to check the Cisco website at http://www.cisco.com/go/netflow. Specifically, the Cisco Feature Navigator tool lists NetFlow features per platform and IOS version. Table 7-11 offers an overview of the most important NetFlow features separated by platform families: the software-based platforms (7500 and below), the 12000 router, and the Catalyst 6500/Cisco 7600. This table also demonstrates that most of the NetFlow features are implemented in software initially and are ported in hardware on the different platforms.

Table 7-11   *Supported Features Per Device*

NetFlow Features	Software-Based Platforms	12000	Catalyst 6500
Export Version 5	✓	✓	✓
Export Version 7			✓
Export Version 8	✓	✓	✓
Export Version 9	✓	✓	✓
Flexible NetFlow	✓	12.0(33)S	
Sampled NetFlow	Random	Deterministic	Flow-based
Input Filters	✓		
MPLS-Aware	✓	✓	
BGP Next Hop	✓	✓	✓
Multicast	✓		✓
Layer 2 Security	✓		✓*
Top Talkers	✓		
SCTP	✓		

*Without MAC addresses support

CHAPTER 8

BGP Policy Accounting

This chapter describes the BGP Policy Accounting features in Cisco IOS. You will see how to apply this feature for a source- and destination-sensitive billing scheme, and you'll see the practical configuration details on the routers. Furthermore, you will understand the similarities between BGP Policy Accounting and the destination-sensitive billing feature.

Border Gateway Protocol (BGP) Policy Accounting measures and classifies traffic to and from different BGP peers. It allows accounting for IP traffic differentially by assigning counters based on BGP community list, BGP Autonomous System (AS) number, and/or AS_PATH, on a per-interface basis. This policy classification is performed via a Cisco IOS policy-based classifier that maps the traffic into one of the possible buckets, representing different traffic classes. Packet and byte counters are incremented for each bucket per interface and per direction (ingress or egress). A user can access the counters either through the CLI or via SNMP.

Even though the Cisco documentation refers to it as a single feature, this chapter divides BGP Policy Accounting into different variations for the sake of clarity:

- Input BGP Policy Accounting is the incoming feature applied on the interface where the traffic arrives, with a classification on the destination (according to the route the traffic will take). This is the initial BGP Policy Accounting variation developed, called BGP Policy Accounting in the Cisco documentation.

- Output BGP Policy Accounting is the outgoing feature applied on the interface where the traffic exits the network element, with a classification on the source (according to the route the traffic comes from). Refer to "Output BGP Policy Accounting" in the documentation for further details.

- The section "Summary of All Four BGP Policy Accounting Combinations" completes the remaining possibilities of the input versus output interface combination with the source versus destination lookup classification. Those extra combinations were developed as improvements to the initial BGP Policy Accounting feature.

This chapter also covers the destination-sensitive billing feature, which is quite similar to BGP Policy Accounting. It is available on only specific platforms. The Destination-Sensitive Traffic Shaping (DSTS) feature is addressed briefly because it takes the BGP Policy Accounting statistics as input to shape the traffic.

This chapter concludes by comparing the BGP Accounting features to the questions raised in Chapter 2, "Data Collection Methodology":

- What to collect?
- Where and how to collect?
- Who is the user?
- Potential scenarios

Input BGP Policy Accounting

When classifying the BGP traffic sent to different BGP peers (destination lookup), BGP Policy Accounting allows accounting for traffic according to the route it traverses.

Input BGP Policy Accounting gives Internet service providers (ISP) the means to charge their customers according to the route that the traffic flows through: traffic routed domestically, internationally, terrestrially, or via a satellite. After the traffic classification is applied, different destination-sensitive billing schemes can be applied.

Leveraging this, the ISP can identify and account for all traffic on a per-customer basis, as shown in Figure 8-1.

Figure 8-1   *Network Diagram Example*

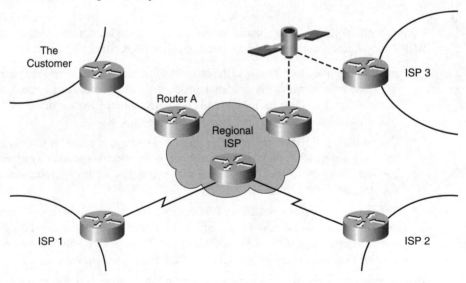

In this example, BGP Policy Accounting enabled in Router A measures the packet and byte volumes in buckets. The buckets represent ISP1, ISP2, and the satellite link to ISP3.

The classification per bucket can be done per BGP AS, assuming that each of the three exits has a different BGP AS.

All traffic destined for a particular set of autonomous systems could be accounted for at one rate, and traffic going to destinations that are more distant could be billed at a second rate. Differentiated billing for different parts of the Internet is a good idea, because it allows the ISP to offer various destination-sensitive billing scenarios.

Note that "billing back" the customer for differently priced upstream providers (passing one's own cost structure to customers) might not be the best model for ISP pricing. There are no incentives for the ISP to lower the costs, and it could confuse the customers, who have no influence on which path packets are routed.

Output BGP Policy Accounting

In Figure 8-1, where an ISP deploys a destination-sensitive billing scheme, imagine a case in which a customer downloads some huge files from the Internet. Destination-sensitive billing, configured with Input BGP Policy Accounting, tracks only the initial small FTP requests. The bulk of the returned data, which is sent in the opposite direction, is tracked with only an additional configured source-sensitive billing scheme.

To use source-sensitive billing, the ISP must apply a traffic classification on the (sub)interface facing the customers on Router A, for the egress traffic. This traffic classification is based on the route that the traffic took before arriving at the customers, which is a source classification.

The question "Does the traffic come from ISP1, from ISP2, or via the satellite link from ISP3?" can now be answered. Therefore, the customers are charged according to the path of the information's source.

The similarities and differences between Input and Output BGP Policy Accounting can be deduced from the similarities and differences between destination- and source-sensitive billing:

- In case of destination-sensitive billing (Input BGP Policy Accounting), the router looks at the traffic when it enters the interface. The router looks at the traffic when it leaves the interface for source-sensitive billing (Output BGP Policy Accounting).

- In case of destination-sensitive billing (Input BGP Policy Accounting), the router executes a destination lookup classification to deduce where the traffic will be sent. For source-sensitive billing (Output BGP Policy Accounting), the router executes a source lookup classification to deduce where the traffic comes from (from which peering point the traffic enters the ISP network).

- The same traffic classifications are used in both source- and destination-sensitive billing (both Input and Output BGP Policy Accounting), based on BGP community list, BGP AS number, and/or AS_PATH on a per-interface basis.

NOTE	A general concern related to any accounting mechanism that performs a source lookup also applies in the case of Output BGP Policy Accounting. A source lookup in the routing table results in the path that this router would take to reach the source. In case of asymmetric routing, where the forwarded traffic path is different from the return traffic path, the deduced routing information is incorrect. Therefore, caution should be taken with Output BGP Policy Accounting (and, as a consequence, with source-sensitive billing), because BGP asymmetry is a common occurrence in ISP environments.
	Some ISPs have an interesting alternative that avoids the issues of asymmetric BGP routes. If an ISP has only a few customers (a maximum of 64, which is the maximum number of buckets in BGP Policy Accounting), and the customer routes are in (I)BGP on the external border routers (those with "upstream" connections), the ISP could map each customer into a bucket on those routers and use ingress BGP Policy Accounting on every interface to an upstream ISP.

Summary of All Four BGP Policy Accounting Combinations

Initially, BGP Policy Accounting was available only on an input interface—that is, for ingress traffic. The Output BGP Policy Accounting feature introduces several extensions: the possibility to account for egress traffic and also accounting based on source addresses for both ingress and egress traffic. Table 8-1 summarizes the four possibilities of source versus destination lookup combined with ingress versus egress traffic.

Table 8-1 *Four Different Combinations of BGP Policy Accounting*

Source lookup classification on the ingress traffic **Example 1**: Checking the peering and transit agreement for the ingress traffic	Destination lookup classification on the ingress traffic **Example 2**: Destination-sensitive billing
Source lookup classification on the egress traffic **Example 3**: Source-sensitive billing	Destination lookup classification on the egress traffic **Example 4**: Checking the peering and transit agreement for the egress traffic

Combining Examples 1 and 4 from Table 8-1 allows ISPs to monitor and verify their peering agreements with neighbor ISPs. In Figure 8-2, classifying the ingress and egress traffic per BGP AS_PATH on the external interface of Router A could indicate that all the traffic back and forth to ISP2 is actually targeted for ISP4. Therefore, directly peering with ISP4 may be the better option in this example, assuming that there is an option for direct peering between ISP1 and ISP4.

Figure 8-2   *Verifying the Peering and Transit Agreements*

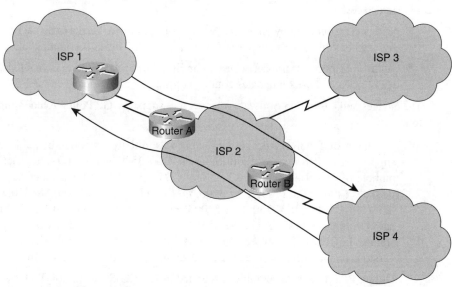

Fundamentals

Figure 8-3 illustrates the different steps that are processed at the router. Router B sends BGP routing updates to Router A, where they are passed through a table-map statement. The table-map uses a route-map statement, which checks for criteria (such as AS number, AS-PATH, and BGP community) in BGP routing updates. The route entries in the Forwarding Information Base (FIB) (generated by Cisco Express Forwarding [CEF]) are extended with BGP Policy Accounting-specific traffic indexes. Ingress or egress traffic is then monitored for the FIB entries. Each time a packet takes a specific route, the associated traffic index (bucket) counters for the (sub)interface are updated.

The BGP Policy Accounting principles can be summarized as follows:

- Account the number of packets and bytes, per (sub)interface, for the different combinations of input/output traffic and source/destination FIB lookups.

- Only the traffic following the BGP routes is accounted. For example, you cannot account for the traffic issued from your local autonomous system.

- It can track up to a maximum of eight different buckets for each (sub)interface. Note that some platforms and IOS releases support up to 64 buckets. The buckets are globally defined for the router.

- CEF or distributed CEF (dCEF) must be enabled for BGP Policy Accounting to work.

- The statistical results can be read via SNMP with CISCO-BGP-POLICY-ACCOUNTING-MIB, but the BGP Policy Accounting configuration is available only via the CLI.

- BGP Policy Accounting is available on the Virtual Routing and Forwarding (VRF) interfaces.

- The packets blocked by an access list are not accounted, because the packets are blocked before the FIB is accessed, where the traffic index accounting takes place.

- A CPU performance impact occurs when BGP Policy Accounting is enabled, because each forwarded packet updates counters during the entry lookup in the FIB.

The devices and Cisco IOS Software releases that support BGP Policy Accounting are as follows:

- The Input BGP Policy Accounting feature was initially supported by platforms that support Cisco IOS release 12.0(9)S: Cisco 7200, 7500, and 12000 series routers. The number of supported platforms in Cisco IOS release 12.2(13)T is much larger. This includes 1400, 1600, 1700, 2600, 3600, 7100, 7200, 7500, AS5300, AS5350, AS5400, AS5800, AS5850, ICS7750, IGX 8400 URM, MGX 8850, and uBR7200. All line cards from the 12000 (except the ATM line cards and the line cards with engine 4) support Input BGP Policy Accounting. Because it was introduced in different IOS versions on the different line cards, you should check the documentation.

- Output BGP Policy Accounting was added in 12.0(23)S and 12.3(4)T. On the 12000, the engine 3 line cards support Output BGP Policy Accounting.

- Today, most platforms supporting CEF also support some variations of BGP Policy Accounting.

- 64 buckets are supported in 12.0(23)S, 12.0(23)ST, and 12.2(9)T for all software implementations: 1400, 1600, 1700, 2600, 3600, 7100, 7200, 7500, AS5300, AS5350, AS5400, AS5800, AS5850, ICS7750, IGX 8400 URM, MGX 8850, uBR7200, 7200, 7500, and 12000 (engines 0, 1, and 2). For hardware implementations (such as engine 3 [and above] line cards on the 12000), the number of buckets varies between eight and 64.

BGP Policy Accounting Commands

The command-line interface (CLI) commands that you need to configure and verify BGP Policy Accounting are as follows:

- router(config-if)# **bgp-policy accounting** [**input** | **output**] [**source**] enables BGP policy accounting for the interface.
  - Use the optional **input** or **output** keyword to account for traffic either entering or exiting the router. By default, BGP policy accounting is based on traffic entering the router (input).
  - Use the optional **source** keyword to account for traffic based on source address (source lookup classification).

- Router(config-route-map)# **set traffic-index bucket-number**
  Applied under the route-map submenu, this command indicates where to collect output packets that pass a **match** clause of a route map for BGP policy accounting.

- Router(config-router)# **table-map route-map-name**
  Applied under the BGP process submenu, this command classifies BGP prefixes entered in the routing table and sets the traffic index next to the entries in the FIB.

- Router# **show cef interface** [*type number*] **policy-statistics** [**input** | **output**]
  displays the per-interface traffic statistics. You can display BGP accounting policy statistics based on traffic traveling through an input interface (**input**) or output interface (**output**) by using the appropriate keyword.

- Router# **clear ip bgp** [**ipv4** | **ipv6** | **vpnv4**] **table-map**
  reassigns the traffic indexes in case of change or removal. Note that this command does not clear the BGP Policy Accounting counters.

NOTE   It is recommended that you consult the specific documentation for your specific IOS release to better understand **route-map** commands as well as other regular expressions. They are very useful in conjunction with the BGP Policy Accounting feature.

SNMP Operations

The cbpAcctTable table, which contains five variables, is the only object in the BGP-POLICY-ACCOUNTING-MIB MIB. It contains all the BGP Policy Accounting packet and byte counters for each (sub)interface and for both the input and output directions:

- **cbpAcctTrafficIndex** is an integer value greater than 0 that uniquely identifies the bucket (also called traffic-type in the MIB).

- **cbpAcctInPacketCount** is the total number of packets received for a particular bucket on an interface.

- **cbpAcctInOctetCount** is the total number of octets received for a particular bucket on an interface.

- **cbpAcctOutPacketCount** is the total number of packets transmitted for a particular bucket on an interface.

- **cbpAcctOutOctetCount** is the total number of octets transmitted for a particular bucket on an interface.

The table indexes are ifIndex, which provides the (sub)interface identifier, and cbpAcctTrafficIndex, which references the bucket identifier.

Note that all counters are type Counter64 (64-bit), so SNMPv2 or SNMPv3 is required to access these counters.

Examples (CLI and SNMP)

The following examples introduce configuring and monitoring Input BGP Policy Accounting with destination lookup classification. They also describe the Output BGP Policy Accounting with source lookup classification using both source and destination lookups based on BGP community-list criteria. These correspond to Examples 2 and 3 in Table 8-1, where the objective could be to apply source- and destination-sensitive billing or to generate the core traffic matrix of an ISP core network. Referring to Figure 8-3, the **configuration** and **show** commands detailed in the following sections are executed on Router A.

Figure 8-3 *BGP Policy Accounting Example*

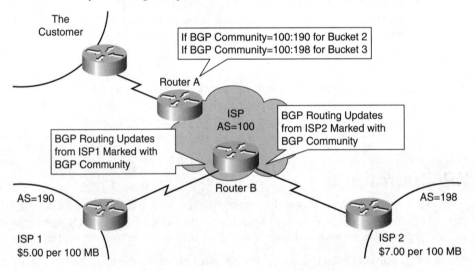

Initial Configuration

In Router B, the BGP routing updates from ISP 1 and ISP 2 are marked with BGP community of 100:190 and 100:198, respectively. However, the detailed configuration of this prerequisite is beyond the scope of this example.

Specify communities in community lists that classify traffic for accounting:

```
ip community-list 20 permit 100:190
ip community-list 30 permit 100:198
```

Define a **route-map** to match community lists, and set appropriate bucket numbers:

```
route-map set_bucket permit 10
match community 20
set traffic-index 2
!
route-map set_bucket permit 20
```

```
match community 30
set traffic-index 3
!
```

Use the **table-map** command under BGP to modify the bucket number when the IP routing table is updated with routes learned from BGP:

```
router bgp 100
table-map set_bucket
network ...
neighbor ...
!
ip bgp-community new-format
```

Enable the BGP policy accounting feature on the customer-facing interface of Router A:

```
interface POS7/0
ip address ...
bgp-policy accounting input
bgp-policy accounting output  source
```

Collection Monitoring

To inspect which prefix is assigned to which bucket and which community (or communities), use the **show ip cef** and **show ip bgp** commands:

```
Router#show ip cef 198.162.5.0 detail
198.162.5.0/24, version 21, cached adjacency to POS7/2
0 packets, 0 bytes, traffic_index 3
  via 10.1.1.1, 0 dependencies, recursive
    next hop 10.1.1.1, POS7/2 via 10.1.1.0/30
    valid cached adjacency

Router#show ip bgp 198.162.5.0
BGP routing table entry for 198.162.5.0/24, version 2
Paths: (1 available, best #1)
  Not advertised to any peer
  100
    10.1.1.1 from 10.1.1.1 (32.32.32.32)
      Origin IGP, metric 0, localpref 100, valid, external, best
      Community: 192:198
```

To look at per-interface traffic statistics, use the **show cef interface policy-statistics** command:

```
LC-Slot7#show cef interface policy-statistics input
POS7/0 is up (if_number 8)
Bucket    Packets                Bytes
1            0                       0
2           20                     2000
3           50                     5000
4            0                       0
5            0                       0
6            0                       0
7            0                       0
8            0                       0
LC-Slot7#show cef interface policy-statistics output
Bucket    Packets                Bytes
1            0                       0
2           40                    200000
3          100                    500000
```

```
4               0                        0
5               0                        0
6               0                        0
7               0                        0
8               0                        0
```

The corresponding MIB table shows the identical entries. The router is accessed with
SNMP2c (SNMP version 2c), the read community string is public, and the SNMP tool net-
snmp is used. Note that only the relevant entries of the cbpAcctTable are shown in the
following MIB table—only buckets 2 and 3, and only the POS/7 interface that corresponds
to the ifIndex 19:

```
SERVER % snmpwalk -c public -v 2c <router> cbpAcctTable
cbpAcctInPacketCount.19.2 = Counter64: 20
cbpAcctInPacketCount.19.3 = Counter64: 50
cbpAcctInOctetCount.19.2 = Counter64: 2000
cbpAcctInOctetCount.19.3 = Counter64: 5000
cbpAcctOutPacketCount.19.2 = Counter64: 40
cbpAcctOutPacketCount.19.3 = Counter64: 100
cbpAcctOutOctetCount.19.2 = Counter64: 200000
cbpAcctOutOctetCount.19.3 = Counter64: 500000
```

Destination-Sensitive Services

Destination-Sensitive Services (DSS) is available only on the Cisco 7600 series router and
Catalyst 6500 series. It allows traffic accounting and traffic shaping to get the BGP
autonomous system numbers to better engineer and plan network circuit peering and transit
agreements.

DSS consists of two separate services:

- **Destination-Sensitive Billing (DSB)**—Similar to BGP Policy Accounting.

- **Destination-Sensitive Traffic Shaping (DSTS)**—Combines the traffic-index
  classification with the traffic shaping action.

Destination-Sensitive Billing

The DSB feature on the Cisco 7600 series router and Catalyst 6500 series is similar to BGP
Policy Accounting. Exactly like BGP Policy Accounting, DSB allows accounting based on
destination traffic indexes and provides a means of classifying customer traffic according
to the route that the traffic travels. Transpacific, transatlantic, satellite, domestic, and other
provider traffic can be identified and accounted for on a destination network basis when the
customer traffic is on a unique software interface. DSB provides packet and byte counters,
which represent counts for IP packets per destination network. DSB is implemented using
route maps to classify the traffic into one of seven possible indexes, which represent a traffic
classification. DSB is supported on ingress and egress ports on the Packet Over SONET
(POS) and Gigabit Ethernet Optical Services Modules (OSM).

To summarize, the DSB feature is equivalent to BGP Policy Accounting with regard to the capabilities, the principles, and even the configuration, because the DSB feature requires the BGP Policy Accounting configuration. Unfortunately, the new feature name DSB sometimes leads to confusion or unnecessary feature comparison between BGP Policy Accounting and DSB.

Destination-Sensitive Billing Example

The **ingress-dsb** command plus all BGP Policy Accounting commands enable the DSB feature. The following DSB example sets a traffic-index of 1 for traffic whose destination is in the BGP AS 100. It also sets a traffic-index of 2 for the traffic whose destination is in the BGP AS 200. Finally, it sets a traffic-index of 7 for the rest of the traffic.

```
Router(config)# router bgp 1
Router(config-router)#  table-map buckets
Router(config-router)#   ...

Router(config)# ip as-path access-list 1 permit _100$
Router(config)# ip as-path access-list 2 permit _200$
Router(config)# route-map buckets permit 10
Router(config-route-map)#  match as-path 1
Router(config-route-map)#  set traffic-index 1

Router(config)# route-map buckets permit 20
Router(config-route-map)#  match as-path 2
Router(config-route-map)#  set traffic-index 2

Router(config)# route-map buckets permit 70
Router(config-route-map)#  set traffic-index 7

Router(config)# interface interface
Router(config-if)# ingress-dsb
Router(config-if)# bgp-policy accounting
```

The monitoring of the collected statistics is ensured by the BGP Policy Accounting **show** commands and the CISCO-BGP-POLICY-ACCOUNTING-MIB, which were explained previously in the chapter.

Destination-Sensitive Traffic Shaping (DSTS)

DSTS performs inbound and outbound traffic shaping based on the destination traffic-index configuration. In other words, DSTS benefits from the traffic-index classification, which was set up by DSB (BGP Policy Accounting configuration) to apply an action—the traffic shaping. Note that the classification based on DSTS is supported with ingress DSS only.

The reasons to use traffic shaping are to control access to available bandwidth, to ensure that traffic conforms to the established policies, and to regulate traffic flows to avoid congestion that can occur when the traffic exceeds the access speed of its remote target interface. Shaping has the effect of buffering the output traffic so that when traffic exceeds a defined threshold, buffering takes place. As long as the burst rate stays within a predefined limit, buffering has the effect of smoothing the output; hence, it is called "shaping."

Because the DSTS feature is only indirectly related to the accounting and performance subjects of this book, this small DSTS section is included for completeness. It is one of the very few accounting features that allows an automatic policy action in conjunction with collection of accounting data.

Destination-Sensitive Traffic Shaping Example

With DSTS, you can shape the traffic per specific BGP AS, per specific BGP AS-path, per specific BGP community, or per specific BGP prefix. This example is built on top of the DSB example in the previous section (which means that all BGP Policy Accounting commands from that example are preserved). It limits the traffic classified with traffic index 1 to 20 Mbps, the traffic classified with traffic index 2 to 80 Mbps, and the rest of the traffic to 120 Mbps. When mapping the traffic index to destinations, this example shows how to achieve the following policies:

- Shape to 20 Mbps the traffic whose destination is in the BGP AS 100.
- Shape to 80 Mbps the traffic whose destination is in the BGP AS 200.
- Shape to 200 Mbps the rest of the traffic.

```
Router(config)# class-map match-all bgp_bucket_1
Router(config-cmap)#  match bgp-index 1

Router(config)# class-map match-all bgp_bucket_2
Router(config-cmap)#  match bgp-index 2

Router(config)# class-map match-all bgp_bucket_7
Router(config-cmap)# match bgp-index 7

Router(config)# policy-map bgp-qos
Router(config-pmap)# class bgp_bucket_1
Router(config-pmap-c)# shape average 20000000 8000 8000
Router(config-pmap)# class bgp_bucket_2
Router(config-pmap-c)# shape average 80000000 32000 32000
Router(config-pmap)# class bgp_bucket_7
Router(config-pmap-c)# shape average 120000000 48000 48000

Router(config)# interface interface
Router(config-if)# bgp-policy accounting
Router(config-if)# service-policy input bgp-qos
```

Applicability

Table 8-2 relates the BGP Policy Accounting properties to the fundamental questions discussed in Chapter 2.

Table 8-2   *Comparison of the Different BGP Policy Accounting Features*

Criterion	BGP Policy Accounting
What to collect (data collection details)?	Total traffic (packets and bytes): • Per (sub)interface • For ingress or egress • For source or destination lookup criteria
Where to collect?	Edge of the network, on the BGP-enabled routers
How to configure?	CLI commands or scripts
How to collect?	Pull model: CLI commands or scripts SNMP
How to identify the user?	With the (sub)interface, because the counters are distinctive per (sub)interface
Use case example	Destination-sensitive billing Source-sensitive billing Network-wide capacity planning Traffic profiling and engineering Peering and transit agreements
Additional details	64-bit SNMP counters Number of buckets: 8 or 64, globally defined, depending on the platforms and Cisco IOS version

CHAPTER 9

AAA Accounting

This chapter describes authentication, authorization, and accounting (AAA), with an emphasis on accounting. It starts with a general introduction to AAA, RADIUS, and Diameter, and then the various standards are discussed, along with voice-specific extensions. You will learn how to identify which AAA functions to use for which requirements and what Cisco has implemented.

With authentication, authorization, and accounting, each "A" describes a specific set of tasks to perform:

- **Authentication** verifies that the users are who they say they are.
- **Authorization** limits the user's activities to a set of policies, such as hours of operation, idle timeouts, filters, limiting service and connection access, and so on.
- **Accounting** generates usage records that log the user's activities.

AAA was invented long before broadband and wireless Internet access became pervasive. It provides a mechanism for user access over dial-in connections, Telnet, SSH, and PPP. Remote access to the network occurs over a modem and a phone line to the Internet service provider (ISP). Users provide their username and password during the authentication process to a Network Access Server (NAS). It usually does not store these details locally but instead forwards the request to a database server that has the user credential information. RADIUS became the standard communication protocol between the NAS and the user database server, defined in RFC 2865 through 2869.

A typical AAA concept is based on a three-tier model, including a user, a client, and a server. With today's networks, the RADIUS RFC terminology can be slightly confusing, because the access server is called the "client," the back-end application is called the "server," and the user is not mentioned at all. A better terminology was introduced by RFC 2753, *A Framework for Policy-Based Admission Control*, distinguishing between a Policy Decision Point (PDP) and a Policy Enforcement Point (PEP). The PEP is the client component, equal to the RADIUS NAS, and the PDP describes the server component, similar to the RADIUS server. Because neither RADIUS nor Diameter uses the RFC 2753 terms, and to avoid the mingling of terminology, we use the RADIUS terms, even though in some scenarios they do not match perfectly, such as with controlling Telnet login into a router.

From an implementation perspective, the user connects to the network element (NAS)—in this case, a Cisco router. The NAS is responsible for passing user information to a RADIUS server, typically running on UNIX or Windows systems. The server is responsible for receiving the NAS requests and returning responses, indicating that it successfully received the initial request.

Figure 9-1 shows the different RADIUS components. The RADIUS naming convention is used, and the RFC 2753 terminology appears in brackets.

Figure 9-1   *RADIUS Components*

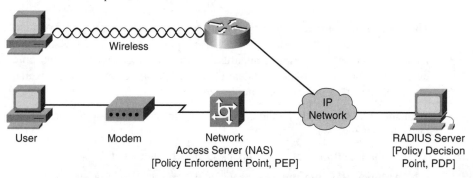

Because of the long history of AAA, you might consider it a legacy technology that was appropriate for only modem dial-in sessions; however, the opposite is true! Even though the analog dial-in model is kind of the exception these days, the latest network technologies still leverage AAA. Think about high-speed Internet connectivity in hotels (usually DSL-broadband networks) or public wireless hotspots at airports or Internet cafes. Users normally get free access to the provider's web page. If they want to surf the Internet or connect to their corporate intranet via VPN tunnels, an access fee is charged first, based on connectivity time. For these scenarios, the AAA server is linked to the billing system, which authenticates and authorizes the user. The NAS establishes and terminates the connection when the contract expires. For broadband networks, the classic dial-in NAS has been replaced by a broadband remote-access server (B-RAS, such as the Cisco 10000 router), but the concept remains the same. In IP telephony environments, especially the accounting component of AAA is extensively used by the gateways to generate Call Detail Records (CDR) for creating billing details. The Internet Protocol Detail Record (IPDR) format is an IP-centric example of a CDR.

NOTE	For more details on IPDR, visit www.ipdr.org/.

To feed the CDRs into a billing system, accurate time stamps are required. Best practice suggests deploying the network time protocol (NTP) in the network, which synchronizes the system clocks on network elements with an authoritative time source.

NTP is defined in RFC 1305. NTP servers can be organized as a symmetric mesh topology or a hierarchy or a combination. In the classic NTP design, the servers are organized as a symmetric peer-to-peer topology or a hierarchy. Each level in the hierarchy is called a *stratum*, which defines the distance from the reference, which is an atomic source, referred to as Stratum 0. In large networks, a hierarchical structure increases consistency, stability, and scalability. A Cisco router can act as the NTP source and receive updates from public sources via the Internet. However, for increased accuracy, it is advised that you consider investing in a GPS appliance with Ethernet or AUX ports that can be connected to a Cisco router.

Because of this book's focus, the rest of this chapter focuses on the accounting part of AAA.

Fundamentals of AAA Accounting

The following principles apply for AAA:

- AAA is an improved logging system used for authentication, authorization, and accounting. In PPP, SLIP, and dial-in networks, AAA is not enabled primarily for accounting, but for authentication and authorization instead. In contrast, for voice scenarios, AAA is primarily used for accounting. For example, in H.323 voice signaling networks, H.325 instead of AAA is used for authentication. In a Session Initiation Protocol (SIP) voice signaling network, HTTP basic or digest is used for authentication, not AAA.

- AAA collects incoming and outgoing packets/bytes.

- Each session can generate start and stop records:
    - "Accounting request start" with the start time
    - "Accounting request stop" with the stop time and a full accounting record

- AAA is adequate for billing because the username gets reported.

- AAA is supported on all switching paths.

It is relevant to note that AAA is not limited to controlling user access; it can also control the operator's access to network devices or even command execution at a network element. Consequently, several types of accounting are possible with AAA; Cisco IOS Software supports five different kinds:

- **Network accounting** collects usage records for network access (over dial-in, broadband, or wireless).

- **Connection accounting** provides information about all outbound connections made from the NAS, such as Telnet and rlogin.

- **EXEC accounting** gathers information about user EXEC terminal sessions (user shells) on the NAS, including username, date, start and stop times, the access server IP address, and (for dial-in users) the telephone number the call originated from.

- **System accounting** provides information about all system-level events (for example, when the system reboots, or when accounting is turned on or off).

- **Command accounting** supplies information about the EXEC shell commands for specified privilege levels that are being executed on a NAS. Each command accounting record includes a list of the commands executed for that privilege level, as well as the date and time each command was executed and the user who executed it.

NOTE	The authors think that in the preceding list, the RADIUS terminology (in particular, the NAS term) is inadequate. However, in an attempt to reduce the potential for confusion, we decided to use RADIUS terms.

High-Level Comparison of RADIUS, TACACS+, and Diameter

Whereas AAA describes the *concept* of authentication, authorization, and accounting, RADIUS and TACACS *implement* AAA solutions. Remote Authentication Dial-In User Service (RADIUS) provides the communication between a NAS and a RADIUS server. The Terminal Access Controller Access Control System (TACACS) implementation of AAA existed before RADIUS and is still applied today. RADIUS is an IETF standard, and TACACS is described in RFC 927 and RFC 1492 as an informational standard only. Cisco extended the TACACS definition by adding security features and the option to split the AAA server into three separate servers; this new definition was called TACACS+. Although the TACACS+ and RADIUS protocols provide similar functionality, they have several key differences, such as the transport mechanism (UDP, TCP), performance impact, standard definition, and packet encryption. The most fundamental difference is the network transport protocol: RADIUS uses UDP to exchange information between the NAS and the AAA server, whereas TACACS+ uses TCP. On one hand, RADIUS is well suited for user authentication and accounting to network access and services. On the other hand, TACACS+ provides additional features such as per-command authorization. An example is a policy defined by a network administrator in which operators need to authenticate before accessing network devices and authorization is required for configuration changes.

Table 9-1 compares TACACS+ and RADIUS functionality.

Table 9-1   *TACACS+ and RADIUS Comparison*

Criterion	TACACS+	RADIUS
Transport	TCP (reliable; more overhead)	UDP (unreliable; higher performance)
Authentication and Authorization	Can be separated (more flexible)	Combined
Multiprotocol Support	Supported (IP, Apple, NetBIOS, Novell, X.25)	IP only
Access to Router CLI Commands	Supports two methods to control the authorization of router commands on a per-user or per-group basis	Not supported
Encryption	Packet payload	Passwords only

As mentioned, RADIUS was developed with a dial-in infrastructure in mind. New technologies, such as broadband and high-speed wireless, combined with new applications, such as IP telephony and video, significantly enhance the requirements for authentication and authorization. The informational RFC 2989 summarizes AAA protocol requirements for network access, with input taken from documents produced by the IETF Network Access Server Requirements Next Generation (NASREQ), Roaming Operations (ROAMOPS), and IP Routing for Wireless/Mobile Hosts (MOBILEIP) working groups, among others.

At this point, Diameter becomes relevant, because it addresses these requirements. The Diameter protocol is an enhanced version of RADIUS that provides multiple enhancements while still being backward-compatible. Details on the Diameter protocol appear in the separate "Diameter Details" section at the end of this chapter.

This chapter's focus is on RADIUS and Diameter, as it is the IETF standard protocols for accounting records in dial-in, broadband, wireless, and IP telephony networks.

RADIUS

In 1997, the Internet Engineering Task Force (IETF) finalized the RADIUS protocol specification as RFC 2058. It was superseded by RFC 2138 and later RFC 2865. RFC 2059 was the first RADIUS accounting standard; it was made obsolete by RFC 2139 and later RFC 2866. Note the difference between the RADIUS protocol specification (RFC 2865) and the RADIUS accounting specification (RFC 2866). Although both are IETF standards, RFC 2866 is an informational standard only, and RFC 2865 is a formal IETF standard.

The RADIUS specification contains client and server roles, where the NAS performs the client role. Splitting the functionality provides the foundation for scalability, because a single RADIUS server can serve multiple clients (NASs), resulting in a single data store for user credentials. Two different RADIUS packet types exist: authentication and accounting packets. The NAS sends authentication requests to the RADIUS server to check the user's identity. This request consists of the user credentials and NAS IP address or identifier. The RADIUS server sends authentication replies that include the reply code and a set of additional attributes. An accounting request is sent to the server when the NAS reports an event, such as the session start and termination. For each successfully processed accounting request, the RADIUS server returns an accounting acknowledgment, which informs the NAS that the information was received. This handshake mechanism avoids packet loss over the UDP protocol. Authorization takes places after successful authentication. For example, your company may have policies for prohibiting access to sensitive information (such as finacial data or source code) over the Internet. In this case, even successful authentication would not grant access to sensitive data.

A typical user session occurs as follows: When a user connects to a NAS, first it verifies that the user is actually registered and that the supplied credentials are correct: this step is called authentication. The NAS forms an authentication request and sends it to the RADIUS server, which then verifies the user's credentials against the database. The acknowledgment packet is returned to the NAS. The server reply advises the NAS to assign an IP address to the user and to establish a connection between the user and the server that the user intends to connect to, assuming that the authentication was accepted.

As the second step, the NAS determines which services the user is permitted to use and optionally applies specific resource limitations for an individual or group. This step is called authorization. Authorization can be implemented in several ways, such as applying a preconfigured access control list (ACL) to restrict the user's access to resources and services based on one or more metrics (time of day, transport type, user group).

After a successful authentication and authorization, the NAS establishes a connection between the user and the application server. Now application data can be transmitted, while so far only access and authorization control traffic was exchanged. At this time, accounting starts as follows: the NAS stores the session's start time and generates an accounting-requests packet for the AAA server. The initiating packet is called "accounting-start," and the terminating packet is called "accounting-stop." During the session, optional accounting update packets can be sent. For each request, the AAA server replies with an accounting-response. A usage record typically consists of the session's start and stop times, duration, and number of input and output octets and packets transferred. Each AAA session consists of at least two report messages:

- Accounting-start request message with the start time
- Accounting-stop request message with the stop time and full accounting details

Figure 9-2 illustrates the interaction between the NAS and the RADIUS server.

Figure 9-2   *RADIUS Interaction*

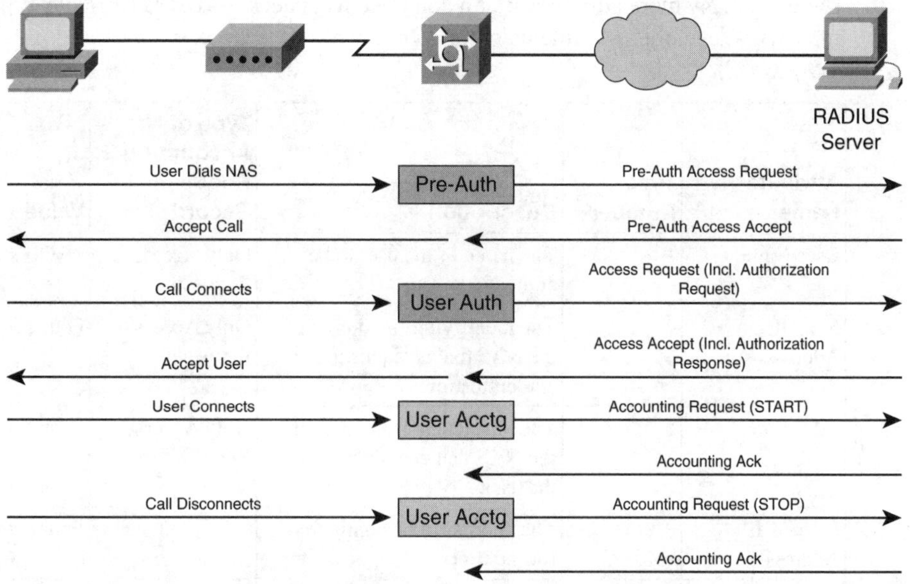

RADIUS Attributes

RADIUS attributes carry the specific authentication, authorization, accounting, and configuration details for the request and response. Attributes are exchanged between the NAS and the server. Each attribute is associated with a set of properties that specifies how to interpret it. The most important property is the data type, which declares the type of data that the attribute identifies (character string, integer number, IP address, or raw binary data). The information to be transmitted with the request is packaged in a set of attribute/value pairs (AV pairs, or AVP), which consist of attribute numbers and the associated data. RFC 2865 describes the RADIUS protocol and defines the different AAA attributes. Note that RFC 2865 defines attributes 1 through 39 and 60 through 63, whereas 40 through 59 are reserved for accounting and are not defined in RFC 2865. The informational RFC 2866 extends this specification by defining the accounting-specific attributes (40 through 59). RFC 2869 is another informational RFC that extends RFC 2865 by specifying attributes 52 to 55. In summary, RFC 2865 (Standards Track) defines authentication and authorization, and the accounting part is defined in the informational RFCs 2866 and 2869.

Table 9-2 describes the significant RADIUS attributes from an accounting perspective. There are many more attributes. For a complete list, check RADIUS Attribute Types at http://www.iana.org/assignments/radius-types.

Table 9-2   *RADIUS Attributes*

Attribute Name	Type Number	Description	Type of Accounting Request Record	Value
User-Name	1	The name of the user to be authenticated.	Only Access-Requests	ASCII string
NAS-IP-Address	4	The identifying IP address of the NAS that is requesting user authentication.	Only Access-Requests	Four octets
NAS-Port	5	The physical port number of the NAS that is authenticating the user.	Only Access-Requests	Four octets
Framed-IP-Address	8	The address to be configured for the user.	—	Four octets
Vendor-Specific Attribute (VSA)	26	Allows vendors to support their own extended attributes that are not suitable for general usage.	—	>= 7 bytes (the vendor-string field must be at least 1 byte)
Called-Station-Id	30	Allows the NAS to send in the Access-Request packet the phone number that the user called, using Dialed Number Identification Service (DNIS) or a similar technology. This number may be different from the phone number the call came from.	—	ASCII string, DNIS phone number
Calling-Station-Id	31	Allows the NAS to send in the Access-Request packet the phone number that the call came from, using Automatic Number Identification (ANI) or a similar technology.	—	ASCII string, ANI phone number

Table 9-2   *RADIUS Attributes (Continued)*

Attribute Name	Type Number	Description	Type of Accounting Request Record	Value
Acct-Status-Type	40	Indicates whether this Accounting-Request marks the beginning (Start) or the end (Stop) of the user service.	—	1 Start 2 Stop 3 Interim-Update 7 Accounting-On 8 Accounting-Off
Acct-Delay-Time	41	Indicates how many seconds the client has been trying to send this record for. Can be subtracted from the time of arrival on the server to find the approximate time of the event generating this Accounting-Request.	—	Four octets
Acct-Input-Octets	42	Indicates how many octets the reporting device has received from the port over the course of this service being provided.	Only Accounting-Request records with Acct-Status-Type = Stop	Four octets
Acct-Output-Octets	43	Indicates how many octets the reporting device has sent to the port in the course of delivering this service.	Only Accounting-Request records with Acct-Status-Type = Stop	Four octets
Acct-Session-Id (overload field)	44	A unique Accounting ID to make it easy to match start and stop records in a log file. This field is also used to transfer vendor-specific information elements (ASCII string; maximum 256 characters).	—	ASCII string; maximum 256 characters

continues

Table 9-2 *RADIUS Attributes (Continued)*

Attribute Name	Type Number	Description	Type of Accounting Request Record	Value
Acct-Authentic	45	Indicates how the user was authenticated—by RADIUS, the NAS, or another remote authentication protocol.	—	1 RADIUS 2 Local 3 Remote
Acct-Session-Time	46	Indicates how many seconds the user has received service for.	Only Accounting-Request records with Acct-Status-Type = Stop	Four octets
Acct-Input-Packets	47	Indicates how many packets have been received from the port over the course of this service being provided to a framed user.	Only Accounting-Request records with Acct-Status-Type = Stop	Four octets
Acct-Output-Packets	48	Indicates how many packets have been sent to the port in the course of delivering this service to a framed user.	Only Accounting-Request records with Acct-Status-Type = Stop	Four octets

Table 9-2 *RADIUS Attributes (Continued)*

Attribute Name	Type Number	Description	Type of Accounting Request Record	Value
Acct-Terminate-Cause	49	Indicates how the session was terminated.	Only Accounting-Request records with Acct-Status-Type = Stop	1 User Request 2 Lost Carrier 3 Lost Service 4 Idle Timeout 5 Session Timeout 6 Admin Reset 7 Admin Reboot 8 Port Error 9 NAS Error 10 NAS Request 11 NAS Reboot 12 Port Unneeded 13 Port Preempted 14 Port Suspended 15 Service Unavailable 16 Callback 17 User Error 18 Host Request
Acct-Multi-Session-Id	50	A unique Accounting ID to make it easy to link several related sessions in a log file. Each linked session would have a unique Acct-Session-Id but the same Acct-Multi-Session-Id.	—	ASCII string

continues

Tab'e 9-2 *RADIUS Attributes (Continued)*

Attribute Name	Type Number	Description	Type of Accounting Request Record	Value
Acct-Link-Count	51	Gives the count of links that are known to have been in a given multilink session at the time the accounting record was generated.	—	The Value field is four octets. It contains the number of links seen so far in this multilink session.
Acct-Input-Gigawords	52	Indicates how many times the Acct-Input-Octets counter has wrapped around 2^32 over the course of this service being provided. Defined by RFC 2869.	Only Accounting-Request records with Acct-Status-Type = Stop or Interim-Update	Four octets
Acct-Output-Gigawords	53	Indicates how many times the Acct-Output-Octets counter has wrapped around 2^32 in the course of delivering this service. Defined by RFC 2869.	Only Accounting-Request records with Acct-Status-Type = Stop	Four octets
Unused	54	—	—	—
Event-Timestamp	55	Included in an Accounting-Request packet to record the time that this event occurred on the NAS, in seconds since January 1, 1970 00:00 UTC. Defined by RFC 2869.	—	—

NOTE The AVP Acct-Delay-Time is especially useful in situations in which the NAS creates duplicate accounting records. This can happen during timeouts in the conversation between the NAS and the RADIUS server. A duplicated record is an exact copy of the previous one, except for the Acct-Delay-Time, which indicates how many seconds the client has been trying to send this record. When the accounting record is sent for the first time, this value is always 0, whereas a resend record has a different value. An accounting application can search for accounting records in which all fields are equal, except for Acct-Delay-Time, and eliminate all but one of the records.

RADIUS CLI Operations

This section, which mainly focuses on the accounting part of RADIUS, covers only the most important commands. For the complete list of RADIUS commands, consult the Command Reference document.

- router(config)# **aaa new-model** enables the AAA access control model.

- router(config)# **aaa group server radius** *group-name* defines the AAA server group with a group name. It groups different RADIUS server hosts into distinct lists and distinct methods.

- router(config-sg-radius)# **server** *ip-address* [**auth-port** *port-number*] [**acct-port** *port-number*] configures the IP address of the RADIUS server for the group server.

- router(config)# **aaa accounting** {**auth-proxy** | **system** | **network** | **exec** | **connection** | **commands** *level*} {**default** | *list-name*} [**vrf** *vrf-name*] {**start-stop** | **stop-only** | **none**} [**broadcast**] **group** *groupname* configures the accounting for different features:

  - **system** performs accounting for all system-level events not associated with users, such as reloads.

  - **network** runs accounting for all network-related service requests, including Serial Line Internet Protocol (SLIP), PPP, PPP Network Control Protocols (NCP), and AppleTalk Remote Access Protocol (ARAP).

  - **exec**—Runs accounting for the EXEC shell session.

  - **connection**—Provides information about all outbound connections made from the network access server, such as Telnet, local-area transport (LAT), TN3270, packet assembler and disassembler (PAD), and rlogin.

- router(config)# **aaa accounting update** [**periodic** *number*] enables periodic interim accounting records to be sent to the accounting server, where the *number* interval is specified in minutes.

The following example configures the RADIUS authentication and accounting for a user initiating a shell connection to the router. Accounting requests are sent with the start, stop, and periodic (every 1 minute) options. Note the default RADIUS accounting port of 1646. The following examples include the port number for completeness; this information is optional when using the default port.

```
router(config)# aaa new-model

router(config)# aaa group server radius MyAdmin
router(config-sg-radius)# server 10.48.66.102 auth-port 1645 acct-port 1646

router(config)# aaa authentication login default group MyAdmin
router(config)# aaa accounting update periodic 1
router(config)# aaa accounting exec OpsAcctg start-stop group MyAdmin

router(config)# radius-server host 10.48.66.102 auth-port 1645 acct-port 1646
  key 7 01100F175804

router(config)# line vty 0 4
router(config-line)# accounting exec OpsAcctg
```

The RADIUS server would report the following information: Date, Time, User-Name, Group-Name, Calling-Station-Id, Acct-Status-Type, Acct-Session-Id, Acct-Session-Time, Service-Type, Framed-Protocol, Acct-Input-Octets, Acct-Output-Octets, Acct-Input-Packets, Acct-Output-Packets, Framed-IP-Address, NAS-Port, and NAS-IP-Address. The following configuration example shows a leased-line PPP client that uses RADIUS for authentication and accounting:

```
router(config)# interface Serial2/0
router(config-if)# encapsulation ppp
router(config-if)# ppp accounting SerialAccounting
router(config-if)# ppp authentication pap
router(config)# aaa accounting network SerialAccounting start-stop group MyAdmin
```

Voice Extensions for RADIUS

The preferred accounting solution for voice over IP is RADIUS. Most voice-specific MIBs are limited to legacy telephony environments. This section examines voice-specific extensions to the RADIUS protocol.

Concept of Call Legs

A call leg is a logical connection between the router and a classic telephony endpoint or another IP telephony endpoint using a session protocol, such as SIP or H.323. For an end-to-end connection, a separate call leg is generated for each segment that lies between two points of the connection. A call processed through a voice gateway, commonly referred to as just a gateway, consists of an outgoing (originate) and incoming (answer) call leg. A voice gateway is a device that allows telephone calls over a high-speed Internet connection. Its primary functions include voice and fax compression and decompression, packetization, call routing, and control signaling. Call leg directions (such as answer or originate) are named and described from the gateway's perspective. An end-to-end call going through an originating and terminating gateway consists of four call legs. Two are from the perspective of the source originating gateway (answer telephony, originate VoIP), and the other two are from the perspective of the destination terminating gateway (answer VoIP, originate telephony). Start-stop accounting has a separate start record and stop record for each call leg. Assuming that a call is established between two voice gateways, start-stop accounting generates four discrete start records and four discrete stop records, in which all eight records have the same ID. Depending on the device configuration, this unique ID is either specified in RADIUS attribute 26 as h323-conf-id or overloaded in RADIUS attribute 44:

- **h323-conf-id value in RADIUS attribute 26 VSA**—h323-conf-id is a RADIUS attribute exported regardless of the voice protocol between the voice gateways. h323-conf-id is sent not only with H.323 configured between the voice gateways, but also when SIP is configured, which might be somewhat confusing. However, with SIP, this value is not identical for all the call legs. Instead, Call-id must be used.

- **Connection ID in RADIUS attribute 44 "Acct-Session-Id"**—Acct-Session-Id works only when the H.323 protocol is used, as opposed to SIP.

- **Call-id values in RADIUS attribute 26 VSA**—Call-id is the way to correlate call legs when SIP is used between voice gateways.

Figure 9-3 illustrates the four different call legs as they are generated through the voice call.

Figure 9-3 *Call Leg Naming Convention*

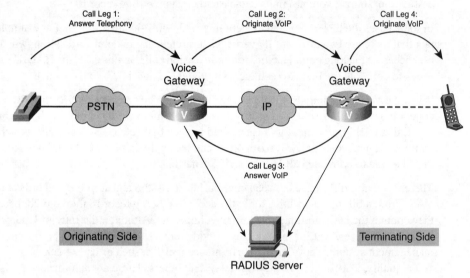

The four call legs are as follows:

- Call leg 1 goes from the originating device (telephone, PC, fax machine) to the originating gateway. It is called answer telephony.

- Call leg 2 is from the originating gateway over the IP cloud to the terminating gateway. It is called originate VoIP.

- Call leg 3 is the mirror image of call leg 2. It is called answer VoIP from the perspective of the terminating gateway. The direction of the arrow in call leg 3 represents the call leg pointing to the originating gateway. This signifies that it is from the perspective of the terminating gateway and is the other half of a matching pair of VoIP dial peers for a single call.

- Call leg 4 is from the terminating gateway to the terminating device. It is called originate VoIP.

An accounting system collects data for all calls, both legacy voice and VoIP. The most important elements of the data, other than the call's duration, are h323-conf-id and incoming-h323-conf-id, because they are required to correlate the different call legs. These two ID values are identical most of the time. This allows the correlation of the answer telephony call leg 1 (characterized by incoming-h323-conf-id) with the following originate VoIP call leg 2 (characterized by h323-conf-id). Because the h323-conf-id value is sent between the VoIP gateways as part of the H.323 protocol, the next VoIP gateway reports the same h323-config-id value for its call legs. Therefore, the RADIUS server correlates all the call legs of the same call. The billing system can combine the data from multiple call records with the same h323-conf-id value and store the call attributes (direction, duration, destination, source, volume) in its database to create a billing record.

In some cases the h323-conf-id and incoming-h323-conf-id are different. For example, the fact that there are two different ID variables has relevance in debit card calling when the user accesses the long pound facility for multisession calls. In this case, the RADIUS server needs to correlate the first two call legs with the incoming-h323-conf-id value.

When the VoIP signaling protocol between the two voice gateways is SIP, the Cisco AVP containing the Call-id value represents the unique conference ID, similar to h323-conf-id. The Call-id field is a mandatory header field in each call-related SIP message, which requires the next voice gateway to report its call legs with the same Call-id. Therefore, Call-id is the way to correlate call legs in a SIP scenario.

There is a major difference between configuring start-stop and stop-only records at the NAS. From a billing perspective, only the accounting-stop records are required, because they contain the call duration, transmitted volume, etc. Although the Interim-Update packets are not relevant for billing, they provide remarkable details for a performance management system. They contain performance metrics, such as early-packets, h323-voice-quality, lost-packets, round-trip-delay, and others. These are significant details for voice performance management, generated per call. This illustrates another intersection of accounting and performance management.

RADIUS VSAs   The latest IETF RADIUS standards (RFC 2865 and RFC 2866) specify that you can use RADIUS attribute 26 to communicate vendor-specific information between a RADIUS client (NAS) and a RADIUS server. Attribute 26 is the VSA in RADIUS records.

The idea of VSAs is to offer vendors the opportunity to create new functions without going through the IETF standards process. This also implies that VSA records are not standardized, which means that different vendor implementations of VSAs might not be interoperable.

The concept of attributes is based on the X.500 definition, in which each attribute consists of a type identifier and one or more values. A VSA is an attribute that has been implemented by a particular vendor. It encapsulates the data as AVPs. The format is

vendor-specific = protocol:attribute = value

For example, *cisco-avpair* = *timezone* = *UTC* is an AVP in which *timezone* identifies the attribute and *UTC* is the value.

RADIUS Accounting with the Vendor-Specific Attribute

Cisco voice-specific VSAs are included in requests and responses between the voice gateway and the RADIUS server. The voice gateway, as a RADIUS client, sends and receives VSAs to and from a RADIUS server. Each Cisco voice-specific VSA conforms to the RADIUS specification for attribute 26. Figure 9-4 shows the format of RADIUS VSAs and Cisco voice-specific VSAs.

Figure 9-4   *RADIUS VSA Format*

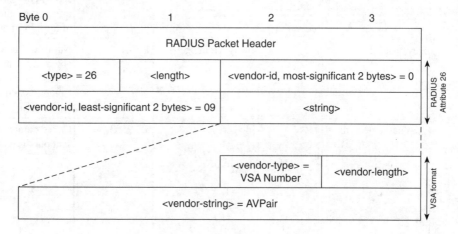

Table 9-3 describes the fields in the VSA.

Table 9-3   *RADIUS VSA Fields*

VSA Field	Definition
Type	26 (vendor-specific)
Length	>= 7 bytes (the vendor-string field must be at least 1 byte)
Vendor-ID	9 (or, in binary, 0000 0000 0000 1001). The high-order octet is 0. The three low-order octets are the vendor's structure of management information (SMI) network-management private-enterprise code in network byte order, as defined in RFC 1700, *Assigned Numbers*. In this case, the value 9 stands for Cisco Systems.
String	Field of one or more octets, such as Vendor-type = VSA number Vendor-length <= 247 bytes Vendor-string = AVP sent as an ASCII string

Table 9-4 lists selected Cisco VSAs for accounting and performance management purposes.

Table 9-4 *Cisco-Specific VSA Fields*

AVP	VSA Number (Decimal)	Format for Value or Text	Sample Value or Text	Description
Charged-units	1	Unsigned integer	0	Number of charged units for this connection. For incoming calls or if the switch doesn't supply charging information, the value of this object is 0.
Early-packets	1	Unsigned integer	1	Number of received voice packets that arrived too early to be stored in the jitter buffer during the call.
gw-final-xlated-cdn	1	Integer Values: *ton:d* *npi:aa* *#:e* where: d = 0 to 7 aa = 0 to 15 e = number in E164 format	8539663	Called number to be sent out the gateway.
gw-rxd-cdn	1	Integer Values: *ton:d* *npi:aa* *#:e* where: d = 0 to 7 aa = 0 to 15 e = number in E164 format	4085268222	Called number as received by the gateway in the incoming signaling message before any translation rules are applied.

Table 9-4   *Cisco-Specific VSA Fields (Continued)*

AVP	VSA Number (Decimal)	Format for Value or Text	Sample Value or Text	Description
h323-billing-model=*value*	109	0 = credit customer (postpaid) 1 = debit card (prepaid) 2 = limited service (prepaid)	1	Type of billing service for a specific call.
h323-call-type=*value*	27	Telephony VoIP VoFR	VoIP	Protocol type or family used on this leg of the call.
h323-conf-id=*value*	24	16-byte number in hexadecimal notation with a space between each 4-byte integer	3C5AEAB9 95C80008 0 587F34	Unique call identifier generated by the gateway. Used to identify the separate billable events (calls) within a single calling session.
h323-connect-time=*value*	28	*Hh:mm:ss:mmm ZON DDD MMM ## YYYY*	14:27:31:098 PST Fri Nov 17 2006	Connect time in Network Time Protocol (NTP) format.
h323-credit-time=*value*	102	Integer in decimal notation	300	Number of seconds for which the call is authorized.
h323-disconnect-time=*value*	29	*hh:mm:ss:mmm ZON DDD MMM ## YYYY*	14:28:03:030 PST Fri Nov 17 2006	Disconnect time in NTP format: hours, minutes, seconds, microseconds, time_zone, day, month, day_of_month, year.
h323-gw-id=*value*	33	Character string	test.cisco.com	Domain name server (DNS) name or local name of the voice gateway that is sending the VSA.

continues

Table 9-4   *Cisco-Specific VSA Fields (Continued)*

AVP	VSA Number (Decimal)	Format for Value or Text	Sample Value or Text	Description
h323-incoming-conf-id=*value*	1	16-byte number in hexadecimal notation with a space between each 4-byte integer	33C5AEAB9 95C80008 AF27092C 587F34 and 3C5AEAB9 95C80008 0 587F34	Unique number for identifying a calling session on a gateway, where a session is closed when the calling party hangs up. It is used to do the following: Match the outbound and inbound call legs for a session on a particular gateway. Collect and match all records for multiple calls placed (within the bounds of a session) on the gateway.
h323-setup-time=*value*	25	*hh:mm:ss:mmm ZON DDD MMM ## YYYY*	14:27:30:007 PST Fri Nov 17 2006	Setup time in NTP format: hours, minutes, seconds, microseconds, time_zone, day, month, day_of_month, year.
h323-time-and-day=*value*	105	Decimal number: *hh:mm:ss*	10:36:57	Time of day at the dialed number or at the remote gateway in the format hours, minutes, seconds.
h323-voice-quality=*value*	31	Decimal numbers from Impairment/ Calculated Planning Impairment Factor (ICPIF) table of G.113	5	Value representing ICPIF of the voice quality on the connection provided by lower-layer drivers (such as the digital-signal-processor). Low numbers represent better quality.

Table 9-4   *Cisco-Specific VSA Fields (Continued)*

AVP	VSA Number (Decimal)	Format for Value or Text	Sample Value or Text	Description
lost-packets	1	Unsigned integer	0	Number of lost voice packets during the call.
round-trip-delay	1	<#> ms	2 ms	Voice-packet round-trip delay, in ms, between the local and remote system on the IP backbone during the call.
session-protocol=*value*	1	String	SIP	Session protocol being used, such as SIP or H.323.
subscriber=*value*	1	String from T1/CAS (Channel Associated Signaling) or E1/R2 line/signal	Coin	T1/CAS or E1/R2 signal information about subscribers.
Tx-duration	1	<#> ms	300 ms	Duration, in ms, of the transmit path open from this peer to the call's voice gateway.
voice-tx-duration	1	<#> ms	100 ms	Duration, in ms, for this call. The Voice Utilization Rate can be obtained by dividing this by tx-duration.

RADIUS Accounting with the Overloaded Acct-Session-Id

To take advantage of standard RADIUS implementations that do not support VSAs, a different method is defined. It embeds the unsupported information elements in the RADIUS Acct-Session-Id (RADIUS value 44 from RFC 2865). The Acct-Session-Id field has a maximum length of 256 characters. It is defined to contain ten discrete fields, separated by a / as the delimited ASCII string. The overloaded Acct-Session-Id also contains connect and disconnect times, remote IP address, and disconnect cause. The following is the string format for the Acct-Session-Id field:

session id/call leg setup time/gateway id/connection id/call origin/call type/connect time/disconnect time/disconnect cause/remote ip address

One of these fields is the RADIUS *connection id,* which is a unique identifier that links accounting records associated with the same login session for a user. The internal representation of the connection-id field is 128 bits in hex format. This string can vary in appearance. An example is 3C5AEAB9 95C80008 0 587F34—denoted as a four-octet string, a space, a four-octet string, a space, a 0, a space, and a three-octet string.

Table 9-5 describes the overloaded Acct-Session-Id fields.

Table 9-5   *Overloaded Acct-Session-Id Fields*

Field	Description
session id	The standard (RFC 2139) RADIUS account-session-id.
call leg setup time	The setup time for this connection in NTP format.
gateway id	The name of the underlying gateway, as a string of the form *gateway.domain_name*
connection id	A unique global identifier used to correlate call legs that belong to the same end-to-end call. The field consists of four long words (128 bits). Each long word is displayed in hexadecimal value and is separated by a space.
call origin	The call's origin relative to the gateway. Possible values are originate and answer.
call type	The call leg type. Possible values are Telephony and VoIP.
connect time[*]	The connect time for this call leg in NTP format (stop only).
disconnect time[*]	The disconnect time for this call leg in NTP format (stop only).
disconnect cause[*]	Documented in the Q.850 specification. The value can be in the range of 1 to 127 (stop only).
remote IP address[*]	The IP address of the remote gateway used in this connection (stop only).

[*] The last four attributes (connect and disconnect times, disconnect cause, and remote IP address) in the overloaded Acct-Session-Id are available only in the stop packets. In start packets and update packets, these fields are blank.

Comparing the Vendor-Specific Attribute and the Acct-Session-Id

As a summary, consider the following rules for choosing between RADIUS attributes 26 and 44 for VoIP accounting:

- The use of attribute 26 (VSA) is recommended whenever available, because it provides a superset of accounting information. After you enable VSAs, the Acct-Session-Id is no longer overloaded, because the information sent in the session ID is captured in VSAs.

- Attribute 44 (overload) should be used only if VSA is not supported, because it provides a limited set of information. Furthermore, this attribute works only when the H.323 protocol is used, as opposed to SIP.

CLI Operations for VoIP Accounting with RADIUS

This section covers only the most important commands related to VoIP accounting with RADIUS. For the complete list of commands, consult the Command Reference document.

- router(config)# **gw-accounting aaa**
  enables VoIP gateway accounting. Previous IOS versions used the **gw-accounting** {**h323** [**vsa**] | **syslog** | **voip**} CLI command for the same purposes.

- router(config)# **radius-server vsa send** [**accounting**] [**authentication**]
  allows the network access server to recognize and use VSAs as defined by RADIUS IETF attribute 26.

- router(config-gw-accounting-aaa)# **acct-template callhistory-detail**
  sends all voice attributes for accounting. It is valid only for RADIUS IETF attribute 26 VSA, not overloaded RADIUS IETF attribute 44, Acct-Session-Id.

- router(config)# **aaa session-id** [**common** | **unique**]
  specifies whether the same session ID is used for each AAA accounting service type within a call or whether a different session ID is assigned to each accounting service type. The default value is **common**.

The following configuration examples highlight the minimal configuration options that are necessary to carry out accounting in a voice environment.

Example 1: Using RADIUS Attribute 44, Acct-Session-Id

```
router(config)# aaa new-model
router(config)# aaa accounting connection MyMethod start-stop group radius
router(config)# aaa session-id common
router(config)# gw-accounting aaa
router(config-gw-accounting-aaa)# method MyMethod
router(config-gw-accounting-aaa)# acct-template callhistory-detail
router(config)# radius-server host 172.18.192.154 auth-port 1645 acct-port 1646
router(config)# radius-server retransmit 1
router(config)# radius-server key lab
```

A typical example of the overloaded Acct-Session-Id is

session id/call leg setup time/gateway id/connection id/call origin/call type/connect time/disconnect time/disconnect cause/remote IP address

For example:

> Acct-Session-Id = "2006/Bellem.vsig.cisco.com/293BDA58 CD2011D9 80A1CA93
> 1717A7D4/answer/VoIP/15:23:42.236 CEST Thu May 25 2006/15:23:48.906 CEST
> Thu May 25 2006/10/10.48.84.18"

The disconnect cause value of 10 in hexadecimal means normal call clearing.

Example 2: Using the Overloaded RADIUS Attribute 44

```
router(config)# aaa new-model
router(config)# aaa accounting connection MyMethod start-stop group radius
router(config)# aaa session-id common
router(config)# gw-accounting aaa
router(config-gw-accounting-aaa)# method MyMethod
router(config-gw-accounting-aaa)# acct-template callhistory-detail
router(config)# radius-server host 172.18.192.154 auth-port 1645 acct-port 1646
router(config)# radius-server retransmit 1
router(config)# radius-server key lab
router(config)# radius-server vsa send accounting
```

The report RADIUS packet looks like this:

```
Thu May 25 17:47:31 2006
Acct-Session-Id = "000002B8"
Calling-Station-Id = "90003"
Called-Station-Id = "3714"
h323-setup-time = " 17:49:11.626 CEST
    Thu May 25 2006"
h323-gw-id = " Bellem.vsig.cisco.com"
h323-conf-id = " 0A41D482 CAD911D9 803900D0 BA187BD0"
h323-call-origin = " answer"
h323-call-type = " Telephony"
Cisco-AVPair = " 0A41D482 CAD911D9 803900D0 BA187BD0"
Cisco-AVPair = "subscriber=RegularLine"
Cisco-AVPair = "gw-rxd-cdn=ton:0,npi:0,#:3714"
Cisco-AVPair = "calling-party-category=9"
Cisco-AVPair = "transmission-medium-req=0"
h323-connect-time = " 17:49:12.342
    CEST Thu May 25 2006"
Acct-Input-Octets = "84720"
Acct-Output-Octets = "84800"
Acct-Input-Packets = "353"
Acct-Output-Packets = "530"
Acct-Session-Time = "11"
h323-disconnect-time = " 17:49:23.198 CEST Thu May 25 2006"
h323-disconnect-cause = " 10"
Cisco-AVPair = "h323-ivr-out=Tariff:Unknown"
Cisco-AVPair = "release-source=1"
h323-voice-quality = " 0"
Cisco-AVPair = "in-trunkgroup-label=2"
Cisco-AVPair = "gw-rxd-cgn=ton:0,npi:0,pi:0,si:0,#:90003"
Cisco-AVPair = "charged-units=0"
Cisco-AVPair = "disconnect-text=normal call clearing
    (16)"
Cisco-AVPair = "peer-address=90003"
Cisco-AVPair = "info-type=speech"
Cisco-AVPair = "peer-id=9000"
Cisco-AVPair = "peer-if-index=148"
Cisco-AVPair = "logical-if-index=12"
```

```
Cisco-AVPair = "acom-level=0"
Cisco-AVPair = "coder-type-rate=g711alaw"
Cisco-AVPair = "noise-level=0"
Cisco-AVPair = "voice-tx-duration=5840 ms"
Cisco-AVPair = "tx-duration=5840 ms"
User-Name = "90003"
Acct-Status-Type = "Stop"
NAS-Port-Type = "Async"
NAS-Port = "0"
NAS-Port-Id = "ISDN 0:D:1"
Service-Type = "Login-User"
NAS-IP-Address = "10.48.88.121"
Acct-Delay-Time = "0"
Client-IP-Address = "10.48.88.121"
Acct-Unique-Session-Id = "495e4d5f519cdb44"
Timestamp = "1116866851"
```

Enabling the following extra command would report some extra information in the
RADIUS attribute 26 VSA:

```
router(config)# gw-accounting aaa
router(config-gw-accounting-aaa)# acct-template callhistory-detail
```

Example 3: RADIUS Records from the SIP Proxy Server

In an H.323 voice-signaling environment, the gatekeeper's role is to translate the phone
numbers into IP addresses. This tells the H.323 endpoints where to send the H.225 packets
and establishes a VoIP connection. In a SIP voice-signaling environment, the SIP proxy
server has a similar role. However, it does not translate telephone numbers. Instead, it
localizes the destination IP address or the next hop to the destination based on the To:
header of the incoming INVITE message.

When the SIP proxy server is configured for record-route (as defined in RFC 3261, it
instructs the endpoints to send all SIP signaling through the proxy. Therefore, the SIP proxy
server sends the call stop record.

Cisco IP phones running SIP send the call accounting information (packets, bytes, and call
duration) in the SIP BYE message. Therefore, the Cisco SIP proxy server adds the SIP
phone accounting information to the stop record. The following example shows such a stop
record example, where sip-hdr=RTP-RxStat and sip-hdr=RTP-TxStat are of special interest
for accounting:

```
NAS-IP-Address = "10.48.80.149"
NAS-Port-Type = "Virtual"
User-Name = ""
Service-Type = "Login-User"
Acct-Status-Type = "Stop"
Acct-Session-Id = "CA942F10-D68C11D9-811FE469-92178729@10.48.88.121"
Called-Station-Id = "<sip:3714@10.48.80.149>;tag=003094c263c1120d2c180756-
5bc2f0d0"
Calling-Station-Id = "<sip:10.48.80.149>;tag=3E10453C-573"
h323-disconnect-time = "13:06:22.149 GMT
Tue Jun 08 2006"
h323-call-origin = " originate"
h323-call-type = " VoIP"
Cisco-AVPair = "sip-status-code=200"
```

```
Cisco-AVPair = "session-protocol=sip"
Cisco-AVPair = "call-id=CA942F10-D68C11D9-811FE469-92178729@10.48.88.121"
Cisco-AVPair = "method=BYE"
Cisco-AVPair = "prev-hop-via=SIP/2.0/UDP
10.48.88.121:5060;received=10.48.88.121;branch=z9hG4bK25E2E7"
Cisco-AVPair = "prev-hop-ip=10.48.88.121:5060"
Cisco-AVPair = "incoming-req-uri=sip:3714@10.48.80.149:5060;maddr=10.48.80.149"
Cisco-AVPair = "outgoing-req-uri=sip:3714@10.48.79.173:5060"
Cisco-AVPair = "next-hop-ip=10.48.79.173:5060"
Cisco-AVPair = "sip-hdr=From: <sip:10.48.80.149>;tag=3E10453C-573"
Cisco-AVPair = "sip-hdr=RTP-RxStat:
Dur=23,Pkt=0,Oct=0,LatePkt=0,LostPkt=0,AvgJit=0"
Cisco-AVPair = "sip-hdr=RTP-TxStat: Dur=23,Pkt=1148,Oct=183680"
Client-IP-Address = "10.48.80.149"
Acct-Unique-Session-Id = "9369859f1124cfa2"
Timestamp = "1118153527"
```

Sending RADIUS records from the SIP proxy server offers the advantage that the records are generated from a single place. For Cisco IP phones running SIP, this mechanism offers a nice alternative to exporting from all voice gateways that require the call legs correlation.

Diameter Details

Diameter is an enhanced version of RADIUS that provides several enhancements while still being backward-compatible. Diameter bridges the gap between the old world and the new world by being designed as a peer-to-peer architecture while at the same time keeping the client/server concept in place. This is achieved by referring to AAA elements as Diameter nodes, where a node can act as a client, server, or agent. The client node is usually the NAS where a user authenticates by providing credentials, such as username and password. The client forwards the access request to a Diameter server node, where authentication takes place. Depending on the success, a "succeed" or "reject" response message is sent back to the client. Note that the roles can change; in some cases a Diameter server can also act as a client. RADIUS deployments using proxy servers for aggregation and roaming support have been popular in the Service Provider space. Diameter has added enhanced support for such deployments by explicitly defining four types of intermediary agents:

- Relay agents, which aggregate requests from different realms (Administrative domain piggybacked on the DNS domain) toward a central server.

- Proxy agents, which can perform the relay agent role and modify the message content—for example, to apply policies.

- Redirect agents, which act as a centralized repository. This simplifies the client configuration, because a client needs to know only the redirect agent (and potentially backup) instead of all servers in the network.

- Translation agent, which can translate between Diameter and RADIUS or TACACS+.

Diameter is structured as a base protocol (RFC 3588, *Diameter Base Protocol*) upon which applications are layered. The base protocol provides AVP delivery, capabilities negotiation, error handling, basic services including accounting, and an extensibility framework for specific application support. Each application is assigned a unique identifier by the Internet Assigned Numbers Authority (IANA). These are used during capabilities negotiation:

- **NASREQ** (Network Access Server Requirements) provides RADIUS-like functionality between a NAS and the AAA infrastructure.

- **Mobile IPv4** describes AAA services for mobile nodes.

- **Credit control** provides a superset of basic prepaid functionality, including time and volume quota management (RFC 4006).

- **EAP** adds support for Extensible Authentication Protocol to Diameter (RFC 4072).

- **SIP** allows Session Initiation Protocol servers to act as Diameter clients to provide AAA services for SIP users (RFC 4740).

You can find the complete, maintained list of Diameter-based applications at http://www.iana.org/assignments/aaa-parameters under "Application IDs."

Diameter runs only over TCP or SCTP for increased reliability and congestion awareness. Diameter accounting records are provided either as a one-time request (EVENT_RECORD) or as continuous records (START_RECORD, INTERIM_RECORD, STOP_RECORD). Each record contains a Session-ID AVP and an Accounting-Record-Number AVP. The combination of these two fields makes records unique and enables a Diameter agent to de-duplicate records, which means eliminating records that have been collected twice.

Table 9-6 lists relevant AAA protocol characteristics and compares RADIUS and Diameter.

Table 9-6   *Comparing RADIUS and Diameter Characteristics*

Characteristic	RADIUS	Diameter
Transport protocol	Connectionless (UDP).	Connection-oriented (TCP, SCTP).
Transport security	Optional IPsec.	IPsec or Transport Layer Security (TLS) is required.
Client configuration	Static configuration.	Static configuration and peer discovery.
Server status (failover)	The server cannot indicate its status (running, going down).	Supports server status messages (keepalive, running, going down).
Server message acknowledgment	The client does not know whether the server received the request or if the message was silently discarded (because of errors or wrong message details).	The server can send error messages, authentication, and session termination messages.

continues

Table 9-6 *Comparing RADIUS and Diameter Characteristics (Continued)*

Characteristic	RADIUS	Diameter
Security model	Supports only hop-by-hop security. Every hop can modify information that cannot be traced to its origin.	Supports end-to-end and hop-to-hop security. End-to-end guarantees that information cannot be modified without notice.
Attribute data size	1 byte is reserved for the length of a data field (maximum 255) in its attribute header.	2 bytes are reserved for the length of a data field (maximum 16,535).
Vendor-specific support	Supports VSAs only.	Supports both vendor-specific messages and attributes (commands).

Currently, Cisco IOS supports the Diameter Credit-Control Application (RFC 4006), layered on the Diameter-based protocol (RFC 3588).

CHAPTER 10

NBAR

This chapter is an overview of the Network-Based Application Recognition (NBAR) feature in Cisco IOS. It helps you decide in which situations NBAR is the appropriate mechanism for accounting and performance management. Based on concrete examples, you will be able to identify the appropriate CLI commands and MIB functions and quickly get NBAR setups operational.

NBAR provides network traffic classification. NBAR recognizes a wide variety of applications by inspecting the IP packet's payload up to OSI Layer 7. It can identify web-based and other difficult-to-classify applications, which can be static (using fixed TCP or UDP port numbers) or stateful (dynamically assigning TCP or UDP port numbers). Figure 10-1 illustrates the parts of the data packet inspected by NBAR.

Figure 10-1 *Parts of the Data Packet Inspected by NBAR*

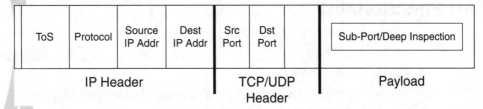

When NBAR recognizes an application, it classifies the traffic for performance and accounting purposes. This enables an operator to invoke services for that specific application, such as offering more or less bandwidth, low- or high-latency queuing, or blocking certain packets. It also enables the operator to define different accounting types for each service. Accounting can use different QoS mechanisms to separate and condition the traffic differently, according to its relative priority. NBAR ensures that network bandwidth is used efficiently by supporting the following QoS features:

- Guaranteed bandwidth with Class-Based Weighted Fair Queuing (CBWFQ). For converged services, you can use Low-Latency Queuing (LLQ), also called Priority Queuing Class-Based Weighted Fair Queuing (PQCBWFQ).

- Policing and limiting bandwidth (ingress function).

- Traffic shaping (egress function).
- Marking (ToS or IP DSCP).
- Increasing or reducing bandwidth.
- Drop policy with Weighted Random Early Detection (WRED).

These additional services are outside the scope of accounting and performance management and therefore are not covered in this book.

NBAR provides a special Protocol Discovery feature that determines which applications and protocols are traversing the network element at any given time by capturing key statistics that are associated with each protocol. The application protocol specifications are defined in a Packet Description Language Module (PDLM). The existing modules can be extended to support emerging application protocols by using the extensible Packet Description Language (PDL). Right now, the use of PDL and the development of PDLMs are limited to Cisco; however, this restriction might be lifted in the future. PDLMs are discussed more thoroughly later in this chapter.

NOTE   NBAR Protocol Discovery can be used independently of or in conjunction with NBAR traffic classification!

NBAR Functionality

The following principles apply for NBAR:

- Network-based application recognition classifies traffic by protocol (Layers 4 through 7). Here are some examples:
  - NBAR extended inspection for HTTP traffic identifies traffic on ports beyond "well known" TCP ports.
  - NBAR Real-time Transport Protocol (RTP) payload classification allows for stateful identification of real-time audio and video bearer traffic. It can also differentiate based on audio and video codecs.
  - Real-Time Streaming Protocol (RTSP)-based applications can work in NAT's PAT configuration mode.
- User-defined custom application classification lets you identify TCP- or UDP-based applications using a string or value to match the type of application within the packet payload.
- Accounting functionality is enabled via the NBAR feature Protocol Discovery. It analyzes application traffic patterns in real time and discovers which traffic is running on the network. Furthermore, it provides bidirectional (input and output) traffic statistics per interface and per application: bit rate (bps), packet counts, and byte counts.

- A maximum of 24 concurrent URLs, hosts, or MIME type matches are supported.

NOTE   Previously, Cisco Express Forwarding (CEF or dCEF) was a prerequisite for NBAR. This limitation has been removed in Cisco IOS Software Release 12.4T. However, turning off CEF has a negative performance impact on the router, so you should enable CEF whenever possible.

Distributed NBAR

Originally, NBAR was not supported on distributed platforms, such as the VIP-enabled Cisco 7500 series routers and the Catalyst 6000 family of switches with a FlexWAN module. The Distributed Network-Based Application Recognition (DNBAR) feature was introduced in IOS releases 12.1(6)E, 12.2(4)T3, and 12.2(14)S. On these distributed platforms, DNBAR implements NBAR functionality on a VIP or FlexWAN module. Packets entering an interface on the VIP or FlexWAN are classified by NBAR, and separate reports are available on these modules. It is important to note that the DNBAR feature is identical to NBAR. Therefore, the term NBAR is used to describe both the NBAR and DNBAR features.

NBAR Classification Details

NBAR can classify applications based on the following characteristics:

- Statically assigned TCP and UDP port numbers.
- TCP and UDP protocols that assign port numbers dynamically and therefore require stateful inspection. This includes packets that require subport classification and classification based on deep packet inspection. This is further explained later in this chapter.
- Non-UDP and non-TCP IP protocols (EGP, EIGRP, GRE, ICMP, IPINIP, IPsec).
- HTTP traffic classified by URL, host, or Multipurpose Internet Mail Extension (MIME) type. NBAR also classifies application traffic using subport information, which combines matching of HTTP traffic and the hostname in addition to classification by MIME type or URL.
- Identifying worms in the packet payload, which is very useful for security mitigation. After you have identified unique match values signatures for a specific attack, use NBAR to block this traffic immediately while establishing a defense plan against the attack. For example, Code Red was identified by an "*.ida" URL in the HTTP GET request.
- Peer-to-peer traffic, such as Napster, Kazaa, Morpheus, Gnutella, Grokster, WinMX, eDonkey, eMule, BitTorrent, and so on.

- Heuristic and holistic classification. NBAR classifies an application based on the information of the whole packet and makes a determination based on the behavior of the whole packet. The RTP Payload Classification feature is based on this algorithm; the packet is classified as RTP based on multiple attributes in the UDP and RTP headers. Note that heuristic and holistic classification functions are limited to the PDLMs and cannot be used to customize applications!

- Citrix Independent Computing Architecture (ICA) traffic classification by application name.

NBAR offers additional capabilities that help classify applications:

- User-defined protocols. Operators can define names for their custom protocol applications. The user-named protocol can then be used by the Protocol Discovery CLI and MIB, and CLI commands such as **match protocol** or **ip nbar port-map** as an NBAR-supported protocol.

- Ten custom applications can be assigned using NBAR. Each customer application can have up to 16 TCP and 16 UDP ports, each mapped to the individual custom protocol. The real-time statistics per custom protocol can be monitored using the Protocol Discovery function.

- Matching the use of multiple ports to one application is a unique benefit of NBAR. A simple example demonstrates this: FTP uses TCP ports 20 and 21. NBAR consolidates traffic from both ports into one record. In comparison with NetFlow, FTP creates two separate flows, which need to be aggregated at a NetFlow collector afterward.

- Payload inspection matching string patterns at a specific offset.

- Inspection for custom protocols by traffic direction, such as traffic heading toward a source or destination instead of collection traffic in both directions.

The following sections explain some of the features in this list in more detail. They describe features that are advanced or not intuitive, compared to evident features such as identifying applications by port number.

Classification of HTTP by URL, Host, or MIME

NBAR can classify application traffic by looking beyond a packet's TCP/UDP port numbers. This ability is called subport classification. NBAR looks at the TCP/UDP payload and classifies packets based on content within the payload, such as transaction identifier, message type, or other similar data. Classification of HTTP by URL, host, or MIME type is an example of subport classification. NBAR classifies HTTP traffic by text within the URL or Host fields of a GET request using regular expression matching. NBAR uses the UNIX filename specification as the basis for the URL or host specification format. The NBAR engine then converts the specified match string into a regular expression. NBAR does not classify packets that are part of a pipelined request. With pipelined requests, multiple requests are pipelined at the server before previous requests are serviced. For HTTP requests, in-depth analysis can be performed.

For request messages (client to server), the following HTTP header fields can be identified:

- **User-Agent**—A value in the HTTP header field, also known as "Browser ID," such as "Mozilla/4.0"
- **Referrer**—The reference to the previous visited website
- **From**—Indicates the initiator of the request, such as the e-mail address

For response messages (server to client), the following header fields can be identified:

- **Server** contains information about the software used by the origin server that handled the request, such as "Server: CERN/3.0 libwww/2.17."
- **Location** is used to redirect the recipient to another location.
- **Content-Encoding** is used as a modifier to the media type, such as "gzip."

Classification of Citrix ICA Traffic by Application Name

NBAR can classify Citrix Independent Computing Architecture (ICA) traffic and perform subport classification of Citrix traffic based on Citrix published applications. NBAR can monitor Citrix ICA client requests for a published application destined for a Citrix ICA Master browser. After the client makes a request to the published application, the Citrix ICA Master browser directs the client to the server with the most available memory. The Citrix ICA client then connects to this Citrix ICA server for the application. NBAR statefully tracks Citrix ICA client/server messages and classifies requests for given Citrix application names and traffic. NBAR performs a regular expression match using a user-specified application name string on the contents of the Citrix ICA control packets carrying the published application name.

NBAR Packet Description Language Module (PDLM)

Even though NBAR supports a long list of static and stateful protocols, new transport protocols will always be developed, and they will require extensions to the existing definitions. Recent examples are new peer-to-peer applications as well as new voice applications and others. NBAR PDLMs, which can be downloaded from the Cisco website, let you add support for new protocols without requiring an IOS release upgrade or a router reload. A PDLM can be loaded at runtime.

NBAR Scope

NBAR does not support certain scenarios:

- MPLS-labeled packets, because NBAR classifies only IP packets. As a workaround, you can use NBAR to classify IP traffic before the traffic is handed over to MPLS. Use the Modular QoS CLI (MQC) to set the IP DSCP field on the NBAR-classified packets and map the IP DSCP settings to the MPLS EXP settings.

- IP Multicast.

- Pipelined persistent HTTP requests.

- URL/host/MIME classification with secure HTTP.

- Asymmetric flows with stateful protocols.

- Packets originating from or destined for the network element running NBAR.

- Custom protocol traffic can be inspected for only the first 255 bytes of the payload.

- IPv6.

- Egress WAN links where tunneling or encryption is configured. As a workaround, NBAR should be configured on ingress interfaces to perform input classification before the traffic is switched to the WAN link for output. Even though NBAR is not supported in these environments, the NBAR Protocol Discovery function is supported on interfaces where tunneling or encryption is used. You can enable Protocol Discovery directly on the tunnel or on the interface where encryption is performed to gather key statistics on the various applications that are traversing the interface. The input statistics also show the total number of encrypted/tunneled packets received in addition to the per-protocol breakdowns.

Supported Devices and IOS Versions

Here is some of the more notable information about devices and IOS versions supporting NBAR:

- NBAR was introduced in Cisco IOS Software Release 12.0(5)XE2 and initially supported the Cisco 7100 and 7200 series routers.

- DNBAR was introduced with IOS releases 12.1(6)E, 12.2(4)T3, and 12.2(14)S. It supported the VIP-enabled Cisco 7500 series routers and Catalyst 6000 family switches with a FlexWAN module.

- NBAR was introduced on the Cisco 800 series routers running IOS release 12.3 T.

- Real-Time Protocol Payload Classification was added in IOS 12.2(8)T and 12.1(11b)E.

- Dialer interfaces are supported since IOS release 12.2(4)T.

- Matching beyond the first 400 bytes in a packet payload was not supported initially. IOS release 12.3(7)T removed this restriction, and NBAR now supports full payload inspection. The exception is that custom protocol traffic can be inspected for only the first 255 bytes of the payload.

- NBAR-supported platforms include the Cisco 800 (12.3T), 1700, 2600, 2800, 3600, 3700, 3800, 7100 (12.0(5)XE2), 7100uBR, 7200 (12.0(5)XE2), 7200 uBR, 7300, 7500 (VIP), and Catalyst 6500 (with or without a FlexWAN card).

- On the Catalyst 6500, NBAR support differs between the various supervisor cards:

  — Sup2: traffic is sent to the control plane (MSFC), which bypasses hardware forwarding.

  — Certain WAN modules such as the FlexWAN and SIP-200 support NBAR.

  — The Sup720 and Sup32 do not support NBAR.

  — The new Programmable Intelligent Services Adapter (PISA) supervisory card (sup32-PISA) integrates the functionality of the MSFC2a into the card. This card implements NBAR in hardware and enables Sup32 to support NBAR.

For up-to-date information, check the Cisco Feature Navigator home page at http://www.cisco.com/go/fn and www.cisco.com/go/nbar.

NBAR Protocol Discovery (PD) MIB

NBAR provides the Protocol Discovery feature as an easy way to discover application protocols that are transiting an interface by displaying various traffic statistics. The NBAR PD MIB expands the capabilities of NBAR Protocol Discovery by providing the following functionalities through SNMP:

- Enable or disable Protocol Discovery per interface

- Monitor ingress and egress traffic

- Display the following per-protocol statistics: total number of input and output packets and bytes and input and output bit rates

- Configure and view multiple Top-*N* tables that list protocols by bandwidth usage

- Configure thresholds based on traffic of particular protocols or applications, and send notifications when these thresholds are crossed

- Maintain a history table of notification events, with a maximum of 5000 entries

- Record the time when Protocol Discovery was enabled

The fundamental principles behind the NBAR PD MIB are as follows:

- NBAR PD MIB was introduced in IOS release 12.2(15)T.

- NBAR functionality can be configured via SNMP (read-only and read-write objects).
- The MIB contains 32-bit and 64-bit SNMP counters.
- Full NBAR functionality is not supported on interfaces where tunneling or encryption is used. See the workaround described in the "NBAR Scope" section.

Table 10-1 summarizes the NBAR PD MIB content.

Table 10-1   *NBAR PD MIB Details*

Table	Description	SNMP Access
cnpdSupportedProtocols	List of all supported protocols	Read-only
cnpdAllStats	All NBAR statistics per interface	Read-only
cnpdTopNStats	Top-*N* table statistics	Read-only
cnpdThresholdhistory	History of falling or rising events	Read-only
cnpdStatus	Enable or disable NBAR per interface, including time stamp	Read-write
cnpdTopNConfig	Configure the Top-*N* table by interface	Read-write
cnpdThresholdConfig	Protocol threshold configuration	Read-write
cnpdNotificationsConfig	Enable traps	Read-write
cnpdMIBNotifications	Rising or falling events	—

NBAR Supported Protocols

The supported protocols can be displayed by accessing the following objects. Note that a new module (PDLM) is required to extend the currently supported protocols.

- **cnpdSupportedProtocolsTable**—Lists all the protocols and applications that NBAR can recognize.
- **cnpdSupportedProtocolsEntry**—An entry in the supported protocols table reflecting key information about a protocol.
- **cnpdSupportedProtocolsName**—Reflects the valid string of a protocol or application that NBAR recognizes.

NBAR Protocol Discovery Statistics

The Protocol Discovery statistics group has two tables. cnpdStatusTable enables Protocol Discovery, and cnpdAllStatsTable stores the Protocol Discovery statistics. Because NBAR predefines a large list of protocols and applications, in most cases only the initial configuration is required to display relevant application traffic. Here are some details from the group:

- **cnpdStatusPdEnable**—This read-write object is used to enable and disable Protocol Discovery on an interface. Values are true and false.

- **cnpdStatusLastUpdateTime**—This is the sysUpTime value when Protocol Discovery was enabled on an interface. This value is 0 if the interface does not have Protocol Discovery enabled.

- **cnpdAllStatsEntry**—The following NBAR Protocol Discovery statistics are gathered:

  — **cnpdAllStatsInPkts, cnpdAllStatsHCInPkts**—The packet counters of inbound packets (32-bit, 64-bit)

  — **cnpdAllStatsOutPkts, cnpdAllStatsHCOutPkts**—The packet counters of outbound packets (32-bit, 64-bit)

  — **cnpdAllStatsInBytes, cnpdAllStatsHCInBytes**—The byte counters of inbound octets (32-bit, 64-bit)

  — **cnpdAllStatsOutBytes, cnpdAllStatsHCOutBytes**—The byte counters of outbound octets (32-bit, 64-bit)

  — **cnpdAllStatsInBitRate**—The inbound bit rate

  — **cnpdAllStatsOutBitRate**—The outbound bit rate

An SNMP example is provided later in this chapter.

NBAR Top-*N* Statistics

The Top-*N* statistics group displays a list of consumed bandwidth per application over a specified interval. The user can select the interface, sample period, and statistic used to base the table on. A maximum of 1024 Top-*N* tables can exist across all interfaces. Tables are ordered by applications using the most bandwidth. Some relevant objects are as follows:

- **cnpdTopNConfigIfIndex**—Select the interface for configuring a Top-*N* table

- **cnpdTopNConfigStatsSelect**—Select the statistic used for the order of the Top-*N* table (bit rate, byte, or packet-based)

- **cnpdTopNConfigSampleTime**—The interval in seconds at which the bit rate is sampled if the cnpdTopNConfigStatsSelect object is set to bitRateIn, bitRateOut, or bitRateSum

- **cnpdTopNConfigRequestedSize**—The number of requested entries in the associated cnpdTopNStatsTable (read-create)

- **cnpdTopNConfigGrantedSize**—The actual size of the associated cnpdTopNStatsTable entry (read-only)

- **cnpdTopNConfigTime**—The value of sysUpTime when the associated cnpdTopNStatsTable entry was created

- **cnpdTopNStatsRate, cnpdTopNStatsHCRate**—The amount of change in the selected statistic (cnpdTopNConfigStatsSelect) during this sampling interval (32-bit, 64-bit)

NBAR Protocol Discovery Thresholds, Traps, and History

Multiple thresholds for individual protocols on an interface can be defined. When a threshold is exceeded, the information is stored and a notification (SNMP trap) is generated, including a summary of the related threshold information. A hysteresis mechanism stops multiple traps from occurring for the same breached threshold within a sample period. The following list summarizes interesting MIB objects in this context:

- **cnpdThresholdConfigEntry**—Contains configuration information to set thresholds for the purpose of notifications. The following details can be configured:

  — **cnpdThresholdConfigIfIndex**—Selects the interface to apply thresholds to.

  — **cnpdThresholdConfigInterval**—The interval in seconds over which the data is sampled and compared with the thresholds cnpdThresholdConfigRising and cnpdThresholdConfigFalling.

  — **cnpdThresholdConfigSampleType**—The method of sampling the selected statistic and calculating the value to be compared to cnpdThresholdConfigRising or cnpdThresholdConfigFalling. Possible entries are absoluteValue and deltaValue.

  — **cnpdThresholdConfigProtocol**—Selects the protocol where the threshold should be placed.

  — **cnpdThresholdConfigProtocolAny**—Provides the option to check *any* protocol that meets the threshold (value=true) or *only* the protocol defined by cnpdThresholdConfigProtocol (value=false).

  — **cnpdThresholdConfigStartup**—The startup value (rising, falling, risingOrFalling) for monitoring the threshold.

- **cnpdThresholdHistoryTable**—Because SNMP traps are sent over the unreliable UDP protocol, this table provides a history of the last 5000 threshold breached events.

- **cnpdNotificationsEnable**—Used to enable or disable notifications on a global basis (value=true or value=false).

- **cnpdThresholdRisingEvent**—The notification that a rising counter has breached the defined threshold.

- **cnpdThresholdFallingEvent**—The notification that a falling counter has breached the defined threshold.

NBAR Configuration Commands

The CLI commands that you need to know to configure NBAR are as follows:

- router(config-if)# **ip nbar protocol-discovery**
  configures NBAR to discover traffic and keep traffic statistics for all protocols known to NBAR on a particular interface.

- router(config)# **ip nbar port-map**
  configures NBAR to search for a protocol or protocol name using port number(s) other than the well-known port. A protocol can be represented by up to 16 different ports.

- router(config)# **ip nbar custom** *protocol-name* [*number* {**ascii** | **decimal** | **hex**}] [**destination** | **source**] [**tcp** | **udp**]
  configures NBAR to classify and monitor additional static port applications. The parameters for this command are defined as follows:

  — *protocol-name* specifies the name of the user-defined protocol.

  — *number* is the byte location of the value to be searched in the payload (0 to 255).

  — **destination** inspects destination flows only (optional).

  — **source** inspects source flows only (optional).

  — **tcp** defines up to 16 explicit TCP port numbers *or* a range of a maximum of 1000 TCP ports.

  — **udp** defines up to 16 explicit UDP port numbers *or* a range of a maximum of 1000 UDP ports.

- router(config)# **ip nbar pdlm**
  extends the list of protocols by loading a new PDLM (providing the full path to the PDLM). New PDLM versions are provided on the Cisco website at http://www.cisco.com/go/nbar.

- router(config)#**ip nbar resources** *10-86400*
  configures memory usage for tracking the max-idle time (in seconds) of stateful sessions.

NBAR show Commands

The **show ip nbar protocol-discovery** command displays the statistics gathered by the NBAR Protocol Discovery feature. By default, statistics for all interfaces on which Protocol Discovery is enabled are displayed. The default output includes bit rate, byte count, packet count, and protocol name. Protocol Discovery monitors ingress and egress traffic and can optionally be applied with a service policy.

Egress traffic statistics are gathered *before* policing features (such as QoS, access lists, or queue drops) at the interface. Therefore, the egress counters might be higher than the actual traffic being forwarded by the interface.

Some of the more detailed **show ip nbar** command options are as follows:

- router# **show ip nbar** [**filter** | **pdlm** | **port-map** | **protocol-discovery** | **resources** | **trace** | **unclassified-port-stats** | **version**]
  displays a variety of statistics based on the keyword used:

  — **filter** displays the current NBAR's filter criteria.

  — **pdlm** displays the currently installed PDLMs.

  — **port-map** displays the TCP/UDP port numbers NBAR uses to classify a given protocol.

  — **protocol-discovery** displays the statistics for all interfaces on which Protocol Discovery is enabled.

  — **resources** displays the memory configuration for tracking stateful sessions.

  — **unclassified-port-stats** displays NBAR's port statistics for unclassified packets.

  — **version** displays currently installed PDL Module Version Info.

The more complex commands are explained specifically:

- router(config)# **show ip nbar protocol-discovery** [**interface** *interface-spec*] [**stats** {**byte-count** | **bit-rate** | **packet-count** | **max-bit-rate**}][{**protocol** *protocol-name* | **top-n** *number*}]
  displays the statistics gathered by the NBAR Protocol Discovery feature. The parameter details are as follows:

  — *interface-spec* specifies an interface to display.

  — **stats** specifies that the byte count, bit rate, or packet count is to be displayed:

    byte-count specifies that the byte count is to be displayed.

    bit-rate specifies that the bit rate is to be displayed.

    packet-count specifies that the packet count is to be displayed.

    max-bit-rate specifies that the maximum bit rate is to be displayed.

  — **protocol** specifies that statistics for a specific protocol (defined by *protocol-name*) are to be displayed.

  — **top-n** *number* specifies that a Top-*N* (*number*) of most active protocols is displayed. For instance, if **top-n 3** is entered, the three most active NBAR-supported protocols are displayed.

- router# **show ip nbar port-map** [*protocol-name*] [**tcp** | **udp**] *port-number*
  displays the current protocol-to-port mappings in use by NBAR.

- router# **show ip nbar unclassified-port-stats** [*number of top talkers*] [**ip** {*starting protocol number* | *top-n talkers*}] [**tcp** {*starting tcp port number* | *bottom-talkers* | *top-talkers*}] [**udp** {*starting udp port number* | *bottom-talkers* | *top-talkers*}] displays NBAR port statistics for unclassified packets.

NBAR Examples (CLI and SNMP)

The following examples provide a systematic introduction to configuring and monitoring NBAR via the CLI.

Basic NBAR Configuration

In this configuration, NBAR Protocol Discovery is enabled on the VIP card of a Cisco 7500 router on serial port 6/1/2. Note that Distributed NBAR does not require different commands than NBAR.

```
router(config-if)#interface serial 6/1/2
router(config-if)#ip nbar protocol-discovery
```

This **show** command displays the discovered protocol, ranked by number of packets:

```
router# show ip nbar protocol-discovery interface serial 6/1/2 top-n
  Serial6/1/2
                         Input                    Output
                         -----                    ------
          Protocol       Packet Count             Packet Count
                         Byte Count               Byte Count
                         5min Bit Rate (bps)      5min Bit Rate (bps)
                         5min Max Bit Rate (bps)  5min Max Bit Rate (bps)
          --------------  ----------------------  ----------------------
          netbios        154540                   0
                         13981136                 0
                         0                        0
                         0                        0
          rtp            54015                    9
                         6059862                  1384
                         0                        0
                         0                        0
```

Some optional parameters to **show ip nbar protocol-discovery**, such as **bit-rate**, **byte-count**, **max-bit-rate**, and **packet-count** statistics, allow more precise display.

To monitor the NBAR Protocol Discovery results with SNMP, the first step is to retrieve cnpdAllStats parameters, where protocols are classified by two indexes:

- **cnpdTopNConfigIndex** uniquely identifies an entry in the cnpdTopNConfigTable table.

- **cnpdTopNStatsIndex** uniquely identifies an entry in the cnpdTopNStatsTable table.

In this example, we are interested in the netbios entry:

```
SERVER % snmpwalk -c public -v 2c martel cnpdAllStatsTable | grep netbios
```

```
CISCO-NBAR-PROTOCOL-DISCOVERY-MIB::cnpdAllStatsProtocolName.15.26 = STRING:
  "netbios"
```

The next example displays all entries that contain two indexes. The first one (15) represents the ifIndex of the interface where NBAR is enabled. ifIndex 15 corresponds to serial 6/1/2 in this example (taken from the IF-MIB table). The second index (26) represents a unique NBAR protocol index. The index 26 corresponds to the netbios entry. As a result, all NetBIOS traffic on the serial interface 6/1/2 is displayed. The cnpdAllStatsTable table contains the input packet count, byte count, 5 min Bit Rate, and 5 min Max Bit Rate from the previous **show** command:

```
snmpwalk -c public -v 2c martel cnpdAllStatsTable | grep 15.26
CISCO-NBAR-PROTOCOL-DISCOVERY-MIB:: cnpdAllStatsProtocolName.15.26 = STRING:
  "netbios"
CISCO-NBAR-PROTOCOL-DISCOVERY-MIB:: cnpdAllStatsInPkts.15.26 = Counter32: 154540
packets
CISCO-NBAR-PROTOCOL-DISCOVERY-MIB:: cnpdAllStatsOutPkts.15.26 = Counter32: 0
packets
CISCO-NBAR-PROTOCOL-DISCOVERY-MIB:: cnpdAllStatsInBytes.15.26 = Counter32: 13981136
bytes
CISCO-NBAR-PROTOCOL-DISCOVERY-MIB:: cnpdAllStatsOutBytes.15.26 = Counter32: 0 bytes
CISCO-NBAR-PROTOCOL-DISCOVERY-MIB:: cnpdAllStatsHCInPkts.15.26 = Counter64: 154540
packets
CISCO-NBAR-PROTOCOL-DISCOVERY-MIB:: cnpdAllStatsHCOutPkts.15.26 = Counter64: 0
packets
CISCO-NBAR-PROTOCOL-DISCOVERY-MIB:: cnpdAllStatsHCInBytes.15.26 = Counter64:
13981136 bytes
CISCO-NBAR-PROTOCOL-DISCOVERY-MIB:: cnpdAllStatsHCOutBytes.15.26 = Counter64: 0
bytes
CISCO-NBAR-PROTOCOL-DISCOVERY-MIB:: cnpdAllStatsInBitRate.15.26 = Gauge32: 0 kilo
bits per second
CISCO-NBAR-PROTOCOL-DISCOVERY-MIB:: cnpdAllStatsOutBitRate.15.26 = Gauge32: 0 kilo
bits per second
```

All counters are duplicated in the table: once for the 32-bit counters, and once for the 64-bit HC counters (HC stands for High Capacity).

Finally, the following command monitors the NBAR resources:

```
Router# show ip nbar resources
NBAR memory usage for tracking Stateful sessions
   Max-age               : 120 secs
   Initial memory        : 1751 KBytes
   Max initial memory    : 5837 KBytes
   Memory expansion      : 68 KBytes
   Max memory expansion  : 68 KBytes
   Memory in use         : 1751 KBytes
   Max memory allowed    : 11675 KBytes
   Active links          : 36
   Total links           : 25753
```

Custom Application Example

If the traffic of interest is not monitored by Protocol Discovery, the NBAR custom application is the option. For example, the custom protocol myapp looks for TCP packets with a destination or source port of 9999:

```
router(config)# ip nbar custom myapp tcp 9999
router# show ip nbar port-map myapp
port-map myapp                     tcp 9999
```

In the following example, the custom protocol media_new identifies TCP packets with a destination or source port of 4500 and that have a value of 90 at the sixth byte of the payload:

```
router(config)# ip nbar custom media_new 6 decimal 90 tcp 4500
```

In this case, NBAR examines packets containing source or destination port 4500. If the sixth byte contains decimal 90, a session cache entry is made, and all subsequent packets of that specific session are classified in "media_new" until a FIN or RESET is detected. For fragmented packets, NBAR looks at the first fragment of a fragment set to see if it contains the value. The rest of the fragment set is classified the same without actually looking into the fragmented packets.

In the last example for the NBAR custom application, the custom protocol app_sales1 identifies TCP packets that have a source port of 4567 and that contain the term SALES in the fifth byte of the payload:

```
router(config)# ip nbar custom app_sales1 5 ascii SALES source tcp 4567
```

These custom applications generate entries in Protocol Discovery, both in the output of **show ip nbar protocol-discovery** and in the NBAR MIB.

Limiting Peer-to-Peer Traffic

These example analyzes Gnutella, which uses six well-known TCP ports: 6346, 6347, 6348, 6349, 6355, and 5634. The configuration and the **show** output are as follows:

```
router(config)# ip nbar port-map gnutella tcp 5634 6346 6347 6348 6349 6355
router# show ip nbar protocol stats byte-count
FastEthernet0/0
                Input                  Output
Protocol        Byte Count             Byte Count
------------------------------------------------
gnutella        43880517               52101266
```

Creating a QoS service policy using the commands of the modular QoS CLI (MQC) allows policing the traffic classified by NBAR, which is Gnutella in this example:

```
router(config)# class-map gnutella
router(config-cmap)# match protocol gnutella
router(config-cmap)# exit
router(config)# policy-map sample
router(config-pmap)# class gnutella
router(config-pmap-c)# police 1000000 31250 31250 conform-action drop exceed-action
drop violate-action drop
```

HTTP Requests Payload Inspection

This example classifies the HTTP traffic according to the URL's content. If the keyword "ebay" is discovered in the URL, the traffic is classified and accounted. Furthermore, MQC allows actions such as policing, rate-limiting, and adjusting the precedence. In this case, a new precedence of 5 is assigned to all eBay traffic:

```
router(config)# class-map match-all ebayclass
router(config-cmap)# match protocol http url "*ebay*"

router(config)# policy-map ebaypolicy
router(config-pmap)# class ebayclass
router(config-pmap-c)# set ip precedence 5

router(config)# interface Serial6/1/2
router(config-if)# ip nbar protocol-discovery
router(config-if)# service-policy input ebaypolicy
router# show policy-map interface serial 6/1/2
 Serial6/1/2
  Service-policy input: ebaypolicy
    Class-map: ebayclass (match-all)
      4 packets, 495 bytes
      5 minute offered rate 0 bps, drop rate 0 bps
      Match: protocol http url "*ebay*"

      QoS Set
        precedence 4
          Packets marked 4

    Class-map: class-default (match-any)
      104 packets, 9590 bytes
      5 minute offered rate 0 bps, drop rate 0 bps
      Match: any
```

The NBAR HTTP possibilities go well beyond what this example shows. Indeed, NBAR is not limited to inspecting the URL's content, but also the server accessed by the HTTP requests, or the MIME type in the HTTP payload can be taken into account. For example, you could classify all traffic containing jpeg or mpeg files.

NBAR Applicability

Table 10-2 relates NBAR to the fundamental questions discussed in Chapter 2, "Data Collection Methodology."

Table 10-2   *NBAR Summary*

Criteria	NBAR
What to collect (data collection details)?	Total traffic (packets, bytes, bit rate) per identified protocol/application: Ingress traffic Egress traffic
Where to collect?	Edge or core, LAN or WAN (any interface type)
How to configure?	CLI (scripts) or SNMP set
How to collect?	Pull model: CLI (scripts) SNMP
How to identify the user?	Not applicable
Use case example	Network monitoring and planning, application monitoring, QoS policy monitoring
Additional details	32-bit and 64-bit SNMP counters

CHAPTER 11

IP SLA

Cisco IP SLA is an embedded feature set in Cisco IOS Software that allows you to analyze service levels for IP applications and services. It is one of those Cisco device instrumentation features with a long history. IOS 11.2 introduced the Response Time Reporter (RTR), which supported three functions: ICMP Ping, ICMP Echo Path, and SSCP (IBM SNA native echo). In those days, multiple customers migrated their dedicated IBM SNA infrastructure to an IP network and realized how limited IP reporting functions were compared to IBM's SNA network. RTR addressed this issue and significantly increased functionality over the years. Cisco renamed RTR Service Assurance Agent (SAA) in Cisco IOS Software Release 12.0(5)T. New features were continuously added and, in 2004, Cisco changed the name to IP SLA. Despite the name changes, the basic principle of IP SLA remained the same: an active measurement that uses injected test packets (synthetic traffic) marked with a time stamp to calculate performance metrics. The results allow indirect assessment of the network, such as Service-Level Agreements (SLA) and QoS class definitions. IP SLA consists of two components, both implemented in Cisco devices:

- Mandatory source device, which generates, receives, and analyzes the traffic.

- The IP SLA Responder, which is optionally used to increase accuracy and measurement details. By adding time stamps to the measurement packets at the destination device, the IP SLA Responder allows the elimination of the measurement packet processing time on the destination device. The IP SLA Responder listens on any standard or user-defined port for UDP, TCP, and Frame Relay packets generated by the IP SLA source.

IP SLA is an example of a device instrumentation technique that does not overlap between accounting and performance, because it is dedicated to performance measurement. Therefore, it is a complementary solution to accounting features such as NetFlow.

IP SLA allows you to measure the performance characteristics of the existing infrastructure. It offers valuable information for network architects to redesign traffic within the network and confidently build end-to-end application-aware SLAs. IP SLA is applicable to both service providers and enterprises for performance management.

Highlighted features of IP SLA are as follows:

- **Network performance monitoring**—Measures delay, jitter, packet loss, packet ordering, and packet corruption in the network.

- **SLA monitoring**—Provides service-level monitoring and verification.

- **IP service network health assessment**—Verifies that the existing QoS settings are sufficient for new IP services.

- **Edge-to-edge network availability monitoring**—Provides proactive verification and connectivity testing of network resources (for example, indicates the network availability of a web server).

- **Voice over IP (VoIP) performance monitoring**—Analyzes critical parameters for a VoIP deployment, which are not only jitter and packet loss, but also the Mean Opinion Score (MOS) and Impairment/Calculated Planning Impairment Factor (ICPIF) values. ICPIF was defined by ITU-T G.11. The ICPIF value represents predefined combinations of loss and delay.

- **Application-aware monitoring**—IP SLA can emulate traffic up to the application level—for example, DNS, DHCP, and web server requests—and can measure the related performance statistics.

- **Accuracy**—Microsecond granularity for jitter delay measurements offers the required precision for business-critical applications.

- **Flexible operations**—Offer various kinds of scheduling, alerting, and triggered measurements.

- **Pervasiveness**—IP SLA is implemented in Cisco networking devices ranging from low-end to high-end routers and switches. This avoids the deployment and management of dedicated measurement boxes.

- **Troubleshooting of network operation**—Provides consistent, reliable measurement that proactively identifies performance and connectivity problems.

Because the terms *probe*, *operation*, and *packet* in the official Cisco IP SLA documentation might lead to confusion, this book uses these terms as follows:

- **Test packets**—Synthetic traffic generated by the IP SLA devices (Source and/or Responder). Packets can contain a single request (DHCP) or can consist of a stream of packets (jitter measurement).

- **Operation**—An action performed by the IP SLA source. An operation consists of one or multiple test packets, resulting in a single result (such as round-trip time [RTT]) or a series of results (such as buckets of distributions). The Cisco documentation calls these probes.

- **Frequency of operations**—The interval between two successive executions of the same operation instance. For an ad hoc measurement, an operation can run once, whereas monitoring performance trends requires continuously running operations.

The fundamentals of active versus passive monitoring were introduced in Chapter 2, "Data Collection Methodology." This section builds on the theoretical foundation and applies it to IP SLA, which uses an active monitoring approach to measure network performance. Cisco IP SLA sends test packets across the network to analyze performance between multiple network locations or across multiple network paths. It simulates network and application services and collects network performance data in real time. The operations have configurable IP and application layer options such as source and destination IP address, UDP and TCP port numbers, type of service (ToS) byte (including Differentiated Services Code Point [DSCP] and IP precedence bits), virtual private network (VPN) Virtual Routing and Forwarding (VRF), and HTTP web address. Results are stored in the Cisco device and are available through the CLI and SNMP MIBs. Multiple performance monitoring applications support IP SLA, such as CiscoWorks Internetwork Performance Monitor (IPM), IP Solution Center (ISC), and many products from other vendors.

IP SLA collects the following performance metrics:

- Delay (both round-trip and one-way)
- Jitter (one-way)
- Packet loss (one-way)
- Packet sequencing (packet ordering)
- Packet corruption detection
- Path (per hop)
- Connectivity (one-way)
- FTP server or HTTP website download time
- Voice quality scores (MOS, ICPIF)

The various IP SLA operations can be classified as follows:

- ICMP-based operations for Echo, Path Echo, and Path Jitter.
- UDP-based operations, such as echo, jitter, DNS, and DHCP.
- TCP-based operations, such as TCP Connect, FTP, HTTP, and DLSw+.
- Layer 2 operations, such as Frame Relay, ATM, and MPLS.
- VoIP-related operations, such as VoIP Jitter, VoIP Gatekeeper Registration Delay Monitoring, and VoIP Call Setup (Post-Dial Delay) Monitoring. The new RTP-based VoIP operation was introduced in Cisco IOS Software Release 12.4(4)T.

Measured Metrics: What to Measure

Identifying the correct measurement metrics can be a challenging task. When customers consider deploying SLA, they usually look for guidance on standard parameters. Unfortunately, these standard parameters exist only partially. ITU-T recommendation G.114 defines a maximum of 150-ms end-to-end transmission time (mouth to ear) for voice applications and an upper limit of 400 ms for most other applications. However, most customers' requirements are as individual as their network design; therefore, customization of SLA parameters might be required in some cases. For a jump start, some basic principles exist for choosing generic performance metrics. If SLAs are already in place, best practice suggests monitoring the agreed-upon SLA parameters if possible. If SLAs are negotiated between a service provider and a consumer, they should be measurable with services such as IP SLA.

The most common and generic metrics are delay (one-way and round-trip), jitter, and packet loss. Specific considerations are related to measurement accuracy. Finally, application-specific metrics related to network services can be included in your SLA statements, including DNS, DHCP, TCP connect, and HTTP. The following sections describe these metrics in more detail.

Network Delay

Network delay describes how long it takes packets to traverse the network and reach the destination. The total network delay consists of network transmission, serialization, and processing delay at the source and target devices. If the destination device is not heavily loaded, you can assume that for long-distance connections or a connection with low-bandwidth links, the network delay dominates the results of the total round-trip delay. In a symmetric routing design where all packets traverse the same hops for both directions, the network delays in each direction should be almost consistent. In this case, round-trip delay measurement could be appropriate. Because round-trip delay does not measure delay per direction, it has limitations in networks where asymmetric routing is applied. In this case, packets from source to destination take a different path than the return traffic. This can be measured with one-way delay operations, which might identify that the delay in one direction is considerably different from the delay in the reverse direction. However, even with a perfectly symmetric route, you may have queuing delays. Those delays are almost never symmetric; instead, they typically occur predominantly in one direction. Therefore, for problem diagnosis or troubleshooting, it is advisable to have one-way delays.

Round-trip times are much easier to measure, so many performance applications report them. Therefore, round-trip measurement is the initial choice for general monitoring, and one-way delay is the right choice for in-depth analysis.

Jitter

Jitter, also known as *IP Packet Delay Variation (IPDV)*, measures the delay variation between packets. It is a relevant parameter for interactive voice and video applications. Jitter describes interpacket delay variation. When multiple packets are sent consecutively from the source to the destination device, such as 10 ms apart, under ideal circumstances in the network, the destination should be receiving them 10 ms apart. Under realistic circumstances, delays in the network, such as queuing and arriving through alternate routes, cause the arrival delay between packets to be greater than or less than 10 ms. Using this example, a positive jitter value indicates that the packets arrived more than 10 ms apart. For example, packets arriving 12 ms apart cause positive jitter of 2 ms. If the packets arrive 8 ms apart, they cause negative jitter of 2 ms. For delay-sensitive applications such as VoIP, positive jitter values are undesirable, and a jitter value of 0 is ideal. Jitter is covered in more detail in Chapter 15, "Voice Scenarios," together with voice measurement standards, such as MOS and ICPIF scores.

Applicability of the term *jitter* is much broader than packet transmission performance, with "unwanted signal variation" as a general definition. Indeed, jitter has been used to describe frequency or phase variations, such as the data stream rate variations or carrier signal phase noise. The term IP Packet Delay Variation (IPDV) is almost self-describing and is more precise. This is why both RFC 3393 (*IP Packet Delay Variation Metric for IPPM*) and ITU-T Y.1540 (*IP packet transfer and availability performance parameters*) prefer this term. To be consistent with the Cisco documentation and CLI, this chapter uses the term jitter.

Packet Loss

Packet loss happens when a network element drops packets instead of forwarding them. This could occur because of overload situations when a router or switch cannot accept any incoming data. Alternatively, based on QoS or security-related policies, the network element might intentionally drop packets with specific characteristics. The impact of packet loss differs with each type of application. TCP-based data transmission suffers from performance degradation due to packet retransmission, and voice sessions seem chopped under heavy packet loss.

Measurement Accuracy

Measurement accuracy is affected by the processing delay at the network elements (typically on the order of milliseconds), the system clock accuracy of the measurement devices, and the method of time synchronization between peers. The Network Time Protocol (NTP) and Global Positioning System (GPS) are common methods for system clock synchronization. The use of GPS is recommended over NTP for time synchronization, specifically for measurement across a WAN. NTP focuses on clock accuracy over long-time scales, which can come at the expense of short-term clock skew and drift. Errors on the order of milliseconds, such as those generated by NTP-based synchronization, primarily affect the precision of one-way metrics where the accurate synchronization of the clocks between the two devices is essential. However, several performance metrics, such as round-trip time, interarrival time, and delay variation, are less sensitive to clock synchronization accuracy.

TCP Connect

TCP connect describes how long it takes a TCP request to be served at the destination server. This is an essential part of application sessions over TCP. This metric focuses on the network and application level. The result is the sum of the network delay and the processing time at the destination to serve the TCP request.

DHCP and DNS Response Time

DHCP and DNS response time are service layer metrics. Even though requesting an IP address through DHCP is usually limited to one operation per user session, it is critical, because in case of a DHCP server failure, users get no network connectivity. For cable and DSL providers that use DHCP for dynamic address allocation for users, monitoring the DHCP server is vital for the users' network access. In contrast to DHCP, DNS requests occur multiple times per session because web pages are usually designed to retrieve information from multiple servers. Even a network with underutilized high-speed links appears dramatically slow if the DNS serves requests slowly. DHCP and DNS monitoring are significant components of an SLA.

HTTP Response Time

The HTTP response time links to business services by providing the display time for specific websites. In the Internet, your competitor is just a mouse click away. Therefore, identifying performance issues with your public website can have an immediate impact on the organization's revenue.

Linking Metrics to Applications

From a practical perspective, you probably want to link the metrics to applications next. The following list offers guidance and direction:

- **Data transmission**—Measure delay and packet loss—if possible, per class of service.

- **VoIP**—Measure jitter and voice quality scores (such as MOS and ICPIF) and monitor voice server and gateway response times.

- **Streaming video**—Measure one-way delay, packet loss, and out-of-sequence arrival of packets.

- **Network services**—Measure DHCP and DNS server response times.

Operations: How to Measure

Based on the previous suggestions, by now you probably have an idea which performance metrics to start monitoring. Next, you want to identify which IP SLA operation types fit best for a given set of requirements and which parameters to configure.

Operations Parameters

Besides identifying the appropriate IP SLA operations to measure performance metrics, an important step is to define the correct parameters. Is a frequency of 5 minutes accurate enough for the average user's performance requirements? What is the optimal packet size and interpacket interval for a jitter test? There is no perfect answer to these questions, because different services have different requirements. However, some best practices are addressed in the following sections. Figure 11-1 illustrates some of the IP SLA parameters and their relationships.

Figure 11-1 *IP SLA Parameters*

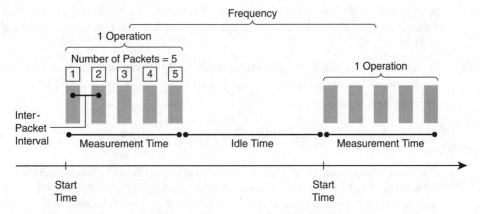

Frequency

Frequency sets the rate at which a specified IP SLA operation is sent to the network. A maximum frequency of one operation per minute and a minimum frequency of one operation every 5 minutes should be sufficient in most networks. The measurement time divided by the measurement interval is called the spectrum of test. For example, running an operation for 30 seconds every minute is equivalent to a 50 percent spectrum of test, because the network is under test 50 percent of the time. The higher the spectrum of test is, the greater the coverage and the larger the amount of test traffic plus performance effect at the source and destination devices. Increasing the frequency also increases the probability of catching an abnormality in the network, but it does not increase the overall accuracy.

Number of Packets

This parameter defines the operation's size. The more test packets an operation generates, the larger the population of measured results becomes. The alternative to running one operation with a large number of packets is to run two or three operations with a smaller number of packets. Because IP SLA aggregates the results per measurement, running more operations with fewer packets increases the granularity over time in comparison to one operation with many packets. Unfortunately, it also means more frequent polling of the device elements to gather results.

Interpacket Interval

The interpacket interval indicates the delay variation between test packets at the receiver side (interpacket delay variance). When a set of packets are generated, they are sent with the same delay value between packets. This delay value changes during the transmission in the network. The receiver calculates the delay variation between packets, resulting in the jitter value. For IP SLA jitter operations, you can define the total number of packets per operation (the default is 10 ms) and the interval between packets (the default is 20 ms). Best practice suggests modeling the desired application's parameters, such as 20 ms in the case of VoIP.

Note that the interpacket interval defines the interval between sending packets within an operation, not the interval between the end of the first transmission and the beginning of the second one.

Packet Size

The main impact of packet size is the device serialization delay, which is relevant for slow network links only. In this case, packet loss can be related to packet size. On fast links, serialization delay can be ignored in comparison to the propagation delay, so the packet size on fast links only consumes bandwidth without adding relevant details.

Timeout

Timeout defines how long an operation waits for the return test packet before considering it lost. This parameter can be used for threshold monitoring. Timeout mainly depends on the measured services and the distance between source and destination. In a LAN environment, a timeout of 5 seconds can be sufficient, whereas monitoring a remote server via a slow link might require timeout values of up to 1 minute.

Lifetime

Lifetime is the total time an operation runs. For SLA validation, lifetime could be configured as "forever." Starting operations during troubleshooting usually limits this value, such as to one hour. Depending on the requirements, a mixture of both ad hoc and scheduled operations might be the right choice.

Start Time

This parameter offers an alternative to running operations forever or just once. You can specify a start time for an operation, let it run for a certain amount of time, and start it again the next day at the same time (recurring function). Note that the start time specifies only the operation's initial start time.

In summary, the selection of operation parameters is a compromise between high measurement accuracy, low bandwidth consumption, and device and network resource usage, such as memory and CPU utilization.

MPLS VPN Awareness

Enhancements to IP SLA allow operators to monitor Multiprotocol Label Switching (MPLS) VPNs and to configure operations on an MPLS VPN PE router by specifying a VPN routing/forwarding (VRF) name to which the operation belongs. The VRF table can be considered a routing table for different VPNs to support overlapping IP addresses in the provider edge (PE) router. If you specify a VRF table when configuring an IP SLA operation, test packets can be sent from one PE to another PE using only the appropriate VPN. The IP SLA Responder is also VRF-aware.

These IP SLA operations can be configured to measure the response time of an MPLS VPN:

- ICMP Echo
- ICMP Path Echo
- UDP Echo
- UDP Jitter
- UDP Path Jitter

The MPLS VPN-aware operation is supported on Cisco platforms that support multi-VRF or VRF-lite and IP SLA.

IP SLA Responder

Although the IP SLA source device can be considered a "packet generator" for synthetic test traffic within a Cisco network element, the optional receiving component is called IP

SLA Responder. This component anticipates and responds to IP SLA request packets and is well embedded in a Cisco network element. Compared to round-trip operations, the IP SLA Responder increases measurement accuracy by time-stamping the test packet as soon as it arrives on the IP SLA Responder, allowing one-way measurements.

To provide useful performance information to an operator, computation of the network response time should distinguish between the "network flight time" and delays introduced by the network elements. Routers may take tens of milliseconds to queue and process incoming packets, which affects the overall response times significantly. The result is that the total response time does not accurately represent the network delay. The IP SLA Responder allows the target device to take a time stamp when the test packet arrives on the ingress interface and another time stamp after processing the request at the Responder.

This allows calculation of the processing time at the receiver. Time stamps offer a granularity of milliseconds for most operation types and microseconds for jitter operations.

Although it is important for troubleshooting to separate network delay and processing delay, for an end-user report they need to be combined, because the user traffic experiences both. A major difference between user traffic and IP SLA synthetic traffic is that IP SLA is implemented as a software process. It does not use the router's forwarding plane (implemented in ASICS), but uses the control plane instead, which is typically slower. Due to the time-stamping at the Responder, subtracting the processing time provides results that are closer to the user experience. Therefore, the distinction between network delay and processing delay is relevant for the Responder!

Figure 11-2 shows how the Responder works.

Figure 11-2 *IP SLA Responder Time-Stamping*

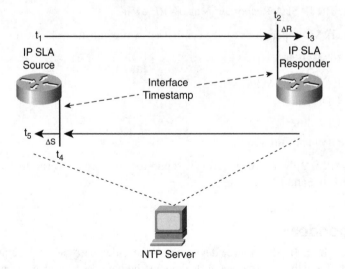

Four time stamps are taken for round-trip time calculation. At the target router (Responder), time stamp 2 (t_2) is taken at the ingress interface, and time stamp 3 (t_3) is taken after the packet is processed. Time stamps are included in the IP SLA test packet payload. Notice that the same principle is applied on the source router. Time stamp 1 (t_1) is applied when the packet is created, and the incoming time stamp 4 (t_4) is taken at the interrupt level to increase accuracy. Time stamp 5 (t_5) is taken at the IP SLA engine after processing at the source device. Next, the source router subtracts t_2 from t_3 to construct the Responders packet processing time. This is represented by $\Delta R = t_3 - t_2$. The same calculation is done for the source device's processing time, where $\Delta S = t_5 - t_4$. The Δ (delta) values are then subtracted from the overall round-trip time ($t_5 - t_1$).

Note that the queuing delay at the source and target router cannot be measured separately. Interface time stamps are applied at the ingress interface only when test packets are received, not at the egress interface before the test packet is sent. Queuing delay can be neglected under normal circumstances; however, this might be an issue on highly utilized interfaces.

An additional benefit of time stamps on the IP SLA Responder is the ability to track one-way delay, jitter, and directional packet loss. Note that for one-way delay measurements the use of Network Time Protocol (NTP), or any time synchronization protocol, is required for both the source router and the Receiver for synchronizing the system clocks. One-way jitter measurements do not require clock synchronization.

IP SLA can specify the IP address and the port number on which the Responder listens to IP SLA test packets. By not using a fixed port, the network element can avoid denial-of-service (DOS) attacks on well-known ports. However, the IP SLA Responder listens on a specific port number (UDP/1967) for control protocol messages sent by an operation. The control message carries information such as protocol, UDP/TCP port number, and duration of the operation. Upon receipt of the control message, the IP SLA Responder enables the specified port for only the specified duration, accepts the requests, and responds to them. The Responder disables the port after completing an operation or if the duration timer expires. For increased security on IP SLA control messages, you can apply Message Digest 5 (MD5) authentication, which is explained in the "Security" section of this chapter. The IP SLA Responder can reply to multiple operations from multiple sources simultaneously. Using the IP SLA Responder is mandatory for the UDP Jitter operation but is optional for the UDP Echo and TCP Connect operations. ICMP operations do not support the Responder.

The following steps occur for each IP SLA operation that uses the IP SLA Responder:

1 The source device initiates the operation by specifying a target device, operation, and port number, as defined in the configuration of the IP SLA operations.

2 The source device sends a control message to port 1967 of the IP SLA Responder, with the specified port number and duration.

3 If MD5 message authentication is enabled, the MD5 checksum is sent with the control message.

4 If MD5 message authentication is enabled, the Responder verifies it. If the authentication fails, the Responder returns an *authentication failure* message.

5 If the source device does not receive a reply from the Responder, it retransmits the control message up to three times and eventually times out.

6 If the Responder cannot process the control message, it returns an *error* message. If the Responder successfully processes the control message, it sends an *OK* reply to the source router and starts listening on the specified port. Note that the Responder can respond to multiple operations from multiple sources that connect to the same port number.

7 If the control message's return code is OK, the source device sends IP SLA test packets to the Responder.

8 Based on the type of operation, the Responder adds time stamps on the return packets for accurate measurement. The source device performs the computation of response time measurements.

9 After responding to the test packets or after the message duration timer expires, the Responder disables the specified monitoring port.

Figure 11-3 illustrates these steps.

Figure 11-3 *IP SLA Responder Communication*

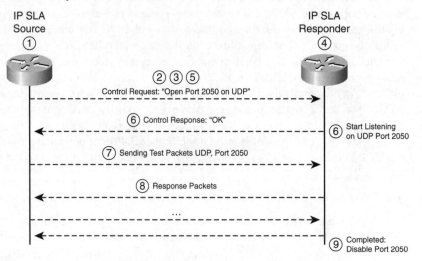

Operation Types

Figure 11-4 depicts an overview of the various IP SLA operations.

Figure 11-4   *IP SLA Operations*

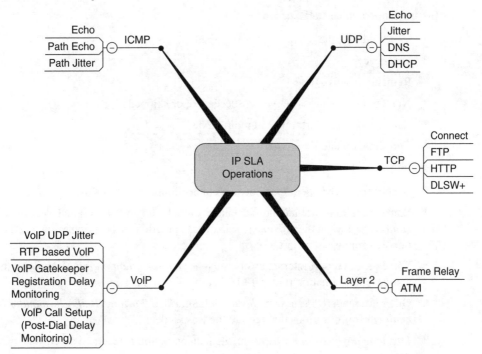

In addition to the structure shown in Figure 11-4, you can apply a different approach when distinguishing the operations:

- **Responder-based operations** offer the capability of unidirectional measurements and improved accuracy compared to round-trip operations. In the replies to the IP SLA source, the Responder includes information about processing delay at the target Cisco device. The IP SLA source device can then separate network delay and destination processing time in its final performance calculation. Use of the Responder is optional for the UDP Echo operation and the TCP Connect operation. It is required for the UDP Jitter, VoIP Jitter, and Frame Relay operations.

- **Non-IP SLA Responder-based operations** are used to monitor specific traffic types, such as HTTP, FTP, DHCP, and TCP Connect. The destination device can be any IP device that supports the protocol being monitored. However, in most cases the targets are not Cisco devices but a server. This explains why those operations are called "non-IP SLA Responders." The most important metric for this group is the server response time, because it reflects the service performance.

The following sections describe all the IP SLA operations in detail. These operations provide a rich set of reports. Some details are generated by all operations, and others are specific. Because the following points are provided by all operations, they are listed only once; the additional details are listed here per operation.

Common operational statistics are

- Time and date the operation was modified
- Frequency
- Remaining active time
- Number of operations activated, succeeded, or skipped
- Latest operation start time and return code
- Threshold counter

Common error statistics are

- Number of *failed* operations due to a connection loss or timeout.
- Some operations provide more details about why an operation failed, such as a *busy status* report when the previously scheduled operation was not finished when the next one was supposed to start.
- Some probes report internal errors, such as an *authentication failure* between the source and destination router if MD5 authentication is applied but fails.
- Other internal error types are *destination interface down* or *IP SLA Responder is not enabled* (for operations that require the Responder).
- *Last time the operation was reset*: when an operation is reset, all saved statistics are deleted.

ICMP Operations

The Internet Control Message Protocol (ICMP) is also called a "ping test." This is usually the first troubleshooting tool for a network operator to verify connectivity between two points in the network. The destination device can be any IP host. In ICMP operations, the source device sends several ICMP packets to the destination, which echoes the ICMP replies. ICMP operations should mainly be used to verify connectivity and for troubleshooting, because ICMP was not designed as an accurate delay measurement tool. Uncertainties can be caused by *low priority processing* of ICMP packets in routers, so the absolute delay results might not be representative of the actual packet delay of user traffic.

NOTE   Note that *low-priority processing* refers to the router *receiving* and *originating* ICMP packets, not to *forwarding* them. By default, routers forward ICMP packets with the same priority as any other traffic.

In an operational network, administrators usually rate-limit ICMP traffic—in particular, at the provider edge—in an attempt to limit the impact of certain types of DoS attacks. Pinging hosts through long network paths is fine and provides useful results. Pinging routers for accurate results requires knowledge of their configuration—for example, to know if ICMP traffic is rate-limited.

IP SLA supports three different ICMP operations:

- ICMP Echo
- ICMP Path Echo
- ICMP Path Jitter

ICMP Echo Operation

The ICMP Echo operation monitors end-to-end response time between a Cisco router and network elements or IP hosts. Response time is computed by measuring the time between sending an ICMP Echo request message to the destination and receiving an ICMP Echo reply. Because it measures only the packet's complete round-trip time, including the test packet's processing time at the destination, the exact results are of limited value. No general statement can be made if a problem occurred in the network or at the destination host. The ICMP Echo operation conforms to the IETF specifications for ICMP ping tests, and the two methods result in the same response times.

ICMP Echo operation reports include the following additional details: performance statistics, such as number of operations; RTT statistics in milliseconds (latest, average, minimum, maximum); and sum and sum of the squares of the RTT measurements, which is useful in statistical analysis, such as calculating the standard deviation.

ICMP Path Echo Operation

The ICMP Path Echo operation collects statistics for each hop along the path that the IP SLA operation takes to reach its destination. The ICMP Path Echo operation determines this hop-by-hop response time between a Cisco router and any IP device in the network by discovering the path using the traceroute tool. As a result, the round-trip delay for the full path is displayed. If a network has multiple equal-cost paths, it can be useful to measure the response time on a specific path. The strict and loose source routing options in the IP header force ICMP echo packets to follow a particular path. However, this option has some disadvantages. The operator needs to know the topology to be able to set up different paths for the operations, and intermediate hops might not support IP source routing. Furthermore, packets with IP options typically require more processing time per hop, because option processing generally is not part of the optimized data-switching path. This results in an increased response time compared to actual data packets without the option set.

ICMP Path Echo operation reports include the following additional details:

- Operational conditions such as target IP address and hop in the path index
- Performance statistics are reported as the latest RTT in milliseconds
- Error statistics including busy status and internal errors

Default settings for the ICMP Path Echo operation are as follows:

- Number of test packets (n) = 10
- Interval between sending test packets = 20 ms
- Frequency of the operation = once every 60 seconds

So, by default, every 60 seconds the ICMP Path Echo sends a set of ten test packets separated by 20 ms. Figure 11-5 illustrates the ICMP Path Echo operation. In this case, the default route from the source to the destination host goes via hop 1 and hop 2, so traceroute discovers both hops. A ping (ICMP echo) is then used to measure the response time between the source IP SLA device and each subsequent hop in the path to the destination IP device. If the metrics for the path going through hop 3 should be measured, the source routing IP option must be specified, assuming that this hop supports it.

Figure 11-5 *IP SLA ICMP Path Echo Operation*

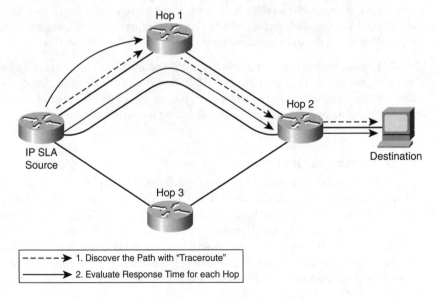

ICMP Path Jitter Operation

The ICMP Path Jitter operation works much like the Path Echo operation. It provides additional metrics, such as hop-by-hop jitter and packet loss. The ICMP Path Jitter operation complements the UDP Jitter operation, which provides total one-way data and total round-trip data. For example, results from the UDP Jitter operation may indicate unexpected delays or high jitter values. The ICMP Path Jitter operation could then be used to troubleshoot the network path and determine if traffic is bottlenecking in a particular segment along the transmission path. First, the operation discovers the hop-by-hop IP route from the source to the destination using traceroute. Then it sends ICMP echo messages to determine the response times, packet loss, and approximate jitter values for each hop along the path. The obtained jitter value for the ICMP Path Jitter operation is the cumulative jitter with noise reduction (RFC 1889).

ICMP Path Jitter operation reports include the following additional details:

- Performance statistics are reported as the latest RTT in milliseconds. The following details are stored per hop:
    — Number of successful round-trip measurements
    — Sum and sum of the squares of the RTT values in milliseconds
- Minimum and maximum positive and negative jitter and the sum and square sum of these values (in milliseconds)
- Error statistics: number of packets lost; number of packets returned out of sequence; sequence errors, verify errors, or internal errors

---

NOTE   The ICMP Path Jitter operation is not supported in the RTTMON MIB; configuration and performance data can be obtained only using the CLI.

Summary of ICMP Operations

In contrast with other IP SLA operations, ICMP operations do not require the IP SLA Responder on either the target device or intermediate devices. ICMP-based operations can compensate for source processing delay but cannot compensate for target processing delay. The jitter values obtained using the ICMP Path Jitter operation are approximate because IP SLA does not use the ICMP TIMESTAMP REQUEST message that allows a responding router to put in receive-time and response-send-time time stamps. If the target router treats ICMP packets with a low priority, it can potentially add significant processing delay. In general, ICMP operations are very good tools for troubleshooting situations. For more robust monitoring and verification, use of the UDP Jitter operation is recommended.

UDP Operations

The results of a UDP Echo operation can be useful for troubleshooting business-critical applications by determining the round-trip delay times and testing connectivity to both Cisco and non-Cisco devices. The round-trip time is computed by measuring the time between sending a UDP Echo request message from the IP SLA source router to the destination device and receiving a UDP Echo reply from the destination device. The source device must be a Cisco router, whereas the destination device can be any IP host.

Compared to ICMP operations, the UDP operations offer more detailed reporting, such as one-way delay measurement, when used in conjuction with the IP SLA Responder.

IP SLA supports three different UDP operations:

* UDP Echo
* UDP Jitter
* VoIP UDP Jitter

UDP Echo Operation

UDP Echo accuracy can be enhanced by optionally using the IP SLA Responder if the destination device is a Cisco network element. The UDP Jitter and VoIP UDP Jitter operations require the IP SLA Responder.

UDP Echo operation reports include the following additional details:

* Performance statistics are reported as the latest RTT in milliseconds
* Error statistics including the number of corrupted packets; sequence errors, verification errors, or other errors

UDP Jitter Operation

The UDP Jitter operation was primarily designed to diagnose network suitability for real-time traffic applications such as voice, VoIP, or real-time conferencing. However, the IP SLA UDP Jitter operation does more than just monitor jitter, because it also includes the statistics of the UDP Echo operation. The generated UDP test packets carry sending and receiving sequence information as well as sending and receiving time stamps from the source and target.

Default settings for the UDP Jitter operation are as follows:

* Number of test packets (n) = 10
* Packet payload size (S) = 32 bytes
* Interpacket interval = 10 ms
* Frequency of the operation = once every 60 seconds

UDP Jitter operation reports include the following performance statistics:

- Number of successful round-trip measurements
- Number of successful one-way measurements
- Sum and sum of the squares of the RTT values in milliseconds
- Minimum and maximum positive and negative jitter from source to destination (absolute values in milliseconds)
- Number of positive jitter values from source to destination (which means network latency increases for two consecutive test packets) and the sum and the square sum of those positive values (in milliseconds)
- Number of negative jitter values from source to destination (which means network latency decreases for two consecutive test packets) and the sum and square sum of those values (in milliseconds)
- One-way delay between source and destination or destination and source (in milliseconds)
- Minimum and maximum time from the source to the destination and the sum and square sum of these values (in milliseconds)
- Error statistics: number of packets lost (from source to destination, or from destination to source, or with an undefined direction); number of packets returned out of sequence; number of packets that arrived after a defined timeout value (late arrival); connection loss; and failed operations due to busy, disconnect, timeout, or other errors.

VoIP UDP Jitter Operation

A VoIP-specific implementation of the UDP Jitter monitoring operation simulates specific voice codecs and calculates voice quality scores. The VoIP UDP Jitter operation uses UDP traffic to generate approximate Voice over IP quality scores. Note that the RTP-based VoIP operation supports Real-time Transport Protocol (RTP). It is explained in detail in the section "RTP-Based VoIP Operation."

The VoIP UDP Jitter operation modifies the UDP Jitter operation by adding the capability to estimate MOS and ICPIF scores in addition to the metrics already gathered by the UDP Jitter operation.

VoIP UDP Jitter operation reports include the following additional details:

- Performance statistics are the same as reported by the UDP Jitter operation, with the addition of the ICPIF and MOS scores for the latest/minimum/maximum values
- Error statistics: number of corrupted packets, failed operations due to busy, sequence errors, verification errors, or other errors

NOTE	ICPIF and MOS values provided by the VoIP UDP Jitter operation are estimates and are intended for only relative comparisons. The values may not match values determined by using other measurement methods. Predictions of customer opinion (such as the E-Model transmission rating factor R and derived MOSs) are intended for only transmission planning and analysis purposes. They should not be interpreted as reflecting actual user opinions.

TCP Connect Operation

The TCP Connect operation is useful for measuring the response time of a server running a particular TCP-based application or general connectivity testing for server availability. TCP Connect is used to test virtual circuit availability or application availability by simulating Telnet, FTP, and other types of connections. TCP Connect measures the response time taken to perform a TCP Connect operation between a Cisco router and any IP device. The destination device can be any IP device or an IP SLA Responder. If the destination router is a Cisco router, IP SLA makes a TCP connection to any specified port number. If the destination is not a Cisco IP host, a known destination port number such as 21 for FTP, 23 for Telnet, or 80 for HTTP must be used.

TCP Connect operation reports include the following additional details:

- Operational conditions such as memory used (number of octets used) and the latest IP destination address

- Performance statistics are reported as the latest RTT in milliseconds

FTP Operation

The FTP operation measures the round-trip time between a Cisco device and an FTP server to retrieve a file. This is the time taken to download the entire file from the source device. Therefore, this operation does not use the IP SLA Responder. The results of an FTP operation to retrieve a large file can be used to determine the network's capacity. However, carrying a significant amount of data traffic can also affect your network's performance. Both active and passive FTP transfer modes are supported, where passive mode is enabled by default. Only the FTP GET (download) operation type is supported.

FTP operation reports include the following additional details:

- Operational conditions including the size of the retrieved file (in bytes).

- Performance statistics are reported as the latest RTT in milliseconds. For this specific FTP operation, RTT is the total time to complete the FTP transaction.

- Error statistics, such as number of failed operations due to disconnect, busy status, sequence errors, verify errors, or internal errors.

DHCP Operation

The Dynamic Host Configuration Protocol (DHCP) operation measures the round-trip time taken to discover a DHCP server and obtain a leased IP address from it. DHCP provides a mechanism for allocating IP addresses dynamically so that addresses can be reused when hosts no longer need them. IP SLA releases the leased IP address immediately after the operation. The DHCP operation has two modes. By default, the DHCP operation sends discovery packets on every available IP interface from the IP SLA source router to identify all DHCP servers in the network. If a specific server is configured, discovery packets are sent to only that DHCP server.

In addition to monitoring DHCP servers, IP SLA can work in conjunction with a DHCP relay agent. A DHCP relay agent is any host that forwards DHCP packets between clients and servers. Relay agents are used to forward requests and replies between clients and servers when they are not on the same physical subnet. Relay agent forwarding is distinct from the normal forwarding of an IP router, where IP packets are switched between networks somewhat transparently. Relay agents receive DHCP messages and then generate a new DHCP message to send out on another interface. The IP SLA DHCP operation contains relay agent option 82, which is inserted by the DHCP relay agent when forwarding client-originated DHCP packets to a DHCP server. The DHCP server echoes the option verbatim to the relay agent in server-to-client replies, and the relay agent strips the option before forwarding the reply to the client.

DHCP operation reports include the following additional details:

- Performance statistics are reported as the latest RTT in milliseconds. For this specific DHCP operation, RTT is the total time to obtain an IP address.

- Error statistics, such as number of failed operations due to a busy status, no connection to the destination, sequence errors, verify errors, or internal errors.

DNS Operation

The DNS operation measures the amount of time between a request sent to a Domain Name System (DNS) and the received reply. DNS is used to translate names of network nodes into IP addresses and vice versa. This operation is a critical element for determining a network's overall performance, because most IP services heavily depend on DNS name resolution. In most cases, faster DNS lookup times translate to a faster server access experience. The DNS operation queries for an IP address if you specify a hostname or queries for a hostname if you specify an IP address. The connection response time is computed by measuring the difference between the time taken to send a request to the DNS server and the time a reply is received. This operation does not depend on the IP SLA Responder.

DNS operation reports include the following additional details:

- Performance statistics are reported as the latest RTT in milliseconds. For this specific DNS operation, the RTT is the total time to obtain a translation from the DNS server.

- Error statistics, such as number of failed operations due to disconnect, busy status, no connection to the destination, sequence errors, verify errors, or internal errors.

HTTP Operation

The HTTP operation monitors the response time between an IP SLA source device and an HTTP server to retrieve a web page. The HTTP server response time measurement consists of the sum of three values:

- **DNS lookup** is the RTT taken to perform a Domain Name Server lookup.

- **TCP Connect** is the RTT taken to perform a TCP connection to the HTTP server.

- **HTTP transaction time** is the RTT taken to send a request and get a response from the HTTP server. It is split into the time for the first HTML byte retrieved by the HTTP operation and the RTT to retrieve the full page. Note that images are not downloaded.

An HTTP request can be made through a proxy server. The HTTP operation supports both the normal HTTP GET requests and the customer HTTP raw requests. For HTTP GET, IP SLA formats the request based on the specified URL. For raw requests, IP SLA requires the entire content of the HTTP request. A raw request is more flexible and allows you to control fields such as authentication. Figure 11-6 shows each step of the HTTP operation.

HTTP operation reports include the following additional details:

- Operational conditions such as the URL of the destination web server, message size of the web page retrieved by the HTTP operation (in bytes), and memory utilized (number of octets)

- Performance statistics, such as RTT (total, minimum, maximum, DNS resolution, TCP connection, HTTP transaction); sum and sum of the squares of the total RTT measurements, all in milliseconds

- Error statistics, such as number of failed HTTP and DNS operations (including authentication failure, or the destination interface is down); number of failed operations due to a DNS, TCP, or HTTP connect timeout; or internal errors, and some diagnosis text

Figure 11-6 *HTTP Operation*

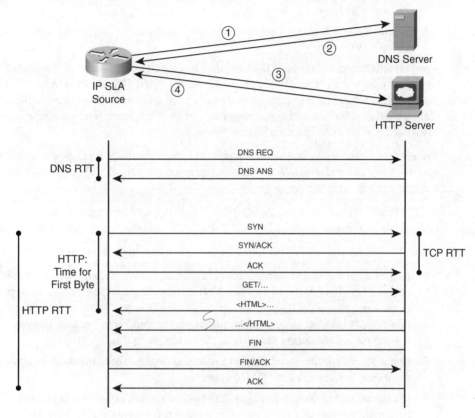

Frame Relay Operation

The IP SLA operation for Frame Relay provides detailed monitoring statistics for physical links or circuits of Frame Relay connections. It provides a variety of metrics for traffic analysis, such as round-trip time, bandwidth usage, throughput, packet loss, burst analysis, delivery ratio, utilization, total frames transmitted, total frames received, and more. The IP SLA function is required on the source device, and the IP SLA Responder at the destination device has to be enabled for Frame Relay. There is no SNMP support for the Frame Relay operations. A vendor-specific XML interface exists; however, specifications currently are not published.

The Frame Relay feature introduces new IP SLA monitoring functions:

- **Physical Interface**—This operation provides physical layer (Layer 1) data for serial interfaces and T3 (DS3) or E3 controllers.

- **Frame Relay Link**—This operation provides Frame Relay link (Layer 2) data for a Frame Relay interface.
- **Frame Relay Circuit**—This operation provides Frame Relay permanent virtual circuit (PVC) data.

The Frame Relay operation uses the enhanced history function, where performance statistics are stored in "buckets" that keep the accumulated data separate from each other. Each bucket consists of data accumulated over a fixed interval of 15 minutes. In the case of the Frame Relay operation, this parameter cannot be configured. Note that there is no SNMP support for this enhanced history function.

Because the Frame Relay operation is testing the connection of a PVC, you do not have to specify an operational target. When specifying the DLCI number, only one target device is possible—the IP SLA Responder.

For the Frame Relay operation, the Responder inserts special frames for statistics measurement. These are returned from the IP SLA Responder to the IP SLA source device.

Frame Relay Monitor operation reports include the following additional details:

- Link state of the Frame Relay access channel: up, down, network-down, user-down, or spoof network up/down (the agent has been spoofing for the user over some portion of the sampling interval while the network side of the access channel has been up/down over the entire sampling interval). Also, the number of seconds this circuit has not been available during the current 15-minute interval is reported.

- Frame Relay-specific interface performance statistics. These measure the absolute number of frames, not just IP SLA frames.

- Maximum and minimum throughput in bps, maximum utilization in percent, maximum number of frames per second per direction (receive, transmit).

- Total number of transmitted frames and octets (including error frames) per direction (receive, transmit), depending on the interface speed. These are 64-bit counters.

- The number of 1-second intervals in which traffic was detected and the traffic rate was below the configured burst limit.

- The total number of frames per direction (receive, transmit) with FCS errors, aborted frames, and too-long or too-short frames; the number of seconds that the network side of the circuit has been down or unavailable; the number of drop events (where a frame was not analyzed and potentially was dropped).

- The number of Forward Explicit Congestion Notification (FECN) seconds that occurred for the circuit since it was created. A FECN second is defined as a second during which one or more nonerror frames were received with the FECN bit set.

- The number of Backward Explicit Congestion Notification (BECN) seconds that occurred for the circuit since it was created. A BECN second is defined as a second during which one or more nonerror frames were received with the BECN bit set.

- The total number of frames and octets transmitted on the circuit that have exceeded the Committed Information Rate (CIR) during the current 15-minute interval.

- The number of frames with the Discard Eligible (DE) bit set, per direction (receive, transmit).

- IP SLA operations performance metrics include one-way and round-trip measurement. The distribution statistics consist of the sum of completion times (used to calculate the mean), the sum of the completion times squared (used to calculate standard deviation), the maximum and minimum completion times, and the number of completed attempts.

- Error statistics, such as number of failed operations due to disconnect, busy status, no connection to the destination, sequence errors, verify errors, or internal errors.

ATM Operation

The IP SLA operation for ATM provides detailed monitoring statistics for physical links or circuits of ATM connections. The ATM interface link statistics are used to monitor the basic health of an ATM interface, such as traffic-, error-, and performance-related counters. The metrics include round-trip time, bandwidth usage, throughput, packet loss, burst analysis, delivery ratio, utilization, total frames transmitted, total frames received, and more. The IP SLA function is required on both the source and the destination device; however, unlike other IP SLA operations, you do not enable the IP SLA Responder at the destination device. Instead, you configure the same ATM operation on both the sending agent and the destination agent to get the full monitoring statistics for ATM connections.

For the ATM operation, the Responder inserts special frames for statistics measurement. These are returned from the IP SLA Responder to the IP SLA source device.

There is no SNMP support for the ATM operations. A vendor-specific XML interface exists; however, specifications currently are not published.

The ATM feature introduces new IP SLA monitoring functions:

- **Physical Interface**—This operation provides physical layer (Layer 1) data for T1 (IMA) interfaces and serial interfaces.

- **Physical Controller**—This operation provides physical layer (Layer 1) data for T1 or E1 controllers configured for ATM.

- **ATM Link**—This operation provides Layer 2 data for an ATM interface.

- **ATM Circuit**—This operation provides ATM PVC data.

The ATM operation uses the enhanced history function, in which performance statistics are stored in "buckets" that keep the accumulated data separate from each other. Each bucket consists of data accumulated over a fixed interval of 15 minutes. In the case of ATM, this parameter cannot be configured.

ATM Monitor operation reports include the following additional details:

- ATM-specific interface performance statistics. These measure the absolute number of frames, not just IP SLA frames, and are collected per direction (receive, transmit).

- Total number of cells and breakdown in AAL 1, 2, and 5 cells.

- Number of Physical Layer Convergence Procedure (PLCP) framing and errors.

- Number of corrected and uncorrected cells.

- Number of Out of Cell Delineation (OCD) seconds.

- Number of Alarm Indication Signal (AIS) seconds.

- Number of Remote Defect Indicator (RDI) seconds.

- Maximum cells per second.

- Number of cell replacement and unanalyzed data events.

- Maximum and minimum throughput in bps, maximum utilization in percent, maximum number of frames.

- Total number of transmitted frames and octets per direction (receive, transmit).

- Five different counters per direction for burst traffic, as a percentage (in seconds).

- IP SLA operations performance metrics include one-way and round-trip measurement. The distribution statistics consist of the sum of the completion times (used to calculate the mean), the sum of the completion times squared (used to calculate standard deviation), the maximum and minimum completion times, and the number of completed attempts.

- Error statistics, such as number of failed operations due to disconnect, busy status, no connection to the destination, sequence errors, verify errors, or internal errors.

NOTE   The ATM operation is supported on only the following platforms: Cisco IAD2420 Smart Integrated Access Device (IAD), Cisco 2600 series with T1 or E1 interfaces, Cisco 3660 series with T1 or E1 ATM interfaces, Cisco MC3810 Multiservice Access Concentrators, and Cisco 7200 series.

VoIP Gatekeeper Registration Delay Monitoring Operation

The IP SLA Gatekeeper Registration Delay Monitoring operation provides statistical data on the amount of time taken to register a gateway to a gatekeeper. To measure VoIP gatekeeper registration response time, the IP SLA Gatekeeper Registration Delay operation sends a lightweight Registration Request (RRQ) from an H.323 gateway to an H.323 gatekeeper. It also records the time taken to receive the Registration Confirmation (RCF) from the gatekeeper. The IP SLA VoIP Gatekeeper Registration Delay Monitoring feature focuses on the function of the call control H.323 stack. Statistics include aggregated totals and median or average data; these can be viewed through the command line or SNMP.

VoIP Gatekeeper Registration Delay Monitoring operation reports include performance statistics, which are reported as the latest RTT in milliseconds.

VoIP Call Setup (Post-Dial Delay) Monitoring Operation

The IP SLA VoIP Call Setup (Post-Dial Delay) Monitoring operation measures the response time for setting up a synthetic VoIP call. By supporting H.323 and the Session Initiation Protocol (SIP), this operation measures the total time between an originating gateway sending a call setup message (containing a call number) and receiving a message from the terminating gateway (destination). The trigger for the timer to stop can be configured as the destination to ring or the called party to answer the call.

Before configuring the IP SLA VoIP Call Setup (Post-Dial Delay) Monitoring operation, you need to prepare the source and destination side:

- Enable the VoIP test-call application on the *originating* gateway, which is the IP SLA source router. This application contains the required scripts to generate call messages for H.323 or SIP; the configuration for the call setup operation is essentially the same for both protocols.

- An IP phone can be set up at the *terminating* gateway to respond to the generated test call. A more convenient alternative is to enable the IP SLA VoIP Responder application in the terminating gateway, which responds to incoming call setup messages from the originating gateway using H.323 or SIP. Note that the configuration of the IP SLA VoIP Responder is different from the IP SLA Responder, even though the concept is similar.

NOTE   If a gatekeeper or directory gatekeeper is involved in the H.323 call signaling, additional control messages are exchanged between the originating and terminating gateways before the call message is actually sent. The additional time required for these messages is included in the total response time measurement. Likewise, if a proxy server or redirection server is involved in the SIP call signaling, any additional time required for control messages exchanged before sending the call message is included in the response time measurement.

RTP-Based VoIP Operation

The Real-time Transport Protocol (RTP)-based voice over IP (VoIP) operation lets you set up test calls and use voice gateway Digital Signal Processors (DSP) to gather network performance-related statistics for a VoIP call. Available statistical measurements for this operation include jitter, frame loss, Mean Opinion Score for Conversational Quality (MOS-CQ), and Mean Opinion Score for Listening Quality (MOS-LQ). This VoIP operation provides the largest set of statistics compared to the VoIP UDP Jitter operation. Whereas the UDP Jitter operation estimates only MOS and ICPIF scores, the RTP-based VoIP probe measures VoIP statistics accurately and uses the same transport protocol as the VoIP calls: RTP. SNMP and Syslog notifications provide proactive threshold violation for constant VoIP quality monitoring. The difference between this operation and the VoIP Call Setup (Post-Dial Delay) Monitoring operation is that this one generates real voice data, whereas the previous one measures details about the call setup. This operation has a number of restrictions and prerequisites:

- Both the source and destination routers must be running Cisco IOS Release 12.4(4)T or later and have an IOS image with the Cisco IOS IP Voice or a higher-grade feature package.

- The IP SLA Responder must be enabled on the destination gateway.

- The source router must have a network module with a c5510 or c549 DSP. The destination router needs to have a network module with a DSP. Depending on the type of DSP, the statistics measured by the IP SLAs RTP-based VoIP operation vary.

- The RTP-based VoIP operation gathers the statistical information only from the DSP of the source router. For source-to-destination measurements, the RTP-based VoIP operation does not obtain statistical information from DSPs.

- The voice port used by the IP SLAs RTP-based VoIP operation is unavailable for other calls.

Table 11-1 describes the different measurement types of the RTP-based VoIP operation and shows which functions require the DSP.

Table 11-1 *Statistics Gathered by the RTP-Based VoIP Operation*

Statistic	Description	DSP Involved in Measurement?
Interarrival jitter (destination-to-source and source-to-destination)	Interarrival jitter is the mean deviation (smoothed absolute value) of the difference in packet spacing for a pair of packets. The source-to-destination value is measured by sending RTP packets to the IP SLA Responder. The calculation is based on RFC 1889.	No
Estimated R factor (destination-to-source and source-to-destination)	Estimated transmission rating factor R. This value is based on one-way transmission delay and standard default values, as well as values obtained from the DSP. The calculation is based on ITU-T G.107.	Yes

Table 11-1   *Statistics Gathered by the RTP-Based VoIP Operation (Continued)*

Statistic	Description	DSP Involved in Measurement?
MOS-CQ (destination-to-source and source-to-destination)	Mean Opinion Score for Conversational Quality. The source-to-destination value is measured by sending RTP packets to the IP SLA Responder. This value is obtained by converting the estimated R factor to the MOS using ITU-T Recommendation G.107 conversion tables.	No
Round-trip time latency	RTT latency for an RTP packet to travel from the source to the destination and back to the source.	Yes
Packet loss (destination-to-source and source-to-destination)	Number of packets lost. The source-to-destination value is measured by sending RTP packets to the IP SLA Responder.	No
Packets missing in action (source-to-destination)	Number of missing packets. The source-to-destination value is measured by sending RTP packets to the IP SLA Responder.	No
One-way latency (destination-to-source and source-to-destination)	Average, minimum, and maximum latency values. These values are measured by sending RTP packets to the IP SLA Responder. The RTP data stream is then looped back from the destination to the source gateway.	Yes
Frame loss (destination-to-source)[*]	Number of DSP frame loss events. A frame loss can occur because of such events as packet loss, late packets, or a jitter buffer error.	Yes
MOS-LQ (destination-to-source)[*]	Mean Opinion Score for Listening Quality.	Yes

[*]Available for only c5510 DSPs

DLSw+ Operation

The DLSw+ operation measures the Data Link Switching Plus (DLSw+) protocol stack and network response time between DLSw+ peers. DLSw+ is the Cisco enhanced version of RFC 1795, *Data Link Switching*. DLSw+ tunnels nonroutable Layer 2 traffic such as IBM Systems Network Architecture (SNA) traffic over IP backbones via TCP. The networking devices performing the tunneling are called DLSw+ peers. DLSw+ peers normally communicate through TCP port 2065. Network response time is computed by measuring the RTT taken to connect to the remote DLSw+ peer. The destination device can be a Cisco router or any other network element that supports RFC 1795. This operation does not require the IP SLA Responder.

DLSW+ operation reports include the following additional details:

* Performance statistics are reported as the latest RTT in milliseconds
* Error statistics, such as number of failed operations due to disconnect, busy status, no connection to the destination, sequence errors, verify errors, or internal errors

IP SLA CLI Operations

This section describes the most important configuration commands to enable the IP SLA feature on the Cisco routers. It explains configuring the operations and their characteristics (type, frequency, precision, ToS, VRF), operation scheduling, operation reactions, and the IP SLA Responder and its optional authentication. After the name change from "SAA" to "IP SLA," the CLI commands were modified extensively. The following list summarizes the changes, starting with Cisco IOS Software Releases 12.4(2)T, 12.2SX, and 12.2SB:

* The **rtr** keyword has been changed to **ip sla**.
* The removal of the **type** keyword lets you enter operations directly under the IP SLA definition.
* The number of CLI sublevels has been reduced so that individual operations are easy to configure. For example, the **protocol** keyword for Internet Control Message Protocol (ICMP) operations has been removed.
* History features are grouped under the **history** keyword.
* The **monitor** keyword (**ip sla monitor**), which was introduced as an interim solution, has been removed. For example, **router(config-sla-monitor-***type***)** became **router(config-ip-sla-***type***)**.
* The keywords **destination-ip** and **destination-port** are now optional, but **source-ip** and **source-port** are still mandatory.
* The new **show ip sla statistics** [**details**] command replaces the **show rtr operational-state** command.
* The new **show ip sla statistics aggregated** [**details**] command replaces the **show rtr collection-history** command. This command is very similar to the **show ip sla monitor statistics** command. In addition, it includes distribution statistics and an aggregated view of data.
* The previous CLI formats are accepted in configuration mode. Note that a **show run** or **show start** command outputs the new CLI formats. This allows backward compatibility.

NOTE	The configuration commands explained in this section were taken from the latest available image—Cisco IOS Software Release 12.4(11)T.

The most important configuration commands to enable the IP SLA feature on the Cisco routers are as follows:

- router(config)# **ip sla** *operation-number*
  configures an IP SLA operation, where the *operation-number* specifies the operation instance of interest. When configured, the IP SLA Monitor configuration mode is entered, as indicated by the (config-ip-sla) router prompt.

- router(config-ip-sla)#*type*
  configures the type of IP SLA operation. The possible IP SLA types are **dhcp**, **dns**, **frame-relay**, **ftp**, **http**, **icmp-echo**, **icmp-jitter**, **path-echo**, **path-jitter**, **slm**, **tcp-connect**, **udp-echo**, **udp-jitter**, and **voip**. When configured, the IP SLA Monitor configuration mode for the specific type is entered, as indicated by the (config-ip-sla-type) router prompt. Note that SLM stands for Service Level Monitor and configures the Layer 2 operation for Frame Relay and ATM. The following examples are configured with **udp-jitter** type operation.

- router(config-ip-sla-*type*)# **frequency** *seconds*
  sets the rate at which a specified IP SLA operation repeats. The default is 60 seconds.

- router(config-ip-sla-*type*)# **precision** {**milliseconds** | **microseconds**}
  sets the level of accuracy at which the statistics for an IP SLA operation are measured. Note that this command applies only to the jitter operation.

- router(config-ip-sla-type)# **timeout** *milliseconds*
  sets the amount of time the IP SLA operation waits for a response from its test packet.

- router(config-ip-sla-type)# **tos** *number*
  defines the type of service (ToS) byte in the IP header of IP SLA operations.

- router(config-ip-sla-type)# **vrf** *vrf-name*
  allows monitoring within MPLS VPNs using IP SLA operations.

- router(config-ip-sla-type)# **request-data-size** *bytes*
  sets the payload size of the IP SLA operation's test packet. This applies to the UDP Jitter, UDP Echo, and ICMP Echo operations.

- router(config)# **ip sla responder**
  is used on the destination device for IP SLA operations to enable the sending and receiving of IP SLA Control packets. Enabling the IP SLA Responder allows the generation of packet loss statistics on the device sending IP SLA operations.

- router(config)# **ip sla group schedule** *group-operation-number operation-id-numbers* **schedule-period** *schedule-period-range* [**ageout** *seconds*] [**frequency** *group-operation-frequency*] [**life** {**forever** | *seconds*}] [**start-time** {*hh:mm*[*:ss*] [*month day*

| *day month*] | **pending** | **now** | **after** *hh*:*mm*:*ss*}]
performs group scheduling for IP SLA operations. (The group scheduling function is explained in the later section "Scheduling.")

- router(config)# **ip sla key-chain** *name*
  enables IP SLA control message authentication and specifies an MD5 key chain.

- router(config)# **ip sla logging traps** enables the generation of system logging SNMP notifications (Syslog traps) specific to IP SLA thresholds.

- router(config)# **ip sla reaction-trigger** *operation-number target-operation*
  defines a second IP SLA operation to make the transition from a pending state to an active state when one of the trigger action-type options is defined with the **ip sla reaction-configuration** command. (The triggers are explained in the "Thresholds and Notifications" section.)

- router(config)# **ip sla reaction-configuration** *operation-number* [**react** *monitored-element*] [**threshold-type** {**never** | **immediate** | **consecutive** [*consecutive-occurrences*] | **xofy** [*x-value y-value*] | **average** [*number-of-probes*]}] [**threshold-value** *upper-threshold lower-threshold*] [**action-type** {**none** | **trapOnly** | **triggerOnly** | **trapAndTrigger**}]
  configures certain actions to occur based on events under the control of the IP SLA. The possible events, configured with **react** *monitored-element*, are connectionLoss, jitterAvg threshold, jitterDSAvg threshold (jitter from destination to source), jitterSDAvg threshold (jitter from source to destination), mos threshold (Mean Opinion Score), PacketLossDS threshold (from destination to source), PacketLossSD threshold (from source to destination), and timeout threshold. The possible actions are trapOnly, triggerOnly (activate the target operation configured by the **ip sla reaction-trigger** command), and trapAndTrigger.

SNMP Operations with the CISCO-RTTMON-MIB

The CISCO-RTTMON-MIB, whose name still contains the initial feature-naming convention RTT, lets you configure most of the operations described in this chapter. Furthermore, the CISCO-RTTMON-MIB lets you monitor the operation results. The only exceptions, for both configuration and monitoring, are the Frame Relay and ATM operations.

The CISCO-RTTMON-MIB defines managed objects that enable a network administrator to do the following:

- Query the supported operation types on the agent (similar to the output of the **show ip sla application** command), along with some administrative information such as the low-memory watermark and the estimated number of configurable operations.

- Configure an operation along with all its parameters (type, frequency, interval, number of packets, packet size, tag, owner, timeout, target IP address, type of service, VRF, precision). The configuration of operation-specific details is also possible: the URL and HTTP version for the HTTP operation, the codec type for the VoIP operation, and so on.

- Configure the operation scheduling, including the Recurring Function, Multiple Operation Scheduling, and Random Scheduling.

- Configure the notification/trigger generation (see the "Thresholds and Notifications" section). Previous versions of the MIB specified four different notifications; these are now deprecated: rttMonConnectionChangeNotification, rttMonTimeoutNotification, rttMonThresholdNotification, and rttMonVerifyErrorNotification. The new MIB version specifies the generic notification rttMonNotification, which is used for any violation on any metric of interest.

- Monitor the operational state of all operations, and collect the results. Two extra tables, specific to the HTTP and jitter operations, contain the detailed results of the last operation.

- Configure the history and collect its results. The MIB limits the hours-of-statistics kept for the UDP Jitter operation to 2 hours. Configuring a larger value using the hours-of-statistics hours global configuration change does not increase the value beyond 2 hours. However, the Data Collection MIB can be used to collect historical data for the operation. The enhanced history feature is currently supported only with the CLI. SNMP support will be added later.

- Configure and monitor the MD5 Authentication for Control Protocol.

Note that, when the rttMonCtrlAdminNvgen MIB variable is set to true, its associated operation is shown in the output of the **show running** command and therefore can be saved in nonvolatile memory (NVRAM). The default rttMonCtrlAdminNvgen value is false.

Application-Specific Scenario: HTTP

Before you configure IP SLA operations, the **show ip sla application** command lets you verify the supported IP SLA functions on the router:

```
router#show ip sla application
        IP Service Level Agreements
Version: Round Trip Time MIB 2.2.0, Infrastructure Engine-II
Time of last change in whole IP SLAs: 17:13:51.307 UTC Wed Dec 20 2006
Estimated system max number of entries: 72877

Estimated number of configurable operations: 72874
Number of Entries configured  : 3
Number of active Entries      : 0
Number of pending Entries     : 0
Number of inactive Entries    : 3

        Supported Operation Types
```

```
Type of Operation to Perform: dhcp
Type of Operation to Perform: dns
Type of Operation to Perform: echo
Type of Operation to Perform: frameRelay
Type of Operation to Perform: ftp
Type of Operation to Perform: http
Type of Operation to Perform: icmpJitter
Type of Operation to Perform: jitter
Type of Operation to Perform: pathEcho
Type of Operation to Perform: pathJitter
Type of Operation to Perform: rtp
Type of Operation to Perform: slm controller
Type of Operation to Perform: slm frame-relay interface
Type of Operation to Perform: slm frame-relay pvc
Type of Operation to Perform: slm interface
Type of Operation to Perform: tcpConnect
Type of Operation to Perform: udpEcho
Type of Operation to Perform: voip

IP SLAs low memory water mark: 99839841
```

The following example shows how to configure an IP SLA with an operation that monitors the reachability of a NetFlow collector at the http://colfish:8080/nfc/ URL. This operation does not require the IP SLA Responder to be enabled:

```
Router(config)# ip sla 1
Router(config-ip-sla)# http get url http://colfish:8080/nfc/ version 1.1
```

At this point, the operation exists but is not yet enabled, because scheduling is a compulsory task.

```
Router(config)# ip sla schedule 1 start-time now life forever
```

At this point, the operation is active.

The output of **show ip sla configuration 1** displays the entry's status, equivalent to the SNMP RowStatus Textual Convention RowStatus: notInService:

```
Router#show ip sla configuration 1
IP SLA Monitor, Infrastructure Engine-II.
Entry number: 1
Owner:
Tag:
Type of operation to perform: http
Target address: 10.48.71.129
Source address: 0.0.0.0
Target port: 8080
Source port: 0
Operation timeout (milliseconds): 60000
Type Of Service parameters: 0x0
HTTP Operation: get
HTTP Server Version: 1.1
URL: http://colfish:8080/nfc/
Proxy:
Raw String(s):
Cache Control: enable
Operation frequency (seconds): 60
Next Scheduled Start Time: Start Time already passed
Group Scheduled : FALSE
Life (seconds): Forever
```

```
Entry Ageout (seconds): never
Recurring (Starting Everyday): FALSE
Status of entry (SNMP RowStatus): Active
Threshold (milliseconds): 5000
Number of statistic hours kept: 2
Number of statistic distribution buckets kept: 1
Statistic distribution interval (milliseconds): 20
Number of history Lives kept: 0
Number of history Buckets kept: 15
History Filter Type: None
```

From the **show** command, you can clearly see the characteristics. This operation is based on IP SLA infrastructure II, which increases measurement accuracy. The operation is an HTTP get on the URL http://colfish:8080/nfc/, with a default operation frequency of 60 seconds and a default threshold of 5000 ms.

However, the output from **show ip sla statistics 1** displays **Latest operation return code: DNS query error**. At this point, the Domain Name Server (DNS) must be configured on the router:

```
Router(config)# ip name-server 10.10.10.10
Router(config)# ip domain-list cisco.com
Router(config)# ip domain-name cisco.com
```

The **show ip sla statistics 1** output now displays the following:

```
Router # show ip sla statistics 1
Entry number: 1
Modification time: 23:51:04.664 CET Fri Oct 20 2000
Number of Octets Used by this Entry: 2656
Number of operations attempted: 7
Number of operations skipped: 0
Current seconds left in Life: Forever
Operational state of entry: Active
Last time this entry was reset: Never
Connection loss occurred: FALSE
Timeout occurred: FALSE
Over thresholds occurred: FALSE
Latest RTT (milliseconds): 352
Latest operation start time: 23:57:04.909 CET Fri Oct 20 2000
Latest operation return code: OK
Latest DNS RTT: 4
Latest TCP Connection RTT: 4
Latest HTTP time to first byte: 148
Latest HTTP Transaction RTT: 344
Latest HTTP Status: 301
Latest HTTP Message Size: 405
Latest HTTP Entity-Body size: 179
```

The HTTP server response time measurements consist of three types:

- **DNS lookup** is the RTT taken to perform domain name lookup—in this case, 4 ms.

- **TCP Connect** is the RTT taken to perform a TCP connection to the HTTP server—in this case, 4 ms.

- **HTTP transaction time** is the RTT taken to send a request and get a response from the HTTP server—in this case, 344 ms. The operation retrieves only the HTML home page.

Even if this operation does not require NTP, a good network practice is to set the clock accurately so that the operation start time is reported correctly.

Finally, a reaction threshold can be configured. Its objective would be to send a trap in case of connection loss for operation 1. The section "Thresholds and Notifications" explains the technical details as well as the configuration.

Application-Specific Scenario: VoIP

The goal of this example is to monitor a G.729a VOIP call, to the specific 10.48.88.121 destination where the IP SLA Responder is configured (**ip sla responder**):

```
Router(config)# ip sla 1
Router(config-sla-monitorconfig-ip-sla)# type udp-jitter dest-ipaddr 10.48.88.121
dest-port 1648 codec g729a
Router(config-ip-sla-jitter)# frequency 30
Router(config)# ip sla schedule 1 start-time now
```

The default settings of a 32-byte test packet size and an interpacket interval of 20 milliseconds are used in this example:

```
Router# show ip sla configuration 1
IP SLAs, Infrastructure Engine-II
Entry number: 1
Owner:
Tag:
Type of operation to perform: jitter
Target address: 10.48.88.121
Source address: 0.0.0.0
Target port: 1648
Source port: 0
Operation timeout (milliseconds): 5000
Codec Type: g729a
Codec Number Of Packets: 1000
Codec Packet Size: 32
Codec Interval (milliseconds): 20
Advantage Factor: 0
Type Of Service parameters: 0x0
Verify data: No
Vrf Name:
Control Packets: enabled
Operation frequency (seconds): 30
Next Scheduled Start Time: Start Time already passed
Group Scheduled : FALSE
Life (seconds): 3600
Entry Ageout (seconds): never
Recurring (Starting Everyday): FALSE
Status of entry (SNMP RowStatus): Active
Threshold (milliseconds): 5000
Number of statistic hours kept: 2
Number of statistic distribution buckets kept: 1
Statistic distribution interval (milliseconds): 20
Enhanced History:

Router# show ip sla statistics details 1
Entry number: 1
Modification time: 08:57:19.702 CET Mon Jul 11 2005
Number of Octets Used by this Entry: 14896
```

```
Number of operations attempted: 61
Number of operations skipped: 1
Current seconds left in Life: 1759
Operational state of entry: Active
Last time this entry was reset: Never
Connection loss occurred: FALSE
Timeout occurred: FALSE
Over thresholds occurred: FALSE
Latest RTT (milliseconds): 2
Latest operation start time: 09:27:19.709 CET Mon Jul 11 2005
Latest operation return code: OK
Voice Scores:
ICPIF Value: 11 MOS score: 4.06
RTT Values (milliseconds):
NumOfRTT: 992    RTTAvg: 2        RTTMin: 1        RTTMax: 5
RTTSum: 2761     RTTSum2: 8089
Packet Loss Values:
PacketLossSD: 6 PacketLossDS: 2
PacketOutOfSequence: 0  PacketMIA: 0      PacketLateArrival: 0
InternalError: 0         Busies: 0        PacketSkipped: 0
Jitter Values (milliseconds):
MinOfPositivesSD: 1       MaxOfPositivesSD: 2
NumOfPositivesSD: 192    SumOfPositivesSD: 194    Sum2PositivesSD: 198
MinOfNegativesSD: 1       MaxOfNegativesSD: 2
NumOfNegativesSD: 192    SumOfNegativesSD: 194    Sum2NegativesSD: 198
MinOfPositivesDS: 1       MaxOfPositivesDS: 2
NumOfPositivesDS: 233    SumOfPositivesDS: 256    Sum2PositivesDS: 302
MinOfNegativesDS: 1       MaxOfNegativesDS: 2
NumOfNegativesDS: 237    SumOfNegativesDS: 256    Sum2NegativesDS: 294
Jitter Avg: 1    JitterSD Avg: 1 JitterDS Avg: 1
Interarrival jitterout: 0       Interarrival jitterin: 0
One Way Values (milliseconds):
NumOfOW: 992
OWMinSD: 1        OWMaxSD: 3       OWSumSD: 1749    OWSum2SD: 3289
OWMinDS: 0        OWMaxDS: 3       OWSumDS: 1012    OWSum2DS: 1354
OWAvgSD: 1        OWAvgDS: 1
```

The convention in this output is that a term containing SD implies a direction from source to destination, and a term with DS implies the reverse direction. The output of this **show** command might not be intuitive; however, it is verbose. It contains the MOS score 4.06, the ICPIF value 11, the minimum/maximum/average RTT, the packet loss in each direction, the out-of-sequence packets, the Missing In Action packet (packetMIA), a lot of statistical jitter, and one-way values for both directions.

A new command, **show ip sla statistics**, and its variant, **show ip sla statistics detail**, have been introduced in the latest IOS version. The advantage is clear visualization of the most important parameters. That means the minimum/average/maximum values of the round-trip time, one-way delay, jitter, packet loss for both directions, and the MOS and ICPIF scores:

```
Router# show ip sla statistics 1
Round trip time (RTT) Index 1
Latest RTT: 1ms
Latest operation start time: *16:21:32.539 PST Wed Sep 27 2006
Latest operation return code: OK
Over thresholds occurred: FALSE
RTT Values
Number Of RTT: 6253
RTT Min/Avg/Max: 1/1/2 ms
Latency one-way time milliseconds
```

```
Number of one-way Samples: 0
Source to Destination one way Min/Avg/Max: 0/0/0 ms
Destination to Source one way Min/Avg/Max: 0/0/0 ms
Jitter time milliseconds
Number of Jitter Samples: 6253
Source to Destination Jitter Min/Avg/Max: 1/1/1 ms
Destination to Source Jitter Min/Avg/Max: 1/1/1 ms
Packet Loss Values
Loss Source to Destination: 0 Loss Destination to Source: 0
Out Of Sequence: 0 Tail Drop: 0 Packet Late Arrival: 0
Voice Score Values
Calculated Planning Impairment Factor (ICPIF): 0
Mean Opinion Score (MOS): 0
Number of successes: 23
Number of failures: 0
Operation time to live: 3496 sec
```

NOTE   The new **ip sla statistics detail** command displays an extended version of **ip sla statistics**, with statistical information such as sum and square sum of the different metrics.

Finally, note that the information can be retrieved via SNMP with the RTTMON-MIB.

Advanced Features

The following features describe enhanced reporting functionality, such as scheduling, statistics, history collection, working with thresholds, and using enhanced object tracking for automated actions.

Scheduling

You define IP SLA operations using two steps:

Step 1   Configure the explicit test packet parameters, such as packet size, packet interval, destination address, and so on.

Step 2   Define the operational parameters, including start time, lifetime, recurring operations, and so on. An operation can start immediately or start at a certain month, day, and hour. An alternative is to use the **pending** option to set the operation to start later. This is also used when an operation is a reaction (threshold) operation waiting to be triggered.

Normal scheduling of IP SLA operations lets you schedule one operation at a time. If no start time is configured, the operation starts immediately, which is no problem if an operation is defined and activated by an operator using the CLI. The situation changes if multiple operations are defined without a specific start time and the network element reloads. Imagine that you have defined 1000 operations at one device with an immediate start. After a reboot, all operations start immediately. This results in a CPU spike at the device and potentially a sudden burst of IP SLA test traffic in the network. Neither of these effects is beneficial to accurate network measurements.

As a workaround, three IP SLA features were introduced to solve the issue:

- Recurring Function
- Multiple Operation Scheduling
- Random Scheduling

Recurring Function

The Recurring Function allows you to define an operation's exact start time. For example, you could start a DHCP operation at 8 a.m. every day. However, if you have large networks with thousands of IP SLA operations on which to monitor network performance, scheduling each operation individually is time-consuming and inefficient.

The following example tests reachability of the DNS server every day at 7 a.m. When combined with the "trap option" of the threshold reaction feature, the network operators are alerted in case of an issue and have a chance to fix it before the majority of users arrive.

```
Router(config)# ip sla 9
Router(config-ip-sla)# dns dns.cisco.com
Router(config)# ip sla schedule 9 recurring start-time 07:00:00
```

Multiple Operation Scheduling

The Multiple Operation Scheduling feature offers, using a single CLI command or the CISCO-RTTMON-MIB, the option to schedule multiple IP SLA operations to run at evenly distributed times over a specified period. A reboot of the router does not affect the scheduling functionality. The following parameters can be configured for the Multiple Operation Scheduling:

- **Group operation number** defines the group configuration or group schedule number of the IP SLA operation to be scheduled. The IP SLA operations must be configured before they can be scheduled as a group.

- **Operation ID numbers** defines the list of operation IDs to be scheduled in an operation group.

- **Schedule period** defines the amount of time for which the operation group is scheduled.

- **Age out** specifies how long the operation is kept in memory when it is not actively collecting information (the default is indefinitely).

- **Frequency** sets the period of time that passes before the operation group is started again (repeated). The frequency statement on the group schedule rewrites the operation frequency of all operations belonging to the group. Note that if the group frequency is not specified (this is optional), the frequency is assumed to be equal to the "schedule period" parameter.

- **Life** configures the total amount of time for the operation to collect information. The operation can be configured to run indefinitely (the default is 1 hour).

- **Start time** sets the starting time for the operation; this can be immediately or an absolute start time.

The Multiple Operation Scheduling functionality plans the maximum number of possible operations. However, this functionality skips IP SLA operations that are already running or those that are not configured. The total number of operations is calculated based on the number of operations specified in the command, irrespective of the number of operations that are missing or already running. Besides keeping multiple operations from starting at exactly the same time after a reboot, another benefit of the Multiple Operation Scheduling function is the equal distribution interval, which offers more consistent monitoring coverage. To illustrate this scenario, consider configuring 60 operations to start at the same 1-minute interval over a 1-hour period. Each operation tests connectivity to a different remote site and runs for 30 seconds, so it tests the reachability within the network once every hour. If all operations start at the same time, connectivity is tested only during the first 30 seconds of every hour for the whole network. If a network failure occurs after all 60 operations have completed, and the network is restored before the operations are due to start again, this failure is not detected by any of the 60 operations. However, if the 60 operations are distributed equally at 1-minute intervals over a 1-hour period, you test connectivity to one site each minute. This increases the chances of detecting a major network outage, because operations are running continuously, and not all tests are performed at the same time.

NOTE   You cannot use the Multiple Operation Scheduling feature in conjunction with the Recurring Function.

The following example schedules all operations from 1 to 11 to be equally distributed every 120 seconds. This means that each new operation starts 12 seconds after the previous one. The group scheduling is repeated every 10 minutes. Note that if individual operations had a frequency configured, this value is overwritten with the new frequency of 120 seconds.

```
Router(config)# ip sla group schedule 1 1-11 schedule-period 120 frequency 600 start-
time now life forever
Router # show ip sla group schedule 1
Group Entry Number: 1
Probes to be scheduled: 1-11
Total number of probes: 11
```

```
Schedule period: 120
Mode: even
Group operation frequency: 600
Status of entry (SNMP RowStatus): Active
Next Scheduled Start Time: Start Time already passed
Life (seconds): Forever
Entry Ageout (seconds): never
```

Random Scheduling

The Random Scheduling feature offers more randomness in the operation schedule. The Multiple Operation Scheduling feature imposes a frequency for the operations belonging to the group. If by chance this frequency perfectly matches the repetition of particular traffic patterns or network behavior (such as traffic load and queue full), the observed metrics might be biased. With the IP SLAs Random Scheduler feature, you can schedule multiple IP SLAs operations to begin at random intervals uniformly distributed over a specified duration of time and to restart at uniformly distributed random frequencies within a specified frequency range. Therefore, the Random Scheduling improves the statistical metrics for assessing network performance.

The following example schedules all operations from 1 to 11 to be equally distributed on a *first* schedule period of 120 seconds. This means that each new operation starts 12 seconds after the previous one. After the initial schedule, each operation chooses a random interval upon every invocation of the probe, over the interval 540 to 660 seconds (9 to 11 minutes).

```
Router(config)# ip sla group schedule 1 1-11 schedule-period 120 frequency range
540-660 start-time now life forever
Router# show ip sla group schedule 1
Group Entry Number: 1
Probes to be scheduled: 1-11
Total number of probes: 11
Schedule period: 120
Mode: random
Group operation frequency: 540-660
Status of entry (SNMP RowStatus): Active
Next Scheduled Start Time: Start Time already passed
Life (seconds): Forever
Entry Ageout (seconds): never
```

Distribution of Statistics

IP SLA provides a variety of operations that can meter very specific performance monitoring details. Although it is useful to have a large number of detailed metrics, this also leads to the challenge of storing the data records at the device. Storing every result of each operation would require large amounts of memory and additional network bandwidth for exporting them. Currently, operations results are stored at the device and retrieved via a pull model, which can be CLI (Telnet or scripts) or SNMP. An important concept to reduce memory consumption is to aggregate the collected performance metrics. Instead of keeping results of all test packets, only those values used for statistical performance analysis are stored. Consider the response time results: from an SLA perspective, you are probably interested in the minimum and maximum value and a distribution curve. In addition, you want to collect the sum of completion times to calculate the mean value and the sum of the squares of completion times to calculate the standard deviation. Ideally, the percentile collection would be a desirable output; however, IP SLA does not yet provide this.

The distribution of statistics feature offers a statistical distribution of response times, which can be thought of as a set of counters that hold the results of test packets. The operator defines a number of response time buckets, IP SLA aggregates the individual results into these buckets, and the result is a response-time distribution curve. Each bucket holds a counter for the number of completed operations that fall into that specific time interval. For example, if the distribution interval is 20 ms and the number of buckets is three, the following buckets are defined:

- Bucket A = < 20 ms
- Bucket B = 20 to 40 ms
- Bucket C = >40 ms

Assuming that five operations are performed with response times of 10 ms, 15 ms, 30 ms, 40 ms, and 80 ms, the counters are incremented as follows: bucket A = 2 (10 and 15 ms), bucket B = 2 (30 and 40 ms), and bucket C = 1 (80 ms).

NOTE   Statistics distribution collection is supported for the ICMP Echo, ICMP PathEcho, UDP Echo, VoIP UDP Jitter, TCP Connect, DNS, and DLSW+ operations. By default, the statistics distribution is kept for the last 2 hours. Note that the history collection feature, described in the next section, lets you change this default value.

Several statistics can be collected:

- Number of statistic distribution buckets sets the number of buckets or statistical distributions kept during the operation's lifetime. Size is the number of buckets that contain data counts for their intervals. This applies to the following operations: ICMP Echo and PathEcho, UDP Echo, TCP Connect, DNS, and DLSw+.

- Statistical distribution interval sets the time interval for each statistical distribution. This applies to the following operations: ICMP Echo and PathEcho, UDP Echo, TCP Connect, DNS, and DLSw+.

- Number of statistic paths collects statistical distributions for multiple paths between source and destination. The size parameter specifies the number of paths for which statistical distribution buckets are maintained per hour for each operation. This applies to the ICMP PathEcho operation only.

Table 11-2 illustrates the assignment of multiple samples into the defined buckets (in this case, buckets are defined in increments of 20 milliseconds) and the resulting total number of items per bucket.

Table 11-2   *IP SLA Statistics Distribution*

Response Time	Response Time Buckets						
	0–20	>20 to 40	>40 to 60	>60 to 80	>80 to 100	>100 to 120	>120
63				✓			
47			✓				
19	✓						
181							✓
96					✓		
29		✓					
101						✓	
55			✓				
91					✓		
103						✓	
66				✓			
82					✓		
41			✓				
Number of Entries	1	1	3	2	3	2	1

The following example displays the configuration of a udpEcho operation type, for which the distribution of statistics feature is enabled. Similar to Table 11-2, the distribution contains seven buckets, and the distribution interval is kept to its default value of 20 ms.

```
Router(config)# ip sla 1
Router(config-ip-sla)# udp-echo 10.48.71.7 65000 source-ip 10.48.71.24
Router(config-ip-sla-udp)# distributions-of-statistics-kept 7
Router(config)# ip sla schedule 1 life forever start-time now
Router# show ip sla statistics aggregated detail
        Captured Statistics
Entry    = Entry number
StartT   = Start time of entry (hundredths of seconds)
Pth      = Path index
Hop      = Hop in path index
Dst      = Time distribution index
Comps    = Operations completed
OvrTh    = Operations completed over thresholds
SumCmp   = Sum of RTT (milliseconds)
SumCmp2L = Sum of RTT squared low 32 bits (milliseconds)
SumCmp2H = Sum of RTT squared high 32 bits (milliseconds)
TMax     = RTT maximum (milliseconds)
TMin     = RTT minimum (milliseconds)

Entry StartT   Pth Hop Dst Comps OvrTh SumCmp SumCmp2L SumCmp2H TMax TMin
1     4951858  1   1   1   28    0     82     382      0        11   1
```

1	4951858	1	1	2	0	0	0	0	0	0	0
1	4951858	1	1	3	0	0	0	0	0	0	0
1	4951858	1	1	4	0	0	0	0	0	0	0
1	4951858	1	1	5	0	0	0	0	0	0	0
1	4951858	1	1	6	0	0	0	0	0	0	0
1	4951858	1	1	7	0	0	0	0	0	0	0

From the **show ip sla statistics aggregated detail** output, the conclusion is that the first bucket (from 0 to 20 ms) contains all the test-packet results. Note that **Dst**, referenced by the **Time distribution index**, basically refers to the bucket number.

History Collection

In addition to gathering aggregated statistics, IP SLA can store the exact results from previous operations. This is useful for troubleshooting purposes to identify when a performance degradation or network outage occurred. With history collection enabled, IP SLA stores data samples for a given operation; these samples are called history data and are stored in buckets. Each bucket contains one or more history entries from the operation. By default, history data is not collected. Instead, the result of every operation is added to the aggregated statistics buckets, as described in the section "Distribution of Statistics."

Related to history is the concept of lives. A life is defined as an operation's lifetime, and entries related to the life are stored. A maximum number of buckets can be configured for each life. When the number of buckets reaches the limit, no further history for this life is stored. The valid range is from 1 to 100, with a default of 100 buckets. Each time IP SLA starts or restarts an operation, a new bucket is created until either the number of history buckets matches the maximum size or the operation's lifetime expires. History buckets wrap, which means that the oldest entry is overwritten by the newest entry.

History collection is supported by the following operations: ICMP Echo, ICMP PathEcho, UDP Echo, TCP Connect, DNS, and DLSW+. In case of UDP PathEcho, an entry is created for each hop along the path that the operation takes to reach its destination. History collection is not supported for HTTP and UDP Jitter because of the large data volume required for these operations.

Starting with IOS 12.2(11)T, history enhancements were added to IP SLA, where the operator can specify the compilation interval and number of groups of data to be collected and stored in buckets. The purpose of the history feature is to compare current network performance with a configurable compilation interval. For example, if you configure 96 buckets, each containing 15 minutes (900 seconds) of aggregated measurements, you can store 24 hours of performance information: 24 hours * (60/15 minutes) = 96:

```
Router(config)# ip sla 1
Router(config-ip-sla)# udp-echo 10.48.71.7 65000 source-ip 10.48.71.24
Router(config-ip-sla-udp)# history enhanced interval 900 buckets 96
```

Enhanced history is supported for TCP Connect, UDP Jitter, Frame Relay, and ATM operations only. In the case of Frame Relay and ATM, the default bucket settings are 15 minutes with a total of 100 buckets. The operator cannot modify these defaults. The IP SLA Jitter operation does not support history of statistics because of the large amount of collected data. Enhanced history statistics do not include voice scores.

NOTE   Collecting history increases memory usage. Collect history only for troubleshooting and analysis purposes. For measuring performance metrics, use the statistics collection function.

A *proposal* to overcome the memory limitations for both statistics and history collection is to use the IPFIX protocol as an export mechanism. This would add a push model to IP SLA, where the device sends ("pushes") the data records to a collection server. This could increase the level of collected details, especially for history collection, and could offer IP SLA a similar flexibility of exporting functions as NetFlow has today. Right now, IP SLA supports only the pull model, in which data is stored locally and retrieved from an NMS system.

Thresholds and Notifications

IP SLA supports threshold monitoring to react to certain network conditions; this includes the capability to trigger SNMP notifications based on defined thresholds. For example, if IP SLA measures too much jitter on a connection, it can generate a notification to a network management system. This allows proactive network monitoring instead of constantly polling the MIB. Especially when gathering the IP SLA performance statistics primarily for fault management purposes, threshold monitoring can decrease the time to identify violation of SLA parameters and at the same time reduce SNMP polling significantly. Threshold conditions can define an upper and lower threshold value as a hysteresis function, so a notification is sent only once when crossing the threshold. Figure 11-7 shows the result of an RTT operation with upper (100-ms) and lower (50-ms) thresholds defined and shows when events are generated.

Figure 11-7 *IP SLA Hysteresis Function*

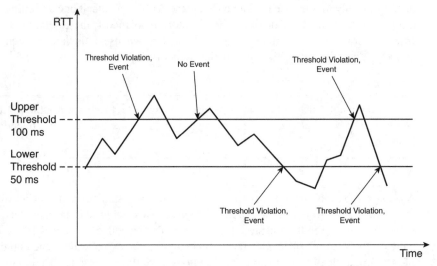

In addition to sending a notification, a threshold violation can activate another IP SLA operation for further analysis. For example, an additional operation can be initiated for troubleshooting. An example would be to run a basic ICMP Echo operation to measure RTT every 5 minutes and, in case of a threshold violation, to start additional ICMP Path Jitter operations for troubleshooting purposes. If the measured value drops below the defined threshold, the additional operation is stopped. You can configure multiple thresholds for the same operation. For example, you could configure a VoIP UDP Jitter operation and define a one-way delay threshold, and additionally configure a MOS threshold for the same operation.

IP SLA reactions are defined in the following sequence:

Step 1 Configure the monitored elements (connection loss, timeout, RTT, jitter, packet loss, MOS). Thresholds can be defined for the following parameters:

— connectionLoss: Connection loss

— ICPIF: Impairment/Calculated Planning Impairment Factor

— jitterAvg: Jitter average in both directions

— jitterDSAvg: Jitter average from destination to source

— jitterSDAvg: Jitter average from source to destination

— maxOfNegativeDS: Maximum negative jitter from destination to source

- maxOfNegativeSD: Maximum negative jitter from source to destination

- maxOfPositiveDS: Maximum positive jitter from destination to source

- maxOfPositiveSD: Maximum positive jitter from source to destination

- MOS: MOS score

- packetLateArrival: Packets arriving late

- packetLossDS: Packet loss from destination to source

- packetLossSD: Packet loss from source to destination

- packetMIA: Missing in action

- packetOutOfSequence: Packets arriving out of sequence

- RTT: Round-trip time

- timeout: Timeout

- verifyError: Verify error

Step 2   Configure the threshold violation types (immediate, consecutive, x of y, averaged).

Step 3   Specify the reaction event (none, trap, trigger, trap and trigger).

Threshold violation defines the trigger or combination of events that activate an action. IP SLA supports the following triggers:

- **Immediate** triggers an event immediately when the value for a reaction type (such as response time) exceeds the upper threshold value or falls below the lower threshold value, or when a timeout, connection loss, or verify error event occurs.

- **Consecutive** generates an event after a violation takes place a number (n) of times consecutively. For example, this type would be used to configure an action to occur after a timeout is repeated three times, or when the RTT exceeds the upper threshold value n times. The default value is $n = 5$.

- **x of y** triggers an event after a number (x) of violations within another number (y) of operations. The default value for x and y is 5. Example: generate an event if the jitter exceeds 30 ms for 10 (x) times during 100 (y) UDP Jitter operations.

- **Average** triggers an event when the averaged totals of a value for a number (n) of operations exceeds the specified upper threshold value or falls below the lower threshold value. This function avoids alarming for peak values, because only the average value of a number of operations is monitored. The default value for n is 5.

The reaction event specifies the action type to be taken when a threshold is breached. Four options exist:

- **None**—No action is taken.
- **Trap only**—Sends an SNMP trap when the specified violation type occurs.
- **Trigger only**—Transits one or more predefined operations from pending" to "active" when the violation conditions are met. Each activated operation continues until its life expires. A triggered operation must finish its life before it can be triggered again.
- **Trap and trigger**—Triggers an SNMP trap and starts another IP SLA operation.

In addition to generating SNMP traps (with the rttMonNotification notification), IP SLA can generate system logging (Syslog) messages when the reaction threshold is crossed for criteria such as *packet loss (unidirectional), jitter (unidirectional),* and *MOS*. These logging messages can then be forwarded to the NMS as Syslog messages or SNMP notifications.

The threshold and notifications concept was enhanced even further with Enhanced Object Tracking for IP SLA, which is described in the next section.

The following example configures a jitter operation for which a trap is fired immediately after the maximum negative delay from source to destination crosses the maximum value of 10 ms and the minimum value of 2 ms:

```
Router(config)# ip sla 2
Router(config-ip-sla)# jitter 10.48.71.7 430
Router(config)# ip sla reaction-configuration 2 react maxOfNegativeDS threshold-
value 10 2 threshold-type immediate action-type trapOnly
Router(config)# snmp-server enable traps rtr
Router# show ip sla reaction-configuration
Entry number: 2
Index: 1
Reaction: maxOfNegativeDS
Threshold Type: Immediate
Rising: 10
Falling: 2
Threshold CountX: 5
Threshold CountY: 5
Action Type: Trap only
```

The following example measures the RTT toward the destination 10.10.10.10 with an ICMP Echo message. Whenever three consecutive results exceed the value of 100 ms, not only is a trap fired, but operation number 6 is started. Operation 6 measures the RTT for each hop of the path, allowing faster troubleshooting of the bottleneck.

```
Router(config)# ip sla 5
Router(config-ip-sla)# icmp-echo 10.10.10.10
Router(config)# ip sla reaction-configuration 5 react rtt threshold-value 100 20
threshold-type consecutive action-type trapAndTrigger
Router(config)# ip sla reaction-trigger 5 6
Router(config)# ip sla 6
Router(config-ip-sla)# path-echo 10.10.10.10
Router(config)#snmp-server enable traps rtr
Router# show ip sla reaction-configuration 5
Entry number: 5
Index: 1
Reaction: rtt
```

```
Threshold Type: Consecutive
Rising (milliseconds): 100
Falling (milliseconds): 20
Threshold CountX: 5
Threshold CountY: 5
Action Type: Trap and trigger
Router#show ip sla reaction-trigger 5
Entry number: 5
Target Entry Number: 6
Status of Entry (SNMP RowStatus): active
Operational State: pending
```

Enhanced Object Tracking for IP SLA

Enhanced object tracking for IP SLA is a new feature introduced in Cisco IOS Software Releases 12.3(4)T and 12.2(25)S. It creates a link between performance monitoring and routing protocols, directly at the network element. In the past, the only relationship between the IP SLA monitoring results and routing decisions in the network existed at the NMS application level. If a certain network connection did not perform according to the SLA definitions, a performance management application could have modified a router's forwarding table. Because this is a complex approach, it was not widely deployed. Enhanced Object Tracking (sometimes called EOT) solves this issue right at the network element. It allows the tracking of state and reachability of IP SLA operations and allows the insertion or deletion of static routes, depending on the state of the tracked object.

Before Enhanced Object Tracking was introduced, only HSRP had a simple tracking mechanism that allowed tracking the interface state. If the interface's line-protocol state went down, the router's HSRP priority was reduced, allowing another HSRP router with a higher priority to become active. Although this mechanism is effective for link-down situations, it cannot be used in conjunction with performance monitoring. The Enhanced Object Tracking feature overcomes this limitation by providing complete separation between the tracked objects and the initiated action when an object state changes. Although it offers more functionality than just IP SLA support, because of this book's focus, the other tracking features are not described here. The results of IP SLA operations can be used to change routing decisions for so-called "first-hop routing protocols" (FHRP), such as Hot Standby Router Protocol (HSRP), Virtual Router Redundancy Protocol (VRRP), and Gateway Load-Balancing Protocol (GLBP). These protocols can register and track objects with the tracking service, and each can take different actions when the state of an object changes. A unique number, specified by using the tracking command-line interface in IOS, identifies each tracked object. Client processes use this number to track a specific object. The tracking service periodically polls the objects and notes any value changes; these changes are communicated to interested clients, either immediately or after a specified delay. The object values are reported as either up or down. Every IP SLA operation maintains an operation return-code value, which is interpreted by the tracking process. Examples of return codes are OK, OverThreshold, and specific operation values. Two aspects of an IP SLA operation can be state and reachability, where the difference between the two relates to the OverThreshold return code. Table 11-3 shows the state and reachability aspects of IP SLA operations that can be tracked.

Table 11-3 *IP SLA Enhanced Tracking Operations*

Tracking	Return Code	Tracking State
State	OK	Up
	Not OK (everything else)	Down
Reachability	OK, OverThreshold	Up
	Not OK (everything else)	Down

Figure 11-8 illustrates using Enhanced Object Tracking in a network.

Figure 11-8 *IP SLA Enhanced Object Tracking*

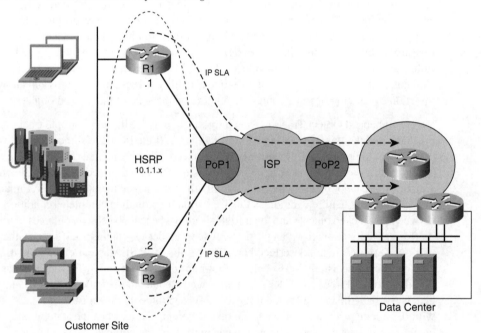

The customer site on the left is connected to the ISP. For redundancy reasons, two routers are grouped with HSRP. An SLA is defined for connectivity, delay, and jitter between the customer site and the data server site. In this setup, a hardware or link failure at R1 would result in a switchover to R2 and vice versa; this is the basic HSRP function. In addition, two IP SLA operations are defined to measure the SLA in conjunction with Enhanced Object Tracking. If one IP SLA operation returns a threshold violation, Enhanced Object Tracking influences the local HSRP priority, which in turn switches the traffic via the alternate router.

In other words, the result of the IP SLA operation influences the HSRP process to select the exit router with the well-performing link toward the data center. This is an interesting fault management scenario as well. If one link is disabled (for connectivity or performance reasons), a notification should be sent to the central fault management application, and the operator can start the troubleshooting process immediately. This avoids outages and increases a service's uptime.

In the following example, EOT object 100 tracks the result of operation 1, which runs an icmp-echo to the server address 10.10.10.100. If operation 1 changes its status, which indicates that reachability to the data center is lost, HSRP on R1 decrements its priority by 10. As a consequence, R2 is chosen as the default gateway for the customer site.

```
R1(config)# ip sla 1
R1(config-ip-sla)# icmp-echo 10.10.10.100
R1(config)# ip sla schedule 1 start-time now life forever
R1(config)# track 100 rtr 1 state
R1(config)# interface FastEthernet0/0
R1(config-if)# standby 1 ip 10.10.10.10
R1(config-if)# standby 1 priority 105
R1(config-if)# standby 1 preempt
R1(config-if)# standby 1 track 100 decrement 10
```

Implementation Considerations

The next sections provide an overview of IP SLA features related to various Cisco IOS versions and also address the impact of implementing IP SLA operations. The performance aspect is discussed, as well as measurement accuracy and security considerations.

Supported Devices and IOS Versions

As illustrated in this chapter, IP SLA offers a variety of features that are related to the different operations, as well as several additional functions, such as Multiple Operation Scheduling and VRF support. Some of these features, such as MPLS, ATM, and Frame Relay, support platform dependencies, and others have Cisco IOS version dependencies. Listing all the different features along with the IOS releases and platforms would take up a lot of space, would offer limited value, and would risk listing obsolete information. For the latest IP SLA information, go to http://www.cisco.com/go/ipsla. Specifically, the Cisco Feature Navigator tool lists IP SLA features for each platform and IOS version. Table 11-4 offers an overview of the IP SLA operations and IOS versions.

Table 11-4   *IP SLA Operations and IOS Versions*

Feature/ Release	11.2	12.0(3)T	12.0(5)T 12.0(8)S	12.1(1)T 12.2	12.2(2)T	12.2(11)T (Engine II)	12.3(4)T	12.3(11)T	12.4 IP Base Feature Set*	12.4 Advanced Feature Set
Responder	✓	✓	✓	✓	✓	✓	✓	✓	✓	✓
ICMP Echo	✓	✓	✓	✓	✓	✓	✓	✓	✓	✓
ICMP Path Echo	✓	✓	✓	✓	✓	✓	✓	✓		✓
UDP Echo		✓	✓	✓	✓	✓	✓	✓		✓
TCP Connect		✓	✓	✓	✓	✓	✓	✓		✓
UDP Jitter			✓	✓	✓	✓	✓	✓		✓
DHCP			✓	✓	✓	✓	✓	✓		✓
DNS			✓	✓	✓	✓	✓	✓		✓
HTTP			✓	✓	✓	✓	✓	✓		✓
DLSw+			✓	✓	✓	✓	✓	✓		✓
UDP Jitter (with one-way delay)				✓	✓	✓	✓	✓		✓
FTP Get			✓	✓	✓	✓	✓	✓		✓
MPLS/VPN-Aware					✓	✓	✓	✓		✓
Frame Relay					✓	✓	✓	✓		✓
ICMP Path Jitter					✓	✓	✓	✓		✓
ATM					✓	✓	✓	✓		✓
VoIP UDP Jitter (with MOS and ICPIF score)							✓	✓		✓
VoIP Call Setup (Post-Dial Delay) Monitoring								✓		✓
VoIP Gatekeeper Registration Delay Monitoring Operation								✓		✓

*Starting with IOS Release 12.4, there is a split of IP SLA functions in the different feature sets. Starting with 12.4(2)T, the IOS IP Base image has only the Responder and ICMP Echo operation. An Advanced IOS feature set is required for the sender capabilities. In IOS 12.4(7) and 12.2(25)SEE, the base package contains only the Responder and no sender functionality. The sender function requires any of the Advanced IOS feature sets. This model will be used in 12.5 and subsequent releases.

Performance Impact

As with any other device instrumentation feature implemented at the network element, IP SLA's performance impact is an important aspect. Routers and switches were not primarily designed for network monitoring tasks; hence, the impact of network management features needs to be analyzed. IP SLA stores each operation's results locally in a hierarchical structure, so the processing time increases with the number of configured operations. The IP SLA scheduling function can help reduce the CPU impact, because a large number of operations starting at the same time can lead to CPU utilization spikes. For absolute figures, you need to distinguish between IP SLA Engine I and Engine II implementation, because there is a significant difference from a performance perspective. Engine II is implemented at IOS 12.2(11)T and later; all previous versions have implemented Engine I. The following new features were added in Engine II:

- 20 to 50 percent reduction in memory consumption per operation.

- Backward compatibility. Any operation supported by Engine I can be achieved by Engine II.

Table 11-5 illustrates the CPU impact. Table 11-6 shows the memory consumption on a Cisco 7200VXR NPE225.

Table 11-5   *IP SLA CPU Impact (Engines I and II)*

Number of Operations per Second	Number of Operations per Minute	Engine I IOS 12.2(8)T5 500 Active Jitter Probes	Engine II IOS 12.3(3) 2000 Active Jitter Probes
4	240	1 percent	4 percent
20	1200	1 percent	3 percent
40	2400	15 percent	7 percent
60	3600	35 percent	11 percent

Table 11-6   *IP SLA Memory Consumption (Engines I and II)*

Operation	Engine I IOS 12.2(8)T5	Engine II IOS 12.3(3)
UDP Jitter	< 24 KB	< 12 KB
UDP Echo	< 19 KB	< 3.5 KB
ICMP Echo	< 17 KB	< 3.2 KB

Figure 11-9 illustrates the relationship between CPU load (in %) and the total number of jitter operations per second. The three lines represent 500, 1000, and 2000 active operations. The test was performed on a Cisco 7200VXR/NPE-225 with IOS 12.2(8)T5. In the test, the additional UDP Jitter operations are activated sequentially, and each operation sends ten 64-byte packets, each with 20-ms spacing.

Figure 11-9   *IP SLA Responder Communication*

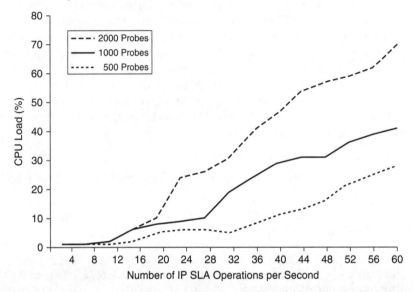

Accuracy

Because IP SLA is used for SLA validation, accuracy is a significant attribute, because it can have an immediate monetary effect. Most SLAs have a penalty or remedy defined, so it is important for both the service provider and the customer to have accurate measurement functions in place. IP SLA is an embedded feature in the network element, so it "competes" with other processes for system resources, such as CPU, memory, queuing, packet forwarding, ACLs, and more.

A significant factor for IP SLA accuracy is the device CPU utilization; the higher it is, the lower the accuracy becomes, if no IP SLA Responder is used. Using the IP SLA Responder has a major impact as well. Tests revealed interesting results when comparing an ICMP Echo operation (without the IP SLA Responder) and a UDP Echo Probe (with the IP SLA Responder) under two different conditions. In the first scenario, the target device's CPU utilization was low; in the second scenario, CPU utilization was 90 percent on average. In the test setup, two routers were connected back-to-back, and the destination router received traffic from other interfaces, so the link between source and destination device remained unchanged for the two test conditions. The results were as follows:

- ICMP Echo operation

  — RTT with unloaded target device was 15 ms.

  — RTT with target device CPU utilization of 90 percent was 59 ms.

Note that the receiver spends excessive CPU time on processing the ICMP Echo Request and generating the ICMP Echo Reply. Because the ICMP Echo operation does not include time stamps at the Responder, the target device's processing time cannot be subtracted from the total response time.

- UDP Echo operation
    — RTT with unloaded receiver was 15 ms.
    — RTT with target device CPU utilization of 90 percent was 15.3 ms.

Because the IP SLA Responder applies time stamps, the processing delay is subtracted in the calculation of the results.

In a separate setup, the IP SLA Responder was loaded with a CPU-intensive interrupt load, such as packet forwarding on centralized platforms. In this case, IP SLA time-stamping routines compete with the forwarded traffic that is processed at the interrupt level; this has a negative effect on the accuracy. The RTT with an unloaded target device was 100 ms, and the RTT with 90 percent CPU utilization at the target device, loaded by forwarded traffic, was 110 ms.

TIP   For RTT accuracy, always use the UDP Echo or UDP Jitter operation in conjunction with the IP SLA Responder. In this case, processing time on the target router is subtracted, and the results are more accurate, regardless of the sender and receiver CPU utilization.

IP SLA results may be inaccurate with an IP SLA Responder on a router loaded with heavy forwarding traffic, because interrupt level code (such as interface traffic) always gets precedence over normal code (in this case, IP SLA). The IP SLA results have good accuracy if the router's forwarding CPU load is below 30 percent. If the router's forwarding CPU load is above 30 percent, the proposed solution is to use a dedicated, nonforwarding router (also called a shadow router) for the source and/or target device.

The process load has a negligible effect on UDP operations with the IP SLA Responder; it can be neglected if the CPU load is below 60 percent. The results become less accurate when the target device CPU load reaches or exceeds the 60 percent utilization due to extensive forwarding traffic. If the router process load exceeds 60 percent, the proposed solution is to use a shadow router.

On distributed platforms, such as the Cisco 7500, 10000, and 12000, another detail needs to be considered. These platforms have various components such as the route processor (RP) and line cards (LC) where each component has its own clock. IP SLA applies transmit (sending) time stamps at the RP, and the receiving time stamps are applied by the LC. This could create inaccurate results on platforms if the system clocks on the RP and LC are not synchronized.

IP SLA granularity was in the range of submilliseconds until accuracy enhancements added the capability to increase the granularity to the microsecond level. In addition, you can specify the packet priority of an IP SLA operation, set the NTP clock synchronization offset tolerance, and monitor the NTP clock synchronization status of an active IP SLA operation. These features were introduced in IOS 12.3(14)T and are currently supported by UDP jitter operations only; codec types are not supported.

To have more details about the accuracy of IP SLA operations and to provide guidance to operators about which operations are best suited for certain requirements, Cisco funded a research project (IP SLA URP).

This project assessed the level of accuracy feasible with active end-to-end measurements of traffic. Details included traffic QoS, delay, delay variation, and packet loss. Because active probing does not assess the quality of all the customer's traffic, the overall traffic quality was assessed with a certain confidence, close to 100 percent. The challenge was to find a suitable trade-off between packet probing overhead, the desired confidence level, and the results' accuracy.

The outcome of the study was encouraging. It proved that accurate statistical assessment of traffic is possible with active probing if test traffic does not receive special treatment and if enough probe packets are used per measurement interval. The confidence interval is the most relevant factor. For example, starting from a confidence of 99 percent, you can approximate that the increase in needed probe packets is roughly 80 percent for each additional 9 percent of confidence.

Security Considerations

Two main aspects are relevant to IP SLA security considerations:

- Exposure or disclosure of measured parameters and measurement components
- Attacks against the Responder

The exposure of measured parameters and measurement components means that an operator should ensure that the measurement design and metrics are not published. Observation of IP SLA data might provide an attacker with information about the paths in the network and communication endpoints. If a hacker knows where measurement is applied in the network and what metrics are measured, he or she can launch an attack against the network elements. Alternatively, users could plan to forge traffic with specific patterns or burst characteristics to fake the SLA measurements, which can be considered fraud.

A completely different attack scenario would be sending measurement requests to a Responder with a victim's spoofed source address, with the goal that the Responder then "attacks" the victim. The difference compared to the scenarios just mentioned is that this is an attack against a third party, not against the Responder.

Dealing with IP SLA Responder attacks is easier compared to keeping the infrastructure secret. The IP SLA Responder must keep a port open for control messages (UDP port 1967); therefore, it can be detected with a port scanner tool. However, the router can identify the port scanning and generates an **RTR responder: bad format** message when the **debug ip sla error** is enabled.

Unauthorized communication with the Responder can be addressed by using the MD5 option, in which the communication between the IP SLA source and the Responder is authenticated. This means that requests are accepted only from authenticated senders and replayed messages are trashed by the Responder. MD5 authentication is defined in RFC 1321. It produces a 128-bit message digest ("fingerprint") as a digital signature. Note that MD5 only authenticates the sender; it does not encrypt the traffic! Encrypting management traffic between the NMS server and the network element is considered a best practice, and not specific to IP SLA, so it is not covered in detail here.

On top of MD5 authentication and packet encryption, you can configure a generic access control list (ACL) to restrict access to the IP SLA source and destination device and only allow the NMS system to configure and retrieve data. Applying an ACL to the Responder's UDP port (1967) can restrict the access to certain IP addresses. This is also part of general security design and is not addressed here.

IP SLA Deployment

When deploying IP SLA, it is suggested that you follow these five steps:

Step 1   Identify SLA metrics (as described in the section "Measured Metrics: What to Measure").

Step 2   Select the appropriate IP SLA types (see the section "Operation Types" for details).

Step 3   Define the operational parameters (see the section "Operations Parameters" for details).

Step 4   Select where to place the IP SLA source and destination in the network (see the section "IP SLA Architecture and Best Practices" for details).

Step 5   Choose an application to configure operations and retrieve and represent the IP SLA results (see the section "NMS Applications").

The following sections describe a proposed architecture for placing IP SLA source and destination devices, setting up operations, composing SLAs, and selecting NMS applications.

IP SLA Architecture and Best Practices

When choosing the best places for the IP SLA operations, you can choose between a full-mesh and partial-mesh design. Full mesh means that you set up an operation between all possible end nodes. This is the most accurate approach and is representative from an end-user perspective. Unfortunately, it does not scale well in large networks, because the number of operations is proportional to the square of the number of nodes. For example, a very small network with five nodes requires ten operations. For 100 nodes, 4950 operations are required. For 5000 nodes, 12,497,500 operations are needed to perform a full measurement.

The alternative to a full mesh is a partial mesh. First you identify the critical network paths and apply full-mesh measurement on only those links. Examples could be the connections from branch offices to headquarters or the core devices in your MPLS network. This approach dramatically reduces the number of operations and still provides accurate performance monitoring results. Figures 11-10 and 11-11 present two design scenarios. The first one is a partial mesh with hierarchical polling, and the second one shows central polling of the core links. Note that these approaches can be combined.

For the hierarchical setup shown in Figure 11-10, full-mesh measurement is applied in the core, and each PoP or branch access area applies the local measurement for the branch office (in the case of an Enterprise network) or the customer site (in the case of an ISP). The SLA metrics for this partial-mesh design are composed, which means that the overall metrics, such as delay or packet loss, are compiled as the sum of multiple submetrics. The total delay between site 1 and site 2 is the sum of the delay values between the source and the destination: $t_{delay1} + t_{delay2} + t_{delay3}$. This approach is very flexible, because the creation of new SLAs and the addition of new sites can be easily integrated into the existing calculation. However, the results are less accurate, because each measurement carries its own error tolerance, which is typically ±1 ms per measurement. Although the composite approach works well for metrics such as delay, packet loss, and packet sequencing, it does not apply to jitter measurements. This has multiple reasons. For example, jitter has positive and negative values, which cannot just be summed up. In the case of composed metrics, jitter is the exception where full measurement is required.

NOTE   Composite metrics cannot be applied to jitter measurements!

The magnified view of PoP1 in Figure 11-10 illustrates the use of a shadow router, which is a dedicated router for network management purposes.

Figure 11-10   *Hierarchical IP SLA Design*

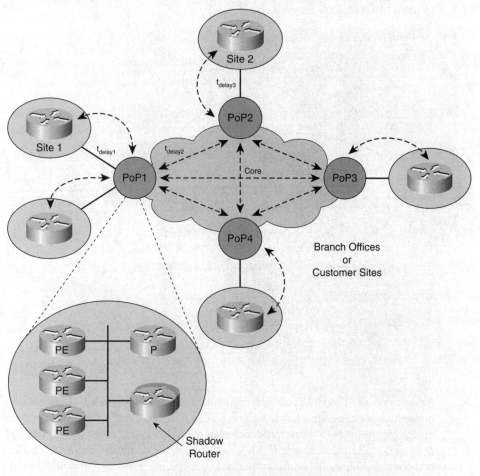

In this case, the shadow router is used for IP SLA monitoring, and all operations and the IP SLA Responder are defined on this device. Using a shadow router offers a number of benefits, such as increased accuracy, because no forwarding traffic competes with the monitoring tasks at the device. In addition, you can run the latest Cisco IOS versions on the shadow router and update them whenever Cisco offers new functions in IOS. This is not a recommended approach for the core network nodes, where stability is more important than new features. Shadow routers can be connected via different technologies, such as MPLS VRF, tunnels, and 802.1q. All core operations in Figure 11-10 are defined between the shadow routers, which monitor the locally connected sites.

The alternative to a hierarchical design with composite metrics is the central IP SLA design, in which a central dedicated router applies the monitoring to the key sites. Figure 11-11 shows a potential setup, in which two shadow routers at the central Network Operations Center (NOC) monitor the network.

Figure 11-11 *Central IP SLA Design*

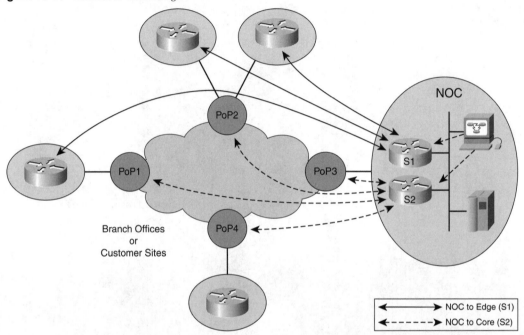

Shadow router S1 monitors all core components, and shadow router S2 monitors connectivity to the edge sites. Even though one shadow router could probably handle all operations, this is not a recommended design, because it introduces a single point of failure. If S1 or S2 fails, at least some IP SLA data is gathered to monitor the network's key components. You should consider two additional points. First, the proposed design monitors only the connectivity between the NOC and the core and remote sites. There might be network outages that are not identified, and the collected IP SLA data may not represent customer performance data. In addition, attention should be given to the scheduling of the operations. Although the IP SLA Multiple Operation Scheduling feature can help distribute the operations equally on one device, only the operator or the NMS application can ensure equal scheduling across the two shadow routers.

An important design aspect is having a single time in the network (as opposed to each network element having its own time). This is useful for accounting and performance management, and it applies to fault and security management as well. Although only the one-way IP SLA measurements mandate using NTP, current best practices suggest implementing the Network Time Protocol (NTP) consistently across the network. NTP is defined in RFC 1305. It is used to synchronize system clocks on network devices with a reference time source. NTP uses the concept of a stratum, which describes the "logical distance" between a client and the master clock, where one stratum is added for each NTP component between the client and the time source. A stratum 1 time server typically has a radio or atomic clock directly attached, a stratum 2 time server receives its time via NTP from a stratum 1 time server, and so on. UTC is the reference time zone for NTP, and each device translates UTC into its local time zone. NTP has a resolution of less than a nanosecond and offers fault-tolerant features. For example, when a network connection is temporarily unavailable, it uses previous measurement polls to estimate the current time and offset. Although stratum 0 NTP sources are very expensive, stratum 1 devices such as GPS appliances are less expensive. The cheapest approach is to synchronize with public NTP sources from the Internet. Which NTP source you select mainly depends on your accuracy requirements. Another source of clock synchronization is the Global Positioning System (GPS), which is more accurate. However, GPS is more expensive than NTP.

NMS Applications

IP SLA gathers performance data and thus offers valuable input for performance management applications. A number of network management applications from partners such as Agilent, CA/Concord, Crannog, HP, IBM/ Micromuse, Infovista, MRTG, and others support Cisco IP SLA. The CiscoWorks Internet Performance Monitor (IPM), Cisco IP Solution Center (ISC), and Cisco InfoCenter (CIC) also leverage IP SLA. Table 11-7 summarizes the various types of IP SLA operations and assigns them to key applications. It also describes what each operation measures and for what purpose the operation can be used.

Table 11-7 *IP SLA Operations Summary*

IP SLA Operation	What It Measures	Key Applications	Comment
ICMP Echo	Measures round-trip delay for the full path	Troubleshooting, connectivity measurement	—
ICMP Path Echo	Measures round-trip delay and hop-by-hop round-trip delay	Connectivity measurement, identify bottlenecks in the path	—
ICMP Path Jitter	Measures round-trip delay, hop-by-hop jitter, packet loss, and delay measurement	Troubleshooting, hop-by-hop analysis	—
UDP Echo	Measures round-trip delay of UDP traffic	Accurate response-time measurement for UDP traffic	—

continues

Table 11-7   *IP SLA Operations Summary (Continued)*

IP SLA Operation	What It Measures	Key Applications	Comment
UDP Jitter	Measures round-trip delay, one-way delay, one-way jitter, one-way packet loss, and connectivity	VoIP and data network performance	One-way delay requires time synchronization between source and target routers
VoIP UDP Jitter (with MOS and ICPIF score)	Measures round-trip delay, one-way delay, one-way jitter, and one-way packet loss for VoIP traffic. Calculates MOS and ICPIF voice quality scores. Codec simulation: G.711 u-law, G.711 a-law, and G.729A.	VoIP performance monitoring	One-way delay requires time synchronization between source and target routers
TCP Connect	Measures the time taken to connect to a target device with TCP	Server and application performance	—
FTP	Measures round-trip time to transfer a file	FTP server performance and troubleshooting. Monitors path quality to and from the FTP server to the measurement node.	—
Dynamic Host Configuration Protocol (DHCP)	Measures round-trip time to get an IP address from a DHCP server	DHCP server performance and troubleshooting	—
Domain Name System (DNS)	Measures DNS lookup time	DNS server performance and troubleshooting	—
HTTP	Measures round-trip time to retrieve a web page	Web server performance and troubleshooting, path quality monitoring	—
Data Link Switching Plus (DLSw+)	Measures peer tunnel response time	Response time between DLSw+ peers	—

Table 11-7   *IP SLA Operations Summary (Continued)*

IP SLA Operation	What It Measures	Key Applications	Comment
MPLS VPN	Adds VRF measurement to other IP SLA operations: ICMP Echo, ICMP Path Echo, UDP Echo, UDP Jitter	MPLS performance monitoring and troubleshooting	—
Frame Relay	Measures circuit availability, round-trip delay, and frame delivery ratio	WAN service level agreement performance	This operation does not have SNMP support
ATM	Measures physical links or circuits of ATM connections	WAN service level agreement performance	This operation does not have SNMP support
VoIP Call Setup (Post-Dial Delay) Monitoring	Measures the response time for setting up a synthetic VoIP call	VoIP performance monitoring	Requires the VoIP test-call application on the source router
VoIP Gatekeeper Registration Delay Monitoring Operation	Measures the amount of time taken to register a gateway to a gatekeeper	VoIP performance monitoring	—

CHAPTER 12

Summary of Data Collection Methodology

This chapter serves two purposes. First, you can read it as a summary of the chapters in Part II to get an overview of the accounting and performance device instrumentation features. With that in mind, this chapter *summarizes* the high-level technical characteristics of all features discovered in the previous chapters and provides a way to structure, categorize, and compare the features.

Second, this chapter offers an *entry point* into the accounting and performance features. So that you won't read all the chapters and then discover that some of the accounting and performance features are not suitable for your specific scenario, the two matrixes in this chapter guide you toward the features of interest.

The previous eight chapters offer many details about the Cisco different device instrumentation features for accounting and performance management. Because the variety of functions could make it difficult to choose the "right" feature, this chapter offers you some guidance in the selection process. Two matrixes compare the features from a technical and business perspective.

Applicability

Tables 12-1 and 12-2 assess the accounting and performance features described in Part II. Table 12-1 offers answers to the fundamental questions:

- What to collect?
- Who is the user?
- How to collect (metering method)?

Here are some comments for clarification:

- Collection details relate to IP address, MAC address, interface counters, BGP autonomous system number, ToS/DSCP, and more. Because this is a summary table, only the most important parameters are described.

- SNMP has two rows because most features support SNMP read operations but only some have writable MIB objects. Note that only a subset of available MIBs is listed.

- Most features meter observed traffic, which is the actual network traffic. Metering observed traffic does not have an impact on the network traffic, compared to synthetic traffic, which is generated specifically for measurement purposes.

- The session start and stop time parameters are explicitly required for billing solutions.

- The metering interface (ingress or egress) and the traffic destination are distinguished. Transit traffic passes the network element and has a remote destination, whereas destined traffic targets the collection device. Originated traffic is generated at the metering device itself. Note that destined traffic can be collected only at the ingress interface and originated traffic is captured only at the egress interface. Figure 12-1 illustrates the different metering options per traffic direction.

Figure 12-1 *Metering Direction and Interface*

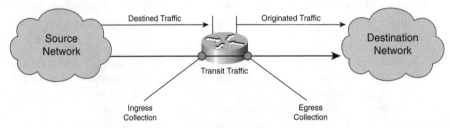

- The Security Options row considers SNMPv3 as security for the listed MIBs and MD5 authentication for IP SLA.

- SNMP is the protocol to transfer the MIB variables' content and therefore is independent of their type. Thus, the SNMP protocol cannot answer the questions "What to collect?" and "Who is the user?" This is why Table 12-1 shows several "not applicable" (NA) cells. These two questions are answered in Table 12-2 for the most important MIBs covered in this book.

Table 12-1   *Overall Functional Area Comparison Related to the Collected Details*

Area	Data	SNMP	IP Accounting	MAC Address IP Accounting	Precedence IP Accounting	ACL IP Accounting	NetFlow	BGP PA	AAA	NBAR	IP SLA
What to collect?	DSCP/ToS	NA			✓		✓			✓	
	MIB	NA									
	Memory	NA									
	Response time	NA									✓
	BGP AS number	NA					✓	✓			
	Applications/type	NA								✓	✓
	Availability	NA									✓
	Session start time	NA					✓		✓		
	Session stop time	NA					✓		✓		
Who is the user?	Interface counters	NA	✓	✓	✓		✓			✓	
	MAC address	NA	✓	✓			✓				
	IP address	NA	✓				✓	✓	✓	✓	✓
	Username	NA							✓		
How to collect (metering method)?	Observed traffic	✓	✓	✓	✓	✓	✓	✓	✓	✓	
	Synthetic traffic										✓
	Sampling						✓				
	Direction: ingress	✓	✓	✓	✓	✓	✓	✓	✓	✓	
	Direction: egress	✓	✓	✓	✓	✓	✓	✓	✓	✓	
	Originated traffic	✓	✓				✓	✓		✓	
	Destined traffic	✓	✓				✓	✓	✓	✓	
	Transit traffic	✓	✓	✓	✓		✓	✓		✓	
How to collect (collecting method)?	SNMP read	✓	✓	✓	✓		✓*	✓	✓*	✓	✓
	SNMP write	✓	✓				✓*	✓		✓	✓
Security options		✓									✓

*Partly supported

Table 12-2   *MIB-Specific Functional Area Comparison Related to the Collected Details*

	MIB-I, II; IF-MIB	PING-MIB	PROCESS-MIB	ENVMON-MIB, MEMORY-POOL-MIB	DATA-COLLECTION-MIB	CB-QOS-MIB	FRAME-RELAY-MIB	MLS-TE-MIB	Expression and Event MIB	RMON, SMON, DSMON, ART MIB
DSCP/ToS						✓				✓[*]
CPU Utilization			✓						✓	
Memory			✓	✓					✓	
Response Time		✓								✓
BGP AS Number										
Applications/ type										
Availability	✓	✓							✓	✓
Session Start Time										
Session Stop Time										
Interface Counters	✓						✓	✓		✓
MAC Address										✓
IP Address										✓

*Partly supported

Table 12-3 assigns accounting and performance features to the different business cases. The idea of this table is to help you choose the feature that offers exactly the level of detail you need. An alternative would be to select a feature that collects all the details and keep only the required fields. Even though this is a valid option, it is not an economical approach, because more data is collected than is actually required. For example, if you are interested in only the total amount of traffic per interface, the SNMP interface statistics provide sufficient details. Of course, alternatively you could collect all NetFlow records and aggregate the flows afterwards, but this is not suggested. Current best practice advises that you meter exactly the level of detail that fulfills your requirements.

Because Table 12-3 does not provide specific details on how to apply a feature to a solution, the next chapters assign techniques to scenarios and explain where to enable a function, how to collect the details, and how to process and combine results from multiple metering instances.

Table 12-3   *Functional Area Comparison Related to Business Cases*

	MIB-I, II; IF-MIB	PING-MIB	PROCESS-MIB	ENVMON-MIB, MEMORY-POOL-MIB	DATA-COLLECTION-MIB	CB-QOS-MIB	FRAME-RELAY-MIB	MLS-TE-MIB	Expression and Event MIB
Device Performance Monitoring	✓	✓*	✓	✓	✓	✓	✓		✓
Network Performance Monitoring and Baselining	✓	✓			✓	✓	✓	✓	✓
User Monitoring and Profiling	✓*				✓				✓
System and Server Performance Monitoring			✓	✓					✓
Application Performance Monitoring and Profiling					✓	✓*			
Link Capacity Planning	✓	✓			✓	✓	✓	✓	✓
Network-Wide Capacity Planning					✓			✓	
Traffic Profiling and Engineering					✓	✓		✓	
Peering and Transit Agreements					✓				
Source- and Destination-Sensitive Billing									
Generic Service Monitoring		✓							✓
Class/Quality of Service Billing						✓		✓	
Application- and Content-Based Billing									
Time- and Connection-Based Billing									
VoIP Billing									
Security Analysis									
Fault Management									✓

*Partly supported

Table 12-3 *Functional Area Comparison Related to Business Cases (Continued)*

	RMON, SMON, DSMON, ART	IP Accounting	MAC Address IP Accounting	Precedence IP Accounting	ACL IP Accounting	NetFlow	BGP PA	AAA	NBAR
Device Performance Monitoring	✓	✓	✓			✓		✓	✓
Network Performance Monitoring and Baselining	✓					✓	✓	✓	
User Monitoring and Profiling	✓	✓	✓			✓		✓	
System and Server Performance Monitoring	✓								
Application Performance Monitoring and Profiling	✓					✓		✓	✓
Link Capacity Planning	✓	✓				✓		✓	
Network-Wide Capacity Planning						✓	✓		
Traffic Profiling and Engineering	✓					✓	✓		
Peering and Transit Agreements						✓	✓		
Source- and Destination-Sensitive Billing		✓	✓			✓	✓		
Generic Service Monitoring									
Class/Quality of Service Billing	✓			✓		✓			
Application- and Content-Based Billing								✓	✓
Time- and Connection-Based Billing						✓		✓	
VoIP Billing								✓	
Security Analysis					✓	✓		✓	✓
Fault Management									

*Partly supported

Assigning Technologies to Solutions

CHAPTER 13

Monitoring Scenarios

This chapter illustrates some of the performance and accounting features explained in Part II of this book. The structure is based on a series of questions that network operators ask:

- "How do I check the device's health in the network?"
- "How do I evaluate the link capacity?"
- "When should links be upgraded?"
- "How do I verify network connectivity?"
- "How do I evaluate the response time between locations?"
- "How do I ensure VoIP quality?"
- "How do I determine the application types in the network?"
- "How do I discover the traffic sent to and received from the Internet?"

These questions start with the simple ones about device and link availability and go up to the complex ones related to network-wide connectivity, type of applications in the network, and VoIP quality assessment. This chapter answers these questions by applying the mechanisms proposed in Part II of this book. In some cases, the example tells you the related chapter where detailed examples are given. In other cases, a full example including the configuration illustrates the point. Sometimes screenshots of network management applications display the answer to the question.

Network Blueprint for Monitoring

Figure 13-1 serves as the basis for this case study. It represents the different components of an enterprise network from a high-level point of view: a connection to the Internet with a potential backup, different branch locations connected over a wide-area network (WAN), a series of enterprise-wide application servers in the data center, the Network Management Station (NMS), and some VoIP traffic.

Figure 13-1 *Network Blueprint*

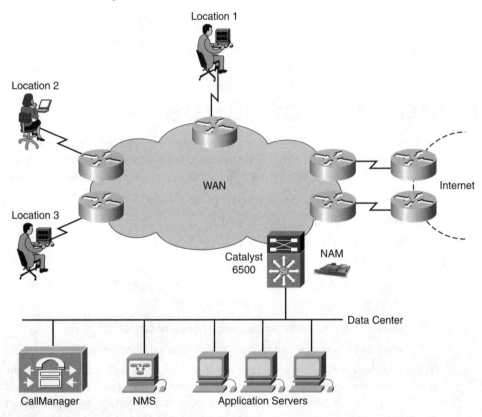

Device and Link Performance

The initial step is monitoring device and link availability. Tools such as CiscoWorks and HP OpenView discover the network topology and report connectivity problems. SNMP polling of router interfaces and the Cisco Discovery Protocol (CDP) Management Information Base (MIB), plus syslog messages and SNMP notifications for linkUp/linkDown, are useful techniques for detecting connectivity issues. Because availability is part of fault management, it is excluded in this case.

The next question relates to the monitoring of device and link performance. The NMS can monitor one aspect of device performance by polling device CPU utilization from the CISCO-PROCESS-MIB. However, instead of regular SNMP polling to discover a potential CPU spike, the router can monitor the local CPU with RMON event and alarm mechanisms and send an SNMP notification in case of a threshold violation. A typical example is the cpmCPUTotal5sec.1 CPU MIB variable (for the first CPU instance on the router), monitored every 20 seconds, for a rising threshold of 90% and a falling threshold of 60%:

```
Router(config)#rmon alarm  1 1.3.6.1.4.1.9.9.109.1.1.1.1.3.1 20 absolute rising-
   threshold 90 1 falling-threshold 60 2 owner me
Router(config)#rmon event 1 log Trap public description "cpu busy" owner sysadmin

Router(config)#rmon event 2 log description "cpu not too busy" ower sysadmin
```

NOTE	Different Cisco IOS trains and platforms interpret the MIB name to a different depth. For example, a 7200 router running 12.4(11)T would not understand cpmCPUTotal5sec.1 or cpmCPUTotalEntry.3.1. You would have to enter cpmCPUTotalTable.1.3.1. To make sure that the command always works, you should always use the full numeric OID. The cpmCPUTotal5sec CPU MIB variable has been deprecated in favor of cpmCPUTotal5secRev, which adds the percentage as units. cpmCPUTotal5secRev, in turn, is deprecated in favor of the cpmCPUTotalMonIntervalValue, which is the overall CPU busy percentage in the last cpmCPUMonInterval period. Before using the right MIB variable, you should check the support of these MIB variables on the platforms of your choice. All those MIB variables are part of the CISCO-PROCESS-MIB.

In the case of a rising threshold, an **event 1** SNMP notification and a syslog message are fired. In the case of a falling threshold, a syslog message **event 2** SNMP notification is sent.

Next to the example of CPU utilization, good practice leads to monitoring other MIB variables, either by direct polling or using RMON event/alarm monitoring. For example, leverage the CISCO-MEMORY-POOL-MIB or the CISCO-ENHANCED-MEMPOOL-MIB for memory monitoring and the CISCO-ENVMON-MIB for environment monitoring.

With link performance, an NMS station can poll the interface statistics, such as ifInOctets and ifOutOctets, for relevant links in the network. These typically are the interfaces toward the Internet, between different locations, or toward the data center, as shown in Figure 13-1. If high-capacity counters such as ifHCInOctets and ifHCOutOctets are available, they should be used, because this avoids the issue of counter32 wrapping up too fast. Figure 13-2 shows the CiscoView application, which displays nice graphs from the interface statistics, such as utilization, traffic types, and errors.

Figure 13-2 *Interface Statistics Monitored with CiscoView*

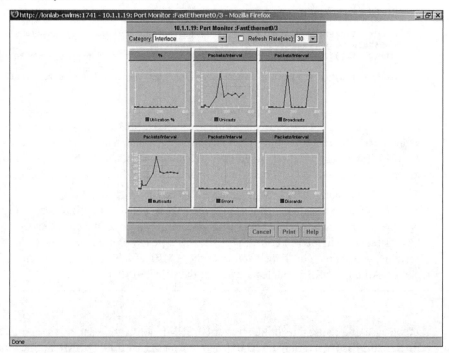

Next is the question "When should a link be upgraded?" Because no MIB variable contains the link utilization ad hoc, calculation is required. In this case, the interface statistics should be related to the interface bandwidth to calculate the link utilization. The interface bandwidth is available from the ifSpeed or ifHighSpeed variables in the IF-MIB, which contain the bandwidth value for each interface.

NOTE   For each interface on the router and switch, the bandwidth is set by default. However, the network administrator should ensure that the default value corresponds to the actual physical speed and configure the bandwidth if appropriate. A typical example is the serial interface bandwidth that is per default set to 1.544 Mbps, the value of a T1 circuit.

Although the interface statistics and link utilization graphs are useful, they suffer from one drawback: the NMS application needs to poll them regularly to extract information. From a graph, either a continuous trending or a threshold violation would lead to a link upgrade.

An alternative to constant polling of performance parameters is to use the EXPRESSION-MIB and EVENT-MIB or RMON-MIB. A new "link utilization" MIB variable is created with the EXPRESSION-MIB, and whenever this value breaches a threshold, the EVENT-MIB or RMON-MIB report an alarm. The full example is provided in Chapter 4, "SNMP and MIBs."

Relying only on SNMP notifications has the potential to miss important events. The UDP protocol is unreliable, and failed network elements might not be able to send a notification, especially during power outages. Although SNMP notifications sent as informs increase the reliability based on a handshake concept, they are transported over UDP. Fully reliable SNMP informs require infinite message queues at the network elements. Therefore, current best practice suggests combining polling of the router's reachability in conjunction with local device monitoring and sending SNMP notifications.

Another alternative to constant SNMP polling of performance parameters from the NMS application every couple of minutes is leveraging the DATA-COLLECTION-MIB mechanism. This MIB can store multiple MIB values locally, enabling the NMS server to retrieve longer intervals with a bulk upload. Chapter 4 explains the CISCO-DATA-COLLECTION-MIB in detail.

The following example collects the ifInOctets and ifOutOctets variables for the Serial0/0 and FastEthernet1/0 interfaces every minute. The results are stored at the router in a file that is transferred every 5 minutes to the ftpserver host via FTP. The username is **ftpuser**, with a password of **ftppassword**:

```
Router(config)# snmp mib bulkstat object-list ifmib
Router(config-bulk-objects)# add ifInOctets
Router(config-bulk-objects)# add ifOutOctets
Router(config-bulk-objects)# exit
Router(config)# snmp mib bulkstat schema interface-stats-fasteth0
Router(config-bulk-sc)# object-list ifmib
Router(config-bulk-sc)# poll-interval 1
Router(config-bulk-sc)# instance exact interface FastEthernet1/0
Router(config-bulk-sc)# exit
Router(config)# snmp mib bulkstat schema interface-stats-serial0
Router(config-bulk-sc)# object-list ifmib
Router(config-bulk-sc)# poll-interval 1
Router(config-bulk-sc)# instance exact interface Serial0/0
Router(config-bulk-sc)# exit
Router(config)# snmp mib bulkstat transfer interface-stats-transfer
Router(config-bulk-tr)# schema interface-stats-fasteth0
Router(config-bulk-tr)# schema interface-stats-serial0
Router(config-bulk-tr)# url primary ftp://ftpuser:ftppassword@ftpserver/tmp
Router(config-bulk-tr)# format schemaASCII
Router(config-bulk-tr)# transfer-interval 5
Router(config-bulk-tr)# retain 30
Router(config-bulk-tr)# retry 5
Router(config-bulk-tr)# buffer-size 1024
Router(config-bulk-tr)# enable
```

The following output is the display from the exported file:

```
Schema-def interface-stats-fasteth0 "%u, %s ,%s ,%u, %u"
        epochtime ifDescr instanceOID ifInOctets ifOutOctets
Schema-def interface-stats-serial0 "%u, %s ,%s ,%u, %u"
        epochtime ifDescr instanceOID ifInOctets ifOutOctets
```

```
Schema-def GLOBAL "%s, %s, %u, %u, %u, %u, %u"
        hostname date timeofday sysuptime cpu5min cpu1min cpu5sec
interface-stats-fasteth0: 980626825, FastEthernet1/0, .9, 167878375, 681136794
interface-stats-serial0: 980626825, Serial0/0, .1, 45228030, 93252495
interface-stats-fasteth0: 980626885, FastEthernet1/0, .9, 167923745, 681142145
interface-stats-serial0: 980626885, Serial0/0, .1, 45228500, 93253512
interface-stats-fasteth0: 980626945, FastEthernet1/0, .9, 167972581, 681143070
interface-stats-serial0: 980626945, Serial0/0, .1, 45228954, 93254513
interface-stats-fasteth0: 980627005, FastEthernet1/0, .9, 168024079, 681149575
interface-stats-serial0: 980627005, Serial0/0, .1, 45229424, 93255530
Global: <Router>, 20010127, 202425, 5866517, 1%, 0%, 0%
```

Finally, the following two CLI commands complete the solution by sending SNMP notifications when a transfer attempt occurs or when the data collection could not be carried out successfully (due to insufficient memory, for example):

```
Router(config)# snmp-server enable traps bulkstat collection
Router(config)# snmp-server enable traps bulkstat transfer
```

Network Connectivity and Performance

The next question is "How do I check connectivity *proactively*?" In Figure 13-1, this means ensuring that all locations have access to the data center, can connect to each other, and can reach the Internet. Note the emphasis on "proactively," because it assumes that services in your network are business-critical. As an operator, you are expected to fix issues within defined service contracts, ideally before end users notice anything. Therefore, "proactive" reduces manual troubleshooting with tools such as ping, traceroute, routing table investigation, and built-in web servers at routers to exceptional situations, because they are reactive features. In addition, a proactive tool is required to recognize connectivity problems. The solution of choice is the Cisco IP SLA function, as described in Chapter 11, "IP SLA."

Identifying the network element on which to enable the IP SLA operations in the network depends on the level of monitoring. Simple network connectivity monitoring requires less effort than service monitoring.

Looking at Figure 13-1, valid options are as follows:

- Configure an IP SLA operation between each remote location and the central Catalyst to test access to the Data Center LAN. This monitors WAN connectivity only, excluding monitoring of network services.

- Configure an IP SLA operation between each remote location and the servers in the Data Center. This measures server availability up to the TCP or UDP port level. It also verifies the servers' return path to the different locations.

- Configure an IP SLA operation between each remote location and the Internet access routers.

Knowing that there is VoIP traffic in the network, an IP SLA operation calculating the jitter metric in addition to network delay offers an advantage. Indeed, connectivity, delay, and jitter values can be quantified with a single IP SLA operation.

Because Chapter 11 describes all IP SLA operations, they are not repeated here. The following example displays a typical IP SLA operation for VoIP call monitoring with the following desired parameters:

- Jitter operation with a G.711 a-law codec and 1-microsecond precision. Note that the μ-law algorithm is used in North America and Japan, whereas the a-law algorithm is used in Europe and the rest of the world.

- Generate a SNMP trap when the connection is lost.

- Generate a SNMP trap when the ICPIF value crosses the value of 30,000 in five out of ten operations.

- Generate a SNMP trap when the round-trip time crosses 120 ms for three times consecutively.

```
Router(config)# ip sla 1
Router(config-ip-sla)# udp-jitter 10.10.10.10 16384 codec g711alaw
Router(config-ip-sla-jitter)# precision microseconds
Router(config-ip-sla-jitter)# frequency 30
Router(config-ip-sla-jitter)# exit
Router(config)# ip sla schedule 1 start-time now
Router(config)# ip sla reaction-configuration 1 react connectionLoss threshold-type
immediate action-type trapOnly
Router(config)# ip sla reaction-configuration 1 react icpif threshold-value 30000
30000 threshold-type xOfy 5 10 action-type trapOnly
Router(config)# ip sla reaction-configuration 1 react rtt threshold-value 120 60
threshold-type consecutive 3 action-type trapOnly
```

A tool such as CiscoWorks Internetwork Performance Monitor (IPM) supports the configuration of IP SLA operations, as shown in Figures 13-3 and 13-4.

Figure 13-3   *Internetwork Performance Monitor: Probe Configuration*

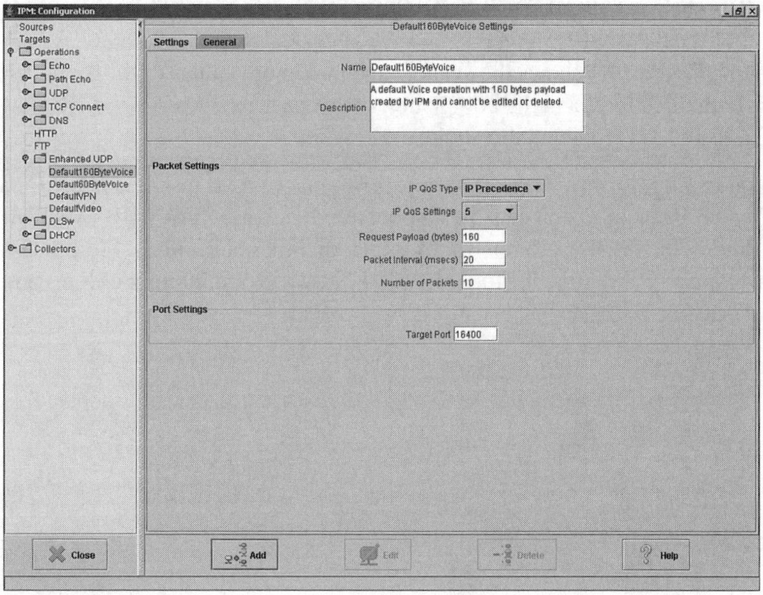

Figure 13-4 *Internetwork Performance Monitor: Event Configuration*

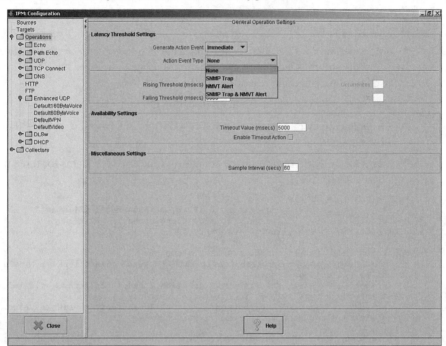

By retrieving the IP SLA results from the CISCO-RTTMON-MIB (or one of the associated MIBs such as CISCO-RTTMON-ICMP-MIB, CISCO-RTTMON-RTP-MIB, or CISCO-RTTMON-TC-MIB), IPM displays the statistical results on a daily, weekly, and monthly basis. Figure 13-5 shows the average and maximum values of the round-trip time, the jitter in both directions, and the completion of test packets. Other reports display the exceptions compared to predefined thresholds.

Figure 13-1 shows a Network Analysis Module (NAM) installed at the Catalyst at the Data Center. Because it supports the Application Response Time MIB (ART-MIB), the NAM displays the response time—for example, of TCP connections. Figure 13-6 shows that the average response time for the server is 17 ms, with a minimum of 5 ms and a maximum of 147 ms.

Figure 13-5 *Internetwork Performance Monitor: Reporting*

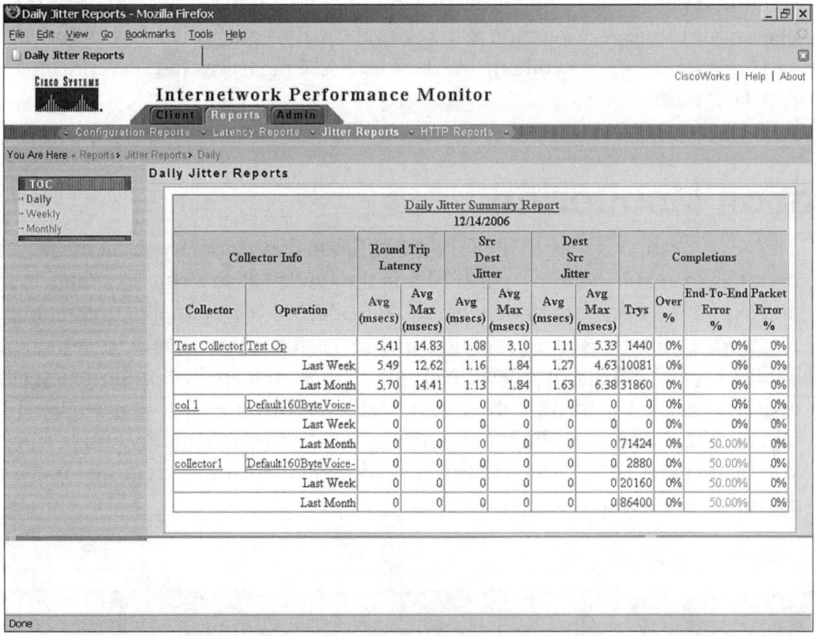

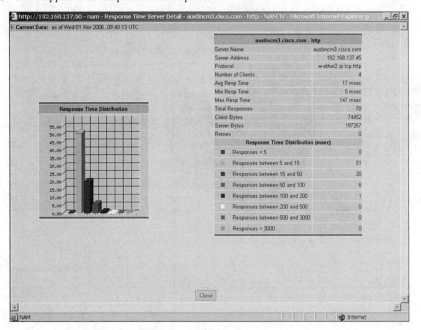

Figure 13-6 *NAM Application Response Time Report*

The combination of IP SLA and ART-MIB/NAM mechanisms offers a complementary solution in the network blueprint shown in Figure 13-1. Indeed, enabling the IP SLA operations from every location to the central Catalyst quantifies the network delay, the jitter, and the packet loss of synthetic traffic. The NAM measures the server response time of the real TCP traffic.

Application Monitoring

The next question is how to identify the different application types in the network. The first option is to enable NetFlow (or IPFIX in the future) at strategic locations in the network and export the flow records to a NetFlow Collector. If just application monitoring is required, a router-based aggregation such as protocol-port would be sufficient. Refer to Tables 7-4 and 7-5 in Chapter 7, "NetFlow," for a complete list of the different router-based aggregations. A report from the Cisco NetFlow Collector, shown in Figure 13-7, can classify the traffic according to the source and destination application port, protocol, and volume in bytes or packets. However, if additional details are required in the report, exporting more information is interesting.

Figure 13-7 *Cisco NetFlow Collector*

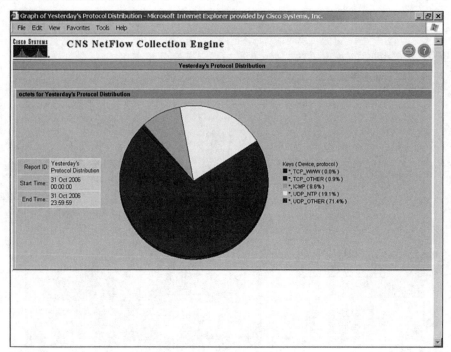

In this case, selecting a router-based aggregation that contains additional parameters is the option of choice. For example, the protocol-port-tos or prefix-port aggregation drills deeper into the packets to discover more flow parameters.

A higher level of flow granularity is obtained when the devices export the full flow records, where the Cisco NetFlow Collector allows monitoring of individual flows classified by IP addresses.

Note that Flexible NetFlow offers some flexibility in the flow record definition required for a specific application.

The collection of NetFlow records is not limited to the Cisco NetFlow Collector. Numerous Cisco partners developed their own NetFlow Collector and monitoring applications. Figure 13-8 shows the NetFlow Tracker from Crannog (acquired by Fluke Networks), which displays the application types and conversations. By clicking a time and an application type, you can see a drilldown, as shown in the popup windows.

Figure 13-8   *Crannog NetFlow Tracker*

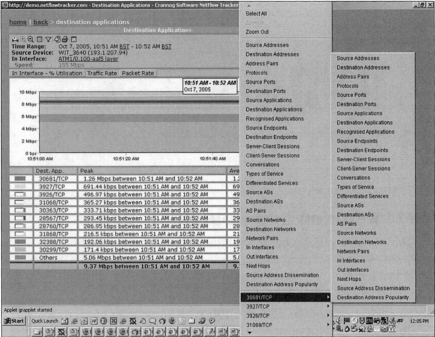

Application type reports typically account for a large amount of HTTP traffic.

However, NetFlow does not support the classification per payload information. For example, NetFlow cannot classify peer-to-peer traffic such as BitTorrent, Kazaa,

Morpheus, Gnutella, and others. Instead of NetFlow, NBAR is the selection of choice for detecting application ports and distinguishing and categorizing traffic per payload information. Figure 13-9 shows an NBAR snapshot from the CiscoWorks QoS Policy Manager (QPM).

Figure 13-9 *QoS Policy Manager: Per-Class Traffic Monitoring*

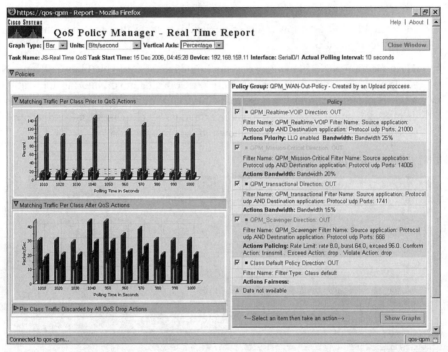

Service Monitoring and Routing Optimization

This section draws attention to a specific feature that is not described in detail in this book—Optimized Edge Routing (OER), another feature in Cisco IOS. OER is not covered in Part II because this feature is really at the edge, between performance monitoring and routing optimization. OER was renamed to Performance Routing (PFR).

Enterprise networks use multiple ISP or WAN connections for reliability and/or load distribution. Existing reliability mechanisms depend on link state or route removal on the border router to select a better exit link for a prefix or set of prefixes. Multiple connections protect an enterprise network from catastrophic failures but do not protect the network from "brownouts" or soft failures caused by network congestion. Existing mechanisms can respond to catastrophic failures at the first indication of a problem. However, brownouts can go undetected and often require the network operator to take action to resolve the problem.

When a packet is transmitted between external networks (nationally or globally), the packet spends the vast majority of its life on the network's WAN segments. Optimizing WAN route selection in the enterprise network can give the end user the greatest performance improvement—even better than LAN speed improvements in the local network.

The OER feature helps enable intelligent path selection at the WAN edge, based on performance-sensitive routing metrics such as response time, packet loss, path availability, traffic load distribution, and cost minimization. If a prefix's performance falls below default or user-defined policy parameters, routing is altered locally in the enterprise network to optimize performance and to route around failure conditions that occur outside the enterprise network. OER is best deployed with multihomed connections to the Internet or WAN intranet connections with two or more possible routes to the destination.

In the enterprise network shown in Figure 13-1, the OER feature, which is located on the border routers, inspects the metrics of the Top-*N* flows that are exchanged with the Internet. NetFlow provides the flow information, and the IP SLA does proactive measuring of the different paths through the network. Figure 13-10, more OER-oriented, displays the different OER components.

Figure 13-10   *Cisco OER Components*

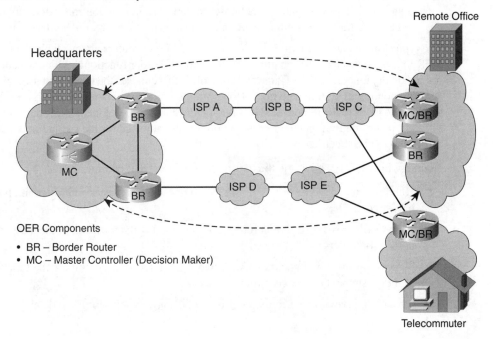

The OER architecture has two main functions:

- **The border controller**—An enterprise edge router with one or more exit links to an ISP or other participating network. At the border router, all policy decisions and changes to routing in the network are enforced. The border router participates in prefix monitoring and route optimization by reporting prefix and exit link measurements to the master controller and then enforcing policy changes received from the master controller. The border router enforces policy changes by injecting a preferred route to alter routing in the network. The border router is deployed on the edge of the network, so it must be in the forwarding path. A border router process can be enabled on the same router as a master controller process.

- **The master controller**—A single router that coordinates all OER functions within an OER managed network. A Cisco router can be configured to run a standalone master controller process. It also can be configured to perform other functions, such as routing or running a border router process. The master controller maintains communication and authenticates the sessions with the border routers. The master controller monitors outbound traffic flows using active or passive monitoring and then applies default or user-defined policies to alter routing to optimize prefixes and exit links. OER administration and control are centralized on the master controller, which makes all policy decisions and controls the border routers. The master controller does not need to be in the traffic forwarding path, but it must be reachable by the border routers.

The typical broadband scenario is when one or two border routers are available, and the OER master controller functionality coexists with the border functionality on the same router. By default, the Border Gateway Protocol (BGP) chooses the best path based on the fewest autonomous system path hops. However, the border routers shown in Figure 13-10 test the two paths to the remote office. Based on the comparison of the metrics between the different paths, the BGP parameters are automatically adjusted for the traffic to take the route with the best metrics.

Note that Figure 3-10 shows the three different possible OER configurations:

- **Headquarters**—Three different routers, composed of a master controller and two border controllers

- **Remote office**—Two different routers, one combining the functions of the master and border controllers

- **Telecommuter**—A single router with two WAN interfaces, combining the functions of the master and border controllers

The website http://www.cisco.com/go/oer is a good starting point for more details.

CHAPTER 14

Capacity Planning Scenarios

The capacity planning case study is divided into two parts: link capacity planning and network-wide capacity planning. Each part uses different accounting features, as described in Part II. Starting simply, the link capacity planning scenario is addressed first. The most important part of this scenario describes network-wide capacity planning, which covers requirements and relationships with network performance monitoring, peering agreements, and traffic engineering. Some aspects and examples of capacity planning were explained in earlier chapters:

- Several sections of Chapter 1, "Understanding the Need for Accounting and Performance Management," are related to capacity planning:
  - "Capacity Planning" justifies the need for capacity planning and explains the interaction between the core traffic matrix and capacity planning.
  - "Traffic Profiling and Engineering" is the companion section on performance optimization of traffic handling in operational networks, with the focus of the optimization being minimizing overutilization of capacity.
  - "Peering and Transit Agreement" is dedicated to the monitoring and capacity planning of BGP peering.
  - "Network Performance Monitoring" deals with the measurement of Service Level Agreement (SLA) data.
- Chapter 4, "SNMP and MIBs," offers an example of link capacity planning with the EVENT and EXPRESSION MIBs.

NOTE   As an introduction to this chapter, read the sections "Capacity Planning" and "Traffic Profiling and Engineering" in Chapter 1.

Link Capacity Planning

Link capacity planning looks at the trending of the link utilization to determine when a bandwidth upgrade will be required.

As explained in the "Device and Link Performance" section of Chapter 13, "Monitoring Scenarios," polling the ifInOctets and ifOutOctets MIB variables allows the computation of the link utilization, assuming that the bandwidth statement is correctly configured for each interface. This parameter can be read and modified at the ifSpeed MIB variable. ifSpeed contains a default value per interface type, but it should be verified. If necessary, you can change it with the IOS **bandwidth** interface command.

Even if constant SNMP polling provides the trending of the link utilization, active trending analysis is recommended to help you find the right time to upgrade the link. The EVENT MIB and EXPRESSION MIB provide a proactive mechanism based on SNMP notifications at the network element. Indeed, as investigated in the "How to Create New MIB Objects" section in Chapter 4, the EXPRESSION MIB lets you create new MIB variables based on existing MIB variables. In this case, a new MIB variable was defined using the ifInOctets, ifOutOctets, and ifSpeed variables from the Interface-MIB, allowing direct monitoring of the interface utilization with a single MIB variable. Associated with the EVENT MIB, this new MIB variable can be monitored for threshold crossing, in which case an SNMP notification is generated. Here's a typical example: If the link utilization rises above 70 percent (or above another specified threshold) during one hour, a notification is sent to the network management station, indicating that it might be time to upgrade the link capacity or at least closely monitor link utilization, including protocols and applications. For further information, refer to Chapter 4, which explains this example in greater detail.

A mechanism based on a threshold-crossing alarm is adequate for short-term planning, but longer-term planning requires an extrapolation of the utilization based on current and future link usage. The input from service management systems is important information to determine the required capacity in the future.

Note that, when a link upgrade is required, the operations team should decide the specific time of the upgrade—so that the maintenance windows can be taken into account, for example.

Although capacity planning monitors link utilization, which is one of the key performance indicators, upgrading the link bandwidth is not always the solution for a better user experience. Indeed, protocols such as HTTP, FTP, and SMTP might consume the additionally available bandwidth very quickly and therefore compete with business-critical applications. The user experience is linked to the specific services used. They have different SLA requirements, with characteristic metrics such packet loss, delay, or delay variation. A proposed solution is to identify the active applications on the link, along with their respective bandwidth utilization, priorities, and SLA parameters (such as business-critical, real-time, and best-effort).

The next step is classifying traffic based on quality of service (QoS) parameters, where specific applications are individually prioritized and potentially rate-limited or blocked. If QoS is deployed, link capacity planning should be decomposed per Class of Service (CoS). In this case, the CISCO-CLASS-BASED-QOS-MIB is the MIB of choice, because it provides the necessary statistics, including summary counters and rates by traffic class before and after the enforcement of QoS policies. For a detailed explanation of MIB capabilities, refer to the Chapter 4 section "Technology-Specific MIBs for Accounting and Performance." Two monitoring solutions exist:

- Immediate polling of the CISCO-CLASS-BASED-QOS MIB from the network management system via SNMP
- Proactive fault management at the network element by setting thresholds on MIB variables at the CISCO-CLASS-BASED-QOS-MIB MIB in conjunction with the RMON event/alarm or the EVENT MIB

Network Blueprint for Capacity Planning

Figure 14-1 serves as the basis for this case study. It represents the different components of a service provider network from a high-level perspective:

- Provider edge (PE) routers connected to the core network
- Customer edge (CE) routers connected to the customers
- Multiple points of presence (PoP) composed of PE and CE routers
- Server farms or data centers
- A core network connecting all the pieces to an intranet
- Different BGP routers (numbered from 1 to 4) for the Internet connections via different providers and the BGP Autonomous Systems (AS) (displayed by AS1 through AS5).

Figure 14-1 *Network Blueprint*

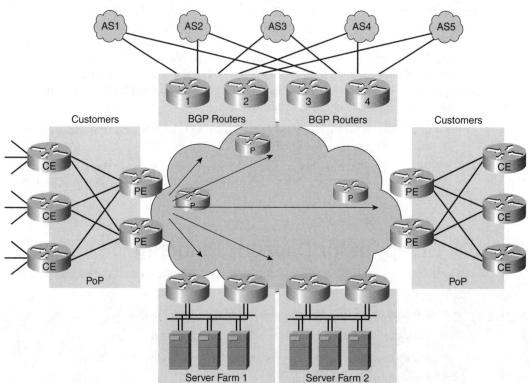

Problem Space

Although at first glance network-wide capacity planning seems to be required for only Internet service providers (ISP), it also applies to any intranet that offers SLAs to customers. The users of the ISP's network are external customers who signed a contract, whereas customers of an intranet are internal users with an implicit contract. In other words, related to capacity planning, the difference between enterprise and service provider networks is merely a question of terminology. Enterprise companies manage *applications* for internal users, where SLAs might have been defined. A service provider manages *services* for external customers with a negotiation on specific SLAs. Although terminology differences between enterprises and service providers exist, the applications/services offered might actually be the same: VoIP traffic, video, business-critical. Figure 14-1, which displays an ISP network, could easily be modified for an enterprise network as follows: the server farms are called data centers, the PoPs are called remote offices, and the core network becomes a Layer 2 or Layer 3 MPLS service offered by an ISP. One observation is that networks designed for specific SLA definitions should ensure that these SLAs are guaranteed—closely monitored, with violations reported.

Network performance monitoring requires knowledge of the core traffic matrix—specifically, to determine if the SLAs are respected during connectivity problems in the network. An ISP that wants to propose SLAs to its customers should first evaluate network performance parameters such as delay, jitter, and packet loss under normal operation. The results, adjusted with extra tolerance (for example, the 95th percentile), are turned into an SLA based on marketing and business requirements. On top of being able to provide specific SLAs at the current time, network-wide capacity planning is required to evaluate whether the SLAs will still be respected in a month, 6 months, or a year based on the new traffic extrapolation.

The next important question is whether the SLAs will still be respected in case of a link or router problem. Even if the Mean Time Between Failures (MTBF) metric improves over time, you can never completely eliminate nonfaulty network modules, malfunctioning routers, link outages, or human errors. A relatively simple software bug can also cause severe performance degradations. Therefore, assuming 100 percent availability at the network elements level is an unrealistic scenario. Note that high-availability functions such as device and link redundancy, backup operations centers, and clear procedures can help you get *closer* to 100 percent availability.

You should evaluate the SLA during network problems by combining the core traffic matrix with a simulation tool. The core traffic matrix is a table that shows the traffic volumes between the traffic origin and destination in a network. The core traffic matrix can either represent the current traffic (based on the current measurements) or consider future needs by multiplying the current core traffic matrix by a factor that represents the traffic growth. By adding this information to an application that takes into account the network topology and routing information, you can visualize the traffic flows related to the topology. If the tool also includes the link speeds, it can deduce and display link utilization with a color scheme. This allows quick visual discovery of (future) bottlenecks in the network. The simulation function of such a tool is another relevant part. When link or router problems are simulated, the routing information is recomputed, and the data from the core traffic matrix is mapped to the new topology and routing information. Next, new potential bottlenecks are calculated, and the question "Will the traffic still reach the destination in case of a network link or router failure?" can be answered. An important question can be answered afterward: "During a network or link failure, will the traffic for certain SLAs still be transmitted with the defined performance parameters?" Indeed, if during a short network outage the traffic of the gold, silver, and bronze classes is unaffected and only the best-effort traffic is influenced, at least the SLAs are respected, and no penalties need to be paid to the customers. Simulating possible what-if catastrophic scenarios in the network is the best way to proactively analyze whether the SLAs are respected during major outages. After the different scenarios have identified the potential (future) weakest points in the network, the administrator should select one or several of the following actions, depending on the defined SLAs and monetary resources:

- Increase the link bandwidths
- Tune the IGP metrics

- Invest in high-availability solutions
- Introduce traffic engineering (see the section "Traffic Profiling and Engineering" in Chapter 1)
- Adjust the BGP exit points (see the section "Peering and Transit Agreements" in Chapter 1)
- Develop load-balancing strategies

Capacity Planning Tools

Several products offer capacity planning capabilities; this section looks at two of them. The goal is not to promote a specific product but to elaborate on the different possibilities of capacity planning applications through a few snapshots.

Note the following:

- Typically, you can associate the notion of SLA with capacity planning by inserting the physical distance of every link. That way, the tools have the knowledge of delay by evaluating the propagation time.
- You can also associate costs per link upgrade, router upgrade, etc. Consequently, the tool can optimize the monetary investment for maximum reliability.
- Today, most products do not collect the core traffic matrix directly from the network. Instead, they import it into the tool, assuming that "someone" generated it, usually in Comma-Separated Value (CSV) format. This creates an additional burden on the operator.
- Most applications are considered offline monitoring tools because they do not retrieve information directly from the devices, nor do they automatically reconfigure the network in case of failures.
- Typically, the tools provide optimization for IGP metrics, MPLS traffic engineering, etc.

Figure 14-2 shows the Cariden MATE capacity planning tool, where the color scheme codes the different level of bandwidth utilization in each direction. Note that this figure displays a different network than the one shown in Figure 14-1. The possible failure types are as follows:

- Link
- Router
- Shared Risk Link Group (SRLG)

SRLG is a group of circuits that may be taken down by a single event. For example, a fiber cut would fail all the circuits traversing the fiber. After the simulation is run, the worst-case scenario of a single failure is displayed, along with its consequences in the network in terms of link utilization and SLAs.

Figure 14-2 *Cariden MATE Capacity Planning Tool*

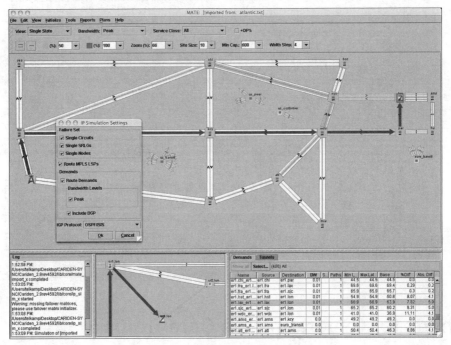

Figure 14-3 shows another network topology represented by the Cisco Network Planning Solution, which is based on OPNET applications and modules. It models the network infrastructure for behavior analysis and presents traffic flow simulations visually to clarify routing dynamics and end-to-end connectivity. The product also shows which traffic flows will be affected by outages and where resulting bottlenecks are likely to occur. Furthermore, it automates capacity planning, resilient link dimensioning, and topology design by validating proposed network changes before deployment.

Figure 14-3 *Cisco Network Planning Solution*

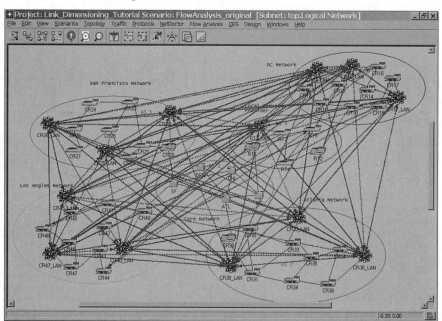

Methods for Generating the Core Traffic Matrix

As explained in the preceding section, the core traffic matrix is the first requirement for network-wide capacity planning. Note that the core traffic matrix is relevant for capacity planning and also for traffic engineering. Traffic engineering is the process of traffic optimization for a fixed network design. Before traffic can be optimized, it must be analyzed, resulting in the core traffic matrix. Before introducing the different solutions described in the following subsections, this section discusses the considerations when generating the core traffic matrix: granularity, internal versus external traffic matrix, and retrieving the data.

What are the criteria for selecting a specific method for generating the core traffic matrix? The answer to the following questions naturally include or exclude some of the methods presented in this section.

First, you need to define the granularity of the core traffic matrix:

- The entry points of the core traffic matrix can be a PoP, a router, a specific interface of a router, or even a source prefix.

- The exit points can be a PoP, a BGP next hop or MPLS Forwarding Equivalent Class (FEC), or a destination prefix.

The lowest granularity is a classification according to the incoming PoP, resulting in high traffic aggregation. The highest granularity creates more entries in the core traffic matrix, which leads to better capacity planning analysis at the cost of generating more traffic and processing more data. In their paper "A Distributed Approach to Measure IP Traffic Matrices," Konstantina Papagiannaki, Nina Taft, and Anukool Lakhina calculated the number of flows for the different granularities per observation period. Even though the paper assumes specific network characteristics in terms of number of PoPs, routers per PoP, and customer interfaces per router, the comparison of the different scales is interesting:

- PoP to PoP matrix: 351 flows
- Router to router matrix: 729 flows
- Link to link matrix: 6561 flows
- Source prefix to destination prefix: 5.5 million flows

These numbers imply that the number of flows is proportional to the granularity of the core traffic matrix.

If the core traffic matrix requires classification per Class of Service (CoS), all numbers are to be multiplied by the number of existing Differentiated Services Code Point (DSCP) values.

Secondly, do you want the capacity planning analysis to be combined for all traffic, or do you want to separate it per class of service?

Next, you should evaluate whether you need the external traffic matrix, which also contains information on where the traffic comes from when entering your network and where it goes when exiting your network. Typically, the external core traffic matrix requires the previous/next BGP AS in the path, or the source/destination BGP AS, or the source/destination IP address or prefix. "Hot potato routing" optimizes the routing decisions by identifying the ISP's nearest exit point.

In the same way as you pass a hot potato quickly to avoid burning your fingers, an ISP hands over the traffic to another ISP as quickly as possible, reducing network utilization in its own network. In Figure 14-4, the traffic from PoP1 to BGP AS3 takes Path1, exiting this way via the nearest BGP, Router 1. To optimize all traffic and lower the link utilization, a possible alternative is to send the best-effort traffic from PoP1 to the BGP AS3 via the suboptimal Path2, exiting via the BGP Router 3, while the high-importance traffic linked to the SLA takes the optimal Path1. As explained with this example, knowledge of the external traffic matrix allows more flexibility to optimize the traffic by tuning the BGP exit routers.

Figure 14-4 *External Core Traffic Matrix*

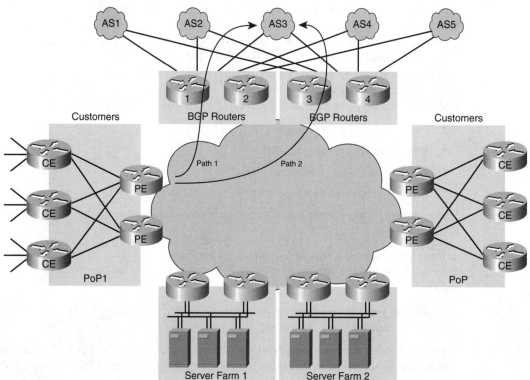

Is the core network a pure IP network or an MPLS network? Some monitoring features allow monitoring of only IP packets, and others are dedicated to MPLS packet monitoring. For example, because only the MPLS labels are relevant in the middle of an MPLS core, it is unnecessary to determine the source and destination prefix of the IP packets encapsulated in the MPLS packet.

Which mechanism is required to collect the core traffic matrix? The first solution is a push model that exports the accounting information from the network element. A typical push model example is the NetFlow export, in which UDP and SCTP are possible transport protocol options. The second solution is the pull model, in which the accounting information is retrieved from the network element, as done by the SNMP protocol. SNMP MIB polling offers the advantage that the polling interval can be configured, effectively retrieving the information only when needed.

The next sections describe both the push model with NetFlow and the pull model with SNMP. It covers four different mechanisms: NetFlow BGP Next Hop type of service (ToS) aggregation, MPLS-Aware NetFlow, BGP passive peer on the NetFlow Collector, and BGP policy accounting. The answers to the preliminary questions in this section will lead to a natural selection of one or maybe two features for a specific scenario.

NetFlow BGP Next Hop ToS Aggregation

Because the BGP next hop is the network's exit point, NetFlow BGP Next Hop ToS aggregation is a simple approach to export the core traffic matrix with NetFlow records.

Table 14-1 lists the NetFlow BGP Next Hop ToS key fields for the core traffic matrix. The inbound interface offers a high level of granularity (potentially the previous router in case of point-to-point links). The BGP next hop presents the network's exit point. The source and destination BGP AS deliver the external traffic matrix. The ToS offers the classification per class of service. Finally, the outbound interface could be useful in case of load balancing within the provider network, because two flow records are created, each with its respective outgoing interface.

Table 14-1   *Key Fields and Nonkey Fields for the BGP Next Hop ToS Aggregation*

Key Fields	Nonkey Fields
Inbound interface	Number of flows
Outbound interface	Number of packets
BGP next hop	Number of bytes
Source BGP AS	Flow start sysUpTime
Destination BGP AS	Flow end sysUpTime
ToS	

The NetFlow BGP Next Hop ToS aggregation is enabled at the BGP routers, on all interfaces toward the core. In Figure 14-1, it would be on all CE-facing interfaces of the PE routers. This mechanism, which observes the IP packet, is suited for both a pure IP network and an MPLS backbone.

Because the traffic is observed as it enters the router, the reported ToS values are related to ingress. In case of "recoloring" (changing the ToS value) at the router, the new ToS values are not reported.

The biggest drawback with this mechanism is that only the prefixes in the BGP table are monitored. Indeed, a route not known in the BGP routing protocol would report 0.0.0.0 as the BGP next hop.

For further details, such as configuration examples, refer to the "BGP Next-Hop Information Element" section in Chapter 7, "NetFlow."

Flexible NetFlow

BGP Next Hop TOS aggregation can be improved using Flexible NetFlow. Indeed, some of the key fields from Table 14-1 are not essential for the generation of the core traffic matrix:

- The outbound interface is of interest only in the case of load balancing. Even then, interest is limited, because the capacity planning tool would simulate the IGP routing and deduce the load balancing.

- The source BGP AS gives some more granularity to the core traffic matrix. However, tuning the BGP parameters to force the entry point for a specific BGP AS is not realistic in practice.

Reducing the number of key fields for the outbound interface and the source BGP AS would reduce the number of flows, the router CPU utilization, and the bandwidth requirements for exporting. In addition, this reduces the NetFlow Collector's workload.

The bandwidth requirements for exporting flow records could be reduced further by excluding some of the nonkey fields from Table 14-1:

- The number of flows is not required by capacity planning.

- The number of packets is of limited interest, because the number of bytes is the factor of choice for accounting applications.

After applying the simplification according to Table 14-1, the key fields and nonkey fields are reduced to the ones listed in Table 14-2. This is a concrete example for the flexibility provided by Flexible NetFlow.

Table 14-2 *Key Fields and Nonkey Fields with Flexible NetFlow*

Key Fields	Nonkey Fields
Inbound interface	Number of bytes
BGP next hop	Flow start sysUpTime
Destination BGP AS	Flow end sysUpTime
ToS	—

Further reduction in the key fields is possible, but it depends on the network characteristics and the required granularity of the core traffic matrix. For example, if no QoS is implemented in the network, the ToS key field is superfluous. For example, the classification per inbound interface might not be required if the router exporting the flow records sufficiently identifies the entry point in the core traffic matrix.

The selection of key fields and nonkey fields in Table 14-2 results in the following configuration:

```
flow record traffic-matrix-record
   match routing destination as
   match interface input
```

```
    match ipv4 dscp
    match routing next-hop address ipv4 bgp
    collect counter bytes long
    collect timestamp sys-uptime first
    collect timestamp sys-uptime last

flow monitor traffic-matrix-monitor
    record traffic-matrix-record
    cache entries 10000
    cache type normal
    exporter capacity-planning-collector

interface pos3/0
    ip flow monitor traffic-matrix-monitor
```

MPLS-Aware NetFlow

In case of MPLS backbones, the MPLS-Aware NetFlow feature is well suited for gathering the core traffic matrix. It monitors the MPLS traffic entering the P routers that is, (router in the previous core) and can offload busy PE routers. An alternative to the ingress collection at the P router is MPLS egress collection at the PE router.

MPLS-Aware NetFlow offers several monitoring flavors, such as monitoring MPLS packets and IP packets, monitoring the underlying IP fields of the MPLS packets, and monitoring multiple labels in the stack. The relevant feature for capacity planning is *MPLS-Aware NetFlow Top Label Aggregation*, which is chosen for the rest of this section. MPLS-Aware NetFlow Top Label Aggregation monitors only the top label (not any other labels) and does not monitor any fields from the underlying IP packet.

Table 14-3 illustrates the important key fields for the core traffic matrix: the inbound interface offers a high level of granularity (potentially the PE router in case of point-to-point links), the FEC field provides the IP address of the network exit point, and the top incoming "label" represents the class of service inserted in the 3 EXP bits. The "label," as exported by MPLS-Aware NetFlow, consists of the 24 most significant bits of the 32-bit quantity, referred to as the "label stack entry" in RFC 3032, *MPLS Label Stack Encoding*. It contains the 20 bits of the MPLS label, the 3 EXP bits for experimental use, and the S bit for the bottom of the stack. Note that the 20 bits of MPLS label are not useful as such, because only the corresponding FEC is a field of interest.

Table 14-3   *Key Fields and Nonkey Fields for the MPLS-Aware NetFlow Top Label Aggregation*

Key Fields	Nonkey Fields
Outbound interface	Forwarding Equivalent Class of the top label
The top incoming "label"	Number of flows
	Number of packets
	Number of bytes
	Flow start sysUpTime

continues

Table 14-3 *Key Fields and Nonkey Fields for the MPLS-Aware NetFlow Top Label Aggregation (Continued)*

Key Fields	Nonkey Fields
	Flow end sysUpTime
	Type of the top label (LDP, BGP, VPN, etc.)
	Output interface

MPLS-Aware NetFlow is typically enabled on the P routers. In Figure 14-1 it would be on all PE-facing interfaces of the P routers. This mechanism is suitable for only MPLS backbones.

The biggest advantage of this method is the low overhead, because only a few records are exported to a NetFlow Collector: one record per P router multiplied by the number of interfaces where NetFlow is enabled, multiplied by the number of FECs in the network.

However, this method cannot produce the external traffic matrix, because only the correlation with the exiting PE allows the determination of the packet's destination, because the P routers do not know this information.

For further details, such as configuration examples, refer to the "MPLS-Aware NetFlow" section in Chapter 7.

BGP Passive Peer on the NetFlow Collector

The NetFlow records have been augmented with many new information elements, resulting in a more complex NetFlow metering process and increased resource consumption. The BGP passive peer feature, introduced in Cisco NetFlow Collector 5.0, establishes a BGP connection to one or several routers in the ISP network. The BGP peer listens to all the BGP routing updates without injecting any updates into its peers—hence the name "passive." After receiving the NetFlow records, the NetFlow Collector looks up the destination IP address in the retrieved BGP routing table, exactly as the NetFlow metering process would do locally on the router to determine the BGP route. It also adds new BGP-related information elements to the NetFlow flow records at the NetFlow Collector.

As shown in Table 14-4, the new nonkey fields added to the flow records consist of any information that can be retrieved from the BGP table by performing a lookup on the flow IP address or prefix.

Table 14-4 *Key Fields and Nonkey Fields for the BGP Passive Peer in the NetFlow Collector*

Key Fields	Nonkey Fields
Any key fields used by the NetFlow metering process in the network elements	Any nonkey fields sent in the flow records
Any BGP-related key field (BGP next hop, source BGP AS, destination BGP AS, full AS path, BGP community, etc.)	Any BGP-related key field (BGP next hop, source BGP AS, destination BGP AS, full AS path, BGP community, etc.)

The most interesting nonkey fields for the core traffic matrix are as follows:

- **BGP next hop**—Provides the network exit point.
- **BGP AS (configured as source, destination, or full path)**—Offers the external traffic matrix.
- **BGP community**—In a network where BGP communities are deployed, a BGP community provides the network exit point.

Note that those extra BGP-related fields can also be used as new key fields, because the Cisco NetFlow Collector allows further flow record aggregation based on any information element present in the flow records.

Imagine that in Figure 14-1 the BGP community is set as a unique value per PoP: each generated internal BGP routing update from this PoP contains a specific BGP community value. Because a specific value of the BGP community represents a specific destination PoP, a classification per BGP community implies a classification per destination PoP. The destination IP address or prefix, exported in the NetFlow record, is looked up in the BGP table on the Cisco NetFlow Collector. From this lookup, the BGP community is extracted. At the Cisco NetFlow Collector, the flow records are first augmented with the BGP community value. Then the flow records are aggregated per BGP community value, producing entries for the core traffic matrix.

BGP Policy Accounting

The full configuration, show commands, and MIB variables of the BGP Policy Accounting feature are covered in detail in Chapter 8, "BGP Policy Accounting." Therefore, this section mainly compares BGP Policy Accounting with the other methods.

In Figure 14-1, BGP Policy Accounting would be enabled on the CE or PE routers. The only two constraints are that the routers must be running BGP and that only IP traffic is observed. Therefore, this feature does not apply to the monitoring of MPLS packets. The first constraint leads to the same limitation as the NetFlow BGP Next Hop Aggregation solution, where only the BGP traffic accounts for the generation of the core traffic matrix. A disadvantage of this solution is that the core traffic matrix cannot be generated per CoS, because the routing table does not contain different entries per ToS. However, the BGP Policy Accounting method presents a real advantage, because the data is retrieved via SNMP with the BGP-POLICY-ACCOUNTING-MIB. This reduces the overhead remarkably compared to NetFlow, because high SNMP polling times such as one hour, several hours, or one day are possible. The only constraint when selecting an extended polling time is to verify that the MIB counters do not wrap twice between two polling cycles.

Other Methods

Several research topics propose different approaches to deduce the core traffic matrix based on various mechanisms: MIB interface counter polling, partial collection of NetFlow and interface counters, IGP metric changes, and the gravity model.

Polling MIB interface counters permits estimation of the core traffic matrix based on the total interface traffic. This method provides a rough estimate only, because the granularity of the counters is an order of magnitude lower than the entries in the core traffic matrix. The addition of a NetFlow collection at specific elements in the network can improve the accuracy of the core matrix traffic estimation.

Some research papers specify that the traffic flows in the network can be observed by the delta of interface counters when modifying the IGP metrics. However, network administrators are reluctant to change the routing information, which may lead to suboptimal routing.

The gravity model explains that the migration between two cities is proportional to the product of the two cities' populations and is inversely proportional to the intervening distance. In other words, the higher the population and the closer the distance, the more people will commute. Taking into account the number of users in the Internet and their location, this theory could be applied to Internet traffic, deducing that the required bandwidth between two cities should be proportional to the product of the two cities' Internet users and inversely proportional to the intervening distance. However, the introduction of network vitualization such as data centers somehow breaks this theory. Indeed, even if they are composed of only a few devices, the data centers exchange high volumes of traffic.

Another research paper proposes to calculate the core traffic matrix for only a short period and then infer the changes by looking at the interface counters, which are directly proportional to the core traffic matrix.

Although all these methods tend to ease the generation of the core traffic matrix, the authors think that the introduction of Flexible NetFlow is currently the most accurate solution. Flexible NetFlow offers the best trade-off: the minimum number of flow records for a required level of granularity.

For completeness, three extra methods need to be mentioned: the switching counters in MPLS Label Distribution Protocol (LDP) network, the statistics in the MPLS Label Switching Router MIB (RFC 3813), and the direct measurement of byte counters in a full mesh of MPLS traffic engineering label-switched path.

Additional Considerations: Peer-to-Peer Traffic

Today, peer-to-peer traffic, boosted with file-sharing applications, becomes an ever-increasing part of Internet traffic. There is no clear answer to what to do with peer-to-peer traffic from an ISP perspective. Basically, it depends on the billing model the ISP offers. Some ISPs consider peer-to-peer as just another sort of traffic, increasing the revenues if the billing model is based on the total amount of traffic. Other ISPs consider peer-to-peer traffic an unprofitable increase of the customer bandwidth requirements, especially in case of a flat-rate billing model. In the latter case, the possible options are to block or rate-limit the peer-to-peer traffic. An alternative is moving to special billing models, such as offering special tariffs for peer-to-peer traffic. In any case, it is desirable to monitor the peer-to-peer traffic. The issue in identifying the latest peer-to-peer applications is that their protocols are embedded in the payload of HTTP port 80, preventing the use of any traffic classification based on the Layer 4 port. The payload inspection for peer-to-peer recognition naturally implies the use of Cisco Network-Based Application Recognition (NBAR). As explained in Chapter 10, "NBAR," it inspects not only the Layer 4 port to classify the traffic, but also the payload, offering a new dimension of traffic monitoring. The section "Limiting Peer-to-Peer Traffic" in Chapter 10 explains monitoring and rate-limiting Gnutella peer-to-peer traffic.

Summary

The link capacity planning scenario is straightforward, because the MIBs such as the IF-MIB and the CISCO-CLASS-BASED-QOS offer all required counters. In contrast, network-wide capacity planning requires generating the core traffic matrix, for which some mechanisms were described in this chapter. The core traffic matrix can be generated with BGP Policy Accounting and NetFlow, especially since the implementation of Flexible NetFlow. Indeed, Flexible NetFlow offers configuration of flexible key fields, which allows any level of granularity. Note that a generation of the core traffic matrix using only BGP next hop as the NetFlow key field offers a simple core traffic matrix and reduces the number of flows to a minimum. The only accuracy approximation with the NetFlow-based solutions stems from packet sampling, which is almost compulsory when metering packets on high-speed interfaces. This introduces some inaccuracy in the measurements. However, those flow inaccuracies can be quantified.

After the core traffic matrix is generated, it should be introduced, along with the IGP information, into a simulation application. This capacity planning approach graphically visualizes the current bottlenecks, simulates the future traffic growth and consequences, and applies what-if scenarios to verify if the SLAs such as delay and packet loss are still respected in case of link or router failure.

CHAPTER 15

Voice Scenarios

The objective of this chapter is to illustrate scenarios in the area of Cisco voice accounting and performance measurement. It describes the technical background of this topic, which is a combination of device instrumentation features and management applications, such as Cisco CallManager and others.

Today's data networks originated in traditional voice networks. In 1875, Alexander Graham Bell invented the telephone. The first telephone company was founded in 1877 as the Bell Telephone Company. Since then, multitudes of books have been written on the subject of accounting and performance management in traditional voice networks.

NOTE   For more information on legacy voice systems and SS7, consult the following resources:

- *Signaling System No. 7 (SS7/C7): Protocol, Architecture, and Services* (Cisco Press, 2004)

- *Signaling System #7*, Second Edition (McGraw-Hill, 1998)

In contrast, this chapter's focus is on voice accounting and performance management in data networks, with an emphasis on IP telephony. In the past, voice traffic was transported over a separate voice infrastructure, and the data network infrastructure was established in parallel so that voice and data traffic did not interfere with each other. Traditional voice accounting and performance functions are standardized within the SS7 system (Common Channel Signaling System No. 7), the global standard for telecommunications, defined by the ITU-T. The success of data networks led to the development of techniques to encapsulate voice traffic in IP packets, and thus Voice over IP (VoIP) was born.

During the initial phase of VoIP, the Public Switched Telephone Network (PSTN) switches remain in the network and take full control over the voice calls. Instead of a dedicated voice trunk between the PSTN switches, gateways to an IP data network now interconnect them by encapsulating voice streams in IP packets. Accounting records and performance statistics are still gathered by the PSTN switches, as defined by SS7. In addition, the gateways provide further details from an IP transport point of view. This scenario is not covered here, because it is only an interim step toward IP telephony.

Consequently, the next step was the development of voice technologies that no longer require PSTN components. Instead, a software switch or IP telephony server delivers the PSTN switch functionality. Alternatively, peer-to-peer applications (such as Skype for voice over the Internet) connect the IP phones without central call control. H.323 (ITU-T) and Session Initiation Protocol (SIP) (IETF) became the standards for voice call signaling and control in an IP network. Relevant data sources for accounting and performance purposes are IP telephony applications as well as voice gateways and network elements. The following sections focus on accounting and performance management for VoIP.

Network Blueprint for IP Telephony

Voice-related performance and accounting data can be collected at multiple places in the network. Figure 15-1 illustrates possible components.

Figure 15-1 *Metering Direction and Interface*

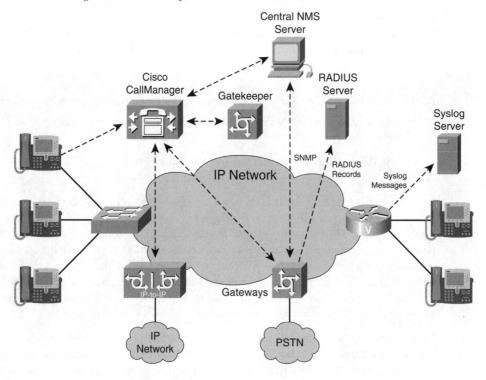

A good starting place is the phone; because it initiates the communication, it should be able to meter statistics. In fact, Cisco IP phones gather Real-time Transport Control Protocol (RTCP) report statistics during a call and send these to the Cisco CallManager (CCM) when the call is completed. CCM provides additional reporting capabilities for both performance and accounting purposes. Additional metering sources are IP telephony gateways and gatekeepers. Gateways provide access to the PSTN as well as Private Branch Exchange (PBX) interoperability. They are involved if a call setup targets a destination outside of the local perimeter; therefore, gateways can meter call details. Gatekeepers perform call control and routing in conjunction with address translation and are a good place to meter statistics. Additional sources are network management applications that collect MIB details, Remote Authentication Dial-In User Service (RADIUS) servers, and Syslog servers.

In case of voice transmission, the differentiation between performance and accounting is extremely relevant. Voice accounting is a primary source for traffic engineering or billing applications in service provider networks, and performance statistics are related to voice quality assurance. These two areas of performance and accounting are considered separately here because the metering processes and data representation are different.

Voice Performance Measurement

Measuring voice performance is fundamental for delivering voice services. From a user perspective, the service quality aspects of e-mail delivery and Internet surfing are nice to have. In a voice environment, quality of service (QoS) is a requirement from day one. As human beings, we are used to a certain voice quality from direct (that is, face-to-face) conversations, and we expect similar voice quality over the phone as well. In the absence of this quality, we tend to hang up the phone and use alternative telephony services such as cell phones, if available. Therefore, voice performance management needs to be considered before metering accounting records becomes relevant.

Standards and Technology

Several standards exist for metering voice performance. The following are relevant for gathering standard compliance data:

- ITU-T standards:
  - P.800 is the Mean Opinion Score (MOS).
  - G.113 is the Impairment/Calculated Planning Impairment Factor (ICPIF), which measures transmission impairments by defining a loss/delay busy out threshold. G.113 was superseded by G.107 (E-Model).
  - G.114 is the network one-way transmission time recommendation:

    0 to 150 ms is acceptable for most applications (toll quality).

    150 to 400 ms is acceptable if the users are aware of it (best-effort quality, e.g. for free Internet calls).

    >400 ms is unacceptable for most applications and users.

— Y.1541 (network performance objectives for IP-based services) defines six different QoS classes, where a one-way mouth-to-ear transmission time of 150 ms is suggested for voice applications.

— G.107 E-Model calculates and evaluates end-to-end connection voice quality.

— P.862 is Perceptual Analysis Measurement (PAMS) and Perceptual Evaluation of Speech (PESQ). These are metrics for voice quality measurement.

- IETF standards from the IP Performance Metrics (IPPM) working group:

— RFC 2879, *A One-Way Delay Metric for IPPM*

— RFC 2680, *A One-Way Loss Metric for IPPM*

— RFC 2681, *A Round-Trip Delay Metric for IPPM*

Mean Opinion Scores (MOS)

The dilemma of measuring the quality of transmitted speech is that it is subjective to the listener. In addition, each VoIP transmission codec delivers a different level of quality. A common benchmark to determine voice quality is MOS. With MOS, a wide range of listeners have judged the quality of voice samples on a scale of 1 (bad quality) to 5 (excellent quality). Table 15-1 shows MOS ratings and their corresponding descriptions.

Table 15-1 *MOS Scores*

Score	Quality	Description of Quality Impairment
5	Excellent	Imperceptible
4	Good	Just perceptible, but not annoying
3	Fair	Perceptible and slightly annoying
2	Poor	Annoying but not objectionable
1	Bad	Very annoying and objectionable

As the MOS ratings for codecs and other transmission impairments are known, an estimated MOS can be computed and displayed based on measured impairments. The ITU-T calls this estimated value Mean Opinion Score–Conversational Quality, Estimated (MOS-CQE) to distinguish it from objective or subjective MOS values.

Note that the initial MOS measurement was based on the round-trip time (RTT) only. The Cisco IOS implementation takes RTT delay and packet loss into the MOS calculation. However, jitter is not yet included.

Impairment/Calculated Planning Impairment Factor (ICPIF)

ICPIF originated in the 1996 version of ITU-T Recommendation G.113. ICPIF attempts to quantify the impairments to voice quality that are encountered in the network. It is the sum of measured impairment factors minus a user-defined access advantage factor (*A*) that is intended to represent the user's expectations based on how the call was placed (for example, a mobile call versus a fixed line call). ICPIF values are expressed in a typical range of 5 (very low impairment) to 55 (very high impairment). ICPIF values numerically less than 20 are generally considered adequate.

ICPIF is calculated by the following formula:

ICPIF = Io + Iq + Idte + Idd + Ie – A

where:

- **Io**—Impairment caused by nonoptimal loudness rating
- **Iq**—PCM quantizing distortion impairment
- **Idte**—Talker echo impairment
- **Idd**—One-way delay impairment
- **Ie**—Equipment impairment
- **A**—An Advantage or expectation factor that compensates for the fact that users may accept quality degradation, such as with mobile services

The Delay Impairment Factor (*Idd*) is a number based on the measured one-way delay. The original G.113 definition was superseded by G.107. The G.107 table is used as a lookup table for the measured delay to compute the Idd value. For example, a delay of 50 ms equals an Idd of 1.5, 200 ms equals an Idd of 7.4, and a 400-ms delay equals an Idd of 31.

The total one-way delay is the sum of the codec delay, look-ahead delay (from compression algorithms), one-way network delay, DSP processing delay, and receive jitter buffer playout delay.

The Equipment Impairment Factor (Ie) measures the distortion introduced by the codecs, related to the amount of measured packet loss. The percentage of packet loss results in a specific Ie factor per codec. For example, 4 percent packet loss equals an Ie factor of 12 for G.711 and 26 for G.729A.

NOTE   The Advantage factor considers the type of access and the user's expectation of quality for this particular service. A conventional wire line has a value of 0, whereas mobile service in a geographic area has a value of 10. The latest version of the ITU-T G.113 recommendation no longer includes the ICPIF model; instead, it refers implementers to the E-Model, described in ITU-T G.107. ICPIF is still a valid measurement approach, and not all management tools and features have implemented the E-Model yet.

Network Elements in the Voice Path

This section examines voice-related metering options that are available at the network elements. There are two fundamental approaches for leveraging device instrumentation for voice measurement: passive and active measurements. Passive measurement functions are available at voice components, such as the gateways; at metering devices, such as the Cisco Network Analysis Module (NAM); and at routers and switches, such as MIBs, NBAR, and NetFlow. Note that NetFlow offers more benefits from an accounting perspective; consequently, it is addressed in that section. IP SLA offers active measurement, which means that tests can be performed independently of existing voice traffic.

Passive Voice Performance Measurement

Cisco voice gateways calculate the ICPIF factor, which can be retrieved by polling the cvVoIPCallHistoryIcpif MIB object in the CISCO-VOICE-DIAL-CONTROL-MIB. If this value exceeds a predefined ICPIF threshold, an SNMP notification is generated. The call durations must be at least 10 seconds for the gateway to calculate the ICPIF value for the call.

Cisco IOS computation of the ICPIF value simplifies the formula and only takes the network components of ICPIF into account—the one-way delay impairment (Idd), the equipment impairment (Ie), and the advantage factor (A). The simplified IOS formula is ICPIF = Idd + Ie – A. Cisco Gateways use this formula to calculate the ICPIF for received VoIP data streams and Cisco IP SLA for VoIP operations.

One-way delay at the Cisco Gateway is calculated by dividing the MIB variable cvVoIPCallHistoryRoundTripDelay by a factor of 2. This variable is part of the callHistoryTable in the CISCO-VOICE-DIAL-CONTROL-MIB.

Because voice quality is measured only from the IP phone to the gateway, any unidirectional network QoS issues in the direction from the gateway to the IP phone are not included in the ICPIF calculation of the Cisco Gateway.

The NAM is a dedicated monitoring blade for the Catalyst 6000 and 4000 switches. A smaller NAM version for the Cisco 2600, 2800, 3660, 3700, and 3800 series access routers also exists. IP telephony-specific statistics are available, such as delay and jitter. The NAM can report VoIP protocols, including Skinny Client Control Protocol (SCCP), Real-time Transport Protocol (RTP), Real-Time Control Protocol (RTCP), Media Gateway Control Protocol (MGCP), H.323, and SIP. Note that RTCP is a subset of RTP.

Network-Based Application Recognition (NBAR) can also identify voice applications. With RTP Payload Type classification, NBAR looks for the RTP Payload Type field within the RTP header to identify voice and video bearer traffic. See Chapter 10, "NBAR," for more details on NBAR.

Active Voice Performance Measurement

Cisco IOS IP SLA uses synthetic traffic to measure performance between multiple network locations or across multiple network paths. It simulates VoIP codecs and collects network performance information, including response time, one-way latency, jitter, packet loss, and voice quality scoring. The following IP SLA operations are targeted toward VoIP measurement:

- VoIP jitter
- VoIP gatekeeper registration delay monitoring
- VoIP call setup (post-dial delay) monitoring (H.323 or SIP)
- RTP-based VoIP operation

The IP SLA VoIP UDP operation feature supports ICPIF, the transmission-rating factor R, and MOS values, but it does not support the E-Model. For more details on IP SLA, refer to Chapter 11, "IP SLA."

Cisco CallManager (CCM)

Cisco CallManager is an IP-based PBX that controls the call processing of a VoIP network. CCM is a central component in a Cisco Communication Network (CCN) system. A CCN comprises multiple regions, with each region consisting of several CallManager groups with multiple CallManagers.

CCM establishes voice calls and gathers call detail information in a VoIP environment. It generates records for each call placed to and from IP phones, conferences bridges, and PSTN gateways. Two different types of call records are produced:

- Call Detail Records (CDR) store call connection information, such as the called number, the date and time the call was initiated, the time it connected, and the termination time. In addition, CDRs include call control and routing information.
- Call Management Records (CMR) store information about the call's audio quality, such as bytes and packets sent or dropped, jitter, and latency. CMRs are also called diagnostic records. Voice quality trends can be discovered by inspecting the CDR's corresponding CMRs. The two records are linked by the GlobalCallID_callManagerId and GlobalCallID_Called fields in the CDR and CMR.

CCM generates a CDR when a call is initiated or terminated or if significant changes occur to an active call, such as transferring, redirecting, splitting, or joining a call. When diagnostics are enabled at the CCM, a CMR is stored for each call, separately for each IP phone involved or each MGCP gateway. The number of records written varies according to the type of call and the call scenario. For example, two CMRs occur for a call between two IP phones, and multiple CMRs are created in case of a conference call or videoconference. CDRs and CMRs are stored in the subscriber SQL database.

NOTE	CCM disables CDR generation by default. You can enable and disable CDRs without restarting the system.

Tables 15-2 and 15-3 describe a selection of CDR and CMR fields. For a list of all fields, see the latest CCM documentation on CCO.

Table 15-2   *CDR Fields*

Field Name	Description
globalCallID_callManagerId	Designates a unique Cisco CallManager identity.
globalCallID_called	Designates a unique call identity value that is assigned to each call.
origLegCallIdentifier	Identifies a call's originating leg.
dateTimeOrigination	The date and time when the user goes off hook or the date and time when the setup message is received for an incoming call. UTC specifies the time.
origNodeId	Identifies the node to which the call's originator is registered at the time the call is made.
origIpAddr	Identifies the IP address of the device that originated the call signaling.
callingPartyNumber	For incoming calls, this field specifies the number of the calling party.
origMediaTransportAddress_IP	Identifies the IP address of the device that originated the medium for the call.
	For Cisco IP phones, this field specifies the address of the Cisco IP phone.
	For PSTN calls, this field specifies the gateway's address.
destLegIdentifier	Identifies the terminating leg of a call.
destNodeId	Identifies the node within a cluster to which the call's terminating party is registered at the time the call is made.
destIpAddr	Identifies the IP address of the device that terminated the call signaling.
dateTimeConnect	Identifies the date and time that the call connected. UTC specifies the time.
dateTimeDisconnect	Identifies the date and time when the call was cleared. This field gets set even if the call never connected.

Table 15-2   *CDR Fields (Continued)*

Field Name	Description
duration	Identifies the difference between the connect time and disconnect time. This field specifies how long the call remains connected, in seconds. This field remains 0 if the call never connected or was connected for less than 1 second.
origDeviceName	Specifies a text string that identifies the name of the originating device.
destDeviceName	Specifies a text string that identifies the name of the destination device.
destConversationID	Specifies a unique identifier that is used to identify the parties of a conference call.

Table 15-3   *CMR Fields (Diagnostics)*

Field Name	Description
cdrRecordType	Specifies the type of this specific record: 0: Start call detail record (not used) 1: End call detail record 2: CMR (default)
globalCallID_callManagerId	Designates a unique Cisco CallManager identity.
globalCallID_callId	Designates a unique call identity value that is assigned to each call.
callIdentifier	Specifies a call leg identifier that identifies the call leg to which this record pertains.
directoryNumber	Specifies the directory number of the device from which these diagnostics were collected.
dateTimeStamp	Represents the approximate time that the device went on hook.
numberPacketsSent, numberPacketsReceived	Designates the total number of RTP data packets the device transmitted (send, receive) since starting transmission on this connection.
numberOctetsSent, numberOctetsReceived	Specifies the total number of payload octets (excluding header or padding) that the device transmitted (send, receive) in RTP data packets since starting transmission on this connection.

continues

Table 15-3 *CMR Fields (Diagnostics) (Continued)*

Field Name	Description
numberPacketsLost	Designates the total number of RTP data packets that have been lost since the beginning of reception. This number designates the number of packets that were expected, less the number of packets that were actually received, where the number of packets that were received includes any that are late or duplicates. Thus, packets that arrive late are not counted as lost.
jitter	Provides an estimate of the statistical variance of the RTP data packet interarrival time, measured in milliseconds. RFC 1889 contains detailed computation algorithms.
latency	An estimation of the network latency, expressed in milliseconds. This value represents the average value of the difference between the NTP time stamp that the RTP Control Protocol (RTCP) messages indicate and the NTP time stamp of the receivers, measured when these messages are received.

Cisco CallManager supports administrators to monitor their IP telephony environment. A web-based tool called Serviceability provides multiple functions. From a performance and accounting perspective, the following are relevant:

- **Real-Time Monitoring Tool (RTMT)** displays real-time monitoring of the components in a Cisco CallManager cluster, such as device discovery and status, call activities, and system and services performance. RTMT continuously monitors a set of management objects, generates daily reports, and sends alerts if values breach thresholds. RTMT is a Microsoft Windows-based application that is installed at the client PC. Figure 15-2 shows a report from RTMT. The summary screen shows the main server parameters (memory and CPU usage) in conjunction with the number of registered phones, number of calls in progress, and active gateway ports and channels. A drilldown function offers comprehensive details.

- **Quality Report Tool (QRT)** provides voice quality and general problem reporting for Cisco IP Phones. QRT combines input from the various collection sources and displays the results with the QRT Viewer application:

  — Information collected from the source device, such as IP address, codec, number of packets, jitter, and packets lost. QRT collects streaming data only once per call.

  — Information collected from the destination device. It's the same as just described if the destination device is also a Cisco IP phone within the same CallManager cluster. Otherwise, this information includes only the IP address, device name, and device type.

Figure 15-2 *Cisco CallManager RTMT Report*

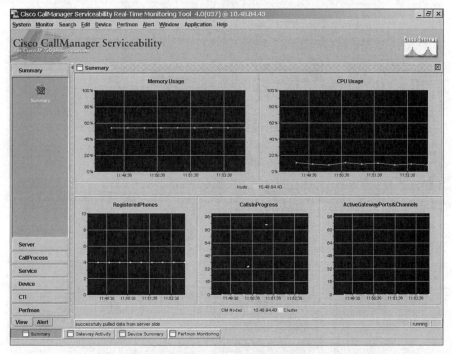

— Information collected from the Cisco CallManager includes the source device name (MAC address), calling and called party number, CallManager ID, and call state.

— Information collected from the Real-Time Information Server (RIS), which maintains CallManager details such as source device type, model, and user. RIS also provides an interface for the CallManager SNMP Agent.

- **CDR Analysis and Reporting (CAR)** generates reports for quality of service, traffic, and billing information from CDRs and CMRs:

    — User reports, such as individual and department bills; Top-*N* reports by charge, duration, and number of calls

    — System reports, such as QoS by gateway and call type, traffic summary, system overview, and CDR errors

    — Device reports, such as utilization by gateway, route group, route list, route pattern, conference bridge, and voice mail

    — CDR search functions to verify the details of a call in the CDR database and to track the quality of a call leg

Figure 15-3 shows a Cisco CallManager CAR report.

Figure 15-3 *Cisco CallManager CAR Report*

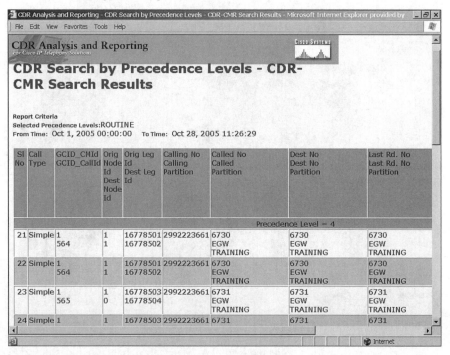

In addition to the reporting tools, Cisco CallManager includes an SNMP agent that provides detailed information about connected devices via the CallManager MIB (CISCO-CCM-MIB). The MIB contains phone tables and counters, and CallManager and other applications can use it to present provision and statistical information.

Besides the server-based Cisco CallManager, a software feature called Cisco CallManager Express (CCME) is implemented in Cisco IOS. CCME is an optional software feature that enables Cisco routers to deliver PBX functionality for enterprise branch offices or small businesses. The related MIB is the Cisco CallManager Express MIB (CISCO-CCME-MIB), which provides a comprehensive set of functions related to configuration, monitoring, and notifications.

Application Examples

In addition to the Cisco CallManager reporting functionality, two other applications are relevant: the integrated web reports of the Cisco NAM and the CiscoWorks Unified Service Monitor.

Network Analysis Module

The Catalyst NAM Traffic Analyzer provides a comprehensive set of voice reports:

- **Voice protocol overview**—The "Aggregate Statistics" table contains basic troubleshooting information for the voice protocols, such as number of calls monitored, average and worst packet loss, and jitter.

- **Worst-quality calls**—This table displays the Top-N worst calls based on packet loss and jitter.

- **Known phones**—This table gathers details for a specific phone (SSCP or H.323), including the phone number, the phone details, aggregated statistics, and Last-N calls.

- **Active calls**—This table displays information for all calls currently being monitored by the NAM.

Packet loss is included in the reports. If the NAM is located at the data center, in most cases it does not analyze the VoIP packets between the sender and receiver. Instead, the call setup and communication statistics messages are monitored. Therefore, the NAM should be placed near the Cisco CallManager (as opposed to being in the path between the caller and receiver) to intercept the CMR.

Figure 15-4 shows a NAM phone details report.

Figure 15-4 *Cisco NAM VoIP Report*

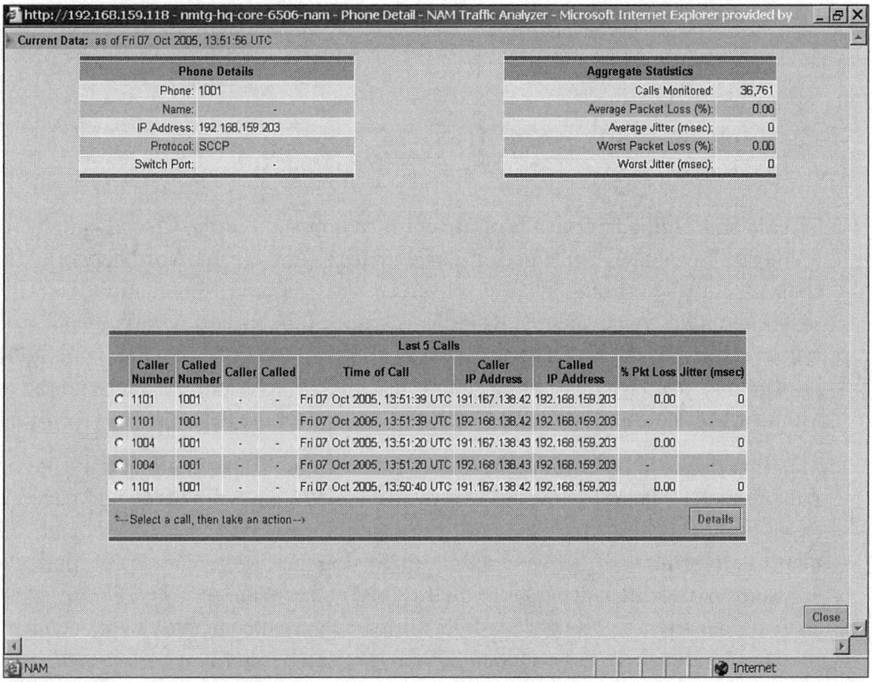

CiscoWorks Unified Operations Manager

CiscoWorks Unified Operations Manager provides a set of functions required to monitor VoIP network components, such as IP phones, gateways, Cisco CallManager, and Cisco Contact Center. Figure 15-5 shows the service level view.

Figure 15-5 *CiscoWorks Unified Operations Manager Service Level View*

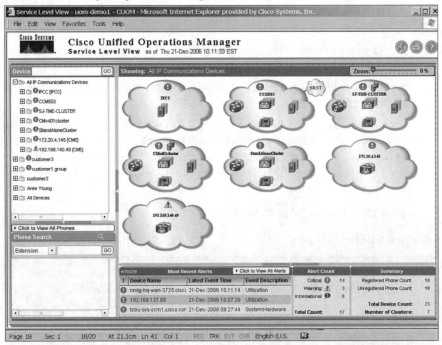

CiscoWorks Unified Service Monitor is one component of the Cisco Unified Operations Manager. It evaluates voice performance metrics for calls in a VoIP network. The product consists of two elements: a hardware sensor and a software application. The Cisco 1040 sensor monitors voice-specific RTP data streams. It behaves similarly to a Cisco IP phone: it uses either the IEEE or Cisco Power over Ethernet (PoE), retrieves configuration information from a TFTP server, and it uses SCCP to communicate with the Service Monitor application. Figure 15-6 shows a sensor report from the Service Monitor.

The sensor should be installed on a switch next to the IP phones that are being monitored. It captures RTP data streams based on voice codecs, analyzes them, and generates a MOS based on the ITU-T G.107 standard. The calculation occurs every 60 seconds. The quality metrics reporting to the server are through Syslog messages. The server application optionally summarizes the voice quality metrics and stores them in a data file for subsequent analysis and reporting. Reported MOS values are evaluated against a user-defined threshold. In case of a threshold violation, an SNMP trap can be sent to a fault or performance management application.

Figure 15-6 *CiscoWorks Unified Service Monitor Sensor Report*

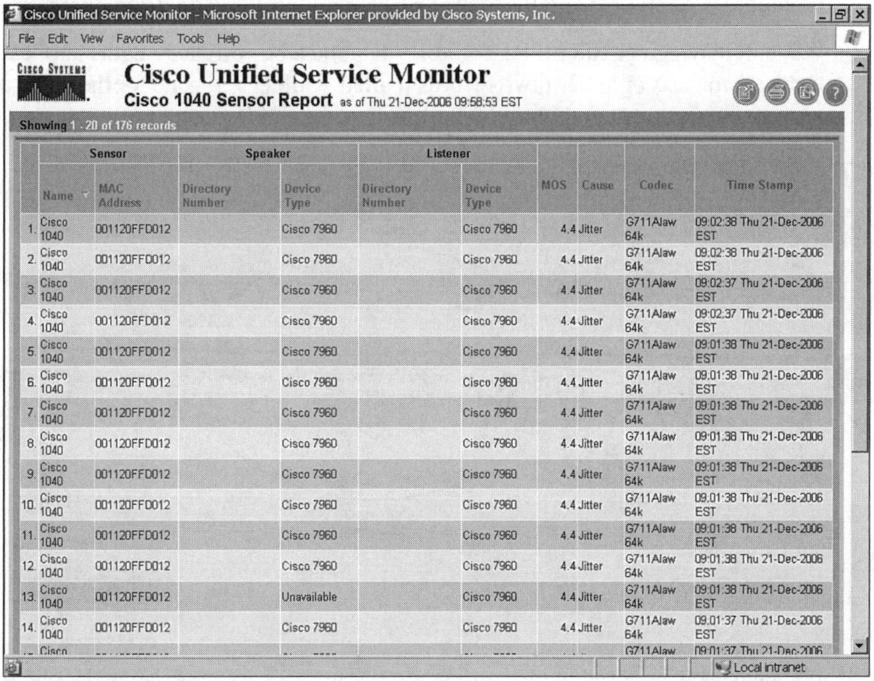

Voice Accounting

Voice-related accounting records are usually gathered as input for network design, capacity planning, or billing purposes. As described, voice performance management ensures the voice quality and is the foundation of voice services. Voice accounting makes it possible to design and charge for the service. Traditionally, voice billing was time-based; VoIP in the Internet probably will lead to changes in this business model. An alternative is volume-based accounting, where voice is considered just another IP application, and the user is charged for the total traffic.

From a business perspective, charging for single VoIP calls is not an economical approach in most cases because of the necessary investments for metering and processing all call records. An alternative is flat-rate billing or billing based on the total transmitted volume.

Standards and Technology

When distinguishing between time- and volume-based accounting, standards are relevant for both approaches. Even though no ITU-T or IETF standard for volume-based VoIP accounting exists yet, the IPDR consortium has developed a framework called Internet Protocol Detail Record (IPDR) to capture network data usage information in IP networks.

When deploying per-call billing for VoIP, data must be correlated at the application level. One call consists of at least two records (called "call legs")—one for the call's originator and one for the receiver. Figure 15-7 illustrates the call leg concept.

Figure 15-7 *Cisco NAM VoIP Report*

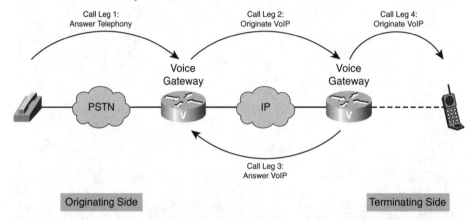

If a gateway is involved in the conversation, four call legs are generated—one from the originating IP phone, one from the PSTN gateway, and two additional for the reverse direction. If these records are created from completely different systems, the result can be a com-bination of records from CallManager, SS7, RADIUS, etc. This increases the requirements for the billing application and illustrates the need for accounting standards that cover the combination of VoIP and PSTN.

For traditional signaling, SS7 is the global standard, defined by the ITU-T. Although VoIP has no global accounting standard, IPDR and TMOC (ATIS Telecom Management and Operations Committee) have proposed a collaboration document to ITU-T study group 3 (SG3). Telcordia has also defined some accounting and billing standards, such as GR-508, GR-1100, and GR-2844.

Network Elements in the Voice Path

Multiple metering techniques gather voice traffic, such as NBAR, RMON, NetFlow, and the CLASS-BASED-QOS-MIB; Part II of this book covers them in detail. Depending on the requirements, some fit better than others. For example, if voice accounting is collected for billing, start and stop time stamps are required, which makes NetFlow a good candidate for metering. Alternatively, if voice traffic is assigned to a dedicated class of service and voice accounting provides input into a traffic planning application, the Cisco-CLASS-BASED-QOS-MIB fulfills these needs.

Gateway, Gatekeeper, Multimedia Conference Manager

An alternative is to use RADIUS for accounting. Chapter 9, "AAA Accounting," describes the voice extensions for RADIUS, supporting H.323 and SIP. If you enable AAA on the Cisco voice gateway or gatekeeper, a RADIUS accounting record is generated when an endpoint registers or unregisters and each time a call is initiated or disconnected.

For videoconferencing scenarios, the Cisco Multimedia Conference Manager (MCM) generates H.323 videoconferencing call records. MCM is a Cisco IOS feature that works in conjunction with Cisco VoIP gateways and routers.

Cisco CallManager (CCM)

The CCM details of CDR and CMR were described earlier. Therefore, this section addresses the collection of Call Detail Records (CDR) in the context of accounting for billing. Because CDRs contain information about call origination, destination, and duration, they can be a source for an accounting or billing application.

CCM stores CDRs in a SQL database for post-processing activities. Each regular call between two parties logs one CDR end-call record, which contains the fields listed in Tables 15-2 and 15-3. When supplementary services are involved in a call, more end-call records may be written. In addition to the CDR end-call record, one CMR per endpoint may be involved in a call. In a regular call between two parties, each using a Cisco IP phone, two CMRs are written: one for the originator and one for the call's destination. Depending on the various call types, such as normal calls, abandoned calls, forwarded calls, and calls with busy or bad destinations, different database fields are populated. CCM does not provide tools for call correlation or distinguish between chargeable calls and nonchargeable calls.

Application Example

Figure 15-3 displays a Cisco CallManager CDR report from CAR. In addition to GUI reports, CDRs can be generated as PDF files and CSV files. Table 15-4 was created from a CDR file in CSV format.

Table 15-4 *Cisco CallManager CDRs*

Originating Time	Terminating Time	Duration (Seconds)	Origination	Destination	Call Classification	Originating Codec	Destination Codec	Originating Device	Destination Device
03:45:21	03:45:41	13	6730	9195299222361#	Internal	G729	G729	SEP003094C306C3	device-trunk-to-gk-sever
10:57:48	10:58:02	1	6730	91924738#	Internal	G729	G729	SEP003094C306C3	device-trunk-to-gk-sever
14:31:51	14:32:23	17	6730	919529926230 1#	Internal	G729	G729	SEP003094C306C3	device-trunk-to-gk-sever
17:42:56	17:45:04	123	4831	6732	Internal	G729	G729	device-trunk-to-gk-sever	SEP003094C306C3

Is Your Network Ready for IP Telephony?

If you are ready to deploy IP telephony, and you wonder if your network is ready as well, there are at least three ways to find out. Simply deploying it and hoping it works is probably not the best choice, so here are two better options.

Chapter 14, "Capacity Planning Scenarios," describes a capacity-planning scenario that could also be used for VoIP analysis. The other option is to leverage IP SLA and run specific VoIP operations, ideally at 5-minute intervals for a couple of days. These operations should be initiated at different locations in the network, such as a branch office, the data center, employees' home offices, and so on.

The results of both methods should clearly indicate the network's bottlenecks.

CHAPTER 16

Security Scenarios

This chapter illustrates a security scenario related to accounting and performance measurement. It describes how to leverage metering information to identify and block security attacks and use performance management to proactively secure the network. This chapter is not an introduction to networking security in general; neither does it explain how to protect a whole network or access to networking devices. Instead, it describes the metering that is provided by accounting and performance management as a relevant building block for security solutions, because security management and incident mitigation depend entirely on information about the network's state. Some of the details can be monitored with seperate devices, such as intrusion detection systems or sniffers. Nevertheless, the various network management techniques explained in the section "Security Management Process" give security operators the facts they need for attack detection and analysis as well as tracing an attacker. Without SNMP monitoring, accounting record examination, flow analysis, and other network management techniques, security operators would have limited visibility of attacks and their impact on the network. This chapter illustrates how the various device instrumentation techniques build the foundation of a security framework.

Because this book focuses on accounting and performance management, security applications are out of scope. For complete security solutions, you should investigate in applications such as Cisco Security Device Manager (SDM), Cisco Security Monitoring Analysis and Response System (CS-MARS), and intrusion detection systems.

Note that there is a close relationship between security and fault management, because security-related notifications can indicate outages. Based on the subject of this book, fault management is addressed at only a high level in this chapter.

The following Cisco Press books offer a good overview of security architectures and troubleshooting:

- *Self-Defending Networks: The Next Generation of Network Security*
- *Network Security Architectures: Cisco Network Security Troubleshooting Handbook*

Network Blueprint for Security Management

Figure 16-1 illustrates the network blueprint for security management. It shows multiple branches and remote offices, regional offices, the central data center, and the Network Operations Center (NOC). Various device instrumentation functions are enabled at strategic locations, such as NBAR for application recognition and NetFlow for traffic analysis. Security functions, such as integrated firewall, are enabled at remote-access routers. At the Internet access, dedicated firewalls protect the network from external attacks in conjunction with Intrusion Detection Systems (IDS). They all report to central network management applications such as CS-MARS and NetFlow Collector at the NOC. Note that a dedicated Syslog server is installed at the NOC. Even though security applications provide Syslog server functionality, this one is used only for logging purposes. Syslog messages from all network elements are stored and archived for troubleshooting purposes. This can be very helpful to analyze the history of issues, such as "When was this event seen for the first time?" and resulting questions such as "Did the number of messages increase over time?"

The security scenarios in this chapter are related to network security, mainly securing network device access and transport of metering data.

It should be mentioned that storing all Syslog messages for years might lead to a storage issue. In this case, a suggestion is to keep the messages from the last three months at the management server and store historical messages on DVDs.

From a high-level perspective, security attacks in the network can be grouped into three categories:

- **Reconnaissance**—Describes the inspection of a network to find active hosts and network elements. The first step for an attacker is to identify potential victims.

- **Intrusion**—A hacker breaks into a system and starts manipulating it. This part relates to securing the operating system against someone logging into it or bypassing the logon routine. It includes everything from choosing secure passwords up to installing the latest bug fixes and following Computer Emergency Response Team (CERT) advisories. Network management applications can identify intrusion indirectly, such as by monitoring log files and ACL violations.

- **Denial-of-service (DoS) attack**—The attacker uses the compromised system to attack other servers, such as public web servers or others. DoS attacks aim at resource starvation, where a "resource" can be anything in the network, such as CPU utilization, bandwidth, memory, or disk space. The commonality of all DoS attacks is that they aim at one or multiple victims, such as routers, servers, or PCs, with the intention to overwhelm the target systems. Sometimes attacks are combined, such as first attacking a router and then an application server. Identifying these activities is a complex problem that requires intelligent analytics about the current activities related to previous or expected behavior.

Figure 16-1 *Network Blueprint for Security Management*

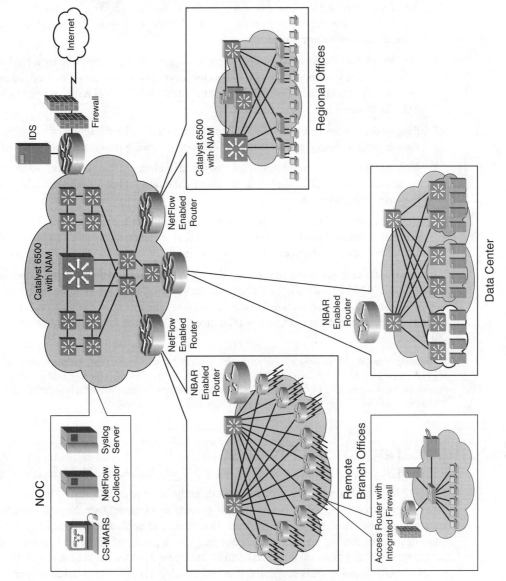

In cases such as these, traffic characteristics can be very similar:

- Ping sweeps perform an ICMP ping to complete ranges of IP addresses, either systematically or randomly. After an ICMP reply message is received, which means an active IP address was found, port scanning takes place. Port scanning searches a system for open TCP or UDP ports as preparation for the attack afterwards. Ping sweeps and port scanning have a common characteristic—abnormal operations. Besides a network management server during network discovery, no application should search for active hosts on the net. In addition, port scanning should not take place under any circumstances.

- DoS attacks are actions that prevent parts of a system from functioning in accordance with its intended purpose. This includes any action that causes unauthorized delay of service. In network operations, flooding a device with TCP SYN requests might cause a denial of service.

- Ping of death is an attack that sends large ping packets with the intent of overflowing the destination device's input buffers, potentially causing it to crash.

- Multiple flows monitored by NetFlow might have identical "fingerprints," such as the same values for the IP header identification field or the packet-length field. This is not the case with normal flows.

- Receiving several NetFlow flows with the same value for the time-to-live (TTL) field, number of packets per flow, or average packet size can be a possible attack indicator. Under normal circumstances, flows have a variety of values in the NetFlow records.

It is wrong to assume that most attacks come from the Internet and therefore monitoring of the intranet can be neglected. In fact, the opposite situation is more often the case. Reconnaissance and intrusion attacks often come from the inside. A quote from John Stewart, a vice president in the Cisco CTO office for Corporate Information Security, illustrates this:

"The insider threat is still the largest one irrespective of competitive and otherwise. We use traffic analysis to generate the stats from outbound denial of service attacks versus inbound attacks against us. These attacks are based on infected lab kits, machines, and devices which are misconfigured or infected, and also 'lingering' viruses that don't really cause harm but haven't been fully eradicated."

Security Management Process

A good illustration for security management is a picture puzzle. It consists of many different pieces, it fits together perfectly if combined correctly, and the overall result depends on every single piece. If one piece is missing, the picture looks incomplete. Security solutions are also a combination of multiple features, functions, and applications. This chapter identifies the accounting and performance management pieces of the security puzzle and puts the magnifying glass on them. Especially in large networks, the potential for attacks exists at multiple points. It is suggested that you develop a multifaceted defense approach. This led Cisco to develop a six-stage security operations model, as shown in Figure 16-2. This framework also provides the structure for this chapter. It positions accounting and performance management for both device instrumentation and management applications in relationship to security.

Figure 16-2 *Six-Stage Security Operations Model*

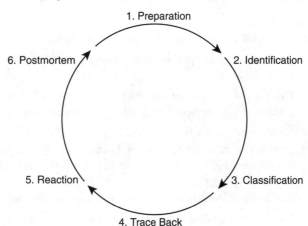

Chapter 1, "Understanding the Need for Accounting and Performance Management," briefly introduces the concept of baselining and security analysis. For consistency purposes, the same concept is applied in this chapter. On top of the basic concept, this chapter applies technologies and products to the six stages and therefore is an extension to Chapter 1.

Preparation

The ability to identify an attack quickly is critical to minimizing the damage a virus or worm can ultimately cause. Aside from waiting for users to complain or the network management alarms to begin flashing in the NOC, how can you detect attacks?

Preparation for attacks includes a set of policies that define who is allowed to do what in the network. From an accounting and performance perspective, preparation means having the right device instrumentation and management applications in place. One technique to spot the possibility that an attack is occurring is to compare the current network performance figures with the expected ones. This requires a performance monitoring system, a performance trending application, and a metering process to identify deviation from normal. This relates to the concept of *baselining*, which was described in previous chapters (such as the "Baselining" section in Chapter 1). Taking the preparation one step further, the performance monitoring system needs sufficient device instrumentation functions at the network elements to meter the required performance details. SNMP MIBs and NetFlow are examples of metering functions at the network element. Note that baselining is a statistical indicator only. There might be legitimate reasons for traffic patterns to deviate.

In summary, the following steps are a good preparation for a network administrator to protect the network in advance:

- Define a policy that describes which protocols, applications, transactions, and connections are permitted and denied in the network.

- Activate accounting and performance management features at the network elements, such as the following:

    — Full NetFlow should be enabled at the edge of the network. It can be combined with Sampled NetFlow at the core network.

    — SNMP read access should be configured at all network elements. Trap destinations are required as well. From a security perspective, leveraging SNMP version 3 is the best approach. If that is not applicable, secure SNMP device access with access control lists (ACL) or a dedicated network for management purposes (data communications network [DCN]).

    — Enable Syslog at the devices. Syslog message severity can be customized from critical to debugging, resulting in few or many messages. Critical devices should get a closer monitoring level (severity level "info" or "notice"), and less-critical devices can be configured with Syslog level "critical" or "alert."

- Analyze flow records for abnormalities to identify reconnaissance, especially ping sweeps and port scans. Advanced attacks do not use sequential scanning; they take a randomized approach or a list of ports. By tracking flow records and correlating them, you can identify these scanning activities; however, this is not as simple as detecting a massive DoS attack. In this case, security management applications are required and must have flow-monitoring capabilities included.

- NBAR is the tool of choice for network protocol discovery up to the application level. However, because of the CPU impact, it should be used with care and only if alternatives such as SNMP, NetFlow, and BGP PA do not provide sufficient details. Hardware-based NBAR implementations, such as the sup32-PISA in the Catalyst 6500, address these performance implications effectively.

- IP SLA is the final function to verify network, server, and application response time. Using IP SLA to assess the network before, during, and after an attack is a great way to measure the impact of an attack and document how long the remedy took.

- Deploying security management applications that collect, store, aggregate, correlate, and present potential threats is the final step during the Preparation stage.

Chapter 13, "Monitoring Scenarios," describes performance management, which is one of the building blocks of security management.

Identification

In a perfect world, preparation would result in blocking all attacks against the network. However, we live in a real world, so attacks will happen eventually! The next logical step is to detect and identify an attack. Some attacks are easy to detect, especially if their goal is to paralyze the users completely. Attacks that try to snoop for passwords or business knowledge are much harder to detect, because they do not leave massive footprints.

Therefore, a critical task is to identify a potential attack quickly. The detection or identification process is a walk between the two extremes of too many "false positives," which are false attack warnings, and "false negatives," which are missed alerts. If operators get too many false alerts, they will soon ignore the messages, whereas suppressed warnings result in a lack of the operator's trust in the security management application. The challenge is to find the right balance!

A successful approach for increasing the accuracy of alerts is to combine multiple sources of information, such as NetFlow and MIB variables. NetFlow at the routers and switches provide valuable information about the current traffic flows. Constantly analyzing the flows is the first step toward identifying an abnormal situation. For example, a sudden increase in the total number of flows, or a large number of flows with the same destination IP address and port number, combined with few or no payloads, can be an attack signal. MIB counters, such as interface traffic and CPU utilization, offer an at-a-glance view of the network and devices. An increase in the number of ACL violations is a useful hint to drill deeper.

Each of these symptoms alone can have a normal reason, such as burstiness of traffic. However, chances are low that multiple indicators of abnormal situations will occur at the same time without a good reason.

Various applications help an operator identify attacks. Examples are the Cisco Security Monitoring, Analysis, and Response System (CS-MARS) and Arbor's Peakflow SP anomaly-detection system. Both applications take the fully automated approach of combining multiple sources of information and displaying the result in a graphical user interface. An alternative approach is writing scripts. You can collect NetFlow records with an open-source application such as flow-tools (see http://www.splintered.net/sw/flow-tools/ for more details) and monitor the total number of flows, either continuously or every couple of minutes. As soon as you have an average value of flows per time interval, you can define a flow threshold value. If the number of current flows exceeds this value, the script should initiate a notification. This can trigger another script that checks device CPU utilization and interface traffic. Note that any correlation is possible only if continuous monitoring of all components is applied! By defining thresholds for these values, you have multiple indicators daisy-chained, allowing you to interact at each step. The collected NetFlow records are a good starting point for further analysis in the Identification stage, which leads to the classification of the attack.

An alternative approach to collecting accounting data for security purposes is to set up a "honeypot." This is a router or computer that is installed by the security operator merely for surveillance and security analysis, but to the outside world it appears to be part of the network. The idea is to provide a limited "open door" for hackers while carefully monitoring their activities. Note that honeypots can be a risk to the network if they are not properly shielded from the production network!

Due to the performance impact of collecting NetFlow records the question arises of whether NetFlow is applicable for the Identification part of the process. There are two valid answers to this question. First, NetFlow is a crucial building block for the classification step. Because you will need the NetFlow records later anyway, why not use NetFlow for identification as well? Second, the NetFlow MIB offers an at-a-glance view of NetFlow statistics, which can point out a potential attack. Because the NetFlow MIB is a relatively new feature, it has limited support from security manage-ment applications. It is nice to notice that it was built because of security requirements. Chapter 7, "NetFlow," covers the NetFlow MIB as well.

For intrusion detection, monitoring logging messages is a key to success. The following list of event logs can serve as a starting point:

- Failed login attempts at the network element result in Syslog messages and SNMP traps.

- High number of ACL violations.

- High number of uRFP drops. Unicast Reverse Path Forwarding (uRPF) is a feature that drops packets with malformed or spoofed IP source addresses. The router examines all received packets to verify that the source address and interface appear in the routing table and match the interface on which the packet was received.

Related to traffic baselining, threat identification also includes monitoring traffic that deviates from normal. Fault management features such as RMON alarms and events or a combination of the Expression MIB and Event MIB can help identify unusual traffic patterns quickly. The challenge for a security architect is combining the number of events to provide information and root-cause analysis to an operator.

In summary, the following steps are suggested as preparation for detecting attacks:

- Baseline the network and define thresholds for significant events. Examples could be NetFlow (number of flows per hour and day) and MIB counters (CPU utilization, minimum free memory, interface utilization). Thresholds can be monitored at the central NMS or locally at the network element by using the Expression MIB and Event MIB.

- Enable logging at the network elements (SNMP traps, Syslog) and at the network servers (Syslog) and also define thresholds, such as for the total number of messages per hour and day, as well as filtering for severe log messages.

- Deploy applications that monitor and analyze network activities and utilization. These tools calculate a utilization trend and deviation from normal, which can be quite handy to quickly identify abnormal situations.

Classification

After identifying an abnormal situation in the network, classifying the kind of attack comes next. It is tricky to block an attack without a clear understanding of the attack's characteristics. You need answers to questions such as these:

- Is this an attack against the network, or the servers, or the services?

- Is it a security threat or a denial of service, such as one caused by a worm?

- Is the attack distributed, or is a single source causing it?

Intelligent device instrumentation features can decrease the time for classifying a threat's kind and scope.

NetFlow

NetFlow is also instrumental in the Classification stage. Two approaches apply when leveraging NetFlow for categorizing an attack: traffic baselining and in-depth flow inspection. Baselining for security is applied with two flavors. The first is for the identification step, where unusual traffic behavior is observed. The second flavor relates to classification, where the attack is classified.

Through NetFlow baselining, you can identify the Top-N traffic volume or number of sessions per host. This can help you identify hosts that suddenly generate much more traffic than they normally do. This can indicate that an attacker broke into that system and used it for a DoS attack or that a user initiated a lot of peer-to-peer traffic by sharing multimedia files. This can be detected as follows: First, you gather a list of known application servers in your network—e-mail servers, application servers, web servers, and so on. Then you retrieve the NetFlow Top-N hosts and compare the two lists. Under normal circumstances, the application servers should be the top talkers in the network. Unless major changes occur in the network, this list of top talkers should be relatively stable. If suddenly a client IP address generates similar volume or more volume than network servers, a flag should be raised.

A similar analysis can be applied to the number of active sessions per host. It is normal for to have a network server thousands of active sessions. But for a client PC, this would be an exceptional situation. A likely reason would be a network scan, a worm, or an attack.

NetFlow for security analysis can be used in two phases. The NetFlow *collection* gathers traffic statistics, and the NetFlow *export* sends the accounting records to a NetFlow collector. If only the summary information is required, the NetFlow MIB (CISCO-NETFLOW-MIB) is the right tool, because it displays traffic summary information, such as the top flows (cnfTopFlows) and packet statistics (cnfProtocolStatistics) such as packet size distribution and number of active or inactive flows.

In-depth flow inspection relates to, for example, TCP flags and TCP or UDP port numbers. Even though NetFlow records do not include payload data, TCP session characteristics gathered by NetFlow are valuable to identify attacks. A three-step handshake process establishes a TCP session. The initial client request contains the SYN (synchronize) TCP flag, to which the server replies with a SYN/ACK (acknowledge) packet. After the client acknowledges the server's acknowledge, the session is established. A TCP session is closed by sending a packet with a FIN (finished) flag set. NetFlow records contain the session's TCP flags, aggregated by a cumulative OR operation. Normal flows have a combination of flags, but a large number of SYN flags without an ACK can point out a DoS attack. Certain combinations of flags should never occur normally and are a clear sign of an anomaly. A security management application should cautiously monitor the NetFlow flag field.

For application server monitoring, it can be useful to analyze the relationship between servers and port numbers. If you know which UDP or TCP ports are used per application, you can identify if someone installed a new application that uses different port numbers. Port monitoring creates a lookup table for active UDP and TCP port numbers per server and compares traffic patterns against this table. If traffic is sent to or from ports that are not listed, generate a notification.

Packet size is another relevant NetFlow parameter. The average packet size on the Internet is greater than 300 bytes. If a large number of flows are significantly below or above that size, raise a flag. Table 16-1 illustrates a DoS attack in which flows from multiple source IP addresses target a single destination IP address with random port numbers and very small packets.

Table 16-1   *NetFlow Records During a DoS Attack*

Source IP Address	Destination IP Address	Input I/F	Output I/F	Source Port	Destination Port	Packets	Bytes	Port
10.1.1.69	10.44.4.245	29	49	1308	77	1	40	6
10.1.1.222	10.44.4.245	29	49	1774	1243	1	40	6
10.1.1.108	10.44.4.245	29	49	1869	1076	1	40	6
10.1.1.159	10.44.4.245	29	49	1050	903	1	40	6
10.1.1.54	10.44.4.245	29	49	2018	730	1	40	6
10.1.1.136	10.44.4.245	29	49	1821	559	1	40	6
10.1.1.216	10.44.4.245	29	49	1516	383	1	40	6
10.1.1.111	10.44.4.245	29	49	1894	45	1	40	6
10.1.1.29	10.44.4.245	29	49	1600	1209	1	40	6
10.1.1.24	10.44.4.245	29	49	1120	1034	1	40	6
10.1.1.39	10.44.4.245	29	49	1459	868	1	40	6
10.1.1.249	10.44.4.245	29	49	1967	692	1	40	6
10.1.1.57	10.44.4.245	29	49	1044	521	1	40	6
...	...	...	...	...	...	...	...	...

To display only certain entries from the potentially large NetFlow cache at the router, use the **include** or **exclude** function:

```
router# show ip cache flow | include 10.44.4.245
```

You can draw two conclusions from Table 16-1:

- Every flow consists of only one packet, and they all have the same packet size (40 bytes). Because the length of the IP and TCP headers are 40 bytes in total, these packets have no payload!

- The source and destination port numbers look like a random mix.

As you can see, none of these symptoms considered alone would be an issue. However, if they all come together, and this traffic pattern is different from normal, a notification should be generated. Again, this points to the need for baselining! In this specific case, a SYN flood attack might be taking place. You could confirm this by inspecting the TCP flags in the NetFlow record.

Network-Based Application Recognition (NBAR)

NetFlow records contain traffic and session characteristics, but no payload data. A complementary feature to NetFlow is the Cisco Network-Based Application Recognition (NBAR) utility. NBAR is a classification engine that applies stateful packet inspection to identify applications based on characteristics such as static and dynamic port numbers and payload details, such as application URLs. This enables NBAR to detect attacks, such as worms, from their payload signatures. As soon as specifics about new worms or attacks exist, NBAR can identify these packets and apply traffic policies, such as blocking only the specific packets. NBAR can be used inbound and outbound to mitigate the effects of attacks immediately. NBAR's advantage over ACLs is the flexibility of blocking only some applications, not all traffic.

During the initial phase of the classification, when the attack's fingerprints are not identified, NBAR can help keep network services operational by prioritizing business-critical applications. Because NBAR understands the details of e-mail, VoIP, SAP, and Citrix applications, these can be prioritized in the network, and all "unknown" traffic can be rate-limited. Even though rate-limiting traffic that is unknown to NBAR might also limit user traffic, it guarantees the availability of the most important services, which is a major achievement when a network is under attack.

Network Analysis Module (NAM)

Even though Cisco did not design the NAM primarily as a security management tool, it can provide useful at-a-glance views of network traffic and help classify traffic. Because the NAM supports RMON, ART, NetFlow, VoIP, and QoS monitoring, it is a valid source for traffic analysis and classification, and it can help an operator to identify abnormal traffic patterns.

Based on the analysis resulting from the identification and classification section, you can define rising and falling thresholds for the following conditions, where actions include logging and trap generation:

- Network layer hosts
- Network layer conversations
- MAC layer hosts
- MAC layer conversations
- Application statistics
- Server response time
- Server-client response time
- DiffServ traffic statistics
- DiffServ host statistics
- DiffServ application statistics

Monitoring these characteristics is related to baselining, so it is important to ensure that generated traps are also sent to the security management application.

Other Attack Classification Features

NetFlow, NBAR, and the NAM offer significant value for traffic classification, but other tools need to be mentioned as well:

- With a "sinkhole," a portion of the network is designed to accept and analyze attack traffic. It can be used to divert attack traffic, monitor for worm propagation, and monitor other potentially malicious traffic.
- "Honeypots" emulate a server or service in the network and are designed to be probed, attacked, or compromised by hackers. This gives the security operator insight into the hacker's plans by observing and analyzing his or her activities. Typical intruder interactions with a honeypot are reconnaissance and intrusions.
- Intrusion Detection Systems (IDS) can be implemented as host-based and network-based solutions. Both methods are based on the assumption that an intruder's activity is different from the characteristics of a regular user or traffic. For host-based IDS, a software agent runs on the server and analyzes log files, access to applications, configuration files, e-mail activities, and more. An example is the Cisco Security Agent, which can be installed on client and server PCs. Network-based IDSs are

usually implemented on dedicated hardware boxes that monitor and analyze all layers of network communications. In addition, the operator can write rules to describe common attack techniques and apply traffic patterns that describe attack "signatures."

- Packet sniffers are external devices for packet inspection.

Trace Back

After identifying and classifying the attack, you need to trace back the source(s) of the attack and isolate them. For this task, you need answers to questions such as these:

- Did the attack come from inside or outside the network?
- Did a special segment of the network initiate the attack, or did it come from all over the network?
- Did servers or client PCs distribute, such as notebooks that were infected outside of the network?
- Are the source IP addresses real or spoofed?

Depending on the answers, different actions need to be taken.

An *IP spoofing attack* occurs when an attacker outside of your network pretends to be a trusted computer. This can be done by using an IP address that is within the range of your network's IP addresses. Or someone could use an authorized external IP address you trust and to which you want to grant access to specified resources on your network. Detecting whether a specific IP address is spoofed is not an easy task.

Different mechanisms are available to locate the source IP address:

- Search the routing table(s).
- Check the Internet Routing Registry (IRR).
- Use NetFlow to trace the packet flow through the network.
- Identify the upstream ISP if the source is outside of your network. From there, the upstream ISP needs to continue tracing to block the source.

The first classification separates valid IP source addresses from spoofed source addresses. If you use a private IP address space (RFC 1918), the existence of a local IP address can be identified with network utilities such as ping, traceroute, and DNS lookup. Public addresses can be validated with tools such as WHOIS via the IRR. This information is distributed globally:

- Europe: whois.ripe.net
- Asia-Pacific: whois.apnic.net
- Latin America: whois.lacnic.net
- U.S. and everywhere else: whois.arin.net

Unfortunately, the IRR does not work in case of spoofed IP addresses. By modifying the source IP address, an attacker can make an IP packet appear to come from a completely different source than it actually does. Because the spoofed packet does not return to the attacker's IP address, it is hard to trace it back.

Fortunately, NetFlow can also help in case of spoofed addresses. Because the source IP address field in the NetFlow record is not useful in this case, the Ifindex field becomes relevant, because it identifies the actual router interface where the flow comes from. If NetFlow is already enabled on all routers' ingress interfaces, you can identify the attacker's path immediately. Otherwise, you can enable NetFlow ad hoc and take the hop-by-hop approach, as explained next.

The following CLI output relates to the data from Table 16-1, where the victim's address is 10.44.4.245:

```
router1#sh ip cache flow | include 10.44.4.245
    Se1 10.1.1.69 Et0 10.44.4.245 ...
```

Se1 identifies Serial Interface 1 as the source interface. The following CLI command displays the flow's upstream router:

```
router1#sh ip cef se1
Prefix              Next Hop            Interface
0.0.0.0/0           10.10.10.2          Serial1
10.10.10.0/30       attached            Serial1
```

Therefore, the upstream router is 10.10.10.2, and the trace back process needs to be continued there. These steps are repeated up to the LAN segment or service provider interface where the traffic originated. A MAC-based ACL can be put in place at that interface to block all traffic from this source.

In case of spoofed IP addresses, the client needs to be identified by the MAC address in the LAN segment. NetFlow enhancements for Layer 2 can provide these details:

- Layer 2 IP header fields.
- Source MAC address field from frames that are received by the NetFlow router.
- Destination MAC address field from frames that are transmitted by the NetFlow router. The MAC address is also needed when tracing back over Internet Exchange Points (IXP), because they connect multiple ISPs with Layer 2 switches.
- Received VLAN ID field (802.1q and Cisco ISL).
- Transmitted VLAN ID field (802.1q and Cisco ISL).

Cisco CS-MARS and Arbor Peakflow Traffic and Peakflow DoS anomaly-detection system leverage NetFlow for the detection of an attack's path through the network and offer a proposal for blocking it.

Because the NetFlow features for Layer 2 are not yet deployed consistently across all Cisco platforms, an alternative is the IP Accounting MAC Address feature. It is considered an interim solution because it collects only a subset of the NetFlow details.

Reaction

As soon as the attack's characteristics and sources have been identified, a remedy can be initiated. Possible solutions range from configuring an ACL up to leveraging sophisticated security management applications.

After you identify the source of an attack, a simple way to block all traffic from the attack toward the victim is to define an ACL at a router, next to either the attacker or the victim. Deploying ACLs through a configuration management tool such as CiscoWorks can be a quick way to block an attack. For example, during the outbreak of the SQL Slammer virus, the Cisco internal IT department immediately blocked it within the Cisco intranet by configuring ACLs at all Internet access points worldwide.

If only a limited number of hosts are targets of the attack, an alternative is to propagate BGP drop information to all routers in the network. If you set the next hop of the target IP addresses to the Null interface, all packets destined for the victims are dropped into the so-called "black hole."

An alternative to dropping traffic from a source or toward a destination is to block only traffic from nonexistent sources. The uRPF feature in Cisco IOS discards IP packets of IP source addresses that cannot be verified, such as spoofed addresses. Note that uRPF creates additional overload on the router, which might be contradictory during an attack where the network is already under heavy load.

NOTE   The "IP source guard" feature prevents IP spoofing by allowing only the IP addresses that are obtained through DHCP snooping on a particular port.

Instead of blocking or verifying all traffic, you can use QoS features such as rate-limiting packets. The committed access rate (CAR) feature can define a limit for certain traffic types. For instance, if a high rate of FTP traffic overutilizes the network capacity, a rate limit can be applied.

NBAR plays an important role in threat mitigation because it works in conjunction with QoS features to block or rate-limit undesirable traffic. When a match value unique to the attack is identified, deploying NBAR can be an effective, tactical first step to block malicious worms while preparing a strategy against the attack. For example, with the Code Red worm, NBAR matched "*.ida" URLs in the HTTP GET request. With Blaster, NBAR looked for SQL packets of a specific length. The following example shows how NBAR can be used with a QoS policy to mitigate the effects of the Code Red and Slammer worms at the network edge. To be complete, the example contains two parts: classification (Steps 1 and 2) and the reaction (Step 3):

Step 1   Create a custom protocol definition to identify all SQL traffic:

```
Router(config)# ip nbar port-map custom-01 udp 1434
```

Step 2   Create a QoS class map to identify SQL packets that are 404 bytes long and Code Red virus packets:

```
Router(config)# class-map match-all slammer-worm
Router(config-cmap)# match protocol custom-01
Router(config-cmap)# match packet length min 404 max 404
Router(config-cmap)# exit
Router(config)# class-map match-all code-red
Router(config-cmap)# match protocol http url "*.ida"
Router(config-cmap)# exit
```

Step 3   Use the QoS **drop** action to discard the matching packets at the ingress interface:

```
Router(config)# policy-map mitigate-worms
Router(config-pmap)# class slammer-worm
Router(config-pmap-c)# drop
Router(config-pmap-c)# exit
Router(config-pmap)# class code-red
Router(config-pmap-c)# drop
Router(config-pmap-c)# exit
```

NOTE   Because NBAR has an impact on the router's CPU performance, it is recommended that you use NBAR on the access links rather than on the core links. Alternatively deploy the sup32-PIS supervisory card in the catalyst 6500.

Postmortem

Assuming that the steps and actions described in the previous sections helped identify and block an attack against your network, the next step is crucial (but still is neglected by some operators). The postmortem examines the situation to identify why the network was vulnerable and what lessons can be learned from the situation. However, the postmortem sometimes requires a decision from upper management to assign time and people to analyze the past situation. Most people are good at firefighting, but only a few like digging into the past.

Postmortems are conducted internally first. If possible, they should include information from other enter-prises or service providers. Especially after a major attack against multiple corporations and organizations, teamwork between the affected groups can increase a postmortem's value and results.

Start the process by reconstructing the attack as precisely as possible to establish a "footprint" for the attack. The different steps are related to the different stages of the Cisco six-stage security operations model:

- The first place to inspect is fault management reporting. If you configured SNMP traps and performance thresholds properly, several conclusions can be drawn from the reported notifications. The baselining information that was initiated during the Preparation stage is useful, as well as the data gathered during the Identification stage.

- Check log files, such as Syslog messages from the network elements and application logs from the servers, and relate them to the fault and performance reports. They are gathered during the Identification stage.

- Performance monitoring and accounting records should provide an idea about the attack's path through the network. If you use security management applications such as CS-MARS or Arbor Networks, these reports can be created easily. This is related to the Trace Back stage.

- Analyze configuration changes at network elements before, during, and after the attack. Applications such as CiscoWorks Resource Manager Essentials (RME) or other configuration applications offer easy ways of comparing configuration files. Distinguish between configuration changes resulting from the Reaction stage and other configuration changes.

With the footprint in place, answer the following questions:

- Did you monitor and collect the right level of details? This is linked to changes in the Preparation stage.

- Were all network parameters, such as flow records, CPU, and interface load, easily accessible during the event? Which other parameters could have helped in the incident? With the answers in mind, modify the Identification stage.

- Was the network security level as strong as possible?

- Were the correct patches applied at both the network element and application server level?

- Did you get enough details during the attack to classify the attack? If not, extend the Classification stage.

- Was the trace back successful? Maybe additional methods are required in the Trace Back stage.

- How long did it take to initiate a reaction?

- Did you gather enough information to complete the Postmortem stage successfully?

Remember, as soon as the postmortem is complete, the Preparation stage for the next attack should start. The following questions can serve as a link between the analysis of the previous security threat and the Preparation stage for the future:

- What worked well during and after the attack?
- What needs to be improved? How can it be improved?
- Who discovered the attack(s)—a user, the operator, or a management tool?
- How long did it take to identify, classify, and trace back the attack?
- How long did it take to block the attack?
- Did the existing tools help support the operators?
- Were the tools used at all? In which of the six stages of the process were tools used? What was their contribution to solving the issue?
- How well did the different teams, such as network operators, data center administrators, and the security group, cooperate? How can the cooperation be improved?
- What additional resources, processes, training, or tools are required?
- Did you find a single point of failure in the network?
- What is the most important lesson learned?
- What will you do differently next time?

With answers to all these questions, you are ready for the Preparation stage, where you can prioritize action items and implement lessons learned to ensure future success.

Summary

This chapter was organized around the Cisco six-stage security operations model:

1 Preparation

2 Identification

3 Classification

4 Trace Back

5 Reaction

6 Postmortem

Most of the different functions and features described in this chapter can be used in more than one stage. For example, just the number of generated NetFlow records can be an indicator in the Identification stage, and the NetFlow record details can be used in the Classification and Trace Back stages.

Table 16-2 summarizes this chapter by creating a mapping between the security management process and device instrumentation features and functions as well as security management applications.

Table 16-2   *Comparison of Features and Scenarios*

Feature/Tool	Baselining and Validation	Reconnaissance	Intrusion	Denial of Service
SNMP MIBs	✓			✓
SNMP traps			✓	✓
Syslog			✓	
ACL	✓	✓	✓	✓
uRFP	✓		✓	
BGP-PA	✓			
NetFlow collection	✓	✓		✓
NetFlow MIB	✓	✓		✓
NBAR	✓			✓
IP SLA	✓			✓
IDS			✓	
Cisco NAM	✓			✓
Cisco SDM		✓	✓	✓
Cisco CS-MARS	✓	✓	✓	✓
Arbor	✓	✓	✓	✓

CHAPTER 17

Billing Scenarios

This chapter highlights how accounting and performance management technologies can be used for billing.

Merriam-Webster's Online Dictionary defines the term billing as the "total amount of business or investments within a given period." In the world of information technology, billing can be defined as the process in which a provider of a service creates an invoice to a customer, related to the usage of that service. In this case, a service provider can be a corporation that delivers internal services to employees, an ISP offering Internet access, a data center operator delivering hosting services, and others. A simple definition of billing is "Creating an invoice related to the use of infrastructure and services."

The focus of this chapter is billing from the network infrastructure perspective (Layer 3 services). Therefore, application server-based billing is not covered in detail, because it requires different account mechanisms.

The rating function at the billing application transforms accounting records into billing records. A monetary tariff is applied to the data volume, duration, and type and quality of service. The major difference between accounting and billing is that accounting collects the usage details (also known as metering), and billing applies the tariffs. Note that the tariffs applied may also depend on the particular customer. This means that the same accounting records may result in different bills, depending on what pricing scheme and tariff are applied.

Therefore, network elements always collect accounting records, not billing records.

Chapter 1, "Understanding the Need for Accounting and Performance Management," describes the relationship between accounting and billing in more detail. The focus of this chapter is applying the technologies and products associated with accounting and performance management.

Network Blueprint for Billing

Figure 17-1 shows the network blueprint for the billing use case. Multiple billing scenarios are shown:

- ISP 1 delivers Internet access to Company A (Sites 1 and 2) and Company B (Site 2).

- ISP 1 and ISP 2 have a peering agreement.

- ISP 2 offers wireless access at public sites, such as at airport lounges or cafes.

- ISP 2 also provides dial-in access and broadband services to private users.

- ISP 2 supplies Internet connectivity services to Company B's Site 1.

- Company A charges departments for Internet usage, but intranet access is free.

This figure also demonstrates that ISPs need to exchange traffic with each other. An example is Company B's VPN service that spans both ISPs. This situation occurs if ISP 1 is not present at Company B's Site 1 or Company B chooses two ISPs for redundancy purposes. The described situation is a simplified scenario; it gets more complex if inter-provider QoS or MPLS services across multiple ISPs are considered.

In addition to Internet access, ISP 1 offers accounting services to Company A. The accounting records distinguish user traffic within the intranet from traffic to the Internet. The billing records are provided in two groups: an aggregated total amount of traffic for intranet services and a detailed list for Internet access.

From a technology perspective, the ISPs might use different metering techniques:

- ISP 1 implements NetFlow services at the provider edge (PE) routers.

- ISP 2 uses Interface MIBs at the PE routers to meter the total amount of traffic both from Company B and at the peering point to ISP 1.

- In addition, ISP 2 deploys access servers for dial-in, a AAA server for wireless access connectivity, and the Cisco Service-Selection Gateway (SSG) for end-user access to video on demand (VoD) and other services.

Figure 17-1   *Network Blueprint for Billing*

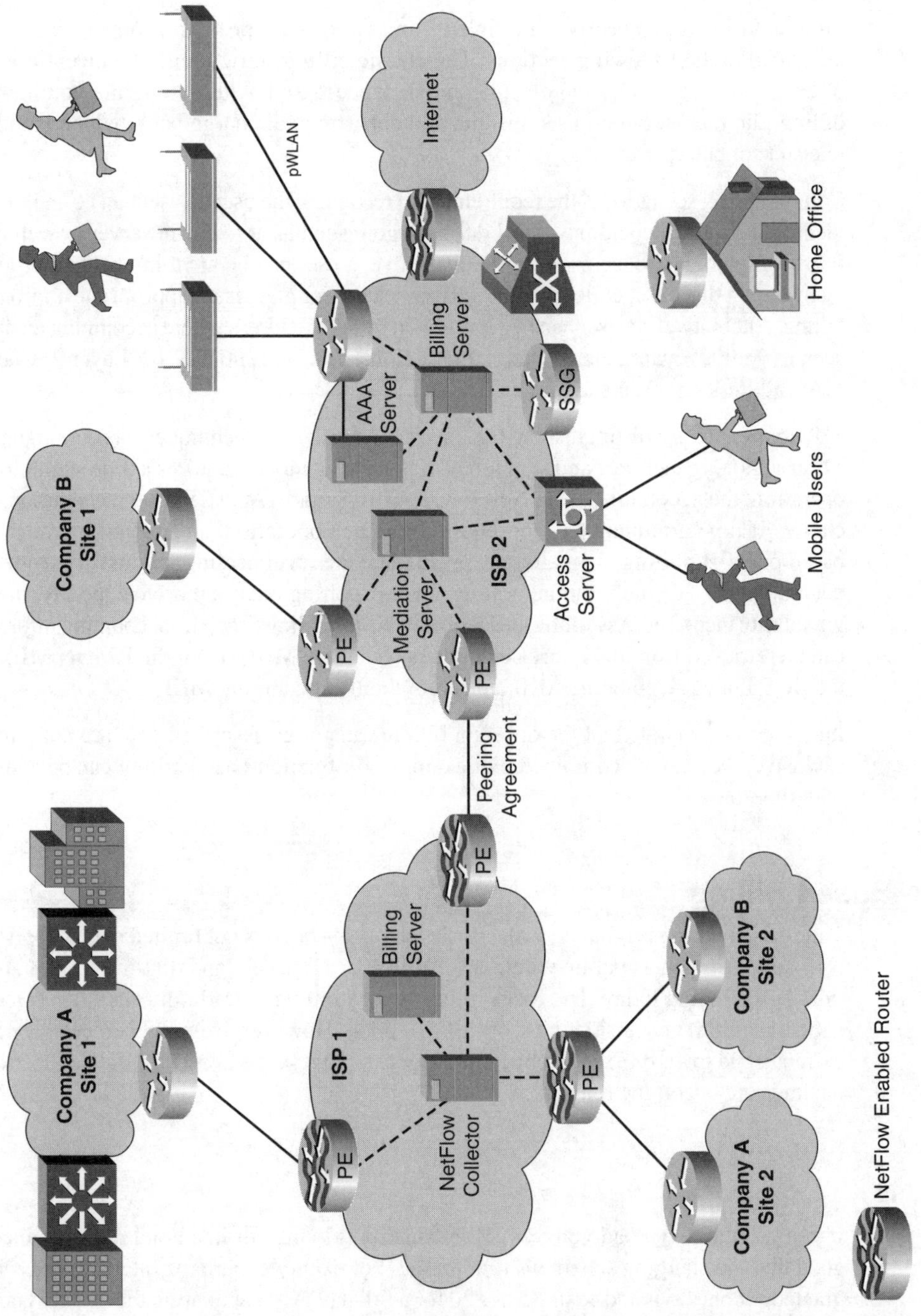

Billing Approaches

From a business perspective, multiple billing options are possible; some of them are described in the following sections. The classic billing started with the invention of telephony, a combination of time- and distance-based. Alternatives are volume-based billing, flat rate, service-based billing, and departmental charge back, which is more relevant for enterprises.

Common to all scenarios is the requirement to recognize the user. A user can be an individual identified by a name and password during logon, such as at a dial-in server or web portal. From an Internet service provider's perspective, a user can be anything behind a router interface. In this case, collecting the MIB interface counters is an appropriate approach for billing. Alternatively, a user can be represented by an IP address where accounting techniques such as NetFlow can meter the user transactions. The same applies for Layer 2, where a MAC address represents an individual host.

The time stamp is a distinguishing parameter for accounting techniques, because it identifies a transaction's exact start and stop times. If the billing model requires a time stamp for each operation, the accounting from NetFlow, RADIUS, and TACACS+ are the solutions of choice. If time granularity is not required for each operation, an accounting mechanism based on MIB polling is an alternative. Indeed, the level of time granularity from MIB counters is based solely on the polling time: if polling occurs more frequently, the time granularity increases. Assuming an adequate SNMP polling time, the accounting information can be retrieved from the interface counters (Interface MIB), from the RMON MIB, from the BGP Policy Accounting MIB, and from the IP Accounting MIB.

It is important to note that the different billing categories described here are not mutually exclusive; they can be combined. For example, destination-based billing can be combined with time-based billing.

Time-Based Billing

Time-based billing originated with classic telephony, but it is not limited to that application. New services such as public wireless LAN (pWLAN) access and dial-in services apply time-based billing today. The focus of time-based billing in traditional cellular voice networks (GSM) is outside the scope of this book. However, from the perspective of the current trend toward Fixed Mobile Convergence (FMC), the described data collection methods are becoming relevant.

pWLAN

If you want to download your e-mails at an airport lounge or in a hotel room, chances are good that the charging scheme is time-based. For example, perhaps Internet access is granted for one hour and costs $5 or $20 for a full day. After activating the wireless network adapter, a DHCP server provides an IP address. After you start the browser, an HTTP redirect command points you to the provider's web kiosk, where you choose the amount of online time and pay by credit card. The timer counts down, independently of user activities, and at the end of the purchased time, the connection is cut off.

Dial-In

Even though pWLAN can be considered the successor to dial-in services, dial-in services still exist as an alternative at locations without wireless coverage. The concept is simple: A user dials into an access server that has multiple phone lines. The access server connects to AAA server (usually RADIUS), where the user is authenticated and authorized. The access servers collect accounting details, which are stored on the AAA server. User credentials can be stored on a local RADIUS server or a central directory server. As users provide a username and password, the provider can aggregate them on a monthly basis. This approach requires the user to preregister with the provider. An alternative is to charge for each call. The user pays a higher access fee to the phone company, which gives a percentage of the fee to the service provider. Chapter 9, "AAA Accounting," explains the AAA concept and RADIUS in detail.

Volume-Based Billing

In contrast to time-based billing, volume-based billing accounts for the total transmitted and received traffic. The most common use-case scenarios are residential broadband access and service provider peering agreements. A relatively new area is peer-to-peer (P2P) traffic. Although some providers try blocking or rate-limiting P2P traffic, evolving the business model and deploying P2P-based services is probably a better option. Subscribers pay for the bandwidth usage and as a result get satisfying service.

Residential Broadband Access (DSL or Cable)

DSL providers and cable operators offer multiple tariffs, from a starter package that includes, for example, 1 GB of traffic per month up to a flat rate for professional users. Combinations of volume- and time-based billing are possible. For example, a provider might offer a package with 8 GB of traffic and 100 hours of online time per month. Additional time and volume are charged for separately.

Multiple metering techniques are applicable in this scenario. Digital Subscriber Line Access Multiplexers (DSLAM) and cable modems have MIB counters on each subscriber interface. These are frequently polled by the accounting application, which consolidates data records and sends them to the billing application afterwards. For cable environments, a performance management solution is being developed at the IETF in the IP over Cable Data Network (IPCDN) working group, which develops MIBs for IPCablecom/PacketCable and Data

Over Cable Service Interface Specification (DOCSIS). RFC 4639 defines the DOCSIS MIB and obsoletes RFC 2669. The CISCO-CABLE-METERING-MIB offers an interim solution on platforms that do not yet support RFC 4639. Accounting for billing is addressed by the DOCSIS 2.0 SP-OSSI (Operations Support System Interface) specification, which defines the Subscriber Account Management Interface Specification (SAMIS). The Internet Protocol Detail Record (IPDR, http://www.ipdr.org) organization provides an industry standard for IP-based usage data records. It can distinguish on-net versus off-net traffic, which is also relevant for destination-sensitive billing. The SAMIS specification is based on the Business Solution Requirements (BSR) specification version 3.5 from IPDR.

Alternatively, NetFlow can be leveraged at the provider edge router. Although this offers flexible charging, it requires a fixed IP address per user. Otherwise, additional overhead for correlating users to IP addresses occurs. To generate billing data, NetFlow records need to be correlated with the user information, such as IP address, router interface, or CPE device.

Both IPDR and NetFlow version 9 offer reliable export. IPDR takes it a step further with built-in application-level acknowledgments. Although this has a potential memory impact on the network element, it guarantees reliable delivery of accounting records, even in case of connectivity issues between the device and application.

Transit and Peering Agreements

Both peering and transit agreements describe formal contracts between service providers for exchange of traffic. Historically, a transit agreement refers to a scenario in which voice calls originated in operator A's network, are carried across operator B's network and potentially other operators' networks, and are terminated in operator C's network. Figure 17-2 illustrates this approach.

In case of a transit agreement, each party pays a fee to send traffic into the other's network. Either A pays B and C separately (direct accounting) or A pays B and B pays C (cascaded accounting). The concept of transit and peering agreements is described in more detail in Chapter 1.

Figure 17-2   *Transit and Peering Agreements*

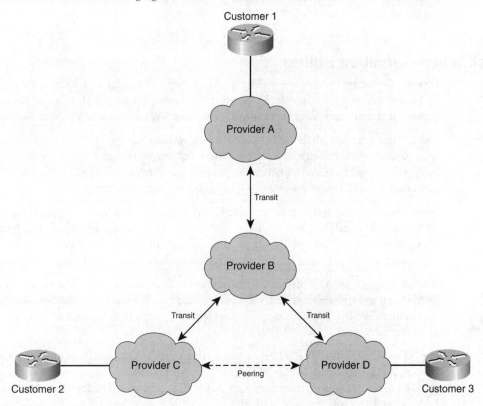

A peering agreement (also called an interconnect) is a bilateral agreement that describes the reciprocal traffic exchange between two provider networks. Because transit costs are a major operating expense for ISPs, peering agreements are a way to reduce costs. In Figure 17-2, traffic from customer 2 to customer 3 can be transported through provider B's network, resulting in transit fees. If C and D sign a peering agreement, they avoid the transit costs. A peering agreement is most economical for equal parties if the amount of traffic is almost the same in both directions. In contrast to transit, both parties agree to exchange traffic without a fee. Therefore, only the total amount of traffic in both directions per day or month is relevant to verify that the peering agreement still reflects the traffic characteristics. Even though transit costs can be eliminated in the preceding example, this is a corner case and is not meant as a general assumption. Metering techniques such as Interface MIB counters, IP Accounting, and BGP Policy Accounting are examples for this use case. If an ISP uses a Layer 2 interconnection (Internet Exchange Point), accounting records including MAC addresses need to be collected. Techniques such as IP Accounting for MAC addresses and NetFlow offer metering of Layer 2 MAC addresses. The related technical details are explained in Chapter 6 for IP Accounting and in Chapter 7 for NetFlow. Alternatively, BGP

Policy Accounting, described in Chapter 8, allows the accounting per traffic index, which can be set per BGP peer.

Destination-Sensitive Billing

Charges for Internet access are usually based on the total volume or flat rates, not on the traffic destination. This might not be the most profitable billing model for service providers, because it is more expensive to transport traffic over long distances than short distances.

The ISP needs to find a balance between the two options. Setting the price too high for the total volume or flat rate drives away customers, but setting the price too low reduces the margin. The right balance is a bet on the percentage of traffic that stays within the ISP's perimeter and that is sent via other providers and creates transit costs.

An alternative is the destination-sensitive billing approach, in which charging is based on the traffic's destination. However, this model is difficult to sell for Internet traffic, because the location of servers is usually unknown to the user. Instead, a provider can offer destination-sensitive billing for specific services, such as voice over IP.

Another example is an ISP offering VPN services to Enterprises, with a low price for traffic within the provider's scope (usually in-country) and a higher rate for traffic that is delivered via another ISP. This business model is appropriate for an ISP, because transit traffic generates additional costs.

For ISPs offering MPLS VPN Carrier Supporting Carrier (CsC) services, distance-based billing becomes relevant. MPLS VPN CSC is an MPLS feature that allows a service provider to act as a transport network for other MPLS networks. The fact that traffic crosses multiple providers is transparent to the end customer; however, the costs need to be aggregated from these multiple providers. MPLS-aware NetFlow is the preferred accounting technique in this environment.

Relevant accounting techniques for destination-sensitive billing are BGP Policy Accounting at the network element. Note that Flexible NetFlow offers traffic aggregation per traffic index; these are the same indexes used by BGP Policy Accounting. Therefore, NetFlow can be used as an alternative to BGP Policy Accounting, with the advantage of extra information elements.

Time- and Distance-Based Billing

For completeness, the time- and distance-based billing option is mentioned here. However, it applies to the legacy telephony environment, in which phone calls are charged based on the call's time and duration and the distance, such as local calls, national calls, and international calls. This model is well known and therefore is not covered in more detail here.

Service-Based Billing

Instead of the "one size fits all" model, billing can be applied per service. An example is differentiated Internet access, offering a best-effort class and a business class with guaranteed service parameters. At the application level, access to selected servers can be free, whereas value-added services require a subscription fee or charging for using the services.

Figure 17-3 illustrates a typical scenario for broadband access in a hotel or at a public hotspot. The user turns on his or her PC or PDA, connects to the wired or wireless network, and starts the browser. For user authentication, HTTP redirection to the web portal's login page takes place. Without any related fees, the user can access the "open-garden" content, such as the provider or hotel's web server. For Internet access, the user logs into the portal and is authenticated and authorized, either by credit card, the hotel room number, or prepaid access cards. In addition to Internet access, the provider can offer value-added content services, such as financial data, music downloads, or video on demand (VoD). These services are offered in the "walled garden" and are charged for separately. The key network element in this scenario is the Service-Selection Gateway (SSG), a Cisco IOS-based feature that works in conjunction with a service management application. It enables users to access different services based on their connectivity or profile with the providers. SSG provides RADIUS authentication and accounting per user and supports prepaid and postpaid billing models.

Figure 17-3 *Billing for Service Selection*

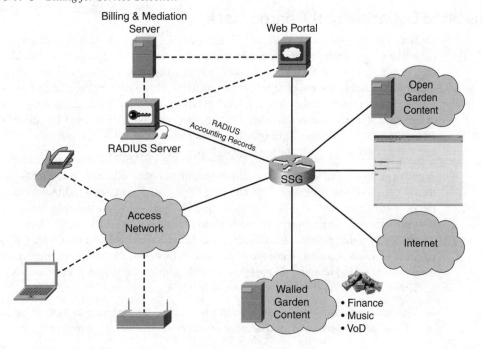

Video on Demand (VoD)

Video on demand is an example of service-based billing, in which a user has broadband Internet access and selects additional services.

The video service can be provided directly by the ISP or by a special content service provider. In case of two separate providers, they can cooperate to increase customer satisfaction, such as by automatically increasing the bandwidth during a video transmission. Alternatively, the ISP can offer a "turbo button" that users can use to increase the bandwidth ad hoc for a certain amount of time.

On the technology side, the provider's web page offers a service selection function. The user chooses a video and pays for it, and a unicast transmission starts. Alternatively, a user can join a live broadcast, such as a football game, concert, or business videoconference. In the scenarios, the user's PC gets an IP multicast address and joins a multicast video transmission.

In the case of the increased-bandwidth option just described, the service-selection server needs a link to the Network Management System's (NMS) provisioning application, which then modifies the link bandwidth parameters for an individual user immediately or at a later scheduled time.

Enterprise Departmental Charge Back

Even though this option is not a real billing solution, it is described here because several enterprises have deployed an accounting solution for charging departments. The idea is to offer a fair assignment of costs to the users and departments. Because intranet access usually has fixed costs, the charge back needs to be related only to the cost of Internet access. This is relatively simple to implement; however, it requires an accounting technique at the Internet access router that identifies the user, such as NetFlow does by collecting the IP source and destination address per flow. Afterwards, the accounting records are aggregated for each month and are assigned to users or departments.

A prerequisite for this solution is a unique assignment of IP addresses to users to identify them by their IP address range. This can be a fixed association, such as the association of the PC's MAC address to an IP address at the DHCP server. Unfortunately, this scenario does not apply to roaming users, because different locations use different IP address ranges. Alternatively, a link between the DHCP and DNS server can associate a unique DNS entry per user, which is independent of the IP address. In this case, the NetFlow collection server needs to replace the IP address in the flow records with the DNS name. The Cisco NetFlow Collector can perform this action immediately when a flow record is received.

NetFlow also supports MAC address accounting at the device level, so it could be used as an alternative. However, the total number of gathered data records could be huge.

Flat Rate Billing

A flat rate is possible with all the scenarios just described. In general, this is not the operator's preferred choice, because time-, volume-, or destination-based billing can generate more revenue. However, providers have to find a balance between pricing and implementation costs. In some cases, such as per-transaction charging, the costs of deploying and operating a complex accounting and billing solution are so high that a flat rate is the best option to make a service profitable. An example is a VoD service where customers subscribe to the service, pay a monthly fee, and watch as many movies as they want.

Alternatively, a provider can offer a flat rate for best-effort traffic combined with volume-based billing for business services that have guaranteed service level parameters, such as bandwidth, latency, and jitter.

Summary

Table 17-1 summarizes the use cases covered in this chapter. For each scenario, the technical requirements are listed (for example, if a time stamp is necessary), followed by the proposed accounting technique.

Table 17-1 *Comparison of Accounting Scenarios*

Use Case	Applicability	Requirements and Prerequisites	Technique
Time-Based Billing	Dial-in Legacy voice pWLAN	Clock synchronization between the servers and an external NTP source	AAA infrastructure Voice switch Billing server SS7 infrastructure
pWLAN	Broadband for roaming users	Subscriber registration or credit card payment, etc.	AAA infrastructure Billing server
Dial-in	Low-speed modem access	Subscriber registration or pay-per-call services	AAA Billing server
Volume-Based Billing	Broadband access Transit and peering agreements	Metering of all conversations	Interface MIBs NetFlow IP Accounting IPDR
Residential broadband access (DSL or cable)	Broadband for residential users	Metering at access point	DOCSIS MIB SAMIS IPDR

continues

Table 17-1 *Comparison of Accounting Scenarios (Continued)*

Use Case	Applicability	Requirements and Prerequisites	Technique
Transit and peering agreements	Service provider interconnect	Identify traffic source and destination (on-net/off-net traffic)	Interface MIBs NetFlow IP Accounting MAC address
Destination-Sensitive Billing	Destination-Sensitive billing	Identify path and providers between source and destination; traffic correlation between user request and server response	BGP Policy Accounting NetFlow Mediation server Billing server
Time- and Distance-Based Billing	Legacy voice	Voice infrastructure	SS7 infrastructure
Service-Based Billing	Content provider, service selection, VoD	Application-based accounting and billing	Service application SSG SAMIS Billing server
VoD	Broadband for residential users	Subscriber registration or credit card payment	AAA infrastructure Content server Billing server
Enterprise Departmental Charge Back	Sharing Internet access	Aggregate users to departments	Interface MIBs NetFlow
Flat Rate	"All you can eat"	Sufficient bandwidth	Nothing

INDEX

Numerics

E

P

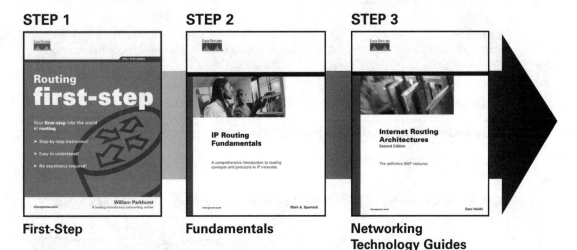

Cisco Press

CISCO CERTIFICATION SELF-STUDY
#1 BEST-SELLING TITLES FROM CCNA® TO CCIE®

Look for Cisco Press Certification Self-Study resources at your favorite bookseller

Learn the test topics with **Self-Study Guides**

Gain hands-on experience with **Practical Studies** books

Prepare for the exam with **Exam Certification Guides**

Practice testing skills and build confidence with **Flash Cards and Exam Practice Packs**

Visit **www.ciscopress.com/series** to learn more about the Certification Self-Study product family and associated series.

Learning is serious business.
Invest wisely.

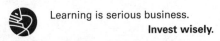

BOOKS ONLINE

ENABLED

THIS BOOK IS SAFARI ENABLED

INCLUDES FREE 45-DAY ACCESS TO THE ONLINE EDITION

The Safari® Enabled icon on the cover of your favorite technology book means the book is available through Safari Bookshelf. When you buy this book, you get free access to the online edition for 45 days.

Safari Bookshelf is an electronic reference library that lets you easily search thousands of technical books, find code samples, download chapters, and access technical information whenever and wherever you need it.

TO GAIN 45-DAY SAFARI ENABLED ACCESS TO THIS BOOK:

- Go to **http://www.ciscopress.com/safarienabled**

- Complete the brief registration form

- Enter the coupon code found in the front of this book before the "Contents at a Glance" page

If you have difficulty registering on Safari Bookshelf or accessing the online edition, please e-mail customer-service@safaribooksonline.com.